Brief Contents

For information:

Sage Publications, Inc.
2455 Teller Road
Thousand Oaks, California 91320
E-mail: order@sagepub.com

Sage Publications India Pvt. Ltd.
B 1/I 1 Mohan Cooperative Industrial Area
Mathura Road, New Delhi
India 110 044

Sage Publications Ltd.
1 Oliver's Yard
55 City Road
London EC1Y 1SP
United Kingdom

Sage Publications Asia-Pacific Pte. Ltd.
33 Pekin Street #02-01
Far East Square
Singapore 048763

Printed in the United States of America

Library of Congress Cataloging-in-Publication Data

Fatehi, Kamal.
Managing internationally: Succeeding in a culturally diverse world / Kamal Fatehi.
    p. cm.
Includes bibliographical references and index.
ISBN 978-1-4129-3690-3 (cloth : alk. paper) 1. International business enterprises—Management—Social aspects. 2. Corporate culture. 3. Intercultural communication. I. Title.

HD62.4.F38 2008
658′.049—dc22   2007002080

This book is printed on acid-free paper.

07 08 09 10 11 10 9 8 7 6 5 4 3 2 1

Acquisitions Editor:	Al Bruckner
Associate Editor:	Deya Saoud
Editorial Assistant:	MaryAnn Vail
Production Editor:	Diane S. Foster
Copy Editor:	QuADS Prepress (P) Ltd.
Typesetter:	C&M Digitals (P) Ltd.
Indexer:	Will Ragsdale
Proofreader:	Scott Oney
Cover Designer:	Candice Harman
Marketing Manager:	Nichole M. Angress

MANAGING INTERNATIONALLY

Succeeding in a Culturally Diverse World

KAMAL FATEHI

Kennesaw State University

SAGE Publications

Los Angeles • London • New Delhi • Singapore

MANAGING
INTERNATIONALLY

Detailed Table of Contents_____

Preface _____

Globalization is well under way. There is no exaggeration if we claim that we have arrived at the "global village." The arrival is not celebrated by the villagers and there is not a welcome mat. Instead, the arrival is marked with a note of caution and a reminder.

The caution note warns us that there are unanticipated outcomes to globalization such as heightened security concerns due to rising acts of violence and terror instigated by, among other things, the stark awareness of value differences. These value differences are brought forth by globalization forces that threaten the possibility of preserving separate ethnic identities and the prospects of assimilation of all by the forces of modernity. The isolation of cultures, nations, and markets of the previous period has been replaced by close interaction, intermingling, and integration among them, actually or virtually. International business and international management have significant roles in all this. To move cautiously in the uncharted waters of global business, and to mitigate unanticipated consequences of globalization, necessitate the study of international management.

The reminder is to shake us up from the comfortable complacency that is an attribute of success. The past technological progress in product developments and processes has lulled firms from industrialized nations into the false assumption that past success can continue unabated into the future. This is far from the true reality. The challenge to this comfortable position comes from business corporations from the emerging markets of Asia, the Middle East, and Latin America. Business enterprises from emerging markets that are going global pose formidable challenges to existing rivals from industrialized countries. In these markets, which are home to the majority of the world population, the emerging global firms have an advantage of being insiders. These are the future firms in the future markets. These markets are growing at much faster rates than their counterparts in developed countries. Supplying these markets successfully requires understanding their uniqueness, which is due to systemic and cultural differences. It is international management that can teach us about the complexity and intricacy of these markets and their people that often are as exotic as they are mysterious to the uninitiated.

Globalization and vanishing national borders have influenced almost everything that we do, particularly in business organizations. Although conflicts between nations have not disappeared, commonality of interest among them in creating a better life for their people is amply evident. This commonality of interest, in part, is manifested through international business. While national governments are obligated to take a nationalistic posture, multinational companies (MNCs) are slowly but inexorably forced to transcend national boundaries. They have the difficult task of integrating the varied values of their diverse workforce in establishing a vision and setting goals for the whole corporation. They have to manage people whose values and expectations are dissimilar. The responsibility of managing across national borders and competing in a culturally diverse world can be satisfied if these managers assume a multicultural perspective. This book offers such a perspective.

The world economy, particularly with the advent of the Internet, is moving ever faster toward a highly interrelated, interdependent state, in which no nation will be immune from the forces of the global market. Increased interdependency, however, does not mean market uniformity or universality of management practices. Cultural, political, and, to some extent, economic diversity differentiates nations and creates unique market segments. Managing a business, be it domestic or international, in such a milieu requires understanding of these diversities.

Realizing the impact and the influence of the global market in managing the firms, most business schools, following the mandate of the Association for the Advancement of Collegiate Schools of Business—International, are offering an international management course, along with other international business courses, to cover the worldwide dimension of business. This book is for use in such a course. It deals with the fundamental concepts of managing from an international perspective. Although the book is primarily for business students, managers will find it useful as well. The book offers conceptual frameworks and theoretical explanations useful for the daily challenges of a practicing manager. The insight thus gained could provide managers with added competitive advantage in the culturally diverse global market.

The scope and intensity of operations that expand and exceed national domestic markets vary among firms and industries. This variation determines different levels of commitment by a firm to the global market. Nomenclaturally, however, most scholars have not differentiated among these varied levels of commitment. All business activities beyond the domestic market are commonly referred to as international, multinational, transnational, and global. Strategy differentiation such as multidomestic versus global is, however, acknowledged. These terms, nonetheless, are beginning to acquire specific meanings, though there is no consensus on their usage.

Among these terminologies, *international* is more popular. Many scholars have used the term *international* to connote all business activities that go beyond the domestic market, regardless of the size or scope of the operation. Almost all business schools use the label "International Management" for the title of the course that covers the management concepts of such an operation.

Also, they use "International Business" as a major field of study. For this reason, in this book, the terms *multinational company* and *international management* are used to describe a firm that operates beyond the domestic market and the management of such a business operation, respectively. Throughout the text, however, to differentiate among firms with various levels of commitment to the world market, whenever necessary, other terminologies have been applied.

The book emphasizes the importance of cultural differences and the difficulties of working with people of diverse cultural backgrounds. It provides its readers with the understanding that international management involves not just conducting international business transactions abroad but also working with people who may not share our basic values and assumptions. There are case studies at the end of each section, which can be used as an anchor for discussion of topical material. These cases are long enough to provide sufficient material for the coverage of the relevant issues but short enough to be discussed in one class session.

The 12 chapters of this book are divided into 4 parts. The first part is an introduction; it elaborates on the importance of international business and management in the first chapter and the critical implications of ethical, social, and environmental aspects of international operations in the second chapter. The three chapters of the second part discuss cultural and behavioral dimensions, cultural influences, communication and negotiation, and leadership and motivation. The five chapters of the third part present operational aspects: international strategic planning, legal issues, organization and structure, control factors, and information systems management of international firms. Industrial relations topics are in the last part, which includes two chapters. One chapter deals with human resource management and the other with labor relations topics.

Acknowledgments

Many people at various stages of the development of this book have provided me with their support, assistance, and opinions. Their useful recommendations are reflected throughout the book. I am grateful for the support and encouragement provided by my friends, V. Baba, former Dean of the Michael G. DeGroote School of Business at McMaster University, Canada; Fariburz Ghadar, William A. Schreyer Chair of Global Management Policy and Planning and Director of the Center for Global Business Studies at Penn State University; and H. Safizadeh, former Interim Dean of the School of Management at Boston College.

I would also like to express my appreciation to the following friends and colleagues. I have benefited from their insights on various international topics: Gussein Bagirov, former Rector of Western University and Minister of Ecology and Natural Resources of the Republic of Azerbaijan; Hikmat Mumenov, Director of the Physical-Technical Institute, Dushanbe,

Tajikistan; Bolat Tatibekov, Head of the Department of Labour Market and Employment, the Institute of Economics of the Ministry of Education and Science, Kazakhstan; and Erzahn Zhatkanbaev, Dean of the Economic Department, Talgat Seitov, Head of International Cooperation Services, Kaziola Kubaev, Chief of the Management and Business Department, and Gulnar Sadykhanova, coordinator of doctoral programs, all at Al-Farabi Kazakh National University.

I am thankful to my dear friends of many years, Arvik Beigomian, Abbas Mo'tamedi, Mostafa Asadi, Babak Kazemi, Mehdi Taghavi, and Foad Derakhshan, who have shared with me their understanding of cultural issues pertinent to developing countries. In particular, I am grateful to Babak, who, while carrying a heavy load of teaching at Aazaad University of Teheran, Iran, with the assistance of his colleague, Mohammad Koloobandy, translated my previous book into the Persian language. Also, a special note of appreciation to my dear friend Mehdi Taghavi, with whom I spent many hours on Persian literature during my undergraduate education and who wrote an introduction for the Persian translation of the book.

A special note of gratitude to my colleagues and good friends at the International Academy of Business, Alma Ata, Kazakhstan: Olga Kuznetsova, Rector of the Academy; Tatyana Urmanova; Liliya Timoshenko; and Zailaubay Kopbassarov. During my Fulbright assignments, I benefited from their hospitality and intellectual stimulation.

I am thankful to Gabrielle Hicky, who was my graduate student at Monash University, Australia, for her useful comments, and Luis Alvarez and Virna Loggidoice, my graduate assistants at Kennesaw State University, who provided me with computer graphics and library research.

The editorial staff at Sage Publications—Al Bruckner, the senior editor; his associates Deya Saoud and MaryAnn Vail; along with Diane Foster, the project editor, and the QuADS copyediting group—all deserve my especial gratitude. Their professionalism and friendliness made preparation of this book an enjoyable and rewarding experience.

I would like to thank the following scholars who reviewed different chapters and offered many helpful comments: Abbas J. Ali, Indiana University of Pennsylvania; Ron Abernathy, University of North Carolina, Greensboro, Elon University, and High Point University; Rabi S. Bhagat, University of Memphis; Charles M. Byles, Virginia Commonwealth University; Meera Chawala, Golden Gate University; Dharma deSilva, Wichita State University; Meredith Downes, Illinois State University; Scott R. Gallagher, James Madison University; Cecile W. Garmon, Western Kentucky University; Mike Geppert, University of London; James Giermanski, Belmont Abbey College; Robert Goddard, Applachian State University; Guenther Kress, California State University, San Bernardino; Laurent Muzellec, University of Dublin; and Lauryn Migene, University of Central Florida.

—Kamal Fatehi
Al-Farabi Kazakh National University
Alma Ata, Republic of Kazakhstan

PART I

Introduction

1 The Management of International Business

T his chapter proposes that we are in the midst of a transition period in which economic competition and international business are the new arenas for international rivalry. International business is the instrument, multinational companies (MNCs) are the force, and international managers are the strategists with which nations attempt to gain a competitive advantage. In such an environment, it is vital for us to understand and learn how to manage international business. Eleven major factors underline the importance of international business and the management of such an operation. These factors are discussed in detail.

To study international management, we need to know what international business is. Therefore, we will briefly describe various forms of international business operations. These operations range from the simple import/export activities to the most challenging foreign direct investment (FDI). The first step in learning how to manage international business is to understand why firms internationalize. We will discuss theories of international expansion to illuminate this issue. The chapter argues that international management is similar to management of domestic operations, because both are concerned with achieving organizational objectives through the proper utilization of organizational resources. International and domestic management differ in managerial mentality, the complexity of the business-host government relationship, culture, and environment. A short discussion of these issues concludes the chapter.

Chapter Vignette

Wine War

France is well-known not only for its rich culture and architecture but also for its wine. Traditionally, French wines used to be the first choice of many connoisseurs of fine wines, and the French were very proud of this distinction. This proud tradition is under siege. The French wine industry is facing a problem that is brought about by globalization and is thus losing its allure and profitability. A dramatic blind wine tasting in 1976 in Paris did not help either. That event was attended by France's elite wine experts. Much to France's horror and America's delight, two California wines scored top honors. The shocking result transformed the wine industry worldwide. The problem, of course, is not limited to France, but France is more seriously affected by it than other countries. Family-owned vineyards are struggling to survive. Some countries, such as Australia and the United States (mostly the state of California), are spending millions to create brands recognized around the world. The majority of wine consumers prefer the fruity flavors offered by producers in California, Australia, and Chile rather than wait for fine Bordeaux wines to mature. These new vintners are concentrated in the markets where wine consumption is growing steadily. "We are in the front lines in the fight against Australian and American wines," says Thierry Berthelot, commercial director of the Quinsac Wine Cooperative.

In recent years, a series of takeovers and mergers have created new multinationals. For instance, Australia's beer baron, the Melbourne-based Foster's Group, bought America's Napa Valley–based Beringer Blass Wine Estates. Another Australian winemaker, Southcorp, took over the family-owned premium winemaker Rosemount. "We've converted from being a cottage industry into a competitive consumer luxury-goods industry," says the chairman of Robert Mondavi Corporation, one of the world's largest winemakers.

Today, of the 10 largest wine companies, only one is French. French wine companies no longer have a dominant share in other markets. For example, three Australian companies are dominating 80% of their home market. French wine producers are reluctant to consolidate, modernize, and standardize a recipe for efficiency. Bordeaux by itself possesses 20,000 different producers. "We stick to our own home regime just when we must begin to compete in a universe of consumers who dress in Nikes, eat Big Macs, and drink Coca-Cola," expresses Jacques Berthomeau, a critic of the French wine industry, who has published a report by the French Agriculture Ministry highlighting their problems. The new wine producers enjoy many advantages over France, including new facilities and the use of modern management techniques. Another advantage for Australian, American, and Chilean winemakers is that these countries work in steady, hot climates that produce regular harvests and consistent wines, while the Bordeaux and Burgundy producers have to deal with unpredictable weather.

Introduction

From the end of World War II until recently, many countries, and particularly the United States, were preoccupied with the threat of communism and the danger of another world war. The United States served as a great security force against communism and provided the much needed stability for world trade to flourish. From 1950 to 1972, world trade increased at an average of 5.9% per year after adjusting for inflation.[4] In the last quarter of the past century, world exports grew almost seven times.[5] Of course, new technologies, falling transportation costs, improvements in education, and increased opportunities for international business contributed to economic growth. Without political stability, however, world trade could not have flourished at a steady and healthy rate. During this period, the United States acted as the police force of the world, and it was preoccupied with the task of containing communism. To maintain this political stability, the United States spent a relatively large amount on defense. The actions of the United States allowed the world, excluding the communist countries, to enjoy economic development at rates that were higher and persisted longer than in any previous period in history.[4]

While the attention of the United States was focused on fighting communism, other nations were able to devote comparatively more time and capital to developing their economies. Under the security umbrella provided by the United States, and the resulting stability, nations engaged in international trade and export. At a time when other countries, such as Japan, were expanding their markets globally, the United States was busy fighting communism. The commitment of the United States to heavy military expenditure was freeing resources and providing opportunities to other nations, particularly Western Europe and Japan, to directly challenge the U.S. share of the world market.

In military affairs and politics, except for the communists, other countries acquiesced to U.S. leadership. Economically, however, they found much more room and opportunity to contest U.S. leadership, and they often assumed a prominent position. In the past, military might would often secure economic domination and wealth for the superior nation. In this period, the fruits of U.S. military power, however, accrued to other nations too. The relatively safe and secure environment following World War II allowed world trade to expand. Increased world trade produced a higher degree of interdependence among nations. Economic interdependencies and the unacceptable consequences of a nuclear war produced a new mentality. For the first time, many nations began de-emphasizing brute force as an acceptable means of conflict resolution. The buildup of the most powerful military force in human history was making military domination less appealing to other countries. Economic competition and international business become the arenas for future rivalry.

The world is still going through some fundamental changes. The threat of a major military confrontation among the world superpowers is diminishing. The conditions that forced the United States to seek military supremacy are gradually disappearing. The former adversaries are seeking help from each other, and old friends are now posing as serious competitive challengers. In short, political and military rivalries are losing ground to economic competition among countries. Global markets and international business are becoming the new battlegrounds. Some governments, for example, spend heavily to support their industries and help them achieve global competitive positions.

Faced with the reality of losing markets to these countries, some are debating the need for a U.S. industrial policy to help secure current market share and to regain lost market shares. They point out the close relationships between government and industry in Japan, China, and other countries that have promoted the expansion of their industries globally. This debate brings into sharp focus the importance of international business. We may question whether the United States needs the type of industrial policy used by other countries, but we certainly need to understand international business and how to manage it. The complexity of international business and the difficulty of managing it were reflected in the French winemakers' problems presented in the vignette at the beginning of this chapter.

Gaining a competitive advantage in the global market is possible only if we understand the underlying forces and concepts of international management. The application of these concepts in managing the cultural and operational diversity of international business is a challenging task.

The Changing Profile of the Global Business Environment

There are many factors that increase the impact of international business, and consequently the role of MNCs, in our lives. The increased volume of international business heightens the importance of international management. The world economy is moving ever faster to a highly interrelated, interdependent state, in which no nation will be immune from the forces of the global market. In such an environment, it is vitally important that we know how to manage international business operations. Eleven major factors underline the significance of international business (see Figure 1.1).

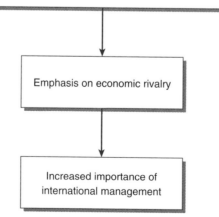

Changes in the global business environment

1. Decreasing trade barriers
2. Developing countries' attitude toward FDI
3. Developing countries' export-oriented strategies
4. Spread of regional trade agreements
5. Technological development
6. Increasing demand for capital
7. Diminishing effectiveness of national borders
8. R&D investment requirements
9. Increasing interdependency among nations
10. The advent of the Internet
11. International terrorism

Emphasis on economic rivalry

Increased importance of international management

Figure 1.1   The Changing Profile of Global Business

Decreased Trade Barriers

The tendency of most countries is to strive for free world trade and the removal of trade barriers. A very good indication of this tendency is the expansion of world trade. During the last quarter of the past century, world trade expanded more than 19 times (see Table 1.1).

The supporters of free trade believe that free world trade is vital to their economic prosperity. Since World War II, countries that have been more open to international business and free trade have grown faster than countries that were less open to the global economy (p. 233).[8] Some, however, would like to take advantage of the open markets of other countries without reciprocating and allowing others free access to their domestic markets. A few have been fairly successful in such practices. The imposition of trade and nontrade restrictions has created friction among the European countries, Japan, and the United States. The handling of such friction, however, suggests the willingness of all to solve these problems in a mutually acceptable and amicable manner. Of course, totally free world trade will not arrive overnight. But there is an inexorable movement toward the removal of most trade restrictions and barriers.

Certain transitory arrangements are already developing. For example, Europe has created an integrated economic and monetary system. An integrated Europe could produce a market larger than the United States. The United States, Canada, and Mexico have created the North America Free Trade Agreement (NAFTA), which removes most of the trade restrictions

Table 1.1   World Trade Trends: 1970 to 2000

Year	1970	1980	1990	2000
Exports (FOB), billions of U.S. dollars				
World	298.8	1,945.9	3,438.6	6,310.1
Industrialized countries	223.0	1,265.1	2,454.1	3,984.7
Developing countries	75.8	680.8	984.6	2,325.4
United States	42.7	225.6	393.6	781.1
Imports (CIF), millions of U.S. dollars				
World	313.5	2,015.6	3,532.2	6,512.8
Industrialized countries	232.4	1,400.4	2,573.3	4,317.0
Developing countries	81.1	615.3	956.9	2,195.8
United States	42.4	257.0	517.0	1,257.6

SOURCE: References 6, pp. 128–135; 7, pp. 130–141.

NOTE: The data prior to 1995 exclude Eastern Europe and the former USSR. FOB, freight on board; CIF, cost, insurance, and freight.

among them and creates the largest free trade bloc. A free trade agreement between the United States and the Central American countries (CAFTA) was signed. Members of CAFTA are the United States, Costa Rica, the Dominican Republic, El Salvador, Guatemala, Honduras, and Nicaragua. Similar events may occur in the Australasian region.

Developing Countries' Attitude Change

The attitudes of many developing countries toward MNCs and FDI have changed. Before the mid-1970s, most developing countries took a dim view of FDI. Expropriation, the forced divestment of foreign assets, and nationalization, the host government seizure of MNC assets, were frequently used as a policy choice by many developing countries in their disputes with MNCs. The large number of pre-1970s expropriations has been attributed to certain problems that developing countries were experiencing. Among them were the lack of administrative capability, the low level of economic development, and an inability to service foreign debts.[9] Also, the East-West conflict was fueling the flames of disputes between the MNCs and the developing countries. After the mid-1970s, however, there has been a dramatic decline in the number of expropriations and nationalizations. This was due to two factors: (1) the improved capabilities of developing countries as discussed below and (2) the realization that a significant relationship exists between FDI and economic growth.[10]

As developing countries improved their economic and political capabilities, the need for ownership control through expropriation and nationalization diminished. Now they can achieve their objectives through taxation and performance requirements rather than by direct control. The changing attitudes of developing countries toward FDI have led some to argue that the attractiveness of foreign investment is growing and its supply is decreasing. Consequently, competition to attract FDI should escalate, and governments may outbid each other with packages of investment incentives and inducements.[11] This may result in increased international trade and may open up previously inaccessible markets.

Adoption of Export-Oriented Strategies by Developing Countries

Hoping to duplicate the success achieved by Japan, Korea, and other Asian nations, many developing countries are adopting an export-oriented strategy of economic growth. The circumstances under which Japan, and to some extent Korea, employed their export-oriented strategies have changed. During the period in which these countries used export-oriented strategies, the U.S. market absorbed the bulk of their exports. This resulted in a substantial trade deficit in the United States. Since this trend cannot continue unabated, and the United States is determined to reverse it, other nations may not fully succeed in emulating Japan. If these countries do not succeed in keeping their markets relatively closed to others, global exports will increase, international trade will expand further, and international management will gain more prominence.

Export-oriented strategy, in part, involves MNCs' participation. As Lecraw and Morrison[12] have noted, 30% to 40% of industrialized countries' imports are through intrafirm trade by MNCs. As more countries view MNCs as an instrument for achieving this goal, we must understand how these firms operate and how they are managed.

Spread of Regional Trade Agreements

Regional trade agreements and pacts are reducing trade restrictions among the members and increasing intraregion trade. Membership in regional trade agreements is on the rise.[13] The most notable trade agreements are NAFTA, the European Union (EU), the Association of South East Asian Nations (ASEAN), and the Andean Pact.

Some speculate that in the future there will be three trading blocks dominating world trade. The first bloc is the EU. The second bloc is the ASEAN, with the expanded membership that could include Australia, India, and Japan. The third bloc is America, with the membership of Argentina, Brazil, Canada, Chile, Mexico, the United States, and Venezuela. There could be relatively free or open trade within these blocs and trade restrictions between them.[3] A strategic response to such a scenario is for firms to have a foothold within each bloc or form strategic alliances with those that already operate within the blocs. Either case results in the expansion of the roles and scope of international management.

Technological Developments

Recent technological developments, particularly in manufacturing, have altered the nature of international business. Robotics, computer-aided design (CAD), computer-aided manufacturing (CAM), and flexible manufacturing have reduced production costs for most products. These technologies have also reduced the labor component of some products. As a result, the low-labor-cost position is less effective as a competitive strategy. Therefore, we expect that the low-labor-cost countries will try to tap MNCs for technology transfer and attempt to move up the supply chain.

Global Demand for Capital

One of the key features of globalization is the increase in capital mobility, which propels national and local governments alike into a heightened competition.[14] Competition for capital will increase further as demand for it rises. Demand for capital from Eastern European countries, and also from the various republics of the former Soviet Union, will likely intensify competition in capital markets. Another important factor in the rising demand for capital is the sovereign debt crisis of the 1980s. In the 1980s, heavily indebted developing countries experienced great difficulty paying back their debts. This resulted in a very serious financial strain on the American and European banks and financial institutions that had given them the loans. Ever since, these institutions have become more cautious, and private sources of capital have become scarce and costly. The financial turmoil during the 1990s in Southeast Asia did not improve matters either. Consequently, more countries are viewing the equity capital from MNCs as a viable alternative. They are realizing the important role of FDI in economic development[15] and its impact on future opportunities for catching up with the developed countries.[16] This is another reason for the changing attitudes of developing countries toward MNCs.

Diminishing Effectiveness of National Borders

Slowly but steadily, national borders are losing their effectiveness in dealing with MNCs. Although we are witnessing a rising national fervor among the subjugated people of the former Soviet bloc, there is evidence that certain new developments are evolving that defy the traditional model. For example, a number of Americans with dual citizenship have served in the governments of Armenia, the former Yugoslavia, and Estonia. In 1998, a U.S. citizen, Vadas Adamkus, was elected president of his native Lithuania. The number of countries that allow dual citizenship is on the rise. Every year, more U.S. citizens claim a second nationality. Overall, the requirement for gaining dual citizenship in these countries is for one to have been born there or have a parent or grandparent as a citizen of those countries. On that basis, and based on the U.S. Census data, it is estimated that at least 500,000 people in the United States are eligible for dual citizenship. This trend has spawned a burgeoning area of study that draws from such diverse disciplines as law, sociology, anthropology, and philosophy. These scholars call the new way of living "flexible citizenship" or "transnationalism." According to them, the old model of nationality is outmoded in this globalizing world.[17]

The top executives of some well-known American firms are foreign citizens. The number of foreign executives in American and European corporations is on the rise. Even staid Japanese firms have not been immune to this trend. After Renault, the French automobile company, took over Japanese car-maker Nissan, it dispatched a Brazilian-born executive as its first foreign chief operating officer.[18] Also, Sony, for the first time, selected Howard Stringer, an American, as its chairman and chief executive officer.[19] For many years, European firms have been preparing for a borderless market in which the nationalities of managers have no bearing on their selection and cross-national career advancement is a norm. Many well-known European firms regularly promote foreigners to their top executive ranks.

The international agreement that created the World Trade Organization (WTO) and empowered it with enforcement authority is a clear indication that, slowly but inexorably, borders are vanishing. It should be noted that for the first time, governments may face the situation where their sovereignty could be curtailed by WTO rules. As the critics of the WTO argue, "The WTO is basically the first constitution (with a global reach) based on the rules of trade and the rule of commerce. Every other constitution has been based on the sovereignty of people and countries" (as quoted by the Indian activist Vandana Shiva in Ref. 20, p. 125). This indicates that trade has assumed a prominent position in our international perspective. Such a view, and the fact that some of the governments' sovereign powers could be challenged by WTO rules, suggests that in the future, nations may face the diminishing effectiveness of national borders and loss of sovereignty.

Investment Requirements of New Technologies

The enormous investment required in new technologies and in research and development and the increasing scale of economies needed for an optimum operation are compelling firms to consider the whole world as a market. In many industries, even the largest and most resourceful firms cannot afford the enormous investment required in today's research and development and new technologies. For example, the estimated U.S.$1 billion needed to develop a new generation of dynamic random access memory chips (DRAMs) forced IBM to form a joint venture with Toshiba Corporation of Japan and Siemens AG of Germany.[21] Similarly, because of the huge cost of developing new drugs, giant pharmaceutical companies such as Glaxo Welcome, Smith Kline Beecham, and American Home Products are forced to look for merger partners.[22] The immense operations and marketing costs of new high-technology products, along with other requirements, have been the driving force behind the increased internationalization and cross-border corporate mergers. Even the U.S. defense industry has been forced to adjust due to the skyrocketing costs of new technologies. Recently, for example, a number of European countries were invited to join in producing the radar-evading Joint Strike Fighter jet. The Joint Strike Fighter project spans more than two decades, is considered the biggest military project in history, and could cost U.S.$200 billion. The interesting aspect of this deal is that not only have other nations accepted involving the U.S. defense contractors in their military operations, but the United States has also invited the other countries to participate in a U.S. military project.[23]

Increasing Interdependence Among Nations

International linkages among countries are creating a higher degree of interdependency, characterized by the increasing volume of FDI. Tables 1.1 and 1.2 illustrate the increase in FDI during the 1970 to 2000 period. While U.S. FDI has been increasing, other countries' investment in the United States has been on the rise also. From 1970 to 2000, U.S. FDI increased more than 15 times. In contrast, FDI in the United States expanded more than 93 times. By 2000, U.S. investment abroad was only slightly larger than FDI in the United States.

In three phases, international linkages have been growing since World War II:

1. The first phase began with the successive reduction of international trade restrictions, which increased world trade. In the mid-1980s, trade was 33% of the gross domestic product of developing countries. It rose to 43% in the mid-1990s.[24] The WTO estimates that due to trade liberalization, real-world income could increase by U.S.$510 billion annually.[25]

2. In the second phase, interdependency through trade was followed by financial integration, which was aided by recycling of the Organization of Petroleum Exporting Countries' surplus during the 1970s. The revenue generated by rising oil prices created a huge surplus, which was invested in Western economies. For such an immense amount of money, the Western economies were the best and safest places for investment. This increased interdependence further.

Table 1.2   The U.S. Direct Investment Position Abroad and the Foreign Direct Investment Position in the United States, 1970 to 2000 (in Millions of U.S. Dollars)

Year	1970	1980	1990	2000
Total U.S.	78,178	215,578	424,086	1,244,654
All countries	13,270	68,351	396,702	1,238,627

SOURCE: Reference 4.

3. Now we are experiencing the third phase of international linkage, which is often referred to as globalization. Globalization is the integration, across borders, of markets for capital, goods, services, knowledge, and labor.[26] The characteristics of this phase include FDIs made by MNCs and technological alliances among them.

A large and growing portion of world trade involves intrafirm trade. For example, in the case of the United States and Japan, more than half the total trade flow is related to intrafirm transactions.[27] These are signs of changing times and the globalization of business. The introduction of market forces, freer trade, and widespread deregulation is happening all over the world. It is signaling that, more than ever before, international trade and investment play an eminent role in our lives. Products are produced everywhere and sold and consumed everywhere. It is becoming very difficult, if not impossible, to identify the national origin of many products. Today, products are assembled from parts produced all over the globe. When the U.S. government was questioning if Honda automobiles had more than 50% U.S. contents, it became clear that General Motors, Ford, and Chrysler were not in a much better position. The issue of national origin is becoming an international trade problem.

Not only are capital, products, and services moving across borders with ease, but people are also moving around the globe at an increasing rate. Two factors related to corporate needs and human aspirations encourage immigration: (1) MNCs are promoting the best employees to higher positions and transferring them to places around the world where they can best serve the expanding, globally integrated firm (see Factor 7, page7) and (2) educated, skilled, and cosmopolitan people in search of a better life find a relatively hospitable reception in many places where their skills and knowledge are needed. Of course, the issue of low-skill labor immigration is a separate matter. This movement exposes people, and particularly employees of MNCs, to diverse ways of thinking, behaving, and problem solving. This builds a closer relationship between MNCs, the host governments, and people from diverse cultures. People in host countries are exposed to cultural diversity and ethnic heterogeneity without traveling away from their homes. The end result is further globalization and an increase in the pace of the march toward a "global village."

One More Step Toward the Global Village

Bank of New York, along with Deutsche Bank, devised the structure of global shares to create an alternative for foreign companies to the American depository shares and receipts (ADSs and ADRs). Global shares are ordinary shares traded in multiple currencies around the world. ADSs and ADRs are not direct shareholdings. They are derivatives of foreign shares created by a U.S. custodial bank. To sell them outside the U.S. banks, they must be converted back to ordinary shares. Their holders may lack the same voting privileges as ordinary shareholders. For these reasons, many foreign issuers consider global shares as an alternative.

In November 1998, DaimlerChrysler began trading as a global share in the United States, Germany, Japan, and five other countries. The financial services giant UBS and the German chemical company Celanese have followed DaimlerChrysler in issuing global shares.

The costs and complexities involved in global shares, however, have kept other potential issuers on the sideline. Linking the home country's clearing and settlement systems with those of the United States and harmonizing local regulations with those of the Securities and Exchange Commission are not simple tasks. We can claim to have arrived at the global village if and when we overcome these hurdles (adapted from Ref. 28).

The Effect of the Internet

In addition to the nine factors already discussed, the development and widespread use of the Internet is a force that greatly influences internationalization of business activities. The advent of the Internet is akin to a revolution. It has permeated many aspects of our lives in ways no one could have anticipated. It has affected many business practices, transformed some, and created new ones.

The Internet reduces business entrance barriers and production costs and increases productivity. Above all, it greatly affects developing and expanding international business activities and presents a significant challenge to traditional internalization arguments. Traditionally, companies would start small and be locally focused, growing gradually. The final stage of growth and expansion would take the firm to the international arena. With the use of the Internet, businesses can be designed from the beginning with the global market in mind. This type of organization is discussed in the chapter on organizational structure.

The Internet affects international business in the following ways:[29,30]

1. It increases global commonality in consumer needs and tastes. This, in turn, makes it possible for MNCs to use more global strategies (discussed in the chapter on strategy) through offering standardized products and services. This is possible because the appeal of globally recognized brands will increase as a result of the worldwide use of the Internet. At the same time, it creates more opportunities for less recognized products and companies in international markets. Dell

Computer, for example, by shifting its marketing and sales efforts to the Web, transformed itself from a contender to a leader in the personal computer industry.

2. It enables MNCs to centralize or coordinate their purchasing globally. In effect, it provides the opportunity to MNCs to become global customers. At the same time, it allows regional firms such as United Parcel Service and DHL to grow faster. Before the advent of the Internet and the Web, globally centralized purchasing required complex, expensive paper-based coordination of dispersed subsidiaries and suppliers. In the case of the Internet, more efficient global sourcing is possible.

3. It drives down global economies of scale, reducing the minimum efficient size of operation. Many physical activities are replaced by Web-based virtual activities. Also, the availability of global distribution channels allows companies to spend much less on international distribution systems or eliminates the need for such systems altogether. Therefore, as a result of reduced economies of scale and transaction costs, well-managed, smaller companies can effectively compete with larger MNCs. By substituting or supplementing physical activities, the Internet makes it easier for firms to participate at the global level. This feature has a couple of ramifications: (1) it allows for companies to be present in smaller markets, which were previously not economically feasible for them, and (2) it enables smaller companies to be global players. With the Internet, it is possible to have a global strategy and at the same time to be responsive to the particular needs of local markets.

International Terrorism

Globalization has provided economic benefits to most nations. The vanishing effectiveness of national borders, increased international trade, the information explosion, including the use of the Internet, and increased immigration have also, however, made it easier for various groups to engage in terrorism. This adversely affects international business. But like the previous 10 factors, it increases the importance of international management. Business is always in search of lower risk and higher return on investment. Sociopolitical strife usually negatively influences business. An important component of strategic planning is the assessment of political risk, which deals with the negative consequences of sociopolitical instability and strife.[31] Because terrorism is a recent phenomenon, it has yet to be systematically incorporated into the business planning process. It is clear, however, that terrorism adversely affects national security.

The preceding 10 factors positively affect international business. International terrorism, however, negatively influences international business. It creates a unique form of nonbusiness risk. Nonbusiness risks are commonly discussed under the topic of country risk or political risk. This topic has been explored by international scholars,[32] who maintain that it adversely affects FDI. The risk due to international terrorism is a recent issue. Its impact on business and the reaction to it are yet to receive scientific and scholarly scrutiny.

The issue of national security as it relates to more frequent acts of terrorism has become a very sensitive matter to industrialized countries. It has become very important particularly to the United States after the tragedy of September 11, 2001. Experts have been sounding alarms about securing the U.S. borders and particularly the ports.[33] The issue of port security drew a very strong uproar after the purchase of a British firm, which operated five terminals at U.S. ports, by Dubai Ports World (DPW). DPW is located in the United Arab Emirates, a country to the south of the Persian Gulf. Some argued that this event would create in the minds of international investors a country risk similar to those of politically volatile developing countries. Such a development could disrupt an increasingly interdependent world economy. It might discourage foreign investment in the United States, on which the nation is heavily dependent. An outcry against similar big acquisitions in Europe stirred concern over a rise in economic nationalism and a backlash against globalization.[34]

MNCs may be forced to react to terrorism against their assets and personnel by (1) forming armed security forces to protect their interests in foreign countries;[35] (2) increasing advance training[36] and proper employee selection for foreign assignments (see the chapter on international human resources); and (3) following experts' recommendations to the intelligence community[37] to improve and expand international management education and training for those assigned to foreign operations.

The Imperatives of the Globalization of Business

In this section, we will discuss the imperatives of globalization of business. First, we will elaborate the need for going international. Then, we will present theories of international trade and FDI. Finally, within the framework of product life cycle, we will explain the firm's expansion into international markets.

Why Do Businesses Expand Their Operations Abroad?

International competition affects most businesses and results in the globalization of many industries. The unprecedented information explosion has greatly contributed to international competition. Technological developments have also reduced transportation costs. Consequently, the physical distance between producers and consumers is no longer much of a competitive hindrance. Domestic firms with unique products or services, or with a competitive advantage, can expand beyond their home market easily.

In today's environment, going international is either an extension of successful domestic business operations or a requirement for remaining competitive. Increased worldwide interdependencies, if continued at the present pace, would make internationalization a requisite for survival. Until that time, many organizations operate at national and international levels as if these two were totally independent. Given this crude assumption, scholars argue on the motives and reasons for firms going international.

Three major theories—international trade, FDI, and product life cycle—have attempted to explain the reasons and motives for international expansion (see Figure 1.2). These theories provide the following explanations.

Theories of International Trade

International trade theorists propose that nations gain from international trade (exports and imports). The gains are the consequences of exploiting relative comparative advantage. **Comparative advantage** is derived from exporting those goods for which a nation holds a superior position in regard to production costs. This superiority could stem from natural resource endowments, such as climate, quality of land, or differences in the cost of labor, capital, technology, and entrepreneurship. Opportunity cost plays an important role in comparative advantage. To produce one product, a country has to give up production of another, and this entails an opportunity cost. Nations benefit from international trade when they export products that they specialize in, because they have the greatest comparative advantage, and import those products in which they have the greatest comparative disadvantage. Free trade does not require that one country gain at another country's expense. Free trade is a win-win deal (p. 266).[8]

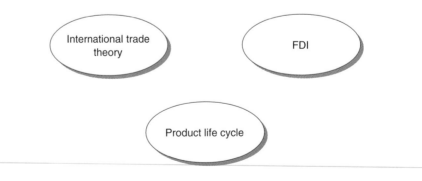

Figure 1.2   Major Theories of the Firm's International Expansion

Foreign Direct Investment Theory

Theories of FDI suggest that four factors influence MNCs' expansion abroad:

1. A change in geographical horizons[38]

2. The possession of an ownership-specific advantage[39]

3. The exploitation of the firm's internal market[40]

4. The effect of locational advantages of host countries

A Change in Geographical Horizons. As firms grow and expand abroad, under the influence of external and internal forces, their geographical horizons widen. The changes in their horizons let them notice international opportunities and stimulate them to invest and expand internationally.

Ownership-Specific Advantage. Compared with local firms, MNCs face certain disadvantages. These disadvantages are the lack of knowledge about the economic, political, legal, and social situations of foreign countries. Geographical distance, currency exchange risk, and language barriers create further difficulties. The established relationships between domestic firms and their suppliers, customers, and regulatory agencies put MNCs at additional disadvantage. When a firm acquires a global horizon and goes international, it can benefit from investments in foreign countries if it has an ownership-specific advantage to offset the disadvantage of its foreignness. The ownership-specific advantage, which is also called strategic advantage, could be a patented technology, product differentiation, economies of scale, brand names, managerial skills, or possession of knowledge.

To Exploit the Firm's Internal Market. A firm's strategic advantage could be licensed, franchised, or traded to local firms. Therefore, ownership-specific advantage alone is not sufficient for a firm to go international. An *internal market* should allow for more effective use of strategic advantages than would contractual agreements with other firms. *Internal market* refers to organizational capabilities, scattered throughout the firm, that could employ the firm's strategic advantages better than would outside business partners. Specifically, the firm's internal market can best exploit the strategic advantages in the firm's intermediate products. Some of these strategic advantages, such as knowledge and expertise, which may ultimately result in a patent, could best be capitalized using the firm's internal market. Unless such knowledge and expertise culminate in products, there is no ready market for them in their intermediate states. The creation of an internal market through international expansion ensures full exploitation of these strategic advantages.

Locational Advantage. Building organizational capabilities and the use of strategic advantages through international expansion do not determine the location of foreign investment. MNCs must justify the choice of investment location. In which foreign countries should MNCs expand? The answer is very simple. MNCs should locate their operations in countries that offer certain locational advantages, such as sources of raw materials, large markets, or low-cost labor.

In summary, four factors determine international expansion: an awareness of international opportunities, the firm's strategic advantage, the rationalization of strategic advantage through an internal market, and the foreign country's locational advantage.

Other Factors. Once a firm, for whatever reason, expands abroad, there is the likelihood that it will develop scanning and learning capabilities. Its presence in many markets enables the firm to locate alternative low-cost production sources and new technologies or learn about market needs that could trigger new product development.[41] In effect, scanning and learning capabilities enhance the firm's competitive advantage. The worldwide presence could also be used as a competitive weapon and for cross-subsidization of markets. Taking the competition head-on, by penetrating into their home turf, forces foreign competition to allocate resources for defensive purposes. Subsidizing losses in one market with funds from another profitable market could hamper the competitive position of rivals.[42] The penetration of rivals' home markets and cross-subsidization could adversely affect the competition. Competition may suffer from significant cash drain, reduced income, and lost opportunities. This could impair the competitors' ability to expand into new markets.

Revised International Product Life Cycle

International product life cycle, first proposed by Raymond Vernon,[43] and expanded on by Adler and Ghadar,[44] suggests a sequential progress for the firm's expansion into the international market, which follows the life cycle of products. Vernon proposed a three-stage model of product life cycle, which was useful in explaining the expansion of post–World War II manufacturing investment abroad. But recent changes in the international environment have reduced the model's appeal. Adler and Ghadar's addition of a fourth stage, which accounts for recent international environmental changes, has improved the model.

The three stages proposed by Vernon are new product stage, mature product stage, and standardized product stage. The model suggests that high-income, economically developed countries are the home for most new products and innovations.

Stage 1: New product: In the first stage, innovating firms in developed countries produce new products for the home market. These products are manufactured at home. Foreign markets, which are other high-income countries, are served through exports. At this stage, since products are new, the firms do not face serious competition.

Stage 2: Mature product: The maturity phase is the second stage, where products have been perfected and sufficiently standardized. As more firms enter the market, price competition forces them to establish manufacturing facilities in other high-income countries, to serve foreign markets with local production. Recent technological developments in industrializing countries are forcing firms to bypass this stage and directly move to the next stage.

Stage 3: Standard product: Heavy price competition characterizes the standardized product stage. The emphasis on price compels firms to move production to low-cost countries. The home market and other high-income countries are served by exports from these locations.

The three-stage international product life cycle is a useful model that explains internationalization of firms for the 20-year period following World War II. Technological developments, however, have accelerated the life cycle of products, where most products become obsolete much faster. Furthermore, the world has become an integrated market that requires mass customization of products to meet individual needs. This brings us to the fourth stage.

Stage 4: International product: According to Adler and Ghadar, we are in the fourth stage of the international product life cycle. This stage is characterized by technological diffusion, high costs of research and development, a global market, mass customization of products, and intense competition among firms from developed and newly developing countries.

In the first three stages, internationalization was in response to specific needs, such as market extension or low-cost production. Adler and Ghadar's argument implies that in the fourth stage, firms go international because the line between domestic and foreign markets, for many manufactured products, is blurring. By the fourth stage, the global market is the source of new technology, capital, and other factors of production at low costs. Internationalization is not an extension of the previous stages but a stage unto itself. It is the diversity and resources of the global market, the immense consumer base, and the necessity of tapping them that instigate FDI and international trade. Due to the unique characteristics of this stage, global operation is the only answer to the pressure of intense competition. As Adler and Ghadar[44] assert,

[In the fourth stage,] . . . top-quality, least-possible-cost products and services become the minimally acceptable standard. Competitive advantage comes from sophisticated global strategies based on mass customization. Firms draw product ideas, as well as the factors and locations of production, from worldwide sources. Firms tailor final products and their relationship to clients to very discrete market niches . . . [T]he product, market, and price orientations of prior phases almost completely disappear, having been replaced by a strategic orientation combining responsive design and delivery with quick, least-possible-cost production . . . {At this stage} strategic orientation requires firms to develop global R&D, production, and marketing networks. (p. 189)

The preceding discussion highlighted various reasons and motivations for the internationalization of the firm. We should add, however, that rarely is the decision to expand abroad based on a solitary reason or motive. The search for enhancing their competitive position entices firms to explore global opportunities. The more adaptable and successful firms usually dare venturing into uncharted waters of the global market. Once there, through first-hand experience, they learn about the expanse of the market and the variety of choices. The wide range of opportunities creates many more reasons to expand further.

Types of International Business Operations

The internationalization process covers a variety of transactions and activities. Imports and exports are two of the simplest forms of international business. The most complex form is managing FDI abroad. These activities can be differentiated based on the perspective of the activities or the types of investment commitment (pp. 3–6).[45]

Perspectives on International Business Activities

International business activities can be viewed from two different perspectives: (1) inward looking and (2) outward looking. These two perspectives are the mirror images of each other.

Inward looking: The inward-looking perspective covers a range of transactions that starts from a foreign location and ends up at home. It consists of imports at one end and the management of a wholly owned foreign subsidiary at the other end.

Outward looking: The outward-looking activities have their beginning at home and their ending at a foreign market. Export is the least demanding of the outward-looking transactions, while establishing operational facilities in a foreign country is the most difficult one.

As mentioned above, the firm's internationalization process begins when it starts to buy from or sell to foreigners. The most serious aspect of the process, however, does not start till the firm commits resources to international activities. The type of foreign investment commitment that a firm may make to international business could be analyzed across three dimensions (see Figure 1.3):

1. Scale of investment

2. Ownership arrangement

3. Type of partners

Investment scale could be small or large. An example of small investment is that of opening a sales office abroad for exporting. Establishing a full-scale production facility abroad is an example of a large-scale investment. The ownership level could vary from minority ownership to wholly owned operations. Partners in an international business could be from local public, local government, or private entities or from other foreign firms.[44] MNCs may choose a combination of these alternatives in their quest to capitalize on the global opportunities available to them.

Direct Investment

There are various options for business expansion beyond the home country market. When a firm explores whether to expand abroad, the first choice and the simplest is export and its mirror image, import. The most demanding and complex form of international business operation is direct investment in the host country, which is called FDI.

FDI involves the ownership and management of physical facilities for producing goods in foreign countries. FDI could be a part of the overall strategy of the firm, or it may be due to trade restrictions imposed by foreign governments. To overcome these restrictions, MNCs find it advantageous

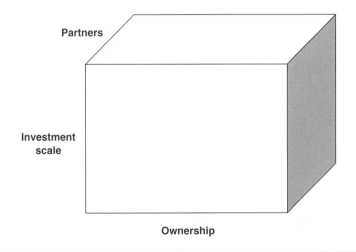

Figure 1.3   Dimensions of International Business Involvement

to invest directly in a country and establish a subsidiary. When a firm establishes production operations abroad, it creates a long-term commitment and obligation and assumes the associated risks and rewards. Having physical facilities such as mining operations, manufacturing plants and equipment, and real estates requires a higher level of financial and human resources commitment. The firm must contend with foreign governments, their policy changes, and local market forces to reap the benefits of operating internationally.

The size and scope of FDI and the choice of strategies for expansion abroad create different types of international firms. These firms may be referred to as international, multidomestic, multinational, transnational, and global. Different scholars have used each term to refer to a specific type of international firm. In this book, we generally use the term *international* for all firms that expand abroad and cross the boundaries of their domestic market. For "industry" identification, however, we distinguish between multidomestic, international, and global industries. We will discuss the differences among them in the chapter on international strategic planning. At this point, it is enough to know that global firms are those enterprises that operate at the global level and treat the whole world as one market.

International Business and International Management

International business deals with business activities and transactions that are carried out across two or more national borders. The management of organizations that are involved in international business is called *international management*. A couple of decades ago, only large and very resourceful firms could operate successfully at the international level. While many international businesses still involve large-scale operations, recent improvements in technology, transportation, and communications and the advent of the Internet have made the size of operations less relevant.

Small companies are using new technologies to penetrate markets that previously were the domain of big business. The success of small firms is not limited to any particular industry or market. Semiconductors, medical equipment, laundry equipment, and wastewater treatment systems are among the many industries that have entered the global market as small businesses. For example, Sharper Finish, Inc., of Chicago, a maker of commercial laundry equipment, deals with 300 distributors in 30 countries, using modern communication technologies. Another example is Midwest Tropical, Inc., of Chicago. Tropical is earning half its revenues from export.[46] A third example is DSP Group, Inc., of San Jose, California, a producer of specialty semiconductors. Nearly half of DSP's sales are to Japan. Although they are from diverse industries, these firms have in common an understanding that managing an international business operation is different from managing a domestic firm. They are all effective in adapting to the requirements of their foreign customers and the requirements of the host country.[47] This newer form of organization, which from its inception caters to the world market, is discussed in the chapter on the organizational structure of an MNC.

Most of the U.S. management know-how, as Richman and Copen[48] observed more than three decades ago, if modified properly, is transferable to other environments (p. 5). The assumption of universality of management concepts and practices, however, could result in utter failure in international business. In other words, there are as many differences as there are similarities between the management of an international enterprise and a domestic business. The differences have less to do with the size of the assets, the earnings, the complexity of the technology employed, or the number of employees. Although all these factors play a role in the success of an enterprise, the differences are primarily due to environmental factors and cultural variations. International management involves greater environmental diversity, complexity, and uncertainty than managing domestic operations. Social, political, legal, economic, and cultural variations of multiple environments require more careful planning and preparation and also a greater diligence in implementation and control.

When a firm ventures abroad into international business, it leaves behind familiar and tested business practices. Everything about the forces that govern the market has to be learned anew. The consumers, competition, suppliers, government, labor market, capital market, and, above all, culture are unfamiliar. While a domestic firm has to deal with only one set of rules regarding market forces, an international operation requires understanding of the interaction between all these forces in multiple markets. International business, especially doing business with developing countries, may offer attractive market opportunities and significant profits, but it also presents many unexpected challenges. Those working in the developing markets may have to deal with disease, civil unrest, difficult living conditions, impossible bureaucracies,[49] and terrorism.[50,51,52]

Although going international may appear fraught with many problems and difficulties, at the same time, it offers many opportunities not available in a purely domestic operation. For example, one of the complexities of international business is doing business in multiple currencies. Exchange rates for foreign currencies fluctuate due to local and global economic forces. Two major forces affect the exchange rate: (1) supply and demand for a foreign currency and (2) domestic conditions, such as the inflation rate, balance of payments, economic growth, and political factors. Exchange rate fluctuation can create additional risk, while at the same time it may offer opportunities. MNCs could use their unique position of operating across national borders to benefit from favorable exchange rates. They could add to the benefits of favorable exchange rates with intrafirm business transactions to boost their profits. Research on firms' performance indicates that internationalization increases financial returns. Firms can extend the product life cycle by shifting sales of outdated products in industrialized countries to developing countries. Also, by operating in many countries, firms can reduce their exposure to environmental risks and increase their bargaining power with their host countries.[29]

In the following pages, we will examine the outstanding features of managing international business operations that distinguish them from domestic businesses.

Major Elements of Managing International Business Operations

The management of international business is very similar to, and very different from, the management of domestic business. The management of international business and that of domestic operations are similar in that both require the attainment of organizational objectives through coordination of activities and utilization of resources. They are different because of the differences in their respective environments and cultural settings. These differences increase the costs and the risks of operating far-flung foreign operations.[53]

The difference is also due to managerial attitudes and mentality. International business has a multi-environment, multicultural framework. The cultural and environmental diversity adds more complexity and uncertainty to international business. This makes the management of such an operation more difficult. Three factors make the management of international business difficult (see Figure 1.4):

1. Management view of international business

2. Host country environment

3. MNCs and host government relationships

The difficulty of managing an international business operation is also due to a mismatch between the managerial mentality and the progression of business from a domestic to an international position. When expanding from a domestic position to an international status is not accompanied by a commensurate change in managerial mentality, the firm may not succeed in international competition. For example, a firm that has expanded to many markets and is dealing with the people from many cultures no longer can operate with the mentality of a domestic company. Ignoring the expanded role of the firm as a corporate citizen of multiple countries results in a tarnished image and operational restrictions. The consequences may ultimately be failure.

Management View of International Business

In the past, some scholars have suggested that the truly international firms could offer the best hope for creating world peace and improving the

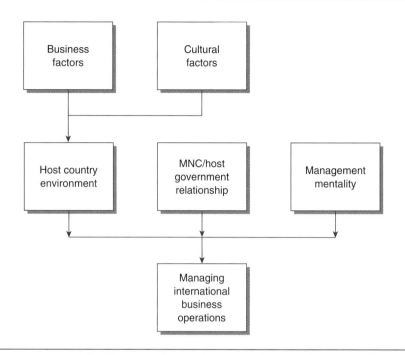

Figure 1.4   Major Elements of Managing International Business Operations

economic conditions of the people. They were asserting that such firms, with supranational frameworks, could conceivably make wars less likely, on the assumption that bombing customers, suppliers, and employees is in nobody's interest.[54] We are now witnessing the emergence of such supranational firms that could rightly be called global. The executives of these firms have a global view and mentality. They focus on worldwide objectives, as well as local objectives. They are globally integrated and locally responsive. The relationship between headquarters and subsidiaries is based on mutual understanding and support. Subsidiaries are neither satellites nor totally independent. They always ask the question, "Where in the world shall we raise money, build our plant, conduct R&D, get and launch new ideas to serve our present and future customers?" (p. 13).[54] Globalization is rendering the traditional way of doing business, and along with it, the parochial mentality, irrelevant. To be globally competitive, managers need to develop a global perspective.[55]

Of course, not all the firms that are engaged in international business have developed a supranational framework and mentality. There appears to be an evolutionary pattern of internationalization that determines executives' state of mind. This state of mind has to do with the attitude of the executives toward foreign people, ideas, and resources, at home and abroad. This attitude differentiates not only between the executives of international and domestic firms but also among executives of MNCs.

Perlmutter proposed that the degree of internationalization of a firm could be estimated by the mentality and orientation of its executives.[54] He identified three states of mind or attitudes toward key decisions on products, functions, and geography. By supplementing the three-stage framework identified by Perlmutter[54] with ideas presented by others (Refs. 56, pp. 71–86; 57, pp. 11–14), the evolutionary process of multinational firms and their executives' mentality could be categorized in four stages. The four stages are *ethnocentric* (or home country mentality), *polycentric* (or host country mentality), *centocentric* (or classical global mentality), and *geocentric* (or supranational mentality). They represent the managerial mentality and attitudes of MNCs.

Ethnocentric Mentality

The ethnocentric firm views foreign markets as an extension of the domestic market. It treats everything from the home country as superior and everything foreign as inferior. Products are produced for the home market and are exported abroad as an additional source of revenue. The firm headquarters and affiliates are identified by the nationality of the home country. Key managerial positions, both at the headquarters and at the subsidiaries, are reserved for home country executives. A foreign assignment is not considered a very desirable appointment and does not advance the professional career of a manager. In short, an ethnocentric firm views itself as a domestic firm with foreign extensions.

Polycentric Mentality

In a polycentric firm, the prevailing attitude is that foreigners are different and difficult to understand. The assumption, therefore, is that the management of foreign affiliates should be left to local people. Products are produced for local consumption in facilities that are operated by host country personnel. Headquarters' control is exercised through financial reports. The firm could best be characterized as a confederation of loosely connected, semiautonomous affiliates.

Although on the surface it may appear that a polycentric firm operating in multiple markets and acting as a local company in every market is a highly internationalized enterprise, this is far from the truth. In a polycentric firm, local managers are not treated as equals to home country managers and are considered somewhat less trustworthy and competent. They cannot aspire to a high-level executive position at the headquarters. Consequently, local managers, who detect headquarters' ignorance of local conditions in its management of subsidiaries and resent the treatment they are receiving, are pulled into a virulent ethnocentric mentality.

Centocentric Mentality

The local responsiveness of polycentric firms results in inefficient operations. Attention to local markets and the demands of local governments creates a system within each subsidiary that ignores internal market opportunities. Manufacturing facilities are often underutilized, and the full benefits of economies of scale are not realized.

Decreasing trade barriers and improvements in telecommunication technologies and transportation allow the use of classical global strategies, viewing the world as one market. We label such an attitude centocentric. Treating the world as one market enables the firm to take advantage of economies of scale in the design, manufacturing, and marketing of products and in research and development. Quite often, products are designed and manufactured at home for the world market. A centocentric firm assumes that nations are more similar in tastes and preferences than they are different. The assumption is that the differences could be made inconsequential by providing better-quality products at lower prices compared with domestic products. Therefore, uniform products could be produced at centers for distribution to all. Centocentric firms require more central control than others. Headquarters maintains control by assigning products or business managers with global responsibilities. The firm is still identified with the home country, and business managers are home country nationals, as are other key executives. The home country culture and the culture of the headquarters permeate the firm and all the subsidiaries. Only local managers who identify with the dominant culture of the headquarters are promoted to key positions. Important strategic decisions are made at the headquarters, and subsidiaries are expected to implement them.

Geocentric Mentality

The success of centocentric MNCs and the power they exert on the local market cause resentment and apprehension. Central control over subsidiaries that dictates major decisions from the home office and identification with the home country produce additional concerns. To offset the perceived power and control exerted by global firms on the local market, host governments are restricting their operations. They also pressure MNCs for more local investment and technology transfer by enacting local content laws. Some governments demand changes in MNCs' personnel policies to allow for local representation in managerial ranks. Moreover, the global market is proving to be more heterogeneous than centocentric MNCs had assumed. The volatility of the global economic and political environment is another reason for global firms to become locally responsive. Add to all this the improvements in manufacturing technologies that have enabled more efficient flexible manufacturing and smaller batch production, and the stage is set for localized strategies.

There are two simultaneous demands on global firms. On the one hand, they are expected to be locally responsive. On the other hand, maintaining worldwide competitiveness requires a higher degree of efficiency, which is possible only with a globally integrated operation. This gives rise to emerging geocentric firms. Geocentric firms view themselves as global companies with no geographic center, in which no nationalities dominate. Viewing the world as their home, geocentric firms strive for flexibility and efficiency globally. Successful geocentric firms think globally and act locally. They integrate an interdependent network of decentralized and specialized companies worldwide. Perhaps the best way to describe a geocentric firm is to look at the operation of one. An example of a geocentric firm is Asea Brown Boveri (ABB), a global electrical systems equipment company.[58] ABB started as a Swedish firm that later merged with a Swiss company and made Zurich its headquarters. The chief executive officer (CEO) of the company described ABB as follows:[59]

> ABB is a company with no geographic center, no national ax to grind. We are a federation of national companies with a global coordination center. Are we a Swiss company? Our headquarters is in Zurich, but only 100 professionals work at headquarters and we will not increase that number. Are we a Swedish company? I'm the CEO, and I was born in Sweden, and only two of the eight members of our board of directors are Swedes. Perhaps we are an American company. We report our financial results in U.S. dollars, and English is ABB's official language. We conduct all high-level meetings in English.
>
> My point is that ABB is none of those things—and all of those things. We are not homeless. We are a company with many homes. (p. 92)

MNCs and Host Government Relationships

The relationship between business and government has always been an area of considerable concern. Governments in their quest for economic development and social programs enact regulations that may restrict business activities or affect earnings. Often, government economic policies and social agendas do not coincide with the goals and objectives of business. Particularly, governments are skeptical of foreign subsidiaries, which are controlled by headquarters outside the country. Influencing the strategies of such foreign affiliates is not as easy as influencing those of domestic firms. Governments can, nonetheless, affect the local subsidiaries of MNCs through their public policy decisions. In dealing with MNCs, the sovereign power of a government renders objections from MNCs mute. This is not to say that governments always have an upper hand in their dealings with MNCs. Usually, the ability of integrated MNCs to acquire capital, material, technology, and labor globally reduces the effectiveness of most government policies.

Global Regulator?

The recent dynamism of global finance has been attributed to fewer regulations on the movement of capital across borders. Capital has been
free to move where it could produce the highest return. As a result, most
countries have improved their regulations to attract mobile capital. This
has produced the convergence of regulations around common international standards. But certain problems remain. National regulatory agencies are no match for global financial firms such as General Electric
Capital, the Citigroup, or Deutsche Bank, which operate at the global
level. Also, there are too many national and local regulators, particularly
in the United States, with no agreement among them. The idea of a single global regulator is on no one's agenda. What the regulators want is
the guarantee that good information is available about the state of global
markets and about financial firms' global operations.

   The three multinational institutions, the International Monetary
Fund, the Bank for International Settlements, and the Financial Stability
Forum, play an important role in advancing the idea of a single global
regulator. But there is no consensus on what should be regulated.
Until now, America's awkward regulatory system does not seem to
have delayed the development of its markets, but in the long run, it
may prove costly if the EU succeeds in fully integrating its capital
markets and introducing appropriate regulation. In fact, it is possible
that pressure from the EU will help make the U.S. regulations uniform
and advance the idea of a global consensus on the issue (adapted
from Ref. 60).

Host governments would like foreign firms to invest in the country,
create jobs, facilitate technology transfer, and help with balance of payment
through exports. Foreign firms with limited operations abroad are forced
to comply with government policies more readily. Their subsidiaries can
comply more easily because they do not face the conflicting demands of
multiple governments. But integrated MNCs, due to the nature of their
operations, may not be able to respond favorably to host government
demands. The demands of one government may differ from the requirements of another.

For example, many developing countries, to earn hard currency, are
emphasizing exports. To give in to the pressure by one government to
increase exports is to jeopardize the relationship with others. Moreover, the
flexibility of a globally integrated operation enables these MNCs to withstand the demands of local governments by capitalizing on their internal
market. Globally integrated MNCs could supplement the operational

restrictions imposed on them in one country with increased business in the other countries.

The foregoing argument may give an exaggerated impression of the power and flexibility of globally integrated firms. Host government relationships with MNCs are very complex and do not lend themselves to simple generalizations. For instance, it is true that reallocation of resources among subsidiaries, shifting of production between various locations, and the use of the firm's internal market are very effective tools for foiling unfavorable policies of the host government. If a host government applies serious pressure on the MNC to severely hamper its business, the MNC's choices are not many. The size of investment and the commitment of the MNC to a host country reduce its flexibility. FDI in plants, production equipment, and physical facilities that are not readily mobile reduces the flexibility of integrated strategies, at least in the short run. In the short run, accommodating the host government may be a wise choice.

Host government subsidies to domestic firms, or the use of the government's purchasing power to give preference to domestic firms, could create unfavorable business conditions for MNCs. Changes in tax laws and labor laws, repatriation of profits, and a host of other regulations and restrictions are sources of additional risk. Political risk increases the cost of doing business abroad and makes FDI a challenging and demanding proposition. Foreign governments have had a history of such practices. The political risk of operating in a foreign country is a reality that MNCs have to deal with. A sudden and dramatic change in government policy toward FDI, though less frequent in recent years, is a distinct possibility that MNCs have to consider when going abroad.

The most troublesome feature of managing across national borders is dealing with the public policies of the home government that are in conflict with host government policies. Complying with the policies of either government could create legal problems for the executives. Consider the quandary of Caterpillar executives during the construction of the Soviet pipeline to Western Europe in the early 1980s. The U.S. government, to punish the Soviet Union for its expansionist policies, ordered Caterpillar to stop selling earthmoving equipment to the Soviet Union. Caterpillar executives complied and stopped shipping equipment from the Peoria, Illinois, plant. The French subsidiary of Caterpillar, however, under the order of the French government, continued delivery of equipment to the Soviets. Caterpillar executives, though following U.S. policies, were not able to satisfy the mandate of the U.S. government.

Host Country Business Environment

Besides the complexity of relationships with the host government, MNCs have to deal with the local workforce, domestic and international competition, and local suppliers and customers, which are different from those in the home country. Cultural differences are a major source of difficulty in managing a global firm. Faced with multiple cultures, MNCs have to adjust and adopt their managerial practices to accommodate the differences among various cultures. Fluctuations in the exchange rate create an additional burden for MNCs. These issues will be discussed in other chapters.

In short, managing an MNC is not managing a larger domestic firm. It involves a change in management mentality and greater attention to the requirements of doing business. The different requirements for managing global firms are a result of the multiple environments of foreign countries and the additional complexity of operating across national borders.

Summary

This chapter explained why international business and management are important to us and why we should learn about them. It was suggested that the prolonged peace after World War II has changed the nature of international rivalry. The diminishing threat of large-scale military conflict between the superpowers has shifted the emphasis from military supremacy to economic competition. The changing attitudes of nations toward global relationships facilitate increased international business. Therefore, understanding the concepts and theories of international business and management has gained added importance.

To learn about international management, the question of why businesses go international was examined. Included in the examination were theories of international trade, FDI, and international product life cycle.

International business operations cover a spectrum of activities, ranging from exporting to direct investment. Various types of international business operations were described. It was proposed that management of these varied business operations is not the same as that of domestic business. The differences between international management and management of domestic business are due to the complexity of the international environment. Internationalization of the firm involves not only the expansion of the operations abroad but also a change in management mentality. The management view of international business is categorized into four stages: ethnocentric, polycentric, centocentric, and geocentric.

The business-host government relationship is a major source of difficulty for MNCs. The flexibility and resourcefulness of integrated global firms, when paired with the sovereign power of host governments, create a challenging and demanding proposition for management. Other factors that make international management different from managing domestic operations are cultural differences and currency exchange fluctuations. These issues will be covered in other chapters.

Discussion Questions

1. Why is it important to learn about international management?

2. What factors contribute to the increased role of international business in our lives?

3. Explain the reasons for firms' international expansion.

4. Raymond Vernon proposed a three-stage international product life cycle. Describe these stages. Adler and Ghadar suggested the addition of a fourth stage. What are the characteristics of the fourth stage?

5. What is the difference between the inward-looking and outward-looking perspectives of international business?

6. How many different types of international business operations can you identify? Describe in detail a major international business operation.

7. Describe international management.

8. In what ways are international management and the management of domestic operations similar? What are their differences?

9. The author asserts that a major differentiating factor among executives of domestic businesses and those of MNCs is managerial mentality (their view of business). This attitude also differentiates among MNC executives. Explain the four stages of managerial mentality.

10. Why do host governments have less influence on integrated global firms?

11. The relationships between the host government and MNCs is more complex than government-domestic business relations. Why?

12. What aspects of international business are affected by the Internet?

13. Review the vignette of this chapter more carefully, and explain the problems of the global wine industry. Use library resources and other material to elaborate on these problems. Explain how international business is transforming the industry and forcing it to consolidate.

References

1. W. Echikson, F. Balfour, K. Capell, L. Himelstein, & G. Khermouch (2001, September 3). Wine war. *Business Week*, 54–60.
2. This moment in history. *Smithsonian* (2006, May), *37*(2), 36.
3. R. Ehrlich (2006, June 18). My round; California vs France: The great wine war. *Independent on Sunday* (London), p. 249.
4. A. H. Meltzer (1991). U.S. leadership and postwar progress. In *Policy implications of trade and currency zones* (pp. 237–257). Kansas City, MO: Federal Reserve Bank of Kansas City.

5. U.S. Department of Commerce, Bureau of Economic Analysis (1966–1992 and 2000). *Survey of current business*. Washington, DC: Author.

6. International Monetary Fund (1999). *International financial statistics yearbook* (Vol. 52). Washington, DC: Author.

7. International Monetary Fund (2001). *International financial statistics yearbook* (Vol. 54). Washington, DC: Author.

8. U.S. Government Printing Office (2004). Economic report of the president. In *Executive Office of the President and the Council of Economic Advisors*. Washington, DC: Author.

9. M. Minor (1990, September). Changes in developing country regimes for foreign direct investment. *Essays in International Business, 8*, 30–31.

10. L. Xiaoying & L. Xiaming (2005). Foreign direct investment and economic growth: An increasingly endogenous relationship. *World Development, 33*(3), 393–408.

11. D. Encarnation & L. T. Wells Jr. (1985). Sovereignty en garde: Negotiating with foreign investors. *International Organization, 39*, 47–78.

12. D. J. Lecraw & A. J. Morrison (1991, September). Transnational corporation-host country relations: A framework for analysis. *Essays in International Business, 9*, 29.

13. S. Urata (2002). Globalization and the growth of free trade agreements. *Asia-Pacific Review, 9*, 20–33.

14. K. Thomas (2003). Geographic scales and the competition for economic growth. *American Behavioral Scientist, 46*(8), 15–17.

15. S. Lall & R. Narula (2004). Foreign direct investment and its role in economic development: Do we need a new agenda? *European Journal of Development Research, 16*(3), 447–465.

16. L. Mytelka & L. A. Barclay (2004). Using foreign investment strategically for innovation. *European Journal of Development Research, 16*(3), 531–561.

17. G. P. Zachary (1998, March 25). Dual citizenship is double-edged sword. *Wall Street Journal*, pp. B1, B2.

18. E. Thornton (2001, November 15). Remaking Nissan. *Business Week*, 70–76.

19. B. Saporito (2005, April 18). Howard Stringer. *Time, 165*(16), 73–74.

20. H. French (2000). *Vanishing borders*. New York: W. W. Norton.

21. L. Hoper & M. W. Miller (1992, July 13). IBM, Toshiba, Siemens form venture to develop DRAMs for next century. *Wall Street Journal*, p. B7.

22. E. Tanouye & R. Langreth (1998, February 2). Genetic giant: Cost of drug research is driving merger talks of Glaxo, Smith Kline. *Wall Street Journal*, pp. A1, A8.

23. A. M. Squeo & D. Michaels (2002, July 22). Joint efforts: U.S. woos allies with unique deal on new fighter jet.*Wall Street Journal*, pp. A1, A10.

24. A. Qureshi (1996). Globalization: New opportunities, tough challenges. *Finance and Development, 33*(1), 30–33.

25. K. M. McGowan (1997). The effects of trade liberalization on consumer in flow, choice alternatives and redress. *Consumer Interests Annual, 43*, 183–185.

26. D. Ernst (2002, May). Digital information systems and global flagship network: How mobile is knowledge in the global network economy. Working page No. 48, East-West Center, Honolulu, Hawaii.

27. S. Ostry (1992). The domestic domain: The new international policy arena. *Transnational Corporation, 1*(1), 9.

28. C. Karmin (2001, August 20). What in the world? Global shares may leave obscurity. *Wall Street Journal*, p. C1.

29. J. W. Overby & S. H. Min (2001). International supply chain management in an Internet environment: A network-oriented approach to internationalization. *International Marketing Review, 8*(4), 392–419.

30. G. S. Yip (2003). *Total global strategy.* Upper Saddle River, NJ: Prentice Hall.

31. K. Fatehi (1994). Capital flight from Latin America as a barometer of political instability. *Journal of Business Research, 30*(2), 187–195.

32. K. Fatehi & M. H. Safizadeh (1994). The effect of sociopolitical instability on the flow of different types of foreign direct investment. *Journal of Business Research, 31*(1), 65–73.

33. J. Giermanski (2006). Boxing clever. *Cargo Security International, February–March,* 40–44.

34. G. Hitt & S. Ellison (2006, March 9). Dubai firm bows to public outcry. *Wall Street Journal,* p. 1.

35. P. Tucker (2006). Redefining national security. *Futurist, 40*(2), 6–7.

36. Doing business in dangerous places (2004, August). *The Economist, 372,* 11.

37. K. G. Busch & S. H. Weissman (2005). The intelligence community and the war on terror: The role of behavioral science. *Behavioral Science and the Law, 23,* 559–571.

38. Y. Aharoni (1966). *The foreign investment decision process.* Boston: Harvard Business School.

39. S. H. Hymer (1976). *The international operations of national firms: A study of direct investment.* Cambridge: MIT Press.

40. P. J. Buckely & M. Casson (1976). *The future of multinational enterprise.* New York: Holmes & Meier.

41. R. Vernon (1980). Gone are the cash cows of yesteryear. *Harvard Business Review, November/December,* 150–155.

42. C. M. Watson (1982). Counter competition abroad to protect home markets. *Harvard Business Review, January/February,* 40.

43. R. Vernon (1966). International investment and international trade in the product cycle. *Quarterly Journal of Economics, 80*(2), 190–207.

44. N. J. Adler & F. Ghadar (1990). International strategy from the perspective of people and culture: The North American context. In A. M. Rugaman (Ed.), *International business research for the twenty-first century* (pp. 179–205). Greenwich, CT: JAI Press.

45. P. W. Beamish, J. P. Killing, D. J. Lecraw, & H. Crookell (1991). *International management* (pp. 3–6). Homewood, IL: R. D. Irwin.

46. W. J. Holstein & K. Kelly (1992, April 13). Little companies, big exports. *Business Week,* 70–72.

47. C. J. Chipello (1992, July 7). Small U.S. companies take the plunge into Japan's market. *Wall Street Journal,* p. B1.

48. B. M. Richman & M. Copen (1972). *International management and economic development.* New York: McGraw-Hill.

49. D. Hammond (2001, May 31). Dangerous liaisons. *People Management,* pp. 24–29.

50. K. E. Klein (2005, May 12). Big concerns of small business. *BusinessWeek.* Retrieved July 9, 2005, from www.businessweek.com/magazine/content/05_12/html

51. A. J. Ali & N. Prashanth (2002). The virtue of the liberating spirit: Positive response to violence and terrorism. *Competitive Review, 12*(1), i–iv.

52. T. Addison & M. S. Mansoob (2005). Transnational terrorism as a spillover of domestic dispute in other countries. *Defense and Peace Economics, 16*(2), 14–18.

53. P. Ghemawat (2001). Distance still matters. *Harvard Business Review, September,* 137–147.

54. H. V. Perlmutter (1969). The tortuous evolution of the multinational corporation. *Columbia Journal of World Business, January–February,* 9–18.

55. B. L. Kedia & A. Mukherji (1999). Global managers: Developing a mindset for global competitiveness. *Journal of World Business, 34*(3), 230–251.

56. D. A. Heenan & H. V. Perlmutter (1979). *Multinational organizational development.* Reading, MA: Addison-Wesley.

57. C. A. Bartlett & S. Ghoshal (1992). *Transnational management* (pp. 11–14). Homewood, IL: Richard D. Irwin.

58. R. C. Morias (2000). ABB reenergized. *Harvard Business Review, January,* 47–48.

59. W. Taylor (1992). The logic of global business: An interview with ABB's Percy Barnevik. *Harvard Business Review, March/April,* 92.

60. The regulator who isn't there (2002, May 18). *The Economist,* pp. 12–16.

2

Socio-ethical Issues and International Management

Businesses are expected to be socially responsible and conduct themselves ethically. While there are some emerging agreements, at least in the United States, regarding the social responsibilities of domestic firms, social responsibility and the ethical aspects of international management are being hotly debated. Disagreements arise due to the nature of international business and the different perspectives that nations hold regarding these issues. National priorities and cultural differences confound the problems further. This chapter examines these issues and highlights these differences.

The major topics covered in this chapter are the problems of corruption and bribery and their effect on international management, the ecological aspects of international business, the special concerns of developing countries, the problems of expanding free trade, and the backlash against globalization. In this chapter, we also discuss the role of supranational organizations, such as the World Trade Organization (WTO), the United Nations (UN), the International Monetary Fund (IMF), and the World Bank, in resolving international trade disputes and promoting global prosperity.

Chapter Vignette

Banana Bribes

Chiquita Brands International, formerly the United Brands Company, has a corporate responsibility officer. Its plantations are certified according to the dictates of Rainforest Alliance, a New York–based international conservation organization with a mission to protect the ecosystem and the wildlife and people that live within it. Chiquita has a 6-year, $20 million environmental improvement campaign. It has come a long way from its tainted past. The company has played a huge role in the economics, politics, and natural environment of Central America for a century. According to the news media, United Brands used bribery to get favorable terms, disregarded the natural environment, fomented wars, and helped overthrow governments to increase its profits.

It was in the mid-1970s that the major misdeeds of United Brands were made public. In 1974, when an attempt was made by the seven banana-producing countries to increase the price of exported bananas, the company reacted surreptitiously. The participating countries were Colombia, Costa Rica, Ecuador, Guatemala, Honduras, Nicaragua, and Panama. They wanted to establish the Organization of Banana Exporting Countries (OBEC), a banana cartel modeled on the Organization of Petroleum Exporting Counties (OPEC). At that time, banana production and exports were controlled by the big three fruit firms, United Brands Company, Standard Fruit Company, and Del Monte Corporation, and prices had not been increased for nearly 20 years. The objective of the seven countries was to fix the price and curtail the production of exported bananas.

While the attempt failed, each country began imposing its own export tax on bananas. These taxes and the increased labor costs would add nearly $19 million to United Brands's expenses annually. Soon after, United Brands made a secret deal with the Honduran government to reduce the banana tax. In exchange, a payment of $2.5 million was made to the Honduran minister of economy.

It was during the investigation of the Watergate scandal that the story of the bribes and the involvement of top executives of United Brands became public. It was disclosed that in addition to payments to banana-exporting countries, United Brands had paid $750,000 to Italian government officials. Concerns over these bribes and other similar cases of corporate corruption led to the passage of the Foreign Corrupt Practice Act of 1977. A sad note on the misdeeds of United Brands: On February 3, 1975, United Brands's CEO, Eli Black, distressed over the publicity surrounding the payoffs, jumped to his death from his 44th-floor office.[1-4]

Introduction

Corruption, bribery, and the demand for large illegal payoffs are not uncommon in the international marketplace. While some cases of misdeeds receive wide publicity, many others go unnoticed. Besides grand briberies, there is widespread petty corruption perpetuated by functionaries at the lower levels of many government institutions. With the rising volume of international trade and increased interdependencies among nations, corruption and bribery are but two of many socio-ethical issues that international managers have to deal with. Additionally, international managers are faced with many ecological problems stemming from worldwide industrial activities that threaten life on earth.

No other issues are more challenging to international managers than socio-ethical and ecological problems. The complexity and interdependency involved in the operation of multinational corporations (MNCs) spill over into the area of social responsibility as well. While the impact, obligations, and responsibilities of a domestic business are limited to its home environment, those of MNCs cross national boundaries and create a web of interdependent and often conflicting responsibilities that are not easily resolved.

Often, what appears on the surface is far from the actual reality. Each subsidiary, for example, is governed by the laws, customs, norms, and business practices of the host country. As long as a subsidiary is able to operate independently of other subsidiaries, it can meet its minimal legal, ethical, and social responsibilities by observing the local standards. Of course, these standards govern overt behavior, leaving covert behavior to the conscience of the manager. The dilemma that international managers experience stems from the interdependency of MNC operations. Actions and decisions by a subsidiary in one country may have repercussions for the rest of the MNC. Further complications arise from the differences in norms and standards of behavior, in general, and managerial behavior, in particular.

Not only are there no clear answers to most international ethical dilemmas; there are no commonly accepted bases for resolving many of the legal problems of MNCs either. This does not mean that there is no order in international business and that international management operates chaotically. It, however, does mean that for international management there is a wider area of potential misunderstanding, disagreement, and dispute. Recently, much progress has been made in establishing standards and codes of conduct to govern MNCs' operations globally. In what follows, we will review the problem areas and discuss the efforts that could lead to their resolution.

Social Responsibilities of MNCs

The term *corporate social responsibility* refers to the obligations of business organizations toward society. Society allows organizations to operate within certain parameters. These parameters are defined by society and, therefore, may vary across nations. The variations, however, are typically not in substance but in procedures. Business is expected to operate in a manner consistent with society's interests. This is true for all nations and all businesses; MNCs are no exceptions. In the United States, while some believe that the social responsibility of business is limited to the economic sphere, the majority accept that business has noneconomic obligations as well. Although the domain of corporate social responsibility is not very well-defined, there are certain areas of agreement. For instance, in addition to providing employment for people and goods and services to consumers, business is expected to help preserve the environment, sell safe products, treat its employees equitably, and be truthful with its customers. In some cases, business is also expected to train the hardcore unemployed, contribute to education and the arts, and help revitalize urban slum areas (p. 64).[5]

Obviously, there is lack of agreement, even *within* a given society, about what an organization's social responsibilities should be, and even beyond the ambiguities in domestic corporate social responsibility, there are uncertainties regarding the social responsibility of MNCs. The uncertainties are due to the differences in norms and value systems with which the MNCs must deal when they conduct business in different countries, not to mention the variations in political and economic systems that they face. The uncertainty is also partly due to the fact that for domestic businesses, certain implicit and explicit codes of conduct guide managerial decision making, while there is much less guidance in the international arena. Although a few international organizations have issued guidelines for some aspects of MNC activities, other aspects are very much open to the discretion of individual firms. Additionally, unique MNC characteristics are a confounding factor. The operation of an international firm spans the globe and transcends national boundaries. As De George[6] puts it,

A global company internalizes the worldwide division of labor and stands ready to move its operations as necessary to take advantage of lower wages, attractive interest and tax rates, and available resources. Such companies loosen their national roots and identification, and assume a global stance . . . they owe primary allegiance to no particular nation. American workers have no special claim on the jobs such companies make available; and their owners are as likely to be non-American as American. Although we can still speak of Ford, General Motors, IBM, Hewlett-Packard, and Johnson & Johnson as American corporations, the sense in which they are American is becoming more and more tenuous. . . . As the corporate ability to escape national constraints increases, the need for multinational and global restraints becomes more pressing. (pp. 3–4)

And at present, due to the lack of global constraints and guidelines, MNC executives are forced to rely more on personal judgment and corporate policies. Many MNCs develop and publish some sort of social responsibility report, which gives an overview of the social and environmental programs in which they are involved.[7]

While it is very difficult to make any definitive statement on what precisely MNC social responsibility is and how it should be determined, certain positions are emerging. These positions are discussed below.

The Stakeholder Perspective

One way of analyzing MNC social responsibility is the stakeholder approach. Similar to a domestic firm, an MNC has stakeholders, whose prosperity and fortune are directly tied to the operation of the company. Actions taken by the company will have a direct impact on its stakeholders.

The major stakeholders of a typical firm are stockholders, customers, suppliers, creditors, employees, the community within which the firm exists and from which it draws its inputs, and the general public. The firm, be it domestic or international, is answerable to its stakeholders. Each stakeholder expects, and often demands, that the firm satisfy its claim in a responsible manner. Stockholders want higher returns on their investment in the firm. Customers want good-quality products that are worth their money. Suppliers depend on the firm for their continued operation and are interested in a dependable business partner. Creditors want the firm to safeguard their capital with sound business practices. Employees want jobs that are economically and psychologically rewarding and secure. The local community expects the firm to act as a good neighbor and to be a responsible member of the community through its participation and contributions to various civic causes and activities. The general public is interested in the firm's continuous contributions to society as a whole and in its assumption of a fair share of the burden of government and society. The general public also wants the firm to safeguard the ecosystem through environmentally safe business practices.

In addition to the above list, the stakeholders of a typical MNC include the host governments and nongovernmental organizations (NGOs). NGOs expect that MNCs will safeguard the natural environment, act with integrity, be fair to all with whom they deal, help poor countries, respect human rights, apply the same standards of conduct used at home to all other countries, and contribute to the economic development of the host countries. Host governments' demands include increased employment and advancement for locals, a fair share of taxes, transfer of technology, obeying of local laws and respect for local customs and culture, fair competition with local firms, and negotiation of equitable business agreements. Often, these claims are in conflict with one another. Satisfying one claim has an impact on others. Reconciliation of these claims is a difficult task. Table 2.1 summarizes the major expectations and demands of the stakeholders of MNCs.

Table 2.1   Multinational Companies: Stakeholders and Their Major Demands

Stakeholders	Major Demands
Stockholders	Increased profits, return on investment
Customers	Quality and safe products at reasonable costs
Suppliers	Continued good business relationships, prompt payment
Creditors	Ability to pay back debts, profitability, sound business practices
Employees	Higher pay, security, good and safe working conditions, good benefits, opportunity for advancement, no discrimination
The community	Benefits to the community, clean environment, philanthropies, community involvement, good citizenship, respect for local culture
General public	Good citizenship, trustworthiness, clean image
Nongovernmental organizations	Safeguarding the environment, acting with integrity, being fair to all, helping poor countries, applying home country standards abroad, contributing to the development of the host countries, respecting human rights, respecting local culture
Host governments	Employing locals, paying fair share of taxes, contributing to economic development of host country, technology transfer, training local personnel, obeying local laws and customs, competing fairly with local firms, equitable contracts

For those aspects of the business that could reasonably be confined to a single nation, the social responsibilities of an MNC and a local firm are identical. There are, however, many facets of MNC operations for which a single-nation perspective is insufficient. Many business activities of MNCs are not limited to a single country. The impact of these activities spills over national borders. In pursuit of profit, plants are relocated, suppliers are replaced, and resources are reallocated, all of which may benefit one country while causing problems for others. From this perspective, MNC social responsibility is a broader, more complex concept than the social responsibility of a domestic business. The broader concept of an MNC's social responsibility embraces its world citizenship.

The World Corporate Citizen

Kenichi Ohmae[8] tells us that MNCs are operating in a borderless world: "Over the political map, the boundaries between countries are as clear as ever. But on a competitive map, a map showing the real flows of financial and industrial activity, those boundaries have largely disappeared" (p. 8). While local variations in tastes abound, information flow has transformed the people of the world into global citizens: They demand the best, and they buy from whoever provides the best products, be it an American, a British, or a Japanese firm. Supplying goods and services to these global citizens is the task of the increasing numbers of MNCs. These MNCs are "the world corporate citizens." If they owe primary allegiance to no particular country, they owe it to the people of the world and to "Mother Earth."

Ensuring that MNCs fulfill their social responsibility to the world community requires guidelines or a code of conduct, and it also requires some form of regulating and monitoring. Today, there exist no comprehensive guidelines governing the behavior of MNCs, and there is no global institution for monitoring them. Given the complexity of issues involved, it is doubtful that either will be developed soon. The monitoring aspect represents a less pressing problem. At present, national governments are doing this job. However, while developed countries are well equipped to monitor and force compliance, developing countries do not have the infrastructure to do so. In the absence of comprehensive guidelines, there are several institutions, both private and governmental, that have assumed a limited role in dealing with the conduct of MNCs. An exception is the passage of the Tort Claims Act, which extends the jurisdiction of U.S. courts concerning human rights violations by MNCs outside the United States.[9] Guidelines that have been established by these institutions cover many aspects of the conduct of MNCs. These guidelines vary in their specificity and scope, and some essentially express the "ideals" toward which a firm aspires. None contains exclusively or specifically ethical guidelines.[6] Often, compliance with these codes is voluntary or indirect.

Among the institutions that have assumed leadership in promoting ethical conduct and establishing codes and guidelines are the International Chamber of Commerce (ICC), the Organization for Economic Cooperation and Development (OECD), the International Labor Organization (ILO), and the UN Commission on Transnational Corporations (Figure 2.1).

Most nations are members of these institutions. The membership of national governments in these institutions obligates the MNCs to comply with the codes. This is an indirect type of enforcement, since there are no direct measures for ensuring compliance. The codes themselves deal with both the behavior of MNCs and the activities of national governments. The major areas that these codes cover are the relationship between national governments, the public, and the MNCs; environmental protection; consumer protection; employment practices; and human rights. MNCs are morally bound to recognize these codes and consider them in their international activities. The incentive to do so is both moral and economic.[10] Some researchers, among them McGuire, Sundgren, and Schneeweis, for example, have found a positive correlation between socially responsible corporate behavior and profitability.[11]

While we do not have comprehensive guidelines for the conduct of MNCs, some scholars have specified certain kinds of MNC behavior as appropriate for the conduct of business in developing countries.[12] De George has suggested that MNCs should act with integrity in their dealings with the people of the world (Table 2.2). Acting with integrity necessitates taking six steps (Refs. 6, pp. 23–58; 13, 521–523).

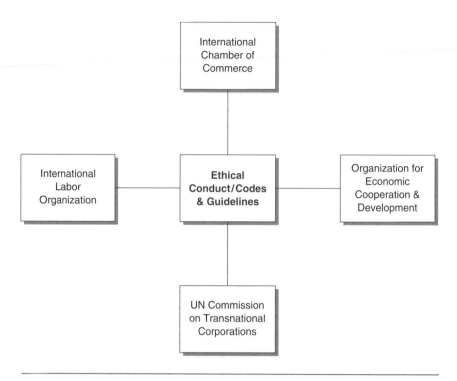

Figure 2.1   Major International Institutions Promoting Ethical Conduct

First, the firm should act in accord with its own self-imposed values, which cannot be less than an ethical minimum but may well exceed it. For example, a firm may neither give nor accept bribes.

Second, in addition to satisfying the basic moral norms applicable everywhere, the firm should uphold other equally obvious moral rules. For example, not only does one not kill a competitor, but one also does not maim or otherwise harm that person.

Third, the firm should enter into business agreements by building on these rules. Business agreements should be fair and should benefit both sides.

Fourth, because developing countries are poor in infrastructure, MNCs have special obligations toward them. We will deal with this aspect of MNC conduct in more detail later.

Fifth, the firm should consider the ethical dimensions of its actions, projects, and plans before acting, not afterward. This means that the ethical dimensions should be an integral part of strategic planning.

Finally, each person should be given his or her due. The firm should be open and receptive to complaints from those affected and address their claims with justice.

Because of its potential impact on the overall corporate performance and long-term survival of the firm, there is an evolving consensus about the fifth step, as De George has suggested. The social responsibility of business

Table 2.2 DeGeorge's Six Steps: Multinational Companies (MNCs) Acting With Integrity in Dealing With the People of the World

Steps/Actions	Examples
First, MNCs should act in accord with their own self-imposed values. This cannot be less than an ethical minimum but may well exceed it.	When abroad, apply the nondiscrimination policies of the home office. Neither give nor accept bribes.
Second, in addition to satisfying the basic moral norms applicable everywhere, other equally obvious moral rules should be upheld.	Do not use unfair business practices and your immense resources to hurt local firms.
Third, the firm should enter into business agreements by building on these rules.	Use integrative methods to negotiate business agreements that are fair and beneficial to both sides.
Fourth, because developing countries are poor in background institutions (e.g., labor unions), MNCs have special obligations toward them.	Assist locals in developing appropriate regulations, establishing nongovernmental institutions and labor unions.
Fifth, the firm should consider the ethical dimensions of its actions, projects, and plans before acting, not afterward. This means that the ethical dimensions should be an integral part of strategic planning.	Establish guidelines for supplier selection so that the pressure for lower costs does not lead to labor abuse by suppliers.
Sixth, each person should be given his or her due.	Be open and receptive to complaints from those affected and address their claims with justice.

SOURCE: Based on References 6 and 13.

should be included in strategic planning. No strategic decision should be made without considering its social responsibility ramifications. These suggestions are echoed by the recommendations and guidelines issued by the OECD, the ILO, and the UN.[14]

To deal with the special case of developing countries, De George[13] suggests seven guidelines (pp. 521–523). These rules are not supposed to form an exhaustive list (see Figure 2.2). Other rules could be added to them. The rules provide the basis for conducting business with developing countries, which do not have infrastructures, institutions, and resources matching those of MNCs. When operating in, and doing business with, developing countries, MNCs should follow these guidelines:

1. They should do no intentional harm. This includes showing respect for the integrity of the local ecosystem and consumer safety.

2. They should do more good than harm for the host country.

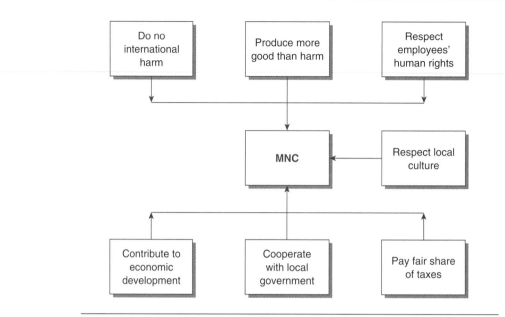

Figure 2.2   Minimum Rules for Multinational Companies (MNCs) Operating in Developing Countries

SOURCE: Reference 13.

3. They should contribute by their activities to the host country's development.

4. They should respect the human rights of their employees.

5. To the extent that local culture does not violate ethical norms, MNCs should respect the local culture and work with and not against it.

6. They should pay their fair share of taxes.

7. They should cooperate with the local government in developing and enforcing just background (infrastructure) institutions (i.e., laws, governmental regulations, unions, and consumer groups, which are means of social control).

By following these rules, an MNC sets a high moral standard and provides a sound basis for mutually beneficial business relationships. Ignoring them negatively affects the MNC for many years. As an example, let us apply these rules to extractive industries in developing countries. Critics have accused MNCs of past and some present exploitation of developing countries. The charges are that the MNCs extract minerals at low costs, pay very low prices, and ship them abroad, where they are sold at handsome profits. Frequently, these raw materials are processed into products that are sold back to developing countries at inflated prices. In this way, these countries are exploited twice: once when their natural resources are bought for a pittance and again when the products made from them are sold back to them at higher prices than those in developed countries, where competition is greater. When applied to extractive industries in developing countries, for example, the first rule obligates MNCs to use environmentally safe extractive methods that preserve natural habitats and do not harm ecosystems. In negotiations for exploration and mining rights, MNCs should not take advantage of the lack of administrative capability in developing countries. A contract that does not give the developing country a fair market price for these rights is clearly in violation of Rules 1 and 2 and possibly Rule 3.

Following these rules is not only moral; it is also practical. Consider the case of oil-producing countries before the formation of OPEC. These countries were asserting that they were being exploited by MNCs. The assertion of exploitation was based on the fact that international oil companies were paying about $2 for a barrel of crude oil. According to these countries, their oil was worth much more than the artificially low price of $2 a barrel. The large international oil companies in industrial countries, acting as a cartel, were collectively imposing low prices and conditions for the sale of crude oil instead of negotiating equitable agreements or allowing market forces to prevail. To these oil-exporting countries, the choice was clear: Fight fire with fire. They countered this unfair pricing by the oil companies by forming a cartel of their own and hiking the prices considerably. This sent a shock wave throughout the world and caused much financial difficulty for all. Eventually, however, market forces brought prices to a level lower than what OPEC desired but considerably higher than prior to the formation of OPEC.

Problem Areas

The most pressing social responsibility and ethics issues arising from the operations of MNCs are the ecological impact of industrial operations, along with bribery and corruption (Table 2.3). These issues are concerns of all nations, and their resolution requires worldwide cooperation by national governments. International cooperation is also needed for the resolution of other major problems. These include the exploitation of global commons,[a] free trade, and the special concerns of developing countries.

Ecological Concerns

The most pressing and thorny international management problem is the ecological impact of industrialization around the globe. All modern industries affect the environment to some degree. For generations, industrialization has taken place without much concern for its environmental consequences.

Table 2.3   Major Social and Ethical Issues Arising From the Operations of Multinational Corporations (MNCs)

Ecological impact of industrial operations

Deforestation
Desertification
Pollution
Poverty resulting from environmental degradation

The use of global commons

The oceans
Outer space
Antarctica

Bribery and corruption

Whitemail bribe
Lubrication bribe

The issue of free trade

Industrialization can be viewed as occurring in two waves. The first wave of industrialization concerned itself only with economic development. The developed countries of today, the first group of nations to industrialize, either were not completely aware of the negative impact of industrialization on the environment or considered the impact so negligible that they were not much worried about the consequences. Either way, the course of industrialization continued unabated with minimal concern for the environment. But after decades of industrialization and economic development, the resulting adverse environmental impact is very much evident.

It appears that at the beginning of the 20th century, population growth and technology had minimal impact on planet Earth. Today, the vastly increased population and expanded industrialization are threatening the earth's fragile ecosystem. Major, unintended changes are occurring around us. Human activities are radically disturbing the symbiotic relationship between the atmosphere, soil, water, plants, and animals. Desertification, deforestation, pollution, and the poverty associated with environmental degradation are posing life-threatening problems to developing countries. The disappearance of rain forests in the tropics, the loss of plant and animal species, and changes in rainfall patterns are disasters for the entire human race and for life on earth. An increase in toxic chemicals, toxic wastes, and acidification is creating life-threatening challenges to industrial nations. Regardless of their level of economic development and geographical location, all nations suffer from the release of carbon dioxide and other gases into the atmosphere due to industrialization. These fumes react with the ozone layer and may produce irreversible damage to the ecosystem (p. 22).[15]

Effects on the Ecosystem

To protect the environment and people from the unintended consequences of industrialization, the developed countries, and particularly the United States, have established numerous regulations and enacted specific "environmental" legislation. The U.S. Environmental Protection Agency (EPA) has used antipollution requirements, clean air and water standards, hazardous waste disposal guidelines, and even free-market forces, to cite just a few measures, to combat pollution. (A market-oriented solution to the problem of acid rain and the trading of pollution permits has contributed to a significant drop in sulfur dioxide emissions from major polluters).[16] Although these measures are useful, they are not sufficient to halt the deterioration of the environment. In developing countries, the story of environmental protection is quite different. Developing countries have neither the administrative sophistication to establish similar protective measures nor the resources to monitor compliance with those measures. Many people in developing countries are not well-informed about the health and ecological consequences of modern industries. The ignorance of the general population and the unpreparedness of their governments mean that the potential for exploitation by the unscrupulous is large.

Today, because of increased knowledge concerning the environmental impact of industrialization, there are worldwide pressures and demands to curb the damage to the environment. The second wave of industrialization, occurring now with the industrialization of developing countries, is faced with these demands. Developing countries that are beginning to industrialize are expected not to follow the practices of the past, which were employed by the present developed countries. They are expected to use methods that are much more environmentally friendly. Of course, the use of these methods has a price. Many of the methods that are ecologically oriented require more investment in technology and equipment than developing countries can afford. The more urgent needs of these nations are eradication of widespread disease and poverty, employment, education, and development of infrastructure. Without economic development, at a cost they can afford, ecological issues may not receive proper attention. Ecological matters are luxuries beyond the reach of these nations. The irony is that the careless exploitation of natural resources, which is less expensive, may harm the environment and deplete natural resources in such a way that it results in further impoverishment. This point has not been lost on world leaders, who, in 1992, convened the Rio conference called the Earth Summit. They called for sustainable development in which the special needs of developing countries are considered. The conference acknowledged that these countries are environmentally vulnerable and, therefore, deserve special priority in terms of international assistance.

Before the Earth Summit was convened, the World Commission on Environment and Development,[15] set up by the UN to address the major challenges of the world community on environmental issues, asserted that ecology and economy are becoming ever more interwoven—locally, regionally, nationally, and globally—into a seamless net of causes and effects. . . . Over the past few decades, life-threatening environmental concerns have surfaced in the developing world. Countrysides are coming under pressure from increasing numbers of farmers and the landless. Cities are filling with people, cars, and factories. . . . Dryland degradation sends environmental refugees in their millions across national borders. Deforestation in Latin America and Asia is causing more floods, and more destructive floods, in downhill, downstream nations. Acid precipitation and nuclear fallout have spread across the borders of Europe. Similar phenomena are emerging on a global scale, such as global warming and loss of ozone. . . .

The recent crisis in Africa best and most tragically illustrates the ways in which economics and ecology can interact destructively and trip into disaster. Triggered by drought, its real causes lie deeper. They are to be found in part in national policies that gave too little attention, too late, to the needs of smallholder agriculture and to the threats posed by rapidly rising populations. Their roots extend also to a global economic system that takes more out of a poor continent than it puts in. Debts that they cannot pay force African nations relying on commodity sales to overuse their fragile soils, thus turning good land to desert. (p. 5)

No matter where it takes place, environmental damage resulting from industrialization and abuse of nature are harmful to all of us. We all live on the same planet, breathe the same air, and drink the same water. Poorly regulated imports, for example, can bring to developed countries contaminated agricultural products grown with harmful chemicals, which are sold in developing countries by firms who take advantage of their less stringent or nonexistent environmental regulations. Pollution in both developed and developing countries becomes the world's problem.

Some MNCs have established manufacturing facilities in developing counties that have more lenient, or are totally lacking in, environmental regulations. Since they are not required to abide by the stringent requirements that are common in many industrialized nations, most of these facilities are operating at lower costs. Others have used developing nations as dumping grounds for hazardous materials that are generated in their home countries. These practices may initially save some money, but considering the associated ecological and human costs, ultimately they are indeed quite expensive. A glaring example was the Bhopal factory, a subsidiary of Union Carbide in India, and the infamous accident that cost thousands of Indian lives. While Bhopal-type accidents are exceptional and isolated violations, when they happen, the resultant tragedies underline the fragility of the ecosystem.

Compared with isolated, grand incidents of abuse by unscrupulous MNCs, environmental damage resulting from poverty, overpopulation, and ignorance is widespread, and its impact on the environment is very severe.

Poor countries can barely feed their people, let alone worry about protecting the environment. Their ecological problems, however, do not remain localized. We are all affected by them.

Inattention to the environment, in the long run, is a luxury that not only poor countries but all of us cannot afford. Nevertheless, the fact remains that wealth and efficient use of natural resources go together. Below a certain level of earnings, people will be concerned only with short-term survival and postpone the issues of their long-term welfare. Therefore, economic growth is needed to combat poverty. "A world in which poverty is endemic will always be prone to ecological and other catastrophes" (p. 8).[15] But in the long run, unrestrained growth that harms the environment would be a self-defeating endeavor. What is needed is sustainable development that preserves "natural capital." Air, water, and other ecological treasures are natural capital that we have to preserve for ourselves and future generations. Sustainable development balances human activity with nature's ability for renewal.

To practice sustainable development, developing countries need assistance from the rich countries and MNCs. Huge investments are needed to protect ocean resources, promote sustainable agricultural practices, control toxic wastes, and reduce adverse impacts on the climate (greenhouse effect and loss of the ozone layer). Developing countries need a huge amount of money annually to implement the recommendations of the Earth Summit.[17] These countries not only need capital for sustainable development; they also need information and transfer of technology to achieve and manage such development. MNCs are in the best position to do this and have a special responsibility to provide the assistance needed:

> Multinational companies can play an important role in sustainable development, especially as developing countries come to rely more on foreign equity capital. But if these companies are to have a positive influence on development, the negotiating capacity of developing countries vis-a-vis transnationals (MNCs) must be strengthened so they can secure terms that respect their environmental concerns.[15] (p. 18)

Of course, MNCs cannot be relied on to provide the required negotiating capacity to developing countries. This is where the UN and other supranational, not-for-profit organizations can be, and traditionally have been, very helpful. The convergence of political and technological changes has created rules, actors, institutions, and expectations that are new, permanent, and global.[18]

In recent years, NGOs such as Greenpeace, Human Rights Watch, and Friends of the Earth have been instrumental in forcing MNCs to act more responsibly. Using the Internet and public media, NGOs have exposed the activities of MNCs in developing countries. They have been successful in pressuring MNCs to be more cautious in dealing with developing countries and to be mindful of the effect of their activities on the environment and the local people.[19] To construct an oil pipeline from the central African country of Chad across Cameroon, for example, NGOs were instrumental in persuading Exxon to make a complex four-way agreement with the host governments, activists, and the World Bank. As part of this agreement, Exxon built schools, funded health clinics, dug water wells, advised entrepreneurs, provided health services and advice to the locals, and observed local traditions and cultural norms along its construction routes. As part of this agreement and to alleviate poverty, the World Bank lent $93 million to the governments of Chad and Cameroon, enabling them to participate as equity investors in the project. The government of Chad passed a law to hold 10% of the oil revenues in a trust fund for future generations. The bulk of the remainder is earmarked for education, health, and rural development. Also, some funds go to the oil-producing regions.[20] Similarly, after a group of women occupied the Chevron facility in Nigeria for 10 days and brought its operations to a standstill, it was forced to reach a settlement with them. The agreement included more jobs for the locals and spending on infrastructure.[21]

One area where MNCs can contribute is transfer of technology. Through technology transfer, MNCs can provide developing countries with the necessary knowledge and capability for using environmentally sound production methods. If practiced properly, such a technology transfer could be mutually beneficial. Many case examples attest to the practicality and profit potential of the transfer of technology that is environmentally friendly. In Poland in the 1990s, for example, mining operations employed 700,000 people, and coal exports constituted 10% of hard currency revenues. Coal also accounted for 90% of domestic energy consumption. The operation of its mines, however, was polluting the Polish rivers and causing serious ecological harm. The Axel Johnson Group of Stockholm, Sweden, a worldwide trading, distribution, and retailing firm, supplied the Polish mines with antipollution technology. A total investment of $60 million provided a consortium of Polish companies with the necessary technology, including water purification and desalination equipment. The treatment of dirty saltwater produces freshwater and salt, both of which are sold commercially. The technology not only eliminated water pollution but also could generate nearly $9 million in additional revenues.[22]

The Use of Global Commons

Developing countries have long complained about their relationship with developed countries. They assert that the relationship is more favorable to developed countries. They feel that rich nations are taking advantage of their lack of technological sophistication. Developing countries claim that not only are their natural resources being exploited to the benefit of industrialized countries, but also the "global commons" are exploited disproportionately by MNCs from rich nations. The global commons most in contention are the oceans, outer space, and Antarctica. At present, the ability to exploit these resources is limited to the MNCs from developed countries. As more nations industrialize and develop technological capabilities, the rate of exploitation will increase. The consequences of unrestricted exploitation of these resources can be disastrous.

The Oceans.

> In the Earth's wheel of life, the oceans provide the balance. . . . they play a critical role in maintaining its life-support systems, in moderating its climate, and in sustaining animals and plants. . . . The oceans also provide the ultimate sink for the by-products of human activities. Huge closed septic tanks, they receive wastes from cities, farms, and industries.[15] (p. 262)

We have to devise ways of protecting the oceans from excessive contamination and abuse. The rich fishing areas and the large deposits of minerals under the seas are the subject of many conflicts among nations. Many of these minerals are far from the limits of territorial waters. Without an international ecosystem approach to protecting the oceans from excessive exploitation, contamination and abuse may endanger life as we know it on earth. Excessive fishing in the North Atlantic, for example, has reduced the catch of tuna, haddock, flounder, and other desirable fish by more than half. If fishing continues at this rate, these fish could disappear.[23] As certain fish species are depleted, frequent fishing disputes and clashes between nations are not uncommon. Tensions and disputes develop not only between neighboring nations, such as the United States and Canada, but also between nations that are far apart, such as Japan, Norway, Chile, Spain, and Denmark, over fishing in or near territorial waters.[24,25]

Many nations claim 3-mile coastal territorial waters and do not allow outsiders within that limit. Some have adopted a 200-mile Exclusive Economic Zone (EEZ). The 1982 UN Convention on the Law of the Sea has given this expanded territorial zone its blessing. Many undersea mineral deposits, however, fall outside the expanded 200-mile territorial waters. Until there is an international agreement for mining the seabeds, disputes and disagreements will arise. Who owns this wealth? How should it be tapped? At what rate should the ocean floor wealth be exploited? The UN Convention on the Law of the Sea has a provision for creating an International Seabed Authority. The authority would control all mining activities in seabeds beyond the 200-mile EEZs. This is the most ambitious attempt ever to provide an internationally agreed-on regime for the management of the oceans and to prevent overexploitation. Many countries have signed the convention, but not all have ratified it. A small number of nations have indicated that they are unlikely to ratify it. Without an international treaty, overexploitation and life-threatening abuse of the oceans may continue (pp. 273–274).[15]

At present, capital requirements and technological barriers limit the exploitation of the oceans. Today, only a few nations have the technology and resources to exploit deep-sea minerals. In 1994, for example, the Shell oil company successfully drilled an oil well in the Auger field, at a water depth of 2,860 ft, 137 miles south of Louisiana's shoreline. Not too many companies can match the technological sophistication and the capital needed for such an operation. Deepwater drilling is not cheap. The Auger platform cost some $780 million and involved the labor of 740 American companies and 33 foreign contractors. The deck is the size of two football fields and weighs about 23,000 tons. It houses 132 workers and supervisors in a five-story dormitory.[26]

While today only a few companies and fewer nations can accomplish what the Shell company is doing, this exclusivity will not last long. As more nations join the ranks of industrialized countries, they may participate in the exploitation of natural resources beyond their own territories. At that time, MNCs' operations may not go uncontested. Without international treaties regulating exploration and exploitation of deep-sea minerals and fishing, simple problems could easily develop into a full-scale conflict. An example is East Timor's attempt to enforce control over the 200-mile territorial waters where Royal Dutch/Shell Oil Group and Phillips Petroleum Company are developing two oil and gas fields. This has created a dilemma for these companies, which had negotiated contracts with Australia before East Timor separated from Indonesia in 1999 and became an independent country.[27]

A few years ago, another interesting conflict arose in the South Pacific. Similar to the United States and some other countries, the island nations of Solomon, Kiribati, and Vanuatu have all claimed EEZs of 200 miles around their coasts. This is mainly to protect the tuna fish in their coastal waters. Tuna fish is to them what oil is to Saudi Arabia. It is a major natural resource. However, these countries do not have navies to protect their coasts. This fact has not gone unnoticed by fishing vessels from other countries, and they often fish around these islands with impunity. The country that these islanders are most bitter about is the United States. Americans have long fished in the Pacific coastal waters and see no reason to stop. A few years ago, an American fishing vessel was spotted by a light aircraft flying around the Solomon Islands' exclusive zone. Unconcerned about its violation, the vessel continued fishing, fully aware that there was no force to stop it. Coincidentally, a privately owned Australian patrol boat was in the Solomon Islands on a sales demonstration tour. Tallyho! The Solomon Islands' crew of armed police on the Australian boat arrested the astonished U.S. "pirate." The Solomon Islands fined the owner and impounded the boat. In retaliation, the United States stopped importing Solomon Islands fish, a major part of its export trade. The American sanction infuriated the Solomon Islands. Eventually, a compromise was reached whereby the fishing vessel was sold back to its original owner for $700,000 and the U.S. trade sanction was lifted.[28]

Outer Space. Telecommunications and the use of space are other areas of contention between the rich and poor countries. As new technologies are

developed, international management will have to deal with additional difficulties. Radio frequencies and space are becoming crowded. Every day, a
new satellite is launched into space to orbit the earth. These satellites are
used for various purposes, from weather forecasting to crop estimation
to telecommunication. In particular, the geostationary orbit 22,300 miles
above the equator is a hotly contested property in space. Competition for
available positions and frequencies in space is resulting in resentment on
earth. Most of the satellites belong to the Western world, Russia, and Japan.
Except for a few nations, developing countries have no satellites, and many
fear that the geostationary orbit will be crowded by the time they have the
technology or the money to launch them. A satellite in the geostationary orbit
travels at the earth's rotational speed and, therefore, is a fixed target for
radio signals. At a lower or higher orbit, satellites go faster or slower than
the rotational speed of the earth. The physical position is not as important
as the frequencies used by these satellites. Overlapping and garbling of radio
beams carrying messages to and from the earth can happen in crowded locations. Every country is interested in positioning satellites in the geostationary orbit. The question is on what basis the orbital positions and frequencies
should be allocated. Developed countries favor the first-come-first-served
basis, while developing countries would like rationing of the available frequencies and orbital positions.[29]

Antarctica. Antarctica is a desolate and inhospitable place. Extreme cold
and heavy winds create a very hostile environment for life. Antarctica's
temperature can reach below −88 °C (−126 °F). Winds of up to 200 miles
per hour create extremely dangerous conditions. It has a very harsh environment, where a person without protective gear can freeze to death in a
few moments.

Except for a few bird species, especially the penguins, and a few scientific expeditions, no one would dare venture into this frigid land. Yet there
are global ownership disputes over Antarctica. Seven nations—namely,
Argentina, Australia, Chile, France, Great Britain, Norway, and New
Zealand—have made territorial claims on Antarctica. These claims, however, are not recognized by other nations.

Because of the extreme cold and its isolation from the rest of the world,
Antarctica's geological composition is not well-known. It is believed, however,
that it has large deposits of minerals. Coal and iron deposits are estimated to
be large enough to be worth commercial exploitation. Antarctica's continental
shelf may contain large deposits of oil and natural gas. The waters surrounding Antarctica support rich marine life, including krill, a tiny shrimplike animal. Large numbers of whales around Antarctica feed on these creatures.

Scientific and commercial interest in Antarctica has prompted many
debates. Since 1959, it has been managed under the Antarctic Treaty, which
was signed by representatives of 12 nations in Washington, D.C. The treaty
dedicated the entire continent to scientific and peaceful uses. It suspended all

territorial claims. In 1991, a protocol to the treaty was approved by 24 nations, prohibiting exploration for oil and other minerals for at least 50 years. The treaty is open to all nations who can demonstrate concrete interest in Antarctica by conducting substantial scientific research.

The present arrangement and the treaty on Antarctica are considered unacceptable by many developing countries. Many developing countries lack the resources and technology to participate in the scientific exploration of Antarctica. While the treaty's signatories claim to manage the continent in the interest of all people, developing countries assert that these interests should not be defined by self-appointed parties. It is, however, highly unlikely that we will see the commercialization of Antarctica any time soon. Legal ambiguities and technological barriers, not to mention the enormous investment needed, make commercial endeavors close to impossible at the present time.

Bribery and Corruption

Often, in the course of doing business and carrying out normal daily transactions abroad, there is no escaping from encounters with bribery and corruption. Bribery and corruption are commonplace when doing business in many places. No geographic location or country has a hold on corruption. Business and political scandals in the United States, Europe, and Japan are testimony to this fact. The practice, however, is pervasive in some countries. Publicity around illicit payments by U.S.-based MNCs in the mid-1970s culminated in the passage of the Foreign Corrupt Practices Act of 1977 (FCPA). When the act was passed, the legislators expected that other nations would follow suit. They did not. Research indicates that the act has weakened the competitive position of U.S. companies and has not reduced bribery in international business deals. The political scandal of the early 1990s in Japan and the illegal practices of some large companies such as Enron[30] may give the impression that corruption is on the rise. In reality, business and government practices have never been so closely monitored by the people and the media. It follows, therefore, that corruption probably is on the wane. Certainly, a reading of the history of the world provides some encouraging notes that our time is not unique in the course of civilization. Polybius, the Greek historian living in the 2nd century BC, summarized Carthage's decline in a single sentence: "At Carthage, nothing that results in profit is regarded as disgraceful." During the Renaissance, corruption was rampant, and business historian Jacob van Kalveren suggested that 16th- and 17th-century Europe should be characterized not as the age of mercantilism but as the age of corruption.[31]

Besides its harmful effect on the moral fabric of society, corruption has economic costs. The bribes that bureaucrats receive to approve licenses inflate business costs. Tax officials who take bribes and allow incomes to go unreported deprive the national treasuries of significant revenues. Bribery is also responsible for depressed investment and economic growth.[32] It is estimated, for example, that fewer than half of the taxes due are collected in Argentina, and 28% of economic activities are not reported. By some accounts, one reason for the government's inability to balance the budget has been this rampant corruption.[33] Government officials who purchase expensive equipment with foreign aid money to receive a kickback from the seller divert resources from useful projects into useless ones. Additionally, corruption has a negative effect on foreign direct investment. Studies indicate that foreign investors generally avoid corrupt markets because corruption is considered morally wrong and, economically, it creates operational inefficiencies.[34] The real cost of corruption must also include the loss of confidence in the system and the stifling of entrepreneurial initiatives. The cost of bribes and illegal payments, for example, has been estimated to be 3% to 5% in China. In Italy, it is estimated that corruption has inflated the total outstanding government debt by as much as 15%. A few years ago, the Chinese government reported that state assets had fallen by more than $50 billion in value. They attributed this primarily to deliberate undervaluation by corrupt officials, who were trading off big properties to private interests or to overseas investors for payoffs.[35]

How to Deal With Petty Extortionists

Here is some advice from an international traveler who would gladly spend $100 to avoid paying a $20 bribe—if there is a chance of succeeding. In some situations, there are no ways to avoid making illicit payments short of abandoning whatever you were trying to do. For example, if you want to leave the West Central African country of Cameroon, the choice is to give the border guard the $20 he demands or else stay in Cameroon for God knows how long.

If you are going to pay the illicit money they demand of you, do it right. Never admit it is a bribe. Say you understand that your case requires additional efforts on the part of the official and you are willing to pay a fee for the extra work.

Do not be afraid to haggle and bargain. If you bargain, you often wind up paying less than what was initially demanded.

Never be rude and insult the functionaries, even though this may make you feel better. You may be arrested for that and end up paying much more, not to mention the time lost in the process.

Under the right circumstances, ask for a receipt. This may scare the extortionists and expedite your case. Otherwise, back home you could present the receipt to their consulate and demand a refund. Be ready to have a good laugh anyhow if your receipt turns out to be like the one the international traveler got from a Chinese policeman, written in Chinese. Back in the United States it was translated to mean "stick it in your ear" (adapted from Jim Rogers's advice to Stratford Sherman, which appeared in Ref. 36).

There are two types of bribes: the whitemail bribe and the lubrication bribe or "speed money." The lubrication bribe is paid to facilitate the process of normal bureaucratic functioning, such as the processing of a visa, clearing of import papers, or issuing of a driver's license. It does not involve any act that is not allowed by law. It is facilitation money and is given in situations where delay could disrupt normal business functions and, therefore, be costly. The lubrication bribe has been almost institutionalized in some developing countries. Even the FCPA does not prohibit it.[37]

Everybody does it and everyone expects it. It is referred to in various parts of the world by various terms. In West Africa, it is *dash*; in Mexico, *mordida* (the bite); in Honduras, *pajada* (a piece of the action); in Brazil, *jeitinho* (the fix); in some former British colonies in Asia, *kumshaw* (thank you); and in the Middle East, *bakhshesh* or *an-aam* (gift).

While lubrication money is paid to low-level bureaucrats, the whitemail bribe is elicited by high-level government officials. There are also other differences between the two types of bribes. The differences are in the method, the amount of payment, and the outcome.

Lubrication money is a relatively small amount, and transactions take place directly between the client and the functionary for the purpose of starting the bureaucratic wheel rolling. Except for the payment, it involves no illegal act.

The whitemail bribe involves large amounts of money and generally includes an elaborate system for concealing it. The recipients of whitemail are high-level government officials, and often, it involves illegal transactions. Because of their illegality, the MNCs making these payments hide them with false accounting, fictitious bookkeeping entries, and bogus documentation. Sometimes payments are funneled through subsidiaries abroad, as consulting fees. In other cases—for example, in Italy and South Korea—these payments take the form of contributions to political parties. Often, the whitemail bribe takes place with the assistance of a go-between, who acts in other capacities too and helps bridge the cultural gap. As Nehmkis suggested, if the Middle East's intermediaries didn't exist, they would have to be invented. For Western business executives, the intermediaries are useful in many ways: They overcome the formidable language barriers and facilitate getting access into the power centers. Many Middle East rulers are still suspicious of, and uneasy with, financial and business transactions with foreigners. Moreover, in the Middle East, the networks of powerful families are the repositories of economic, financial, and political intelligence. The West does not have an equivalent system with which to compare them. Those with connections with these powerful families can provide a sense of confidence for the organizations that deal with foreigners.

Evidence suggests that MNCs are both victims and culprits when it comes to corruption.

Corporate Taxes: Italian Style

A leading American bank opened a subsidiary in a major Italian city. At the end of the first year of operation, the firm's local lawyers and tax accountants advised the bank to file its tax return "Italian style," meaning to understate its actual profit significantly. The American general manager of the bank, who was in his first assignment abroad, refused to do so, because he considered it dishonest and unacceptable. A few months after filing its "American-style" tax return, the bank was invited to discuss its taxes with Italian tax authorities. They suggested that the bank's taxes were at least three times higher. It is a customary practice that Italian corporations understate their profits by anywhere between 30% and 70%. Italian tax authorities, aware of this practice, usually assess taxes owed by the corporations based on what they assume the actual earnings should be. Of course, this amount is open to negotiation, which opens up room for the work of tax negotiation agents called *commercialista*. The *commercialista*'s fee, a lump sum known as the *bustarella*, is included in the payment to the government. Corporations never learn how much of the money paid was *bustarella* and how much of it was the fee. The total amount, however, is a deductible expense on the firm's tax return for the next year.

SOURCE: Adapted from Reference 38.

MNC executives should take certain steps to combat bribery and corruption. The first recommendation is to flatly reject the practice of bribery. Indulging in bribery has a corrosive effect on the business and the people. In response to suggestions and demands for illegal payments, you could say that you have a great respect for your counterpart but you risk prosecution under the law if you pay. When a West African minister, for example, during a break in a negotiation session, poetically told a U.S. executive that the minister was "the first tree in the forest and needed water," the American replied in friendly but blunt terms, "If I pay you, I will go to jail." Considering the personal relationship they had developed during the negotiations, the official certainly would not have wanted to see that happen (pp. 101–102).[39] If you are asked to do something that violates your moral beliefs or your company's code of ethics or that is against the law, do not do it. There is an advantage in gaining a reputation as a person who will not make moral compromises.

Sometimes, it is possible to please government officials with worthy community projects instead of a bribe. Building a school, a road, or a sports facility for the youth, for which a bureaucrat can take the credit, could go a long way in securing a government contract that otherwise would have been denied. Finally, keep in mind that in many cultures, gifts and payments are an essential part of building relationships between persons and groups. To reject abruptly and moralistically any suggested request for a gift may be interpreted as a rejection of the relationship that the other side considers necessary for doing business with you (p. 101).[39] As De George reminds us, "Basic morality does not vary from country to country, even though certain practices may be ethical in one country and not in another because of differing circumstances. Getting this subtle difference straight is the crux of the matter" (p. 11).[6]

While corruption is widespread internationally, it is more prevalent in developing countries. Why is corruption so rampant in many developing countries? One explanation, of course, is simple human greed and the breakdown of moral values. Some argue that the low salaries of government workers are partly responsible for widespread bribery in most developing countries. Studies have found that corruption is significantly correlated to GNP per capita.[40] While no two nations are similar, poor countries that pay subsistence-level salaries to government bureaucrats are sowing the seeds of corruption. Without sufficient income, when opportunities for generating additional money arise, not too many functionaries can resist the temptation. This is especially the case in many developing countries, where people make a distinction between morality and the law. In their view, delaying paperwork for a wealthy foreign company so as to extract a fee may be illegal, but it is not an evil act. Another explanation takes into account cultural differences and value orientations. What one culture considers a normal facilitation of a business transaction, another may call a bribe.

Many issues that make sense in one culture, when viewed through a different cultural perspective, would appear inappropriate and sometimes even wrong. The following anecdote vividly illustrates the cultural differences regarding ethical concerns:

> The cannibal was having a conversation with an educated and sophisticated man from the Western world. The Westerner asked him, "how exactly do you go about finding your food?" "When we run out of food," answered the cannibal, "we declare war on a neighboring tribe. We kill as many people as we want, bring them back and eat them. How about you? I heard that there was a huge war in your part of the world a few years ago. How many did you kill?" Visibly embarrassed, the Westerner said, "Millions." "Wow!" the cannibal could not hide his surprise. "And did you eat them all?" "Certainly not! We do not eat people," answered the shocked companion. It was the cannibal's turn to look surprised and confused, even a little disgusted. With a puzzled voice he inquired, "What a waste; why did you kill them in the first place then?"[b]

If bribery were the rule that everyone followed, it would cease to be bribery and instead become a cost of doing a certain kind of business. Tipping in the United States is an example. It is widely and openly practiced. While tipping is customary in the United States, it is considered demeaning and insulting in other countries. Similarly, in some countries, civil servants are known to earn a part of their salaries from the small payments made by clients. These payments ensure better and more timely service. Since Americans do not tip civil servants, it does not mean that others view the practice similarly everywhere. Management theorists widely acknowledge the importance of cultural differences in business, but ethical differences are not fully understood. Researchers have documented, for example, the individualism of Americans and the collectivism of the Japanese or the time sensitivity of the Swiss and the laxity of South Americans but not the differences in ethical issues.[41] The distinction may involve the prevalence of the practice and the openness with which it is followed. Unless the payment is truly a common and open practice, it is ethically questionable.[6] (p. 13)

Lobbying is another example of an action that is sanctioned in one country but frowned on in others. In the United States, lobbying legislators and government agencies is an accepted legal practice. Even foreign countries are involved in lobbying. Some other nations consider it influence peddling and a mislabeling of buying votes and favors. Japan is on the top of the list of countries that spend the most money on lobbying in the United States. Why do the Japanese spend so much money? Some say that they want to tie up the country's talented trade lawyers, making them unavailable for cases that are brought against them. Others say that they take a long view of their relationship with Washington and are well aware that today's lawyer may be tomorrow's senior official.

The Colonial Legacy

They are tall and narrow featured, and during the colonial era . . . [a] minority among the majority Hutu, the Tutsi not only administered Rwanda and neighboring Burundi, but the Germans and, later, the Belgians celebrated them with a kind of Wagnerian romanticism, assuring them the best kind of jobs and favored treatment. . . .

. . . [A]fter the Belgians left Africa and Rwanda began to grapple with the uncertainty and turbulence of majority rule, the Tutsi sinecure unraveled. Tribal uprising among the Hutu singled out the Tutsi for reprisal; hundreds of thousands fled, tens of thousands were massacred. . . . Beyond central Africa, . . . much of the developing world has been struggling for nearly half a century to come to terms with grinding ethnic and tribal rivalries that remain, in a way, one of the most enduring legacies of their colonial past. . . .

(Continued)

(Continued)

> . . . [T]o administer their far-flung holdings, the European powers
> needed locals to rule in their place. . . . In superimposing what in
> some cases was a new hierarchy atop an existing social system, colo-
> nialism gave a new shape and tension to relationships between dif-
> ferent ethnic groups, even if it did not reorder them entirely. . . . In
> some ways, the very tribalism or contemporary ethnic politics in
> northern India or parts of Africa were, at root, European inventions.
> (Excerpted from Ref. 42)

Since they had formerly represented Japan, these officials might be more
sympathetic toward the Japanese views and more inclined to support their
interests. "When you represent the Japanese, and your source of income is
Japanese, your perceptions change," a former Japanese lobbyist noted.[43]

Besides poverty and cultural differences, other reasons have been given
for the rampant corruption in developing countries. Kolde,[44] for example,
has traced the cultural and historical roots of bureaucratic corruption and
bribery in some developing countries to the clashes of cultures and the colonial legacy (pp. 152–153).

Many developing countries were colonies of the West. Kolde asserts
that confused loyalties, weak identification with nationhood, and a lack of
internal cohesion are common to most ex-colonies. In these countries,
tribes were not integrated into nations under the rule of Western powers.
They were kept in tribal minisovereignties. To prevent the formation of
anticolonial coalitions among tribes, intertribe conflicts and rivalries were
fomented and cultivated. When these ex-colonies gained their independence, they lacked the substance of nationhood. The problem was compounded by the fact that the Western powers had ruled indirectly through
native chieftains and community elders. These native leaders were, therefore, viewed by the general population as agents of the colonizing authority. Their traditional authority and legitimacy were weakened in the eyes
of the local people. At the time of independence, the traditional sources of
social order were not in place.

Moreover, Western legal systems that were superimposed on tribal
structures resulted in the breakdown of discipline in indigenous societies. In
these societies, legal technicalities and multitudes of regulations replaced
simple honesty and personal accountability, which in most preindustrial
societies served as the main instruments of order and control. Many of
these regulations were a matter of relabeling and redefining the old practices. If previously witchcraft was sanctioned by the indigenous system as

legitimate, for example, the newly imported law declared it a crime. Gift giving to chiefs and elders, which the natives considered not only right and proper but purifying and sanctifying, was declared as payment of bribes by the imported Western law. Moreover, to deal with the natives, the foreign rulers relied on go-betweens. The go-betweens, while themselves natives, had learned the ways of the rulers and were often the lawyer-translator-opportunists who exploited the ignorance of both the rulers and the ruled.

> When the independence came, the colonial legacy was often a lawyer-ridden bureaucratic system deluged with favoritism and corruption. Highly repugnant to the native population, this colonial inheritance greatly increased the difficulty of building confidence between the new national government and the people. . . . National authorities have had but modest success in restructuring this colonial legacy and in changing public perceptions of government.[44] (p. 152)

The Issue of Free Trade

The premise of expanding international trade is that all participants will benefit from it. To increase international trade, we have to remove the barriers to free trade. To begin to do this, bilateral and multilateral trade agreements have been established. The most important multilateral trade agreements take place under the auspices of the WTO. These agreements are aimed at reducing tariff and nontariff trade barriers.

Free trade and open markets have consequences for domestic industries. Foreign competition forces inefficient domestic businesses out of the market and out of being. This creates displacement of jobs in the host country. In the long run, most analysts believe that the resultant efficiency creates more jobs, but in the short run there will be pockets of unemployment in declining industries. The short-run consequences put pressure on the host country's government to protect inefficient industries. Because of the trade agreements, however, the government cannot protect inefficient domestic firms against efficient foreign competition as far as tariffs are concerned. Some governments, therefore, use less obvious measures, such as subsidies to domestic firms and regulations and tariffs on foreign companies. These measures make it very difficult for foreign firms to establish a foothold in the country. There are other problems, too. Environmental protection measures are not uniform around the world. In countries with more stringent regulations, industries are forced to invest in capital equipment for ecologically cleaner production. Such an investment adds to production costs and puts businesses at a competitive disadvantage relative to firms from other countries with less demanding regulations or no regulations at all.

Invisible Trade Barriers

For many years, American and European companies have complained that the Japanese market is closed to foreigners. While there are not many visible barriers to trade with Japan, invisible obstacles are many. Foreign businesses, and particularly American companies, are often blamed for not trying hard enough and giving up easily when they face difficulties in Japan. While this might be true, experience is a very powerful teacher. American construction firms, for example, after many attempts and apparent success in the beginning, learned that the clubby environment of the industry in Japan could not be penetrated. By a gentleman's agreement, foreigners are excluded from the construction industry. Then why try at all? In retailing, the story is totally different. A tightly controlled Byzantine distribution system keeps foreign competition out of many consumer products and inflates prices for consumers. The laws that are designed to protect thousands of small shops prevent the establishment of discount stores and supermarkets. Foreign competitors face a very difficult task cracking the system. Because of long-standing exclusive agreements between the wholesalers and retailers, it is almost impossible to find a distributor. There are many layers to this distribution system, and products change many hands before they get to the final consumer. Each layer adds more to the price of the product without adding any value to it. How could an exporter build a customer base with so many roadblocks?[45-48]

Concerns of Developing Countries

There is a division in the world economy. The world is divided into two camps of "haves" and "have-nots," or North and South. These two groups not only live under different socioeconomic conditions but have different approaches and orientations to world problems as well. The have-nots, many of them old colonies of industrialized countries, based on their past experience, believe that the North is attempting to hold them down and exploit them. At the Earth Summit, for example, the North was trying to build a consensus, and probably an agreement, that would limit the destruction of rain forests, reduce pollution, and safeguard nature. The South saw the meeting as an opportunity to get the North to commit to resources for the protection of nature. In their opinion, the North, by its unrestrained industrialization, had endangered the planet and would have to pay for its cleanup. If the South was going to forego cheap and dirty technology and stabilize the population, the North would have to assist and pay at least part of the bill. To Brazil, China, India, Malaysia, and Mexico, for example, the unfettered ability to industrialize was essential, and pollution, in their opinion, was an unavoidable consequence.

The tendency of developing countries to follow easy and less expensive economic development strategies and the reluctance of developed countries to assist in the use of more expensive but environmentally safer methods will have grave consequences for the world. Consider the scenario of increased car ownership by the people of developing countries. UN demographers estimated that the world population was 5.7 billion in 1994 and that it will double to more than 10 billion by 2050. If we extrapolate the rate of car ownership by the people of developed countries to the rest of the world, the increased pollution from additional cars certainly will have an adverse effect on the planet. Safeguarding the ecosystem calls for population control and environmentally friendly means of transportation; these, in turn, require investment in education and family planning and a coherent approach to economic development globally. At present, the UN is supporting programs and attempts that are aimed at stabilizing the earth's population at 7.8 billion by the year 2050.[49]

Many years ago, Perlmutter stated that increased international trade is the best hope for world peace: Bombing customers, suppliers, and employees is in nobody's interest.[50] We should add that the worst enemy of peace is poverty. No international trade is possible with destitute people, and poverty cannot be eradicated without equitable world trade. The intellectuals of many developing countries believe that MNCs are partly to blame for the plight of poor nations. They cite examples of past flagrant exploitation and point to statistics that indicate that not only did these countries not benefit from their relationship with MNCs, but they actually suffered. Between 1960 and 1968, for example, profit remittance to MNCs by Latin American countries exceeded $6.7 billion.[51] The belief that developing countries are heavily dependent on developed countries and draw decreasing benefit from the relationship is called "dependencia." The dependencia school of thought paints an exploitative picture of the world, in which MNCs move wealth and benefits away from poor, developing countries to rich, developed countries. The process of wealth transfer is assisted by an "unequal exchange," in which commodities incorporating high-value labor are purchased by consumers whose labor has been sold at a low value. In this way, global inequalities are built into the prices we pay in the open market.[52] Consider, for example, New Guinea villagers who produce coffee for the world market. After coffee beans leave their village, they are transported overseas, change hands many times, go through several processes, and finally end up in the form of processed coffee in jars and cans in the world market. The villagers receive just enough cash to support a local store, which sells, among other things, cans of Nescafé coffee. The price paid to the villagers for their coffee is a factor of 48 less than the price they have to pay for the cans of Nescafé (p. 35).[53] In this way, dependencia is increasing the gap between the rich and the poor.

Frequently, to expand to developing countries, MNCs build close relationships with the governments and the elites of those countries. Unfortunately, these governments often are not representative of the people and are not acting in their best interests. In particular, international bankers have had their share of acquiescing to the schemes of governments and the elite, who were lining their own pockets at the expense of the people. Many attribute many of the economic problems of developing countries and their huge external debts to these relationships. Some have suggested a circular relationship between capital flight, political instability, and economic hardship in these countries.[54] There are some indications that international bankers and financiers have had an active role in and contributed to capital flight from developing countries.[55-57] Thus, international bankers, through their participation in capital flight, may have contributed to the plight of these countries. De George describes this peculiar relationship:

> [International b]anks in less developed countries face a dilemma: the best prospect for large loans are the government and the country's elite. But the government and the elite do not always use their loans for the good of the country; indeed, they tend to use them for themselves and their own narrowly conceived interests. . . . Banks do not only lend money; they also receive money. Offering customers secret unnumbered accounts and evincing a willingness to accept deposits without question make banks accomplices to exploitation, crime, and the flight of investment capital from less developed countries.[6] (p. 71)

Such relationships perpetuate the dependency of developing countries on technology and capital from developed countries. The dependency phenomenon has been the subject of much debate. Many have argued that if this pattern continues, developing countries may never attain a level of economic development comparable with that of the United States and the more prosperous European nations. The experience of a few Asian countries, such as Korea, Taiwan, Singapore, and Malaysia, however, indicates otherwise. While these countries are not comparable with the United States now, continuation of their present rate of growth and industrialization could bring them to that level. Nevertheless, the abject poverty of many developing countries leaves ample room for worry and concern.

While acknowledging the past unscrupulous practices of some MNCs, and the potential for abuse, no one denies that MNCs can play a very constructive role in assisting developing countries. The nature of their involvement and assistance, however, remains an open question. Probably, what we all need to understand is that the problems of poor nations cannot be solved with approaches that have worked for the rich. Insistence by the World Bank and the IMF of fiscal restraint and export push by these countries, while all that is available for exports are raw materials, falls into this category. We need new ideas and practical solutions. Recent efforts at alleviating the debt burden of developing countries and preserving rain forests are good examples. In this case, environmental groups have initiated a drive to retire the external debt of developing countries in exchange for saving forests, the natural habitat of wildlife. This exchange works as follows: A private conservation organization purchases the commercial debt of a developing country at a steep discount from a bank or in the secondary market and agrees to cancel the debt in exchange for setting aside a nature area for conservation. Based on similar ideas, the World Bank now incorporates environmental concerns into its loan programs. An example is a 20-year environmental action plan for Madagascar. The plan was jointly developed by the World Bank and the World Wide Fund for Nature. It is aimed at increasing public awareness about environmental issues, establishing and managing protected areas, and encouraging sustainable development.[58]

Globalization Backlash

To the dismay and surprise of its advocates, there is a backlash against globalization. The backlash so far has been manifested through a number of protests and demonstrations, around the world, against the IMF, the World Bank, and the WTO. A coalition of 600 organizations in nearly 70 countries has been formed, which includes many NGOs, such as Amnesty International, the Sierra Club, and the Malaysian-based Third World Network, and labor organizations such as the American Federation of Labor and the Congress of Industrial Organizations (AFL-CIO).

The enthusiastic advocates of globalization ascribed to it every improvement in labor, legal, and environmental standards in most developing countries, including advancement in democracy and human rights. In the words of Robert Kuttner,[59] the last claim would certainly be news to Martin Luther King, Thomas Jefferson, Mahatma Gandhi, and Nelson Mandela, who struggled mightily to build decent, democratic, and humane societies. Equally misguided are claims that globalization is the root of all evils. There is no denying the fact that laissez-faire globalization has negative consequences. It is against these negative effects that many people are revolting. We have to remind ourselves that "capitalism works better as a mixed system than a laissez-faire system. For a century, citizens of Western countries have voted for a mixed system to temper the extreme, and inequalities of raw capitalism" (p. 25).[59] Therefore, the protestors assert that it is appropriate to have a charter for human rights when we have the WTO, which has a charter mostly for property rights.

The backlash against globalization cannot be simplified in a couple of words. Globalization is a system of worldwide economic integration in which capital, goods and services, and labor are free to cross national borders in search of better returns. This system has benefits and some deleterious effects, such as the widening of income gaps within and between countries.

The point is not that global integration is a bad thing. The point is that there should be a discussion . . . about how much power nations should cede to the global marketplace; about the extent to which an economy should sustain a society, as opposed to the reverse. It should be about the trade off between economic security and economic efficiency, between growth and equality.[60] (p. 244)

The backlash against globalization can be summarized as follows:[61]

1. Globalization is not helping many poor countries. The adoption of market-based policies, such as free trade, open capital markets, and privatization, instead of spurring economic growth, has destabilized developing nations.

2. Industrialized countries are not practicing what they advocate to developing countries. They have continued, for example, with agricultural subsidies, which reduce the competitive position of agricultural products from developing countries, while demanding that these countries adopt free-market policies.

3. Just as there is an alliance against terrorism, there should be an alliance for protecting the global environment and a global alliance against poverty. The World Bank estimates that $100 billion per year—double the present level of economic assistance—is needed to achieve the UN goal of reducing extreme poverty by half by 2015. The additional money amounts to less than 0.2% of the GDP of the OECD countries.

Many are surprised that in the midst of unprecedented economic prosperity there is a backlash against globalization, the very phenomenon that is credited for the remarkable economic growth. Those who think this backlash is temporary and will go away will be disappointed. This phenomenon will last longer due to the fundamental nature of the issues that have triggered it. There are five factors behind the backlash (Figure 2.3):[62]

1. *Insecurity:* As companies restructure to become more competitive globally, many operations are moved to lower-cost locations around the world. Workers who lose their jobs often have a difficult time adjusting to the requirements of the new economy. They see globalization as a villain.

2. *Priorities:* Environmental issues and labor standards overseas are a top priority, especially with the young and the educated. People are very concerned about degradation of the ecosystem and unjust treatment of workers.

3. *Mistrust:* Decisions made behind the closed doors of the World Bank, the IMF, or the WTO are not trusted by many people who are accustomed to transparent, democratic institutions.

4. *Policy:* The contractionary policy imposed by the IMF on developing countries during their financial crisis is losing support among their people, especially since the opposite policy is employed in the United States.

5. *Technophobia:* Most people are uncomfortable with genetically modified food. Progress and growth fueled by technological innovations are seen as harmful to people and the environment, especially when they result in the weakening of traditional national values.

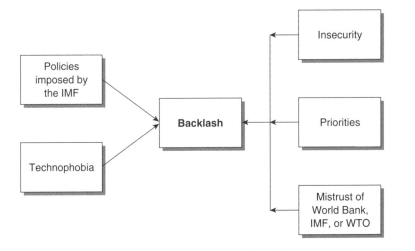

Figure 2.3   Factors Behind the Backlash Against Multinational Companies

SOURCE: Reference 62.

World leaders, in making public policy decisions, and international managers, in making corporate strategic decisions, would be better off if they take the backlash against globalization very seriously. The five reasons that lie at the heart of the backlash are not contrived by lunatics. They are real, and all of them can be constructively addressed. It takes a willingness to see that unrestrained turbocharged globalization can undermine the very foundations of the society it attempts to build.

Supranational Organizations

Civilization has come a long way in conflict resolution. While pockets of regional animosities remain, we are beginning to accept that wars are not the best method of resolving our disputes. We are beginning to see that all members of the "global village" are better off when mutually beneficial solutions are applied to common problems. The harmony and prosperity of a village is directly related to its ability to resolve the differences and disputes among its members in an orderly and peaceful fashion. The chief, the elders, or the village council are usually the arbitrators of disputes among the villagers. Although our global village does not have a chief, there are certain supranational organizations that resemble the village council. While their mandate may be the same as that of the village council, the power and authority of these institutions is not the same. For problems that lie within national borders, these institutions do not have any power at all. The most prominent of these institutions are the UN, the World Bank, the IMF, and the WTO.

All intranational business problems are handled by national governments and domestic legal systems. There is no dispute regarding the power and sovereignty of national governments in domestic conflict resolution. Not all business problems and disputes, however, are of a purely domestic nature. Most MNC operations cross national borders and involve multiple jurisdictions. Certain questions arise for MNC operations that are not confined to one country. For instance, in the case of disputes between firms from two different countries, whose legal system should apply? In some cases, there are no clear jurisdictional demarcations to show where the sovereignty of one country ends and that of the other begins. Moreover, certain issues do not fall within the jurisdiction of any nation. One such example is the use of the global commons. As MNCs expand their operations and as more countries industrialize, the need for and the importance of supranational institutions for resolving international problems will increase.

The United Nations

This section is based on information gleaned from several sources including References 63 through 65. The UN was established in 1945 in the midst of the euphoria and optimism surrounding the end of World War II. The mission of the UN was to ensure peace on earth and to serve as an arbitrator of international conflicts. To carry out its mission, the UN charter provided for the creation of six primary organs, namely, the General Assembly, the Security Council, the Economic and Social Council, the Trusteeship Council, the International Court of Justice, and the Secretariat.

The General Assembly is the organ that reflects the total membership of the UN. It is one of the most influential organs of the UN. All members have equal voting power in the Assembly, and because of this it has been referred to as the "town-hall meeting" of the world. The primary functions of the General Assembly include discussion of and recommendations concerning the issues presented before it, control of finances, election and admission of new members, and initiation of proposals for Charter review and amendment.

The Security Council is responsible for making specific and binding decisions where the issues of peace and security are concerned. Membership in this council includes five permanent members: the United States, Russia, the United Kingdom, France, and China. These five countries were given permanent membership in the Council assuming that they would be responsible for enforcing any binding decisions the Council makes. There are also 10 (originally 6) other countries that are elected by the General Assembly as nonpermanent members. The nonpermanent members are chosen on the following geographical basis: three from Africa, two from Asia, one from Eastern Europe, two from Latin America, and two from Western Europe and other states.

The Secretariat comprises the permanent administrative staff of the UN and is directed by the chief administrative officer, the Secretary-General. The Security Council recommends a nominee for the Secretary-General to the General Assembly for approval. Although the Charter has not specified the term of office, the Secretary-General usually serves for 5 years.

The International Court of Justice, which is composed of 15 judges, is elected by the General Assembly and the Security Council voting concurrently. The court has two functions: It serves as the tribunal for the final settlement of disputes submitted to it by parties, and it also acts in an advisory capacity to all other organs of the UN with regard to questions of a legal nature.

A cluster of some 20 intergovernmental agencies operate around the UN to promote general welfare in the world through economic, social, and cultural programs. Six of these agencies, along with the UN itself, are headquartered in Geneva, Switzerland. They include the International Telecommunication Union (ITU), the World Health Organization (WHO), the ILO, the World Meteorological Organization (WMO), the World Intellectual Property Organization (WIPO), and the WTO. Two agencies, the World Bank and the IMF, are located in Washington, D.C. The rest of the agencies are scattered among various cities, primarily in Europe and North America.

The World Bank and the International Monetary Fund

Information in this section was culled from a variety of sources including References 66 through 71. The World Bank and the IMF were created during the Bretton Woods (New Hampshire) meetings on July 1, 1944. Because of the total dependence of the Allied countries on the United States, the role and influence of the latter on the conference and its outcome were decisive. As a result, both the World Bank and the IMF are strongly influenced by the United States in philosophy and direction.

The World Bank

The original function of the Bank was to provide funds for the reconstruction of Europe. After Europe recovered, the bank shifted its focus and became exclusively a development adviser and financial intermediary between state-sponsored projects and private investors. It borrows on commercial terms by selling bonds and then lends the proceeds to finance development projects around the world.

The World Bank comprises a group of institutions that specialize in various aspects of economic development. The group consists of three internationally oriented institutions and four regionally oriented banks. The three internationally oriented institutions are the International Bank for

Reconstruction and Development (IBRD), the International Development Association (IDA), and the International Finance Association (IFS). Through its triple-A credit rating, the IBRD is able to borrow billions of dollars a year in private capital markets and, thus, is able to fund a substantial portion of the money the World Bank lends out. Its primary focus is financing medium- and long-term projects. The IDA lends only to the poorest countries on concessional (below-market) terms. Some of their typical projects include primary school classrooms and technical assistance and loans to poor farmers. When a country pays back its loans, it becomes a donor and adds to the funds available for loans to others. The four regionally oriented banks are the Inter-American Development Bank (IDB), the Asian Development Bank (ADB), the African Development Bank (AfDB), and the Caribbean Development Bank (CarDB).

Membership in the IMF is a condition for admission to membership in the Bank. Therefore, the Bank's member governments are also members of the Fund. Voting privileges are in proportion to the capital stock owned by the members in the Bank. Slightly more than 20% of the votes belong to the United States. As the largest shareholder, the United States chooses the Bank's president. For this reason and because it is located in Washington, D.C., and its origin goes back to Bretton Woods, some have called it "America's institution" (pp. 4–7).[71] Other large shareholders are the United Kingdom, Germany, France, and Japan. All matters before the bank are decided by majority vote.

The International Monetary Fund

The IMF is not a bank but a club. Member countries pay a subscription and agree to abide by a mutually advantageous code of conduct. The IMF's original objective was to promote trade by creating a reliable and stable exchange rate system. The IMF functioned by providing a pool of money from which members could borrow short term, to adjust their balance of payments with other members.

Over the years, both institutions—the World Bank and the IMF—have changed. The Marshall Plan eclipsed the Bank's role in European reconstruction in the late 1940s. Likewise, when Richard Nixon took the United States off the gold standard in 1971 and switched to floating exchange rates, the IMF's original function disappeared. These developments resulted in a change in priorities for both institutions. The Bank and the IMF focused their attention on world poverty and shifted their operations from serving the rich countries to serving the middle-income and poor nations. Today, the Bank's main goal is to promote long-term economic growth, which reduces poverty in developing countries. To do this, the Bank has become a development adviser and financial intermediary between state-sponsored projects and private investors, corporations, and commercial banks. The Bank primarily sponsors specific infrastructure projects such as roads and dams. It also makes loans for "policy adjustments" that enhance a country's economic, financial, or political environment for private investment.

The IMF started on a new path in 1982 when it came to the aid of Mexico, which had nearly defaulted on its loans from commercial banks. The action seemed consistent with the agency's goal of overseeing the international monetary system and helping member countries overcome short-term financial problems. Since then, the IMF has been operating in a three-way arrangement with heavily indebted countries and commercial banks. Because of their new roles, with the Bank making policy adjustments and the IMF involved in long-term structural loans, the duties of the two institutions overlap.

Criticisms Against the IMF and the World Bank

Critics charge that despite their goals, neither organization has been successful in promoting real market-oriented policy reform. The result of their approach to lending, the critics argue, is massive impoverishment and indebtedness around the globe. They point out that despite the Bank's and the Fund's efforts, and a large amount of lending, there are more people living in absolute poverty than ever before.

Critics cite several problems with the IMF's and the Bank's lending. They charge that the Fund's short-term adjustment lending can do more harm than good when applied to the structural problems of the Third World. According to these critics, the fund focuses on narrow accounting data, ignoring the broad policies that have slowed development. For instance, because the Fund typically demands that a borrowing nation reduce its current account deficit, the country restricts imports; or its insistence that a country cut its budget deficit causes the government to raise taxes, thereby slowing growth. One of the main criticisms leveled at the Bank and the Fund stems from the concept that funds are "fungible" (negotiable in kind, substitutable, or exchangeable). Because of this, critics charge that no matter how conscientiously the Bank examines a project or how well justified it is economically, the project that is actually financed becomes an altogether different one and probably much less sensible. They argue that the truly good projects would have gone ahead anyway, paid for out of the country's own resources, and that the Bank ends up financing marginal projects, those that would not have proceeded without the additional funds.

The concept of fungibility extends to the IMF also. Because the IMF makes loans directly to governments, and not for specific projects, these funds can be redirected. Critics charge that the IMF underwrites any country, no matter how venal or brutal, and that these funds are frequently redirected toward economically nonproductive ends.

Another criticism is that the IMF and the Bank do little to enforce the conditions of their loans. If a country violates its agreement, the organizations will simply suspend the loan and negotiate a new agreement, and funds will flow again. When the country violates the new conditions, the process starts anew. Members are required to consult the IMF annually on their economic and financial policies. These consultations should provide the IMF an opportunity to review and influence the members' policies. Since the IMF has no formal sanctions against noncompliance, it is not clear how effective the consultation process is. As Paul Volcker, the former U.S. undersecretary of the treasury for monetary affairs, has stated,

> When disagreement arose between the IMF and member countries on the need for policy changes, if the country was small, it fell into line; if it was large, the IMF fell into line; if several large countries were involved, the IMF disappeared.[72] (p. 250)

There are a host of other complaints and criticisms. Debtor countries charge that because of the Fund's insistence that to renegotiate a loan, the country must have in hand an agreement with its bankers and also that there should be no interest in arrears, the Fund is simply a collector for the commercial banks. Conservationists charge that the Bank and the Fund collude in their dealings with developing countries and that they support programs that do not work. There are accusations that the Bank and the Fund apply identical remedies, irrespective of a country's circumstances, and that they have a market-oriented, free-enterprise philosophy, which they apply in a doctrinaire way. The 2001 Nobel Prize laureate in economics, Joseph Stiglitz, asserts that the IMF has failed in its mission: Many of the policies the IMF advocated have contributed to global instability. Contrary to the expansionary monetary and fiscal policies used by the United States and other Western countries, when a developing country faces a financial crisis, the Fund insists on a contractionary policy by raising the interest rate and restricting credit availability.[73] Others have recommended that the IMF should get out of long-term development finance and refocus its efforts on short-term emergency lending.[74]

The World Trade Organization

Established on January 1, 1995, as the successor to the General Agreement on Tariffs and Trade (GATT), the WTO is the only international organization dealing with the global rules of trade between nations. Its main function is to ensure that trade flows as smoothly, predictably, and freely as possible.

GATT was a multilateral agreement setting out rules for the conduct of international trade. It was founded in 1948 on a provisional basis to make rules for the conduct of trade among its members. A parallel organization, the International Trade Organization (ITO), was set up to enforce those rules. However, the charter for the ITO was never ratified, leaving GATT as an interim agreement. The goals of the agreement were to create a more predictable environment for international trade and to liberalize trade so that investment, job creation, and trade could flourish.

As an interim arrangement, GATT was very successful. The objective of GATT was the elimination of trade tariffs. Under its auspices, governments cut the average tariff on manufactured goods from 40% in 1947 to approximately 5% in 1991.

In all, there were eight agreements under GATT, each called a Round. The eighth Round, the Uruguay Round, concluded in December 1993, with a signing ceremony in January 2004 in Marakesh, Morocco. It took 7 years to conclude the Uruguay Round. The most recent agreement under the WTO was the Doha Round, which started in 2001 in Doha, Qatar, and provided the mandate for negotiations, including those on agriculture and services. The Doha mandate was refined by work at Cancun in 2003, at Geneva in 2004, and at Hong Kong in 2005.

The WTO's agreements are negotiated and signed by a large majority of the world's trading nations and ratified in their parliaments. These agreements are the legal ground-rules for international commerce. Essentially, they are contracts, guaranteeing member countries important trade rights. They also bind governments to keep their trade policies within agreed limits that are to everybody's benefit. Although the agreements were negotiated and signed by governments, the beneficiaries are international producers of goods and services, exporters, and importers. The purpose of these agreements is to help businesses involved in international trade.

The main decision-making bodies of the WTO are councils and committees consisting of the entire membership. Administrative and technical support comes from the WTO Secretariat in Geneva, Switzerland. Decisions in the WTO are typically made by consensus among all member countries and ratified by members' parliaments. Trade frictions are channeled into the WTO's dispute settlement process, where the focus is on interpreting agreements and commitments and ensuring that countries' trade policies conform with them. In this way, the risk of disputes spilling over into political or military conflict is reduced.

The WTO is intended to be more powerful than GATT. It oversees trade in goods, services, and ideas and has binding authority. GATT was never more than a provisional set of rules with a small office in Geneva. The WTO is the umbrella organization covering the old GATT and all the new agreements. A key function of the new organization is dispute settlement, which was supposed to be the original role of the ITO. Unlike GATT, which had no effective way of imposing sanctions on violators and suffered from continual delays and blockages, the WTO has a dispute settlement panel and an appeals body. If the reports of the panel are challenged, the appeals body makes a final and binding judgment. The judgments of the appeals body will have to be implemented within a reasonable period. Sanctions can be imposed against the recalcitrant country.

While the WTO is an improvement on GATT, developing countries have certain complaints about it. In their opinion, the provisions pertinent to developing countries' trade with developed countries are "soft laws," which hinders their implementation. The general nature of the language used in these provisions, for example, resulted in a number of valid cases where the WTO had to conclude that there was no breach of obligations by allegedly violating parties. "The set of GATT/WTO legal provisions purported to confer benefits to developing countries and LDCs contains a 'birth defect': they are, on the whole, a set of 'soft law' rules. The non-binding and non-enforceable, 'soft law' nature of these rules explain to a large extent why they keep a 'poor track record' as to their effectiveness in implementation."[75]

What Is Next?

We are witnessing a transition period in the world. While we are not quite sure where the transition will exactly take us, it is our hope that nations in leadership roles are keeping their focus on the ideal destination and are selecting their present paths accordingly. We hope that the present path will take us all to prosperity and peace.

Like any transition period, this one is governed by the forces of change. Technological advancement in telecommunications, computers, and the Internet and the increased convenience of travel are reducing physical distances and bringing the countries of the world ever closer to a "global village." Political changes are pushing the world in two different directions. The fall of international communism is changing military-political rivalries to economic-political rivalries and consequently creating ever-increasing market competition. At the same time, ethnocultural differences, which were suppressed by the rivalry between capitalist democracies and communism, are coming into the limelight. Increased understanding of the ecosystem and the impact of people on the environment, coupled with the disastrous consequences of a few blatant cases of industrial negligence, such as the Bhopal disaster and the Chernobyl accident, are galvanizing the forces of environmentalism into demanding better safeguards for the ecosystem. Also, the negative effects of globalization have created a backlash against it.

New players are emerging on a scene dominated by economic and political rivalry, and new aspects of competition are also appearing. No longer can the United States be assured of its undisputed world leadership. These new developments have advantages as well as drawbacks. The period from the end of World War II until the fall of global communism was characterized by U.S. political and economic leadership. Many attribute the success of GATT, the predecessor of the WTO, and the growth of world trade during this period to the dominance of the United States and its willingness to support the emergence of an economically strong Europe and Japan to combat the expansion of international communism. The dominant position of the United States gave it the power to set the rules, which all participants had to follow. With a large market and a dominant position, the United States was able to and did absorb some of the costs. At present, however, the threat of international communism has vanished, and the United States is opting out of its leadership position to look after its own interests.

During this transition period, who is going to set the rules? No matter who sets them and what form they take, why should anybody follow these rules? Since there is no undisputed front-runner and no dominant power to handle disputes, how do we resolve trade conflicts and who will be the arbitrator? Of course, one immediate need is to strengthen supranational organizations such as the UN and the WTO, but doing this is, in itself, a slow and arduous task.

There are certain signs that additional answers are emerging to the questions of leadership and role setting. To answer these questions, we should take into consideration the intertwining of international management and international relations and note four observable trends (p. 237).[65]

First, there is a growing diffusion and ambiguity of power. The hegemony of the United States is on the decline, and other major powers are faced with increasing internal and external problems. Europe is an economically integrated market and is slowly moving toward political unity. Ministates are emerging that are at times capable of frustrating the will of major powers.

Second, international alignments are becoming more fluid. The fall of international communism is bridging the ideological gap between Eastern and Western Europe. The growing number of newly industrializing countries is blurring the line between the haves and have-nots. And there is an increasing localization of politics related to ethnicity and other issues that exist beneath the global level.

Third, the pattern of interdependencies is becoming more intricate. This is due to the expanding agenda of concerns that merges economics, ecology, and politics, leading to a broadening concept of national security beyond traditional military considerations. International terrorism should be mentioned at this point (see Chapter 1). International terrorism is making the control of MNC operations and the provision of security for doing business across international borders very difficult. It is a hindrance to globalization. It endangers free trade and increases the cost of international business. This issue will be the focus of attention for the managers of MNCs and national policymakers alike. Without effective control, if not the eradication, of international terrorism, international business will suffer. International terrorism highlights the importance of nonbusiness risk assessment and management. Consequently, secure markets and safe business practices would reap the benefit of global concerns over international terrorism.

Fourth, the role of nonstate actors is on the rise, and linkages between the activities of local, national, international, and intergovernmental levels are increasing. There are signs of emerging nonterritorial organizations through the growing networks of NGOs (e.g., Amnesty International) and alliances among MNCs. While we may never see a world map defined by MNC logos, their influence may match those of most national governments.

The increased complexity of international management, propelled by these four trends, gives market power and size a new prominence. Some[76] argue that those who control the world's largest markets will be informally writing the rules of international business. If this assertion is true, the Europeans may be writing the de facto rules of international trade in the next century. While the specifics of those rules are not predictable, their directions are discernible from certain observable trends. In world trade, to be considered fair, the rules must apply to all participants. We must have "a level playing field." There must be broadly similar taxes, regulations, and private modes of operation. Many of the benefits that are now local may become global or vanish. German firms, for example, may not be able to continue giving 3 years' leave to new mothers if the rest of the world is not willing to match their generosity. If in one country, such as Japan, commercial laws provide opportunities to businesses to work out common strategies of conquest in home or foreign markets, others will be forced to respond. Similarly, in an open world economy, the high minimum wages of Western countries are threatened by the low minimum wages in Asia. Given the short vacations in Japan, long European vacations are not viable. No nation alone can compel businesses to honor ecological standards. MNCs will simply move production to those parts of the world with no fringe benefits and no environmental regulations. In effect, hidden benefits and covert costs will become overt in wages and prices. Likewise, extreme variations in return on investment cannot last long. Issues that were previously localized will become global.

> The capitalist who is willing to work for the lowest rate of return in the world sets the maximum rate of return for everyone else. If the Japanese capitalist will accept a 3 percent return, Americans cannot have 15 percent.[76] (p. 13)

Summary

Similar to their domestic counterparts, MNCs have social responsibilities. Because of cultural and market diversity, however, MNCs face a much more difficult challenge in fulfilling their social responsibilities. MNCs not only have an obligation to abide by the local laws of the host countries; they must also preserve the ecological well-being of the planet, respect the host culture, and follow overall ethical standards. While basic morality does not vary among nations, due to differing circumstances, certain practices are locally determined. The executives of MNCs need to understand those variations and consider them in their day-to-day business.

While compliance with national laws and ethical norms is a local concern, other issues, such as ecological problems, harvesting the riches of the oceans, the exploration of Antarctica, the exploitation of outer space, and the effects of globalization, are global matters. There are wide areas of disagreement regarding these issues. With the emphasis changing from military-political rivalry to economic-political rivalry among nations, the handling of these issues is gaining added urgency. Supranational organizations such as the UN, the WTO, the World Bank, and the IMF are well positioned to take leadership roles in global conflict resolution in all these issues. The nature of these organizations and the methods they adopt to resolve global differences will be the subject of debate for many years to come. What is clear at this point is that our transformation toward a global village is well under way.

Discussion Questions

1. It is suggested that for many social responsibility issues, the MNCs have a special obligation toward developing countries. Explain the reason for such a special obligation.

2. The newly independent country of Neverland is interested in selling exploration rights to its minerals. Since this is Neverland's first international venture, you can probably negotiate a very lucrative deal for your company. You may be able to negotiate a below-market price for its minerals. In all likelihood, your agreement will become the industry pattern for other MNC negotiations. What will you do? Support your decision on practical and moral grounds.

3. Why are global ecological problems difficult to solve?

4. Do you agree with the claim that we need to develop global standards to protect the ecosystem? Support your opinion.

5. Why should the rule of "first come, first served" not be applied to the use of outer space?

6. In the case of lubrication money, why shouldn't an executive simply follow what everybody else is doing?

7. Explain the reasons for the backlash against globalization.

8. In your opinion, is the backlash against globalization a temporary phenomenon? Why?

9. What are the benefits of the WTO?

10. What are the criticisms against the WTO?

11. Elaborate on the changing mission and strategies of the World Bank and the IMF.

12. Do you agree that the UN should be strengthened?

13. Do you think that the United States can maintain its global leadership role? Explain your reasons. If your answer is no, what type of leadership is likely to emerge?

Notes

a. *Global commons* refers to natural resources such as the oceans, outer space, and Antarctica.

b. Told by my graduate student Parvathy Menon, who had heard the joke in Russia.

References

1. N. Stein (2001, November 26). Yes, we have no profits. *Fortune*, 182–186.
2. P. Kihss (1975, February 4). 44-story plunge kills head of United Brands. *New York Times*, pp. 1, 10.
3. K. H. Bacon, M. Bralove, & S. J. Sansweet (1975, April 9). United Brands paid bribe of $1.25 million to Honduran official. *Wall Street Journal*, pp. 1, 23.
4. P. Nehemkis (1975, Winter). Business payoffs abroad: Rhetoric and reality. *California Management Review, 18*(2), 5–20.
5. P. Wright, C. D. Pringle, M. Kroll, & J. A. Parnell (1994). *Strategic management*. Boston: Allyn & Bacon.
6. R. T. De George (1993). *Competing with integrity in international business*. New York: Oxford University Press.
7. M. Merrifield (2003). Corporate social responsibility. *Baylor Business Review, 21*(1), 2–8.
8. K. Ohmae (1991). *The borderless world*. New York: Harper Collins.
9. L. J. Dhooge (2004). The Alien Tort Claims Act and the modern transnational enterprise: Deconstructing the methodology of judicial activism. *Georgetown Journal of International Law, 35*(1), 3–103.
10. K. A. Getz (1990, July). International codes of conduct: An analysis of ethical reasoning. *Journal of Business Ethics, 9*, 567–577.
11. J. B. McGuire, A. Sundgren, & T. Schneeweis (1988). Corporate social responsibility and firm financial performance. *Academy of Management Journal, 31*(4), 854–872.
12. G. R. Bassiry (1991). Multinational corporations in less developed countries: An alternative strategy. *Human Systems Management, 10*, 61–69.
13. R. T. De George (1999). *Business ethics*. Upper Saddle River, NJ: Prentice Hall.
14. L. J. Felix & A. Boni (2002). The impact of the multinational in development: An ethical challenge. *Journal of Business Ethics, 39*, 169–178.
15. World Commission on Environment and Development (1990). *Our common future*. Oxford, UK: Oxford University Press.
16. J. J. Fialka (1997, October 3). Clear skies are goal as pollution is turned into a commodity. *Wall Street Journal*, pp. A1, A5.
17. Earth summit approves Agenda 21, Rio declaration (1992). *UN Chronicle, September*, 59–65.
18. M. Naim (2004). Globalization: Passing fad or permanent revolution? *Harvard Business Review, 26*(1), 83–84.
19. R. L. Martin (2002). The virtue matrix. *Harvard Business Review, March*, 69–75.
20. Exxon's African adventure (2002, April 15). *Fortune*, 101–114.
21. S. Moore (2002, July 26). Nigeria's new challenge for Big Oil. *Wall Street Journal*, p. A8.

22. A. A. Johnson (1992, December). Traders. *Stanford Business School Magazine*, *61*(2), 16.

23. Over-fishing threatens ocean's future (2002, March 4). *Business Week*, 73.

24. J. Darnton (1999, April 2). Fishing nation's fish stories. *New York Times*, p. 4E.

25. J. Friedland (1997, November 25). Fish stories these days are tales of depletion and growing rivalry. *Wall Street Journal*, p. A10.

26. A. Salpukas (1994, April 24). 2,860 feet under the sea, a record-breaking well. *New York Times*, p. F9.

27. A. Trounson (2002, July 18). New nation, old frustration: Who owns what? *Wall Street Journal*, p. A10.

28. Fishy business in the Pacific (1985, November 16). *The Economist*, pp. 37–38.

29. T. W. Nether (1985, September 15). Third World seeks its place in space. *New York Times*, p. E7.

30. R. Leeds (2003). Breach of trust. *Harvard Business Review*, *25*(3), 76–83.

31. H. Schollhammer (1977). Ethics in an international business context. *MSU Business Topics, Spring*, 56.

32. J. Radmann (2004). Correlates of bribes giving in international business. *International Journal of Commerce and Management*, *14*(2), 1–14.

33. N. D. Schwartz (2002, February 4). The Argentina effect. *Fortune*, 118–120.

34. M. Habib & L. Zurawicki (2002). Corruption and foreign direct investment. *Journal of International Business Studies*, *33*(2), 291–307.

35. K. Pennar, P. Galuszka, D. Lindorff, & R. Jesurum (1993, December 6). The destructive costs of greasing palms. *Business Week*, 133–138.

36. Mr. Rogers takes his dream trip (1992, February 24). *Fortune*, 104–110.

37. J. E. Bahls (2004). Illicit affairs? If you do business overseas, be sure your administrative fees aren't really illegal bribes. *Entrepreneur, September*, 14–16.

38. A. L. Kelly (1984). Case study: Italian tax mores. In T. Donaldson (Ed.), *Case studies in business ethics* (pp. 14–17). Englewood Cliffs, NJ: Prentice Hall.

39. J. W. Salacuse (1991). *Making global deals*. Boston: Houghton Mifflin.

40. B. W. Husted (1999). Wealth, culture and corruption. *Journal of International Business Review*, *30*(2), 339–360.

41. T. Donaldson & T. W. Wunfree (1999, Summer). When ethics travel: The promise and peril of global business ethics. *California Management Review*, *41*(4), 47.

42. W. E. Schmidt (1994, April 17). Once chosen, tribal elites now suffer consequences. *New York Times*, p. E3.

43. S. Engelberg & M. Tolchin (1993, November 2). Foreigners find new ally is U.S. industry. *New York Times*, pp. A1, B8.

44. E.-J. Kolde (1985). *Environment of international business*. Boston: PWS-Kent.

45. J. Sterngold (1993, August 29). Making Japan cheaper for the Japanese. *New York Times*, p. E6.

46. D. E. Sanger (1993, October 11). Discounting finally makes it to Japan. *New York Times*, pp. D1, D2.

47. L. W. Tuller (1991). *Going global: New opportunities for growing companies to compete in world markets*. Homewood, IL: Richard D. Irwin.

48. J. M. Schlesinger (1991, June 10). U.S. contractors find they rarely get work on projects in Japan. *Wall Street Journal*, pp. A1, A9.

49. S. Chira (1994, April 13). Women campaign for new plan to curb the world's population. *New York Times*, pp. A1, A12.

50. H. V. Perlmutter (1969). The tortuous evolution of the multinational corporation. *Columbia Journal of World Business, January–February*, 9–18.

51. A. Pinto & J. Knalkel (1973). The centre-periphery system 20 years later. *Social and Economic Studies, 22,* 34–89.

52. P. J. Taylor (1992, January). Understanding global inequalities: A world-system approach. *Geography, 77,* 17.

53. T. P. Bayliss-Smith (1982). *The ecology of agricultural systems.* Cambridge, UK: Cambridge University Press.

54. K. Fatehi (1994). Capital flight from Latin America as a barometer of political instability. *Journal of Business Research, 30*(2), 187–195.

55. R. T. Naylor (1987). *Hot money and the politics of debt.* New York: Linden Press.

56. W. Ingo (1985). *Secret money: The world of international financial secrecy.* Lexington, KY: Lexington Books.

57. M. R. Sesil, K. Witcher, & D. Hertzberg (1986, May 27). Flight capital's destination often is U.S.: Political security attracts billions of dollars. *Wall Street Journal,* p. 2.

58. M. J. Moline (1991). Debt-for-nature exchanges: Attempting to deal simultaneously with two global problems. *Law and Policy in International Business, 22,* 133–157.

59. R. Kuttner (1999, December 20). The Seattle protestors got it right. *Business Week,* 25.

60. J. Useen (2000, May 15). There's something happening there. *Fortune,* 244.

61. L. D'Andrea Tyson (2001, December 3). It's time to step up the global war on poverty. *Business Week,* 26.

62. What's behind the global backlash? (2000, April 24). *Business Week,* 202.

63. P. R. Baehr & L. Gordenker (1984). *The United Nations.* New York: Praeger.

64. L. M. Goodrich (1977). *The United Nations in a changing world.* New York: Colombia University Press.

65. J. M. Rochester (1993). *Waiting for the millennium.* Columbia: University of South Carolina Press.

66. *The World Bank, IFC and IDA: Policies and Operations* (1962). Washington, DC: International Bank for Reconstruction and Development.

67. A. L. Acheson, J. F. Grant, & M. F. J. Prachowny (1972). *Berton Woods revisited.* Toronto: University of Toronto Press.

68. E. Coady (1992). Global change and the World Bank. *Bankers' Magazine, 3,* 25.

69. P. Mistry (1991). World or wonder-land bank? *Banker, 788,* 40.

70. B. Orr (1990). Are the IMF and the World Bank on the right track? *ABA Banking Journal, March,* 74–82.

71. D. Bandow (1990). The IMF: Forever in its debt. *Business and Society Review, Spring,* 4–7.

72. R. Solomon (1977). *The international monetary system, 1945–76.* New York: Harper & Row.

73. J. E. Stiglitz (2002). *Globalization and its discontents.* New York: W. W. Norton.

74. A. Meltzer (2000, March 8). A Blueprint for IMF reform. *Wall Street Journal,* p. A22.

75. G. Olivares (2001). The case for giving effectiveness to GATT/WTO rules on developing countries and LDCs. *Journal of World Trade, 35*(3), 545–551.

76. L. Thurow (1992). New rules for playing the game. *National Forum, Fall,* 10–13.

Case 1

CONSTRUCTION DILEMMA

Shawn Thelen and Anatoly Zhuplev

Russoconstruct, a privately owned and operated Russian construction firm, is based in Nizhny Novgorod, a medium-sized Russian city on the Volga River. It has been operating since 1996, securing government and private contracts in the *oblast* (the equivalent of a state in the United States) for repair and ground-up construction projects. The number of employees varies depending on the number of sites being developed. For tax purposes, the annual income and number of employees are listed at close to zero—a common practice in Russian accounting to avoid taxes. Recently, Russoconstruct entered into a contract with Studwall Incorporated, a privately owned U.S. firm, to import galvanized steel wall studs to Nizhny Novgorod. The contract is valued at 100,000 USD, to import a quantity sufficient to fill a 40-ft shipping container. Studwall is owned and operated by Russian immigrants who relocated to the United States in 1992, shortly after the fall of communism. The owners of Studwall hold green cards (the right to work and live in the United States) and are seeking United States citizenship. This is the first time Russoconstruct and Studwall are doing business together.

The contract stated that the studs would be delivered to St. Petersburg's port and transported by truck 885 km (550 miles) to Nizhny Novgorod for customs inspection. Studwall was responsible for having the product delivered to Nizhny Novgorod. Russoconstruct paid 100,000 USD when the product was off-loaded in St. Petersburg according to the contract. This is when Russoconstruct's problems with delivery began.

Forty-three days have gone by since the product was delivered at St. Petersburg, and it is yet to be transported to Nizhny Novgorod. Under Russian customs regulations, any product held in the customs warehouse for more than 45 days can be seized and sold at auction. It was the responsibility of Studwall, under the contract, to arrange to have the product transported by truck from St. Petersburg to the Nizhny Novgorod customs warehouse. Studwall has contracted a local Russian trucking firm, Perevozki, to transport the product to Nizhny Novgorod. The problem is that Perevozki is not licensed to take possession of goods not cleared by customs. The customs officials in St. Petersburg will not inspect the wall studs because the shipping documentation states

SOURCE: Used with permission from Shawn Thelen, Assistant Professor at Hofstra University, New York, and Anatoly Zhuplev, Associate Professor at Loyola Marymount University, Los Angeles, California. Personal and company names have been changed.

that the product should clear customs in Nizhny Novgorod. Additionally, the St. Petersburg customs office will not allow any trucking company other than the one indicated on the shipping documents to take possession of the product without Studwall's authorization.

Russoconstruct believes, based on reliable secondhand information, that the managers of Perevozki are in collusion with the managers of Studwall. Based on this information, Russoconstruct also believes that if the product is auctioned off by customs after the 45-day period, Perevozki and Studwall will purchase and resell the studs. Russoconstruct has tried to approach the customs offices in both St. Petersburg and Nizhny Novgorod to have the point of customs inspection changed to St. Petersburg. Neither office has been of great assistance. Customs benefits by receiving the money from the auction if the product is confiscated and resold; however, Russoconstruct does not believe that customs is cooperating with either Perevozki or Studwall in this matter.

Russoconstruct is also responsible for the small storage fees that have been accumulating with the customs warehouse in St. Petersburg. Russoconstruct feels that it can avoid paying these in full by working with the customs officials once the product is released. Russoconstruct has telephoned Studwall in the United States several times, but the calls were not answered, and no one responded to messages left on the answering machine. Russoconstruct has also contacted Perevozki several times. Perevozki has responded that this is not their problem and that it needs to be worked out between Russoconstruct and Studwall. Russoconstruct, feeling that it has already paid for the product once, is not willing to wait for the product to be auctioned off to repurchase it from Russian customs. It does not want to bribe anyone at the customs office in St. Petersburg to have the product released because this would set a bad precedent for future shipments.

Russoconstruct has asked for your advice in resolving the problem.

DISCUSSION QUESTIONS

1. Do you think that Russoconstruct should offer a bribe to the customs officials to have their material released?

2. Would you advise Russoconstruct to sue Studwall? If yes, should it sue in Russia, in the United States, or elsewhere?

3. Are there any unconventional methods that you would recommend to Russoconstruct to solve this problem, given the 2-day time constraint?

REFERENCES

1. R. Apressyan (1997). Business ethics in Russia. *Journal of Business Ethics, 16*(14), 1561–1570.
2. D. Elenkov (1997). Differences and similarities in managerial values between U.S. and Russian managers. *International Studies of Management & Organization, 27*(1), 85–107.
3. T. Taylor, A. Kazakov, & M. Thompson (1997). Business ethics and civil society in Russia (Ethics, trust, and control in Russian organizations: Recent developments). *International Studies of Management & Organization, 27*(1), 5–29.
4. S. Deshpande, E. George, & J. Joseph (2000). Ethical climates and managerial success in Russian organizations. *Journal of Business Ethics, 23*(2), 211.
5. W. Snavely & S. Miassoedov (1998). Cross-cultural peculiarities of the Russian entrepreneur: Adapting to the new Russians. *Business Horizons, 41*(2), 8–15.
6. RealEstate.ru (2006). Russia's building materials industry statistics for 2005. Retrieved May 22, 2006, from www.realestate.ru/eng/article.aspx?id=187

Case 2

Vodka Blues

Anatoly Zhuplev and Shawn Thelen

The demise of the U.S.S.R. in 1991 drastically changed lives, careers, and ways of life for millions of people. Before the collapse of communism, Sergey Krutoi, in his early 40s, married with one child, had an engineering degree and a stable job in Nizhni Novgorod, a medium-sized Russian city on the Volga River. Eleven years later, he is a successful Russian entrepreneur.

In Soviet times, this industrial city was dependent on two or three main manufacturing industries, which began gasping for survival under the new market conditions when capitalism took over in the early 1990s. Sergey figured out that his plant would not be able to survive in the market environment and decided to start his own business. He has been successful in starting up, operating, and expanding retail kiosks for the past 4 years. Initially, he started with one kiosk and then bought the second, third, and fourth, adding one a year. All four kiosks, located in different areas, offer basically the same product line, including candy, soda, snack food, cigarettes, beer, wine, cognac (brandy), vodka, and fortified wines with high (25%) alcohol content.

Russia is the largest vodka market in the world, with consumption reaching an estimated 250 million cases in 1996, compared with the U.S. consumption of 33.4 million cases.[1] Russians have long been famous for heavy drinking. Over centuries, vodka (customarily consumed straight) has been a popular drink of choice in both celebration and grief.[2]

In the late 1990s, beer began to outstrip vodka as Russia's favorite tipple. In 2002, beer consumption had exceeded $6.5 million, compared with $6.3 million spent on vodka.[3] The Russian authorities, similar to their Soviet predecessors, do not classify beer as an alcoholic drink like wine or vodka. The ubiquitous street kiosks, the main outlet for cheap food and drink in Russian cities, underscore the scope of the high alcohol consumption and related health problems[4] (for comparison, please refer to the statistics for alcohol consumption in Russia and the United States, according to which during the period from 2000 to 2005, the per capita alcoholic drinks consumption in Russia grew by 45.7%,[4,5] while in the United States it declined by 1.52%[6]).

SOURCE: Used with permission from Shawn Thelen, Assistant Professor at Hofstra University, New York, and Anatoly Zhuplev, Associate Professor at Loyola Marymount University, Los Angeles, California. Personal and company names have been changed.

Russia: Off-Trade Consumption of Alcoholic Drinks by Sector (in Liters per Capita): 2000 and 2005

	2000	2005	% Growth, 2000–2005
Beer	34.4	55.5	61.5
Flavored alcoholic beverages	1.4	3.8	177.2
Wine	4.7	7.3	55.3
Spirits	14.9	14.0	–6.1
Alcoholic drinks	55.3	80.6	45.7

SOURCE: Reference 5.

United States: Off-Trade Consumption of Alcoholic Drinks by Sector (in Liters per Capita): 2000 and 2005

	2000	2005	% Growth, 2000–2005
Beer	64.3	61.7	–4.01
Cider/perry	104.9	90.3	–13.89
Flavored alcoholic beverages	1.2	1.6	32.46
Wine	5.8	6.6	13.09
Spirits	3.6	3.9	8.36
Alcoholic drinks	75.0	73.8	–1.52

SOURCE: Reference 6.

Russia: Sales of Alcoholic Drinks by Sector (in U.S.$ Million): Total Value for 2000 and 2005

	2000	2005	% Growth, 2000–2005
Beer	6,885.4	13,205.8	191.8
Flavored alcoholic beverages	595.1	1,645.5	276.5
Wine	3,133.3	5,673.5	181.1
Spirits	12,162.6	12,311.4	1.2
Alcoholic drinks	22,776.4	32,836.2	144.2

SOURCE: Reference 7.

Apart from the immense market size and newly found opportunities for entrepreneurship, many people in the early days of the Russian market transformation have gravitated to selling vodka due to the financial payback and their post-Soviet meager economic conditions.

During his several years in the kiosk business, Sergey has developed good relations with the police and local city government officials and is well connected with the local business community. He is also rumored to have a relationship with what is called *krysha* (a "roof") in Russian business practices. In Russian jargon, a roof is an organization that provides protective services and helps in handling problems with government regulations in exchange for a profit cut.[a] Some people would consider it organized crime—the "mafia."

All four of Sergey's kiosks are in great, high-customer-traffic locations adjacent to bus/trolleybus stops. Additionally, his kiosks are the only ones in each of their areas that offer their respective product lines. These locations are difficult to arrange without good connections. There may be other kiosks close by, but they carry noncompetitive products, such as compact disks, dairy products, and pharmaceuticals; therefore, direct competition is relatively low. Recently, Sergey has been offered $2,500 for his second best kiosk, located across from a busy bus stop.

In 1 month's time, the federal government will be implementing a new law prohibiting kiosks from selling hard liquor (anything with an alcohol content over 25%), such as vodka, whiskey, and cognac. In the near future, only walk-in mini markets and stores will be permitted to sell hard liquor. Mini markets cost about $20,000 to purchase and $10,000 to $12,000 to build oneself, and the cost of a store is too high for Sergey to go it alone, although he has the right connections to accomplish this with financial help.

A common business practice of kiosk owners is not to report their total revenue, in order to lower their tax payments. They do this by failing to record some products in their commercial transaction logs. This is done for many products but especially for vodka. In some cases, owners of kiosks either sell illegal homemade spirit (*samogon*) or buy bootlegged vodka from the distillery, which is not recorded in the production logs. This also reduces the taxable revenue of that distillery.[b] It is not

known for certain whether Sergey is involved in either of these practices, but he is believed to be operating like all other kiosk operators.

Vodka makes up approximately 40% of Sergey's annual sales revenue. This has been consistent across all four kiosks. Compliance with this new law will most likely reduce Sergey's revenues from his kiosks by 40% and his profits by an even greater amount. Sergey feels that he can continue to operate without selling vodka, but he will not be able to enjoy the same income or growth that he has in the past. Knowing the Russian government's penchant for haphazard reforms, some of Sergey's competition believe that this law enforcement campaign will soon run out of gas; so they have decided to continue to sell vodka despite the new law, thereby risking fines and forced closure.

To combat this decrease in revenue, Sergey has decided to introduce more varied and well-known lines of beers, wines, and fortified wines high in alcohol. He is hoping that the high-alcohol wines will meet customer demand and make up for the decrease in vodka revenue and profit.

Recently, there has been increased pressure on kiosks by city regulatory agencies. Examples of this include the fining of kiosk owners on account of dirty surroundings and fines for minor infractions in the building code pertaining to kiosks. On the basis of conversations with fellow kiosk owners, Sergey believes that he is not the only businessperson being harassed.

Sergey faces a dilemma and needs to make a difficult decision: He is concerned about the survival of his business, the looming fall in revenue, and the pressure by city law enforcement officials. Sergey also does not want to damage his relations with the roof because that may have serious business and even personal repercussions.

What solution would you offer Sergey in this situation?

DISCUSSION QUESTIONS

1. What is the nature of the Russian market transition, and what does it mean for business?

2. Explain Sergey's motives in quitting his job at a government-owned enterprise and starting his own entrepreneurial venture in retail trade.

3. Why are personal connections so important for business in Russia?

4. Give your critical judgment on the following alternatives, and justify the rationale for Sergey's business solution in this case:

   A. Switch to a legitimate business, be 100% law-abiding, pay all taxes, pay no bribes, and refuse all cooperation with the roof.

   B. Open a mini market with a loan from a bank or other legitimate entity or, possibly, friends and family.

   C. Continue relations with the roof, bribing law enforcement officers and inspectors, but stop selling illegal vodka.

   D. Continue relations with the roof, bribing law enforcement officers and kiosk inspectors, and continue selling illegal vodka.

   E. Borrow money from the roof to construct a mini market and to pay all necessary bribes to government officials for permits and favors.

REFERENCES

1. Absolute frustration: Why foreign distillers find it so hard to sell vodka to the Russians (1998, January 15). *Wall Street Journal*, p. A1.
2. M. MacKinnon (2003, May 15). Vodka turns 500 with toasts to joy and misery. *Globe and Mail* (Canada), p. 1.
3. N. Paton (2002, October 20). Russia lite: Nyet to vodka, da to beer. *Observer* (UK), p. 1.
4. Russia, home of vodka, cracks down on ads for beer. Beer consumption climbs (2002, October 26). Reuters, p. 1.
5. Consumer lifestyles: Russia (2006, October 24). *Euromonitor International*.
6. Consumer lifestyles: US (2006, November 1). *Euromonitor International*.
7. Alcoholic drinks: Russia (2006, May 22). *Euromonitor International*.
8. V. Korchagina (2002, May 22). Study: Bribery a $36 bln business. *Moscow Times*, p. 1.

IVEY

Richard Ivey School of Business
The University of Western Ontario

Case 3

YAHOO VERSUS SURVIVORS OF THE HOLOCAUST[A]

David Wesley

The Net interprets censorship as damage and routes around it.

—John Gilmore, founder of the
Electronic Frontier Foundation

On January 29, 2001, Timothy Koogle, chief executive officer (CEO) of Yahoo Inc. (Yahoo), learned that a group of French Nazi concentration camp survivors had charged him with war crimes for allegedly justifying the Holocaust through his company's Web site, Yahoo.com. The Association of Deportees of Auschwitz and Upper Silesia filed the charges in French criminal court after Yahoo executives refused to obey a French court order requiring the company to block access to neo-Nazi content on its U.S.-based servers. Yahoo claimed that the court order violated U.S. and international laws protecting freedom of speech. Holocaust survivors were angered by Yahoo's apparent support of content that demeaned their suffering and that of millions who died at the hands of Adolf Hitler's Nazi regime. If Koogle were found guilty, he potentially faced incarceration in France.[1]

COMPANY BACKGROUND

In 1995, two Stanford University students posted their Internet bookmarks on a Web site that they called Yahoo.com. The site was simple compared to other Internet search engines, but that simplicity made it popular with new users. By 1999, Yahoo had become the second most popular destination on the Net, behind America Online.

As Yahoo continued to expand its Web index, the company also began offering auxiliary services, such as news, e-mail, shopping, auctions, and Web hosting. In May 1999, Yahoo acquired GeoCities for $55 million. This popular free Web hosting service was primarily supported through advertising revenues (see Exhibit 1).

EXHIBIT 1 Selected Financial Data for Yahoo and Acquired Companies

Components of the consolidated results of operations of Yahoo and the acquired companies, prior to their acquisitions by Yahoo (in thousands):

	2000	1999	1998
Net revenues:			
Yahoo!	$1,104,921	$543,732	$198,981
broadcast.com	—	28,748	17,392
GeoCities	—	12,984	18,227
eGroups	5,257	3,178	32
Others	—	3,144	10,500
	$1,110,178	$591,786	$245,132
Net income (loss):			
Yahoo!	$93,156	$86,766	$30,216
broadcast.com	—	(7,617)	(14,290)
GeoCities	—	(17,249)	(19,759)
eGroups	(22,380)	(13,322)	(967)
Others	—	(767)	(8,841)
	$70,776	$47,811	$(13,641)

The following table sets forth net revenues and gross property and equipment assets for geographic areas (in thousands):

	United States	International	Total
2000			
Net revenues	$941,266	$168,912	$1,110,178
Long-term assets	119,100	62,375	181,475
1999			
Net revenues	$532,731	$59,055	$591,786
Long-term assets	88,500	4,842	93,342
1998			
Net revenues	$228,929	$16,203	$245,132
Long-term assets	45,372	1,938	47,310

In the late 1990s, the Internet had grown from a mainly English-speaking U.S.-based information service to a multilingual global communications and commerce industry. Most analysts expected the number of online users to approach one billion within a few years. The highest levels of growth were expected in non-English-speaking countries throughout Europe, Asia, and Latin America. While English speakers represented a clear majority among Internet users, their majority was quickly diminishing.

Yahoo developed 24 international sites[b] in 13 languages. In each of its international markets, Yahoo built independent directories of local language Web sites and other content. By 2001, approximately 40 percent of Yahoo users were located outside the United States, although no single international location accounted for more than 10 percent of total company revenues.

Yahoo's international success could be traced back to early efforts by founders David Filo and Jerry Yang to hire qualified executives to build the company. One of their hires was Timothy Koogle, a former Motorola executive, who joined Yahoo in March 1995 as company president. After receiving his bachelor of science degree in mechanical engineering from the University of Virginia, Koogle went on to earn master of science and doctor of engineering degrees from Stanford University. In 1999, he was named one of the "Top 25 Executives of the Year" by *Business Week* for his instrumental role in building Yahoo into a $21.4 billion company. That same year, Koogle was elected company chairman. By January 2001, Koogle had accumulated stock options worth $365 million, in addition to receiving a $295,000 annual salary.[1]

As an Internet portal, Yahoo derived most of its revenues from online advertising (see Table 1). In the wake of the dot-com stock market crash in 2000, many companies cut advertising budgets in order to reduce costs. Worse still, 40 percent of Yahoo's advertisers were other Internet companies, many of which faced bankruptcy. By the time Yahoo announced a 42 percent decline in advertising revenues on April 11, 2001, company shares had already fallen 92 percent.[2]

The decline of Yahoo's fortunes prompted a mass exodus of the company's leading executives in early 2001. Fabiola Arredondo, managing director of Yahoo Europe, resigned on February 15 following a sharp downturn in European advertising revenues. Savio Chow of Yahoo Asia resigned one day later. Three more Yahoo executives also quit: Mark Rubinstein, managing director of Yahoo Canada, Dennis Zhang, Yahoo's general manager in China, and Jin Youm, chief executive officer (CEO) of Yahoo South Korea. Finally, on March 7, 2001, Timothy Koogle announced that he too would be replaced, albeit not on such voluntary terms as his international counterparts.[3]

YAHOO FRANCE

Established in 1996, Yahoo France, a 70 percent-owned subsidiary of Yahoo Inc., was the first major French-language Internet portal.[c] The company housed its 56 French developers and company support staff in a spacious three-story office building in an upscale Paris suburb. Despite competition from France Telecom and other leading European media and telecommunications companies, Yahoo had grown to become the most popular portal in France, with 63 percent of France's 7.7 million Internet users accessing the site on a daily basis.[4]

Content was organized in much the same way as on the company's U.S. parent. In

Table 1   Yahoo Advertising and User Trends

	Q1 2001	Q4 2000	Q3 2000	Q2 2000	Q1 2000
Avg. Daily Page Views (millions)	1,100	900	780	680	625
Active Users (millions)	67	60	55	47	
Number of Advertisers	3,145	3,700	3,450	3,675	3,565
Avg. Revenue per Advertiser	$48K	$76K	$77K	$67K	$58K
Retention of Top 200 Advertisers	92%	93%	80%	98%	96%
Avg. Length of Contract (days)	285	252	235	225	230
Percentage of Non-U.S. Revenue	18%	15%	16%	15%	14%
Percentage of Non-U.S. Traffic	33%	29%	29%	27%	22%
Dot-com advertisers—% of Revenue	30%	33%	41%	47%	46%

SOURCE: Deutsche Banc Alex. Brown

fact, all of Yahoo's international sites had the same look and feel, but each tailored its content to suit local tastes. In France, sports categories focused on the Tour de France, World Cup soccer and the French Decathlon; while in the United Kingdom, these categories focused on rugby, cricket, and equestrian events. The challenge was to determine what should remain uniform for global brand building and what should be adapted to suit local tastes.

Yahoo v. La Ligue Contre le Racisme et l'Antisemitisme

> As the most participatory form of mass speech yet developed, the Internet deserves the highest protection from government intrusion.
>
> —Justice Stewart Dalzell,
> Panel Member,
> Communications
> Decency Act (U.S.)

From the start, France presented unique challenges, compared to other countries where Yahoo had local operations. Chief among these was the country's myriad regulations and a tradition of centralized

bureaucracy (an artifact of the French Revolution that had been revived following the Second World War by the protectionist policies of Charles de Gaulle). One example was a language law that required the use of French, even when anglicisms were commonly used among the French population. As such, computers, by law, had to be referred to as "ordinateurs" in all official and commercial documents. Another example was a labor law that made dismissing employees an extremely difficult and involved process. The head of a French business organization did not hold out much hope for the future. "Things are going to change slowly," he noted. "Some companies have moved out of France for this reason."[4]

Although Yahoo was perhaps better prepared to enter France than many other Internet companies with less international experience, no one in the company could have envisioned that Yahoo would become embroiled in the most significant legal dispute over Internet jurisdiction in history. But that is what happened. In April 2000, La Ligue Contre le Racisme et l'Antisemitisme (LICRA), together with the Union of French Jewish Students, filed suit against the U.S. company for allowing users to post Nazi-era memorabilia for sale on Yahoo's auction site.

Yahoo executives believed that they had complied with a French law that prohibited the display or sale of items that incite racial hatred (including most historical items associated with Nazi Germany) by excluding such items from the company's French-language portal (www.yahoo .fr). For LICRA, however, Yahoo had not gone far enough. In LICRA's view, the availability of Nazi content on the company's U.S.-based English-language site constituted a violation of French law, as the items could be displayed on computer screens in France. Yahoo also maintained more than 150 neo-Nazi Web sites through its GeoCities Web hosting service.[d]

On April 5, 2000, LICRA sent a letter to Yahoo's U.S. headquarters in Santa Clara, California, demanding that all Nazi items be removed from the company's auction site within eight days. When Yahoo failed to comply, LICRA filed suit with the Tribunal de Grande Instance de Paris, alleging that Yahoo had violated the Nazi Symbols Act.[5]

Yahoo's lawyers argued that the French court lacked jurisdiction over a U.S. Web site operated from the United States and directed toward U.S. customers. The court disagreed. On May 22, 2000, it ruled that the availability of Nazi items on the company's U.S. English-language site constituted a violation of the law because French users could access the U.S. site. The court ordered Yahoo to block French users from accessing banned content. In the order, Presiding Judge Jean-Jacques Gomez stated:

... YAHOO is currently refusing to accept through its auctions service the sale of human organs, drugs, works or objects connected with pedophilia, cigarettes or live animals, all such sales being automatically and justifiably excluded with the benefit of the first amendment of the American constitution guaranteeing freedom of opinion and expression;

Whereas it would most certainly cost the company very little to extend its ban to symbols of Nazism, and such an initiative would also have the merit of satisfying an ethical and moral imperative shared by all democratic societies;

Whereas it is true that the "Yahoo Auctions" site is in general directed principally at surfers based in the United States having regard notably to the items posted for sale, the methods of payment envisaged, the terms of delivery, the language and the currency used, the same cannot be said to apply to the auctioning of objects representing symbols of Nazi ideology which may be of interest to any person;

Whereas, furthermore, and as already ruled, the simple act of displaying such objects in France constitutes a violation of Article R645-1 of the Penal Code and therefore a threat to internal public order;

Whereas, in addition, this display clearly causes damage in France to the plaintiff associations who are justified in demanding the cessation and reparation thereof;

Whereas YAHOO is aware that it is addressing French parties because upon making a connection to its auctions site from a terminal located in France it responds by transmitting advertising banners written in the French language;

Whereas a sufficient basis is thus established in this case for a connecting link with France, which renders our jurisdiction perfectly competent to rule in this matter.[6]

Yahoo initially argued that the court's measures were not technically feasible since users were not identified by nationality, but by an anonymous Internet Protocol (IP) number. However, a court-convened panel of experts reported otherwise, namely that a number of startup companies had developed geolocation software for the purpose of delivering localized advertising. Such software could be adapted to selectively block 70 percent of French users. If Yahoo were to also ask users for their nationality, the panel concluded that 90 percent of French users could be prevented from viewing Yahoo's questionable content.[7]

On November 20, 2000, the court reconfirmed the May 22 decision, and further stated:

> We order YAHOO Inc. to comply within 3 months from notification of the present order with the injunctions contained in our order of 22nd May 2000 subject to a penalty of 100,000 Francs[e] per day of delay effective from the first day following expiry of the 3 month period;
>
> 1/ YAHOO Inc.: to take all necessary measures to dissuade and make impossible any access via yahoo.com to the auction service for Nazi merchandise as well as to any other site or service that may be construed as an apology for Nazism or contesting the reality of Nazi crimes.
>
> 2/ YAHOO France: to issue to all Internet surfers, even before use is made of the link enabling them to proceed with searches on yahoo.com, a warning informing them of the risks involved in continuing to view such sites;
>
> 3/ continuance of the proceeding in order to enable YAHOO Inc. to submit for deliberation by all interested parties the measures that it proposes to take to put an end to the trouble and damage suffered and to prevent any further trouble.[6]

Yahoo voluntarily began screening items on its auction sites worldwide to exclude some Nazi-era memorabilia,[f] but refused to screen users by nationality. Yahoo also continued to both host anti-Semitic Web sites on its GeoCities Web hosting service, and to provide Web links to similar sites hosted on third-party servers.

LICRA intended to file similar suits against Amazon and eBay. "The combat is only beginning," announced LICRA representative Marc Knobel.[8] In response, Amazon claimed that the display and sale of Nazi products wasn't "an issue" and that the company followed "all the rules of countries" in which it operated.[8]

In reality, both Yahoo and Amazon offered fresh English- and German-language copies of *Mein Kampf* on their U.S. Web sites, as well as used copies on their German auction sites, apparently in violation of German law prohibiting the sale of the book.

That such products were used by hate groups to promote their views was undeniable. Amazon even posted white supremacist reviews for *Mein Kampf* on its Web site, one of which read:

> This is a must-read book for every self-respecting white person to understand why Hitler had to start WWII and stop communists in Russia, which were mostly of Jewish origin. ...If Hitler hadn't stopped them, then today the whole of Europe and probably most of the world would be living under the terror of Bolshevik

communists. . . . Overall, the book shows that [Adolf Hitler was] very smart.[9]

Another reviewer maintained that *Mein Kampf* was an "ingenious work straight from one of the most intelligent minds of our century."

On May 17, 2001, eBay, the most popular auction site on the Internet with more than $5 billion in annual revenues, instituted a policy prohibiting the listing of items "likely to incite violence or perpetuate hate crimes" on its Web site. A company spokesperson stated that eBay was committed to following the laws of the countries where it conducts business. "It's a matter of respecting the communities where we live and work."[10] Despite eBay's policy, hate-crime items continued to find their way onto the auction site. A June 20, 2001, search of the term "Nazi" revealed 3,694 items (about 1 percent of eBay's total listings), including a mix of historical artifacts and neo-Nazi paraphernalia.

THE YAHOO COUNTERSUIT

In Cyberspace, the First Amendment is a local ordinance.

—John Perry Barlow, Electronic Frontier Foundation

On December 21, 2000, Yahoo filed a countersuit against LICRA with the U.S. District Court for the Northern District of California. Yahoo argued that compliance with the French order would violate constitutionally protected free speech in the United States.[11] Yahoo also argued:

The Orders exercise an unreasonable, extraterritorial jurisdiction over the operations and content of a U.S.-based Web service belonging to a U.S. citizen. The Paris Court has extraterritorially imposed on a U.S. corporation the drastic remedy of a prior restraint and penalties that are impermissible under U.S. law, instead of simply enforcing the French Penal Code against French citizens who break French law.[12]

According to Yahoo, the French decision violated a U.S. federal law. The Communications Decency Act provided Internet hosts with immunity from liability for content posted by third parties (see Exhibit 2).[13] It also violated Article 19 of the International Covenant on Civil and Political Rights, Article 10 of the Convention for the Protection of Human Rights and Fundamental Freedoms, and Article 19 of the Universal Declaration of Human Rights (see Exhibit 3).

EXHIBIT 2   Communications Decency Act Title 47 (Abridged)

Sec. 230. Protection for private blocking and screening of offensive material

(b) Policy
  It is the policy of the United States—
    (1) to promote the continued development of the Internet and other interactive computer services and other interactive media;
    (2) to preserve the vibrant and competitive free market that presently exists for the Internet and other interactive computer services, unfettered by Federal or State regulation;

(3) to encourage the development of technologies which maximize user control over what information is received by individuals, families, and schools who use the Internet and other interactive computer services;

(4) to remove disincentives for the development and utilization of blocking and filtering technologies that empower parents to restrict their children's access to objectionable or inappropriate online material; and

(5) to ensure vigorous enforcement of Federal criminal laws to deter and punish trafficking in obscenity, stalking, and harassment by means of computer.

(c) Protection for "Good Samaritan" blocking and screening of offensive material

1. Treatment of publisher or speaker

No provider or user of an interactive computer service shall be treated as the publisher or speaker of any information provided by another information content provider.

2. Civil liability

No provider or user of an interactive computer service shall be held liable on account of—

(A) any action voluntarily taken in good faith to restrict access to or availability of material that the provider or user considers to be obscene, lewd, lascivious, filthy, excessively violent, harassing, or otherwise objectionable, whether or not such material is constitutionally protected; or

(B) any action taken to enable or make available to information content providers or others the technical means to restrict access to material described in paragraph (1).

(e) Effect on other laws

(1) No effect on criminal law

Nothing in this section shall be construed to impair the enforcement of section 223 or 231 of this title, chapter 71 (relating to obscenity) or 110 (relating to sexual exploitation of children) of title 18, or any other Federal criminal statute.

(2) No effect on intellectual property law

Nothing in this section shall be construed to limit or expand any law pertaining to intellectual property.

(3) State law

Nothing in this section shall be construed to prevent any State from enforcing any State law that is consistent with this section. No cause of action may be brought and no liability may be imposed under any State or local law that is inconsistent with this section.

(4) No effect on communications privacy law

Nothing in this section shall be construed to limit the application of the Electronic Communications Privacy Act of 1986 or any of the amendments made by such Act, or any similar State law.

SOURCE: Federal Communications Commission.

EXHIBIT 3   **International Covenants on Free Speech**

International Covenant on Civil and Political Rights

UN General Assembly (1972)

Article 19

1. Everyone shall have the right to hold opinions without interference.

2. Everyone shall have the right to freedom of expression; this right shall include freedom to seek, receive and impart information and ideas of all kinds, regardless of frontiers, either orally, in writing or in print, in the form of art, or through any other media of his choice.

3. The exercise of the rights provided for in paragraph 2 of this article carries with it special duties and responsibilities. It may therefore be subject to certain restrictions, but these shall only be such as are provided by law and are necessary:
   (a) For respect of the rights or reputations of others;
   (b) For the protection of national security or of public order, or of public health or morals.

Convention for the Protection of Human Rights and Fundamental Freedoms

Council of Europe—Rome (1950)

Article 10—Freedom of expression

Everyone has the right to freedom of expression. This right shall include freedom to hold opinions and to receive and impart information and ideas without interference by public authority and regardless of frontiers. This article shall not prevent States from requiring the licensing of broadcasting, television or cinema enterprises.

The exercise of these freedoms, since it carries with it duties and responsibilities, may be subject to such formalities, conditions, restrictions or penalties as are prescribed by law and are necessary in a democratic society, in the interests of national security, territorial integrity or public safety, for the prevention of disorder or crime, for the protection of health or morals, for the protection of the reputation or rights of others, for preventing the disclosure of information received in confidence, or for maintaining the authority and impartiality of the judiciary.

Universal Declaration of Human Rights

UN General Assembly (1948)

Article 19

Everyone has the right to freedom of opinion and expression; this right includes freedom to hold opinions without interference and to seek, receive and impart information and ideas through any media and regardless of frontiers.

SOURCE: UN Office of the High Commissioner for Human Rights.

LICRA responded that the U.S. court did not have jurisdiction over the French organizations, and that defending itself in a U.S. court would result in an undue financial burden. District Judge Jeremy Fogel disagreed. On June 7, 2001, he declared that his court did indeed have jurisdictional authority over the French defendants. In his order, he stated:

> There can be little doubt that most people in the United States, including this court, find the display and sale of Nazi propaganda and memorabilia profoundly offensive. However, while this fact may cause one to sympathize with the Defendant's efforts before the French Court, it is immaterial to this Court's jurisdictional determination. As Yahoo! and others have pointed out, a content restriction imposed upon an Internet service provider by a foreign court just as easily could prohibit promotion of democracy, gender equality, a particular religion or other viewpoints which have strong support in the United States but are viewed as offensive or inappropriate elsewhere.[14]

Other factors that favored U.S. jurisdiction included LICRA's use of a U.S. marshal to serve notice on Yahoo to appear in the French court, sending a cease and desist letter to Yahoo's headquarters in Santa Clara, California, and accessing the U.S. Web site to gather evidence. The order further explained:

> If the non-resident defendant's contacts with the forum state are substantial or continuous and systematic, the defendant is subject to general jurisdiction on the forum state even if the cause of action is unrelated to the defendant's activities within the state.

Fogel also stated that, beyond the direct circumstances, the case was "ripe for adjudication" as precedent to determine future litigation against U.S. Internet companies by foreign jurisdictions. "California has an interest in providing effective legal redress for its residents," particularly in matters that "might infringe upon the First Amendment to the United States Constitution," he argued. Furthermore:

> Many nations, including France, limit freedom of expression on the Internet based upon their respective legal, cultural or political standards. Yet because of the global nature of the Internet, virtually any public Web site can be accessed by end-users anywhere in the world, and in theory any provider of Internet content could be subject to legal action in countries which find certain content offensive.

Finally, LICRA unsuccessfully argued that Yahoo should have challenged the order in a French court. Fogel replied that U.S. courts were a "more efficient and effective forum" for addressing questions of U.S. laws and constitutional concerns. Furthermore, had Yahoo argued its case in the French court and lost, international law would have prohibited Yahoo from resubmitting its case in a U.S. court at a later date. Yahoo's only redress would then have been to appeal the decision to a higher court in France.[15]

PURVEYORS OF HATE

The Internet is a shallow and unreliable electronic repository of dirty pictures, inaccurate rumors, bad spelling and worse grammar, inhabited largely by people with no demonstrable social skills.

—Chronicle of Higher
Education, April 11, 1997

In the early 1980s, neo-Nazis and white supremacists began using computer bulletin boards to disseminate their views. Donald Black, the leader of one of the largest of these groups, had learned to use a computer while serving prison time for plotting to overthrow the government of Dominica in order to establish an Aryan state. After his release in 1985, Black launched the first white supremacist Web site. Black's "Stormfront" was one of the largest hate sites on the Internet, hosting skinheads, Ku Klux Klansmen, and neo-Nazis. By 1999, Black reported more than one million hits to his Web site, with more than 2,000 Internet users accessing the site on a daily basis.[16]

The National Alliance was another of the more popular hate sites. It hosted a fictional novel titled "The Turner Diaries" in which an all-white army successfully establishes a world government and exterminates blacks, Jews, and other minorities. The novel was also available in French and German, and was believed to have inspired several acts of violence, including the April 1995 bombing of the Oklahoma City federal building in which 168 people lost their lives.

Several neo-Nazi sites posted bomb-making formulas that were linked to at least 30 bombings between 1985 and 1996.[16] In April 2001, law enforcement agents uncovered a neo-Nazi plot to destroy Boston's Holocaust Memorial, using the same explosive formula used in the Oklahoma City bombing.[17]

All told, some 800 Web sites promoted Nazism, the majority of which were physically located in the United States. Besides offering anti-Semitic literature, neo-Nazi sites also distributed computer games directed at children. These included KZ, a concentration camp simulator, and Manager, a game in which players selected victims for Nazi gas chambers.[18] More sophisticated sites offered multimedia content, including videos and rock music. Of the 50,000 white supremacist rock CDs sold annually in the United States, most were targeted toward teen listeners and included lyrics that advocated murdering blacks or committing other acts of violence.[19]

White supremacists claimed that the Internet has been very effective for recruiting new members. "We don't have money to have TV and newspaper ads," admitted one neo-Nazi Web publisher. "The Net has allowed us to reach people in a way we never could with our limited resources."[20] Some attributed the increasing popularity of such sites for the year-over-year increase in hate crimes against minorities.[21]

INTERNATIONAL OUTRAGE

Hateful speech did not enjoy the same protection in most countries as it did in the United States. Germany, France, the United Kingdom, Denmark, and Canada have all brought charges against individuals and organizations for posting racist and hateful content on the Internet.

Germany was one of the first countries to vigorously prosecute publishers of electronically delivered hate propaganda. Dr. Frederick Toben, an Australian citizen of German origin, operated a Web site in Australia in which he denied the Holocaust and railed against the supposed "forces of Zionist evil." Although many sites made similar claims, Toben was one of the few to direct his activities toward German users.

Toben published German-language pamphlets that advertised the site and distributed them in Germany. On December 12, 2000, Germany's highest court held that the Australian Web site was subject to German laws against denying the Holocaust, thus confirming a lower court ruling that sentenced Toben to 10 months in prison. A Georgetown University law professor, John Schmertz, explained:

> German criminal law may punish a foreign national if he publishes statements that constitute incitement of hatred among people on a foreign Internet server that is accessible to German Internet users within Germany. Such actions are considered "capable of disturbing the peace in Germany."[22]

Australian lawyer Ronald S. Huttner not only agreed with the German decision, but supported similar measures in Australia:

> In Australia we do not have any legislative equivalent of the First Amendment. On the contrary, we prefer the view that, even in the most free of democracies, the right of minorities to be protected from racial bigotry, vilification and abuse is more important than the so-called "right" of Nazis.[23]

The German interior minister, Otto Schily, criticized the United States for sheltering 90 percent of the Web's hate content publishers. Although illegal under international law, the German government was exploring electronic countermeasures, such as spamming and denial-of-service attacks, against foreign sites that violated Germany's hate laws. In early 2001, in one of its first actions against a commercial site, German prosecutors charged Yahoo Germany for hosting *Mein Kampf* on its GeoCities Web hosting service.[24]

In the United States, anti-hate organizations, such as the Anti-Defamation League (ADL) and the Simon Wiesenthal Center, sought to combat hate and racism through education. These organizations took the position that many Internet users were unable to distinguish between legitimate Web sites and those posting fallacious historical commentary in order to incite hatred toward minorities. They hoped to counter some of the progress made by hate groups by posting their own Web sites to expose the fallacies in Nazi propaganda.

The ADL also developed a filtering program, called the "Hate Filter," that could be downloaded by users. Whenever someone using the filter tried to access a blocked hate site, the user would be redirected to related ADL educational material. Filters were often employed by parents, schools, and libraries, to counter groups intent on capturing "the minds of youngsters."[16] Critics of filters complained that they encouraged young users to access prohibited sites by bypassing the filter. Filters also blocked access to legitimate sites by historians providing information about the Second World War because these sites contained banned keywords such as "Nazi."

EXTRATERRITORIALITY

Until the 18th century, most nations maintained control over citizens and property within their borders, while lacking authority over persons or things outside their borders. When one government wished to assert its authority over another, it usually had to go to war. The Industrial Revolution and mass migrations of the 19th and 20th centuries changed that. Long before the advent of the Internet, the increased mobility of populations and the creation of multinational corporations necessitated the development of internationally accepted rules for cross-border legal disputes.

Extraterritoriality commonly referred to the practice by which one state exercised legal power over conduct that occurred in another state. Nations that exerted these powers usually did so to secure the safety and well-being of their citizens against criminal actions in foreign countries. Such would be the case when a country prosecuted foreign nationals involved in terrorist acts against its citizens. The nation initiating the case relied on the goodwill of the foreign state to enforce its judgments.

Problems of extraterritoriality occurred when both nations had an interest in the outcome of a case. The Internet vastly increased the complexity of these decisions, as content providers usually transacted, in one way or another, with individuals or organizations in multiple states simultaneously. An auction site in the United States, for example, may list an item from a seller in Japan, and then re-list that item through several online partner sites in Europe. As different jurisdictions may hold different opinions about who is actually responsible for the content, decisions over whose laws should apply remain unclear.

Prior to the Internet, businesses had to make an effort to generate sales in foreign markets. They had to set up distribution channels, advertise through local media, and create local infrastructure to transact sales. Internet content providers, on the other hand, had to make an effort to *not* have their businesses accessed by foreign users. Suddenly the default market had become global and Web businesses had become subject to the laws of each country in which they transacted business. This could include a single act, such as the sale of a product to a foreign address, or a continuous presence, such as a foreign-language Web site targeted to residents of a foreign country.

The liability of the Web content provider substantially increased when the site intentionally targeted foreign users, through the use of either local languages or regionally specific content. If a Web site offered content in Malay, for example, one could be certain that it targeted Malaysian Internet users. A common interpretation of extraterritoriality suggested that the site provider could then be required to comply with Malaysian law. The U.S. Department of Justice applied this interpretation when it convicted an Antigua-based sports gambling site of violating U.S. gambling laws in early 2000.[25] The crux of the case rested on the fact that the gambling site knowingly accepted bets placed by U.S. Internet customers, even though sports gambling is legal in Antigua.[10]

A few courts, however, maintained that simply having a site accessible in a given jurisdiction was sufficient for the Web content provider to be subject to the laws in that jurisdiction. In the United States, a Connecticut-based firm sued a Massachusetts firm for using its trademark on the Internet, even though both companies had similar names and could justify claim to the trademark in their respective states. The court reasoned:

The Internet, as well as toll-free numbers, is designed to communicate with people and their businesses in every state. Advertisement on the Internet can reach as many as 10,000 Internet users within Connecticut alone. Further, once posted on the Internet, unlike television and radio advertising, the advertisement is available continuously to any Internet user. [The company] has therefore, purposefully availed itself of the privilege of doing business within Connecticut.[26]

Under the Connecticut court's reasoning, any company doing business through the Internet would be subject to the laws of every jurisdiction where the Internet was accessible, even if the Web provider did not target the foreign state and did not derive any benefit from access to its site by foreign users. Increasingly, regulators in the United Kingdom and several other European Union (EU) nations began to adopt such an interpretation, namely "that if the Web site can be accessed in a particular jurisdiction, the laws of the place where the access takes place will apply and the Web site provider must comply with those local laws."[27]

PROTECTION OF FREE SPEECH

The United States, however, did not extradite individuals for engaging in constitutionally protected speech, even if the activity was a clear violation of another country's law. For this reason, some experts believed that, as more countries began to enforce laws against promoting hatred, the United States would become an offshore haven for foreign hate groups. In at least one case, Ernst Zündel, a German resident of Canada, posted his anti-Semitic views on a California-based Web site in an attempt to avoid prosecution in Canada.[16]

The First Amendment's protection of speech did not prevent Internet companies from instituting an "acceptable use" policy for users. Typically, when users signed up for a service, they signed contracts that included "terms of service." Private contracts of this type were entered into between an individual and a company and therefore did not involve government protected free speech. An "acceptable use" policy could prohibit users from sending racist messages, or posting questionable content on Web pages. Internet providers

relied on company employees and public users to report violations of company policy. When companies banned individuals from using their services, most customers could easily find more liberal Internet providers willing to host their activities.

INTERNATIONAL CONVENTIONS ON JURISDICTION

The international nature of the Internet created a plethora of jurisdictional problems for legislators. Since 1968, Europeans resolved international disputes using a mechanism known as the Brussels Convention. The convention dictated that all EU nations respect and enforce civil and commercial legal decisions handed down by other EU nations. New rules approved in 2000 extended the right of consumers to sue companies in other EU nations that used the Internet to market products in multiple jurisdictions.[27]

The Hague Convention on Jurisdiction and Foreign Judgments was broader still. In the early 1990s, the Convention's 52 member nations, including the United States, sought greater cooperation in international law enforcement. Later, the treaty was expanded to include Internet disputes. If passed, the Convention would require member states to enforce commercial laws of other member states even when the actions were considered legal in local jurisdictions.[28]

NOTES

a. This case has been written on the basis of published sources only. Consequently, the interpretation and perspectives presented in this case are not necessarily those of Yahoo Inc. or any of its employees.

b. This figure includes localized versions of Yahoo in Argentina, Asia, Australia and New

Zealand, Brazil, Canada, China, Denmark, France, Germany, Hong Kong, India, Italy, Japan, Korea, Mexico, Norway, Singapore, Spain, Sweden, Taiwan, the United Kingdom, and Ireland.

c. SOFTBANK, a Japanese software distribution company, held a 30 percent share.

d. The author's June 2001 search of Yahoo's GeoCities Web server using keywords such as "Aryan" and "White Pride" revealed multiple pages of links to GeoCities sites promoting hatred and violence toward minorities (see www.geocities.com).

e. 1 French Franc = US$0.13 (July 21, 2001).

f. Excluded items included flags, uniforms, and badges but not stamps and coins.

REFERENCES

1. "Yahoo's Timothy Koogle," *Forbes*, January 29, 2001.
2. "Inside Yahoo!," *BusinessWeek*, May 21, 2001.
3. "Out of Yahoo!'s hot seat," *Ad Age Global*, March 1, 2001.
4. "Yahoo France," *Fortune*, October 16, 2000.
5. Le Nouveau Code Penal Art. R.645-2.
6. The County Court of Paris, N° RG: 00/05308 N°: 1/kl Interim Court Order, November 20, 2000. Translated by The Center for Democracy and Technology (www.cdt.org).
7. "Welcome to the Web. Passport, please?," *New York Times*, March 15, 2001.
8. "Yahoo ordered to bar the French from Nazi items," *Wall Street Journal*, November 21, 2000.
9. Review from Amazon.com. June 2001.
10. "Yahoo decision in France fuels e-commerce sovereignty debate," *New York Law Journal*, December 12, 2000.
11. "*Yahoo files suit over French ruling*," Mealey's Cyber Tech Litigation Report, January 2001.
12. "First Amendment: Yahoo! v. La Ligue Contre le Racisme et l'Antisemitisme," *Computer and Online Litigation Reporter*, January 3, 2001.
13. Communications Decency Act, 47 U.S.C. § 230.
14. Yahoo! Inc., v. La Ligue Contre le Racisme et l'Antisemitisme, Case No. 00-21275 JF, June 7, 2001.
15. "*Achieving legal and business order in cyberspace: A report on global jurisdiction issues created by the Internet,*" American Bar Association, Unpublished Draft.
16. Statement of the Anti-Defamation League on Hate on the Internet before the Senate committee on the judiciary. September 14, 1999.
17. "*Police: Suspect wanted to start racial war,*" Boston: WCVB TV, June 21, 2001.
18. "A German and U.S. clash over efforts to crack down on neo-Nazi Web sites in the U.S.," *International Enforcement Law Reporter*, February 2001.
19. "Web of hate," *Salon*, October 16, 1998.
20. "*Net group stalks LA gunman,*" *Wired News*, April 11, 1999.
21. "Hate crimes reported to the FBI: 8,759 in 1996, 7,947 in 1995 and 5,932 in 1994. Web of Hate," *Salon*, October 16, 1998.
22. "German High Court decides novel issue . . . ," *International Law Update*, January 2001.
23. GigaLaw.com discussion list, January 5, 2001 (www.gigalaw.com).
24. "It's a brave new world of on-line liabilities," *New York Law Journal*, May 1, 2001.
25. Federal Wire Wager Act, 18 U.S.C. § 1084.
26. 937 F. Supp. 161 (D. Conn. 1996) cited in "Achieving Legal and Business Order in Cyberspace: A Report on Global Jurisdiction Issues Created by the Internet," American Bar Association, Unpublished Draft.
27. Thinking twice about your Web site. (2001, January). *Corporate Risk Spectrum*.
28. Global treaty—Threat to the Net? (2001, June 22). *ZDNet News*. Retrieved from http://news.zdnet.com

Case 4

UNION CARBIDE, BHOPAL

Technological Hazards

Sita C. Amba-Rao

THE ACCIDENT

Union Carbide (India), Limited (UCIL) is a subsidiary of Union Carbide, U.S.A., located at Bhopal in the central part of India. On the night of December 2, 1984, operators at the UCIL plant noticed a rise in pressure in a tank containing methyl isocyanate (MIC), a deadly, potent, and highly volatile gas used to make pesticides. The pressure and a small leak were misinterpreted as harmless, common occurrences. Soon the situation reached a crisis. Because the safety backup systems were not in order, the employees were unable to control the leak and fled from the scene. The gas escaped into the atmosphere before the tank was sealed. The plant had a single manual alarm system, which was sounded once, but few people heard it or could understand its significance.

The cloud of gas quickly spread across the city, resulting in the death of and injury to thousands of people. By the end of the week, an estimated 2,500 people were dead and about 200,000 injured, many of them incapacitated to the point that they could no longer earn a living. Other long-term effects on health were uncertain. Thousands of cattle and other animals also fell victim, and the environment was

polluted. The accident was the worst industrial disaster in history. The plant was closed and the license to operate it was canceled.

UNION CARBIDE CORPORATION (UC)

At the time of the accident, UC had over 99,000 employees worldwide. The company was the third largest chemical company in the United States and the seventh largest in the world; it was the 31st largest of the world's multinational companies. Its subsidiary, UCIL, ranked 25th in total sales in India. The company's products included a number of consumer and industrial items. Its sales in 1983 were $9 billion, down from a high of $10.17 billion in 1981. The company's net income fell from $310 million in 1982 to $79 million in 1983. In December 1983, its assets exceeded $10 billion, with a book value per share of $69.95. However, the company's receipts on pesticides were $14 million in 1983, comprising only 8% of the corporation's total sales of $175 million. Also, the Bhopal plant was operating at less than one third of its capacity.[1]

Union Carbide had a reputation for its environmental concerns and was ranked first by the U.S. National Council of Economic Priorities among the country's eight largest chemical companies in complying with the Occupational Safety and Health Administration's standards between 1972 and 1979.

Union Carbide (India) Limited

Union Carbide's manufacturing operations in India go back to 1934, with its first battery plant. It was one of the few foreign firms in India that could hold majority equity interest, with 50.9% ownership of UCIL, because of its sophisticated technology and its role in agricultural growth and exports. Otherwise, the equity limit for foreign investment in India was 40% under the Indian Foreign Exchange Regulations Act (1973). The Bhopal plant was built in 1969 under a technology transfer agreement, despite the objections raised by experts concerned about its hazardous nature. Manufacturing of MIC began in 1979. At the time of construction, the plant was outside the city of Bhopal, which had a population of 672,000. In later years, many poor people settled near the plant, attracted by its water lines and roads. In 1975, a municipal corporation official had asked that the plant be moved away from the city because of the hazards involved. In response, the official's service was terminated. Later, in 1984, the Department of Environment announced banning the location of plants with hazardous substances near populous areas.

During this period, the Bhopal plant had been having operating problems because of reduced demand, increased competition, and the consequent cost-cutting measures. Further, this plant made an insignificant contribution to the company's profits. Consequently, UC decided in 1984 to sell the plant. Throughout this period, however, the relations between UC, the city, and the

government had been good because of the company's contribution to employment and population growth in the area.

The Chemical Industry and Safety

Despite the high level of potentially dangerous activities in the chemical industry, the safety record of the industry is one of the best and better than that of the manufacturing industry. In 1983, the chemical industry had 5.2 occupational injuries per 100 workers versus 7.5 for all manufacturing. Chemical companies contend that they apply the same standards of safety in foreign operations as at home. However, implementation and enforcement problems made it difficult to maintain standards and avert the possibility of disaster. While the number of environmental agencies in developing countries has risen considerably (11 in 1972 to 110 in 1984), they are understaffed and underfinanced by their governments. In India, the Department of Environment had a staff of 150, while the headquarters of the U.S. Environmental Protection Agency had a staff of 4,400. Further, inspectors in developing countries were found to have a low status, poor pay, and large areas to cover, setting the stage for disasters such as one in Mexico City in which gas tanks exploded in November 1984. Yet such workplaces were adopting complex industrial processes similar to those in the United States without the requisite controls.[2]

Antecedents of the Accident

In addition to the external developments described above, prior to the accident, the Bhopal plant had operational difficulties, employee problems, and technological shortcomings. In 1982, there was an internal audit of the plant's design and operations in which human, technological, and organizational factors needing attention were identified. The company had an action plan to rectify these problems. In 1984, the company reported correcting all deficiencies except two on which work was in progress: malfunction of a safety valve and potential overfilling of the MIC storage tank erroneously.

Employee issues reported in the audit included low morale, lack of staff, and inadequate training and managerial experience. The high turnover of plant managers affected attention to plant maintenance and contingency plans for dealing with such major accidents.

Technological problems needing attention, according to the report, included flaws in the design and operation of the plant, equipment, materials, and operating procedures. Postaccident investigation confirmed various system failures in the MIC production process and neglect of safety and maintenance.

COMPANY RESPONSE

After the accident, Union Carbide immediately mobilized its resources and took several actions worldwide. It was a strategy of damage control and reaction. However, as in any such major event, the company responded in three stages: immediate, short-term, and long-term efforts. The corporate actions, both symbolic and concrete, included the following:

Immediate. The company stopped production and shipment of MIC worldwide. Union Carbide's chairman, Warren Anderson, visited India to provide relief to the victims. A technical investigating team was sent to Bhopal. Money and essential items were contributed. Employees worldwide were informed of the events, thus ensuring the functioning of the safety processes in all plants. The company's overall excellent safety record was publicized. So were the procedures and equipment at the plants in West Virginia. Employees around the world expressed their concern by observing silence. Stockholders were assured of the financial soundness of the company.

Intermediate. Five million dollars' worth of safety improvements were installed at West Virginia, the only other place where MIC was produced. Further, aid was given to the victims in various forms, although it was rejected by the Indian government. The long-term plans included the rehabilitation of the surviving victims and their families. The company proposed major projects, such as building training and rehabilitation facilities and a $10 million hospital.

These steps should be viewed in perspective. Chairman Anderson expressed the company's moral responsibility but not legal liability. While not accepting blame on behalf of UC, he desired out-of-court settlement of compensation. Further, the worldwide reaction from various quarters—the media, international agencies, interest groups, and the chemical industry—had an influence on the company's post-Bhopal response. Many, including senior executives of chemical firms, were critical of UC's inattention to the developing crisis despite internal warnings. They felt that, given such highly hazardous operations, the company had a hierarchical responsibility for safety as the parent corporation and could not rely on foreign infrastructure to enforce legal compliance.

ROLE OF THE INDIAN GOVERNMENT

To gain the proper perspective, the role of the Indian government with regard to UC, both historically and around the period of the accident, should also be noted. The government represents the country's interest while collaborating with domestic and global businesses. The Indian government acted in the interest of the nation's economic growth and industrialization. However, it failed to provide the appropriate structure and environment. Initially, the government insisted on introducing the complex operations against expert advice and without the necessary infrastructure and later permitted manufacturing in a densely populated area, on the basis of its historically good relations with UC. Further, it legalized the occupation of squatters around the plant despite the company's reminder about the risk.

Yet in response to the crisis, the government avoided acknowledging its share of the responsibility in creating the situation leading to the accident, distanced itself from UC, rejected relief efforts by UC, and controlled information to maintain its political legitimacy. Nevertheless, following the Bhopal accident, the government acted swiftly, providing money, food, and medical care, spending $40 million. Legal action was also taken, with plant officials being arrested for negligence.

As explained above, manufacturing with complex technology and plants has to be supported by appropriate levels of infrastructure. The latter refers to both physical and social aspects. In the Bhopal case, the required level of infrastructure was absent. This was evident in various forms. The slums around the company prevented speedy evacuation of people in an emergency. The need for training, or drilling, the employees in the understanding of safe operating procedures and the reasons behind them was not recognized. The constant alertness and discipline required when working under hazardous conditions had not been internalized. Similarly, the plant and government officials concerned with environment, health, and safety had to be sensitized and trained at the point of importing technology as well as in its later use. This was not done. For example, the mayor of Bhopal had no idea of the potential dangers involved in the operation of the MIC plant.[3] Further, as already mentioned, the Department of Environment was understaffed; the state government had 15 inspectors to cover the more than 8,000 plants located in the state.[4] Such gaps existed despite greater efforts toward safety enforcement in India than in most Third World countries.[5]

The tragic events of Bhopal did appear to have an impact on government complacency, because since the accident, environmental legislation and legal actions have been initiated.[6] For example, an Indian petroleum plant was ordered by a state government to relocate for safety reasons, and in another case, the Supreme Court ruled that the parent company has absolute responsibility for the safety of its plant's operations.[7]

LEGAL ISSUES

Besides relief activities, the Indian government took legal action, arresting plant officials for negligence. Top executives were also arrested, including Warren Anderson, immediately on his arrival in India. Later, Anderson was ordered to leave the country. Meanwhile, thousands of lawsuits were filed in the United States and India on behalf of the victims, amounting to over $15 billion. The allegations against UC were that the company was negligent in designing the plant and had not warned the residents about the potential danger of the chemical and that the Bhopal plant lacked a warning system similar to the automatic, computerized system used by its counterpart in West Virginia.[8]

In March 1985, the company and the government began negotiations. The government rejected UC's offer and filed a suit against UC. The suit held UC accountable for "the design, development and dissemination of information and technology worldwide."[9] Further, the suit contended that UC was negligent in the design, maintenance, and safety of the plant, particularly in misrepresenting safety concerns to the government and in storing "dangerously large quantities" of MIC without warning systems. Later, as lawyers for the victims were negotiating, the government intervened and preempted action on behalf of the victims.

A major legal question was whether the case should be tried in the United States, because UC, a U.S. corporation, was the majority owner of UCIL, or in India, where the accident had occurred. The plaintiffs' lawyers and the Indian government preferred the United States because of faster resolution and larger awards. The company preferred that the case be tried in India because India was the site of action and evidence, and the compensation based on the value of lost earnings due to death or disability in India would be far less than the amount set in the United States (p. 55).[8] The company was also concerned about possible punitive damages that are not covered by insurance.

The lawsuits in the United States were referred to the U.S. Federal District Court in New York under Judge John F. Keenan. After unsuccessful efforts to settle the case, Keenan ruled in May 1986 that the case should be tried in India.[10] He viewed the trial in the United States as tantamount to imposing U.S. standards and values on a developing country and stated that the Indian courts were capable of awarding fair and equitable justice. Thus, the case was adjudicated to the Indian Supreme Court.

On February 14, 1989, the parties reached a settlement when the Indian Supreme Court awarded $470 million to the government on behalf of the victims. All criminal charges and civil suits against the company were dropped.[11] The settlement evoked arguments from both proponents and opponents. Proponents believed that this sent a message of multinational parent responsibility for subsidiary liability. Opponents, including activists and the lawyers of the victims, challenged the constitutionality of the settlement, saying that it was very low, considering the number of victims and the level of suffering, and filed petitions on their behalf. The Supreme Court heard their arguments, and in October 1991, the Court upheld the settlement paid by UC but removed the immunity from prosecution granted earlier, leaving the company open to criminal charges.[12] In April 1992, UC's assets were seized by the court as the company had not responded to the criminal charges;[13] and trial was ordered against the UCIL officials in May 1993.[14] As for victim compensation, reports indicate that the compensation process is proceeding at a very slow pace for survivors. Meanwhile, people are dying every day due to the aftereffects.

SOCIAL CONCERNS AND CORPORATE ACTIONS

To enable assessment of the corporation's social responsibility, this section includes relevant corporate behaviors at various times, in order to observe the consistency between the company's espoused commitment and its implementation.

Following the Bhopal accident, the company undertook several affirmative steps to respond to the tragic consequences. To a certain extent, these actions were undoubtedly undertaken on UC's initiative. But external pressure, particularly from the statements of other chemical company executives about parent company responsibility, was inevitable. Chairman Anderson proclaimed that the company was morally responsible for the events at Bhopal and asserted his company's commitment to stay in India and work at the problem until it was resolved. Similarly, historically the company had developed positive relationships with the government, providing economic opportunities to the community. Thus, the company had attempted to establish an image of itself as a good corporate citizen.

Considering the historical and post-Bhopal events, however, there were incongruities in what the company projected and what occurred in effect. These became evident particularly in UC's relationship with its subsidiary and in certain steps taken relative to the two MIC-producing plants in Bhopal and West Virginia. Some of these events, which occurred at different times, are presented in brief as illustrations.

1. As was explained earlier, the corporation commissioned the MIC production plant against the advice of technical experts and later continued to operate in the populous area without adequate infrastructure.

2. The Bhopal community, as a stakeholder, had no influence on what was happening as antecedents to the crisis were developing in and around the plant. The community was not aware of the deteriorating conditions in the plant, the increasing risk, and the emergency procedures, nor could it prevent the slum settlement. They perceived only the beneficial purpose of the product (pesticide). Moreover, the problem posed by the lack of transportation and communication facilities to quickly evacuate such a mass of people in an emergency was overwhelming.[5]

3. As the postaccident events unraveled in 1985, UC attributed the cause of the accident to local mismanagement and distanced itself from the Bhopal subsidiary. Yet over the years, UC failed to provide support to UCIL, despite corporate control of UCIL's governance. This was apparently due to the corporation's decision to sell the pesticide plant because of its strategic insignificance to UC (it provided a low proportion of total profits and faced high competition).[15] Also, it should be noted that following the accident, the UCIL management was caught in the legal battle between the parent company and the Indian government. The plant management was constrained in its movement, actions, and communication with outsiders, although it maintained contact with employees and suppliers.

The following three events illustrate to what extent the company's commissions and omissions in the 1980s led to major and smaller accidents both at Bhopal and at its West Virginia plant: (1) not following up on the safety audit of UCIL in 1982, which revealed chronic operational deficiencies that finally led to the accident; (2) not sharing its findings at the West Virginia plant in 1984 with UCIL about the possibility, and the dire consequences, of an MIC "runaway reaction" prior to the Bhopal accident (which may have reduced the seriousness of the accident); and (3) installing expensive safety features in the West Virginia plant after the Bhopal crisis without appropriate operational training and neglect of operational procedures, resulting in a toxic gas leak and crises affecting 135 people in 1985.

The response of UC to the accident itself was called a "strategy of containment" (p. 557).[16] The intention of the company was to protect its assets at any cost and "downplay the seriousness of the situation, to minimize the adverse impacts, especially to health, and seek to implicate others. . . . It also appears to be a typical, if not standard, industry response" (pp. 40–41).[17]

Post-Bhopal Consequences on the Corporation and Elsewhere

As information about the accident spread, there was widespread reaction. The corporation faced resistance to its business operations elsewhere in the world. There were bomb explosions and public demonstrations against the company in Germany. MIC shipment to France was stopped by its Environment Ministry, and negotiations were stalled on plant construction proposals elsewhere. Other repercussions included bitterness among UC employees at the news that, allegedly, a few Indian workers were responsible for the accident; the employees felt that this blemished the company's and its employees' reputations.[18] The negligent attitude of UC was generalized to the chemical industry as a whole and all U.S. multinationals, as well, by critics. Questions were raised regarding the risks and benefits to companies and countries in such hazardous operations, the need for increasing safety measures, and the importance of informing residents about hazards. Minor accidents after the Bhopal incident increased fear about safety among residents living near chemical plants in the United States. This resulted in the passage of right-to-know laws in several states. And the U.S. Occupational Safety and Health Administration passed a regulation requiring companies to inform all concerned about the nature of the substances used and any precautions required.[19]

More specifically, immediate repercussions were felt on the corporation's financial and market status. The company's share value fell to $35 from $49; the company went through restructuring and sold many of its businesses, including profitable ones, closed plants, and laid off 4,000 employees. In addition, the GAF Corporation attempted a takeover of UC. UC incurred a heavy debt in preventing the takeover.

On the whole, the Bhopal tragedy acted as a catalyst for chemical companies and the U.S. Chemical Manufacturers Association to review and revise their practices in handling, storing, transporting, and using dangerous substances.

Questions

1. Evaluate the social strategy of Union Carbide and the Indian government considering the antecedents and consequences of the Bhopal accident, before and after its occurrence.

2. To what extent should developing countries consider individual rights or social welfare in the use of hazardous technology? Analyze the ethical aspects of the case.

3. What corporate actions or policies could have prevented the Bhopal disaster?

4. Should global firms have a universal policy regarding their business operations? Should this include use of sophisticated technology in developing countries?

5. "Use of hazardous technology in developing countries requires pluralistic involvement by the parties

concerned, namely, the corporations, governments, and communities. The three parties are mutually dependent for resources, finances, and information." Explain this statement, indicating the role of the three parties involved.

6. Can developing countries, which are striving to raise the general standard of living of their population, pay attention to the environment to the same extent as developed countries? Should they? Would this issue be any different with the new privatization and globalization efforts by India and other developing countries?

REFERENCES

1. A calamity for Union Carbide. (1984, December 17). *Time*, Vol. 124, issue 25, p. 38.

2. W. C. Frederick, K. Davis, & J. E. Post (1988). *Business and Society* (6th ed.). New York: McGraw-Hill.

3. J. R. Long & D. J. Hanson (1985, February 11). Bhopal triggers massive response from Congress, the administration. *Chemical and Engineering News*, 63(6), 60.

4. L. R. Ember (1985, February 11). Technology in India: An uneasy balance of progress and tradition. *Chemical and Engineering News*, 63(6), 62.

5. C. Trost (1984, December 13). Danger zone: Chemical plant safety is still just developing in developing nations. *Wall Street Journal*, p. 1.

6. F. Bordewich (1987). The lessons of Bhopal. *Atlantic, March*, 30–33.

7. M. Miller (1987, March 11). Carbide's Bhopal case may be hurt by ruling in India's supreme court. *Wall Street Journal*, p. 1.

8. Union Carbide fights for its life. (1984, December 24). *Business Week*, pp. 53–56.

9. F. Friedman & M. Miller (1985, April 9). Union Carbide is sued by India in U.S. *Wall Street Journal*, p. 14.

10. Nobody wins in the Carbide ruling. (1986, May 26). *Business Week*, pp. 41–42.

11. S. Hazarika (1989, February 15). Bhopal payments by Union Carbide set at $470 million. *New York Times*, p. 1.

12. S. McMurray (1991, October 4). India's High Court upholds settlement paid by Carbide in Bhopal gas leak. *Wall Street Journal*, p. B3.

13. S. Hazarika (1992, May 1). Court in India to seize Union Carbide assets. *New York Times*, pp. C7, D7.

14. S. Kumar (1993, May 1). Union Carbide officials face prosecution. *New Scientist*, 138(1871), 8.

15. Frederick et al. *Business and Society*, p. 585.

16. H. Deresky (1994). *International management*. New York: Harper Collins.

17. W. Morehouse & M. A. Subramaniam (1986). *The Bhopal tragedy: What really happened and what it means for American workers and communities at risk* (a preliminary report for the Citizens' Commission on Bhopal, pp. 40–41). New York: The Council on International and Public Affairs.

18. L. Helm, M. A. Harris, W. B. Globerson, & J. H. Dobrzynski (1985, November 25). Bhopal, a year later: Union Carbide takes a tougher line. *Business Week*, pp. 96–101.

19. U.S. Department of Labor (1988). *Chemical hazard communication* (OSHA #3084). Washington, DC: Author.

Case 5

FOOTWEAR INTERNATIONAL

R. William Blake

John Carlson frowned as he studied the translation of the front-page story from the afternoon's edition of the *Meillat*, a fundamentalist newspaper with close ties to an opposition political party. The story, titled "Footwear's Unpardonable Audacity," suggested that the company was knowingly insulting Islam by including the name of Allah in a design used on the insoles of sandals it was manufacturing. To compound the problem, the paper had run a photograph of one of the offending sandals on the front page. As a result, student groups were calling for public demonstrations against Footwear the next day. As the managing director of Footwear Bangladesh, Carlson knew he would have to act quickly to defuse a potentially explosive situation.

FOOTWEAR INTERNATIONAL

Footwear International is a multinational manufacturer and marketer of footwear. Operations span the globe and include more than 83 companies in 70 countries. These include shoe factories, tanneries, engineering plants producing shoe machinery and molds, product development studios, hosiery factories, quality control laboratories, and approximately 6,300 retail stores and 50,000 independent retailers.

Footwear employs more than 67,000 people and produces and sells in excess of 270,000,000 pairs of shoes every year. The head office acts as a service center and is staffed with specialists drawn from all over the world. These specialists, in areas such as marketing, retailing, product development, communications, store design, electronic data processing, and business administration, travel for much of the year to share their expertise with the various companies. Training and technical education, offered through company-run colleges and the training facility at headquarters, provide the latest skills to employees from around the world.

Although Footwear requires standardization in technology and the design of facilities, it also encourages a high degree of decentralization and autonomy in its operations. The companies are virtually self-governing, which means their allegiance belongs to the countries in which they operate. Each is answerable to a board of directors, which includes representatives from the local business community. The concept of "partnership" at the local level has made Footwear welcome internationally and allowed it to operate successfully in countries where other multinationals have been unable to survive.

BANGLADESH

With a population approaching 110,000,000 in an area of 143,998 sq. km (Exhibit 1), Bangladesh is the most densely populated country in the world. It is also among the most impoverished, with a 1987 per capita gross national product of US$160 and a high reliance on foreign aid. Over 40% of the gross domestic product is generated by agriculture, and more than 60% of its economically active population works in the agriculture sector. Although the land in Bangladesh is fertile, the country has a tropical monsoon climate and suffers from the ravages of periodic cyclones. In 1988, the country experienced the worst floods in recorded history.

The population of Bangladesh is 85% Muslim, and Islam was made the official state religion in 1988. Approximately 95% of the population speaks Bengali, with most of the remainder speaking tribal dialects.

Bangladesh has had a turbulent history in the 20th century. Most of the country was part of the British-ruled East Bengal until 1947. In that year, it joined with Assam to become East Pakistan, a province of the newly created country of Pakistan. East Pakistan was separated from the four provinces of West Pakistan by 1,600 km of Indian territory, and although East Pakistan was more populous, the national capital was established in West Pakistan. Over the following

EXHIBIT 1 Bangladesh

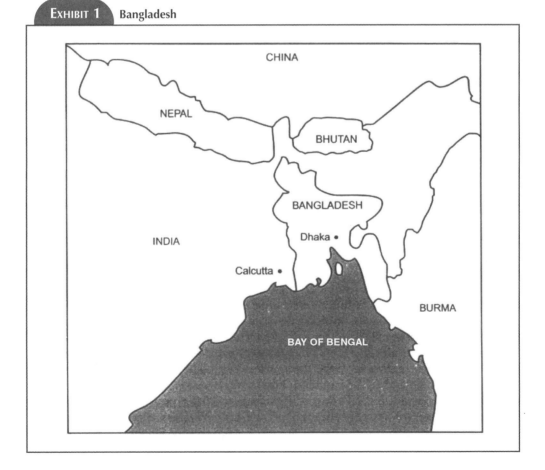

years, widespread discontent built in East Pakistan, whose people felt that they received a disproportionately small amount of development funding and were under-represented in government.

Following a period of unrest starting in 1969, the Awami League, the leading political party in East Pakistan, won an overwhelming victory in the local elections held in 1970. The victory promised to give the League, which was pro-independence, control in the National Assembly. To prevent that happening, the national government suspended the convening of the Assembly indefinitely. On March 26, 1971, the Awami League proclaimed the independence of the People's Republic of Bangladesh, and civil war quickly followed. In the ensuing conflict, hundreds of thousands of refugees fled to safety across the border in India. In December, India, which supported the independence of Bangladesh, declared war, and 12 days later, Pakistan surrendered. Bangladesh had won its independence, and the capital of the new country was established at Dhaka. In the years immediately following independence, industrial output declined in major industries as a result of the departure of many of the largely non-Bengali financier and managerial class.

Throughout the subsequent years, political stability proved elusive for Bangladesh. Although elections were held, stability was threatened by the terrorist tactics resorted to by opposition groups from both political extremes. Coups and countercoups, assassinations and suspension of civil liberties became regular occurrences.

Since 1983, Bangladesh had been ruled by the self-proclaimed president General H. M. Ershad. Despite demonstrations in 1987, which led to a state of emergency being declared, Ershad managed to retain power in the elections held the following year. The country remains politically volatile, however. Dozens of political parties continually maneuver for position, and alliances and coalitions are the order of the day. The principal opposition party is the Awami League, an alliance of eight political parties. Many of the parties are closely linked with so-called opposition newspapers, which promote their political positions. Strikes and demonstrations are frequent and are often the result of cooperation among opposition political parties, student groups, and unions.

FOOTWEAR BANGLADESH

Footwear became active in what was then East Bengal in the 1930s. In 1962, the first major investment took place with the construction of a footwear-manufacturing facility at Tongi, an industrial town located 30 km north of Dhaka. During the following years, the company expanded its presence in both conventional and unconventional ways. In 1971, the then managing director became a freedom fighter while continuing to oversee operations. He subsequently became the only foreigner to be decorated by the government with the "Bir Protik" in recognition of both his and the company's contribution to the independence of Bangladesh.

In 1985, Footwear Bangladesh went public and, 2 years later, spearheaded the largest private sector foreign investment in the country, a tannery and footwear factory at Dhamrai. The new tannery produced leather for local Footwear needs and the export market, while the factory produced a variety of footwear for the local market.

By 1988, Footwear Bangladesh was employing 1,800 employees and selling through 81 stores and 54 agencies. The company introduced approximately 300 new products a year into the market, using their in-house design and development capability. Footwear managers were particularly proud of the capability of the personnel in these departments, all of whom were Bangladeshi.

Annual sales in excess of 10,000,000 pairs of footwear gave the company 15% of the national market in 1988. Revenues exceeded US$30 million, and after-tax profit was approximately US$1 million. Financially, the company was considered a medium contributor within the Footwear organization. With a population approaching 110,000,000 and a per capita consumption of one pair of shoes every 2 years, Bangladesh was perceived as offering Footwear enormous potential for growth through both consumer education and competitive pressure.

The managing director of Footwear Bangladesh was John Carlson, one of only four foreigners working for the company. The others were the managers of production, marketing, and sales. All had extensive and varied experience within the Footwear organization.

THE INCIDENT

On Thursday, June 22, 1989, John Carlson was shown a copy of that day's *Meillat*, a well-known opposition newspaper with pro-Libyan leanings. Under the headline "Footwear's Unpardonable Audacity," the writer suggested that the design on the insole of one model of sandal produced by the company included the Arabic spelling of the word *Allah* (Exhibit 2). The story went on to suggest that Footwear was under Jewish ownership and to link the alleged offense with the gunning down of many people in

---

EXHIBIT 2   Translation of the *Meillat* Story

Unpardonable Audacity of Footwear[1]

In Bangladesh a Sandal with Allah as Footwear trade mark in Arabic designed in calligraphy has been marketed although last year Islam was made the State Religion in Bangladesh. The Sandal in black and white contains Allah in black. Prima facie it appears it has been designed and the Alif "the first letter in Arabic" has been jointly written. Excluding Alif it reads LILLAH. In Bangladesh after the Satan Rushdies[2] Satanic Verses which has brought unprecendented demonstrations and innumerable strikes (Hartels). This International shoe manufacturing organization under Jewish ownership with the design of Allah has made religious offence. Where for sanctity of Islam one million people of Afganistan have sacrificed their lives and wherein occupied Palestine many people have been gunned down by Jews for sanctity of Islam in this country the word Allah under this guise has been put under feet.

   Last night a group of students from Dhaka university came to **Meillat** office with a couple of pairs of Sandal. The management staff of Footwear was not available over telephone. This sandal has got two straps made of foam.

1. The translation is identical to that which Carlson was given to work with.

2. Salman Rushdie was the author of the controversial book *The Satanic Verses*. The author had been sentenced to death, in absentia, by Ayatollah Khomenei, the leader of Iran, for crimes against Islam.

Palestine by the Jews. The story highlighted the fact that the design was on the insole of the sandal and, therefore, next to the foot, which signified great disrespect to Muslims.

Carlson immediately contacted the supervisor of the design department and asked for any information he could provide on the design on the sandals. He already knew that they were from a medium-priced line of women's footwear known as "Chappels," which had the design on the insole changed often as a marketing feature. Following his investigation, the supervisor reported that the design had been based on a set of Chinese temple bells that the designer had purchased in the local market. Pleased with the appearance of the bells, she had used them as the basis for a stylized design, which she submitted to her supervisor for consideration and approval (Exhibit 3).

All the employees in the development and marketing department were Muslims. The supervisor reported that the woman who had produced the offending design was a devout Bengali Muslim who could not speak or read Arabic. The same was true of almost all the employees in the department. The supervisor confirmed to Carlson that numerous people in the

EXHIBIT 3   The Temple Bells and the Design Used on the Sandal

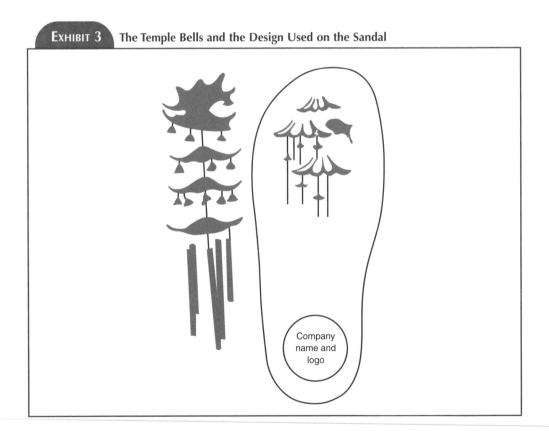

Company name and logo

EXHIBIT 4   The Arabic Spelling of Allah

department had seen the new design prior to its approval and no one had seen any problem or raised any objection to it. Following this conversation, Carlson compared the design with the word *Allah*, which he had arranged to have written in Arabic (Exhibit 4).

Carlson was perplexed by the article and its timing. The sandals in question were not new to the market and had not been subject to prior complaints. As he reread the translation of the *Meillat* article, he wondered why the Jewish reference had been made when the family that owned Footwear International was Christian. He also wondered if the fact that students from the university had taken the sandals to the paper was significant.

As the day progressed, the situation got worse. Carlson was shown a translation of a proclamation that had been circulated by two youth groups calling for demonstrations against Footwear to be held the next day (Exhibit 5). The proclamation linked Footwear, Salman Rushdie, and the Jewish community and ominously stated that "even at the cost of our lives we have to protest against this conspiracy."

More bad news followed. Calls had been made for charges to be laid against Carlson and four others under a section of the criminal code that forbade "deliberate and malicious acts intended to outrage feelings of any class by insulting its religion or religious believers" (Exhibit 6).

A short time later, Carlson received a copy of a statement that had been filed by a local lawyer, although no warrants were immediately forthcoming (Exhibit 7).

While he was reviewing the situation, Carlson was interrupted by his secretary. In an excited voice, she informed him that the Prime Minister was being quoted as calling the sandal incident an "unforgivable crime." The seriousness of the incident seemed to be escalating rapidly, and Carlson wondered what he should do to try to minimize the damage.

EXHIBIT 5   Translation of the Student Groups' Proclamation

The Audacity Through the Use of the Name "Allah" in a Sandal[1]

Let Rushdies Jewish Footwear Company be prohibited in Bangladesh.

Dear people who believe in one God It is announced in the holy Quran Allahs name is above everything but shoe manufacturing Jewish Footwear Shoe Company has used the name Allah and shown disrespect of unprecedented nature and also unpardonable audacity. After the failure of Rushdies efforts to destroy the beliefs of Moslems in the Quran, Islam and the prophet (SM) who is the writer of Satanic verses the Jewish People have started offending the Moslems. This time it is a fight against Allah. In fact Daud Haider, Salman Rushdie Viking Penguin and Footwear Shoe Company all are supported and financed by Jewish community. Therefore no compromise with them. Even at the cost of our lives we have to protest against this conspiracy.

For this procession and demonstration will be held on 23rd. June Friday after Jumma prayer from Baitul Mukarram Mosque south gate. Please join this procession and announce we will not pardon Footwear Shoe Companys audacity. Footwear Shoe Company has to be prohibited, don't buy Jewish products and Footwear shoes. Be aware Rushdies partner.

Issued by Bangladesh Islamie Jubashibir (Youth Student Forum) and Bangladesh Islamic Satrashbir (Student Forum)

1. The translation is identical to that which Carlson was given to work with.

EXHIBIT 6   Section 295 of the Criminal Code

295-A. Deliberate and malicious acts intended to outrage religious feelings of any class by insulting its religion or religious believers. Whoever, with deliberate and malicious intention of outraging the religious feelings of any class of [the citizens . . .], by words, either spoken or written, or by visible representations insults or attempts to insult the religion or religious beliefs of that class, shall be punished with imprisonment. . . .

. . . In order to bring a matter under S. 295-A it is not the mere matter of discourse or the written expression but also the manner of it which has to be looked to. In other words the expressions should be such as are bound to be regarded by any reasonable man as grossly offensive and provocative and maliciously and deliberately intended to outrage the feelings of any class of citizens. . . . If the injurious act was done voluntarily without a lawful excuse, malice may be presumed.

EXHIBIT 7   The Statement of the Plaintiff

The plaintiff most respectfully states that:

1. The plaintiff is a lawyer, and a Bangladeshi Citizen and his religion is Islam. He is basically a devout Moslem. According to Islamic tradition he regularly performs his daily work.

2. The first accused of this . . . is the Managing Director of Footwear Shoe Company, the second accused is the Production Manager of the said company, the third accused is the Marketing Manager, the fourth accused is the Calligrapher of the said company and last accused is the Sales Manager of the said company. The said company is an international organization having shoe business in different countries.

3. The accused persons deliberately wanted to outrage the religion of Muslims by engraving the calligraphy of "Allah" in Arabic on a sandal thereby to offend the Religion of majority this Muslim Country. By marketing this sandal with the calligraphy of "Allah" they have offended the religious feelings of millions of Muslims. It is the solemn religious duty and responsibility of every devout Muslim to protect the sanctity of "Allah." The plaintiff first saw the sandal with this calligraphy on 22nd June 1989 at Elephant road shop.

The accused persons collectively and deliberately wanted this calligraphy under the feet thereby to offend the religion of mine and many other Muslims and have committed a crime under provisions of section 295A of the Penal Code. At the time of hearing the evidence will be provided.

Therefore under the provisions of section 295A of the Penal Code the accused persons be issued with warrant of arrest and be brought to court for justice.

PART II

Cultural and Behavioral

3

International Management and the Cultural Context

To manage a business organization effectively, it is essential to understand people's values and assumptions, which are shaped by their cultures. Cultural norms and values are not universal, although there are some similarities. Among these similarities are a desire to be helpful, respect for authority and power, and the tendency toward comfort. But even those concepts and values that at first glance appear to be universal show vast differences on closer scrutiny.

In this chapter, we learn how cultural differences influence the management of business organizations. The differences between the most prominent American cultural values and those of other nations are used as a framework for the discussion of the managerial implications of cultural differences. The definitions of national culture and corporate culture explain the relationship between the two. A discussion of organizational typology illustrates how cultural diversity in multinational corporations (MNCs) could improve organizational capabilities.

Chapter Vignette

A few decades ago, when MNCs started sending their employees abroad, they learned about a phenomenon called cultural shock. Manifested as a feeling of bewilderment, loss, and anxiety, cultural shock beset people who, in a foreign land, did not find the familiar clues that make everyday life a comfortable exercise. Now, many MNCs are being introduced to another cultural shock. Strategic alliances between large MNCs create multicultural teams and result in many unforeseen problems between these teams that slow down projects.

Cooperative projects combining culturally diverse people should produce synergy. Americans, for example, look at objects and relate them in a linear fashion. Japanese look at the harmony between objects and spatial relationships. To Americans, harmony is a symmetrical balance when every object is balanced by an equal object on the opposite side. To Japanese, harmony is a fit, a match, an asymmetrical balance that creates a coherent pattern without forcing parallels and matching opposites. Combining the two divergent styles could produce new solutions.

Take the case of International Business Machines (IBM) when it began a cooperative project with Siemens AG of Germany and Toshiba Corporation of Japan to develop a new computer memory chip. At the partnership's East Fishkill, New York, facilities, in mostly windowless offices, more than 100 scientists from culturally diverse backgrounds were brought together.[1]

Before getting together for the project, all the scientists were sent for training programs in their home countries. Toshiba, for example, provided language training. Siemens briefed its scientists about "hamburger" managerial styles. They were told that when criticizing a subordinate, Americans start with small talk: "How is the family?" This is the top of the hamburger. Then, they slip in the meat, the criticisms, which are followed by more bun, the encouraging words, such as "I know you can do better." With Germans, all you get is the meat. Japanese offer only the soft bun; you have to smell the meat.

From the onset of the project and before the full realization of potential synergies, problems began to slow the project down.[1] Siemens' scientists were shocked to find that Japanese seemingly fall asleep during meetings. (It is a common practice for overworked Japanese managers to close their eyes and rest when talk does not concern them.) The Japanese found it painful to sit in small, individual offices and speak English. The Americans complained that the Germans planned too much and the Japanese were not making clear decisions.

The toughest adjustment problem for the Japanese Toshiba scientists was in the area of corporate culture. They were accustomed to working in large rooms with a lot of people, constantly overhearing all the conversations, which was like living in a sea of information. IBM's small offices could not accommodate this important information exchange. The Germans were horrified to see windowless offices. They also did not like to step outside the offices for smoking. For a few months, they were all on their best behavior. With the passage of time, however, the three groups grew more isolated. Even softball games and after-hours socializing were marred by cultural differences. The Americans and Japanese knew softball, but the Germans did not. Participation in the project became a frustrating experience for everyone involved.

Introduction

The survival of an organization depends on its ability to respond to environmental changes and societal demands. Corporate culture consists of the assumptions and values created by the manner in which the organization adapts to these changes and demands. To survive, the organization must interact effectively with its environment. This includes the relationship between corporate culture and the cultural environment. Various aspects of national culture are reflected in the culture of the firm. Although the transfer from national culture to the culture of the firm is never complete, it is irresistible. Very seldom can irreconcilable contradictions exist between the two. Any difference is either temporary or a normal variance of the national norms (p. 80).[2] Incongruity between corporate culture and societal values results in the death of the organization. Organizations that survive are those that adopt cultures that reflect the major values of their society and its dominant cultural characteristics.

Cultural Framework

Although the domain of a culture is not limited by national borders, for simplicity and practicality, we will often use national boundaries as the basis for discussing cultural phenomena. National boundaries delineate the social,

legal, and political environments of host countries. It is within these boundaries that MNCs have to operate and may encounter difficulties due to cultural misunderstandings.

While a domestic firm embodies the basic attributes of its national culture,
an MNC is influenced by the multicultural nature of its global market. Each
firm, however, develops its own unique corporate culture, which exhibits

1. the basic values of society;

2. the requirements of its industry; and

3. the shared philosophy and beliefs of its members, particularly the
   values and philosophy of its top management.

Therefore, there are many cultural similarities and also some differences
among firms. Since domestic firms share the same national culture, cultural
variations among firms are attributed not only to the philosophy of their
founders but also to the differences in industry characteristics[3] and the composition of their members. MNCs, however, are not limited to influence
from one national culture. Through their affiliates around the world, they
are exposed to diverse cultures. Similar to domestic firms, MNCs develop
corporate characters that are the representations of the cultural diversity of
their affiliates. Successful MNCs develop an understanding of cultural differences and learn how to take advantage of opportunities that cultural
diversity may provide and how to cope with different national cultures.[4]
Otherwise, problems similar to those that beset the participants in the IBM
project at East Fishkill may plague the operation of MNCs and detract from
the benefits of internationalization.

Cultural Values and Organizational Behavior

Culture is the way people live and relate to each other and their environment. Culture has physical and nonphysical manifestations.

The physical manifestations of culture can be seen in functional objects
and artistic creations such as architecture, crafts, music, dance, literature,
and poetry.

The nonphysical aspects of culture are manifested through the mental
frameworks people use in dealing with their surroundings. Even our most
mundane daily activities, such as our viewing of surrounding objects, are
influenced by cultural assumptions and frameworks. The following[5] is an
example of variations in mental frameworks between two cultures.

When Nissan chose a car design developed by American designers for the
Infinity J30 over the Japanese design, the Americans were naturally elated.
They were, however, surprised by the proposed modifications. Nissan's
Japanese executives liked the low, gently sloping back end, but they hated the

front. The rejection highlighted cultural differences in visual perception. When Westerners conjure up an image of a car, it is a side view. With the Japanese, however, it is the front. The Japanese read personality and expression into the "face" of the car. All discussions for modifications were centered on whether the "eyes" were sleepy or awake and whether the "mouth" gesture was appropriate, a reference to the shape and size of the headlights and grill. In the end, the headlights and grill were redesigned to make for bigger, more expressive "eyes" and a smaller "mouth."

Likewise, a review of advice columns in Japanese newspapers reveals some of the cultural characteristics that distinguish Japanese. The Japanese version of Ann Landers may sound very parochial or even "antifemale" to Americans, but it fits well with the Japanese. Most of the advice given dwells on the maintenance of social harmony, the avoidance of confrontation, and the importance of hard work. The most common piece of advice offered to suffering questioners is *Gaman*, the stoic virtue of endurance, tolerance, and bearing pain without complaint. The following are two samples:

Sample 1: Mrs. T. of Yamagochi complained to the "Jinsei Annai" ("Guide to Life") column of the newspaper *Yomiuri Shimbun* that her husband has no time at all for the children. She wrote, "He leaves home early and comes home late, therefore, he never sees them. Even on his days off, he leaves early and does not return home till late at night, when the children are already in bed. When the children ask him to play with them, he says he will but goes out anyway. My heart aches to see my children play alone on Sundays, while watching with envy the neighborhood kids who are playing with their fathers."

The advice: "Be patient with your husband, please. You did not mention what kind of job your husband has. He could be involved in scientific research. People involved in scientific works often ignore their families. So please treat him warmly and spend more time with the children yourself. We hope that your husband is successful in his work."

Sample 2: Mrs. C. of Ibaragi had a different problem. She was married 3 years ago and now lives in her husband's home. She wrote that the house is always very dirty. Nobody ever cares to clean the house except her. It drives her crazy to see her baby crawl in all that filth. Her request to her husband to move to another house was answered so rudely that she was considering divorcing him.

The advice: "You have to learn to get along with others. If your in-laws are not concerned about cleanliness, you have to be patient. If you respond by smiling brightly and clean the house as well as you can, it may have an impact on them."[a]

A typical American newspaper would offer quite different advice. Hypothetical answers to these troubled women would proceed to deal with the issues more directly as in the following:

Answer 1: "Evidently, he is unable to realize his obligations and fulfill his role as a father/husband and is attempting to find satisfaction in his work. He may not feel comfortable at home, so he avoids spending time at the house. Whatever the reason, you and your husband should seek professional help while the children are young and the marriage is still intact."

Answer 2: "I suggest you find an affordable home of your own. Help your husband see the benefits of living separately from his family. Explain to him how his family will enjoy the additional space and freedom this will provide them. Keep trying, and don't give up. He may come to his senses. After all, everyone wants more privacy, more space, and a clean home."

To continue our discussion of the influence of culture on international management, we should define culture and corporate culture.

Culture Defined

There are many definitions of culture. Culture is a system of knowledge and standards for perceiving, believing, evaluating, and acting. It is a process of socially transmitted behavior patterns that serves to relate people to the environment.[6] Culture develops over time and is constantly and slowly evolving. A simpler definition is offered by Hofstede, who described culture as "the collective programming of the mind which distinguishes the members of one category of people from those of the other" (pp. 389–398).[7] Another simple definition of culture is given by Schein,[8] who states that culture is the way in which a group of people solves problems and reconciles dilemmas.

Language, ethnicity, and religion are the major components of culture. With some exceptions, ethnicity is a geographically based attribute, as are language and religion.

To understand a culture fully, one must have knowledge of its religious foundation. There are several major religions and many minor ones. The major religions are Buddhism, Christianity, Confucianism, Hinduism, Islam, Judaism, and Shinto. Even a cursory examination of their fundamentals would require voluminous discussion. People who are seriously pursuing international careers would benefit greatly by studying these religions.

The three major religions originating from the Middle East—Judaism, Christianity, and Islam—have much in common and share the same basic framework. These three religions believe in one God who is omnipotent, omnipresent, and omniscient. They also believe in life after death and a day of judgment. The Asian religions such as Hinduism and Buddhism, however, have a different structure. Many abstract religious concepts that have shaped Western thoughts and beliefs are alien to followers of these two religions. A characterization of these differences by H. L. Telshaw Jr. is illuminating. Telshaw, who worked for General Motors for many years in international assignments, especially in Asia, asserted that the adherents of Confucius, Buddha and Lao Tsu's Tao have been molded by the thoughts, ideals and teachings of these Oriental philosophers which incidentally tend to concentrate on developing strong personal and family values unencumbered by such intellectual hurdles as "immaculate Conceptions," "Resurrections," miracles, etc. . . .

We in the Occident having been reared on a battleground contested by the forces of good and evil, have developed an unusual capacity for guilt, not found in the same extremes in the Orient. Captivated by the promises of heaven and the threats of hell, we tend to be idealistically and fearfully motivated. Moreover, because of the widely held belief that we are individually accountable at the judgment seat for our deeds, we tend toward self centeredness and egotism. Orientals, on the other hand, see themselves as merely another manifestation of the creation and strive to be "in harmony" with its other elements and therefore tend to be more realistic—more fatalistic, humble, even innocent.[9] (pp. 250–251)

Cultural differences can be analyzed along many dimensions. Two dimensions relevant to international business are complexity and heterogeneity.

Animal Culture

A very popular area of research in science today is the study of animal behavior. For example, scientists at Emory University are hoping, through the study of animals' behavior and cultures, to learn about human behavior. Carel van Schaik of the University of Zurich, who studies orangutans in Sumatra and Borneo, believes that orangutan groups that spend more time together develop richer cultures and learn more. In effect, culture makes them smarter. From a scientific perspective, "culture" is invented by individual animals in a group and then taught and assimilated by other animals within the group. However, it is not shared among populations of the same species elsewhere. This finding is based on animal behaviors of dolphins, humpback whales, chimpanzees, olive baboons, and orangutans. For example, baboons tend to be aggressive and combative, but this behavior was altered among the baboons on a nature reserve in Kenya. In 1982, all the aggressive male baboons of Kenya's Masai Mara Reserve troop died. The deaths were due to a tuberculosis epidemic. Consequently, the only surviving baboons were the sociable and convivial minority. By 1993, the troop had evolved into a more tolerable baboon society with less

(Continued)

(Continued)

aggressive encounters between troop members and fewer female harassments or terrorized subordinates. In addition, new young males joining the troop promptly adapted to the local customs.

With the omnipresent aggressive tendencies in human nature, this study is encouraging as it suggests that aggression could be a result of powerful cultural influences instead of an innate condition. This notion could possibly be extended to other behaviors that are believed to be innate.[10,11]

Cultural Complexity

The amount of inherent background and contextual information that explain a given situation or condition is referred to as *cultural complexity*. Unspoken, unformulated, and inexplicit rules are used by all cultures in interpersonal relationships and communication. Subtle information supplied by these clues is vital to situations and interpersonal behavior. Cultures vary in their use of contextual information. The more the contextual information required for understanding social situations, the more complex the culture. The higher the cultural complexity, the more difficult it is for outsiders to correctly assess and interpret social circumstance. Countries can be categorized as having a high or a low level of cultural complexity, according to the amount of contextual information needed to understand daily life situations. (See Tables 3.1 and 3.2.) Examples of low-context cultures are the United States, Germany, and Switzerland. China, Japan, and the Latin American and Middle Eastern countries are high context, while France is moderate context (p. 16).[12]

In low-context cultures, communication is explicit and direct; the opposite is true for high-context cultures, where much information is transmitted by physical context or internalized in people. It is hard for those unfamiliar with this hidden information to correctly interpret and understand the message. For example, in a business deal, when an American responds affirmatively to a proposal, it means that the proposal is being accepted. A Japanese "yes," however, may not mean acceptance. Depending on the circumstances surrounding the message, it may mean "yes" or maybe "no." Japanese are very reluctant to say "no," fearing the damage they may cause to interpersonal relationships. They are particularly anxious not to embarrass others by saying "no" in public.

There are many more implicit rules and requirements governing the daily life of people in countries with a high level of cultural complexity. These rules and understandings determine the appropriateness of behavior. Violations of these rules are not taken lightly. For example, in Japan, the place of people around a negotiation table is strictly based on their seniority.

Table 3.1   Information Attributes in High- and Low-Context Cultures

High Context	Low Context
Through physical context	Through content of the message
Internalized by people	Not internalized by people
Hidden under the surface	Apparent and embedded with the message
Difficult to interpret by outsiders	Easy to interpret by outsiders
Indirect expression of negative information in public	Direct expression of negative and positive information in public
Implicit rules	Explicit rules
Adherence to rules is enforced	Adherence to rules is not enforced
Warm-up period is needed for serious information exchange	Information exchange can begin immediately

Table 3.2   Interpersonal Relations in Low- and High-Context Cultures

High Context	Low Context
Difficult to form friendships	Easy to form friendships
Long lasting/permanent	Temporary, transient, and casual
High obligation	Low obligation
High duration	Low duration
Trust has to be earned	People are trusted until proven wrong
Long-lasting cultural norms	Cultural norms tend to change
Involved in others' lives	Privacy is valued
Appear to be very polite	Politeness not apparent
High cultural protocol	Low cultural protocol
Adhere to cultural protocol	Tolerate deviations from cultural protocol

The same is true in the Middle East, where no business transaction should begin until participants have exchanged pleasantries and had time to learn about each other and feel comfortable carrying out the business transactions. The desire for efficiency and fast action that prompts Americans to get to the business at hand immediately will be regarded as rude and impolite. In such situations, in effect, the Americans are missing the contextual ingredient they should use to interact with others.

In countries with a low level of cultural complexity, interpersonal relationships tend to be temporary and transient. Friendships are very easily formed and dissolved. The ease and speed with which Americans get to know people often leads visitors to the United States to comment on how "unbelievably friendly" Americans are. There is a worldwide complaint, however, that Americans are capable of only informal, superficial friendships that do not involve an exchange of deep confidences (p. 5).[13] Often, foreigners are surprised and disappointed by the American attitude toward friendship. At first, the initial gesture of friendliness, such as getting invited to an American home, is mistakenly interpreted as a sign of the desire for a close relationship. When such an expectation is not fulfilled, they are disappointed. They are not aware that the American friendship tends to be high spread, low obligation, low duration, and high trust (Du Bois as cited in Gareis, p. 69).[14] Americans offer their friendship readily and trust others easily. This friendship, however, lacks a sense of obligation and permanence. American mobility and advanced institutions can explain the difference between American friendship and that of others. Growing up in families that change residence every few years, Americans either do not sufficiently practice forming close friendships or develop a self-protective, defensive manner. Keeping relationships casual will not result in hurt feelings when it is time to separate and say good bye. In times of need, such as a financial crunch, institutions such as banks and charitable organizations are effective sources of assistance. They reduce the need for or substitute for reliance on close friends.

In contrast, interpersonal relationships are often more difficult to form but are long lasting and much stronger and deeper in countries with high-context cultures. Friendship in these cultures is marked by high obligation and high duration. Their cultural norms tend to have a long life and resist change. People from high-context cultures are inclined to get more involved in each other's lives.

Considering these cultural differences, without proper training and preparation, managers from low-context cultures would face difficulties when dealing with people from high-context cultures, and vice versa. Taking words at their face value, ignoring unspoken signals, and lacking background information embedded in the cultural tradition could result in gross misunderstandings. The tendency of low-context cultures for direct communication and specificity could be interpreted as rudeness and impoliteness. The preference not to meddle in other people's lives could be regarded as cold and indicative of an absence of feelings. Of course, people from high-context cultures experience difficulties of their own in low-context cultures.

Cultural Heterogeneity

Language, ethnicity, and religion are the major components of culture. A relatively large degree of dissimilarity and diversity among cultural components is regarded as *cultural heterogeneity*. A country diverse in language, ethnic makeup, and religion is culturally heterogeneous. Examples are Canada, the United States, and India. These countries are made up of many subcultures. Countries having a relatively low diversity of language, ethnicity, and religion are Japan and Saudi Arabia; they are culturally homogeneous.

It is more demanding and challenging for expatriate managers to function in cultures with a high level of cultural heterogeneity and complexity. To perform managerial functions demands a more careful assessment of situations and an understanding of circumstances. It is more difficult for an expatriate, for example, to manage a firm in India than in the United States. While both the United States and India are culturally heterogeneous, India has a higher level of cultural heterogeneity and complexity. Conducting business transactions in a country with a relatively homogeneous culture is much simpler for a foreigner. Understanding the cultural complexity and heterogeneity of host countries should be a top priority of MNCs. To succeed in the multicultural environment of the world market, MNCs should show sensitivity to their host countries' cultures and try to understand the cultural differences. Also, focusing on the dominant culture in a heterogeneous culture may result in lost opportunities. The losses are due to not recognizing the needs of members of subcultures. For example, only recently have American businesses begun to cater to the Mexican-American subculture.

Exotic Cuisines

When people travel around the world, they may have to try different foods. Some of the exotic cuisines include insects, various plants, and unique animals. In Colombia, for instance, travelers may be offered termites and palm grubs or spread ground-up ants on bread. In the Philippines, the food selection may include beetles, grasshoppers, locusts, and dragonflies.

In Mexico, the custom of eating insects originates from pre-Hispanic inhabitants, who viewed insects as an important source of protein since there were no cows at that time. Now, not only common people eat these exotic foods; they are also found in upper-class restaurants. Some restaurants include in their menus worms, nopales (a small, thick cactus leaf used in salads), huitlacohche (a brainlike fungus that grows on maize), and escamoles (ants' eggs). The worms are lightly fried in olive oil and served in a bowl with tortillas and guacamole. They taste something like pork crackling or fried seaweed. In a small town called Oaxaca, grasshoppers are a popular fast food.

But today, these exotic foods are slowly gaining the status of delicacies and may be priced out of the reach of the poor. A chef lamented these developments saying it is a shame because half a kilo of grasshoppers for a few dollars has more protein than 20 kilos of beef.[15]

Four Dimensions of Culture

While there are similarities among cultures, no two cultures are alike. There are many ways of comparing and contrasting cultures. In the literature on international management, a well-known typology of culture is offered by Hofstede.[16] He compared cultures using four cultural dimensions: individualism/collectivism, masculinity/femininity (gender values differentiation and rigidity), uncertainty avoidance, and power distance. The four dimensions are described in the following. While the validity of these dimensions has been a matter of controversy, they have provided a broad framework that has inspired much research and new theorizing (p. 365).[17]

Individualism. Individualism is the culture's emphasis on personal identity. It encourages self-serving behaviors. In individualistic cultures, it is expected that individuals primarily look after their own interests and those of their immediate family. Therefore, individualistic cultures are loosely integrated. The opposite of individualism is collectivism. Collectivist cultures emphasize groups (e.g., family, neighborhood, organizations, and the country), not individuals. In a collectivist society, the interests and goals of individuals are subordinate to those of the group.[18] Individuals seek fulfillment and happiness in the harmony of the group. Groups provide security to members and protect their interests in exchange for their complete loyalty. Compared with individualistic societies, collectivist societies are tightly integrated (p. 390).[7]

Individualism is directly related to the use of space and accessibility.[19] Individualistic societies heavily emphasize owning space. The heavy emphasis on individual ownership, in turn, tends to distance people from one another, limit sensory stimulation, and promote privacy. Most Western cultures are individualistic, whereas Eastern European and most South American cultures are collectivist. People from individualistic cultures rely on personal judgment, while collectivists value collective judgment and emphasize harmony between people. Collectivists are more interested in living in harmony with nature, while individualists attempt to dominate nature.

Gender Role Differentiation and Rigidity. This dimension refers to the rigidity of socially prescribed gender roles. In some cultures, gender roles are narrowly defined, and people are expected to behave within their socially prescribed roles. Masculinity is identified with traits and behaviors such as strength, speed, assertiveness, competitiveness, dominance, anger, ambition, and the pursuit of wealth. Feminine characteristics and behaviors are associated with emotionality, affection, compassion, warmth, and nurturing of the weak and needy. The emphasis on one or the other set of attributes characterizes the masculinity or femininity of a culture. In societies where gender roles are more clearly specified, masculine manners are expected from men, and women are expected to behave in feminine ways.

Countries can be ranked according to gender role differentiation and rigidity.[16] The 10 countries with the highest masculinity index are Japan, Austria, Venezuela, Italy, Switzerland, Mexico, Ireland, Great Britain, Germany, and the Philippines. The highest feminine value countries on this index are Sweden, Norway, the Netherlands, Denmark, Finland, Chile, Portugal, Thailand, Peru, and Spain. Although not among the 10 highest on the masculinity index, the United States tends to be a masculine society. Compared with the people of most countries, American people of both sexes seem to be loud, aggressive, and competitive. In the United States, feminine people are more expressive, nurturing, and relational and provide more personal information. Masculine people are more dominant, argumentative, assertive, and goal oriented. Emotional expressions such as crying are associated more with femininity.

Power Distance. Variation in the distribution of power among the members of a society is called power distance (PD). It is the difference in the amount of power possessed by the least powerful and the most powerful members of the society. Various degrees of power inequality exist in all cultures. According to Mulder's power distance reduction theory, superiors will try to maintain and increase the PD between themselves and subordinates, and subordinates will try to reduce this distance.[20] Hofstede, however, proposed that there is a culturally based equilibrium level at which both the most powerful and the least powerful persons will find inequality acceptable. Cultures with high PD tend to concentrate influence and control in the hands of a few. Distribution of power and influence tends to be more equal among people of low-PD cultures.

PD can be measured using Hofstede's power distance index (PDI). The 10 countries with the highest PDI are the Philippines, Mexico, Venezuela, India, Singapore, Brazil, Hong Kong, France, Colombia, and Turkey. Cultures with the lowest PDI are found in Western Europe, Israel, New Zealand, the United States, and Canada. There is less emphasis on power among the people of low-PD countries. As Hofstede said of one Swedish university official, "In order to exercise power, he tries not to look powerful" (p. 94).[16] Interpersonal relationships between the people of high-PD countries tend to be more along the hierarchical line. In general, Asian and African cultures maintain hierarchical role relationships.[21]

Uncertainty. Cultures view risk and uncertainty differently. Some cultures have more aversion to risk and uncertainty and avoid situations that are ambiguous and risky. Other cultures can tolerate such situations with less discomfort and anxiety. "Cultures with a strong uncertainty avoidance are active, aggressive, emotional, security-seeking, and intolerant. Cultures with a weak uncertainty avoidance are contemplative, less aggressive, unemotional, accepting of personal risk, and relatively tolerant" (p. 390).[7]

Hofstede found that the top 10 countries that are high on the uncertainty avoidance dimension are, in descending order, Greece, Portugal, Belgium, Japan, Peru, France, Chile, Spain, Argentina, and Turkey. The

10 cultures with the lowest uncertainty avoidance are Singapore, Denmark, Sweden, Hong Kong, Ireland, Great Britain, India, the Philippines, the United States, and Canada (p. 122).[16] Countries that are higher on uncertainty avoidance tend to be Catholic cultures, while Protestant, Hindu, and Buddhist cultures tend to be more tolerant of ambiguity and risk (p. 135).[16]

There are many ways of explaining cultural differences. The application of these four dimensions is only one method. According to Osland and Bird,[22] there are 22 dimensions commonly used to compare cultures. In discussing cultural differences, scholars and researchers have used those dimensions that were considered more relevant to their purpose. For example, in a large-scale study of 62 cultures, the GLOBE Project, at Thunderbird, the Garvin School of International Management, has used nine dimensions: PD, in-group collectivism, institutional collectivism, uncertainty avoidance, future orientation, gender egalitarianism, assertiveness, humane orientation, and performance orientation.[23]

Familiarity with cultural dimensions is useful for understanding cultural differences. Besides the knowledge of cultural dimensions, there are two cultural features with which MNC managers should be familiar: cultural paradox and cultural shock. This will assist them in dealings and interactions with people of different cultures.

Cultural Paradox

Certain situations appear to contradict the values that we associate with a given culture. These situations are called **cultural paradoxes**. Consider the following examples.

According to Hofstede's cultural dimension of uncertainty avoidance, Americans are characterized by high tolerance for uncertainty while Japanese have a low tolerance. Why, then, in business contracts do Americans painstakingly spell out every possible situation while Japanese intentionally incorporate ambiguous clauses? Also, in the United States, autocratic behavior is frequently tolerated from CEOs, even though the United States is identified as an egalitarian culture. In Latin America, status derived from class and family background is more important than achieved status gained through hard work. In professional soccer, however, achieved status trumps class and family distinction.[22]

Osland and Bird[22] assert that in using the aforementioned cultural dimensions, we should be very careful not to stereotype the entire culture. Cultural dimensions are often framed, perhaps inaccurately, as a dualistic, either/or situation. Bipolar patterns make cultural behavior appear paradoxical. What appears to be paradoxical may be variation in behavioral norms for individuals, organizational cultures, subcultures, generational differences, and the changing sections of society. We should keep in mind that cultural values are not uniformly accepted and practiced by all members of the society, nor are they uniformly distributed in all cultural institutions. Also, we should not assume that different cultural values cannot coexist. According to Leung et al. (p. 359),[17] "strong traditional values, such as group solidarity, interpersonal harmony, paternalism, and familism, can co-exist with modern values of individual achievement and competition. A case in point is the findings that Chinese in Singapore and China indeed endorsed both traditional and modern values."

Cultural Shock

Cultural shock, or as it is popularly known, "culture shock," is a psychological condition that a person experiences before adapting and adjusting to a new cultural environment. Facing totally unfamiliar signs and signals in daily social interaction in a new environment creates anxiety, which we call cultural shock. Concerns over necessities that are taken for granted overwhelm the newcomer to a foreign culture. The ordeal of finding out where to buy groceries and how to mail a letter, using public transportation, asking directions to commonly used public places, ordering unfamiliar foods in restaurants, and dealing with local laws and customs in the host country overburdens foreigners. The psychological demands of performing all these tasks without the benefit of prior experience are disorienting and stressful.

In daily life, we learn the cues necessary for dealing with others and with our surroundings. These learned cues are useless in a foreign country, where signs are in a different language; facial expressions, customs, and norms are unfamiliar; and others do not respond to our actions as we expect.

Cultural shock affects people differently. Some are able to deal with it more successfully. As Redden puts it, "Culture shock is a psychological disorientation caused by misunderstanding or not understanding the cues from another culture. It arises from such things as lack of knowledge, limited prior experience, and personal rigidity."[24] Individuals entering a new environment usually go through several fairly predictable stages of adjustment (see Table 3.3) (Oberg, 1979, as cited in Gareis[14] [p. 70] and Black and Mendenhall[25]):

1. *The honeymoon stage:* During this stage, the new place is positively exciting and fascinating to the person.

2. *The crisis stage:* This stage is marked by complaint, hostility, and seeking refuge with fellow nationals. This condition is triggered by the stress and frustration associated with having to live in an unfamiliar environment and interact according to strange rules. Some have called this the "disillusionment or culture shock stage."

Table 3.3   Stages of Adjustment to a New Environment

Stages	Symptoms
Honeymoon	Exciting and fascinating
Crisis	Complaints, frustration, and hostility
Recovery	A feeling of superiority toward the host culture
Adjustment	Ease of communication and acceptance of the host culture

3. *The recovery stage:* This stage is marked by a feeling of superiority toward the host country. Gradually, the individual adapts to the new cultural norms and learns how to behave appropriately in the host country. During this stage, the person regains composure and a sense of humor.

4. *The adjustment stage:* This stage is marked by ease of communication and acceptance of host culture ways as an alternative way of living. This stage has also been called the "mastery stage," characterized by an increase in the individual's ability to function effectively in the new culture.

Cultural Aspects of Management

Managerial concepts such as motivation, superior-subordinate relationships, authority, leadership, and control are rooted in cultural values and norms. The meaning attached to and the application of these concepts varies from one culture to another. The roles and expectations of managers and subordinates are different across cultures. Consider the following conversation between an American manager (A) and a Greek worker (G) (pp. 42–43).[26] Based on his cultural norms, the American manager, who favors employee participation, expects certain initiatives and self-direction from the worker. The Greek worker, however, expects a superior to exercise managerial authority and be direct in giving orders. Both attribute a certain meaning to the dialogue, using their cultural assumptions and frame of reference, and each has certain culturally determined expectations regarding superior-subordinate relationships.

Conversation between them, and how that conversation is interpreted, is depicted in the following (pp. 42–43) (attributions are in parentheses):[26]

A: How long will it take you to finish this report?

(A: I asked him to participate. G: His behavior does not make sense. He is the boss. Why doesn't he tell me?)

G: I do not know. How long should it take?

(A: He refuses to take responsibility. G: I asked him for an order.)

A: You are in the best position to analyze time requirements.

(A: I press him to take responsibility for his own actions. G: What nonsense! I better give him an answer.)

G: 10 days.

(A: He lacks the ability to estimate time; this time estimate is totally inadequate.)

A: Take 15. Is it agreed you will do it in 15 days?

(A: I offered a contract. G: These are my orders: 15 days.)

In fact, the report needed 30 days of regular work. So the Greek worked day and night, but at the end of the 15th day, he still needed one more day's work.

A: Where is the report?

(A: I am making sure he fulfills his contract. G: He is asking for the report.)

G: It will be ready tomorrow.

(Both attribute that it is not ready.)

A: But we had agreed it would be ready today.

(A: I must teach him to fulfill a contract. G: The stupid, incompetent boss! Not only he did give me the wrong orders, but he does not even appreciate that I did a 30-day job in 16 days. I can't work for such a man.)

The Greek walks out in disgust and later hands in his resignation. The American is surprised.

Because of cultural differences, the American and the Greek were unable to understand each other. The consequence of such ineffective interaction is a disappointment for the individuals and a performance loss for the firm.

The interaction between the Greek and the American is probably typical of the encounters that occur when two persons from different cultures, who are not familiar with the norms of the other's culture, interact. Though cultures differ, cultural differences between traditional and modern societies are more noticeable in international business. Many norms of modern societies either do not have equivalents in traditional cultures or are totally different. The concept of time, for example, as a tangible commodity that could be saved, wasted, used, and given away is alien to many traditional cultures. Modern societies have much more differentiation and compartmentalization of various facets of daily interaction. In traditional societies, however, most aspects of daily life blend together. Business transactions, for example, are combined with interpersonal relationships such that separating them may not be possible. For instance, to babysit for a neighbor, an American expects to get paid, while in most Asian countries, since neighborhood children are all part of a big family, an expression of appreciation suffices. An attempt to pay for a favor that requires just a compliment could cause much embarrassment.

The most notable compartmentalization and differentiation are in the separation of individuals' work roles in the organization and the roles outside the organization. Americans leave behind much of the trappings and circumstances of their roles as superiors when they finish their daily work. In a traditional culture, a superior's organizational distinction and status extend far beyond the firm and the work relationship. In the Middle East, for example, superiors are considered as role models even outside the organization. A good boss is someone who is concerned about the family problems of his or her subordinates and lends a helping hand in their resolution. The same is true in Latin America.

Culture influences every aspect of people's daily lives. The influence is pervasive. The underlying cultural values and assumptions are the foundation for accepted and expected managerial practices and corporate culture. These assumptions and values prescribe the way individuals perceive and evaluate the world, themselves, and others.

Cultural Values in Contrast

To appreciate the influence of cultural values and assumptions on management, let us examine some fundamental cultural values relevant to business. In particular, we will start with a discussion of some basic values of U.S. culture that guide decision making and anchor perception of the environment. We will compare and contrast them with those of other cultures. The resultant understanding could safeguard us against cross-cultural mistakes and mishaps.

People of most cultures have a tendency for ethnocentrism. The inclination to display an attitude of superiority is symptomatic of ethnocentrism. When doing business abroad, such a tendency could undermine the competitive position of an MNC. Today, American managers have a much more enlightened understanding of people of other cultures. Previously, American MNCs dispatched their managers to other countries not to learn and understand more about the host culture but to improve and change it for the better. As it was usually put, they wanted to "help introduce modern managerial values" (p. 84).[2] This attitude was more pronounced when dealing with developing countries. As Kolde asserts, because of their material "backwardness," developing countries were assumed to be formless matter waiting to be shaped and developed to American concepts of good management. To the surprise of many, the subsequent interaction with these cultures brought the sobering realization that the social fabric of any society, whether or not it is industrially advanced, can be as tenacious as that of our own (p. 85).[2]

Some assume that mere traveling abroad, participating in popular activities, and following the way of life of foreigners will elevate them to cultural understanding. To them, cultural sensitivity and understanding boil down to three Ds: dining, drinking, and dancing. The three Ds are helpful in breaking the ice and enabling a person to strike up a friendly conversation with foreigners, but they are not a safeguard against cultural misunderstanding. Knowing the culinary variations among nations is useful (see Table 3.4); however, the knowledge and understanding of cultural values, norms, and assumptions is the proper way of increasing our cultural sensitivity.

Most of us do not want to be considered insensitive and ignorant. Learning about other cultures certainly allows us to be sensitive to other people and their perspectives. This is helpful at a personal level and can produce successful business deals and reduce failures in business transactions. We cannot become proficient in the knowledge of all cultures. However, understanding our own basic cultural values could go a long way

Table 3.4   Interesting Food Items Around the World

Food Items	Locations
Monkeys and tarantulas	Amazon
Donkeys and monkeys	China
Rabbits, snails, donkeys, and livestock intestines	France
Horses	Kazakhstan
Grasshoppers, worms, ants, and ants' eggs	Mexico
Camels and livestock brains, eyes, and testicles	Middle East
Locusts	Middle East, North Africa, and the Philippines
Crickets	North Africa
Cats and dogs	South Korea
Rats and snakes	Vietnam
Termites and palm grubs	Colombia
Beetles, grasshoppers, and dragonflies	The Philippines

toward increasing our sensitivity to cultural differences. Let us now examine the basic American cultural values.

The Individual

An organization is made up of a group of people and is the result of their purposeful collective efforts. People are the essence of an organization. All organizational activities are based on assumptions regarding the individuals, their interpersonal relationships, and how they relate to society. These assumptions are culturally determined and differ among nations. There is a big difference, for example, between the Western, particularly the U.S., concept of the "person" and the place of a person in society and the corresponding Asian understanding. According to Richard E. Nisbett,[27] Americans regard personalities as relatively fixed, while Asians regard them as more malleable (pp. 6, 12–127).

Westerners have an isolationist concept of the "person." To them, an individual is a person standing alone and clearly separate from his or her environment. Such a concept of an individual is alien to Japanese. In the Japanese language, there is no equivalent term for the English word *I*, denoting a person isolated from the surroundings. For Japanese, individuals exist only in relation to others. "The individual is a node of interrelations with others around him or her. Each has a special way and meaning in relating with others, which becomes his or her individuality. Without such relations, there is no individuality."[28] Different terms are used to distinguish between these various individualities that identify the person-situational relationships. The "I" of teacher-student, or a superior-subordinate situation (*watakushi*, for male or female), for example, is different from the "I" of parent-child or sibling relationships (*watashi* or *ore*, a female or male about 14 years or older; *atashi* or *boku*, a girl or a boy under 14 years).

The differing views of an individual produce divergent concepts of organizational relationships. In countries with an isolationist view of the individual, such as the United States, an individual is expected to perform certain functions with clearly defined responsibilities. The individual's participation in business organizations is based on a clear demarcation of each person's performance and the importance of the individual's contribution to the organization. Job descriptions clearly specify the domain of each person's responsibilities and the management expectations of a person occupying a position. This situation is totally different in Japan (p. 5).[29] Japanese business organizations do not necessarily define the scope of the job assigned to each individual. The basic unit of work is not the individual's job but the job of a work unit, a section, or a department. This is consistent with the "Japanese vagueness of individual responsibility, the idea of joint group responsibility, and the strong sense of responsibility toward the small, close group" (p. 5).[29] Similarly, the Chinese philosophy of individual rights could be regarded as one's "share" of the rights of the community as a whole, not a license to do as one pleases (pp. 6, 199).[27]

Because of different cultural heritages, the differences between Americans and Japanese are not surprising. However, there are also differences in perspectives between the Americans and other Western cultures. For example, the best way to illustrate the difference between the Germans and the Americans is by using the concept of social distance proposed by Kurt Lewin (pp. 18–25).[30] His explanation of Germans and Americans is valid even today and has reverberated in more recent literature on intercultural studies (pp. 67–80).[14]

Lewin states that an individual could be depicted as having a multilayered personality with two major regions, the peripheral region and the central region, as illustrated in Figure 3.1. Americans have a much larger peripheral region and a smaller central region (the shaded area in Figure 3.1) than Germans. The peripheral region is the "public self" and the central region is the "private self." Americans have more layers of the peripheral, and these layers are easier to penetrate. Their deeper layers of the central region, however, are relatively inaccessible. In comparison, Germans have low accessibility at the peripheral region but share a larger area of the central region with their intimates.

The accessibility of a larger peripheral region means that Americans are more willing to open to others than are Germans. In the United States, it is quite common for strangers to greet each other with a smile. Such behavior is unusual in Germany. The Americans seem more friendly and ready to help strangers. A visitor to the United States is more apt to receive an invitation to dine with people in their homes than someone visiting Germany. It seems that Americans need less privacy in certain aspects of

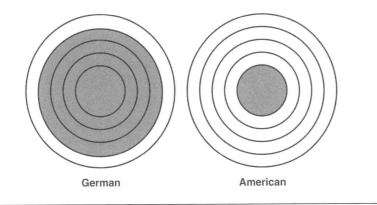

German   American

Figure 3.1   Social Distance

their lives. Many executives of American corporations or government agencies leave the doors of their offices open, and everyone can see their daily
activities. German managers, even those at lower managerial positions,
would find it unthinkable to leave their doors open. To Germans, such
accessibility is an indication of low prestige.

The openness of the peripheral region does not extend to the more
private, intimate region of the American personality. Friendship in the
United States progresses much faster through the layers of the peripheral
region and up to a certain point where the central core of the personality is
reached. It is as difficult to reach the central region of the American personality as that of the Germans. But it seems that the boundary leading to intimate relationships is more clearly marked for Americans than for Germans.
In Germany, the transition from the peripheral region to the very intimate
region is more gradual and more involved.

Interpersonal relationships involve less of the central core of Americans
and more of the central region of Germans. Americans can form relatively
close relations with others without deep personal and emotional involvement. This makes it possible to have less personal friction and fewer disap-
pointments. It also makes it as easy to say good-bye to friends of many
years as to acquaintances of a few weeks.

The size of each region and the number of layers in it may explain certain
behavioral differences among Germans and Americans and American and
German communication patterns. When faced with small difficulties and
misfortunes in daily life, for example, Americans tend to express less open
anger. Their reaction is more from the point of view of an accident taking
place and the remedies needed to prevent a similar occurrence. Germans
react to these difficulties from more of a moral point of view by assigning
blame. These differences in the reaction to events reflect differences in the
layering of the peripheral and central regions for Germans and Americans.
It is less likely that these events will touch the central regions of an American

and more possible that they may touch the Germans' central region. Therefore, the German reaction is more one of anger and moral judgment because it involves more of the private, central core of the person.

The peripheral layers of personality, according to Lewin,[30] include the "executive" region of a person (p. 25). These layers are closer to the environment and correspond to the appearance and the action of a person. It seems that compared with Germans, Americans emphasize achievement more than ideology and status, and in science the emphasis is more on practice than on theory. Americans are pragmatic and Germans are idealistic (see Box 3.1).

Box 3.1   Shoe-Shining Monopoly

Hikmet Kotsch is a Turkish-born, naturalized citizen who has lived in Germany for three decades. He arrived in Germany as a guest laborer. On retirement, he tried to supplement his income through shoe shining, which he had learned at his uncle's shoe-shining parlor in Istanbul. He applied for a license, but it was rejected. To the Germans, shining shoes was not a legitimate occupation.

Several years ago, he moved to Berlin, where he thought he could work as a shoe shiner. He applied again for the license, and once again it was rejected. He tried over and over again but did not have any luck.

For more than 2 years, Cemaltettin Cetin, a social worker, helped Kotsch write over 40 letters to various government agencies appealing for a license. They did not get any response at all. Finally, Cetin had a brilliant idea. Knowing that Germany values credentials like no other country, he wrote to the Istanbul chamber of commerce requesting a certificate for Kotsch. They obtained the certificate indicating that Kotsch's work in his uncle's business made him a master of a recognized profession, a shoe shiner.

With the certificate in hand, he applied for a license again and was granted one just because he had a diploma from Istanbul. He was eventually allowed to do shoe shining in a mall. He became the sole legally sanctioned professional shine in Berlin. But his monopoly has not helped him much. He says the Germans spend all their money on beer.[31]

Ecological Relations

Besides the isolationist view of the individual, Americans also have a different ecological concept of the individual, the relationship between the person, the environment, and other people (see Table 3.5).

Americans believe that people are the masters of their own destiny. They are very optimistic about their ability to shape the future through hard work. They believe that individuals have a considerable choice in what

Table 3.5   The American View of the Individual

1. People are masters of their destinies
2. Optimistic about the ability to shape the future
3. Individuals can influence the events around them
4. Hard work brings a better future
5. Pride in doing things without help from others
6. Strong sense of independence
7. Self-determination and individual responsibility
8. Individual responsibilities are clearly defined
9. Pragmatic realism
10. Cost and benefit analyses guide decision making

happens to them and around them. Americans take pride in doing everything by themselves without help from others and have a very strong sense
of independence. The concept of self-determination has a counterpart of
individual responsibility. Individuals are held responsible for their deeds.
The limits of each person's responsibilities are clearly defined. Business
organizations assign work to individuals and hold them accountable for the
outcome. Personal accomplishment is highly valued in American culture,
and failures are considered stepping-stones to eventual success. Of course,
the American self-determination concept is tempered with pragmatic realism. Cost and benefit analyses serve as guides for making decisions. The
idealism of pursuing a dream for the sake of the pursuit has less appeal
to Americans. An endeavor should have a realistic chance of producing a
tangible outcome; otherwise, it is not worth the effort.

The American concept of the individual as an independent, self-sufficient,
self-reliant, and hardworking person who should be held responsible for outcomes has been an anchor around which other social values were constructed.
Various cultures have different views of the individual and ecological relations. In some cultures, the concept of the individual as a lone entity all by
itself and separate from the surrounding milieu does not have much appeal.
Japanese, Middle Eastern, and Southeast Asian cultures have a concept of
individual responsibility different from the one common in American firms.

In Japan, there is little awareness of "individual responsibility." The
scope of individual responsibility is very small and obscure. Instead, the
responsibility is to the group. As a corollary, there is an exceptionally strong
sense of "solidarity of responsibility" among members of a family, a work
group, and other social organizations. The solidarity of responsibility is a
given. Regardless of an individual's wish, membership in a group puts a person in the position of assuming joint responsibility (p. 2).[29] This sense of
joint responsibility is felt more toward lower-level groups, such as work
groups in which members have closer contact with one another, than to larger
groups. This joint responsibility creates "responsibility of the stronger."

"When the weaker element in the group is in trouble or placed in an awkward situation, it is considered natural in Japan that he or she seek succour, and that the 'stronger' will be considered as being 'irresponsible' should he not respond to and take appropriate measures" (p. 2).[29]

The self-determinism valued in American culture makes little sense to a devout Muslim, who believes in preordained faith based on God's will. It is not uncommon to hear a Muslim responding to a business request with a reply of "Insha Allah," which means "if God is willing." Since the destiny of people and all events are dependent on the will of Allah, it is irreligious for a devout Muslim to think he or she can influence the future. Consequently, planning for the future and striving to succeed in the American sense take on a different meaning for Muslims. In this vein, business strategy and planning are carried out within the context of God's will. Successes are regarded as the blessings of God, and failures are viewed as what God did not mean to be. This does not mean lack of effort or a disbelief in struggle. It means submission without fuss to what has happened.

This fatalist view of life (from the American perspective) is also shared by the Buddhists of Southeast Asia, where people believe that the selfish desire for possession and enjoyment is the source of all suffering. Hard work seems futile, and self-determination has no meaning where forces beyond human control influence events.

The same is true in Latin America, where the culture promotes a strong belief that fate has more to do with success than does effort. Again, this belief is probably rooted in religious teachings and historical experiences.

Class-Rank Relationship

In the United States, being a senior executive of a well-known, large company is tantamount to belonging to "high society." Promotion in business serves as the main path for upward mobility in society. The rank-status correspondence is less pronounced in other cultures. An observation by Kolde in the statistical analysis department of a European organization is an apt illustration: The department was headed by a person from a lower social class who had impeccable credentials as an analyst. In a subunit of the department, there was a titled aristocrat with a prominent social status but modest analytical skills. Although in the organizational setting the commoner was in charge, in nonbusiness settings he was outranked by his aristocratic subordinate. Some of the social functions in clubs and parties that his aristocratic subordinate customarily attended were inaccessible to the commoner because of his low-class status (p. 426).[32]

The status of individuals in American society is based on many factors. Besides family and wealth, the status of an American is largely dependent on level of education, amount of expertise, and his or her accomplishments. In other societies, such as among Arabs, familial links overshadow everything else. Although education level, knowledge, and expertise confer prestige and status on individuals, the status of an Arab in society is largely determined by his or her family position and social contacts.[33] Likewise, the caste system of Indian society will determine the profession a person is expected to pursue. Modernization, however, is weakening the caste structure.

Work and Material Gain

Hard work is considered a requisite for the attainment of a goal. It is not only a requirement for success but also a virtue. The frontier heritage of America has made hard work the gospel. The prolonged siesta of other lands, the leisurely luncheon, and the hour-long teas are frowned on (p. 688).[34] Without hard work, individuals should not expect to achieve their goals, in all likelihood they won't, and if by luck they do, they do not deserve it. Americans take pride in hard work and believe it will eventually pay off. Work permeates all aspects of American life. Social occasions, religious gatherings, and leisure activities are quite often used as opportunities to facilitate or conduct business. Many Americans spend their weekends doing what others consider manual labor, such as painting the house, washing the car, mowing the lawn, or tinkering in the garage. It seems to others that Americans live to work, while others work to live.

To people of many cultures, work is a necessary burden, which if possible should be avoided. Australians, for example, seem to envy the "bludger," a person who appears to work hard while actually doing little work (p. 13).[35] Most Middle Easterners look down on manual work with contempt and consider it undignified to engage in manual labor. The undignified status of manual work may be one reason why some oil-rich nations of the Persian Gulf region traditionally import virtually all their labor force from other countries, notably Pakistan. Manual work is particularly demeaning for the educated and the wealthy. Some Europeans do not share the American attitude toward work. The following story describes the Italian view of a person who is too much consumed by the work ethic. Italians consider such a person as one-dimensional.[35]

An Italian air force officer gave me his impressions of Germans. He likes Germany, but found the Germans very *lineare*, meaning direct, purposeful, and efficient. "Lineare" is not a compliment. It characterizes a one-dimensional person, while Italians feel it is important to develop the whole person, not just the work side. I said I thought the Americans were probably just as bad as the Germans, but he shook his head and grinned. "Worse," he said, "much worse." (p. 13)

While Americans work hard because they consider hard work a virtue and enjoy it as an activity, Japanese work hard for a different reason. Japanese people work hard because of their loyalty and obligation to the group and because of a sense of responsibility to the group. To perform well is considered fulfilling a duty. When the group succeeds, so do the individual members, and when the group fails, its members have failed. The failure of an individual member to do his or her part in a group situation usually results in a deep sense of agony and shame, the loss of face. So people work hard, stay overtime, or come to work even when sick to ensure the group's success.

Japanese work more hours than their American or European counterparts. In Japan, very seldom does anyone refuse to work overtime. Since everybody seems to work hard, most individuals feel obligated to do the same. Doing otherwise could cause collective failure and result in loss of face. It would plunge the individual into a deep personal agony and shame. Japanese feel that if you lose face once, you lose face forever. The pressure to work hard, and the feeling of obligation and duty to do so, critics say, has resulted in a phenomenon called "karoshi," meaning sudden death from hard work.[36]

While wealth has universal appeal, the significance of wealth and wealth acquisition varies among nations. Wealth has two basic dimensions. First, wealth is an instrument for the provision of sustenance and physical comfort for self and others. Second, wealth is a measure of success and accomplishment. The Americans' penchant for wealth is not only aimed at providing material comfort but is also an indication of accomplishment. Often, the Americans focus more on the second dimension. As Billington and Ridge have asserted, the American emphasis on wealth acquisition is a frontier heritage. From the early days of the frontier experience, the abundance of natural resources had resulted in a state of mind in which material progress was the only measure of a person's worth. Wealth was the talisman that would create social status, influence, and political power. Money was the primary objective in the life of many frontier settlers. The contemporary materialistic attitude of Americans is rooted in the affluence of the frontiers (p. 688).[34]

The Failure of an International Joint Venture

After two and a half years of alliance, Corning Company and a Mexican glass manufacturer, Vitro, had to call off their marriage. Corning is the glass and ceramic giant with a long history of successful joint ventures. More than half of Corning's operating income comes from joint ventures. Corning's success in alliance with other companies is mostly due to its ability to cope with the constant give-and-take that joint ventures require.

Not all of Corning's alliances, however, are successful. The joint venture with Vitro is an example. Vitro, Sociedad Anonima, is a well-known glass manufacturer based in Monterrey, Mexico. It has a large, well-educated, and highly trained workforce. While some past failures were due to economic and political factors, this one was attributed to cultural differences. In the beginning, the alliance seemed to be a perfect match. Both had the same corporate philosophy, which emphasized service to customers. On the surface, the companies appeared very similar. Deep down, however, they had some basic cultural differences. Corning managers, for example, were sometimes left waiting for important decisions about marketing and sales. In Mexican culture, only top managers could make those decisions, and at Vitro, those people were busy with other matters. Conversely, Mexicans sometimes saw the Corning managers as too direct, while Vitro managers, in their effort to be very polite, sometimes seemed unwilling to acknowledge problems. Often, the Vitro managers thought that the Corning people moved too fast, while the Corning managers thought that the Vitro people were too slow. The Mexican managers were taking very long lunch breaks, while the Americans had no problem eating lunch at their desks. While the Americans were willing to discuss what went wrong and learn from it, the Mexicans were reluctant to criticize anyone, especially a partner. Therefore, many mistakes were left unattended.[37-39]

Other nations have different perspectives on wealth, money, and status. In contrast to Americans, Germans, for example, consider the intrinsic value of material things. Consider the purchase of books. Americans feel remiss if they buy books but do not read them. The Germans feel that owning books, even if they do not read them immediately, is important. For that reason, hardcover books sell better in Germany, and paperback sales are higher in the United States (p. 46).[13]

Americans have a tendency to display their wealth conspicuously and flaunt their material possessions. They enjoy displaying to others their accomplishments. Some cultures are more subtle about the display of wealth. Americans view wealth more from the consumption aspect. They view wealth as something to be used. Usefulness is a criterion to measure the worth of material things. If something is not useful, it should be thrown away. The American penchant for wastefulness is probably also an indirect result of the frontier mentality. To those settling in the frontiers, it must have seemed that the plentiful resources of America were inexhaustible. Therefore, there was no reason for conservation. The resulting wastefulness is evident in the activities of everyday life. To feel warm and comfortable at home, for example, a typical American, who is wearing only light clothes, may turn up the heat and warm up the whole house. In contrast, a typical European would put on an additional sweater for warmth and comfort.

The worth of a position or an occupation is determined by several primary factors, including honor, power, prestige, and the monetary earnings associated with it, as well as the impact it may have on the family. In some cultures, the nonmonetary aspects of a job are more important. In other cultures, the monetary gains are emphasized more. It is not unusual for an American to set a goal of becoming a millionaire by a certain age and to take on more than one job in pursuit of that goal. This narrow pursuit of material gain is frowned on in many traditional cultures with close family relationships. Faced with an opportunity to earn more money or help a family member, for example, a Hindu may choose the latter. The method and manner of wealth acquisition are of concern to all cultures. However, the Americans' high regard for business and wealth acquisition through business is not universal. In cultures where there is no high regard for business, outsiders often fill the gap in business and commercial activities. The Indians in East Africa and the Chinese in Southeast Asia, for example, have been successful in business and commerce due to the tendency of locals to hold business and commerce in low regard (p. 119).[40]

Informality

Informality is a salient American characteristic that has its roots in the frontier experience (pp. 49–58).[41] When Americans moved West in search of a better life, they left behind much of the complexity of their Old World cultures. There were no rules or protocol and no opportunity to practice old customs. Very soon, a much more informal way of speaking, dressing, and engaging in social relationships developed, reflecting a more relaxed etiquette (pp. 347–350).[42] The Old World's formal social rules, ceremonies, and traditions never took root in frontier America. As Robert Cruden explains, frontier people, under the pressure of hard work and isolation, had to shuck off the grace and amenities of eastern cities. They cultivated only those values necessary for survival: sheer physical strength and courage, pragmatic thinking, assertive egalitarianism, and an obsession with purely material things. They simply evolved their way of life.[43]

This informality has persisted over the years, and Americans have never shown much interest in rules and practices that are impractical, restrict behavior, or limit interaction with others. Americans consider too much formality as unfriendly, and they are ill at ease with it. A striking example of this fondness for informality can be found on the pages of American firms' annual reports. They are full of pictures of smiling executives. In contrast, in other countries, very seldom is a picture of a smiling executive seen on a corporate annual report. To other nations, the smiling face of an executive is not a dignified pose.

This informality has become such a strong American trait that many Americans assume it is universal. In reality, however, many cultures rigidly adhere to customs and ceremonies. Germans, for example, are very much aware of official and formal titles when addressing each other. In Germany, students never call college professors by their first names. Officially, a professor is addressed as *herr* (Mr.), *doktor*, or *professor*. At work and in office situations, Germans always use formal address with each other. German executives call their secretaries by an honorific followed by the last name, such as *Frau Schmidt*. The use of the first name is regarded as too familiar and condescending by Germans (pp. 64–65).[13]

Latin Americans are very much interested in pomp and circumstance. Personal etiquette and hospitality rules are strictly observed. Any failure to observe the ceremonial practices is construed, at best, as a lack of culture and savoir faire and, at worst, as impolite and rude. The practice of keeping family names going back several generations is a means by which Latin Americans can show a relationship to prominent families or to the Iberian peninsula.

Japanese are very much concerned with strict observance of the rules of interpersonal relationships, proper manners, and discipline. In the days of samurai rule, a serious disregard for manners and the failure to show proper respect to a samurai could be punishable by death. They practiced a very precisely prescribed way of eating, greeting, gesturing with hands, wearing clothes, walking, and sleeping. Even today, the daily life of a Japanese is governed by a very strict code of conduct (p. 11).[35] James Mortellaro, an American executive who worked for 10 years for Japanese firms, made the following observations on Japanese formality:[44]

> Employees at a typical Hitachi factory in Tokyo remove their shoes before entering their work areas. They wear slippers, color-coded for different jobs, functions, and departments. There are stripes of many colors painted side-by-side on the floor at the main entrance. Employees follow these stripes into the depths of the plant, each color leading off in a different direction. They must follow the color corresponding to their slippers. This practice constantly reminds them of their place and their position in the company. (p. 66)

A naive foreigner, uninformed about the Japanese code of conduct, for example, may lose a business deal just because of an inappropriate manner of exchanging business cards. When Japanese are handed a business card, they acknowledge each individual and his card, they carefully study them, and then respectfully stow them away. In so doing, they are trying to understand the person's relationship to the organization and his or her position within it. In a way, they create a context for future interaction.

Joking and Fun

Certain American characteristics are closely and directly related to their affinity for informality. In particular, Americans are very exuberant, they like simplicity and brevity of expression, and joking and kidding are common practice on most formal and informal occasions.[41]

Americans work hard and with the same vigor wholeheartedly participate in fun and games. Their open enjoyment of life and hearty expression of pleasure contrasts with the attitude of Latin Americans, who are much more formal and reserved. They never remove their jackets in public and are very careful to preserve a dignified composure. Relaxed manners, unabashed drinking, and hearty laughter are reserved for family and a circle of close friends. Latin Americans, or for that matter, people from many other cultures, would be truly at a loss at a Shriners convention or a college class reunion and would certainly be surprised at a typical college fraternity hazing.

Americans favor simplicity and brevity of expression and frank, open, direct actions. The "bottom line" and "getting to the point" are common currencies of daily language. Americans practice a relaxed form of tact and diplomacy in their interpersonal relationships. The no-nonsense attitude of discussing directly the substance of the business at hand is not correct in other cultures. Where social acceptance, preserving harmony, and saving face are considered important, people refrain from candor and frankness. To avoid embarrassment and hurt feelings, Japanese and many Asians are very reluctant to criticize others publicly, give direct answers, or put others on the spot. Americans, on the other hand, are very much interested in quick and timely feedback of the sort that requires a direct and frank response.

Americans enjoy joking and kidding very much. They use it to break the ice and feel comfortable around people. It also seems to be an equalizer that removes artificial social barriers and brings everyone to the same level. In the rest of the world, the American kidding and joking can be offensive. Outside a close circle of friends, formality and courtesy govern all inter-personal relationships. The practice of roasting, a ceremony in which colleagues affectionately elaborate on the behavioral or physical shortcom-ings of a designated person, would be unthinkable in other cultures and extremely offensive. When a Chinese American consultant, who worked for both U.S. and Chinese firms, met with an American finance chief, he was shocked to observe the following take place. His client's secretary burst into the meeting for a surprise birthday party for her boss. Along with a cake, she had hired a clown who poked fun at the finance chief. The consultant thought to himself, "This can never happen in a Chinese company."[45]

Americans like to lace their speeches and presentations with humor, and many formal presentations are opened with a joke. In other cultures, jokes are not suitable for formal occasions and should be told only among friends and in informal settings. It is considered abnormal to tell a joke in a formal presentation.

An American businessman was preparing for a business trip to Japan. His cultural consultant told him not to use a joke for the opening of his presentation. American jokes, he was told, lose much of their funny mean-ing in translation into Japanese. Besides, Japanese do not use jokes and funny remarks in business presentations. He followed the advice and started his presentation very formally. It seemed to him that the interpreter was translating his presentation very effectively. That gave the American confidence, and in the middle of his presentation when he remembered a very appropriate joke, he could not help telling it. To his surprise, the audience of Japanese managers broke into hearty laughter. When the speech was finished he asked the Japanese interpreter how he had translated the joke. The interpreter answered, "I did not. I told them, your American guest just told you a joke; you are supposed to laugh."

Attitude Toward Time

The phrase *time is money* explains the American attitude toward time. Time is a valuable and scarce commodity that should be employed in useful purposes. Americans are very conscious of time and try very hard to make the most efficient use of their time. In the eyes of many foreigners, Americans are always in a hurry. Foreigners who spend some time in the United States have a common complaint: "There is a deadline for everything" or "From the beginning of everything, Americans look forward to the finish; they do not take time to enjoy life and whatever they do. Everything is instant. Instant coffee, instant pictures, instant messages, instant life." The high value that Americans place on time could explain their penchant for action and their disdain for inactivity. Moreover, Americans typically have a low tolerance for silence in meetings. In contrast, most Asians can remain silent for long periods when nobody utters a word. To them, the silent period is an opportunity for contemplation and for organizing and evaluating one's thoughts.[46] The American dislike for long periods of silence may have gotten many American negotiators into serious trouble. An international vice president of a large U.S. company illustrates this:[46]

> In one of my company's deals overseas, our buyer was sitting across the table from the Japanese manufacturer's representative for the purpose of bidding on an item in which we were interested. Following the usual niceties, our man offered $150,000 per batch. On hearing the bid, the Japanese sat back and relaxed in his chair to meditate. Our buyer, interpreting this silence to be disapproval, instantly pushed his offer higher. It was only after the session was over that he realized he had paid too much.

Time Perspective

Individuals, organizations, and cultures vary in their attitudes and orientation toward time. The time perspective could be considered a continuum, one end of which is monochronic and the other end polychronic.[47] To engage in one activity at a time and finish each activity before beginning the next is monochronic, typical of the American and northern European time perspective. To do two or more activities concurrently or intermittently during a time period is polychronic, characteristic of many traditional societies (pp. 13–22).[13]

Polychronic Time. Industrialization seems to be a major factor influencing time perspectives. We develop time perspectives in relation to the environment. Before the industrial revolution and the emergence of factory work, people in agrarian societies observed natural changes in the environment and used those changes to organize their lives. Life progressed through days, nights, seasons, and years. Time was measured by the occurrence of natural phenomena, not by artificial means. In a circular fashion, day led to night and night to day; spring led to summer, summer to fall, fall to winter, and winter to spring. Important events reoccurred and were interrelated. Work and activities did not have precise deadlines. While there were certain times for planting and harvesting, delaying either by a few days was not disastrous. Interrupting one activity to engage in another did not seriously hamper normal daily life. Unlike today's industrial societies, agrarian life went on without a rigidly imposed structure. In relating to the environment, people developed a time concept very much in tune with the requirements of their daily lives.

Similar to natural events that occur concurrently, polychronic people spend their time according to the dictates of events. As events evolve around them, polychronic people tend to deal with those events according to their importance, without hesitating to postpone less important ones. They may do many things concurrently, moving from one to another, without predetermined deadlines. Rather than being governed by the modern concept of time, the progression of events and activities is more the consequence of momentary urgency and the requirements of interpersonal relationships. The life of a polychronic person centers on people and interpersonal relations, while for a monochronic person, time is the essence.

The industrial revolution with its requirements of working with machines and following a work schedule made **polychronic time** problematic. The natural measures of time were no longer appropriate for factory work and machine operations. A new abstract concept of time based on the movement of a mechanical object, the clock, replaced natural time measurement.

Monochronic Time. Monochronic cultures perceive time in a linear way, like a road that extends from the past into the future. **Monochronic time** is divided into segments, compartmentalized, and scheduled. Monochronic people devote their attention to scheduled activities, one at a time. They assign property values to time. Time could be owned, spent, saved, or given away. Since time is viewed in a linear fashion and activities are scheduled with a clear expectation of starting and finishing times, a request for an unscheduled task or meeting could bring the familiar response, "I don't have time for it." Similarly, monochronic people "spend" their time at work or at home, "save" or "set aside" time for family gatherings, and "waste" time waiting. If their expectations are met, monochronic people "enjoy" their time and have a "good time"; otherwise they have a "hard time" or a "lousy time."

Monochronic cultures emphasize punctuality and promptness. To be late for a meeting or not to finish a task on time can cause considerable annoyance. Therefore, unscheduled interruptions are avoided as much as possible. In contrast, polychronic people consider unscheduled meetings and events a normal part of social interactions where business and nonbusiness activities intermingle. The difference in time perspective for punctuality and strict adherence to timetables and schedules could create problems for international managers. In traditional societies, for example, a combination of polychronic attitudes and concern for interpersonal relationships results in business practices that, from a monochronic perspective, are unacceptable. In the Middle East, for example, changing work schedules and appointments to fit regular visits by clients, friends, and relatives is very common. A northern European or an American manager unfamiliar with the cultural values of the Middle East could interpret such practices as a lack of concern for the business at hand. Similarly, a Latin American may be late for a business appointment due to a preference for finishing a conversation with a friend rather than due to lack of interest or commitment.

Age and Gender

Attitudes toward age and gender vary among cultures. Americans have a special admiration for youth, and females are gaining more equality with their male counterparts. Although in many aspects there is still some division between male and female with regard to rank, the equalization attempts are paying dividends. Laws have made it clear that there should be no discrimination between the sexes in business practice. American cultural values still favor males; however, both sexes are usually treated similarly. Unlike in traditional societies, where females play a subservient role, American females consider themselves the equals of males, and societal values are changing in that direction. Other societies have a different attitude toward females. Except for a few Western societies, in the rest of the world, females are not granted the same opportunities as males and do not enjoy the same privileges. Japanese society, by all accounts, is still a strictly male society. Females do not play a prominent role in business or in government. Women who hold jobs before they are married are expected to quit after marriage. The same is true for other countries in Asia, Africa, and even Australia. In some countries, women are denied the most basic rights, such as holding a job outside the home or voting in an election. In Saudi Arabia or Kuwait, for example, women do not have the right to drive a car; they can only be passengers. In many orthodox Muslim countries, women are expected to adhere to a very rigid code of conduct and personal appearance. They may not be seen in public in any fashion that draws attention to them. Males and females have different status and, consequently, different rights.

While Americans are aware that many countries have different attitudes toward women, they will be surprised to learn that the admiration for youth and youthfulness is not universal either. The United States is a very young country. The vigor and strength of its youth made this country expand and prosper. Unlike the Old World, there were no restrictions and limitations on how far a person could advance. Particularly, the rugged frontier life favored the physical stamina and strength of youth (pp. 68–69).[48] Since then, Americans have come to admire youthfulness and consider young age as a favorable characteristic. Elderly people do not have as high a place in society as in other nations. In other nations, old age is a sign of experience and wisdom, and youth is synonymous with naïveté and lack of sophistication. In many Asian countries, senior citizens are highly respected, and there is a clear ascending order of status according to age. Positions of authority and power, in business and in government, are occupied by mature people. It is very unusual to see younger people in high offices. American MNCs that ignore these cultural values and send the most qualified younger or female managers abroad may not receive a favorable reception. The assignment of a young person or a female is interpreted as an indication of lack of interest and commitment or the low value of the business to the MNC. Traditional societies will place a higher value on seniority than performance in choosing to fill a position.

Corporate Culture

Corporate culture indicates organizationally shared values, beliefs, assumptions, and understandings that are the basis for relevant corporate norms and behavior patterns. A very simplified definition of corporate culture is "the way things work around here" (p. 13).[40]

Cultural phenomena are detectable in organizations at three levels:[8]

1. Overt behavior and other physical manifestations, such as artifacts and literature, are at the first level. Formal communication style and dress code are first-level examples.

2. The second level consists of values, a sense of what "ought" to be. Promoting from within the organization and lifetime employment are examples of the second level.

3. The third level contains the basic assumptions, including methods of coping with the environment. Strategic choices and ways of dealing with competition are third-level examples.

Corporate culture, according to Davis,[49] is based on **internally oriented** beliefs of how to manage and **externally oriented** beliefs of how to compete. Since organizational culture is influenced by societal culture, some organizational values reflect the basic attributes of the cultural environment.[50] Because of differences in national cultures, accepted managerial practices vary around the world, as do the norms of relating to other businesses and how businesses compete. For example, management by objectives (MBO), which was designed based on American cultural values, failed to work in Europe. In the hierarchical organizations of France, superiors and subordinates were uncomfortable negotiating future goals as required by MBO. In Sweden and Holland, MBO procedures were considered too autocratic.[51] What is considered a business gift in other countries might be regarded as a bribe in the United States. In contrast, lobbying, which is regarded by Americans as a normal political practice, is considered to be influence peddling and corruption in other countries.

Corporate culture is a product of the firm's environment and the interpersonal relationships among its members. Initially, the firm's culture is influenced by the culture of the country in which it was established. Once the firm expands its operations outside its borders and the dominance of its home culture, the influence of the host country's national culture becomes a reality.

The performance of business organizations depends on their ability to maintain internal consistency and external compatibility. Internal consistency is the equilibrium and balance between the various internal components of the firm, such as hiring, promoting, and rewarding employees. External compatibility is the harmony of the firm with its host environment, including relations with suppliers and ways of dealing with competitors. Organizations should be careful not to create too much internal inconsistency when creating external compatibility. In an effort to create external compatibility and to represent the cultural diversity of the global market in their corporate cultures, the MNCs may create a morass of cultural mismatch and cause internal inconsistency. The challenge is to bring about external compatibility and at the same time manage a culturally diverse workforce without creating internal conflict.

Many believe that cultural diversity enhances organizational competitiveness. Failure to manage cultural diversity properly, however, could lead to increased conflict and communication breakdowns. Consequently, depending on their approach to cultural diversity, MNCs could either enhance their worldwide competitiveness or fall victim to cultural quagmires.

The Mismatch of Corporate Cultures

Global media mergers, in which products are information, ideas, words, and images, are rarely without major difficulties. The acquisition of Diamandis Communication Inc. by the French magazine empire Hachette S.A. illustrates this point well. Two years after the merger, Diamandis, who was considered a great asset to the firm, and his two top lieutenants severed their relationships with the company. This move followed months of disagreement among the top managers.

(Continued)

(Continued)

> Cultural differences were the root cause of their problems; they were manifested in the managerial styles of the American and French executives. Hachette's executives, like most Europeans, used instinct to guide them; they made most of their decisions on gut-level feelings, without the benefit of meetings or marketing studies. By involving themselves in the tiniest details, suggesting covers and new page designs for magazines, even deciding what pictures should be used and where they should be used, French executives clashed with U.S. editors, who used a more systematic, planned approach. (Adapted from Ref. 52)

When MNCs are unfamiliar with the culture in each environment, they face potential problems associated with the peculiarities of those cultures. Not all areas of the firms are affected in the same way. The extent of difficulties arising from lack of cultural understanding is determined by how much various areas of the firm and the host culture interact with each other. The more the interaction between a functional area and the host culture, the more potential there is for problems. For example, sales and marketing functions interact with the host culture much more than does the research and development (R&D) function. Consequently, sales and marketing have the potential to encounter much more cultural misunderstanding.

The success of an MNC's global expansion, therefore, depends on its ability to adopt the practical aspects of each host country's cultural norms while maintaining the core aspects of its corporate culture that are the basis of its competitiveness. Although cultural adaptation to national cultures is a given, no direct, one-to-one correlation between the MNC's corporate culture and the host country's culture is conceivable. Instead of seeking complete identification with the host country's culture, it is practical to aim for the avoidance of cultural incompatibility. A more realistic expectation is to achieve a certain degree of compatibility, or constructive neutrality, with the host country's culture (p. 82).[2]

Constructive Neutrality. Kolde defines **constructive neutrality** as a positive system of principles and norms to guide the decision-making processes of all the entities and affiliates of an MNC. These principles and norms help the firm avoid or minimize clashes with its various national environments. The aim is to facilitate optimal involvement and participation of the company in the productive systems of its host countries (p. 83).[2]

It is easier to achieve constructive neutrality if MNCs adopt a multicultural composition and orientation. A unicultural organization not exposed to cultural diversity and an ethnocentric firm that believes in the superiority of its own culture may have difficulty relating to the idiosyncracies of other cultures. In the multicultural environment of world business, it is, therefore, advisable for organizations to become multicultural and develop a geocentric mentality. This is done by adopting the best attributes of both local and corporate cultures to function effectively in different cultural environments. What are the characteristics of a muticultural firm? In the following section, we examine the cultural typology of the organization and discuss the attributes of multicultural firms.

Cultural Typology of the Organization

Trompenaars and Hampden-Turner[53] used two dimensions, egalitarian-hierarchical and person-task, to identify four types of corporate cultures (p. 6). The four types are metaphorically named the family, the Eiffel Tower, the guided missile, and the incubator (see Figure 3.2). The four types are "ideal types." In practice, the four types are mixed and overlapping, with one culture dominating.

	Personal/Informal	Task/Formal
Egalitarian/decentralized	Incubator	Guided missile
	Person/fulfillment oriented	Task/project oriented
	Country: Sweden	Country: United States, United Kingdom
	Business: small	Business: large
Hierarchical/centralized	Family	Eiffel Tower
	Power oriented/dominant	Role oriented/dominant
	Country: France, Spain	Country: Germany
	Business: small	Business: large

Figure 3.2   Four Types of Corporate Culture

SOURCE: Reference 53.

The Family Culture

The family culture is both personal and hierarchical, in which the "father" has much more authority and experience than his children. Such a corporate culture is power oriented, and the leader acts like a caring father, who knows what is good for his family and acts accordingly. This type of power is intimate and nonthreatening. The atmosphere of the corporation is much like a home. By working hard and resolving conflicts, employees in this corporate culture derive pleasure from such relationships. Pleasing a superior (the father or elder brother) is a reward in itself. Power is not over the family members but through them. A big punishment is the loss of affection and place in the family. The general happiness and welfare of the family members (employees) is regarded as the concern of the family-type corporation.

The pressure to perform well is moral and social rather than financial. Familial cultures such as those of Greece, Italy, Japan, Singapore, South Korea, Spain, Turkey, and several Asian countries support such a corporate culture. These countries also industrialized late, and many feudal traditions have survived without much change and have become the norms of corporate culture.

To outsiders, the family culture is arbitrary, irrational, cozy, and full of nepotism and favoritism (corruption). Many modern American organizational practices, such as merit-based hiring or pay for performance, will not be popular in a family corporate culture. The reverse is true too. The following is a case in point.

A Dutch company was setting up a $15 million joint venture with a large Brazilian company. The Dutch delegation was surprised when the owner of the Brazilian company introduced a junior accountant as the key coordinator of the joint venture. They were puzzled as to why a junior accountant was given such a weighty responsibility, including the receipt of their own money. The Brazilian told them that this young man was the best choice among 1,200 employees because he was his nephew. Who could be more trustworthy? Instead of complaining, the Dutch should be happy that he was available (p. 168).[53]

The Eiffel Tower

The bureaucratic organization with division of labor and prescribed roles and functions resembles an Eiffel Tower. These roles and functions are coordinated from the top by a hierarchy that is symmetrical and narrow at the top and broad at the base. It is rigid, stable, and robust. However, its hierarchy is quite different from that of the family culture. Each level has a clear function, and roles to perform those functions are prescribed in advance.

The higher authority is an impersonal role that is occupied by a person selected for that position based on his or her abilities and qualifications and how closely those match the requirements of the position. The person occupying that position is not important. He or she could be replaced by anyone with similar qualifications. A new occupant of the position has very little freedom of choice and has to do the job as it has been defined in advance. Not much is left to personal preferences.

Because the authority comes from the roles and positions, it does not extend beyond the boundaries of the organization. Outside the organization, the boss is another person and would be treated accordingly. Both the boss and the subordinates accept this treatment as normal and natural. The boss is powerful only within the confines of the bureaucracy, and the rules sanction his or her organizational actions.

In the Eiffel Tower company, people, or "human resources," are valuable for their effect on organizational goals, similar to capital and cash resources. They are moved around to positions where they can best serve the organizational mission and goals. Personal relationships are avoided because they can warp sound and objective judgment and create favoritism. Organizational logic dictates separating personal preferences and choices from those of the organization.

The Eiffel Tower corporate culture is common to North America, Northwest Europe, and those nations that are task oriented and put roles before people.

The Guided Missile

The guided missile culture is egalitarian and therefore different from the family and the Eiffel Tower culture. It resembles the Eiffel Tower culture more because of its impersonal and task-oriented features. But unlike the Eiffel Tower culture, where "means" are important, in the guided missile culture, the "ends" are vital. Everything must be done to accomplish the strategic mission and reach the target. It is a task-oriented organization in which teams or project groups undertake various jobs. These jobs (tasks) are not fixed in advance but will be determined as new targets are established.

This type of corporate culture and structure was pioneered by the U.S. National Aeronautics and Space Administration. It used project groups working on space probes that resembled guided missiles. A large number of engineers and specialists were engaged in tasks that would change as the projects advanced. Their contributions could not be specified in advance. They had to work together harmoniously; otherwise the projects would not succeed. Because they were all experts and no particular expertise could be regarded as less or more important than another, there could be no hierarchy. Leaders or coordinators who were responsible for the final projects knew less than the specialists, and so they had to respect them and their expertise.

Because it is very costly to have a workforce composed of professionals, guided missile culture is very expensive. The relative value of individual contributions to the project may not be clear as in the Eiffel Tower culture. Groups are project dependent; therefore, they are formed and dissolved as needed. However, a functioning organization requires some degree of permanency. Therefore, in practice, guided missile culture uses the Eiffel Tower culture as a skeleton to give it stability and permanence. This results in an organizational structure that is commonly known as a matrix.

In a guided missile culture, changes are accepted very easily, and they happen regularly. People are moved around from project to project, and loyalties are more to the project and the profession than to the corporation.

Motivation is intrinsic, and team members get enthusiastic about the projects. They identify with the project and work very hard toward its completion. The project becomes a common goal to which all members dedicate themselves.

This type of corporate culture can function where task-oriented relationships and egalitarian attitudes are valued. The United States, Norway, and Ireland are examples of countries in which the guided missile corporate culture could function.

The Incubator Culture

The metaphor of an incubator culture should not be confused with the "business incubator." However, the logic of both is quite similar. In both, the purpose is to enable individuals to be creative by removing the routine and mundane from daily work. The incubator culture is both egalitarian and personal. There is almost no structure and organization; it only serves as an incubator for the individual's self-expression and self-fulfillment. The minimum structure of the incubator is to provide for personal conveniences such as heat, light, and computer services so that individuals can tap their creative potential.

Other people in the incubator culture are important in that they provide the much needed evaluation and criticism of new ideas. They develop, procure, and provide the resources needed to produce innovative products or services that the organization provides to its clients. Typical examples of incubator cultures are found in start-ups in California's Silicon Valley and along Route 128 near Boston. These firms are usually entrepreneurial or founded by creative teams.

With a minimum of structure, the incubators have minimal hierarchies. The authority of the firm's members comes from the nature of their ideas and the inspiration of their vision, which makes others work with them.

In the incubator culture, people often work with an intense emotional commitment. The commitment is more to the work than to the people. To the individuals, the groundbreaking and society-changing nature of their work unleashes the enthusiasm and commitment associated with a discovery trip—a trip to the unknown, in which the reward is the "journey." In the incubator culture, people are motivated by the nature of the task, which may result in revolutionary products or establish new and precedent-setting ideas, methods, and paradigms.

The close and intimate relationship among people serves as an effective nurturance for creative ideas. At its best, it can be a very effective and exciting place in which face-to-face relationships provide honest feedback that helps weed out ineffective ideas. Association in the incubator culture is voluntary and is often undertaken by idealists who are interested in being part of a groundbreaking venture. It can be a most significant and intense experience that would be difficult to sustain or repeat. Its success results in the need to bring in new people who are strangers, which then alters the existing special relationships.

Unlike in the family culture, in which leadership is ascribed, or in the Eiffel Tower culture, in which leadership comes from the roles and rules, in the incubator culture, leadership is achieved. People whose ideas and progress impress others the most are followed. Politics that impedes group achievement is unacceptable and detested. Conflict resolution is either by trying the opposing alternatives to verify their validity or by voluntary departure.

Countries and Corporate Culture Types

Trompenaars and Hampden-Turner have researched the preference of countries for corporate culture types and scored them accordingly. They give the highest score for the guided missile companies to the United States and the United Kingdom and the highest score for the family business culture to France and Spain. The highest score for the incubator is given to Sweden, and the highest score for the Eiffel Tower culture to Germany. They, however, suggest that these findings should be regarded cautiously. Smaller companies, regardless of their location, more likely resemble the family or the incubator culture. Large companies have the Eiffel Tower or the guided missile culture.

Monolithic, Plural, and Multicultural Organizations

On the basis of cultural diversity, business organizations could be categorized as monolithic, plural, or multicultural. We examine these organizations using the following six factors: acculturation, structural integration, informal integration, cultural bias, organizational identification, and intergroup conflict.[54] These factors influence the cultural diversity of the organization and are depicted in Figure 3.3. The following is a brief description of these factors:

1. **Acculturation** is the method of resolving differences between the dominant culture and any minority culture. Acculturation could be by assimilation, the unilateral adoption of the norms and values of the dominant culture by other cultural groups; by pluralism, combining some elements of the dominant and any minority cultures; or by separation, where there is little adoption from either culture.

2. **Structural integration** is the presence of members of different cultural groups at various organizational levels.

3. **Informal integration** is the inclusion of members of minority cultures in informal networks and activities taking place outside the ordinary work activities.

4. **Cultural bias** is the existence and practice of prejudice and discrimination in the organization.

5. **Organizational identification** is the extent to which the workforce identifies with the firm.

6. **Intergroup conflict** refers to friction, tension, and power struggles between various cultural groups within the firm.

Having described the six different factors with which cultural diversity is examined, we now elaborate on the organizational types.

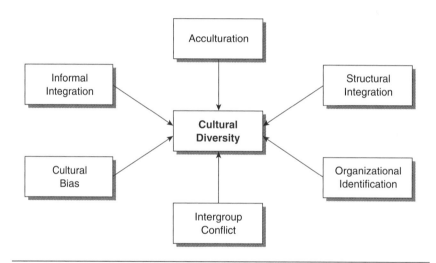

Figure 3.3   Factors Influencing the Cultural Diversity of the Organization

Monolithic Organizations

Monolithic organizations are highly homogeneous with little structural integration. They consist of one dominant cultural group. If members of other cultural groups join the firm, they must adopt the existing cultural norms to survive. There is prejudice and discrimination against the members of the cultural minority because of a lack of structural and informal integration. Consequently, organizational identification among the host country personnel is very low. But there is little group conflict because of the homogeneity of the workforce.

Firms in the early stages of involvement with international business are mostly monolithic. When they expand abroad, they represent the culture of their home country. Their parochial attitudes and ignorance of the host culture prevent them from taking full advantage of the opportunities the host culture could present to them. If the firms expand beyond simple import and export activities, the forces of competition for local talent and pressure from local governments for the inclusion of locals in their operations alter their cultural composition. Therefore, eventually, the homogeneity of the monolithic firm gives way to the heterogeneity of a plural organization.

Plural Organizations

The norms and values of other cultures are usually well represented inside plural organizations because these businesses try to include host country citizens in their workforce. Human resource management practices often change because they need to tap local knowledge to learn about the host market. Also, some governments require employment of local personnel. As a result, MNCs gain a higher level of structural integration than monolithic firms, leading to a plural organization that is culturally heterogeneous. The home country personnel, however, are still dominant in number and occupy key decision-making positions at all organizational levels. The top managers of plural organizations have an ethnocentric attitude, believing that "our way is the best way." Examples of plural organizations include many subsidiaries of U.S. MNCs operating abroad, such as Exxon, Ford, and Apple Computer.

Although structural integration is incomplete in plural organizations, partial structural integration results in some host country citizens being included in the MNCs' informal networks. This informal integration reduces prejudice and discrimination and heightens native workers' identification with the firm. Plural organizations experience more intergroup conflict than do monolithic firms because of the higher numbers of host country personnel. Similar to monolithic organizations, plural firms rely on assimilation for acculturation. Personnel who are not members of the dominant culture of the firm and do not strongly ascribe to its prevailing cultural norms will have difficulty progressing in the organizational hierarchy.

Multicultural Organizations

Both plural and multicultural firms are culturally heterogeneous. Plural organizations, however, do not value their cultural diversity, while multicultural firms do. They recognize the value of cultural heterogeneity and understand the potential contributions of cultural diversity to organizational performance. Multicultural organizations adopt a synergistic approach to management and have overcome the shortcomings of plural firms.

Multicultural organizations are characterized by full structural and informal integration, an absence of prejudice and discrimination, and minimum intergroup conflict. Members of minority cultures identify with the organization, and acculturation happens because all participating cultures are integrated into a synergistic whole. It is doubtful whether many MNCs have reached their goal of multiculturalism, but probably the global market's competitive environment will force MNCs to adopt a multicultural posture. The ability of MNCs to attract and maintain qualified personnel from host countries will depend on an attitude that values cultural diversity. To be competitive in the global job market, MNCs must not only provide good wages, fringe benefits, and a good quality of work life; they should also offer foreign employees the chance to advance their careers through work opportunities in other countries.[55] Effective cross-cultural career advancement in firms that do not value cultural diversity is extremely difficult. Therefore, the future growth and fortune of global firms may depend on their success in forming multicultural organizations. Multiculturalism gives firms certain benefits and improves their organizational capabilities. Asea-Brown Boveri (ABB), a global firm that was originally established as a Swedish company, and Jamont, a subsidiary of James River Corporation operating in Europe, are examples of multicultural organizations. Both these firms are discussed in other chapters.

The Benefits of Multiculturalism

Until recently, most organizations were primarily concerned with the problems and costs created by the ethnic and gender diversity of the workforce. They ignored the potential benefits of cultural diversity. But diversity of the workforce could be a source of competitive advantage. The following are the major potential advantages of multiculturalism:[56]

1. *Reduced costs:* There is evidence that as the cultural diversity of firms increases, so does the cost of poor integration. The experiences of minorities and women at work indicate that when cultural minorities are not fully integrated into the workforce, they tend to have lower job satisfaction and higher absenteeism and turnover. Firms that properly manage cultural diversity could have a cost advantage over those that do not, because of lower absenteeism and turnover rates.

2. *Resource acquisition:* With the increasing globalization of business, competition for qualified personnel has become more intense. Firms with a good reputation for handling cultural diversity attract more and better-qualified personnel. This benefit of cultural diversity is especially critical to an MNC's international expansion. A well-qualified pool of managers adds expertise and knowledge to the firm. In addition, these managers, with their diverse backgrounds, understand the value of cultural diversity and are better suited to nurture it. Consequently, they could set the stage for a mutually reinforcing process.

3. *Marketing advantage:* The insight and cultural sensitivity of the multicultural workforce improves marketing efforts. Multicultural personnel enable MNCs to understand and adopt the cultural perspectives of their multiple markets.

4. *Creativity:* Creativity flourishes when there is a diversity in perspective and less emphasis on conformity. Multicultural organizations are potentially more hospitable to creativity.

5. *Problem solving:* Multicultural firms have access to a broader and richer base of experience. Heterogeneity allows a wider range of perspectives and a more thorough critical analysis of issues. Therefore, heterogeneous groups have the potential for making better decisions.

6. *Organizational flexibility:* Research has demonstrated that bilinguals have a higher level of divergent thinking and cognitive flexibility.[57] MNCs that value cultural heterogeneity actively recruit and employ host country personnel. Many of these employees are bilingual. The inclusion of bilinguals who also have different cultural perspectives enhances the cognitive flexibility of MNCs. Moreover, MNCs broaden organizational policies and procedures to accommodate the inclusion of culturally diverse people. A combination of less standardized norms and a tolerance for culturally different viewpoints should create more flexibility and a feeling of oneness.

These benefits can be realized only in multicultural firms, since by definition, they are fully integrated organizations. Communication problems and conflict could beset a firm that does not fully integrate and take advantage of cultural diversity.

The advantages outlined above could enhance the competitiveness of multicultural firms in the global market. To create a multicultural organization, MNCs should strive to create heterogeneity in their workforce through effective human resource management practices. Proper human resource management is also a function of organizational culture. This subject will be discussed in a separate chapter.

Summary

A firm's global business environment is made up of a multitude of value systems, cultural practices, and nationalistic viewpoints. To operate successfully in this diverse and dynamic environment, the multinational firm must change its frame of reference. The provincial local/national perspective that serves the domestic firm well cannot be effective in a global market and should be abandoned in favor of a global perspective. The firm needs to develop an understanding of cultural forces that could affect its global operations. As the firm learns how to deal with varying cultural forces and sentiments existing in various national markets, it learns to adopt appropriate strategies. These strategies aim to combine the diversity of national markets in an overall corporate plan yet allow it to be responsive to the unique characteristics and demands of each host country. A successful international enterprise is a firm that can be viewed by the host country as an "insider," a firm that understands and responds to the uniqueness of the host country. To gain the status of insider, the MNC is required to understand the host country's national culture and learn how to avoid cultural pitfalls. Such practices should provide it with additional competitive advantage.

Discussion Questions

1. Define culture.

2. Describe cultural complexity. How does cultural complexity affect the management of international business?

3. Why do MNC managers find it more difficult to work in a culturally heterogeneous country?

4. What are cultural paradoxes? Why do cultural paradoxes exist? Give an example of a cultural paradox.

5. Explain cultural shock. When and why does cultural shock happen?

6. List Hofstede's four dimensions of culture.

7. There are differences between the American and Japanese concepts of the "individual." How could such a difference affect the management of a business firm in either country?

8. According to Kurt Lewin, Americans form friendships more quickly and easily than do Germans. Why?

9. Why are Americans more informal than people of other nations? How could this informality cause difficulties for American managers abroad?

10. How could Americans' penchant for informality create problems when doing business abroad?

11. Both Americans and Japanese value hard work, but for different reasons. Explain.

12. Explain why a monochronic manager would have difficulty with polychronic workers.

13. What problems would an American female manager face in foreign assignments?

14. What is corporate culture? Elaborate on the relationship between corporate culture and national culture.

15. Use the explanation of corporate culture provided by Trompenaars and Hampden-Turner and elaborate on the relationship between national culture and corporate culture.

16. How different is the family corporate culture from the Eiffel Tower type?

17. What factors differentiate between monolithic, plural, and multicultural organizations? Describe the differences between multicultural and monolithic firms.

18. Explain the benefits of cultural diversity. How can MNCs gain a competitive advantage through cultural diversity?

Note

a. These examples are based on a news story that appeared in the *Wichita Eagle*, November 26, 1992. The original column was written for the *Los Angeles Times/Washington Post* by T. R. Reid.

References

1. E. S. Browning (1994, May 3). Computer chip project brings rivals together, but the cultures clash. *Wall Street Journal*, pp. A1–A8.
2. E. J. Kolde (1974). *The multinational company*. Lexington, MA: Lexington Books.
3. G. G. Gordon (1992). Industry determinants of organizational culture. *Academy of Management Journal*, 16(2), 396–415.
4. P. C. Early & E. Mosakowski (2004). Cultural intelligence. *Harvard Business Review, October*, 139–146.
5. L. Armstrong (1991, December 2). It started with an egg. *Business Week*, 142.
6. Y. Allaire & M. E. Firsirotu (1984). Theories of organizational culture. *Organizational Studies*, 5, 193–226.
7. G. Hofstede (1984). Cultural relativity of quality of life concept. *Academy of Management Review*, 9(3), 389–398.
8. E. Schein (1985). *Organizational culture and leadership*. San Francisco: Jossey-Bass.
9. H. L. Telshaw Jr. (1985). ABCD—Asian business and cultural disparities. *Conference Proceedings of the American Institute for Decision Sciences*, 250–251.
10. Anonymous (2006, May). Wild things. *Smithsonian*, 37(2), 20.
11. S. Begley (2004, May 7). Cultures of animals may provide insights into human behavior. *Wall Street Journal*, p. A1.
12. E. T. Hall (1977). *Beyond culture*. Garden City, NY: Anchor Books.

13. E. T. Hall & M. R. Hall (1987). *Understanding cultural differences*. Yarmouth, ME: Intercultural Press.

14. E. Gareis (2000). Intercultural friendship: Five case studies of German students in the U.S.A. *Journal of Intercultural Studies, 21*(1), 67–91.

15. R. Lapper (2002, December 14/15). Opening a new can of worms. *Financial Times*, p. III.

16. G. Hofstede (1984). *Culture's consequences*. Beverly Hills, CA: Sage.

17. K. Leung, R. S. Bhagat, N. R. Buchan, M. Erez, & C. B. Gibson (2005). Culture and international business: Recent advances and their implications for future research. *Journal of International Business Studies, 36*(4), 365.

18. H. C. Triandis, R. Comtempo, & M. J. Villareal (1988). Individualism-collectivism: Cross-cultural perspectives on self-grouping relationships. *Journal of Personality and Social Psychology, 54*, 323–338.

19. I. Altman (1975). *The environment and social behavior*. Monterey, CA: Brooks/Cole.

20. M. Mulder (1977). *The daily power game* (pp. 3–5). Leiden, The Netherlands: Marinus Nijhoff Social Sciences Division.

21. W. B. Gudykunst & Y. Y. Kim (1984). *An approach to intercultural communication*. New York: Random House.

22. J. S. Osland & A. Bird (2000). Beyond sophisticated stereotyping: Cultural sensemaking in context. *Academy of Management Executive, 14*(1), 65–79.

23. M. Javidan, G. K. Stahl, F. Brodbeck, & C. P. M. Wilderom (2005). Cross-border transfer of knowledge: Cultural lessons from Project GLOBE. *Academy of Management Executive, 19*(2), 59–76.

24. W. W. Redden (1975). *Culture shock inventory—manual*. Fredericton, New Brunswick, Canada: Organizational Test.

25. S. J. Black & M. Mendenhall (1991). The U-curve adjustment hypothesis revisited: A review and theoretical framework. *Journal of International Business Studies, Second Quarter*, 225–247.

26. H. C. Triandis (1975). Culture training, cognitive complexity and interpersonal attitudes. In R. W. Brislin, S. Bochner, & W. J. Lonner (Eds.), *Cross cultural perspectives on learning* (pp. 42–43). New York: Wiley.

27. R. E. Nisbett (2003). *The geography of thought*. New York: Free Press.

28. M. Maruyama (1989). Epistemological source of new business problems in the international environment. *Human Systems Management, 8*, 71–80.

29. R. Iwata (1982). *Japanese-style management: Its foundations and prospects*. Tokyo: Asian Productivity Organization.

30. K. Lewin (1948). *Resolving social conflict*. New York: Harper & Row.

31. D. Benjamin (1994, September 7). Is Hikmet Kotsch only "Schuhputzer" in all of Germany? *Wall Street Journal*, pp. A1, A5.

32. E. J. Kolde (1985). *Environment of international business*. Boston: Kent.

33. C. Pezeshkpur (1978). Challenges to management in the Arab world. *Business Horizons, August*, 47–55.

34. R. A. Billington & M. Ridge (1982). *Westward expansion*. New York: Macmillan.

35. L. Copeland & L. Griggs (1995). *Going international: How to make friends and deal effectively in the global marketplace*. New York: Random House.

36. K. L. Miller (1992, August 3). Now, Japan is admitting it: Work kills executives. *Business Week*, 35.

37. C. Mitchell (1988, July 2). Partnerships are way of life for Corning. *Wall Street Journal*, p. 6.

38. N. A. Nichols (1993). From complacency to competitiveness. *Harvard Business Review, September/October*, 163–171.

39. A. DePalma (1994, July 10). Still under construction. *Wichita Eagle*, pp. 1E–2E.

40. V. Terpstra & K. David (1991). *The cultural environment of international business.* Cincinnati, OH: South-Western.

41. T. O. Wallin (1976). The international executive's baggage: Cultural values of the American frontier. *MSU Business Topics, Spring*, 49–58.

42. F. S. Philbrick (1965). *The rise of the West, 1754–1830* (pp. 347–350). New York: Harper & Row.

43. R. Cruden (1980). *Many and one: A social history of the United States.* Englewood Cliffs, NJ: Prentice Hall.

44. J. S. Mortellaro (1989, February). Japan's management imperialism. *Business Marketing, 24*(2), 62–72.

45. C. Hymowitz (2005, July 5). Chinese acquisitions in U.S. mean changes for American workers. *Wall Street Journal*, p. A11.

46. A. M. Whitehill (1989). American executives through foreign eyes. *Business Horizons, May/June*, 42–44.

47. A. C. Bluedorn, C. F. Kaufman, & P. M. Lane (1992). How many things do you like to do at once? An introduction to monochronic and polychronic time. *Academy of Management Executive, 6*(4), 17–26.

48. W. Nugent (1981). *Structures of American social history* (pp. 68–69). Bloomington: Indiana University Press.

49. S. M. Davis (1984). *Managing corporate culture.* Cambridge, MA: Ballinger.

50. J. P. van Oudenhoven & K. I. van der Zee (2002). Successful international cooperation: The influence of cultural similarity, strategic differences, and international experience. *Applied Psychology: An International Review, 51*(4), 633–653.

51. G. Hofstede (1971). Do American theories apply abroad? *Organizational Dynamics, 10*(1), 63–80.

52. P. M. Reily (1991, February 15). Egos, cultures clash when French firm buys U.S. magazines. *Wall Street Journal*, p. A1.

53. F. Trompenaars & C. Hampden-Turner (1998). *Riding the waves of culture.* New York: McGraw-Hill.

54. T. Cox Jr. (1992). The multicultural organization. *Academy of Management Executive, 5*(2), 34–47.

55. M. Maruyama (1992). Changing dimensions in international business. *Academy of Management Executive, 6*(3), 88–96.

56. T. H. Cox & S. Blake (1991). Managing cultural diversity: Implications for organizational competitiveness. *Academy of Management Executive, 5*(3), 45–56.

57. W. Lambert (1977). The effects of bilingualism on the individual: Cognitive and sociocultural consequences. In P. A. Hurnbey (Ed.), *Bilingualism: Psychological, social, and educational implications* (pp. 15–27). New York: Academic Press.

4 International Communication and Negotiation

No business transaction can be carried out without communication. International management involves communicating over national borders and dealing with cultural differences. To communicate, we use language, signs, and symbols, all determined by culture. In this chapter, we learn that effective international communication requires understanding of cultural influences. We will learn about cultural differences in verbal and nonverbal communication. Finally, we conclude the chapter with a discussion of cultural differences in international negotiation.

Chapter Vignette

Moda Esphenaaj was an Asian student on a training assignment with a large bank in New York. The bank had extensive business in Moda's home country. Bob Balladur had volunteered to become Moda's mentor and was assisting him during his stay in New York.

It was Moda's second month of stay in New York City when he asked Bob, "Why do people sell their garages? Are parking spaces for cars at a premium in New York?"

Of course, Bob answered "Yes" to the second question, on parking spaces. On many occasions, Bob and Moda had searched in frustration for a spot to park Bob's black Saab. Surely, Moda by now should have noticed New York's parking problem. However, he could not understand what Moda was getting at with the first question. When he asked, Moda's response sent him into roaring, hearty laughter. Moda had seen many signs for "garage sales" and thought that people were selling their garages separately. When Bob explained the meaning of those signs, Moda's face turned red with embarrassment. Being a sensitive man, Bob shared his own experience of many years ago, which was not only embarrassing but also very costly.

The story went like this. Bob was working in an American bank in Paris as a senior manager in charge of "les cambistes," as the fast-and-furious foreign exchange traders are called. One day, a currency exchange trader from the Bourse (the word for "stock and currency market" in French) called to say that the U.S. dollar was sinking fast. Bob yelled a profanity and slammed down the phone so hard that it broke into two pieces. A few seconds later, the trader called him on another phone and dutifully reported the purchase of a large block of U.S. dollars. "You did what?" Bob angrily inquired. To which the protesting trader answered, "But you said 'achet'"—the French word meaning "buy." That afternoon, Bob walked into his boss's office and said, "I've got a funny story to tell you, but it will cost you a quarter of a million dollars to hear it."

Moda could not wait for Bob to finish his story. Before he reached the end, both men were laughing loudly, and Bob was relieved.[a]

Introduction

During the course of a day, we are judged by the effectiveness of our communication. We are appraised by the way we speak, by our accents or dialects, by our body language, by the way we listen, and even by the way we read and write. Communication is a skill that has to be learned and sharpened. As the world constantly changes, we must continue to improve our communication skills. Do you spend most of your time listening, speaking, or writing?

When people get together, communication is inevitable. It is impossible not to communicate in the presence of other people. However, it is guaranteed that the communication taking place is not always accurate, nor does it reflect the intention of the participants. Everything we do, every inadvertent move we make, even our silences are perceived and interpreted by other people. Sometimes, we send erroneous messages by the manner of our dress or the tone of our voice or simply by the condition of our bodies. We may, for example, mistake someone as a successful financial consultant if he or she dresses in a conservative style, carries a leather briefcase, and reads a financial newspaper. However, if the person responds to a finance quiz with a far-fetched answer, it is obvious that we have made a mistake and the person just fits the stereotypic image of a financial consultant.

When managers and workers understand the company's mission and objectives, the organization is more likely to achieve its goals. Communication among organizational members is essential for task accomplishment. Members have to communicate in order to receive and send information. To work in a team, send a message, give an order, assist a coworker, report a task accomplishment, negotiate a business transaction, or do any of the myriad business activities in a typical day, we need to communicate.

As an organization becomes more complex, it becomes even more important for it to have an effective communication system. Because all business activities involve communication and because international management is more complex than domestic business, effective communication is crucial to the success of an international operation. To deal with customers, suppliers, government agencies, and a host of other organizations, it is necessary to communicate across national borders. To manage internationally, effective communication is imperative.

Micro and Macro
International Communication

International communication can be viewed from two different perspectives, the micro and macro levels. The micro level involves communication and information flow between the directors of the firm, its employees, and its external constituencies. At the micro level, intrafirm, interpersonal, and intercultural communication are connected to one another. Of course, multinational companies (MNCs) are more concerned with the communication issues at the micro level.

The macro level deals with the problems and opportunities that arise from the flow of information and communication between countries. At this level, international information is exchanged through mass media, telecommunications, and high-technology transfer, which could have far-reaching political, economic, social, and cultural consequences for nations. The macrolevel issues of international communication and information dissemination may potentially be the source of future difficulties.

According to Mowlana,[2] the macro level of international communication can be viewed from four different perspectives (pp. 180–182):

1. The idealistic-humanistic approach views international communication as a way to bring nations and people together. International communication is considered a source of power that international organizations (e.g., the United Nations) can use to serve the world community. Effective international communication can increase understanding among nations and peoples and improve conditions that are conducive to world peace. The first approach is idealistic and assumes the objective transfer of information and values—an impossible feat. It also assumes a universally accepted view of international order and peace.

2. The political proselytization approach considers international communication as a medium of propaganda and advertising. It is claimed that the political proselytization approach is used by industrialized countries to manipulate the people of the Third World. This has created distrust of the international media and has fueled intolerance and hatred among people and nations.

3. The economic power approach is an increasingly popular view that considers international communication the source of economic power. Weaker nations are dominated by industrialized countries through international business activities that result in technology transfer and "modernization." Developing countries become amenable to being controlled by Western powers once they have adopted the ways of Western industrialized nations. Countries that convert to Western ways may lose their cultural identity and indigenous creative power.

4. International communication may also be viewed as the source of political power. Countries communicate through mass media, literature, films, and data transmission. Increased communication among countries can potentially increase understanding among nations and peoples and improve conditions that are conducive to world peace. International communication through media, films, and so on conveys the cultural content associated with the source too. This, however, may not always be in the best interests of the recipient country. It may lead to cultural domination. The economic and political views have equated international communication with other commodities to be traded and used for manipulation and domination.

All four approaches have been criticized. An integrative view of international communication is more realistic. The integrative view considers international communication encompassing elements of the four approaches and can offer a more practical venue for addressing major cross-cultural and international concerns. Seen from this perspective, a major concern is the widening gap between developed and developing countries' capacity to deal with international communication and information management. While many people in developing countries are waiting for their first telephone, for example, the residents of the developed world are using the Internet to send and receive all sorts of information regardless of their location.

The world is becoming smaller due to the accelerating rate of technological development. This in turn creates interdependencies among nations, resulting in more communication and interaction among them. In this global village, communication technologies are instruments that can be used or misused.[3] "Since information is a resource that can be converted into all kinds of power, there is intense competition and conflict over how information is produced and used" (p. 207).[2]

Developing countries contend that the international flow of information and communication heavily favors the developed countries. They assert that the existing pattern of international communication is creating a dependent relationship similar to business and trade dependency. This means that developed countries are the source and supplier of information and developing countries are the naive consumers. The values, traditions, and cultures of developing countries are slowly and steadily being lost and are being replaced by those of developed countries. As Mowlana[2] puts it, "The nature, pattern, and direction of the world economy more or less parallel and depict the directionality of the world information flow" (p. 198). McPhail[4] argues that the pattern of information flow between developed and developing countries fosters "electronic colonialism":

The dependency relationship [is] established by the importation of communication hardware, foreign-produced software, along with engineers, technicians, and related information protocols, that vicariously establish a set of foreign norms, values and expectations which, in varying degrees, may alter the domestic cultures and socialization processes. (p. 18)

Even if we consider the concerns of developing countries as exaggerated and paranoid, we cannot ignore the fact that the gap in information and communication technology may increase the vulnerability of these countries. Often, there is more information available, for example, about a developing nation in centers that study these countries than in the developing country itself. "When others know more about you than you know yourself, their power to dominate is enhanced significantly" (p. 56).[4]

An international manager must cultivate an appreciation of these views and a familiarity with the concerns of the host nationals. A better understanding of these issues will foster more productive relationships. Sensitivity and empathy with the people of host countries will create a friendlier atmosphere in which to conduct international business transactions.

We next consider the various aspects of cross-cultural communication.

The Classic Communication Model

Communication comes from the Latin word *communis*, meaning "common." When we attempt to communicate with another person, we seek to establish "commonness" by sharing information, knowledge, ideas, or attitudes. Communication is a two-way process and takes place when a person transmits ideas, knowledge, meanings, and feelings to others.

A typical process of communication involves the sender (source) of communication, the receiver (target) of communication, and the feedback loop. A medium, such as a telephone, computer, letter, or face-to-face position, is used to send a message to the target. Communication can take place only if the sender's message falls within the receiver's realm of understanding and knowledge. The commonality in language, experience, knowledge, and culture provides a framework for communication between people. Cultural differences, language diversity, and differences in experience and knowledge create barriers to communication. If the receiver of a message, due to any of these differences, is unable to decode the message and comprehend it, the message will not reach its destination. The three components of the communication process are origination, destination, and feedback.

Origination

As Figure 4.1 depicts, any communication process has three major segments, the origination, the destination, and the feedback loop. The origination segment consists of the sender and his or her field of experience, which includes attitudes, experience, knowledge, environment, sociocultural background,[5] and values that differentiate him or her from others. Also, the origination segment

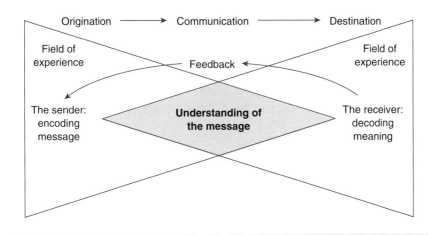

Figure 4.1   **Classic Communication Model**

includes the meaning and the information the sender intends to share. The sender "encodes" the meaning of the message into signs, symbols, and words that the receiver can understand. The sender ensures the accuracy of the information transmitted by composing the message in his or her mind and organizing it in a logical sequence. In doing so and in "encoding" the meaning into an understandable form, a message is created. After encoding the message, the sender channels the message to the receiver.

Destination

The destination segment consists of the receiver, decoding, and the meaning of the message. After receiving the message, the receiver attempts to decipher the meaning of the words, symbols, and nonverbal signals such as the hand gestures and tone of voice. Listening to the composition of words, the manner of presentation, and other signs and signals used in communication, the receivers use their field of experience to interpret the message. They may encounter some "noise," elements that can cause distortion, in the form of confusion and misunderstanding of the message. Many potential sources of noise exist when communicating across cultures. We will consider several of them subsequently.

Noise (Distortion)

Confusion can result when the sender and the receiver have not had the same common experiences. The field of experience is used as a frame of reference to interpret what people encounter in their daily activities. When the sender and the receiver have similar fields of experience, they have much the same frames of reference. Therefore, the information exchanged between them is usually not distorted very much. As Wilbur Schramm[5] described it,

The greater the overlap of the source and the receiver's fields of experience, the greater the probability of successful communication. In other words, they have things in common that facilitate better communication. An individual engaging in communication with another person of a significantly different background should be aware that greater effort may be needed to ensure successful communication. (p. 6)

Commonality of fields of experience between the origin and the destination reduces noise and increases fidelity of communication. Even in a domestic situation, for example, the sender of the message may be a manager who uses technical computer jargon. If the receiver is a new salesperson in the company, he or she may not have much experience with the technical language and may receive limited information from the manager. Consequently, the lack of enough commonality between the sender and the receiver results in some noise, which in turn prevents the receiver from understanding the message.

There might be other reasons for communication noise. The receiver of the message may not pay close attention to the message. He or she might be a new recruit, nervous, and anxious to impress the supervisor. In this case too, the message is distorted and is not the same as the original.

Cultural differences are the major source of communication distortion. Communication difficulties arise from cultural differences because of the lack of commonality of values, beliefs, and norms between people of two cultures. Sometimes, in cross-cultural communication, these differences could lead to misunderstandings and cause serious problems. An example of a serious cross-cultural communication misunderstanding happened years ago at Ain Shams University in Cairo, Egypt.

In the midst of a discussion of a poem, a British professor, explaining the subtleties of the poem to a sophomore class, was carried away by the situation. He leaned back in his chair, put his feet on top of the desk, and continued with his talk. The class felt insulted, became furious, and afterward, the entire student body demonstrated in front of the English Department. The incident even made the headlines of the local newspapers. To a stranger, this innocent act might seem ridiculous, baffling, incredible, incomprehensible, and even funny. But to the natives, the students' behavior was logical and in its context made sense. The indignant students and their supporters were outraged and felt offended because in the Middle East and in some Asian countries, it is extremely insulting to have to sit facing the soles of the shoes of another person.[6]

Misunderstanding can happen even when people from different cultures communicate in the same language. While the language is the same, the choice of words and the way of expressing the thoughts are not. German and Dutch negotiators, for example, will choose their words carefully to be exact and unambiguous. They want the other side to know precisely what is being discussed. Indonesians, Japanese, and Middle Easterners choose their words even more carefully, but for a different reason. They are concerned not to offend anyone. They try their best not to use any blunt words or negative remarks or directly reject and embarrass others. In these cultures, directness and frankness are equated at best with immaturity and naïveté and at worst with arrogance. To them, only children speak out what is on their minds and say exactly what they mean (p. 40).[7]

Feedback

Feedback is a loop connecting the destination segment to the origination segment, providing information about the message to both the sender and the receiver. Through feedback, the receiver sends information back to the sender describing the results of the communication. Without feedback, the sender would not know whether the message had been received or understood. In short, feedback is a response and control mechanism in the communication process. For feedback to be an effective control, however, it must be given by the receiver and must be understood by the sender. The differences in the giving and understanding of feedback can further complicate communication in cross-cultural settings. For example, in a communication between a Japanese and an American, when the Japanese, who desires harmony and wants to save face, politely avoids publicly contradicting the American, the American may take this feedback at face value. In this case, the feedback has not served its purpose.

International Verbal Communication

Like their domestic counterparts, international managers use verbal communication more than other media. What makes verbal communication different for international managers is the use of foreign languages. Often, when discussing the communication process, the assumption is that the sender and receiver are using a common language that they both understand. In MNC operations, this may not necessarily be the case. The most visible and important factor international managers deal with is language diversity. Because of the variety of languages spoken in an MNC, international managers without foreign language skills must rely on interpreters. No matter how competent the interpreter or how accurate the translation, some meaning is always lost in the process. There are always meanings and shades of meanings that cannot be conveyed by translation. Some words cannot be translated at all. The difficulty of translation is but one of the many problems associated with the use of interpreters. Good interpreters are in short supply. A good interpreter is more than a translator of words. There are many characteristics that make a good interpreter, including sensitivity to cultural and social differences, understanding of what makes people laugh in other cultures, and political sensitivity.[8] Sometimes, when using interpreters, people may let their guard down and use less tact. On such occasions, a socially and culturally sensitive interpreter would not faithfully translate verbatim. The following is an example:[8]

> Before addressing a Chinese audience, a Western scientist noticed a number of children were playing and chattering in the aisles. To his dismay, no one was attempting to quiet them down. After impatiently waiting for a while, he exploded angrily at the interpreter, "Will you tell those little brats to shut up!" The interpreter quietly spoke into the microphone in Chinese what roughly translates, "Little friends, would you please be just a bit more quiet, if you don't mind?" (p. 265)

Humor is very difficult to translate. An important attribute of a good interpreter is the knowledge of what is funny in other cultures. Recall the story in Chapter 3 about an American executive in Japan telling his audience a joke. The interpreter probably knew the translation would not do justice to the joke and therefore told the audience, "Your American guest just told you a joke; you are supposed to laugh," and the audience responded with hearty laughter.

In translation, one can avoid potential minefields if one is aware that certain political issues are off-limits. For example, the Middle East is made up of a number of countries and cultures. A frequent mistake is the assumption that all are Arabs. This is politically and culturally a very sensitive matter to Iranians, Turks, and Kurds. A good interpreter would make an appropriate distinction and would refer to each culture accordingly.

Danish and Swedish Communication

In the Danish culture, the main purpose of interpersonal communication is maintenance of a familiar atmosphere and relation of affection. It is impolite to explain things, because such an act assumes that someone is ignorant. It is also impolite to ask questions on anything beyond immediate personal concern, because the respondent may not know the answer. It is often considered aggressive or offensive to introduce new ideas. One prefers to repeat the same old jokes. Discussion of politics or economics is taboo, except in marginal enclaves. Safe topics of intellectual conversation are art, literature, and music, on which people are expected to disagree without embarrassment.

In contrast, in Sweden, the purpose of daily interpersonal communication is transmission of new information or frank feelings. One prefers to be silent unless he or she has an important message, while in Denmark one must keep talking (p. 49).[9]

The reliance on interpreters reduces the amount of information an international manager may collect. It shrinks the circle of sources that could be contacted and increases the time involved in communication. The ability to communicate in the local language allows managers to convey their meaning more accurately than with the use of an interpreter. Choosing your own words and picking your own sentence patterns in a foreign language are superior to relying on someone else to correctly or incorrectly produce your ideas, phrases, and nuances. Foreign language skills also contribute to the international managers' adjustment to the local culture and society. According to Mendenhall and Oddou,[10] language skills can be viewed as a means to create and foster interpersonal relationships or as a means to understand the dynamics of a new culture. Language skills not only allow international managers to communicate with the locals more easily and accurately; they also permit them to be treated more like "insiders," which by itself is a competitive advantage.

We have discussed language differences in communication and have noted that language differences make international communication very difficult. Additional difficulties arise from cross-cultural differences in nonverbal communication. Managers who are assigned to international operations may gain foreign language proficiency. They may, however, experience difficulty comprehending the full meaning of verbal communication unless they can read and understand nonverbal communication cues. We now consider issues in nonverbal communication.

Cultural Differences in Nonverbal Communication

Communication consists of verbal and nonverbal components. Nonverbal communication cues impart meanings that are usually not presented in verbal communication. Just as there are cultural differences among various national groups, so are there differences in communication patterns, especially in nonverbal cues. Differences in nonverbal communication cues can be a source of misunderstanding. International managers could greatly improve their understanding of people from other cultures by learning the subtleties of meanings conveyed by these nonverbal cues.

To elaborate on the differences in nonverbal communication cues among cultures, we could discuss country-by-country differences. This would be a tedious process. Signs and motions using the hands, fingers, eyes, and head, for example, convey different meanings in different cultures. Several examples of these motions are described in Table 4.1. Some of these signs convey just the opposite meanings in two different cultures. Although learning these signs is very beneficial and can prevent embarrassing experiences, it is very time-consuming. While those contemplating an international assignment are well-advised to make a specific study of nonverbal signs in their prospective host

Table 4.1   Implications of Various Nonverbal Behaviors in Different Cultures

Nonverbal Behavior	Country	Meaning
Thumbs up	United States	An approval gesture/O.K./Good job!
	Middle East	A gesture of insult
	Japan	A sign indicating "male"
	Germany	A sign for count of "one"
A finger circulating next to the ear	Argentina	A telephone
	United States	That is crazy!
A raised arm and waggling hand	United States	Good-bye
	India, S. America	Beckoning
	Some Africans	Beckoning
	Much of Europe	A signal for "no"
Showing the back of the hand in a V-sign	England	A rude sign
	Greece, Middle East	A sign for count of "two"
Showing a circle formed with index finger and thumb	United States	Very good!
	Turkey	Insult gesture/accusation of homosexuality
Crossing first two fingers	United States	Good luck!
	Taiwan	No smoking!
Touching a person's head	United States	Affection
	Thailand	A major social transgression
Eye contact, gazing	United States	A sign of attentiveness
	Japan	A rude behavior/invasion of privacy
	Most Asian countries	Sign of disrespect to senior people
Widening eye	United States	An indication of surprise
	Chinese	An indication of anger
	Hispanic	Request for help
	French	Issuance of challenge
Shaking the head side to side	Western countries	A sign for disagreement/no
	Bulgaria	A sign for agreement/yes
Nodding the head up and down	Western countries	A sign for agreement/yes
	Greece, Bulgaria	A sign for disagreement/no
A handshake	Western countries	A greeting action
Bowing	Japanese	A greeting action
Hands placed together in front of the face	India	A greeting action

country, a better alternative is to compare these differences on some common dimensions. We choose the seven most commonly discussed dimensions of culture.[11] The seven dimensions are expressiveness, emotions, individualism, gender role differentiation and rigidity, power distance (PD), uncertainty, and contextual variations. In the following pages, we will discuss cultural differences in nonverbal communication along these dimensions.[12] The four dimensions introduced by Hofstede, which were discussed in the previous chapter, are summarized here. While there are controversial arguments regarding the validity of Hofstede's cultural dimensions, the use of these dimensions is very common among international management scholars, and they are the basis for much research and discussion on cultural differences.[13] Other researchers have offered expanded lists that include these four dimensions.[14] However, the following dimensions are more relevant for our discussion of cross-cultural communication issues. Table 4.2 illustrates the differences between Americans and Japanese based on these dimensions and other cultural factors.

Table 4.2   Comparison Between Americans and Japanese on Communication-Related Cultural Factors

Factors	Americans	Japanese
Emotional intensity	Higher	Lower
Individualism	High	Low
Gender role differentiation and rigidity	Moderate	High
Power distance	Low	High
Uncertainty avoidance	Low	High
Contextual information	Low	High
Communication emphasis	Verbal/direct	Nonverbal/indirect
Nonverbal cues	Few/informal	Many/formal
Purpose of interpersonal relations	Self-satisfaction	Group harmony and compliance
Respect for authority	Moderate	Very high

Expressiveness

If we consider the expressiveness dimension as a continuum, at one end of this continuum are actions that communicate closeness, accessibility, and approach. At the other end are behaviors that express avoidance and distance. In the United States, for example, smiling, touching, eye contact, nearness, open body positions, and more vocal animations are highly expressive behaviors. In a positive relationship, individuals tend to reciprocate expressive behaviors. Cultures in which people exhibit much expressiveness, such as standing closer to one another and touching more, have been labeled as "high-contact"

Table 4.3   Expressiveness and Nonverbal Communication

Less Expressive (Low-Contact) Cultures	More Expressive (High-Contact) Cultures
Distance	Closeness
Avoidance/restraint	Accessibility/open
Detachment	Approach
Less touching	Touching
Not interrupting others in communication	Overlapping communication

cultures.[15] People of low-contact cultures tend to stand apart and touch less (see Table 4.3). South Americans, southern and eastern Europeans, Middle Easterners, and Indonesians are considered to be from high-contact cultures. Asians, North Americans, and northern Europeans are classified as coming from low-contact cultures. Australians and New Zealanders are moderate in their cultural contact level.

Face-to-face communication and interaction between people of high- and low-contact cultures can create moments of uneasiness and anxiety. Americans' preference for keeping their distance during interpersonal communication may be interpreted by South Americans or Middle Easterners as cold, suspicious, and unfriendly. Conversely, Americans may feel anxious and imposed on by the Middle Easterners' habit of staying very close and touching frequently during a conversation. Taiwanese, for example, tend to prefer seating arrangements that allow side-by-side contacts with persons of the same sex. Americans, on the other hand, prefer seating people of the opposite sex side by side.

People from expressive cultures get actively involved in the communication process and are not bothered by interruptions and overlapping conversations. The opposite is true for people from less expressive and more reserved cultures, who consider interruptions rude and impolite. While expressive communicators may interrupt each other, less expressive and more reserved people patiently take turns in communicating. Communication between the very reserved and polite Japanese is punctuated by moments of silence as well.

Emotions

Emotional expressions are important in communication. For many years, scientists assumed that nonverbal communication cues expressing emotions were culture specific and were learned differently across cultures. Evidence gathered recently, however, suggests that there are at least six universal emotional cues: facial expressions for anger, disgust, fear, happiness, sadness, and surprise (Table 4.4). These emotional cues are understood by people of many cultures.[16] There are, however, some cultural differences in the experience and evaluation of emotions. The results of cross-cultural research indicate that the antecedents of emotions vary between cultures. Matsumoto et al.[16] reviewed research findings regarding these differences. Americans and Europeans cited physical pleasures, cultural pleasures, birth of a new family member, and achievement-related situations as the antecedents of joy. World news, permanent and temporary separations, and death brought about sadness for Europeans and Americans. For the Japanese, relationships were more frequent elicitors of sadness, anger, and fear. For Americans and Europeans, strangers and risky situations were more frequent elicitors of fear (Table 4.5).

The intensity and duration of these emotions vary among the three cultures, too. Americans report feeling their emotions more intensely and for longer periods of time than do Europeans and Japanese. Emotion-eliciting events also cause Americans to feel greater positive self-esteem and self-confidence than the Japanese. This may be due to Americans' individualistic tendency, which emphasizes the self more than others. Finally, the Japanese

Table 4.4   Universal Emotional Cues

Facial expression for

1. Anger
2. Disgust
3. Fear
4. Happiness
5. Sadness
6. Surprise

Table 4.5   Antecedents and Elicitors of Emotion

	More Frequently Reported by	
	Americans and Europeans	**Japanese**
Emotions	**Antecedents**	**Elicitors**
Joy	Physical pleasures Cultural pleasures Birth of a new family member Achievement-related situations	
Sadness	World news Temporary or permanent separation Death	Relationships
Fear	Strangers Risky situations	Relationships
Anger	Relationships Situations of injustice	Relationships

appear to be more reluctant than Americans to name the cause of their sadness-producing experiences and usually take no action even when they report strong negative emotions.

The review of cross-cultural research by Matsumoto et al.[16] also revealed a difference in the physiological responses to emotional experience among the three cultures. In contrast to Europeans and Americans, the Japanese respondents reported fewer stomach troubles and muscle symptoms in response to the four emotions; less blood pressure change for joy, fear, and anger; and less feeling of cold for fear. These differences may be related to the differences in intensity and duration of the emotions reported by the people of these three cultures.

Observing nonverbal communication among different cultures provides expatriates an insight into cross-cultural communication. In some situations, the real meaning is not conveyed by the verbal language. Verbal communication might be a convenient way out of a potentially embarrassing situation. In a public discussion, for example, the Japanese may agree verbally to avoid the appearance of insulting others by disagreement. Verbal communication may intentionally be vague, which is an indication of disagreement. Also, the words spoken may be just the opposite of the real message, which is hidden under the surface. In these situations, the real meaning and the true message are conveyed through noncommital phrases, nonverbal silent language, nonverbal behavior, or the context of the communication and the manner of delivery. Paying attention to vague messages and learning these signs, signals, and silent codes of communication could improve intercultural relations and, consequently, influence the managers' performance.

Individualism

Individualism is the culture's emphasis on personal identity. It encourages self-serving behaviors. In individualistic cultures, individuals are expected to primarily look after their own interests and those of their immediate family. The opposite of individualism is collectivism. Collectivist cultures emphasize groups (e.g., family, neighborhood, organizations, and the country), not individuals. The interests and goals of individuals are subordinate to those of the group. Individuals seek fulfillment and happiness in the harmony of the group. Groups provide security to the members and protect their interests in exchange for their complete loyalty.

The nonverbal behaviors of individualistic cultures are different from those of collectivist cultures. The daily activities of people of collectivist cultures demonstrate their interdependence. People in these cultures live in close proximity to each other and synchronize their play, work, and sleep, while individualistic people tend to do "their own thing" separately.[11] Interdependence and socially prescribed interpersonal relationships are reflected in the way collectivist people use time. They tend to schedule more tasks simultaneously and interrupt meetings to tend to the requests of friends, family members, and business associates. In a way, they are more people oriented than the people of individualistic cultures.

Because compliance with norms is central to collectivists, they may suppress emotional displays that are contrary to the group mood. Therefore, people of collectivist cultures seem to be more reserved and formal in their demeanor. This tendency may explain a frequently expressed stereotype that "Orientals are inscrutable." Conversely, since individual freedom is of paramount value in individualistic cultures, these cultures encourage the expression of emotion.

In collectivist cultures, most of the norms governing interpersonal relationships are determined by society, while individuals bear this responsibility in individualistic cultures. Therefore, in individualistic cultures, personal initiatives are used for building many interpersonal relationships, including intimate relationships. In the United States, for example, flirting, small talk, initial acquaintance, and dating are more important than in collectivist cultures (p. 291).[11] In collectivist societies, families often arrange opportunities for young people to meet members of the opposite sex and eventually marry. Arranged marriages are not uncommon in some collectivist societies (pp. 47–66).[17] Consequently, it is easier to meet people and communication is more open in individualistic cultures such as in the United States. The usually transient and casual nature of these relationships, however, may make it appear to collectivists that Americans are noncaring people.

Gender Role Differentiation and Rigidity

This dimension refers to the rigidity and differentiation of socially prescribed gender roles. In some cultures, gender roles are narrowly defined. People are expected to behave within the socially prescribed gender roles. Masculinity is identified with traits and behaviors such as strength, speed, assertiveness, competitiveness, dominance, anger, ambition, and the pursuit of wealth. Feminine characteristics and behaviors are associated with emotionality, affection, compassion, warmth, and nurturing of the weak and the needy. The emphasis on one or the other set of attributes characterizes the masculinity or femininity of a culture.

Power Distance

Variation in the distribution of power among the members of a society is called power distance. It is the difference in the amount of power possessed by the least powerful and the most powerful members of the society. Various degrees of power inequality exist in all cultures. In each culture, there is an equilibrium level at which both the most powerful and the least powerful persons will find inequality acceptable.

PD creates communication barriers among people and affects nonverbal behaviors. When there is a high level of PD, subordinates show more respect and appear to be more polite in the presence of superiors. Possibly, the continuous smiles of many Asians, who are reared in high-PD countries, are attempts to produce social harmony or appease superiors (Anderson & Bowman, 1985, as cited in Ref. 11). Also, compared with low-PD countries, people of high-PD cultures appear to speak in a lower voice, apparently not wanting to disturb others. Conversely, those in low-PD cultures are generally less aware that their loud voices may be offensive to others.

Uncertainty

Cultures view risk and uncertainty differently. Some cultures have more aversion to risk and uncertainty and avoid such situations. Other cultures can tolerate such situations better.

Uncertainty and ambiguity could create stress and anxiety, especially in cultures with less tolerance for them. Since freedom can lead to more uncertainty, to avoid uncertainty, some cultures increase the rules governing behavior. Other cultures are able to tolerate freedom without excess stress or anxiety (p. 175).[12] On this basis, one could speculate that there are more communication formalities and more codification of nonverbal behavior among high-uncertainty-avoidance cultures. Conversely, among people of low-uncertainty-avoidance cultures, there might be fewer communication formalities and less codification of nonverbal behavior. Americans, for example, are less worried about the specifics of eating rituals in informal dinners than are the people of most other cultures.

Contextual Variations

Cultures vary in their use of context in the communication process.[15,18] High-context (HC) cultures pay attention to the surrounding circumstances or the context of an event for interpretation of the message.[19] The physical surroundings, the manner of delivery, the situation, and the nature of the issue at hand are all an integral part of the communication process and serve to impregnate it with information. This subtle information is understood within the culture because people are accustomed to it. In such cultures, words cannot be taken at face value, and not knowing the hidden meaning behind the words may lead to embarrassment and misunderstanding.

People of HC cultures are self-reflective, group oriented, and sensitive to group harmony. They have respect for hierarchy of status and authority. Family honor and obligations are important to them, including respect for one's ancestors. Asians, most Africans, South Americans, the southern and eastern Mediterranean peoples, and Middle Easterners are considered to belong to HC cultures.

In contrast to HC cultures, people of low-context (LC) cultures convey most information explicitly by the message itself. Unambiguity and specificity are characteristics of LC communication, in which messages are spelled out clearly. People of LC cultures are interested in straightforward answers of "yes" or "no" to most inquiries, and they feel uncomfortable in situations where they have to decipher the meaning from the context of the communication.

To people of LC cultures, good communication is direct and does not leave much to personal judgment and interpretation. LC cultures attempt to remove all ambiguity and try to anticipate all contingencies in their contractual relationships. Consequently, most business contracts and agreements are lengthy documents. Conversely, in HC cultures, business contracts are viewed as documents formalizing business relationships that are already built on trust. A few pages would be sufficient as a legal basis for such relationships.

People of LC cultures are direct and outward in their communication patterns and problem-solving style. They do things in sequence, one thing at a time, and tend to be more individualistic. In contrast to the people of HC cultures, people of LC cultures progress better in a planned manner, are technology oriented, and display and reward initiative. LC cultures have a frontier spirit; possess a strong drive toward accumulating knowledge, material products, and capital wealth; need to control the environment to suit their individual needs; and rely on written rules and regulations for social interaction, cohesion, and control (see Table 4.6).

Because of these tendencies, LC cultures are stereotyped by others as selfish, individualistic, work driven, inflexible in dealing with human situations, using more external control, and result oriented. The major attributes

Table 4.6   Cultures and Contextual Variations in Communication

High-Context Cultures	Low-Context Cultures
Convey Information Through	
Physical surrounding, implicit	Message itself, explicit
Ambiguous	Unambiguous, specific
Indirect/evasive	Direct/outward
Facial expression, speed, location, pause/silent	Straightforward, yes/no answer
Contract document is to formalize business relationship	Lengthy legal document to anticipate all contingencies
Family honor and obligations, respect for ancestors	Display and reward personal initiatives
Group oriented, share the credit	Individualistic, self-centered
Relationship above achievement	Strong drive to accumulate knowledge and wealth
Appear to others to be sneaky, mysterious, nondisclosing, inscrutable	Stereotyped: inflexible, efficiency/result oriented, excessively talkative, redundant
Tradition and informal understanding	Written rules
Self-reflective	Self-revealing

that LC cultures are identified with are "things" and "efficiency" over "people." They tend to use one-dimensional thinking in planning and problem solving. Most Westerners, including Australians, Britons, Germans, New Zealanders, North Americans, the Swiss, and Scandinavians, are considered to belong to LC cultures. People of these countries are concerned with specifics, details, and precise timetables for most of their activities.

LC cultures put much emphasis on verbal communication and downplay the value of nonverbal communication. The people of LC cultures are usually perceived by others as excessively talkative, redundant, and belaboring the obvious. Conversely, HC people are described as sneaky, mysterious, and nondisclosing (p. 294).[11] Nonverbal communication is more important to people of HC cultures. People of LC cultures do not perceive many of the contextual communication cues that are common to HC cultures. Much meaning is communicated among the people of HC cultures by contextual cues, such as facial expressions, tension, speed and location of interaction, pause and silent moments, and other subtleties of the occasion. People of HC cultures are more active participants in communication and expect the same from the other party. They will try to interpret and understand the unspoken signs, unarticulated moods, and environmental cues present during a conversation. These cues are often overlooked by most people of LC cultures.

HC and LC cultures have contrasting communication styles. The differences in communication are often the source of misunderstanding and mistrust between people of HC and LC cultures. Understanding these differences can pave the way for better relationships and improved business activities among nations.

Communication Competence

It cannot be overemphasized that international managers must be competent in their communication with the host culture. Expatriates are heavily dependent on their communication skills to bridge the cultural gaps with locals and to overcome the experience of culture shock on foreign assignments.

Spitzberg and Cupach[20] have defined communication competence as the social judgment made by the parties involved in the communication process (interactants) regarding the "goodness" of self and others' communication performance. Communication skills are the basis of communication competence. Verbal and nonverbal behaviors are communication skills, while communication competence is the social judgment made by interactants regarding the possession of these skills.

There are two ways to approach the study of communication competence: one is **culture specific** and the other, **culture general**.[21]

The culture-specific approach views intercultural communication competence as the degree of adjustment to and adoption of the communication patterns and practices of the host country. In other words, skills in and familiarity with communication modes of the host country are considered as communication competence.

The culture-general approach assumes that there is a certain communication competence useful to all cultures. It focuses on those aspects of communication competence that can be generalized to intercultural communication.

In international communication, an integrative view is more practical, in which features of both approaches are combined. While universal communication skills may exist (the claim of the culture-general approach), there might be cultural differences in the behaviors that reflect those skills (consistent with the culture-specific view). Communication skills such as empathy and respect, for example, might be universal. The expressions and interpretations of them, however, might vary across cultures.[22]

The effectiveness of expatriate managers depends on their ability to adapt to cultural and environmental differences. Among the most important skills needed for cross-cultural adaptation are cross-cultural communication skills, the ability to deal with stress, and the ability to establish interpersonal relationships.[10] Cross-cultural research has identified seven communication skills that influence success in foreign countries:[22]

1. The ability to express respect for other persons and their cultures

2. The ability to respond to others nonjudgmentally

3. The recognition of the individual basis of our knowledge

4. Empathy, the ability to see the world through other people's eyes

5. The ability to function in both people-oriented and task-oriented roles

6. The ability to take turns and not dominate the interaction and the relationship

7. The ability to tolerate ambiguity and adjust to a new situation with little discomfort[22]

Mastering these skills prepares expatriate managers for building interpersonal relationships in most cross-cultural situations.

Intercultural communication competence is enhanced by learning the value systems of other cultures and by developing verbal and nonverbal communication skills. Knowing the foreign language alone is not sufficient for communication competence. In Japan, for example, a person speaking Japanese and politely interacting with people may not create a favorable impression if in response to a polite bow of the Japanese, he or she naively extends a hand in greeting.

Sensitivity to cultural differences in communication styles improves intercultural communication competence. To be effective in intercultural communication, for example, one should be aware that the type and pattern of interaction and response are influenced by one's cultural upbringing. Most

Americans' visualization of a classroom is a place in which students are informally dressed and where frequent interaction among the teacher and the students takes place. Asians, on the other hand, think of a classroom as a place with formally dressed students who listen silently to their teacher's lecture.

Interpersonal interactions and responses to the same questions vary even within a country. In the United States, for example, children of middle-class parents are generally taught more elaborate ways of communication at home. Therefore, these children's classroom answers tend to be long and involved. Children of lower-class parents learn more restrictive communication codes at home and are more likely to respond in the classroom with one-word answers. Much back channeling is involved in African American communication and interaction. While the speaker is talking, he or she is encouraged by the listener's back channeling of vocal utterances such as "yeah," "right on," "ahuh," "tell it," "amen," and "go on." A white, middle-class teacher who is uninformed about cultural differences may misinterpret the short answers of these students as an indication of less knowledge. Similarly, such teachers are often offended by back channeling and consider the constant interruption annoying rather than reinforcing.[23]

Dos and Don'ts of Communication With Foreigners

Communication between people of different cultures is more difficult not only due to cultural differences but also due to differences in language. Many people who speak a foreign language may not fully comprehend its subtleties and nuances. Adler offers certain ways to improve communication with someone who is not fully proficient in a language. She has recommended ways of improving understanding when dealing with people whose native language is not English:[24]

Do not confuse foreigners by the use of colloquial expressions. Make it easier for them to understand you by enunciating each word clearly. Use simple vocabulary, and avoid long, compound sentences that require language proficiency. Repeat important ideas as often as you can, and pause frequently to allow time for mental translation and comprehension. Highlight important issues by providing summaries at important junctures in your discussion. Spontaneous translation takes time and energy. Allow listeners enough time to think. Do not rush to fill the silent periods that are normal in bilingual conversations. It is a mistake to equate poor grammar and mispronunciation with the lack of intelligence. Provide verbal and nonverbal encouragement, and do not embarrass novice speakers. (pp. 84–85)

In addition to learning about other cultures, Frank Acuff suggests the following 10 negotiation strategies that will work anywhere (p. 97):[25]

1. Plan the negotiation

2. Adopt a win-win approach

3. Maintain high aspirations

4. Use language that is simple and accessible

5. Ask lots of questions, then listen with your eyes and ears

6. Build solid relationships

7. Maintain personal integrity

8. Conserve concessions

9. Be patient

10. Be culturally literate and adapt to the negotiating strategies of the host country environment

International Negotiations

One of the most difficult and important tasks facing international managers is negotiation. To successfully conclude a business deal, labor agreement, or government contract with foreigners requires a considerable amount of communication skill. International negotiation is very complex and difficult because it involves different laws, regulations, standards, business practices, and above all cultural differences. The popularity of the saying "When in Rome, do as the Romans do" is an indication of our awareness that to succeed in international negotiation, we need to suppress our ethnocentric tendencies. This awareness, however, has not translated into substantial knowledge and understanding. There are two types of negotiation, intracultural and intercultural. Today, much of the literature on negotiation deals with intracultural settings. Only recently has intercultural negotiation received the attention of management scholars.

Acuff has defined negotiation as "the process of communicating back and forth for the purpose of reaching a joint agreement about differing needs or ideas" (p. 21).[25] In any negotiation, we can identify three components: the process, the parties in the negotiation, and the agreement or the outcome of the negotiation. Negotiating entities could be from the same culture or from different cultures. In the following pages, we summarize the elements of negotiation from an intracultural perspective. Next, we study the role of cultural differences in intercultural negotiation.

Negotiation Process

Most writings on negotiation assume similarity in culture and fields of experience among negotiating parties. Based on this assumption, negotiation strategies are devised to influence the other party's position. Writing from a North American perspective, Goldman,[26] for example, suggested that successful negotiation involves accomplishing three tasks (p. 6):

1. Bringing your own perceptions in line with reality

2. Ascertaining the other side's perceptions of the proposed transaction and the available alternatives

3. Finding ways to favorably alter the other side's perceptions

He says that in negotiation what counts is not true reality but the parties' perception of reality. He assumes that negotiating parties are from the same culture and have similar views and perceptions of reality.

There are two extreme negotiating positions, "hard" and "soft." Those taking a hard position see every negotiation as a contest of wills. They believe that by taking extreme positions and holding out longer, they will fare better. Taking a hard position may lead to confrontation, however. Often, the other party responds by taking an equally hard position. This exhausts both parties and damages their long-term relationship. Whereas a hard position is confrontational and adversely affects long-term relationships, a soft position may create a one-sided deal and foster ill feelings. Avoiding confrontation and taking a more accommodating soft position may result in undue advantage for the other party. By making concessions, a soft negotiator often ends up with less than a desirable deal and may feel bitter about it.[27]

Neither the hard nor the soft approach to negotiation is constructive. Fisher and Ury[27] suggest that principled negotiation (PN), or negotiating on merits, is a better alternative. Although PN was proposed for intracultural situations, and although it has been criticized by others,[28] with some modifications, it can be applied to intercultural negotiations as well. Cultural differences, however, render some of its aspects less useful for negotiations that cross cultural boundaries.

Principled Negotiation

The PN method is applicable to all stages of negotiation and involves four basic factors: people, interests, options, and criteria. The three stages of negotiation are analysis, planning, and discussion. In each stage, according to Fisher and Ury,[27] you could consider the four factors of PN (see Table 4.7).

In the following, we will discuss the four factors of PN, which could produce a constructive negotiation process.

Table 4.7   **Principled Negotiation**

	People	Interests	Options	Criteria
Analysis	×	×	×	×
Planning	×	×	×	×
Discussion	×	×	×	×

People. Separate the people from the problem. Often, negotiating parties become emotional, and instead of attacking the problem, they attack each other. This produces defensive behavior, which is not conducive to constructive negotiation. Reducing the emotional overtone and building a good working relationship improves the chances of success. Allow room to express emotions without taking them personally. In reserved cultures, such as those of Asia, negotiations and communication are expected to be free of emotional outbursts. Visible emotional expressions are considered signs of immaturity.

For strangers to reach an agreement, they must communicate well. Try to build a relationship with the other party that encourages good communication. Finally, allow the other party a "face-saving" position.

Interests. Focus on interests, not positions. Sharing information creates understanding. Positions are "what" the parties say they want, and interests are "why" they want them. Try to discover what "interests" are behind the positions of the other participants. Be careful when one party tries to learn the other's interests without revealing its own.

Options. Look for areas of mutual gain, and search for alternatives that give both sides something to gain. Considering multiple options, instead of one option at a time, may provide for more commonality of interests. Before deciding how to cut the pie, increase its size.

Criteria. Insist on objective criteria that can be used in selecting the final option. Agreement on objective criteria, such as market value, expert opinion, custom, precedence, law, and industry practices, eliminates one-sided outcomes.

Do not give in to pressure, and do not permit the negotiation to become a contest of wills. Following these four factors in the three stages of negotiation should lead parties to an agreement that both can accept.

Now, let us consider the three stages of PN.

Analysis. Make certain preparations before arriving at the negotiation table. The analysis stage deals with gathering and organizing information for diagnosing the situation. Review the issues pertinent to the four basic factors of people, interests, options, and criteria. Consider any people problems that might arise during the negotiation, such as perception, emotion, and communication. Define your interests and those of the other party. Review the options already on the table, and identify the criteria and framework suggested for the negotiation. Analysis applied to intercultural negotiation involves learning about other cultures; understanding their communication methods; and knowing their likes, dislikes, and preferences.

Planning. In the planning stage, again you are dealing with the same four factors of people, interests, options, and criteria. Here, you want to generate ideas and decide how to use them and determine how to deal with people problems that may arise. Prioritize your interests, and set realistic objectives. Generate more options, and devise criteria for selecting the best option.

Discussion. Parties communicate back and forth looking for ways to agree on various issues. Discussion is how perceptions, feelings, and difficulties in communication are addressed. Both parties acknowledge each other's interests, identify options that are mutually beneficial, and seek agreements on objective standards that could resolve opposing interests. Applied to intercultural negotiation, the discussion stage can be used to build and improve the relationship and create trust between parties.

PN provides parties to a negotiation with a method of focusing on basic interests and mutually advantageous solutions. Unlike inefficient bargaining within a political framework, PN enables parties to reach an agreement without all the haggling and posturing. By separating the people from the problem, PN makes amicable and efficient agreement possible. Cultural differences, however, make some aspects of PN less viable for intercultural negotiations.

PN makes culturally based assumptions regarding the fields of experience and value systems of negotiators and views negotiations from a North American perspective. While these assumptions may be true for intracultural negotiations, they might not be as effective in intercultural situations. For example, separating people from problems is not realistic in relationship-focused (RF) cultures. People from RF cultures are unable to separate people from the issues. The objective, abstract separation of people from problems or issues leaves them nothing tangible to deal with.

In the following section, we examine the American style of negotiation and its shortcomings. We discuss how these shortcomings could lead to ineffective intercultural negotiation.

The American Negotiation Style

Americans often enter international negotiations assuming their knowledge and experiences at home in dealing with suppliers, buyers, bankers, labor, and U.S. government agencies will be sufficient in securing a good agreement. They take a self-centered, objective, problem-solving approach. Although they are very well aware that it takes two to make a deal, they concentrate on their side and attempt to maximize their gains. In the same vein, Kuhn[29] advises negotiators,

Don't worry what others get. Don't worry what others think. Just know what you want to accomplish. Keep your eye on the ball and don't allow extraneous pressures to distract you. A good deal maker is constantly enhancing his or her perceived power. The trick is track record. Everyone wants to associate with a winner. (p. 27)

Confident of their own skills and believing that most negotiations can be dealt with in a logical and systematic order, Americans venture into negotiations with others while making assumptions that can lead to problems. Most of these assumptions are similar to those made in PN and can lead to ineffective international negotiation. Let us look at some of these assumptions (Refs. 25, pp. 41–66; 30). Table 4.8 highlights characteristics of American and Japanese negotiation.

Table 4.8   Negotiation Factors of the Americans and the Japanese

Americans	Japanese
Self-assured	Group dependent
Win/lose attitude	Win/win attitude
Competitive/distributive outcome	Noncompetitive/integrative outcome
Self-promotion	Group promotion
Lone Ranger (doing it alone)	Rely on group
Efficiency/task oriented	Relationship oriented
Direct/open communication	Subtle/indirect communication
Active	Passive
Silence is avoided	Silence is accepted
Linear thinking	Holistic thinking
Fixed/written contracts/legal	Fluid, flexible contracts
Abstract concepts	Situational concepts
Verbal cues	Nonverbal cues
Ego-preserving attitudes	Relationship-building attitudes
Power-oriented attitudes	Harmony-seeking attitudes
Short-term perspective	Long-term perspective
Deal focused	People focused
Comfortable with strangers	Comfortable with friends and associates
Clarity and openness	Face saving
Avoid small talk	Build relationship through small talk
Impatient	Patient
Act informally	Follow formal protocol

Doing It Alone

The individualistic tendencies of Americans lead them to believe that they can handle any situation alone. Americans often enter negotiations very self-confidently, thinking that they can handle whatever difficulties they encounter. They stress individuality and the importance of asserting the self, and they value autonomy and independence.[31] They take the "Lone Ranger" approach to negotiations (p. 45).[25] From the other party's viewpoint, this may look as if Americans are not taking the negotiation seriously and are not prepared for it. In practice, by going it alone, Americans may find themselves in strange situations, in unfamiliar settings, and outnumbered.

Informality and Open Communication

To Americans, informality is not only a desirable attribute; it is efficient. It allows one to get down to business quickly without wasting time. The assumption is that getting to the point and discussing the "bottom line" saves time and energy. Time spent on formalities and protocol is time taken away from doing business. Americans prefer direct and open communication. They believe that honest information exchange should facilitate negotiation. They like to put all their cards on the table and be direct, sincere, and honest, telling it as it is. The desire for efficiency and getting things done in less time makes them appear hasty and impatient. Many foreigners see open and direct communication as crude. In some cultures, it is offensive and rude to jump into the final issue without proper preparation and without following protocol.

Foreign Language Skills

Most American managers are not proficient in foreign languages. In contrast, their foreign counterparts are often well versed in at least a couple of foreign languages. The inability to communicate in any language but English is a handicap for Americans. Often, American negotiators watch in frustration while foreigners argue among themselves in their mother tongue, aware that the Americans will not be able to comprehend the content of their arguments.

Silence

Unlike Asians, who use silent periods to reflect and organize their thoughts, Americans do not like silence. Because of their concern for time, silent periods appear to Americans as inactivity and a waste of time. They get frustrated in what appears to be a slow-moving negotiation process because of their inability to read the nonverbal, silent language of Asians. The following complaint is a typical example:

> I spent a week in Japan negotiating a deal that seemed to be good for both parties. For the life of me, I could not make any sense, one way or another, if they were interested or not. They just sat there listening

to me, with no expressions on their faces. Yes! They apologized a lot for nothing. I am forced to make another trip just to find out if they like my proposal!

Persistence and Competitiveness

Americans prize persistence and will not give up easily. They do not take "no" for an answer. Their competitive nature and their desire to win make persistence a very valued attribute. "If at first you don't succeed, try and try again" is a hallmark of the American mentality. Americans view negotiations as a win-lose situation. Moreover, they assume that others have the same view of the negotiation. Unfortunately, projecting such unwarranted similarities can lead to disappointment when negotiations get bogged down due to cultural differences.

Legalistic and Linear Approach

Most American negotiators use a linear approach to problem solving. Complex problems are broken down into simpler issues, and each issue is tackled separately. In a linear fashion, one issue at a time is solved until the total problem is settled. Americans prefer precise, written contracts that cover every detail of the business transaction in a legal, formal framework.

Now that we have learned about the American style of negotiation, we can examine intercultural negotiations.

Intercultural Negotiations

Effective communication is the foundation of a successful negotiation. Intercultural negotiation has all the pitfalls of intracultural communication and is made more difficult by cultural differences. Based on the proposition suggested by Bangert,[32] in the following paragraphs we will examine the influence of culture on various components of negotiation.

Cultural Influences on Negotiation

The complexity of issues in a negotiation may determine the size of the negotiating teams. Negotiations on complex issues such as oil exploration and marketing rights with a foreign country require the use of many specialists. Most negotiations between MNCs and their foreign partners are complex. In these negotiations, MNCs employ many staff specialists. Not all members of the staff need to attend the negotiation session. Negotiating teams may simply benefit from the behind-the-scenes services of the specialist staff. Cultural differences influence the size of the team directly involved in the negotiation. Negotiating teams from collectivist societies tend to be large, whereas in an individualistic culture, a single person can constitute an acceptable negotiating team. The Japanese, for example, prefer to use a large negotiating team, while Americans may send only a couple of persons to the negotiation table. Those two lone negotiators at the table may be overwhelmed by the team of negotiators from a collectivist society.

Collectivist societies consider people very important. Long-term relationships, consensus, and harmony among organizational members are important to them. The blurring of boundaries between people and the environmental situations in collectivist cultures has already been discussed. Contrary to the suggestion of PN, it is difficult for collectivists to separate issues from the people. For the same reason, collectivists are very reluctant to express disagreement openly. They fear that this may cause hurt feelings. Consequently, nonverbal and indirect communication cues play an important role in negotiation with collectivists. To succeed in business in Korea, for example, a person needs an extraordinary skill to read *nunch'i* (noon-chee).[33]

> *Nunch'i* means the look in a person's eyes, the nonverbal reaction of a person to a question, an order, or any interaction with another person. Koreans are very skilled at this subtle art and take it for granted that others are also. (p. 83)

In a classic case of cross-cultural communication failure, a foreign manager learned the role of *nunch'i* the hard way. Paul Dredge, a senior associate of Korean Strategy Associations, recounted the following incident:[33]

> The office of a joint venture company in Seoul, Korea was located in a prestigious but inconvenient area of the city. To make it more convenient for both the visitors and the employees, the foreign manager decided to move the office to a nice down-town location. In his discussion of the issue with his Korean colleagues he did not encounter any objections. All along he assumed they agreed with his choice of the location. He was baffled, however, when at the last moment the Korean president, without any explanation, refused to allow the move. It created an impasse, and a great deal of ill will on both sides.
>
> From the beginning, the Korean president and personnel had opposed the move. They had not directly expressed their opposition, however. They did not want to confront him openly in a contest that they knew the foreign manager could not win. To be polite, in a face saving attempt, they were not specific about their objection to the move. It was up to the foreign manager to ask the right questions and understand the right answers. They had relied on his ability to read *nunch'i*. His failure had caused the loss of face on both sides. (pp. 83–84)

Negotiations between people of **masculine** and **feminine** cultures may also run into difficulties. For negotiators from masculine societies, ego preservation is important. For them to compromise may give the appearance of giving in, which could be considered a sign of weakness. Consequently, they may be in greater danger of taking a rigid position, which may lead to breakdown in the negotiations. Negotiators from a feminine culture may not be aware of the importance of ego to people of masculine cultures. Building the ego of their counterparts and focusing on the task at hand may help advance negotiations faster.

Similarly, negotiation is more difficult between people of different cultures with dissimilar value systems. Compared with **low-PD** cultures, negotiators from a **high-PD** culture may need more information to convince their superiors of the value of the agreement. They may also take more time because they have to clear most decisions with those in positions of power.

Views of the expected outcomes of negotiation may also be culturally based. Specifically, the expected outcomes of any negotiation may be either integrative or distributive.

Integrative outcomes, or win-win situations, produce mutual benefits to both parties. To produce integrative outcomes, both parties must locate and adopt options that reconcile their needs. Integrative negotiations result in great benefits for both parties and stable relationships. By cooperation, the parties increase the size of the pie that they will eventually divide among themselves.[34]

Distributive outcomes are the result of competition among the negotiators, each trying to get a larger share of the same pie without attempting to increase its size. Distributive negotiation is a win-lose scenario, in which negotiators believe that they have opposing interests and incompatible alternative choices.[35]

Similar to most Westerners, Americans view a contract, once it is negotiated and signed, as binding regardless of changed circumstances that might make it less attractive to one of the parties than it had been initially (pp. 65–66).[36] For Americans, a contract should not be modified: "A deal is a deal. For Easterners, agreements are often regarded as tentatively agreed upon guides for the future" (p. 196).[36] Americans tend to have a short-term, distributive view of negotiation. Since Americans are concerned with their own interests and view negotiations competitively, they often arrive at distributive outcomes. In contrast, most Asians view negotiation as a long-term relationship and a cooperative task. Based on laboratory experiments, we can make certain statements regarding intercultural negotiations. Viewing negotiations as win-win propositions tends to produce integrative outcomes. Negotiations between those with distributive views (e.g., Americans) and those with integrative views (e.g., Japanese) tend to produce distributive outcomes.[37]

We know that differences in the fields of experience create barriers to communication and may derail intercultural negotiation. Consider the following case:

A young female interpreter in one of her early assignments ran into a very challenging situation. She had been assigned as an interpreter for the Russian delegations in India. One of her contracts was to be the interpreter for a cultural exchange program. On the Indian side, she was working for an administrative officer, a post held in high esteem in the country. On the Russian side, the head of the delegation was the director of a cultural organization. The day the Russian arrived in India, she and her employer went to his hotel to welcome him to the country. The Russian was overjoyed to see them, and after greetings and introductions, he decided to make them more comfortable by narrating an anecdote of not quite innocent contents. Mistake number one. It was visibly evident that the Indian administrator was not at all amused. The astute Russian realized something was probably wrong and decided to rectify the situation in the true Russian style by pouring a round of vodka for everybody, without even asking them if they would like to have a drink. Mistake number two, and a major one. The Indian administrator, who was a very conservative person, did not drink. She was probably in the worst dilemma. She had lived in Russia for a few years and knew that the best way to insult a Russian is to not drink his vodka. But to drink it would be like slapping her boss in the face. Of course, she decided to keep her job and not even pick up the drink. But after such a head start you can imagine how the rest of the negotiation went.[b]

Deal-Focused and Relationship-Focused People

The people-oriented and task-oriented continuum often discussed in the leadership literature can be used in typology of cultures and negotiation perspectives. According to Richard Gesteland,[7] people of different cultures can be categorized as either deal focused (DF) or relationship focused (RF). DF people are fundamentally task oriented, while RF types are more people oriented.

RF types constitute the vast majority of the world's cultures. Africans, Asians, Pacific Islanders, Latin Americans, and Middle Easterners are RF. They prefer to deal with family, friends, and those well-known to them. In effect, they are more interested in doing business with those who can be trusted. Doing business with strangers makes them uncomfortable unless they are given a chance to get to know and develop trusting relationships with them. They are very interested in preserving harmony. Therefore, very seldom do they bluntly say what is on their mind.

Only a small number of the world's cultures are of the DF type. People of northern Europe, North America, Australia, and New Zealand are DF, and they are relatively open to doing business with strangers. Clarity and sincerity are preferred by DF types over harmony and saving face. It is common for DF types to make initial contacts with prospective business partners without prior relationships or connections. For DF people, the sooner the business negotiations and business deals begin, the better. They prefer to waste no time over what they consider unnecessary, time-consuming small talk and activities that are not directly related to the business at hand.

In doing business with RF types, referrals or introduction by a go-between who can be trusted is helpful. In business negotiations and transactions, RF people spend a great amount of time building relationships with prospective business partners before getting into actual business negotiations.

To be successful in business negotiations, we should recognize the differences between the two types. Negotiations between RF and DF types can run into major difficulties if the idiosyncrasies of each type are not acknowledged and ways for dealing with them are not devised. Consider the following example:[7]

> A northern European executive had been haggling for months in long drawn-out negotiations in Ho Chi Minh City. The deal was to start a joint venture with a Vietnamese company. Toward the end of a very frustrating day, the European manager lost his patience. He was no longer able to mask his irritation from what seemed to be endless inquires and delays. His face began to turn red, very red. He started to shake with anger. Then he clenched his fist so hard that the pencil he was holding in his hand snapped. Instantly, the silence fell over the room at the sound of the breaking pencil. A moment later, all of the Vietnamese delegation got up and stormed out of the conference room. The next day a fax from them informed the European headquarters that Vietnamese would never again sit across the negotiation table with such a rude and arrogant person. To them, openly showing anger had resulted in both sides losing face. (p. 36)

Negotiation Points to Remember

Given the differences in negotiation perspective that can occur between Americans and people of other nations, it is not surprising that international negotiations are marred by many difficulties, misunderstandings, and mistakes. Learning about the cultural perspectives of negotiation can reduce some of the problems of intercultural negotiations. The first step in improving international negotiations is to understand the influence of cultural differences on negotiation styles. Armed with knowledge about various cultural perspectives on negotiation, steps can be taken to reduce the difficulties and increase the chance of success in dealing with people of other cultures. The following examples illustrate style differences in international negotiation and point out the pitfalls to avoid.

We know, for example, that there are differences in time orientation and other cultural values between Americans and other people. These cultural differences influence the objectives, content, and direction of discussion in negotiations. Americans value youth and rely more on expertise and knowledge than on age and seniority in selecting the members of negotiating teams. Younger negotiators are not uncommon among American teams. In other cultures, such as those of the Middle East, South America, and Asia, team members are often selected on the basis of age, seniority, social standing, and family connections. Some foreigners may not look favorably on a negotiation when they sit across the table from a much younger manager representing an American company.

Sometimes, intercultural negotiation fails due to ignorance and unfamiliarity with the cultural values of the host country. The host may consider that ignorance disrespectful and insulting. This was the case with an American salesman who was attempting to secure a multi-million-dollar business in Saudi Arabia. He presented his Saudi client with a business proposal in a pigskin folder. He was astonished when he was unceremoniously tossed out of the country and his company was blacklisted. In many Muslim cultures, anything associated with pigs is considered vile.[38]

The decision-making styles of Asians, and particularly Japanese, are different from those of Americans. The Japanese include more levels of hierarchy and many more people in most decision processes. Involving more people in the decision-making process when the intention is to arrive at a consensus becomes more time-consuming. The implementation of consensus decisions takes less time, however. The American style of proposal-counterproposal negotiation does not fit well with the Japanese consensus-building, group-based decision-making process. Persuasive arguments are not as effective with the Japanese as is detailed information. They would prefer first reaching an agreement informally, then formalizing it with a short, written contract.[39]

Bargaining and negotiation are part of daily life in the Middle East. It is unusual to walk into a shop and purchase merchandise at a specific price. No one expects to complete a deal quickly without bargaining. Patience and protocol are prized. Middle Easterners enjoy flowery prose and poetry and often sprinkle their talk with the recitation of poetry. As RF-type people, they are more concerned with personal integrity and building a relationship than with the formality of concluding an agreement. As it is with the Asians, saving face and preserving their honor and reputation is very important to Middle Easterners. They take pride in their hospitality, are very generous, and appreciate generous people. They have little respect for those who are tightfisted with their wealth. Foreigners who want to establish business relationships in the Middle East should be ready to combine personal relationships with business transactions. In the following paragraph, a foreign negotiator's recounting of his experience is a typical example of the personal nature of doing business in the Middle East.[25]

> The Labour Minister for the United Arab Emirates was in my office to help negotiate an end to a work stoppage by the local Dubai construction workers. The meeting went well until we finished our discussions. While walking with His Highness to the door of my office, I mentioned that he had a beautiful briefcase (mine was in a general state of disrepair). As I reached the door I noticed that he was no longer walking with me. I turned around to see His Highness emptying the contents of his briefcase on my desk.
>
> "Did you lose something?" I tried to ask helpfully.
>
> "No, no," he replied. "I want you to have," he added, as he presented his briefcase to me. "This is for you. You are my friend."
>
> After profusely apologizing, I convinced him that I really couldn't accept the briefcase.
>
> The lesson learned? In that part of the world, don't go around complimenting people on their possessions. You just might end up with them. (p. 57)

In negotiating with people from different cultures, understanding the proper negotiation behaviors and protocol can increase the likelihood of success. Astute negotiators pay close attention to greetings and appropriate ways of addressing people, proper dress, and the norms of formality/informality in various cultures. Along these lines, Table 4.9 summarizes some important points to remember.

In the unfortunate event that a negotiation runs into dispute and deadlock, there are ways of preventing a total failure. Changing the composition of the negotiating team may help, possibly even assigning a wholly new team. A less dramatic action may also be successful. A change of venue, adjournment of the session, or repackaging the deal may be sufficient to break the deadlock. Popular cultural practices may offer opportunities in these situations. Arabs, for example, will take a recess for prayer, Japanese will bring in a senior executive to "see what the problem is, Swedes will go out drinking together, and Finns [will] retire to the sauna."[40]

Summary

Without communication, no organization can function. By communicating, we share information, knowledge, beliefs, and values; we also share our ideas,

Table 4.9   Points to Consider in Intercultural Negotiation

Behavior	Cultural Norms/Values to Consider
Punctuality	Are they polychronic or monochronic?
Greetings	What is the proper way of addressing and greeting people? The role of business cards?
Deal or relationship focus	Should the hosts focus on building a relationship first or accept the American-style business focus?
Formal versus informal	How much informality is accepted?
Dress code	What is the proper dress? What colors should I avoid?
Nonverbal Cues	
Emotion	How reserved should a person appear? How much emotion can be displayed?
Eye contact	Is it polite to keep direct eye contact?
Silence	How is silence reviewed? Is it accepted?
Touching	Is touching a normal behavior?
Personal space	What is the proper distance between people?
Body language	What gestures and forms of body language are rude or insulting?
Dining protocol	What are the eating protocols? What manners should be avoided? What foods are taboo?
Gift giving	Is gift giving expected in business settings? What gifts should be avoided? What price range is acceptable?
Age and gender	How senior should the negotiator be? Are females viewed (un)favorably?

opinions, and feelings with others. It is through communication that we negotiate a deal, buy and sell products, and exchange information. Communication
is complete when the meaning we intended to send with our message reaches
its destination and is understood by the receiver. This requires commonality of
fields of experience between the sender and the receiver. Cultural differences
that create different fields of experience make communication across cultures
very difficult. International managers need to understand the influence of cultural differences on communication. They can improve intercultural communication by recognizing the cross-cultural variations in communication patterns.

Although verbal communication and written communication are the
predominant forms of communication, nonverbal cues are used to supplement or replace the oral and written forms. Similar to differences in languages, there are cultural variations in the nonverbal cues, signs, and signals
used in communication. Because language differences are apparent, we learn
foreign languages to communicate with other people in their mother tongue.
Nonverbal cues, signs, and signals used in communication are less evident;
therefore, fewer attempts are made to understand them. International managers who do not familiarize themselves with the idiosyncrasies of nonverbal communication will face more communication problems. Ignorance of
nonverbal, cross-cultural communication can have serious consequences.
Unfamiliarity in reading the meaning behind the verbal messages could lead
to misunderstanding, confusion, and business failure.

To negotiate a business deal, international managers must recognize the cultural differences in communication and negotiation styles. The skills developed
in intracultural negotiations are insufficient for conducting intercultural negotiations. "Projective similarity," assuming that others negotiate the same way
as we do, could lead to disappointing results. The American view that negotiation is a competitive game is not necessarily shared by other people. Some
cultures view negotiation as a relationship-building exercise. Such a view of
negotiation calls for a different type of negotiation and different skills.
Attempts at maximizing our gains with such a group may produce a short-term
result but may damage the long-term relationship. International managers who
succeed remember the saying "When in Rome, do as the Romans do."

Discussion Questions _____

1. What are the differences between macro and micro international
   communications?

2. Explain developing countries' concerns regarding international
   communication.

3. In what way can cultural differences cause communication problems?

4. Why is understanding nonverbal communication more important to
   international managers?

5. Give an example of an American nonverbal communication that may have a different meaning in another culture.

6. Based on the material in this chapter, how would you advise a person from a culture that is high on the femininity index in negotiations with an individual from a culture that is high on the masculinity index?

7. Why do negotiators from high-PD societies need more information?

8. Use at least two cultural dimensions discussed in this chapter for explaining the assertion that Americans are very legalistic and short-term oriented in negotiations.

9. What is the PN method? How different is PN from other negotiation methods?

10. Compare the American style of negotiation with that of the Japanese.

11. How do you negotiate with RF people?

12. What strategies should be used in negotiation with DF people?

13. What are your recommendations for breaking a deadlocked negotiation?

14. You are planning a trip to Riyadh, Saudi Arabia. The trip is for the purpose of negotiating a business deal with a prospective Saudi partner. As is customary in the Middle East, you are planning to take a couple of gifts for your hosts. Which one of the following should you take with you and which one(s) should you not take with you? Explain.[c]
    a. A 20 to 30 lb whole ham
    b. A bottle of whisky
    c. A book of American landscape paintings
    d. A set of expensive pens with your company logos engraved on them
    e. A Bible

15. A few years ago, before accepting international assignments, you studied a couple of foreign languages, including Spanish. Your 2 years of work in Singapore did not provide you with an opportunity to practice your language skill. Now you are assigned to Brazil. When visiting your host in Rio de Janeiro, is it a good idea to speak in Spanish even though you are not proficient? Explain.

Notes

a. The second part of Bob's story is adapted from Reference 1.
b. Told by Parvathy Menon, my graduate assistant.
c. This and the following question are based on the classroom material used by Betty Jane Punnett and Donald M. Wood, both from the University of the West Indies.

References

1. R. Brown (1983, January 10). The Maverick who yelled foul at Citibank. *Fortune*, 46.
2. H. Mowlana (1986). *Global information and world communication*. New York: Longman.
3. K. Nordenstreng & W. Kleinwachter (1989). The new international information and communication order. In M. K. Asante & W. B. Gudykunst (Eds.), *Handbook of international and intercultural communication* (p. 87). Newbury Park, CA: Sage.
4. T. L. McPhail (1987). *Electronic colonialism: The future of international broadcasting and communication* (2nd rev. ed.). Newbury Park, CA: Sage.
5. W. Schramm (1963). How communication works. In W. Schramm (Ed.), *The process and effects of mass communication* (p. 6). Urbana: University of Illinois Press.
6. F. S. Yousef (1974). Cross-cultural communication: Aspects of contractive social values between North Americans and Middle Easterners. *Human Organization, 33*(4), 383–387.
7. R. R. Gesteland (1999). *Cross-cultural business behavior*. Copenhagen, Denmark: Copenhagen Business School.
8. J. C. Berris (1991). The art of interpreting. In L. A. Samovar & R. E. Porter (Eds.), *Intercultural communication* (pp. 265–269). Belmont, CA: Wadsworth.
9. M. Maruyama (1993). *Mindscapes in management*. Aldershot, UK: Dartmouth.
10. M. Mendenhall & G. Oddou (1985). The dimensions of expatriate acculturation: A review. *Academy of Management Review, 10*(1), 39–47.
11. P. Anderson (1991). Explaining intercultural differences in nonverbal communication. In L. A. Samovar & R. E. Porter (Eds.), *Intercultural communication* (pp. 286–296). Belmont, CA: Wadsworth.
12. M. L. Hecht, P. A. Anderson, & S. A. Ribeau (1989). The cultural dimensions of nonverbal communication. In M. K. Asante & W. B. Gudykunst (Eds.), *Handbook of international and intercultural communication* (pp. 163–185). Newbury Park, CA: Sage.
13. K. Leung, R. S. Bhagat, N. R. Buchan, M. Erez, & C. B. Gibson (2005). Culture and international business: Recent advances and their implications for future research. *Journal of International Business Studies, 36*(4), 365.
14. M. Javidan, G. K. Stahl, F. Brodbeck, & C. P. M. Wilderom (2005). Cross-border transfer of knowledge: Cultural lessons from Project GLOBE. *Academy of Management Executive, 19*(2), 59–76.
15. E. T. Hall (1966). *The hidden dimension*. Garden City, NY: Doubleday.
16. D. Matsumoto, H. G. Wallbott, & K. R. Scherer (1989). Emotions in intercultural communication. In M. K. Asante & W. B. Gudykunst (Eds.), *Handbook of international and intercultural communication* (pp. 225–246). Newbury Park, CA: Sage.
17. M. J. Gannon (2004). *Understanding global cultures*. Thousand Oaks, CA: Sage.
18. E. T. Hall (1959). *The silent language*. New York: Doubleday.
19. C. E. Halverson (1992). Managing differences on multicultural teams. *Cultural Diversity at Work, May*, 10–15.
20. B. H. Spitzberg & W. R. Cupach (1984). *Interpersonal communication competence*. Beverly Hills, CA: Sage.

21. M. R. Hammer (1989). Intercultural communication competence. In M. K. Asante & W. B. Gudykunst (Eds.), *Handbook of international and intercultural communication* (pp. 247–260). Newbury Park, CA: Sage.

22. B. Ruben (1976). Assessing communication competency for intercultural adaptation. *Group and Organizational Studies, 1,* 334–354.

23. J. E. Andersen (1985). Educational assumptions highlighted from a cross-cultural comparison. In L. A. Samovar & R. E. Porter (Eds.), *Intercultural communication: A reader* (pp. 160–164). Belmont, CA: Wadsworth.

24. N. J. Adler (1991). *International dimensions of organizational behavior.* Boston: Kent Publishing.

25. F. L. Acuff (1993). *How to negotiate anything with anyone anywhere around the world.* New York: American Management Association.

26. A. L. Goldman (1991). *Settling for more.* Washington, DC: Bureau of National Affairs.

27. R. Fisher & W. Ury (1981). *Getting to yes: Negotiating agreement without giving in.* Boston: Houghton Mifflin.

28. D. Ertel (2004). Getting past yes: Negotiating as if implementation mattered. *Harvard Business Review, November,* 60–68.

29. R. L. Kuhn (1988). *Dealmaker: All the negotiating skills and secrets you need.* New York: Wiley.

30. J. L. Graham & R. J. Herberger (1983). Negotiators abroad don't shoot from the hip. *Harvard Business Review, 61,* 160–168.

31. H. R. Markus & S. Kitayama (1991). Culture and the self: Implications for cognition, emotion, and motivation. *Psychological Review, 98*(2), 224–253.

32. D. C. Bangert (1993, October). Culture's influence on negotiations. Paper presented at the Academy of International Business, Maui, HI.

33. B. De Mente (1991). *Korean etiquette and ethics in business.* Lincolnwood, IL: NTC.

34. M. H. Bazerman & M. A. Neal (1982). Improving negotiation effectiveness under final offer arbitration: The role of selection and training. *Journal of Applied Psychology, 67,* 543–554.

35. D. G. Pruitt (1981). *Negotiation behavior.* New York: Academic Press.

36. R. E. Nisbett (2004). *The geography of thought.* New York: Free Press.

37. T. R. Lituchy (1993, October). Negotiating with the Japanese: Can we reach win-win agreements? Paper presented at the Academy of International Business Conference, Maui, HI.

38. J. K. Sebenius (2002). Cross-border negotiations. *Harvard Business Review, March,* 76.

39. S. A. Hellweg, L. A. Samovar, & L. Shaw (1991). Cultural variations in negotiation styles. In L. Samovar & R. E. Porter (Eds.), *Intercultural communication: A reader* (pp. 185–192). Belmont, CA: Wadsworth.

40. R. Lewis (1995, August). A clear-cut case for compromise. *Management Today,* p. 72.

5

Managerial Leadership and Motivation in an International Context

E ffective managers lead and motivate their followers to perform their jobs successfully. The ability of a manager to lead and motivate affects his or her ability to manage. Organizational performance is based on the collective contribution of all members. Organizations could suffer without an effective leader to increase and combine these contributions. To attain an organization's goals, managers must be able to guide and direct the organization's members to perform to the best of their abilities.

While leadership and motivation are not easy tasks, they are much easier in domestic firms than in an international enterprise. Providing direction and purpose for a culturally diverse workforce in an MNC is very challenging. Although there are many similarities between MNCs and their domestic counterparts, the operational requirements of MNCs are different in many ways. In a domestic firm, because managers and workers share the same cultural values and heritage, many issues do not require much elaboration and explanation by the managers. Cultural norms provide a basic framework for the fulfillment of duties and a simple means for control. Such a vehicle is not available to an international manager who works with a culturally diverse workforce. In this chapter, we will learn about the difficulties that international managers may experience in leading and motivating such a workforce. Also, we review leadership practices in Europe and Japan.

Like domestic companies, global companies rely on leadership and motivation to energize their employees toward reaching the organization's goals. Companies engaged in international business need to develop extra sensitivity to cultural variations in order to satisfy and motivate their employees. The cultural relativity of major leadership and motivation theories is reviewed in this chapter. The success of Japanese firms in competition with American companies has been attributed to their unique management style. Whether what motivates a Japanese worker will work in other cultures, including American culture, is a question worth investigating. According to some scholars, the fall of the Soviet Union and major developments in communication technology have fostered a trend toward a global culture. These developments, along with the influence of culture on leadership and motivation and their implications for international management, are examined in this chapter.

Chapter Vignette

Inspiring Leaders

South Africa has seen two world-renowned leaders, Mahatma Gandhi and Nelson Mandela, who used different means to achieve a broad common end—freeing their people from oppression and injustice. The means used by both of them to promote their cause included business and economic actions aimed at hurting the purses of their tyrant rulers.

Mohandas Karamchand Gandhi was born on October 2, 1869, in Porbandar, a city in the present state of Gujarat, in India. While he was a legal adviser for an Indian firm in South Africa, he witnessed the widespread denial of human rights to Indian immigrants. It was in South Africa that Gandhi propounded his philosophy of passive resistance and noncooperation as a strategy for opposing tyranny and human rights abuses. When he returned to India, Gandhi began teaching and practicing passive resistance and civil disobedience, which Indians called "satyagraha" (a Sanskrit word meaning nonviolence resistance), He led Indians in a long and difficult struggle against British rule. Knowing the importance of economic pressure, he ordered the complete boycott of all British goods. Finally, under his leadership, India gained its independence in 1947.

Gandhi lived a spiritual and ascetic life. He wore only a loincloth and a shawl, which was how the lowliest Indians dressed. He responded to the abuses, beatings, and jail sentences that British authorities inflicted on him with fasting, prayers, and meditation and urged his followers to do the same. Gandhi was revered by Indians as a saint; they call him Mahatma ("great souled"). He is the symbol of free India and the spiritual leader of the nonviolence movement globally. His teachings and philosophy have influenced and inspired nonviolence movements everywhere.

Rolihlahla Nelson Dalibhunga Mandela, who in 1994 was elected the first black president of South Africa, was born on July 18, 1918, at Mbhashe in Umtata District. His father was a chief, and his mother was one of his father's four wives. In 1942, Nelson obtained his B.A. degree and became a student at the University of the Witwatersrand in the Faculty of Law. In 1944, Mandela joined the African National Congress (ANC), the political party that aimed at eradicating the segregationist practices of the South African government. In 1947, he was elected the ANC's secretary, and in 1951, he became its president. At first, he followed the path of nonviolent resistance against the apartheid policy of South Africa, but dismayed by its apparent failure, he soon joined the armed struggle.

In 1960, police fired at unarmed pass-law protesters, massacring thousands. Consequently, civil strikes ensued, and the government declared a state of emergency. Thousands were arrested, and the ANC was banned. Mandela was forced to go underground in April 1961. He organized military training for armed operations against the apartheid regime. Soon, he was arrested and sentenced to imprisonment for 5 years. In 1963, following the arrest of other ANC leaders, Mandela, while still in jail, was sentenced to life imprisonment for sabotage and attempting to overthrow the state. While in prison, he received many awards, honorary degrees, and even honorary citizenship from other nations. To force the dismantling of the apartheid regime, he pleaded with Western governments to impose economic sanctions against the South African government and urged MNCs to withdraw their investment from South Africa. Finally, the economic measures and worldwide condemnation forced the abandonment of apartheid practices.

When Mandela was released on February 11, 1990, some wondered whether he would be ready for compromise after spending more than a quarter of a century in prison. Some have argued that if he had been bent on vengeance, he could have caused mass riots and massive civil strife. But he, as the leader of South African blacks, set aside his personal feelings. He concluded his first speech after his release from prison by saying, "I have fought against white domination, and I have fought against black domination. I have cherished the idea of a democratic and free society in which all persons live together in harmony and with equal opportunities. It is an ideal which I hope to live for and achieve. But if needs be, it is an ideal for which I am prepared to die."[1-5]

Introduction

Many business failures can be traced to functional deficiencies, such as poor planning or marketing. Many more are due to managers' inability to lead and motivate employees. Effective managers are those who can lead their subordinates toward the accomplishment of organizational goals. This is a feat not easily managed. Among managerial skills, leadership competency and the ability to motivate are two of most difficult to master. While managers can rely on assistance from others in technical matters, they have to resolve leadership problems and motivation issues through personal initiatives. Leadership and motivation skills, therefore, are critical to a manager's success.

If leading and motivating are important determinants of success in a domestic business, they are much more important in an international operation. What constitutes a good leader in one culture may not necessarily hold true in other cultures. Also, what motivates people varies among cultures. Most Americans, for example, prefer democratic leaders who seek inputs from their subordinates. In other cultures, such a leader may be regarded as naive or incompetent. In some cultures, a leader should always know how to take charge and lead his or her subordinates without needing much assistance from them. Any failure to take charge would be interpreted as a sign of incompetence. For Americans, motivation is mostly an individual, personal issue. In some other cultures, however, personal factors are subordinated to the group's benefit.

Besides having technical expertise, international managers must possess the ability to organize and lead a workforce of diverse cultures and to achieve cross-cultural collaboration in spite of multicultural difficulties. They need to be proficient in motivating, coaching, mentoring, and assessing the performance of people with different values, beliefs, and attitudes. The requirements for managerial leadership in international contexts extend well beyond functional management practices and encompass a sensitivity to, and empathy with, cultural diversity. The task of leading under demanding conditions requires an understanding of leadership concepts and the ability to apply them to different cultural circumstances.

Major leadership theories, which have shaped Western managerial thinking and philosophies, have been developed and tested almost exclusively in the West. While these theories are based on Western cultural values and assumptions, they are often implicitly presented as universal theories. Consequently, practicing managers have applied them, along with other Western managerial concepts, to international situations without considering the need to modify them according to the context. Not surprisingly, the results have been less than stellar.

In the following section, we discuss the shortcomings of these theories and examine their applicability to different cultural situations.

The Shortcomings of Leadership Theories

The following discussion is based on the assumption that readers are familiar with the leadership theories presented in Appendix A.

Popular leadership theories assume that the leaders and followers have a lot in common within their value systems and culture and that the roles of leader and followers are universal. These theories, implicitly if not explicitly, advocate democratic, participative leadership behavior as the preferred choice. Almost all theories were developed in the United States and are based on American cultural values. As Reitz[6] has asserted, because the American

> culture has traditionally placed higher values on democratic than on authoritarian leadership, certain biases can be detected in the research on the effects of these leadership styles. A great deal of research is designed to prove that democracy is superior to autocracy, rather than to test that proportion. (p. 524)

Recent research is questioning the validity of these assumptions. We could claim that democratic behavior is "nicer" than authoritarian behavior, but it is not necessarily more productive.[6] Other kinds of leadership behavior, under different circumstances and in different cultures, may be more productive. "A single normative leadership style does not take into consideration cultural differences, particularly customs and traditions as well as the level of education and the standard of living" (p. 79).[7] In developing countries, for example, where most people are preoccupied with scratching out a livelihood, there is less concern for participation in decision making.

Modern leadership theories ushered in by studies at Ohio State University and the University of Michigan established a consensus that leadership skills can be learned. Also, these theories, implicitly or explicitly, assume a democratic environment, where participation in decision making by all involved, including the workers, is favored and expected. They also assume that most of the physiological, lower-level needs of employees are reasonably satisfied. Such an environment provides a fertile ground for participative/democratic leadership practices. For example, Likert proposed that participative management is an effective managerial leadership approach characterized by open channels of communication and the inclusion of inputs by lower-level employees in the decision-making process. He proposed that participative management results in higher productivity and higher job satisfaction.

Other theorists expressed similar views. Tennenbaum and Schmidt, for example, suggested that there is no one best way to lead but made other assumptions pertinent to the work environment in the United States. They suggested that leaders use their power according to the situational demands. To them, the situational demands implicitly took place within an individualistic society and did not involve a multicultural environment. A combination of situational requirements may dictate the full use of power by leaders or involvement of subordinates in the decision-making process. Situational demands include the personalities of subordinates, their willingness to accept responsibility, their expectation about the leader's behavior, and the group's ability to accomplish the given tasks. If individual subordinates are not self-directed and require close supervision, if the work group does not have the ability to solve problems, if they are not willing to take responsibility, and if they expect the leader to take charge, then a directive leadership style may be more productive. In situations contrary to the one described above, a relationship-oriented leadership style would be more appropriate. Situational factors, such as time pressure, the nature and scope of the problem, and organizational circumstances also have an impact on the manager's behavior. All these situational demands are related to work and a work environment that is implicitly American. Tennenbaum and Schmidt assumed that both managers and workers share the same cultural values. They assumed that both have the same perspective regarding work, authority, social interaction, risk taking, and individual-group relationships.

A more recent concept seen in the leadership literature is self-leadership. It advocates the development of individual attributes that could lead to self-control and self-motivation. In effect, according to this theory, instead of managers acting as leaders, they should lead others to lead themselves.[8] The theory encourages empowering employees to identify with work and exercise self-direction and self-motivation. Consequently, through self-leadership, employee and organizational performance is enhanced.

Self-leadership assumes that organizations support self-control and personal initiatives and that the individual is self-directed and self-motivated. It also assumes that employees' value systems and cultural norms accept subordinates taking the roles that belong to superiors (see the discussion on "self" in the section on motivation). We know, however, that managerial leadership differences among nations may be the result of people's implicit assumptions regarding leadership qualities.[9] In most cultures, individuals believe that leaders should have certain personality characteristics, skills, and behaviors. These belief systems are referred to as cognitive categories, mental models, and stereotypes, as well as by other names, and could affect an individual's response to and acceptance of another, or him- or herself, as a leader. For example, in cultures that rank high on uncertainty avoidance, employees are very reluctant to take personal initiatives and look up to managers and leaders for instructions, encouragement, guidance, and support. Participative management is not popular in these cultures. As De Mente asserts (as cited in Ref. 10),

> In China, the primary qualities expected in a leader or executive [are] someone who is good at establishing and nurturing personal relationships, who practices benevolence towards his or her subordinates, who is dignified and aloof but sympathetic, and [who] puts the interests of his or her employees above his or her own.

It is not practical to expect self-leadership in cultures where people have certain assumptions about leadership that preclude subordinates in leadership roles. Also, self-leadership may not be applicable where subordinates are not comfortable in situations that call for self-direction and self-motivation.

Among the theories of leadership, situational theories have the best potential for application in cross-cultural settings. While these theories do not specifically consider national cultures as a situational variable, the underlying theoretical framework allows for such an inclusion. Moreover, since they do not advocate a particular leadership style for all situations, situational leadership theories accept that different leadership styles can be effective in different cultures. They also indicate that leadership effectiveness can be improved by modifying the contingent situational variables, such as the group, the task, the followers' skills, and organizational policies. Still, certain assumptions are embedded in all these theories. By learning about these assumptions, the managers of MNCs will be able to modify them to fit the work environment in different cultures.

The Cultural Relativity of Leadership

Cultural differences have a major influence on the effectiveness of various leadership behaviors. Norms, role expectations, and traditions governing relations between various members of society are strong determinants of effective leadership behavior. These differences are manifested in MNCs whose employees come from different cultural backgrounds. The challenge for international managers working with multicultural employees is to recognize these differences and adapt their relationships accordingly. To learn about these differences, we will review two cultural dimensions: acceptance of authority and dealing with uncertainty. While all cultural values influence the behavior of leaders, these two are of particular importance. Here, we will focus on their influence on leader-follower relationships. Using these two dimensions as a reference, we will discuss the predominant leadership practices in Europe and Japan.

Acceptance of Power and Authority

The use of power and authority is central to managing and leading. Power and authority are universal to all cultures. Hierarchical relations are the mainstay of social interactions. The importance, emphasis, scope, and application of power and authority, however, vary among societies. Hofstede called this variation the *power distance*.[11] In societies where power is more evenly distributed among the members, there is only a small gap between the most powerful members and the least powerful. In others, there is a wide variation in power distribution, and the difference between the most powerful and the least powerful is large. In such societies, the large differences in power are legitimate and acceptable to all members. Members often feel uncomfortable if the distance is knowingly violated. For example, if a superior in a large-power-distance society attempts to reduce the distance by acting more accessible and friendly, his or her subordinates may not willingly accept such openness. They may attribute some ulterior motives to this overture.

Matrilineal Leadership

Mosuo women and Khasi society are among the few surviving female bastions in the world. Mosuo women come from a small village in China called Yongning, and Khasi people live in northeastern India.

Mosuo women lead most of the businesses, head the households, control the family finances, and inherit their clan's assets. They are also the pursuers in relationships. Some of these women are married, and some of them have a lover who visits them at night and is sent home in the morning; this is called *zouhun*, or "walking marriage." It is unbelievable that in a society such as China's, where female babies are often abandoned, women can be in charge of homes, businesses, and relationships.

According to Sunami Anna, who is a Mosuo woman, to run a family well, a woman must be in charge. Sunami has the power of choosing her successor, but it is obvious that her daughter will get the privilege. Men who work in Sunami's clan have to give her all their earnings, and she decides what to do with the money.

The situation is the same in Khasi society, where the youngest daughter inherits the property, and after marriage, her husband moves into the family house. Men have no line of succession, no land, and no business. According to one Khasi man, they play the role of breeding bulls and babysitters.[12,13] (The article in Ref. 13 originally appeared in the *Times of India*, January 28, 1994.)

In small-power-distance societies, people believe in equality and will attempt to minimize inequality. Superiors do not see themselves as being very different from subordinates, and vice versa. With minimum distance among them, superiors are accessible to subordinates. Powerful people do not flaunt their power, and they try to appear less powerful. Changes in small-power-distance societies take place incrementally through the redistribution of power.

People in large-power-distance societies believe in a hierarchical power distribution, where everyone has a rightful place and everyone is protected by this order. Superiors consider themselves different from subordinates, and vice versa. The large power difference between superiors and subordinates leads to superiors being inaccessible. Power entitles people to certain privileges, which include obedience and respect from others. Powerful people will not hide their powers and, in fact, use various trappings to signal their power. Officeholders can be identified by their mode of dress, type of office, and entourage. Meaningful changes take place only through dethroning the powerful. Since other people are seen as a potential threat to one's power, they can rarely be trusted.

Where power distance is large, subordinates may not feel quite comfortable with closer relationships between themselves and the managers. Since leadership is an interactive process that requires subordinateship, the followers' expectation of an ideal leader greatly influences the feasibility of certain leadership practices. To most subordinates in large-power-distance cultures, for example, a benevolent autocrat or paternalist is an ideal superior. Hofstede's research indicates that subordinates in larger-power-distance countries tend to accept authoritarian leadership more readily.

Managers moving to large-power-distance cultures learn that they can be more effective by behaving autocratically. This is borne out by the colonial history of most Western countries. Interestingly enough, among the ex-colonial powers, France, with a larger power distance, enjoys a much better relationship with its old colonies (p. 57).[14] Among the European countries, it was in France, too, that the application of management by objectives (MBO) failed.[15] MBO requires an agreement between managers and subordinates on a set of objectives and the means of achieving them. This means that subordinates must have sufficient independence and autonomy to negotiate with their superiors. Low-power-distance cultures more readily meet these requirements. Both managers and subordinates of high-power-distance cultures, however, have difficulty coping with such arrangements. Hofstede[14] quotes French management scholars asserting that DPO (*direction par objectifs*, the French equivalent of MBO) does not work in France because

> French blue- and white-collar workers, lower-level and higher-level managers, and "patrons" all belong to the same cultural system which maintains dependency relations from level to level. Only the deviants really dislike this system. The Hierarchical structure protects against anxiety; DPO, however, generates anxiety. (pp. 57–59)

Cultures high on power distance and uncertainty avoidance are not fertile ground for participative management. Underlining this point is the French experience with MBO. During the 1980s, the French government implemented laws that were designed to promote workplace democratization from the bottom up. The goal was to promote a new citizenship in the workplace and to make the worker the agent of change. It mandated the creation of "direct expression groups," where employees could freely express their concern and raise questions about the operation of the firm. The government said that French management needed reform because they had lagged behind managers elsewhere in developing productive relations with employees. Neither management nor workers showed much interest in the reforms, however, and the French business community adamantly opposed the reform. Managers saw the expression groups as a potential threat to their authority. Likewise, employees were not interested in the democratization of their workplace. They were more concerned with job security, higher wages, and shorter workweeks.[16] As Hofstede[14] noted, where both power distance and uncertainty avoidance are high, having a powerful superior whom we can both praise and blame is one way of satisfying a strong need for avoiding uncertainty (p. 53).

Managers from low-power-distance cultures find it easy to act and manage autocratically when working in a large-power-distance culture. However, they have difficulty operating in an environment with a power distance lower than their own. U.S. managers, for example, have difficulty in fully accepting industrial democracy (see Chapter 12) as it is practiced in Sweden or Germany. Power sharing and participation in decision making take on a whole new dimension in an industrial democracy. From the American perspective, industrial democracy impinges on the prerogatives of management. American managers do not accept a power-sharing scheme that cuts across all levels of the organization and in which the lower levels have a major role.[17]

Until recently, most leadership research in the West focused on transactional leadership. Transactional leaders use organizational resources to elicit employees' performance in a transaction/exchange process. "Transactional leaders do not generate passion and excitement, and they do not empower or inspire individuals to transcend their own self-interest for the good of the organization" (pp. 559–560).[18] Today, transformational leadership is the most prominent among the theories of leadership.[19] There are four components to transformational leadership: **charisma, inspirational motivation, intellectual stimulation,** and **individualized consideration.**[20] Gifted people who are able to gain the respect, pride, trust, and confidence of their followers by conveying a sense of vision are considered **charismatic.** Through **inspirational motivation,** these leaders communicate high expectations and use symbols to focus efforts on important objectives in a simple way. **Intellectually stimulating** leaders encourage followers to think critically and use careful rationality in problem solving. **Individualized consideration** refers to helping followers grow through personal attention and coaching, with each employee being considered individually.

Walumbwa and Lawler[21] found that in emerging economies such as those of China, India, and Kenya, collectivist orientation had a positive impact on the relationship between transformational leadership and work-related outcomes. On that basis, one could speculate that in collectivist cultures, transformational leaders may be more effective.

Avoiding Uncertainty

To live is to deal with uncertainty. Uncertainty is part of life, and all managers deal with uncertainty in running organizations. A critical aspect of managing and leading is dealing with uncertainty by giving subordinates enough direction and instruction to adequately perform their tasks.

Society's orientation toward the handling of uncertainty is reflected in the management of its institutions and organizations.

Uncertainty avoidance is the extent to which a society feels threatened by uncertain and ambiguous situations and tries to avoid these situations by providing greater career stability, establishing more formal rules, not tolerating deviant ideas and behavior, and believing in absolute truths and the attainment of expertise.[14]

Cultures placing a strong emphasis on uncertainty avoidance consider life's uncertainties a continuous threat that must be fought. They avoid conflict and competition and strive for consensus. Security in life is valued greatly, which leads them to search for ultimate truth and values. People in these countries take fewer risks, worry more about the future, and rely on seniority for advancement in organizations. To avoid uncertainty, there is a heavy reliance on written rules and regulations. Matters of importance are left to the authorities, which relieves subordinates from assuming the responsibility. Hofstede[11] found that in countries high on uncertainty avoidance, loyalty to employers is considered a virtue.

People in cultures with low emphasis on uncertainty avoidance accept uncertainty as an inherent aspect of life and take it in their stride. They are contemplative and less aggressive, avoid expressing their emotions, and are tolerant of dissent and deviant behavior. There is less emphasis on rules and regulations, and people are more willing to take risks. They believe that a certain amount of conflict and competition is constructive for society and devise various mechanisms to promote competition. Authorities are there to serve the people, and if rules cannot be kept, they should be changed. Loyalty to employers is not seen as a virtue, and people do not hesitate to change their jobs if there is opportunity for advancement.

A clustering of 40 countries according to their position on these two dimensions of power distance and uncertainty avoidance is depicted in Figure 5.1. As can be seen from Figure 5.1, the United States, Canada, and most northern European countries are low on power distance and low on uncertainty avoidance. Asians, people from the Mediterranean, and South Americans are high on both dimensions. A few Asian countries are high on power distance and low on uncertainty avoidance (upper left-hand quadrant), and a few European countries are low on power distance and high on uncertainty avoidance (lower right-hand quadrant).

It is important to recognize that the leadership theories referred to in this chapter were all developed in countries that are low on power distance and low on uncertainty avoidance. Both superiors and subordinates in these countries value power sharing. These cultures have a more receptive environment for the practice of democratic-participative management. Therefore, it is not surprising that these theories generally advocate democratic-participative management. Subordinates gain more autonomy and

Uncertainty Avoidance

Hong Kong India Philippines Singapore	Argentina Mexico Belgium Pakistan Brazil Peru Chile Portugal Colombia Spain France Taiwan Greece Thailand Iran Turkey Italy Venezuela Japan Yugoslavia	
Australia Netherlands Canada New Zealand Denmark Norway Great Britain Sweden Ireland U.S.A	Austria Finland Germany Israel Switzerland	

Large — Power Distance — Small

Weak   Strong

Figure 5.1   Country Clusters Based on Power Distance and Uncertainty Avoidance

SOURCE: Reference 11.

NOTE: In each cluster, countries are listed alphabetically, not according to their scores on the two dimensions.

freedom due to their participation in the decision-making process. Those who are low on uncertainty avoidance are better suited to deal with the autonomy thus gained. In these cultures, superiors are comfortable with the subsequent uncertainty associated with granting autonomy to their subordinates. Similarly, subordinates are not uncomfortable with assuming the risk and uncertainty associated with participation in decision making. The lower power distance between members of these societies allows for a closer relationship between leaders and followers.

An essential aspect of leadership is the role and behavior of subordinates. Subordinate employees use various strategies to influence their superiors. Table 5.1 summarizes subordinateships for the two levels of power distance. At each level of power distance, both subordinates and superiors expect certain appropriate behaviors from the leader, and a mismatch poses problems. Which strategy is chosen depends on its perceived appropriateness in a given culture. What an American subordinate may find appropriate may not be viewed similarly by an Asian. This difference was observed in research among Chinese and Americans working in Hong Kong and

Table 5.1   Subordinateship for the Two Levels of Power Distance

Small Power Distance	Large Power Distance
Subordinates have weak dependence needs	Subordinates have strong dependence needs
Superiors have weak dependence needs toward their superiors	Superiors have strong dependence needs toward their superiors
Subordinates expect superiors to consult them and may rebel or strike if superiors are not seen as staying within their legitimate role	Subordinates expect superiors to act autocratically
Ideal superior to most is a loyal democrat	Ideal superior to most is a benevolent autocrat or paternalist
Laws and rules apply to all and privileges for superiors are not considered acceptable	Everybody expects superiors to enjoy privileges; laws and rules differ for superiors and subordinates
Status symbols are frowned on and will easily come under attack from subordinates	Status symbols are very important and contribute strongly to the superior's authority with the subordinates

SOURCE: Reference 11, p. 259.

Americans working in the United States. It was found that a difference exists between the Eastern and Western styles of upward influence. Americans preferred overt tactics involving image management that permit them to showcase their individual skills and abilities. They preferred, for example, to manage an independent project or make sure that important people in the organization heard of their accomplishments. In contrast, Hong Kong Chinese preferred a more covert approach that works behind the scenes, one that may involve using their family and trusted friends to obtain information and influence that may help them to succeed.[22]

Managerial Leadership in Europe

Managerial leadership centers on the relationship between the manager and the followers. The manner of relating to employees, the style of projecting and using power, and the method of dealing with conflicts and crises set the stage for managerial leadership. The boundaries within which one deals with these issues vary among cultures. Americans prefer informality and a moderate use of power. They are pragmatic and practical. While they are conscious of projecting a proper image, they do not sacrifice results for a proper appearance. They allow participation by the lower levels of organization when such participation can lead to improved performance and productivity. Assuming that Europeans, due to a shared cultural heritage, have the same preferences can lead to disappointment.

Cultural Prism: Authority and Leadership

The respect of subordinates depends on appearance of strength and competence, but what comes across as strong and competent is not the same everywhere. In Mexico, machismo is important. In Germany, polish, decisiveness and breadth of knowledge give a manager stature. . . . The point is, you should behave appropriately for your role, or your employees may be confused.

Americans are peculiar in their concentration of interest and effort into a few activities. With few exceptions, industrial leaders in the United States are known only for their corporate identity. Latin American management emphasizes the total person. Leaders are respected as multidimensional social beings who are family leader, business leader, intellectual and patron of the arts. . . . French and Italian industry leaders are social leaders. . . . In Germany, power can be financial, political, entrepreneurial, managerial, or intellectual; of the five, intellectual power seems to rank highest. Many of the heads of German firms have doctoral degrees and are always addressed as "Herr Doktor."

To communicate rank or to estimate the power of a foreigner you have to know the local accouterments of success or position. . . . Appearance and clothing are extremely important to the Latin Americans. Arabs and American businessmen seem to value large offices. . . . Ostentatious displays of power are considered bad form by the Germans.[23] (p. 120)

Britain

On the two dimensions of uncertainty avoidance and power distance, the British are very similar to the Americans. Their high tolerance for ambiguity and low power distance is reflected in their industrial relations practices. Labor-management relations are less codified in England than in any other Western European country, which is not surprising in a country that does not even have a written constitution. While French managers believe in a rigid separation of professional and private life, British executives perceive a fluid and much more obscure boundary between the two spheres. The British are more passive and empathetic, spending time relaxing, doing chores, and simply being together. While the career strategy of the French executive is more defensive, that of his or her British counterpart is more aggressive and involves taking more risks. The British see the most positive characteristics of the boss as persuasive-paternalistic or consultative.[11]

Probably due to a high tolerance for ambiguity, the British prefer a generalized, nonspecialized education for managers. A British manager was quoted as saying, "the more difficult it is to plan, the less you need full-time professional planners" (Refs. 11, p. 118; 24). Centuries of class conflict have left their mark on the workplace. Often, British workers consider their employers to be exploitative, since employers have exploited their ancestors for centuries. Over the years, British labor has developed a socialistic attitude that at times even advocates public ownership of corporations. It has produced a class-war outlook in which workers are not enthusiastic about toiling for the "boss class" (p. 458).[25] The elitist and hierarchical organizational systems prevalent in Britain are not much concerned with nurturing the people in the factories. By and large, the workers carry out what they are told to do.[26]

The British

An American executive advising a young manager who was being assigned to England: "Remember, the United Kingdom is a polyglot of ancient cultural influence—Angles, Saxons, Normans, Vikings, Celts, Picts, Romans, and others. Today this so called homogeneous isle is becoming more pluralistic with the influx of immigrants from the commonwealth nations. . . . Normally, you will find them reserved, polite, and often friendly, but don't take them for granted. For all their simulated modesty, the British can be tough and blandly ruthless when necessary. They are masters at intelligence gathering, political blackmail, and chicanery, as a reading of [the] book *Intrepid* will illustrate. Despite how quaint and eccentric they may appear to you at times, don't sell them short. They are a game people who built an empire with a handful of men and women. Although England and Wales are only the size of Alabama, and the population density is close to the size of France, the British once ruled 14 million square miles and more than 500 million souls. I remember reading once: 'Because their Union Jack once flew over a good portion of the globe, the people have an empire ethos that gave meaning to those who served it.' . . . It explains their effortless superiority in world affairs, and their inward, invisible grace as a people. It produced a tradition of public service and an education and class system that was dedicated to the needs of the Empire. It also spawned a credo that natural leaders, not low-born self-made men and women, should rule among the multitude."[25] (p. 458)

The British are very protective of their "space." Outdoor cafes common in some parts of Europe are absent in Britain. Phillips[26] attributes this to the dislike of the British for being in close proximity to other people. "The worst thing that can happen to a Briton on holiday is for someone else to come and sit next to them on the beach."

France

The French tend to favor formal and ritual activities over informal activities (p. 98).[15] They are idealistic and concerned with the essence of values. While the motto of the French republic is *Liberté, Egalité, Fraternité* ("Liberty, Equality, Fraternity"), the importance of social classes cannot be ignored. The French social classes are the aristocracy; the upper bourgeoisie; the upper-middle bourgeoisie; and the middle, lower-middle, and lower classes. The French are very status conscious. Social status depends on one's social origin. While Americans can aspire to the highest level of society through their own accomplishments and hard work, the best that the French can do is climb one or two stages of the social ladder. Education, a knowledge of literature and the fine arts, a tastefully decorated beautiful house, and the proper ancestral social origins are outward signs of social status (pp. 465–471).[25]

The top French managers are an elite group, very much aware of their *grandes écoles* (great schools/universities) roots. *Grandes écoles* supply almost all the top positions of the well-known and large public and private organizations. Military influence and tradition are very much in evidence in these schools, and therefore, they have maintained their strong male traditions. Mostly engineers by background, the graduates of *grandes écoles* excel in quantitative thought and expression and in the numerical dimensions of strategy. They have a great affinity for written communication, which reinforces a formality that permeates their relationships. To them, the manager should be able to grasp complex problems, dissect and synthesize them, manipulate ideas, and appraise solutions. They would rather be considered intellectuals than practical people, and they are obsessed with grammatical rectitude. French managers tend to have a bias for thought and intellect rather than action. In this vein, the witty detractors of the French inclination for theory have a caricature of one French civil servant telling the other, "That's fine in practice, but it'll never work in theory" (pp. 12–13).[26] French organizations are highly centralized and hierarchical, and decisions are made at the very apex. Educational credentials are the basis of a finely graded distribution of positions and offices. Unlike in U.S. companies, the highly credentialed managers in French organizations are allowed to accumulate all the responsibilities they feel capable of handling.[27]

Managerial Leadership in France

French managers see their work as an intellectual challenge, requiring the remorseless application of individual brainpower. They do not share the Anglo-Saxon view of management as an interpersonally demanding exercise, where plans have to be constantly "sold" upward and downward using personal skills. . . . The design of French organizations reflects and reinforces the cerebral manager. France has a long tradition of centralization, of hierarchical rigidity, and individual respect for authority. French company law resembles the country's constitution in conferring power on a single person. . . . [T]he *president-directeur-general* (PDG) . . . is chairman of the board and chief executive rolled into one. . . . The PDG is not answerable to anyone.[27]

French workers are very much concerned with the quality of life. Very seldom are they willing to sacrifice their free time and vacation for the sake of work. They cherish their 2 to 4 weeks of annual vacation, one of the longest in Europe. French managers' leadership style is predominantly autocratic.[28] However, they tend to avoid face-to-face confrontation and conflict in organizations. Perhaps the social class distinction that separates the workers from the ruling executives leaves less room for face-to-face relationships. Therefore, impersonal rules are devised to protect both the superiors and the subordinates. "From below, one obeys the rules and thus does not submit to the absolute authority of an individual and as a result protects one's independence. From the top, edicting the rules affirms the capacity of sovereign power" (p. 95).[15]

Germany

Small power distance and strong uncertainty avoidance are two characteristics of German society. According to Hofstede,[11] societies that are strong on uncertainty avoidance are intolerant of deviant persons and ideas and consider them dangerous. People of these societies are nationalistic, aggressive, and consensus seeking; have an inner urge to work hard; are concerned with security; and are strong advocates of law and order. Almost all these characteristics are stereotypical of Germans. Germans are known for their industriousness and efficiency. They are an inward people who tend to be very private. They perform better when they are given clear instructions and know what is expected of them.[28] Compared with Americans, Germans seem to take a long time to develop friendly relations with others. Germans are status conscious and idealistic. They are reserved, and to outsiders, they appear to be cold. They are detail oriented and meticulous. When Ford Motor Company started its *world car* concept, integrating the worldwide production of automobiles, they learned firsthand about German precision. The Germans made components that required very fine fitting. Other countries, however, were not accustomed to producing, for example, doors and body parts with the precision of a few millimeters. The result was incompatibility of parts and components produced in Germany with those produced in other countries.

While Americans are satisfied with partial models that leave many questions unanswered, such as various motivational models, control mechanisms, and delegation, Germans have tried to develop more systematic models. This approach to management has produced the "Harzburger model." In this model, managing is done by defining the tasks to be performed, creating job descriptions for the tasks, and defining behavioral roles for their performance.[29] Such a bureaucratic model approaches leadership and motivation from a logical, institutional, and economic perspective. It views the firm as operating in an economic free-enterprise system that "motivates" it to seek profit. Within such a system, individuals are considered as rational persons who seek to maximize their personal profit or utility in a manner consistent with the firm's objectives.[30] Viewed from an institutional perspective, leadership is, therefore, considered as a phenomenon comprising the acquisition, possession, and use of power. This view of leadership, however, is tempered with the institutional participation of employees in the management of the firm through *codetermination* (discussed in Chapter 12). Additionally, it considers leadership's responsibility to improve employer-employee relationships on the basis of voluntary socio-ethical obligations. The aim is to develop a new relationship between capital and labor on a voluntary rather than a legal basis. It advocates consensus-based partnership between unions and management (p. 1390).[29]

Leadership Succession in a German Company

I look carefully at the young people who are brought to my attention by my colleagues. I spend a lot of thought on these people. . . . I invite these young men to my home for dinner. Often I give garden parties for perhaps 60 or 90 people in honor of some visiting foreigners. Then I can see how they behave, how their wives behave, how well they get along with foreign people, the quality of their education. . . . We don't like people who can't behave properly. . . .

We invest a lot in these people. If they have language deficiencies, we train them. If they are to work in Latin America, we send them to Spain for three months so they speak a really good Spanish.

At the moment, I do not know that there is a member of corporate management whom I could propose as my successor. So I look (around) the world a bit, and we have identified two or three people who could qualify. So I might arrange a golf game with some of my fellow chief executives. . . . As we play, I might say to one chief executive: "There is a chap in your organization who, we think, can do things for us. What are his chances with you?" He might respond: "Well, his boss is only three years older, so I can't offer him anything like your opportunity. You can have him."[31] (p. 10)

German managers are predominantly from the engineering disciplines. With very few exceptions, these managers have middle- or upper-class backgrounds.[32] German workers are among the highest paid and best treated in the world. They have one of the shortest workweeks and among the longest paid vacations. While the majority of the German workforce is not unionized, contracts negotiated by labor unions cover both unionized and nonunionized employees. This is due to the fact that about 90% of employers are members of an employers' association, and collective agreements are on regional and industry levels.

Managerial Leadership in Japan Versus the United States

The nature of the decision-making process at the higher levels of organizational hierarchy influences the type of leadership employed throughout the organization. In the United States, of the two components of the decision-making process, decision formulation is the domain of top management, and implementation of those decisions is relegated to the lower levels. In the American system of decision making, fewer levels and smaller numbers of people are involved. Therefore, a shorter time period is needed to formulate a decision. To implement these decisions, however, organizations are compelled to secure the commitment and support of the lower levels and a larger number of people. When successful, this method produces quick results. Securing the commitment and support of the lower levels in implementing these decisions requires certain leadership characteristics and skills that are very akin to those required in selling and marketing. To produce results, leaders have to be very persuasive and have to command resources that the subordinates desire, or they need to have the personal traits (charisma) that would make subordinates follow their directions.

Ringisei: Japanese Decision Making

When an important decision needs to be made in a Japanese organization, everyone who will feel its impact is involved in making it. . . [A] decision where to put a new plant . . . (for example) will often mean sixty to eighty people directly involved in making the decision. A team of three will be assigned the duty of talking to all sixty to eighty people and, each time a significant modification arises, contacting all the people involved again. The team will repeat this process until a true consensus has been achieved. Understanding and support may supersede the actual content of the decision, since the five or six competing alternatives may be equally good or bad. . . .

(Continued)

(Continued)

> When a major decision is to be made, a written proposal lays out one "best" alternative for consideration. The task of writing the proposal goes to the youngest and newest member of the department involved. Of course, the president or vice-president knows the acceptable alternatives, and the young person tries like heck to figure out what those are. He talks to everyone, soliciting their opinions, paying special attention to those who know the top man best. In so doing he is seeking a common ground. Fortunately, the young person cannot completely figure out from others what the boss wants, and must add his own thoughts. This is how variety enters the decision process in a Japanese company.[33] (pp. 44–45)

In contrast to the U.S. decision-making process, the Japanese employ a consensus-building method known as *ringisei*, or *ringi* for short. In fact, the Japanese have no equivalent for *decision making* (p. 27).[11] *Ringiseido* literally means "a system of reverential inquiry about a superior's intentions." In this context, the term means obtaining approval on a proposed matter through the vertical, and sometimes horizontal, circulation of documents to concerned members in the organization (p. 34).[34] In the *ringi* system, everyone who will feel the impact of a decision will be involved in making it.

The system originated in government offices and national enterprises at the beginning of industrialization. In a *ringi* system, the business plan or proposal about important problems that require a budget must be sent from the lower- to the higher-positioned staff and finally decided on by the president. The business plan or proposal must be sent from the lower group head to the head of the next level and, finally, to the department head. If at each succeeding level, the superior cannot consent to the plan, it must be sent back to the original lower-level manager for modification or total revision and then sent to the upper level again.[35]

In a *ringi* system, the demand for information pulls the decision down toward the implementation level. At the same time, the need for decisions to match the corporate strategies pulls it upward. The equilibrium of these two conflicting demands usually takes place at the middle level. The success of the system depends on the competency and leadership skills of middle-level management, which serves as a bridge between the upper and lower levels of the organization. The effectiveness of middle managers depends on their personal relations with other managers. Unless they can obtain the required information from all corners of the organization, they will not be able to perform their job successfully (p. 39).[34] Under the *ringi* system, managerial leadership at the top entails coping with crisis situations or charting new directions for the organization. The chief executive does not alter or disapprove of the decisions reached through *ringi*. The lower levels work hard to make sure that no *ringi* decision reaches the top that will not be approved. After the general direction and strategy of the firm is communicated to the middle and lower levels, operational decisions and methods of implementing those decisions are entrusted to them. In Japanese firms, chief executives spend most of their time in establishing and maintaining close relationships with government officers and other corporate heads (p. 41).[34]

High on both power distance and uncertainty avoidance, Japanese culture favors consensus and shuns deviant behavior. Japanese tend to favor authoritarian-paternalistic leaders. Respect for authority is central to Japanese society. From an outsider's point of view, the *ringi* system of decision making appears to connote an egalitarian practice. Taken in the context of Japanese culture, however, it is another way of removing uncertainty and abiding by the power of authorities. As Prakash Sethi and his associates[34] assert, "The controlling and motivating mechanism[s] in Japanese organizations are not humanism and egalitarianism, but hierarchy, authority, power, and domination. . . . [E]galitarianism as a cultural trait does not exist in Japan" (p. 267). Hierarchical authority relationships are not confined to the corporation but extend to all aspects of Japanese society. The use of authority and submission governs all interactions. Managers rely on the use of authority and its by-product, discipline, to achieve what American managers try to achieve by using other techniques, such as power sharing and MBO. As Bruce-Briggs[36] asserts, Japanese labor discipline was not created by skillful corporate management. Of course, discipline and hierarchy are Western terms. The Japanese speak of expected behavior and "harmonious relations." Discipline and respect for authority have been there all along as part of the Japanese cultural character. Japanese do what is expected of them. They are expected to respect authority, work hard, work right, and not block productivity improvement. Consider the ordinary observation of the visitor to Japan:

> Early in the morning in Tokyo: Along the curb sanitation men carefully polish their tiny Isuzu garbage truck. Imagine the response of American garbage men to such a directive. . . . Just before opening time at a little middle-class shop in Kyoto: Before the main counter stands a young man in a business suit—obviously the manager. To his left and two steps to his rear, a slightly younger man—the assistant manager—listening intently. Lined up before them, in better formation than . . . (any) Army squad, the uniformed shopgirls, the No. 1 girl one pace forward, all in "respect" position—hands clasped before them, head slightly bowed, eyes fixed on the managers, receiving the orders of the day.[36] (p. 41)

While the use of authority is at the center of Japanese leadership, the desire for consensus and the subordination of the individuals to the group minimize its abuse.

Leadership Summary

A critical factor that determines the success of an organization is the leadership ability of its management. A review of leadership theories reveals that there is no one best way of leading. Many situational factors contribute to the effectiveness of managerial leadership. These factors include the leader's characteristics, the followers' characteristics and expectations, the task, organizational policies, and the top management's values and philosophies. An ever-present factor that influences other situational factors is the national culture. Most leadership theories have ignored the influence of national culture on the effectiveness of managerial leadership. The reason for this oversight is researchers' ethnocentric tendencies. The major leadership theories in use today have all been developed in the United States, to be used by American managers. These theories have avoided any discussion of the national culture yet have implicitly assumed American middle-class cultural values as a framework. Based on American values, most of these theories have advocated a participative-democratic leadership style. While the application of these theories could be effective in the United States, it is doubtful that they would be equally effective abroad. If cultural differences are not taken into account, the application of all leadership theories will be limited to their original home culture. Therefore, international managers should consider cultural differences while leading the multicultural workforce of MNCs.

While there are cultural differences among various regions of the world, such as Asia, Europe, and North America, there is diversity within each region as well. Some of the differences are very subtle yet can significantly affect behavioral responses and the leader-follower relationship. Although we certainly appreciate the cultural differences between the British, French, and Germans, we may neglect the differences among some smaller nations. Similarly, it would be a big mistake if we were to label all Asian cultures as Oriental cultures. The difference between Indonesia and Korea, for example, is greater than that between Japan and the United States. According to Maruyama,[37] for example, Danish culture is closer to Indonesian culture than to Swedish culture in terms of the way people organize their thoughts and behavior. In Danish culture, the main purpose of communication is to maintain affection and a familiar atmosphere. In contrast, in Sweden, the purpose of daily interpersonal communication is the transmission of new information or frank feelings.

At present, there is no leadership theory broad enough to cover the values of different cultures. The existing theories, however, can be useful to international managers if they take into account cultural differences. Armed with an understanding of cultural differences, we may be able to chart a safe passage in the sea of international management. From such a perspective, we ask international managers to remember a few caveats. First, the use of authority is regarded differently in different cultures. The conspicuous use of power and authority is frowned on in some cultures and encouraged in others. Second, cultures vary in their practice of delegating authority and responsibility. Subordinates in some cultures are not comfortable with participating in decision making. Third, the meaning of work varies according to the culture. For some, work is a necessary evil; for others, it is a source of pride and purpose. A different leadership approach is required for dealing with each of these attitudes. Finally, when abroad, observe the native management practices for cues as to what works well.

Motivation

Motivation has long been a major concern for management because it is linked to productivity, creativity, job turnover, absenteeism, and so forth. Motivation is defined as the process through which behavior is mobilized to reach certain goals, which in turn satisfies individual or organizational needs. Motivation is the total of all forces within individuals that account for the effort they apply to the job at hand. Motivation begins with the search to satisfy needs. Figure 5.2 shows the three main phases a person undergoes during the need satisfaction process.

Although in their daily activities, managers primarily focus on accomplishing business objectives and satisfying organizational needs, to accomplish this, they must also see that their employees' needs are satisfied. An effective motivational program uses the individual's needs to generate internal energy and to direct energized behavior toward achieving organizational and individual goals. The individual's satisfaction with the job, and ultimately with his or her life, plays an important role in sustaining the desired behavior and achieving the much needed predictability necessary for planning organizational activities.

Job satisfaction is a part of one's overall satisfaction with life and, in turn, is affected by it. Employee dissatisfaction can lead to absenteeism, poor-quality products, accidents, family problems, and deterioration of mental health. Effective managers closely monitor both employee job satisfaction and work performance because they know that job satisfaction can lead to a better working relationship with superiors, peers, and subordinates. A satisfied employee working in a less disruptive work environment will be a more productive worker. For most people of many cultures, work attributes are among the most important motivating factors. In a survey of more than 8,000 randomly selected employees from Belgium, Great Britain, West Germany, Israel, Japan, the Netherlands, and the United States, Harpaz

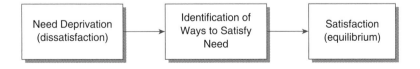

Figure 5.2   Need Satisfaction Process

found that the paramount work goal, by a wide margin, was "interesting work." For these workers, "good pay" and "good interpersonal relations" were second and third in degree of importance.[38]

Motivation and Culture

Human motivation is the product of the interaction between people and the physical and social environment. It is important to recognize, however, that most of the management literature on motivation is psychologically oriented and is based on psychological models developed and tested almost exclusively in the United States. These theories are presented in Appendix B. While psychological models of motivation are very useful for the management of U.S. businesses, they are inadequate for international management. We all accept, in principle, that there are differences among people of different cultures. In studying human motivation, however, U.S.-based researchers have taken a simplistic view by ignoring the cultural influences on people's behavior. To understand human motivation, we need to understand not only the people themselves but also their environment and their culture. More specifically, as D'Andrade[39] puts it, "to understand why people do what they do, we have to understand the cultural constructs by which they interpret the world" (p. 4).

Culture plays an important role in the formation of many of our needs, their relative importance, and the way we attempt to satisfy them. Many human needs, such as security, love, and esteem, are learned through cultural influences. Through socialization with others, people learn acceptable ways of satisfying their needs and follow these norms in pursuit of need satisfaction.

The importance and priorities that people assign to their needs are also determined by their cultures. Americans place a particular importance on individual needs, such as personal comfort and self-actualization. In contrast, Japanese may sacrifice individual comfort to achieve social acceptance. Middle Easterners often sacrifice personal comfort, and even encounter financial hardship, to offer hospitality to their guests. Cultural values are the foundation of socially acquired needs and define the acceptable methods of need satisfaction. Americans, for example, value individualism very much, and it is the basis of many other American values. Even the Declaration of Independence speaks of individualism, where it reads "life, liberty, and the pursuit of happiness."[40] To Americans, freedom of choice and expression is the basis for many individual needs and need satisfaction. Very few Americans, for example, would tolerate interference by others in their choice of a mate. In contrast, in many traditional families in India, China, and the Middle East, such decisions are made by parents, often with little or no consideration of the individual's opinion. Often, respect for parents inhibits children from even expressing their opposition.

In Chapter 3, we learned that culture influences people's perceptions of time and space, as well as attitudes toward work and authority. In turn, the perception of time and space and the attitudes toward work and authority influence people's motivation. Even among subcultures—various groups of the same culture—these differences are noticeable. Nord,[41] for example, identified age, rural versus urban background, ethnicity, and sex as important factors that influence an individual's behavior in work organizations. Research in the United States has found that younger employees are more motivated by money, while for older employees, job security and fringe benefits are more important. In a comparative study of attitudes toward work in China and Taiwan, Derakhshan and Khan[42] found a generation gap in both cultures between younger and older workers, which influenced their work attitudes. There was also a difference between the attitudes of the two samples, with the Taiwanese sample reflecting attitudes closer to Western values.

In a case study, Whyte and Braun[43] identified a group of patterns in socialization and education that appear in less developed economies. Autocratic teachers, glorification of military heroes, and disrespect for businesspersons were among the factors that led to the lack of independence training and, therefore, the lack of motivation. However, in a study of similarities among 14 countries, Haire et al. discovered that countries cluster along ethnic rather than industrial lines.[44] Black and Porter[45] studied the managerial behaviors and job performances of Americans, Hong Kong Chinese, and American expatriates in Hong Kong. They found that those managerial behaviors that were significantly related to job performance in the United States did not seem to be relevant to job performance in Hong Kong. In short, the effect of culture on behavior is complex and cannot be discounted.

Cultural Influences on Motivation

Organizational performance is a function of employees' work contributions to organizational goals. The efforts exerted by employees at work are influenced by their motivation. A motivated worker is a more productive worker. If we consider motivation as a psychological state that compels a person to expend a certain amount of effort to accomplish a job, we are dealing with two main concepts: work and the person, or "self." In studying cross-cultural motivation, we should be careful not to assume that these concepts have a universal meaning. There is a growing body of research that indicates that people of different cultures have different views about these two concepts. The perception of self is a product of cultural upbringing, and so is the meaning of work.

Cultural Definitions of Work

Throughout the history of Western civilization, work has been regarded variously as drudgery, a necessary evil, an obligation, a duty, and a way to salvation. To engage in physical work has been considered undignified and demeaning, on one extreme, and honorable, glorified, and exemplifying piety, on the other. According to Max Weber, a contributing factor to the emergence of modern capitalism, characterized by large organizations, was the value and importance that the Protestant religion accorded to work and the accumulation of wealth.

> Perhaps because of our Puritan work ethic and the basic belief in cause and effect, we take pride in our work; we conduct business at social functions and we take work home with us. . . . Work gives us identity; we often define ourselves and others by what we do; elsewhere identity often stems from religion, family and village.[23] (p. 13)

Thus, personal introductions vary among Americans and the Japanese. In the United States, most individuals will typically talk about *what* they do—that is, the content of their work: "I'm a doctor" or "I'm a machinist." In contrast, in Japan, most people identify themselves by referring to their employer: "Morio of Mitsubishi" or "Tanaka of Toyota."

Regardless of the kind of work a person does, Americans expect the person to be willing to do whatever it takes to do the job. A common expression indicating such an attitude is that "we must be willing to get our hands dirty." Of course, the positive attitude that many Americans have toward work is not universal. In some cultures, a negative attitude toward work is more pervasive. In some South American cultures, involvement in physical work is regarded as demeaning and beneath the dignity of a well-respected person. Work is classified as low or high status depending on what it involves. In extreme cases, college-educated people will not concern themselves with the problems on the shop floor. They consider that type of work degrading. They think that their college degrees should raise them above such low-status jobs.[46] The same is true in some Middle Eastern countries. Kuwaitis, for example, regularly hire non-Kuwaitis to perform most jobs that require physical labor, even the sensitive security tasks. Most, and particularly the educated, Kuwaitis consider physical work demeaning and undignified.

Americans' Faith in Hard Work

William H. Newman[46] has suggested that anyone contemplating a transfer of U.S. management practices to other cultures should understand the premises of these practices. The American faith in rewards for persistent hard work and the value of hard work, for example, are not universal beliefs.

"Both our lore and our experience underscore the necessity for hard work if objectives are to be achieved. Even among those who do not accept the Puritan ethic that hard work is a virtue in itself, there is a strong belief that persistent, purposeful effort is necessary to achieve high goals. Hard work is not considered to be the only requisite for success; wisdom and luck are also needed. Nevertheless, the feeling is that, without hard work, a person is neither likely to achieve, nor justified in expecting to achieve, his objectives.

"This belief in the efficacy of hard work is by no means common worldwide. Sometimes a fatalistic viewpoint makes hard work seem futile. In other instances, it is more important to curry the favor of the right man; and in still other situations, hard work is considered unmanly." (p. 347)

People work for many reasons. The first reason that immediately comes to mind is the instrumentality of work, a term that means that to live a comfortable and dignified life, most of us need to work. Therefore, work is an important vehicle for obtaining what we need to live. To have a comfortable life, we are motivated to work. Taking only this meaning of work into account, organizations devise a variety of techniques, such as pay and fringe benefits, to motivate their employees.

However, work has other meanings. In addition to being a necessity, work can be an attractive activity in itself. It may also provide people with an opportunity to socialize and interact with others and satisfy their gregariousness. Many people will continue to work even if they are financially secure. It is the interesting nature of the activity itself that draws them to work. For others, work is a very important aspect of their life. Without work, they feel that something is missing in their lives. For these people, work assumes a very central position in their lives. We have learned that the centrality of work (its importance) in people's lives varies from culture to culture. In a seven-country study of the meaning of work, for example, researchers found a wide variation in work centrality among the countries studied. They found work centrality to be highest for Japan and lowest for the United Kingdom. The sequence of rank ordering was Japan, Yugoslavia, Israel, the United States, Belgium, the Netherlands, Germany, and the United Kingdom.[47] Jyuji Misumi's[48] research has confirmed that the Japanese consider work to be highly important in their lives. Among the four countries studied, Misumi found that work importance was highest among the Japanese, followed by the Americans, Germans, and Belgians.

The cultural differences in the meaning of work have practical implications for international managers. Since there are variations in the meaning that people of different cultures attach to work, differentiated motivational programs need to be applied. To motivate those who consider physical work undignified, for example, we may have to rely more on the monetary outcomes of the work. For others, making the work more interesting or socially rewarding may be a better choice.

Although there are cultural differences in the meaning of work, cross-cultural research also suggests that there is substantial commonality among cultures about certain facets of work. Among the major features of work that people of many cultures value are "good pay" and "interesting work."[38] The implication for international management is that if the pay is good and if the jobs are interesting, managers will have an easier time motivating people from diverse cultural backgrounds.

Cultural Definitions of Self

Many consider individualism as the most salient feature of American culture. Many American ideals, such as equality and objectivity in treating people based on their own merits and not on their social standing or political connections, are anchored to individualism. To describe Americans as individualistic does not fully explain the cultural differences between Americans and the people of other nations. Individualism only tells us about the societal and external view of an "individual," the view that the society holds with regard to a person and his or her relationship with other members of society. To fully comprehend the difference between Americans and the people of other cultures, we need to explore the concept of "individualism" from the personal aspect of "self."

The concept of self has many facets. Westerners view the individual as a self-contained, autonomous, and independent entity. Based on this understanding, the individual comprises a unique configuration of attributes, such as traits, abilities, motives, and values. These attributes constitute the basis for the individual's behavior.[49]

The three major facets of self are

1. Physiological-ecological[50]

2. Inner-private

3. Public-relational[51]

We assume that people everywhere are likely to develop an understanding of themselves as physically distinct and separate from others. This is the **physiological-ecological** self—the self that is referred to as "I."

The **inner-private** self arises from the sense of awareness that each person has of his or her internal aspects such as dreams, feelings, and the continuous flow of thoughts, which are private and cannot be directly known by others. Some aspects of the inner-private self are probably universal, but many other aspects may be culturally determined.

As we relate to others, we develop an understanding of the **public-relational** self, which is defined by social relationships. People of different cultures see the public-relational self as either *separate from and independent of* others or as *connected to and interdependent on* others.

For most Westerners, the self is an impermeable, free agent, with attributes that are independent of circumstances or a particular relationship, which can move from group to group and situation to situation without significant alterations. In effect, the self can be abstracted from its surroundings. For Easterners (and many other people), the person is connected, fluid, and conditional. The person exists in a web of relationships, such as the family and society. The person is mostly identified in terms of these relationships, and purely independent behavior is impossible. For example, in Chinese, there is no equivalent term for the word *individualism.* An American may describe himself or herself as a "fun-loving and hardworking person," whereas a Japanese, a Chinese, or a Korean may say, "I am fun loving with my friends" or "I am serious at work," which puts the person in relation to others and in a context (pp. 49–51).[52]

Many Westerners, including Americans, believe in the inherent separateness of distinct persons. It is the norm, and people are expected to become independent from others and discover and express their unique attributes. Markus and Kitayama[51] describe the attempt at developing such a self as follows:

Achieving the cultural goal of independence requires constructing oneself as an individual whose behavior is organized and made meaningful primarily by reference to one's own internal repertoire of thoughts, feeling, and action, rather than by reference to the thoughts, feelings, and actions of others. . . . This view of the self derives from a belief in the wholeness and uniqueness of each person's configuration of internal attributes. (p. 226)

The independent view of the self gives rise to concepts such as "self-actualization," "self-esteem," "realizing one's potentials," "being true to one's self," and many other expressions describing and canonizing the self and self-centered activities and concepts.

In contrast to the Western view, many Eastern cultures have maintained an **interdependent** view of the self. These cultures believe in the fundamental **connectedness** of humans to each other. Examples of common American expressions relating to the independent self are "stand up and be counted" and "do your own thing." In contrast, the Japanese saying that "the nail that stands up gets hammered down" represents the concept of the interdependent self. To experience the "interdependent self," one should see oneself as part of an encompassing social relationship. It also involves recognizing that one's behavior is determined by, contingent on, and, to a large extent, organized by what the person perceives to be the thoughts, feelings, and actions of *others* in the relationship.[51]

An interdependent self is not separate from the social context. It is more connected to and less differentiated from others. Such a connectedness motivates people to fit in and become a part of the social context and to fulfill the obligation of belongingness with relevance to others. As Hernandez and

Iyengar[53] put it, the crucial point for such a person is not the inner self but rather the relationships the person has with others. Experiencing interdependence entails seeing the self as a part of an all-encompassing social relationship. Therefore, interdependent persons are more motivated by those contexts that allow them to perceive themselves as fitting in with a social group, which in turn enables them to enhance their relationships with others.

The internal attributes of an **interdependent** self are less fixed and concrete and more situation specific, and they are sometimes elusive and unreliable. In such a case, the attitudes will not directly regulate overt behavior, especially if the behavior implicates significant others. In many social contexts, the interdependent self must constantly control and regulate its opinions, abilities, and characteristics to come to terms with the primary task of interdependence. In an interdependent, collectivist culture, an independent behavior, such as expressing an opinion, is likely to be influenced and somewhat determined by the forces of interdependence. Such behavior has a significance that is different from the one exhibited by an independent self in an independent culture.[51] The contrast between the external source of what Westerners consider inner attributes, such as conscience, and the external source of such attributes for the Japanese is described by Dore:[54]

> The Christian who believes that his conscience is the voice of God within him feels that it is a duty to God to obey its dictates and that he has sinned in the sight of the Lord if he fails to do so. The Japanese who conceives of the voice of his conscience as the voice of his parents and teachers feels it to be a duty towards them to obey it, and if he fails to do so it is they whom he has let down. Even after their death his feelings of guilt may take the form of imagining how displeased these honored parents and teachers would be. (p. 385)

Parsons et al.[55] have suggested that **self-orientation** (independent self) versus **collectivity orientation** is an important variable that determines human action. Giving priority to one's own "private interests, independently of their bearings on the interests or values of a given collectivity," is self-orientation. Taking into account the values and interests of a collectivity before any action is taken is collectivity orientation.

Interdependent cultures assume that a person is mostly defined by situations and by the presence of others. Therefore, a person is inseparable from the situations of others. This interconnectedness, for example, is the basis for the Chinese culture's emphasis on synthesizing the constituent parts of any situation or problem into a harmonious whole. The Japanese word *jibun*, for self, more accurately describes "one's share of the shared life space."[51] For the Japanese, according to Hamaguchi (as cited in Ref. 51),

> a sense of identification with others (sometimes including conflict) pre-exists and selfness is confirmed only through interpersonal relationships. . . . Selfness is not constant like the ego but denotes a fluid

concept which changes through time and situation according to interpersonal relationships. (p. 228)

In contrast to **independent** cultures, in **interdependent** cultures, relationships are often valued for and by themselves, not as a means of achieving personal objectives. People are constantly aware of others and will try to account for others' goals and desires in the pursuit of their personal goals. A reciprocal arrangement exists within which people passively monitor their contributions to others' goals and vice versa. The importance of others to one's life and the resultant relationships and social obligations are limited to persons belonging to "in-groups," such as family members or members of social or work groups. The following excerpt from Dore[54] illuminates this:

> The individual surrenders a part of himself not to a group of which he is a member, but to particular individuals whose leadership he accepts, with whose fortunes he identifies himself, on whose help he depends for securing his own advancement or happiness, on whose goodwill he depends for his emotional security, and whose approval he depends on for his self-respect. (p. 389)

A summary of the key differences between the independent and interdependent selves is presented in Table 5.2. The two different concepts of self have various implications for motivation. An independent self takes pride in its own attributes and accomplishments. In contrast, an interdependent self may be motivated to avoid such a selfish expression. Instead, the overt expression of pride may often be directed at a collective of which the self is a part (p. 237).[51] The following is an example of how Japanese feel proud of the accomplishments of their superiors and how every member of the group experiences a shared pride in those accomplishments.

> In a Tokyo office [a company employee] let me witness a gesture of devotion to his office superior which I had never experienced in the Western world. We were at the end of an interview in his office which, being that of a lower-middle ranking officer, was small and sparsely furnished. But the size and nature of his office were never part of our conversation. As I was preparing to take my leave, he said, "Let me show you the office of my Section Chief." He took me to an office three times as big as his, very well furnished, pointed to the empty chair behind the big desk ornamented with lots of bric-a-brac and proudly said: "This is the desk of my Section Chief."[56] (p. 215)

According to most Western theories, motivation is more a personal phenomenon, and others indirectly influence the process as a means of contributing to individual goal accomplishments. The concept of an **interdependent** self implies a more fundamental and vital role for significant others in shaping and directing the behavior of a person.

Table 5.2   Summary of Key Differences Between Independent and Interdependent Concepts of Self

Feature Compared	Independent	Interdependent
Definition	Separate from social context	Connected with social context
Structure	Bounded, unitary, stable	Flexible, variable
Important features	Internal, private (abilities, thoughts, feelings)	External, public (statuses, roles, relationships)
Tasks	Be unique Express self Realize internal attributes Promote own goals Be direct; say what's on your mind	Belong, fit in Occupy one's proper place Engage in appropriate action Promote others' goals Be indirect; read others' minds
Role of others	*Self-evaluation:* others important for social comparison, appraisal reflected	*Self-definition:* relationships with others in specific contexts define the self
Basis of self-esteem[a]	Ability to express self, validate internal attributes	Ability to adjust, restrain self, maintain harmony with social context

SOURCE: Reference 51. Copyright 1991 by the American Psychological Association. Reprinted with permission.

a. Esteeming the self may be primarily a Western phenomenon, and the concept of self-esteem should perhaps be replaced by self-satisfaction, or by a term that reflects the realization that one is fulfilling the culturally mandated task.

In the preceding discussion, we have implied that in **interdependent** cultures, most of the motives of an individual are shaped by the group. Therefore, there are a number of motives that have more relevance to an **interdependent** self than to an **independent** self. Murray[57] presented a list of such motives, including **affiliation, avoidance of blame, similance** (the need to imitate others), **deference** (the need to willingly follow superiors and those we admire), **nurturance** (the need to nurture, protect, and aid others), **abasement** (acceptance of self-deprecation), and **succorance** (the need to seek aid, sympathy, and dependence).

Since for an **interdependent** self, it is imperative to socially integrate, seek harmony with others, and immerse the self in the collectivist whole, all these needs would be more relevant and even desirable to the **interdependent** self (p. 240).[51] For the interdependent Chinese, for example, the achievement need is more socially oriented. Their achievement goal is to meet the expectations of others who are important and close to the individual.[58]

Cognitive consistency has also been considered as a motivating force. Individuals seek to establish consistency in their cognitions. Cognitive inconsistency creates dissonance,[59] an unpleasant anxiety producing a psychological state that motivates the individual to take an action. An example of cognitive inconsistency is the case of a person who smokes cigarettes and believes that smoking is detrimental to his or her health. In this example, the individual can pursue a number of alternatives to eliminate the dissonance. An **interdependent** person whose internal attributes are more flexible is less likely to quit smoking as long as his or her reference group smokes. For this individual, the confirmation of self-harm comes from the group. In this case, the situational requirements regulate the private feelings of **interdependent** persons. Therefore, there is less room for experiencing inconsistency and dissonance.

Applicability of Major Motivation Theories

One major obstacle in the effective motivation of employees in MNCs is the assumption that the available motivation theories are universal. These theories erroneously assume that human needs are the same everywhere and that people will respond similarly to a motivation program. Of course, the assumption that "one size fits all" is faulty. There are culturally based differences in people's needs and the means they use to satisfy them. Because of the difficulties in understanding other cultures, and perhaps due to ethnocentric tendencies, many studies on motivation have, either explicitly or implicitly, ignored cultural differences. In fact, until recently, most management literature paid little attention to the effect of culture on motivation.

Stereotyping and Ethnocentrism

The roots of the universality assumption can be traced to stereotyping, oversimplified conceptions or beliefs about others, and ethnocentrism, which is the belief in the superiority of one's own ethnic group. When faced with an unfamiliar situation, we rely on stereotypes to simplify our perception of the environment. Stereotypes may be correct or incorrect. When confronted with an unfamiliar culture, people assume similarity with their own culture unless other stereotypes are present. Ethnocentrism leads to the belief that "our way is the best way of doing things." Ethnocentrism is an attitude found in almost any culture. Studies have found that people usually think of their country as disproportionately important in the world. In most countries, maps used in classrooms usually illustrate that country at the center of the world. In Chinese writings, the character for China means the "center of the earth."[60]

Ethnocentrism often leads to prejudiced behavior. Many people of industrialized countries equate lack of industrialization with lack of culture. Equally erroneous is the tendency to equate the materialism of industrial societies with spiritual corruption. As Kolde[61] puts it,

A widely propounded fallacy in the advanced industrial countries holds that all nations evolve in a series of evolutionary steps in a unilinear path. The Americans, British, and French are likely to place their own respective countries at the pinnacle of this path, and look upon all other peoples' cultures as backward and inferior to theirs. Cultural maturity, thus, is rationalized to be a correlate of economic progress. The claim for cultural superiority by members of subindustrial societies, who regard the relatively greater reliance on materialistic considerations in industrial societies as evidence of moral and spiritual degeneration, is similarly irrational. (pp. 78–79)

Incorrect stereotypes and ethnocentric attitudes are often harmful. They can be changed, however, by training and exposure to other cultures. To be effective in motivating an international workforce, managers need to understand the influence of stereotyping and ethnocentrism, and MNC management development and educational programs should attempt to reduce ethnocentrism and stereotyping.

The Shortcomings of Major Motivation Theories _____

A detailed review of major motivation theories is presented in Appendix B. These include Maslow's Hierarchy of Needs, Herzberg's two-factor theory, McClelland's Three Motives, expectancy theory, equity theory, and reinforcement theory (learning theory).

Maslow's Hierarchy of Needs

Maslow identified five categories of human needs, which follow a hierarchical order of importance. Ranging from the lowest to the highest, these need categories are physiological, security, social (affection), esteem (self-esteem and esteem of others), and self-actualization. Each level of need is activated only after the preceding lower-level need has been sufficiently satisfied. The most potent need is self-actualization.

Maslow's need hierarchy has been criticized on the ground that it is only applicable to American culture. Hofstede[62] questioned the applicability of North American motivation theories, including McClelland's (discussed later) and Maslow's. He asserted,

The ordering of needs in Maslow's hierarchy represents a value choice—Maslow's value choice. This choice was based on his mid-twentieth century U.S. middle-class values. First, Maslow's hierarchy reflects individualistic values, putting self-actualization and autonomy on top. Values prevalent in collectivist cultures, such as "harmony" or "family support," do not even appear in the hierarchy. Second, the cultural map suggests that even if just the needs Maslow used in his hierarchy are considered—the needs will have to be ordered differently in different cultural areas.

Most of the interpretations of the need hierarchy theory are made within the individualistic framework of Western cultures, which overemphasize needs such as self-esteem and self-actualization. Redding[63] suggested that it is questionable to apply Western "ego-centered paradigms," which focus on individual needs, to cultures that emphasize relationships. Similarly, Nevis,[64,65] in a comparison of Chinese and American cultures, suggested that society, rather than the individual, determines the four-level hierarchy of needs for Chinese. Ranging from the lowest to the highest, these needs are belonging, physiological, safety, and self-actualization in the service of society. As depicted in Figure 5.3, there are three major differences between Maslow's hierarchy and the Chinese need hierarchy as suggested by Nevis.

First, the need for belonging (social) has replaced physiological needs as the most basic need. Second, self-esteem is not included in the hierarchy. Self-esteem, according to Nevis, as a driving force makes sense for cultures that emphasize individualism. It is not a necessary, universal requirement that is found in all cultures. In particular, as F. L. K. Hsu (as cited in Ref. 64) has pointed out, in the collectivist Chinese culture, the concept of self is quite different from the Western concept:

> The Chinese use a concept of "jen" (man), which is defined as the person plus the salient, intimate societal and cultural environment that makes her or his life meaningful. This implies much less differentiation in the self-concept of individuals and stresses identity as a *social* phenomenon. (p. 261)

Third, although self-esteem is considered unimportant, self-actualization is still present. In China, self-actualization is defined as a moral imperative and a social confluence: "My country needs me to be the best."[64] Therefore, it becomes a duty for the individual Chinese to fully develop the self. Failure in self-development could bring severe shame and loss of face. For the Chinese, achieving the goal of the extended family is more motivating than trying for individualized self-fulfillment.[66] In many cultures, social needs are

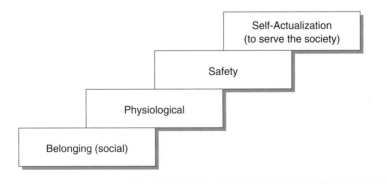

Figure 5.3   **Chinese Need Hierarchy**

much more prominent. It is common to mix business dealings with a heavy dose of socializing.

Within a given culture, ethnic and individual differences also complicate the applicability of Maslow's theory. To remedy this problem, Hofstede has suggested using work-related culture and job levels and categories to map need satisfaction hierarchies. Based on his study, he recommends using physical rewards for lower-level employees, while using challenge, autonomy, and cooperation as motivators for middle and upper managers.[14] Cross-cultural studies have found that managers and professionals are more responsive to higher-order needs in Maslow's hierarchy.[67]

Andean Preference

An American company developing a copper mine in Chile experienced difficulty getting workers. Although it offered good meals, hot water, housing, movies, etc., the workers flocked to the French company. The workers who were employed by the French had the roughest housing and none of the comforts offered by the Americans. Baffled, the American company studied the situation and figured out what was happening. The French offered no perks but paid workers by the hour. The people of the Andes cared more about their time off. It was important for them to be able to come and go without question.[68]

Although there is some support for the universality of the need hierarchy, the support is inconclusive. In an early study of 14 industrial countries, including Japan, Haire et al.[44] found some support for Maslow's theory. Later, in a study of eight countries selected from different parts of the world, Reitz[69] also found some support for the order of satisfaction as suggested by Maslow. The failure to find evidence supporting a universal hierarchy of needs has led critics to argue that the theory may be good only for European, and more specifically Anglo, cultures. They argue that, in studies that found support for Maslow's theory, the research samples were mainly taken from these cultures.

Some studies have shown that there may be a consistent rank ordering of needs in each culture, however. In his study of clusters of needs in several countries, Ronen[70] concluded that there is support for Maslow's contention that groups of needs appear in a sequence rather than simultaneously. Adler[71] suggested similar support for the existence of a need hierarchy in developing countries, but one that emphasizes security and self-esteem needs (pp. 152–153). Recently, other writers have used the two clusters of developing and developed countries to study motivation. They suggest that while higher-order needs (like achievement) are more valued in developed countries, lower-order needs (security and affiliation) are more important in developing nations. Some have gone as far as to suggest that this gap is responsible for differences in economic prosperity (see the discussion later on McClelland's theory).

Finally, according to Maslow, lower-level needs have to be "reasonably satisfied" before the higher level is activated. While the idea of "reasonable satisfaction" and of what it comprises has been the subject of virtually no study to date, it seems logical to expect that what constitutes a reasonable level of satisfaction varies across cultures as well.

Motivators and Hygiene Factors

Herzberg[72,73] identified two groups of factors, hygiene and motivators, that influence individual performance in work organizations. Hygiene factors could only create discomfort if they were not met, but they have no effect on motivation. Hygiene factors are external to the job (extrinsic), such as working conditions, pay, and relations with peers. Motivators include job-related (intrinsic) factors, such as the work itself, achievement, responsibility, and recognition. Herzberg emphasizes achievement as a strong motivator; therefore, the problems associated with its cross-cultural validity become shortcomings of this theory. (See also the discussion of this issue with McClelland's theory.) Additionally, studies have found little evidence in support of a universal list of hygiene factors or motivators. In a study in the Panama Canal Zone, Crabbs[74] found that some hygiene factors satisfied employees. Hines tested the theory in New Zealand and found that interpersonal relationships and supervision, both considered hygiene factors by Herzberg,[75] contributed to employee satisfaction.

Hofstede[62] has suggested that although achievement may be a strong motivator in some cultures, security is more important in countries with a low tolerance for uncertainty. He argued that the word *achievement* does not even translate into many other languages.

> The consequence of country differences along these two dimensions is that management conceptions about the motivation of employees, common in North America, do not necessarily apply abroad. . . . [For example,] the countries in which McClelland's nAch [Achievement need] is strong are characterized by weak uncertainty avoidance [personal risk taking] and strong masculinity. McClelland's nAch may represent one particular combination of cultural choices. (p. 396)

Research findings from several countries, including New Zealand,[76] Israel,[77] Zambia,[78] and the United Kingdom,[79] suggest that although there may be a clustering of two distinct groups of factors with functions similar to what Herzberg suggests (hygiene and motivators), their components vary across cultures.

McClelland's Three Motives

McClelland[67] identified three important individual drives (needs): achievement, power, and affiliation. He suggested that the need for achievement was the most important factor leading to economic success. He proposed that at the national level, the aggregate level of this need was related to the rate of economic development. McClelland believed that the need for achievement, and related attributes, could be taught.

Cross-cultural studies of McClelland's theory have produced conflicting results. Early support for this theory came from a study by McClelland in which he trained a group of entrepreneurs in India and later measured their achievement in terms of increased profits, starting new businesses, and investigating new products. He reported that as a result of his training, the rate of achievement-oriented activities among this group almost doubled.[80] Bhagat and McQuaid[81] have cited a number of studies in both developed and developing countries that support this theory. Hofstede found a positive correlation between the need for achievement and the need to produce and willingness to accept risk. A number of researchers since that time have questioned McClelland's findings. Many studies have not found a link between this need and the rate of economic growth. For instance, Iwawaki and Lynn[82] found similar levels of need for achievement in their Japanese and English samples, despite a higher rate of economic growth for Japan. Two studies found unusually low levels of this need among Chinese and Czechoslovakian managers, which was inconsistent with the level of economic growth (p. 153).[60]

While McClelland's idea does permit cross-cultural theorizing, it assumes only one path to economic development manifested through a high need for achievement, which is characteristic of Western individualistic societies. Recent economic progress in some Asian countries indicates the existence of alternative paths. Moreover, the lack of a common definition for "achievement" restricts research on McClelland's theory. While achievement is measured in financial terms in American culture, in Japan it is determined by other factors, such as affiliation. As stated earlier, some argue that the word *achievement* does not even translate to some languages. Moreover, Bond's[58] summary of several studies leads to the conclusion that for the Chinese, achievement need is socially defined, with the ultimate goal being to meet the expectations of in-group members (p. 5).

The implications of the conflicting findings are clear. Many training and organization development programs exported to other countries to boost employees' achievement needs prove useless. In a study in India, McClelland and Winter[83] reported that their achievement training program had little effect. A follow-up study[84] revealed that the program had instead increased the participants' need for status, which is highly important in that culture. For a program to be successful, it should be designed for the importing culture. Moreover, the link between the increase in need for achievement and performance has to be established in that environment.

Furthermore, these characteristics and motives are the result of cultural conditioning *early* in a person's life and, probably, cannot be changed in a brief training course.

Expectancy Theory

This theory proposes that motivation is a deliberate and conscious choice to engage in a certain activity for achieving a certain outcome or reward. Mathematically expressed, motivation (M) is the product of three variables (p. 6):[85] (1) Valence (V), the value (attractiveness) of the potential reward or outcome; (2) Instrumentality (I), the expectation that performance will lead to receiving the reward; and (3) Expectancy (E), the belief by the individual that exerting a certain amount of effort will lead to accomplishment of the task. This theory can be expressed mathematically by the equation $M = V \times I \times E$.

Cross-cultural research on expectancy theory involves answering two questions. First, does the multiplicative relationship between the three determining variables ($V \times I \times E$) hold for various cultures? Second, what effect does a given culture have on these variables?

There are very few cross-cultural studies that have tested the validity of the relationships among various variables of expectancy theory. The limited research on the issue, however, provides support for the first question. Eden[86] analyzed data collected from 375 male members of an Israeli kibbutz with regard to the relationship among intrinsic, status-oriented, and material rewards and motives. He concluded that the effect of externally mediated rewards on intrinsic motivation was explained on the basis of expectancy theory.

To answer the second question, we need to examine variables individually for cultural effects. Valence, the value of the reward, varies across different cultures. In collectivist societies, social groups play an important role in determining the value of the reward and the expectation of achieving it. It should not be surprising when people in these societies prefer spending more time with family and friends over an increase in pay. To them, work is not the central point in life. Using Adler's[71] terms, "Expectancy theories are universal to the extent that they do not specify the type of reward that motivates a group of workers" (p. 159). Instrumentality and expectancy are based on an individual's evaluation of his or her abilities, past experiences with supervisors and the organization, and belief about what role he or she can play in determining his or her destiny. While Protestant cultures promote the belief that an individual is in charge of his or her destiny, Catholic and Muslim cultures encourage submission to the will of God. The belief that the individual does not have much control over his or her life should lead to lower expectancy scores in these cultures. In Hindu and Buddhist cultures, the emphasis on social relationships and harmony, instead of materialism and competition, is probably the reason for the lower value of individual achievement and the belief in luck.

Equity Theory

According to Adams,[87] the individual's perception of inequity is a motivating force. More specifically, a person compares the ratio of his or her compensation, what he or she gets from the job (outcomes), to his or her contributions to the job (input) with that of others in a similar situation. Compensation comes in many different forms, including pay, job security, opportunity for advancement and promotion, good working relationships, and a safe and pleasant work environment. Inequity in either direction generates tension.

Culture influences our perception of the value of the job outcomes as well as our contributions to the organization. Culture also provides the frame of reference for a comparison of ratios. The sensitivity of people to inequity, and the avenues they use to remedy the problem, is also influenced by culture. For instance, if a less qualified peer receives a pay raise, a Japanese employee is more likely to reevaluate his or her perception of his or her outcome/input ratio compared with that of peers (refer to our earlier discussion on the cultural definition of self). Conformity to group and organizational norms would inhibit more severe action. In a similar situation, an American employee would be more willing to file a formal complaint or even leave the organization.

In their research in an Israeli kibbutz, Yuchtman and Seashore[88] found support for the equity theory. More research is needed, however, to establish its cross-cultural validity. One practical bit of evidence for the validity of this theory is the worldwide practice of pay secrecy. Many organizations follow this policy to avoid unwanted comparisons and unnecessary complaints.

Motivation and Learning

B. F. Skinner and other learning theorists assert that behavior is a function of its consequences. Behavior that is followed by desirable consequences (reinforced behavior) tends to be repeated. In contrast, undesirable consequences have the opposite effect. In this way, we learn to change our behavior to experience desirable consequences and avoid the undesirable ones (e.g., punishment).[89–91] (Also, for a description of the conditioning process, see Ref. 92.)

As in motivation, the two major concerns in learning are finding the right incentives and the correct way, or schedule, to administer them. The values and attractions of rewards vary across cultures. Similarly, cultural factors influence the undesirability of negative incentives. Also, culture is a major determinant of the types of reinforcement and the methods used for their application. Although all cultures use a combination of positive reinforcements and punishment, some tend to use more positive incentives, while others make more use of punishment. Positive reinforcement leads to longer-lasting and more predictable results, but the only effect it has is to make the behavior continue. Punishments cause the behavior to stop, but the effect usually lasts only a short time if the punishment is removed. Also, there are dysfunctional consequences to punishment, such as low self-esteem. While these ideas appear to be universal—consistent laboratory results have been obtained with animals using food as a reward and electric shocks as punishments—the challenge for us in a cross-cultural setting is to find out which rewards *really* reward in a given culture and which punishments *really* punish.

Motivation and Japanese Employees

In recent years, Japanese management and motivation practices have received worldwide attention. The success of Japan's companies, particularly its auto industry, has spotlighted the way Japanese businesses work. According to William Ouchi,[33] there are three fundamental properties of Japanese organizations that distinguish them from American firms: lifetime employment, internal promotion, and nonspecialized career paths. Many large Japanese companies offer lifetime jobs to their employees. While the recent downturn in the Japanese economy has eroded the foundation of this practice, fundamentally, the relationship between employees and employers remains long term. Lifetime employment, although desired by workers and a goal of employers, covers perhaps 35% of Japan's workforce. Promotions are entirely from within the firm. The process of evaluation is very slow and long-term oriented. Because of lifetime employment and internal promotions, employees receive broad-based training. They are moved between functions, offices, and geographical locations so that they become familiar with the whole organization (pp. 11–38).

Not only are there differences between American and Japanese companies; there are differences between employees of the two nations as well. Americans emphasize individualism, nonconformity, and competition, while Japanese promote collectivism, conformity, and cooperation. Japanese employees are under more pressure to conform and work long hours. Long hours and job stress create health-related problems. Recent increases in the rates of heart attacks and suicides among Japanese employees are attributed to increased job stress. There is even a word for death from hard work and stress, *karoshi*, which means sudden death by a heart attack or stroke triggered by overwork. According to some estimates, more than 10,000 Japanese fall victim annually to *karoshi*.[93] The international expansion of Japanese industries has created additional demands on some employees' time and energy.

Global Trends and Motivation

Dramatic technological changes and political restructuring around the world have created new problems as well as opportunities. Acceleration of the rate of change in recent years has made it difficult to predict global trends in motivation. Two major questions have been raised regarding the changes in the management of motivation and human resources.

First, will the collapse of the Soviet system result in the integration of the socialist cultures into the Western cultures? If so, will this integration lead to more emphasis on social needs in Western organizations (i.e., make them more employee centered)? Some scholars of international management believe that this will happen. They argue that there will be more emphasis on relationships in Western companies and more attention paid to work and production in Eastern societies. So far, there is little evidence to support this contention. American companies have been reducing their staffs and lowering employees' benefits despite increases in reported profits. Traditionally, increased profits have led to more hiring and increases in employee benefits. Recent practices, however, have been contrary to historical trends. This "getting lean and mean" strategy has left unemployment and the employee benefit problems for the individual or the government to solve. On the other hand, with the easing of restrictions on businesses in the former communist states, there is a noticeable rise in entrepreneurial attitudes and behaviors. Freed from the communist yoke, these societies have witnessed an explosion of emerging small businesses and privatization of government-controlled industries. Transformation to a market economy, however, has caused new political and economic problems that have yet to be resolved.

Second, will the expansion of global business, advancements in telecommunication technology, and widespread use of the Internet lead to more uniformity among cultures? There are some signs of this development. The popularity of American culture overseas and Americans' rising interest in learning about other cultures are early indications of such a trend. There are some indications to the contrary as well. For example, in a study of the macro-environmental characteristics of 18 industrialized nations over the 1960 to 1988 period, Craig et al.[94] found a diverging pattern. Contrary to the popular assumption, they found that countries were diverging rather than converging. Global economic problems and the resulting protectionist attitudes are major obstacles in the road to a global culture.

Adler[71] believes that employees bring their ethnicity into the workplace and promote or enhance their culture in their work organizations. In her words, Germans become more German, Americans become more American, Swedes become more Swedish, and so forth (p. 58). If the tendency to emphasize one's ethnicity and heritage is on the rise, the future may hold more problems for international managers, who are already burdened with problems and difficulties. An example is the experience of Bridgestone, the Japanese tire company, which bought Firestone, of Akron, Ohio, to gain a foothold in the U.S. market. Soon after the purchase, cultural differences between Akron and Tokyo surfaced. Besides the language difficulty, adjusting to styles of work proved to be an obstacle to smooth operations. "The Japanese, who work until 9 p.m. or later, won't fathom why their American colleagues won't stay that late, too. And the Americans complain about Japanese arrangements such as open offices and desks facing each other."[68]

The convergence or divergence of cultures will have a significant impact on how cross-cultural motivation is managed. Research findings are pointing in both directions.[95] Today's rapid changes call for continuous monitoring of cultural differences for effectively managing motivation.

Motivation Summary

Culture plays an important role in managing motivation in work organizations. Culture affects employee perceptions and the way employees respond to rewards or punishments. For managers who plan to work overseas or have employees from other cultures, cultural understanding is a prerequisite to success. Motivating people without knowledge of their culture is an impossible task. For example, when followers of Herzberg suggest that money is not a motivator, it may be because in Western societies most of the basic needs are reasonably satisfied. In some developing countries where most people are less prosperous by Western standards, money is still an important motivating factor. Money, however, may not be a motivating factor in other cultures for a different reason.

> Money is not an incentive everywhere—it may be accepted gladly, but will not automatically improve performance. Honor, dignity and family may be much more important. Imposing the American style of merit system may be an outrageous blow to a respected and established seniority system. Merit must be defined: "May the best person win" can mean "the most popular person" or "the person from the most aristocratic family."[23] (p. 14)

The cultural diversity of MNCs poses a problem for the universal application of motivation theories. Studies suggest that the need to belong and associate is a strong motivator in societies that emphasize the value of social relationships. In these cultures, the American concept of individualism is not a strong basis for motivation. Although individuals follow a hierarchical order to satisfy needs, this hierarchical order apparently varies across cultures. Unfortunately, the grouping of countries into large categories, such as developed and underdeveloped, without paying attention to cultural attributes, does not provide a good solution to understanding motivation. Understanding important needs and their rank order in a given society requires research designed for that specific culture. To be applicable in international settings, the traditional psychologically based motivation models should also take an anthropological orientation, whereby cultural influences on motivation are taken into account. This would provide international managers with an additional tool for understanding the idiosyncrasies of human behavior.

Discussion Questions _____

1. Discuss the way in which ethnocentric tendencies affect our lives as well as the way in which we run businesses in the United States.

2. Explain how variation in the concept of self could affect a person's motivation.

3. Individualism is a well-known attribute of Americans. Americans are also known to help their neighbors in times of need. Are these two traits in conflict?

4. Work by itself could be a motivating factor for Americans. Do other cultures consider work as a motivator or a necessity? Discuss the meaning of work from the perspective of another culture.

5. Do you know of any example of ethnocentrism in another country? If yes, describe it.

6. Why is Maslow's hierarchy of needs considered ethnocentric? Is there a universal hierarchy of human needs?

7. Are motivators and hygiene factors universal? Explain.

8. Compared with the people of other countries, the Japanese tend to work longer hours. What cultural characteristics of the Japanese could you use to explain this tendency?

9. In your opinion, what are the reasons for the Japanese younger generation's interest in more leisure time?

10. What are the cultural implications of the expectancy theory of motivation? Does individual willingness to take risks make a difference in a person's motivation?

11. What leadership characteristics of Mahatma Gandhi and Nelson Mandela do you consider to be similar?

12. Why should international managers learn about leadership theories that are developed in the United States?

13. Tennenbaum and Schmidt suggested that there are four forces influencing a manager's actions. Describe these forces.

14. How could a leader's philosophy regarding human nature affect his or her relationship with his or her followers?

15. By using Fiedler's contingency model, elaborate on the contention that leadership effectiveness depends on a match between the leader's behavioral inclinations and the favorableness of the situation.

16. What is the meaning of the phrase *the cultural relativity of leadership*?

17. The leadership theories reviewed in this chapter favor a democratic leadership style. Do you think that these theories are valid for non-Western cultures?

18. What are the differences between managerial leadership practices in the United States and France?

19. This chapter refers to the difficulties that the Ford Motor Company experienced when it integrated its European operation of car manufacturing. What were the cultural differences causing those problems?

20. Briefly explain the Japanese decision-making process called *ringi*. In your opinion, why is *ringi* effective in Japan?

21. Elaborate on the statement "There is a functionality in the host country managerial practices."

References

1. J. M. Brown (1989). *Gandhi: Prisoner of hope*. New Haven, CT: Yale University Press.
2. M. Fatima (1990). *Higher than hope: The authorized biography of Nelson Mandela*. New York: Harper Collins.
3. *Nelson Mandela speaks: Forging a democratic nonracial South Africa* (1993). New York: Pathfinder.
4. C. S. Wren (1990, February 13). Mandela sees negotiations soon over political rights for Blacks. *New York Times*, p. A16.
5. F. W. De Klerk (2005, April 18). Seizing the historical moment. *Time, 165*(16), 96.
6. H. J. Reitz (1977). *Behavior in organizations*. Homewood, IL: Richard D. Irwin.
7. P. Hersey & K. H. Blanchard (1972). *Management of organizational behavior*. Englewood Cliffs, NJ: Prentice Hall.
8. C. C. Manz & C. P. Neck (2004). *Mastering self-leadership: Empowering yourself for personal excellence*. Upper Saddle River, NJ: Pearson.
9. J. B. Shaw (1990). Cognitive categorization model for the study of intercultural management. *Academy of Management Review, 15*(4), 626–645.
10. M. Javidan, P. W. Dorfman, M. Sully de Luque, & R. J. House (2006). In the eyes of the beholder: Cross cultural lessons in leadership from Project GLOBE. *Academy of Management Perspective, February*, 67–90.
11. G. Hofstede (2001). *Culture's consequences*. Thousand Oaks, CA: Sage.
12. K. Chen (1995, August 30). Equal opportunity isn't big concern for Mosuo women. *Wall Street Journal*, p. A1.
13. S. Z. Ahmed (1994, February 15). What do men want? *New York Times*, p. A21.
14. G. Hofstede (1980). Motivation, leadership, and organization: Do American theories apply abroad? *Organizational Dynamics, Summer*, 42–63.
15. J. Rojot (1990). Human resource management in France. In R. Pieper (Ed.), *Human resource management: An international comparison* (pp. 95–98). Berlin, Germany: Walter de Gruyter.

16. F. L. Wilson (1991). Democracy in the workplace: The French experience. *Politics and Society, 19*, 439–462.

17. K. Fatehi-Sedeh & H. Safizadeh (1986). Labor union leaders and codetermination: An evaluation of attitudes. *Employee Relations Law Journal, 12*(2), 188–204.

18. L. R. Gomez-Mejia, D. B. Balkin, & R. L. Cardy (2005). *Management: People, performance, change.* Boston: McGraw-Hill.

19. B. M. Bass (1999). Two decades of research and development in transformational leadership. *European Journal of Work and Organizational Psychology, 8*, 9–32.

20. B. J. Avolio (1999). *Full leadership development.* Thousand Oaks, CA: Sage.

21. F. O. Walumbwa & J. J. Lawler (2002, August). Building effective organizations: Transformational leaderships, collectivist orientation, work-related attitudes, and withdrawal behaviors in three emerging economies. Paper presented at the Academy of Management Annual Meeting, Denver, Colorado.

22. D. A. Ralston, D. J. Gustafson, & R. H. Terpstra (1993, October). The impact of Eastern and Western philosophy on upward influence tactics: A comparison of American and Hong Kong Chinese managers. Paper presented at the Academy of International Business Annual Conference, Maui, HI.

23. L. Copeland & L. Griggs (1985). *Going international: How to make friends and deal effectively in the global marketplace.* New York: Random House.

24. M. Marks (1977). Organizational adjustment to uncertainty. *Journal of Management Studies, 14*, 1–7.

25. P. R. Harris & R. T. Moran (1991). *Managing cultural differences.* Houston, TX: Gulf Publishing.

26. N. Phillips (1994). *Managing international teams.* Burr Ridge, IL: Richard D. Irwin.

27. J.-L. Barsoux & P. Lawrence (1991). The making of a French manager. *Harvard Business Review, July–August,* 58–67.

28. R. D. Lewis (1996). How to lead in another language. *Management Today, March,* 82–84.

29. R. Wunderer (1990). Leadership. In E. Grochla & E. Gaugler (Eds.), *Handbook of German business management* (pp. 1390–1400). Stuttgart, Germany: C. E. Poeschel.

30. G. Reber (1990). Motivation. In E. Grochla & E. Gaugler (Eds.), *Handbook of German business management* (pp. 1490–1500). Stuttgart, Germany: C. E. Poeschel.

31. R. Shaeffer (1985). *Developing new leadership in a multinational environment.* New York: Conference Board.

32. K. Bleicher (1990). Management. In E. Grochla & E. Gaugler (Eds.), *Handbook of German business management* (p. 1395). Stuttgart, Germany: C. E. Poeschel.

33. W. G. Ouchi (1981). *Theory Z.* Reading, MA: Addison-Wesley.

34. S. P. Sethi, N. Namiki, & C. L. Swanson (1984). *The false promise of the Japanese miracle.* Boston: Pitman.

35. Y. Takahashi (1990). Human resource management in Japan. In R. Pieper (Ed.), *Human resource management: An international comparison* (p. 218). Berlin, Germany: Walter de Gruyter.

36. B. Bruce-Briggs (1982, May 17). The dangerous folly called Theory Z. *Fortune,* 41–44.

37. M. Maruyama (1992). Changing dimensions in international business. *Academy of Management Executive, 6*(3), 93.

38. I. Harpaz (1990). The importance of work goals: An international perspective. *Journal of International Business Studies, 21,* 75–93.

39. R. G. D'Andrade & C. Strauss (1992). *Human motives and cultural models.* Cambridge, UK: Cambridge University Press.

40. S. M. Lipset (1993). Culture and economic behavior: A commentary. *Journal of Labor Economics, 11*(2, Pt. 2), S330–S347.

41. W. Nord (1972). Cultures and organizational behavior. In W. Nord (Ed.), *Concepts and controversy in organizational behavior* (pp. 205–206). New York: Goodyear.

42. F. Derakhshan & R. Khan (1989). Attitudes towards older employees in PRC and Taiwan: A cross-cultural comparison. *Proceedings of Pan Pacific Conference,* 68–71.

43. W. F. Whyte & P. R. Braun (1966). Heroes, homeworks, and industrial growth. *Columbia Journal of World Business, Spring,* 1–57.

44. M. Haire, E. E. Ghiselli, & L. W. Porter (1963). Cultural patterns in the role of management. *Industrial Relations, 2,* 96–117.

45. J. S. Black & L. W. Porter (1991). Managerial behaviors and job performance: A successful manager in Los Angeles may not succeed in Hong Kong. *Journal of International Business Studies, 22*(1), 99–113.

46. W. H. Newman (1972). Cultural assumption underlying U.S. management concepts. In J. L. Massie, J. Luytjes, & N. W. Hazen (Eds.), *Management in an international context* (p. 347). New York: Harper & Row.

47. MOW International Research Team (1985). *The meaning of working.* London: Academic Press.

48. J. Misumi (1993). Attitudes to work in Japan and the West. *Long Range Planning, 26*(4), 66–71.

49. E. E. Sampson (1989). The challenge of social change for psychology: Globalization and psychology's theory of the person. *American Psychologist, 44,* 914–921.

50. U. Neisser (1988). Five kinds of self-knowledge. *Philosophical Psychology, 1,* 35–59.

51. H. R. Markus & S. Kitayama (1991). Culture and the self: Implications for cognition, emotion, and motivation. *Psychological Review, 98,* 224–253.

52. R. E. Nisbett (2003). *The geography of thought.* New York: Free Press.

53. M. Hernandez & S. S. Iyengar (2001). What drives whom? A cultural perspective on human agency. *Social Cognition, 10*(3), 269–294.

54. R. P. Dore (1958). *City life in Japan.* Berkeley: University of California Press.

55. T. Parsons, E. Shils, & J. Olds (1951). Categories of the orientation and organization of action. In T. Parsons & E. A. Shils (Eds.), *Toward a general theory of action* (p. 81). Cambridge, MA: Harvard University Press.

56. F. L. K. Hsu (1975). *Iemoto: The heart of Japan.* New York: Wiley.

57. H. A. Murray (1938). *Explorations in personality.* New York: Oxford University Press.

58. M. H. Bond (1986). *The psychology of Chinese people.* New York: Oxford University Press.

59. L. Festinger (1957). *A theory of cognitive dissonance.* Palo Alto, CA: Stanford University Press.

60. S. Ronen (1986). *Comparative and multinational management.* New York: Wiley.

61. E. J. Kolde (1974). *The multinational company.* Lexington, MA: D. C. Heath.

62. G. Hofstede (1984). The cultural relativity of the quality of life concept. *Academy of Management Review, 9*(3), 396.

63. S. G. Redding (1977). Some perceptions of psychological needs among managers in South East Asia. In Y. H. Poortinga (Ed.), *Basic problems in cross-cultural psychology* (pp. 338–343). Amsterdam: Swete & Zeitlinger.

64. E. C. Nevis (1983). Using an American perspective in understanding another culture: Toward a hierarchy of needs for the People's Republic of China. *Journal of Applied Behavioral Science, 19*(3), 249–264.

65. E. C. Nevis (1983). Cultural assumption and productivity: The United States and China. *Sloan Management Review, Spring,* 17–29.

66. H. M. Yay (1988). Chinese cultural values: Their dimensions and marketing implications. *European Journal of Marketing, 22*(5), 44–57.

67. D. C. McClelland (1961). *The achieving society.* Princeton, NJ: Van Nostrand Rienhold.

68. T. F. O'Boyle (1991, April 1). Bridgestone discovers purchase of U.S. firm creates big problems. *Wall Street Journal,* p. A1.

69. H. J. Reitz (1975). The relative importance of five categories of needs among industrial workers in eight countries. *Academy of Management Proceedings,* 270–273.

70. S. Ronen (1979). Cross-national study of employee work goals. *International Review of Applied Psychology, 28*(1), 1–12.

71. N. J. Adler (1991). *International dimension of organizational behavior.* Boston: Kent Publishing.

72. F. Herzberg, B. Mausner, & B. S. Snyderman (1959). *The motivation to work.* New York: Wiley.

73. F. Herzberg (1968). One more time, how do you motivate employees? *Harvard Business Review, January–February,* 54–62.

74. R. A. Crabbs (1973). Work motivation in the culturally complex Panama Canal company. *Academy of Management Proceedings,* 119–126.

75. G. H. Hines (1973). Achievement, motivation, occupations and labor turnover in New Zealand. *Journal of Applied Psychology, 58*(3), 313–317.

76. G. H. Hines (1973). Cross-cultural differences in two-factor motivation theory. *Journal of Applied Psychology, 58*(3), 375–377.

77. D. Macarov (1972). Work patterns and satisfactions in an Israeli kibbutz: A test of the Herzberg hypothesis. *Personnel Psychology, Autumn,* 483–493.

78. P. D. Machungwa & N. Schmitt (1983). Work motivation in a developing country. *Journal of Applied Psychology, 68*(1), 31–42.

79. R. N. Kanung & R. W. Wright (1983). A cross-cultural comparative study of managerial job attitudes. *Journal of International Business Studies, 14*(2), 115–129.

80. D. C. McClelland (1965). Achieving motivation can be developed. *Harvard Business Review, November–December,* 120.

81. R. S. Bhagat & S. J. McQuaid (1982). Role of subjective culture in organizations: A review and directions for future research. *Journal of Applied Psychology Monograph, 67,* 635–667.

82. S. Iwawaki & R. Lynn (1972). Measuring achievement motivation in Great Britain and Japan. *Journal of Cross-Cultural Psychology, 3,* 219–220.

83. D. C. McClelland & D. G. Winter (1969). *Motivating economic achievement.* New York: Free Press.

84. U. N. Pareek & V. K. Kumar (1969). Expressed motive of entrepreneurship in an Indian town. *Psychologica, 12,* 109–114.

85. D. R. Hampton, C. E. Summer, & R. A. Webber (1982). *Organizational behavior and the practice of management.* Glenview, IL: Scott, Foresman.

86. D. Eden (1975). Intrinsic and extrinsic rewards and motives: Replication and extension with kibbutz workers. *Journal of Applied Social Psychology, 6,* 348–361.

87. J. S. Adams (1965). Inequities in social exchange. *Advances in experimental social psychology* (Vol. 2). New York: Academic Press.

88. E. Yuchtman & S. E. Seashore (1967). A system resource approach to organizational effectiveness. *American Psychological Review, 32,* 891–903.

89. B. F. Skinner (1971). *Beyond freedom and dignity.* New York: Alfred Knopf.

90. B. F. Skinner (1963). Operant behavior. *American Psychologist, 18,* 503–515.

91. B. F. Skinner (1969). *Contingencies of reinforcement: A theoretical analysis.* Englewood Cliffs, NJ: Prentice Hall.

92. B. M. Bass & J. A. Vaughn (1966). *Training in industry: The management of learning.* Monterey, CA: Brooks/Cole.

93. K. L. Miller (1992, August 3). Now, Japan is admitting it: Work kills executives. *Business Week,* 35.

94. S. S. Craig, S. P. Douglas, & A. Grein (1992). Patterns of convergence and divergence among industrializing nations: 1960–1988. *Journal of International Business Studies, 23*(4), 773–787.

95. D. A. Ralston, D. J. Gustafson, F. M. Cheung, & R. H. Terpstra (1993). Differences in managerial values: A study of U.S., Hong Kong and PRC managers. *Journal of International Business Studies, 24*(2), 249–275.

Case 6

KIWI SAMURAI

SecureFit Industries in Japan[a]

David C. Thomas

Rain streaked the windows of his Christchurch office as Eion Williams, chairman of The SecureFit Group, prepared for his 34th trip to Japan. It was September 29th and spring had yet to arrive in New Zealand, but Eion knew the early autumn weather in Osaka would be very pleasant. He was quite looking forward to his semi-annual trip now that all the preparations had been made. He had just finished reviewing the last six months of correspondence with Masanobu, Inc., SecureFit's major distributor in Japan, and the gift for its president Mr. Kiyomitsu was being crated for the trip. Eion was very pleased with the magnificent hand-blown glass orb that would be his gift to Kiyomitsu-san, this year's part of a ritual that had been going on for over fifteen years now. After so much time, it had been difficult to think of something new, which also reflected the magnitude of SecureFit's business relationship with Masanobu. Japan was the largest export destination for SecureFit's products and was by far the most profitable. The gifts for the three principal managers would be easier. He always picked up a few bottles of the 30 year old whisky that they seemed

to prefer. By telling them that he had simply taken advantage of the airport duty-free shop he had always been able to prevent the traditional[b] return of a gift from each of them that he didn't really want and would only weigh down his luggage.

Eion Williams was a creature of habit and this trip would follow a pattern established many years earlier. He would stick to an established itinerary, stay in the same hotels, take the same airline flights, and even sit in the same seats on the aircraft as he had on previous trips. This, he felt, was one of the advantages of being executive chairman and being able to set your schedule a year in advance. There would be a significant difference on this trip, however. This time he was taking someone with him. That someone was Mark Blyth who, upon Eion Williams's retirement the following year, would assume responsibility for the firm's business in Japan. As Eion Williams prepared for this trip to Japan, his next to last as Executive Chairman of SecureFit, he reflected on the growth of SecureFit over the past 33 years.

Founded on November 24, 1961, as The SecureFit Fence Company, SecureFit Industries was built on an innovative

SOURCE: Used with permission and reprinted from Thomas, David C. (2003). Kiwi Samurai: SecureFit Industries in Japan. In D. C. Thomas (Ed.), *Readings and cases in international management: A cross-cultural perspective* (pp. 246–253). Thousand Oaks, CA: Sage.

retaining wall system, which was designed to withstand the unique New Zealand soil conditions. The wall system, invented by Colin Freeman and marketed by Eion Williams, became an instant success and many examples of the product are still to be found around New Zealand. In the early to mid 1960's, while retaining wall systems remained the principal product, Colin Freeman designed a number of other products many of which were produced by SecureFit. The name of the firm was changed to SecureFit Industries in 1964. In 1967 SecureFit introduced a retraction mechanism for automobile seats that employed a Colin Freeman designed sealed nylon bearing. The product locked the seat-belt position in response to increasing tension. This development, coupled with the introduction of automobile assembly in New Zealand, led to substantial growth in the company as sales of this unique product skyrocketed. Saturation of the domestic market led SecureFit to its first offshore venture, a license to manufacture the product in Australia to Aaron Hinton Pty Ltd. Bolstered by a loan from the Development Finance Corporation of New Zealand based on this export potential, SecureFit was on solid ground. However, Eion Williams was convinced that SecureFit's future depended on developing the export potential for its product. By 1970, SecureFit had established a market for its unique products in England, Singapore, Malaysia, Thailand, and South America.

Eion Williams recalled those early trips overseas. While government export incentives had helped to offset much of the travel costs, it was still necessary to work at a tremendous pace to get the most out of the opportunity. Even for someone who was as fit as he had been in those days, it was arduous work. One of the early trips had involved stops in 27 countries in 10 weeks. The glamour of travel had worn off very quickly on that trip and by the time he had got to South Africa he had become quite irritable and impatient with potential customers. The lower back pain that often emerged after long periods of sitting was a constant reminder of another less than entirely pleasant overseas journey. An aircraft controller's strike at Heathrow had turned a trip from Christchurch to Stockholm into a 54-hour ordeal with no opportunity to rest his back. He had grabbed a heavy bag out of a taxi, seriously injuring his back. And he had to be in 13 different cities in over the next 14 days. On returning to Auckland he had the injury attended to. The operation to repair the crushed disc and subsequent recuperative period had been the only time he had missed work due to illness or injury in over thirty years.

By 1971, all the overseas travel had begun to pay off with 39,000 pairs of seat belt mechanisms shipped in 31 separate consignments. In 1972, this grew to 136,000 pairs. By the late seventies, exports had then taken on an increased significance and accounted for about 20% of all sales.

By 1977, Eion Williams had visited 56 countries to evaluate markets and/or introduce SecureFit's products. SecureFit was exporting regularly to about 10 different countries at this time. While the company had been successful in many areas of the world, others such as South America had presented difficulties because of uneven economic growth or political instability. A report from the British trade office had impressed Eion with the point that the 500 most successful exporters from Britain, while exporting to 160 countries, made 80% of their profits from only 20% of their markets. Thus, began the search for a market that had political stability and economic growth and, in short, would be the best place to be in 10 years. Even in 1977 it became clear to Eion that this would be Japan.

A friend of Eion's, who at the time worked in the Auckland office of the giant Japanese firm Mitsui, provided SecureFit with its first exposure to the Japanese market. Eion had given him samples of products and brochures to be sent off to Japan with an eye toward establishing an agent relationship with Mitsui. About a month later, Eion received a telex from Mitsui saying that they had completed their market survey, and would he come to Japan to learn the results. It was February 1978 and Eion had booked the first available flight to Tokyo. He remembered how impressive the big black, 60 storey Mitsui building had been, how it had dominated the Shinjuku district of Tokyo. He also remembered the smooth English-speaking Japanese junior executives with whom he met. In effect they said that most (90%) of Japanese automobile parts and accessories were manufactured locally and hence there were no opportunities for SecureFit's product in Japan. Then the guy just said, "End of meeting." Eion was irritated at having been brought to Japan just to be told that and recalled that this had been his first and last meeting with fluent English speakers in Japan. He had gone straight around to the New Zealand embassy and borrowed an interpreter. Then, he spent the next several days going around Tokyo showing the product samples he had brought to the major automobile parts manufacturers. He had also taken a video with a Japanese narration that showed SecureFit's product being manufactured in New Zealand. This approach had been helpful in Latin America where it had been difficult to explain that SecureFit made only the retraction mechanism, not the entire seatbelt, and were therefore a supplier and not a potential competitor.

Dealing in the automobile component industry in Japan was very different from other Japanese industries, such as automobiles themselves or electronics, which were much more used to dealing with foreigners. The window manufacturers in Japan sell only to the domestic market and, therefore, had little prior experience with foreign firms. Eion's approach at each facility had been to ask (through his interpreter) who was the best component manufacturer, importer, agent, or distributor in Japan. The name that kept popping up was Masanobu. So, he had contacted Masanobu. Fortunately, their managing director recognized some opportunities for the products and expressed interest in being SecureFit's agents in Japan. After several months of correspondence in which he had prepared a detailed marketing plan Masanobu agreed to be the exclusive distributor in Japan. The plan had included that Eion would make the Japanese market his personal responsibility, visit twice a year, meet their demands for quality and service, ship product within one month of receipt of orders, and airfreight at SecureFit's expense if they missed the first available ship.

It was on his second visit to Japan in October of 1978 that Eion Williams met Ichikawa Kiyomitsu, Managing Director of Masanobu, at their headquarters in Osaka. Kiyomitsu-san, now 75 years old, was an energetic chain smoker and hard drinker without particularly good English language skills. Eion had come to regard him as very intelligent, with a feel for Western ways of doing things. He also seemed to have a keen awareness of what was transpiring around him. On that trip he had arranged for Eion to be taken around the country to meet Masanobu's major customers. One such customer, Kobe Automotive Products, was ultimately the first Japanese company to use SecureFit's products. The general manager of Kobe at the time was a Mr. Tamagawa. Mr. Tamagawa, Eion recalled, was a great believer in testing and more testing. He took SecureFit's seat belt mechanism, which was normally tested to operate a minimum of 360,000 times before failure, and subjected it to 1.8 million operations, the equivalent of 60 years of normal operation.[c] He found that a part failed in the last few operations unless a screw was added on the underside of a hollow aluminium rivet on the mechanism. He demanded that SecureFit incorporate this modification into the product, for which he was willing to pay an additional 20 yen per unit. Actually, it had proved to be more efficient for Masanobu to make the modification in Japan, which they did for five years until Eion was able to prove to Mr. Tamagawa that a new version of the product would last as long or longer without the modification.

By the time the first order had actually been placed from Japan, Eion Williams had made three visits to Japan and established a pattern that has lasted over 15 years. Part of that pattern concerned the Japanese obsession with quality. Every six months on the first Monday in October and April, Eion would be picked up from his hotel and driven to Masanobu's headquarters. The first meeting would inevitably be in the large meeting room with 15 or 16 of Masanobu's managers from around the country in attendance. After the ritual exchange of greetings and calling cards, Mr. Kiyonaga, their quality manager, would come in with a box of faulty SecureFit product and tip it out on the table in front of Eion. It might have been only one fault in 10,000 but it looked terrible. Since Japanese automobile manufacturers guarantee the car and all of its components, faulty components created a big problem for them. While Eion explained what action had or was being taken on each fault the rest of the managers just seemed to glare at him. If a particular fault was ever subsequently repeated all hell would break

loose and they would send rude telexes saying things like don't you train your people or don't they care? Although these meetings put him in a difficult position as a supplier, particularly when he was seeking a price increase, they had also provided some lessons regarding quality control. In fact, it was from this experience that SecureFit had developed its fault report system, which subsequently became a cornerstone of its quality control programme.

The need to maintain quality always had to be balanced against the constant demands for new and innovative designs by the Japanese automobile industry. Large automotive component manufacturers in Japan produce bi-annual catalogues and are constantly looking for something that will differentiate them from their competitors. Eion felt that the Japanese manufacturers had come to depend on SecureFit for new products, but knew he would not sacrifice quality. He had said "no" more than once when asked to rush a product into production in order to meet the deadline of the forthcoming catalogue. Holding hundreds of patents worldwide as well as SecureFit's ability to continuously innovate gave Eion the power he needed to say no to the Japanese. This ability was something he valued very much.

All being said, Eion Williams was pleased with what he and SecureFit had accomplished in Japan. However, he knew that the relationships that had been built over years could not be left unattended. That's where Mark Blyth came in. In June of next year, when Eion Williams will have retired, Mark would take over responsibility for the Japanese market. The transition would begin with this trip on which Mark would take on the role of observer while Eion followed his normal routine. The following spring, Eion would be the observer as well as being the honoured [guest] at a number of functions because of his retirement. Eion intended for this transition to be seamless both at home in Christchurch and in Japan. Steven Campbell would take on most of his remaining duties, as in fact he already had. He had always said that nothing would please him more than after his retirement for someone to say "Where's Eion? I haven't seen his car in the parking lot lately." Of course he will still probably go back to Japan once a year to play golf with Mr. Kiyomitsu, or something like that—just what company presidents are supposed to do.

Mark Blyth was also preparing for the trip to Japan. It had been three and one half years since he had left Japan with Sachiko, his wife, to return to New Zealand. In that time, he had completed his M.B.A. at Canterbury University and found what seemed an ideal situation for someone with his skills. SecureFit had needed someone with an affinity for the Japanese market and an understanding of manufacturing. His eleven years of experience in Japan, fluency in the language, and engineering background made the fit seem obvious. More than that, though, SecureFit seemed to be getting it right in a number of areas. They had won numerous export and quality awards, were an innovator in team-based management, plus the place seemed to have the kind of culture he had been looking for. Halfway through his M.B.A., Mark had drawn up a shortlist of 5 companies who did business in Japan and appeared to have the kind of strategic vision he thought was necessary to compete effectively there. After a three-week trial period at SecureFit he had become convinced that this was the kind of company he was looking for. Also, SecureFit's growth and the fact that the top management team was changing (as a result of Eion Williams's upcoming retirement) suggested that advancement opportunities might be good. An interview with Steven Campbell clinched it. Steven's vision of SecureFit in five to ten years was something that he had really bought in to; something that he had found lacking in the short-term perspectives of other New Zealand firms.

Now, after four months on the job at SecureFit, he was on his way to Japan to be introduced as the new marketing director who would be responsible for the Japanese market. He knew that the title of marketing director was partly a result of the need to assure Masanobu that they would be dealing with a very senior SecureFit executive. He also knew that this did not diminish the importance of his role. He had some concern that the Japanese might think that at age 37, he was too young to hold such a high position. Perhaps his prematurely grey hair would disguise his age. He felt that it was important that the Japanese be convinced that he would be authorized to make decisions. After all, they had been dealing with Eion, who was not only the Executive Chairman (the equivalent to the company president in Japan), he was a founder of the company with an encyclopaedic knowledge of the industry. The transition would be a tricky one, but one that he felt could be managed effectively. The importance of his performance on this trip could not be overemphasized. His career, and to some degree the future of SecureFit, depended on how well these initial meetings went.

Mark Blyth was confident in his ability to deal effectively with the Masanobu executives. His eleven years at Matsushita[d] not only gave him experience with the Japanese: it gave him credibility. He knew through Naoko MacDonald, the Japanese translator employed by SecureFit in Christchurch, that the Japanese were impressed with his credentials. And credentials always overly impress the Japanese. Mark also had some unique connections that he thought might be used to advantage at some stage. One of his wife's relatives, a cousin, was an executive with Nissan. Perhaps he could help fill what Mark perceived as an information gap between SecureFit and their end user, the Japanese automobile industry. Also, the silver symbol for *Ju* that he wore as a tie tack would not go unnoticed in the automotive components industry. *Ju* stands for judo, and Mark Blyth had originally gone to Japan in 1982 because of his interest in judo.[e] He was a 4th *dan*, a level that would garner respect among enthusiasts, and the automotive components industry was full of judo enthusiasts. And if his judo connections weren't a competitive advantage, perhaps his prowess at *shogi*[f] would be. He had often found that playing *shogi* with someone gave him some insight into their character. Certainly his level of Japanese language skill was an advantage that not many foreigners enjoyed. However, he reminded himself that he had to be careful in his use of Japanese on this trip. He almost wished that Eion had not told the Japanese that he was fluent in the language. In the past, he had found it useful to keep his level of language skill hidden until late in a negotiation. This was a tactic that he had learned from the Japanese who often understood English very well but didn't show it. He understood from Naoko that the Japanese were looking forward to being able to converse with someone from SecureFit in their own language. While he felt that his language skills would improve communication with Masanobu in the longer term, it might pose a problem on this trip. Since Eion Williams did not speak Japanese it was important that all the meetings in which Eion participated were conducted through the translator. Direct communication with Mark in Japanese would take

Eion out of the loop and potentially be very confusing. Mark considered that he might revert to the rough Kobe dialect, which was characteristic of the Japanese language he first learned in western Japan. He had always feared slipping into this speech pattern when making formal presentations in Tokyo for Matsushita. However, now this ability to speak "less than perfect" Japanese when needed might be an advantage. He wondered how the executives at Masanobu would react to this tactic.

Mark was excited about the trip to Japan the next day and felt that he had prepared well. After having read the last three years of correspondence with Masanobu (and skimming five years' worth) he felt he knew the relationship fairly well. He also knew that only one of the meetings would be in Osaka with Ichikawa Kiyomitsu and that Kiyomitsu-san would retire in about three years' time. At that time, his son Torii would take over as president. Torii had a marketing background and was described by Eion as very un-Japanese. Torii had acted as Eion's translator for the past seven or eight years. At age 37, he had been promoted very rapidly through the ranks of Masanobu and was now managing director of the firm's Tokyo office. Mark understood that Torii's rapid rise had been against the wishes of the other directors and that something of a power struggle had occurred. However, with Torii's promotion to the Tokyo office, it now seemed clear that he would be the next president. Mark felt that he should use this trip as an opportunity to start building a relationship with Torii. Since he planned to stay in Japan a week longer than Eion, Mark thought he would take the opportunity to visit Torii at Masanobu's Tokyo office. This, he thought, would give the two men an opportunity to get to know each other without the restrictions imposed by the head office environment of Osaka. He might also use this time to explore other issues that interested him about SecureFit's relationship with Masanobu.

As Mark thought about what he wanted to accomplish on this trip to Japan he felt that establishing the relationship with Torii was paramount. He was no use to SecureFit if he couldn't make that relationship work. However, he also felt that he should spend a significant amount of time observing Eion Williams. After all, Eion had cracked one of the toughest markets in the world and managed to stay on top of it for seventeen years.

Mark found Eion Williams to be an intriguing man. He was especially impressed by Eion's apparent ability to control the flow of events in Japan. For example, he would send his agenda for the meetings at Masanobu on the day he left New Zealand for Japan. This, Mark thought, doesn't really give the Japanese much time to prepare. Also, from reading the transcripts of meetings he knew that Eion wouldn't allow smoking at any meeting in which he was in attendance. Mark thought this must have made many of the Japanese, who smoke like crazy, pretty nervous after a time. He also understood that Eion didn't really engage in the after hours drinking and socializing so prevalent in Japan. More importantly, Eion had often been able to say no to the Japanese on issues ranging from local manufacture of products to the timing of new product introduction. In Japan, being able to say no to a customer and make it stick was something that Mark had found to be very unusual. He had also heard, again through Naoko, that many of the Japanese were afraid to tell Eion exactly what they thought. Perhaps this was because of Eion's stature as Executive Chairman or maybe it was because Eion didn't speak Japanese. In any

case, watching how the Japanese reacted to Eion should prove educational.

Also on Mark's agenda was to investigate a number of issues which he thought might suggest the need for change in the relationship with Masanobu in the years to come. These included some changes in market conditions including the breaking down of distribution barriers, increased consumerism, and a change toward safer cars. He felt that communications with Masanobu had not in the past been adequate to keep SecureFit abreast of changes in the Japanese market, which he knew could change very quickly. He wasn't sure if Masanobu just wasn't collecting the information or if it wasn't getting back to Christchurch. In any case, he felt that communications must be improved. Also, part of that improvement in the relationship must involve more visits to New Zealand by technical staff at Masanobu. For example, there was an engineer who accounted for about a third of the faxes that SecureFit got from Japan. Mark felt certain that a visit to Christchurch could sort out some of the issues he was raising. Probably, no one at Masanobu had suggested a visit because his superior had never visited. Again, he thought, that's the kind of thing his knowledge of Japan and the Japanese could help him sort out.

Mark Blyth was confident as he prepared to return to Japan in his new capacity as Marketing Director of SecureFit. However, he also knew that there was a lot that he didn't know, couldn't know, after only four months with the firm. There are things that you just can't learn from reading the files, he thought. He also knew, through Naoko, that Masanobu had some concerns about the relationship and he wondered what those might be. Find out the problems, he thought, that's all he needed to do. After all, he wasn't taking over on this trip.

Eion Williams, who had made a practice of delegating half of his responsibilities every five years, was confident in his plan for handing over his most important responsibility, the Japanese market. He felt that his success had been due, at least in part, to the fact that he was the Executive Chairman and could make commitments that would bind the company. A salesman wouldn't be able to do that. Mark Blyth would go to Japan with the title of marketing director on his cuff and he would be responsible for that market, just as all directors of SecureFit were responsible for markets.[g] Masanobu had been aware of Eion's retirement for years so the timing of the transition would not be a surprise. Also, Mark was extremely well qualified and he certainly knew Japan and the Japanese well. One of Eion's concerns was that perhaps Mark knew Japan too well. His 11 years of servitude, as Eion thought of it, in Japan certainly had to have had an effect. Eion had never really been enamoured with the Japanese, he just respected their business ability. They knew about power relationships, but so did he, and he knew when he could say no. He wondered if Mark Blyth would be able to say no.

DISCUSSION QUESTIONS

1. How do the business practices in Japan, as described in the case, compare with those in your home country?

2. Why do you think that SecureFit Industries and its chairman, Eion Williams, have been so successful in Japan?

3. How will the management transition at SecureFit affect the relationship with their major supplier, Masanobu?

4. What will Mark Blyth have to do to maintain the business relationships in Japan? How might this differ from what Eion Williams would do?

5. How central to Mark Blyth's success is his fluency in the Japanese language? his knowledge of Japanese business practices? his engineering background?

NOTES

a. This case was prepared by David C. Thomas for classroom discussion rather than to illustrate the effective or ineffective handling of an administrative situation. The preparation of this case study was supported by a grant from the Carnegie Bosch Institute for Applied Studies in International Management. The names of individuals and companies in this case have been changed. This case study has been used with the permission of the author.

b. The giving of a gift in Japan places a burden on the other person (*on*) which is lifted when a comparable gift is returned.

c. SecureFit guarantees its products for 20 years.

d. Matsushita is a large manufacturing firm marketing products under the Panasonic and National brand names among others.

e. Mark Blyth had been captain of the New Zealand Judo team that travelled to Japan in 1982.

f. Shogi is a Japanese board game somewhat similar to chess.

g. For example, the accounts director was responsible for Malaysia and the technical director for Australia and Papua New Guinea.

APPENDICES

Patent Protection in Japan

SecureFit Industries depends on innovation to remain competitive and spends about 10% of annual sales on research and development. To protect this innovation SecureFit owns over 300 patents worldwide.

The price of this patent protection is not cheap, costing an estimated NZ$5000 per patent per country.

Two attempts at patent infringement have occurred in Japan. In the first case, one of the largest auto components companies in Japan and a large SecureFit customer, Yoshida, had approached SecureFit about developing locks, a new seatbelt mechanism. SecureFit had advised them that they would be pleased to produce the product, but that it would be six months before they could start the development program. Twelve months later SecureFit learned that the component had appeared on one of Yoshida's products which infringed SecureFit's patent. Through their patent attorneys, SecureFit advised Yoshida that they were infringing the patent and would have to cease. Toyonobu, a Tokyo manufacturer who was making the product on tooling financed by Yoshida, immediately contacted SecureFit. Toyonobu attempted to negotiate a settlement of a 2½% royalty to be paid to SecureFit. SecureFit's response was that if Toyonobu would transfer the tooling and technology to Masanobu (SecureFit's exclusive distributor in Japan) SecureFit would not sue them for damages or back royalties of 10% covering the infringing products they had produced. The matter was complicated by the fact that Yoshida, as part of the new product design, had incorporated and patented an improvement on the mechanism. After several months of negotiations Toyonobu agreed to move the tooling to Masanobu and transfer ownership of the new patent to SecureFit. In return, SecureFit (through Masanobu) would charge Yoshida a 5% royalty on the project whereas the price to all other customers would include a 10% royalty.

A second patent infringement involved an engineering company in Osaka, coincidentally also named Toyonobu but unrelated to the firm mentioned above. This Toyonobu had introduced an almost identical copy of SecureFit's largest selling product. It was made of stainless steel and differed on one small detail, unrelated to function, through which they had sought to circumvent SecureFit's patent. SecureFit was not prepared to accept this particular situation and sought an injunction from the Osaka Patent Court. It took thirteen months but SecureFit finally won and Toyonobu was required to cease manufacture. This being Japan, there were no damages, court costs or royalties awarded. In fact, Toyonobu was allowed several months to continue production while they redesigned the product.

Note: As opposed to being able to patent a single novel feature of a design, as in most parts of the world, the Japanese patent office requires that each and every aspect of a design be detailed in the application. The effect of this is that it is relatively easy for a Japanese infringer to change just one of these details to circumvent the patent. Many business people would argue that it is extremely difficult to beat a Japanese company in a Japanese court on this type of patent infringement case.

SecureFit's Fault Report System

Any fault or complaint on any part or system is recorded on a bright yellow complaint form. The intent of the form is to provide information to prevent the error from occurring again. The form is applied rigorously and the directors and the CEO review all complaint forms on a monthly basis.

SecureFit Corporate Statement

Purpose. To be the leading supplier of our products by determining customers' needs and developing products to meet those needs.

What We Value. We believe in the importance of

- Delighting our customers
- Empowering our people
- Quality and innovation
- Keeping the promises we make
- Teamwork as a way to get things done
- Making work fun
- Being fair
- Celebrating our achievement
- Being willing to take risks

Case 7

FRANK DAVIS COMES TO MADAGASCAR[A]

Antananarivo, Madagascar

Valerie VinCola

Frank Davis entered the cocktail lounge at the Madagascar Hilton Hotel, located in the nation's capital city of Antananarivo, and quickly scanned the room. Behind a cloud of cigarette smoke in the corner there was a table of boisterous French businessmen. A few other tables of two or three people were scattered throughout the lounge. Frank chose a seat at the bar next to a well-dressed white man who looked like he might be American. This was Frank's first visit to Madagascar and he wanted to get the impressions of other Americans doing business there.

"What would you like?" asked the bartender in slightly accented English.

"A beer, please. What kind do you have?" Frank asked.

"Actually the THB isn't bad. It's the local beer," offered the well-dressed gentleman next to Frank.

"Thanks. I'll try a THB," Frank told the bartender.

"Is this your first time in Madagascar?" asked the man after introducing himself as Jean-Paul, an American of French descent.

"Yes. I'm here evaluating the local business climate. I work for a U.S. food processing company, Summit Foods, that is interested in the local spice market. How about you?"

"I head up the operations of a textile company in Madagascar's free trade zone, Zone Franche. I've been here since right after the presidential election in 1993."

Frank was somewhat familiar with the recent political history based on background material he had received from the U.S. State Department. Madagascar was a former French colony that had gained independence in 1960. Since independence, there have been four presidents: Tsiranana, from 1960 to 1972, and Ratsimandrava, assassinated in 1975, were both in power during the First Republic. Then came Ratsiraka, who introduced the country to the Second Republic and socialism, but he was forced to yield to a transitional government in 1991 after a 6-month strike. In February 1993 the current president, Zafy, was elected after a popular referendum which adopted a new constitution establishing a mixed presidential-parliamentary regime. Since the late 1980s and particularly under Zafy's Third Republic, the country was

SOURCE: These materials were developed and published by the Institute of International Education and its Emerging Markets Development Advisers Program with funding from the United States Agency for International Development.

attempting to shift to a free-market economy from a centrally planned one.

"A textile company?" said Frank. "Then you must be pretty familiar with the general investment climate here. My boss is convinced there's a lot happening in this country because he has a distant relative who made a fortune here. But I haven't had a chance to look around yet, except for the ride from the airport to the hotel, and that was pretty depressing. The poverty seems to be so pervasive, and yet we passed several Mercedes and sport utility vehicles that didn't seem to be driven by foreigners. I don't get it."

Jean-Paul laughed and shrugged his shoulders. Although he was smiling, his eyes seemed to be sad. "Investment climate? Investment climate . . . Well, I guess it depends on how you define it, and how badly you want to invest. It also depends on who you know and who you are willing to pay to get things done."

Frank's eyebrows shot up. "Pay to 'get things done'? Like what things?" he thought to himself. He let Jean-Paul continue.

"The Third Republic is about 2 years old. The present administration was elected after a general strike that brought the government and the economy to a standstill. Conditions were bad, wages were low, and people got sick of socialism because it seemed to be benefiting only those in power, not the country. The new administration claims to support free-market capitalism, but according to many of my Malagasy business associates, this crew is almost as bad as the crew they voted out."

"But your company is still here. Obviously you are making money if you're still here, right?"

"Believe it or not, we're making money despite the local business climate and the Malagasy government, not because of it. Thanks to the Zone Franche, we pay no taxes on our export receipts and we can hold our profits in U.S. or French currency. Otherwise all the foreign exchange we earn would have to be directly deposited into local banks and then would be automatically converted and held in Malagasy currency. If we were not in the Zone Franche, each time we needed foreign exchange to do business outside the country, we would have to apply for it and, of course, pay a fee! Our firm is doing okay here due to the low barriers to entry in the textile industry, low labor costs, and the ability of the Malagasy work force to master new skills quickly. But you would not believe all we've gone through to get where we are now." Jean-Paul fell silent and took a long drink of his beer.

Frank was thoughtful. "This guy doesn't seem too optimistic, but he himself said he's making money. I wonder what kinds of problems he ran into."

"Don't get me wrong. This is a beautiful country and the people work incredibly hard. When I first came here after President Zafy took office, I was full of optimism and could see lots of possibilities. I've been in operations management for 20 years. I've dealt with unions, weathered the effects of the energy crisis and foreign competition on the textile industry, as well as the relocation of our company to the southeastern United States from Massachusetts, my home state. I've even helped my company locate a facility in Taiwan. But it hasn't prepared me for some of the things I've dealt with here." He smiled ruefully and pushed back his chair. "Oh, and one more thing," Jean-Paul added.

"What's that?" Frank asked, eager for more information

"Do you have an umbrella?"

"An umbrella? No. Why?" Frank asked, puzzled by the amused expression on Jean-Paul's face.

"Buy one, you'll need it. We're getting into the rainy season here, complete with cyclones. You'll see what I mean soon enough. I wish you luck."

"Cyclones!" Frank thought to himself. "Thanks," he said to Jean-Paul's back as he headed toward the door.

Frank wasn't sure whether Jean-Paul was wishing him luck with his assignment or in weathering the rainy season in Madagascar. He felt a bit discouraged, but at the same time his interest was piqued. He smelled a challenge and envisioned himself as an investment pioneer in rugged territory.

FRANK'S ASSIGNMENT

Frank Davis had been sent to Madagascar on an exploratory mission by his supervisor, Martin Herlihy, a regional vice president of a multinational food processing company, Summit Foods, based in the United States. Frank had been asked to identify potential opportunities for the company to either import agricultural products or set up a food processing operation in Madagascar. He was also asked to assess the country's general investment climate. Even if opportunities could be found, Frank's boss knew there could be several nonquantifiable costs of doing business in a developing country that could render an otherwise profitable project infeasible. Frank's foresight and good judgment had saved the company money in past expansion projects, and Martin knew Frank would be thorough in considering the many factors that could influence a potential investment. Martin was eagerly awaiting Frank's assessment of the situation.

Martin Herlihy was interested in expanding Summit Foods' product offerings to include spices. Due to the heightened health consciousness of U.S. and European consumers, spices were quickly replacing oils and heavy sauces as a natural flavor enhancer in both commercially processed and prepared-at-home foods. Given the increased numbers of dual-income families, consumers cooked at home less often than they did 20 years ago. However, they were using more volume and a greater variety of spices when they did cook at home. Ethnic cooking and ethnic restaurants were extremely popular, and that preparation required many nontraditional spices.

Madagascar was known for its spices, particularly vanilla and cloves. (See Exhibit 1.) Martin asked Frank to find out about other types of spices grown in Madagascar and their current production levels. He felt strongly that the Malagasy government would encourage export of spices because he knew that cloves and vanilla were historically the main sources of foreign currency earnings in the country (Exhibit 2).

The restaurant at the Hilton did not serve dinner for another hour and a half. Frank decided to take a walk around the neighborhood of the hotel. Although he had researched Madagascar as thoroughly as possible before he left the States, he had not found much information beyond the official reports put out by government agencies such as the State Department and the Commerce Department. He had learned that Madagascar was the world's fourth largest island with a population of 12.5 million, 1 million of whom lived in the capital, Antananarivo, where he was staying. The annual population growth rate was estimated to be 3.19%, with a fertility rate of 6.68 children per woman. In economic terms, this could mean a largely untapped consumer market if the people had disposable income to spend. But Frank was not sure how to assess that yet. The annual per capita income was about $230 but he did not know what the

| EXHIBIT 1 | Spices of Madagascar | | |

English Name	French Name	Malagasy Name	Latin Name
Spices currently exported			
Cinnamon	Cannelle	Kanela	*Cinnamonum zeylanicum*
Turmeric	Curcuma	Tamotamo	*Cucuma longa*
Ginger	Gingembre	Sakamal	*Zingiber officinale Roscoe*
Clove	Girofle	Jirofo	*Syzygium aromaticum*
Hot or chili pepper	Piment capsicum	Sakay	*Capsicum frutescens*
Black peppercorn	Poivre noir	Kipoavatra mainty	*Piper nigrum*
Green peppercorn	Poivre vert	Dioavatra maitso	*Piper nigrum*
Vanilla	Vanille	Lavanila	*Vanilla fragrans*
Spices That Have Export Potential			
Pink peppercorn	Baie rose	Voatsiperifery	*Schirus terebenthifolius*
Mace	Macis		*Myristica fragrans*
Nutmeg	Noix de muscade		*Myristica fragrans*

SOURCE: May 1994 Study of Madagascar Exports for Horticultural Products, ATW Consultants for USAID.

NOTES: Black peppercorn and green peppercorn share the same botanical name, probably because green peppercorn is a fairly new recogized plant. Mace & Nutmeg are part of the same plant, so they have the same botanical name. Apparently there are no Malagasy words for these spices. They are grown in the wild, not commercially, so perhaps they are not used in Malagasy cooking and are not known as spices there.

| EXHIBIT 2 | Exports of Nontraditional Spices From Madagascar (1993) | | | |

Customs Code	Spices	Quantity (kg)	Value FOB (1,000 FMG)[a]	Price/kg FOB[a] (1,000 FMG)[a]
090411100	Green peppercorns in brine	371,559	1,616,136	4,350
090411900	Other peppercorns, not ground	1,470,148	2,506,289	1,705
090412000	Peppercorns, ground or crushed	4,824	37,064	7,683
090420000	Chili peppers, dried or ground	20,022	96,635	4,826
090610000	Cinnamon, whole	1,169,319	1,704,081	1,457
090620000	Cinnamon, ground or crushed	46,724	86,310	1,847
090810000	Nutmeg	143	1,725	12,063
090930000	Cumin seeds	150	99	660
090950000	Fennel seeds	245	36	147
091010000	Ginger	17,461	8,682	497
091020000	Saffron	146	194	1,329
091030000	Turmeric	2,256	15,402	6,827
091040000	Thyme	48	81	1,688
091050000	Curry	232	1,518	6,543
091099000	Other spices	476	6,619	13,905
	Total	3,103,753	6,080,871	

SOURCE: State Data Bank (BDE) Antananarivo.

NOTE: Average rate of exchange in 1993: 1 U.S.$ = 1,900 FMG; 1 FF = 330 FMG. FOB, freight on board.

median income was, or what the cost of living was.

He knew Madagascar was approximately the size of Texas and rich in natural resources such as graphite, chromite, coal, bauxite, titanium, salt, quartz, and tar sands, as well as semiprecious stones. His environmentally conscious friends in the States knew that the country was home to many species and even genuses of flora and fauna that were indigenous nowhere else in the world. He also knew that there was widespread soil erosion caused by deforestation and overgrazing, and that this was contributing to desertification of the island. Several species of plant and animal life were endangered.

Frank also knew a little about the Malagasy people. Their ethnic origin was a combination of Malay-Indonesian, African, Arab, French, Indian, and Creole. The religious composition of the population was 7% Muslim, 41% Christian, and 52% indigenous beliefs. A strong emphasis on ancestor veneration characterized most spiritual belief in the country. Over 90% of the Malagasy workforce was employed in the agricultural sector, including fishing and forestry, and the major exports included coffee, vanilla, cloves, shellfish, sugar, and petroleum products. The chief industries were largely agricultural product processing (such as meat canneries, soap factories, breweries, tanneries, and sugar-refining plants) and textile factories, like the company Jean-Paul represented.

The first thing that struck Frank after leaving the grounds of the Hilton Hotel was the poor condition of the infrastructure—streets, sidewalks, and the storm drainage or sewer system (he was not quite sure what the purpose was of the little streams that ran alongside the streets)— and the absence of traffic signals. Come to think of it, he did not remember stopping at a single red light on the way from the airport. An extensive and well-maintained transportation network certainly would contribute to the success of any agriculturally based economy where the producers were geographically dispersed throughout the country.

Frank also recalled that the Madagascar airport was served almost exclusively by Air Madagascar, a state-owned enterprise. The lack of competition would likely keep the cost of freight and passenger travel high, with little incentive to improve service efficiency. Despite the poor roads and lack of traffic signals, there was certainly no shortage of cars in the capital, and almost every third car seemed to be a taxi. The air was hot and hazy, thick with car exhaust. Frank noticed several buses so full of people that the backdoors remained open and two or three people clung to the outside. Exhibit 3 captures a few of the sights that caught his eye along the way.

As he continued down the street, Frank was approached by several people selling a variety of items which they pushed at him: handicrafts, Ray Ban sunglasses, brooms, tire irons, a basketball, and some fruits or vegetables he did not recognize. *"Non, merci,"* he said over and over again, but they continued to walk alongside him displaying their wares.

"Bon marché! Combien, Monsieur?" They were ready to bargain but Frank had no money and no need for a tire iron in Madagascar. He began to feel annoyed and a bit overwhelmed by the entourage of vendors. He decided to turn back after another several minutes of sales pitches in French and another language which he assumed was Malagasy. It occurred to him that he needed to change his money at the hotel before dinner anyway. As he came closer to the hotel, he was approached by a barefooted little boy in dirty rags carrying a baby on his back. "That boy can't be any more than 5 years old," Frank thought, shocked by the sight. "And the

EXHIBIT 3   **Scenes of Madagascar**

Buildings fill the hillsides
around downtown
Antananarivo

A street vendor displays local produce in the market

baby isn't even old enough to walk. Where are the parents?"

"*Monsieur, donnez-moi la monnaie? Donnez-moi la monnaie?*" the boy begged, thrusting his little hand forward. His big brown eyes implored Frank to give him some spare change. His face was dirty and his nose runny. Frank was torn inside but looked away and walked quickly back to the hotel, just as the sky was turning dark and threatening rain. Frank reminded himself to buy an umbrella as he took refuge in the air-conditioned lobby from both the rain and the pitiful scene he had confronted outside. He headed for the cashier to change his money.

THE FLOTTEMENT

The exchange rate was just under 4,000 Malagasy francs (FMG) to a dollar. Frank recalled that when he left the United States 2 days before, the rate was about 3,600 FMGs. "Could the rate have changed that much in 3 days?" Frank asked himself. Then he recalled what he had read about the monetary system. In May 1994, the FMG moved from a fixed exchange rate system to a floating exchange rate. The FMG was untied from the French franc (FF) to fluctuate on its own against hard currencies, but the FF remained the main currency of reference. This step to liberalize the Malagasy currency was referred to as the flottement, and was required by the International Monetary Fund (IMF) in fulfillment of a planned structural adjustment program. As a result of the flottement, the FMG lost about half of its value almost overnight, setting off wide-scale price increases. Because of the weak economy, Madagascar's currency was weak. It had consistently lost value relative to hard currencies since the flottement was instituted.

"Do you need to stamp this?" Frank pushed a small currency declaration form across the counter to the cashier. He had been given the form by the stewardess on his flight into Madagascar and told to declare all his currency, traveler's checks, credit card account numbers, and personal checks. The paper was barely large enough to contain all the information requested, but Frank

complied. He did not want to be unnecessarily detained for not following procedures when he left the country. His tour book had warned him that airport officials would ask him how much he spent in the country and whether he was taking any Malagasy money outside the country with him.

"I'm sorry sir, we don't have a stamp. Only the banks stamp the form if you change money there," the cashier informed him.

"But aren't I required by law to have a stamp? How can the hotel exchange money for me but not stamp my form? I'm not sure I understand." Frank was genuinely puzzled.

"If you want your form stamped, you must go to a bank. But the banks are closed until Monday. If you want to exchange your money here, I'll give you a receipt, but I don't have a stamp. Do you want to change it here?"

Frank hesitated. He wanted to follow the rules but he did not quite understand them, and the cashier did not really clarify it for him. He needed the money now and the banks were closed. Was he expected to wait two days to exchange his money, or would he have to explain his predicament to the airport officials and risk being detained at the airport? He finally decided to exchange only as much money as he thought he would need for the weekend, and hope it would not be an issue later. He did not see any other option.

"For a country that is badly in need of foreign exchange, they certainly make it difficult to convert your money," he thought to himself as he left the counter.

GOVERNMENT APPROVALS

Frank entered the dining room and was seated promptly at a corner table set for one. A short time later Jean-Paul poked his head inside the restaurant and, seeing Frank, waved and approached his table.

"Mind if I join you?" he asked.

"Not at all." Frank gestured towards a chair, "Please, have a seat."

"How are you doing? I barely missed getting caught in the torrential downpour. It's coming down pretty hard out there."

Both men stared out the window at the pouring rain. The sky was dark and ominous. It was hard to believe that just 45 min ago the sun had been shining brightly with barely a cloud in the sky.

After giving their dinner orders to the waiter, Frank decided to broach the topic of Madagascar's investment climate again with Jean-Paul. He felt that although Jean-Paul seemed a bit cynical, there was probably a lot he could learn from his experiences. He planned to try to schedule appointments at the Ministry of Commerce, Ministry of Industry, Energy and Mining, and Ministry of Transport, Meteorology and Tourism during his 1-month visit. He felt that an initial discussion with Jean-Paul would help him put things into a context and develop some meaningful questions for his interviews with the various Ministers.

"So Jean-Paul, I'm interested in hearing more about your experiences in Madagascar, if you don't mind sharing them with me. Tell me about some of the obstacles or problems your company encountered when trying to set up a facility," Frank asked.

"Well, the first thing any company interested in setting up business in Madagascar needs is an *agrèment*, or official approval of the government. The hard part is deciding who to approach to obtain this approval, and how to present your business proposal. You need some type of approval from every ministry which has jurisdiction over any part of your business. For example, in our case, we needed the okay of seven ministries, and each ministry has a set of questions that must be answered and documents

that must be filed. Some ministries asked for the same information, others asked for information which seemed irrelevant or outside their jurisdiction. One ministry lost our dossier, but didn't bother to inform us—and maybe they didn't realize themselves—until we called to inquire about the status of the approval 2 months after submitting everything. The amount of red tape here is mind-boggling."

"Is there some sort of checklist or description of the type of documentation required? I mean, do they want a full-blown business plan? A letter from your financial institution? What do they base approval on?" Frank asked, trying to get a clearer picture of what the Malagasy government would request.

"That's just the problem. No one seems to know. It changes from ministry to ministry, day to day. To the first ministry we approached we gave every piece of documentation we thought they could possibly use. I figured that if I was forthcoming with information and demonstrated a serious willingness to do business in Madagascar, the review process would be shorter because they didn't have to keep asking for additional information. I even gave them the names and resumes of the managers we intended to bring in to manage the new facility," explained Jean-Paul.

"That seems like a reasonable approach. Did it help expedite things?" Frank asked.

"Expedite? That's not quite the word I would use. Try *mora mora*," responded Jean-Paul. "It means slowly, slowly in Malagasy—and is often used to describe the 'Malagasy way,'" he grinned. "That first ministry was the ministry that lost it all. Or at least that's what they told us after 2 months."

Jean-Paul went on to explain that there seemed to be a great deal of overlap between the ministries, and even conflicting information about what types of business activities are encouraged. The laws of one ministry were often superseded by proclamations, decrees, and statutes of that ministry or a different one. There was also a lack of communication between ministries, and Jean-Paul got the feeling there were little rivalries and power plays among the ministries.

"Reasons for denial or disapproval are not given, so it's difficult to address their concerns and try again. I heard from a friend that he knew someone who was denied an *agrément* because they wouldn't offer an interest in their project to people high up in the ministry."

"It sounds like there's a problem with administrative efficiency and consistency. But you could probably find that sort of problem in any large organization in any country, really," Frank remarked.

"That may be true. But if you want to do business in this country and save yourself a lot of time and trouble, I'd suggest you find yourself an influential partner who is highly placed in the government."

The waiter arrived with their dinner. As he laid the plate down in front of Frank, the lights went out and the music stopped. The waiter immediately lit the candle on the table as other waiters circulated around the dining room to light those at other tables.

"Bon appetit!" the waiter said to the two men, as he walked back toward the dark kitchen. Dumbstruck, Frank watched the hotel employees for a few minutes waiting to see if someone would take control of the situation and explain to the customers what was going on. Jean-Paul and many of the other diners began eating as if nothing was awry.

"If you're waiting until the lights come back on to eat your dinner, it'll probably be cold. You might as well eat. The power will come back on eventually. It goes out just about every time there's a big rain.

During the rainy season, that could mean at least once a day."

Frank was surprised. Frequent power outages could obviously cause problems with production schedules and delivery dates. And what about information management? Companies which were highly dependent on data must have to take special precautions to safeguard it. Frank made a mental note to find out what provisions were made for back-up power sources, if any.

"What other types of problems have you dealt with?" Frank asked.

"The property rights laws," Jean-Paul answered. "It's been the policy of our company to purchase land and do the construction ourselves, to very exacting specifications. We have built two factories in other countries in the recent past and have found the best layout and configuration for our machinery and assembly lines. So we prefer to build from scratch rather than lease. But, as you may know, foreigners cannot own land in Madagascar. This posed a problem for us, and frankly our CEO took this to be a signal of distrust by the government."

Frank was not aware of this prohibition against foreign ownership of land. Jean-Paul went on to explain that the Malagasy culture considered the land to be sacred. He had even heard a man once say that to the Malagasy, the land is like their body. It was passed down through the generations from the ancestors, and the fact that Madagascar was an island nation probably contributed to their beliefs. Jean-Paul explained that many people get around this law by using Malagasy partners, but that this arrangement can be extremely costly and risky because the foreigner is beholden to the Malagasy. If there is ever a dispute or the relationship deteriorates, the foreigner has questionable legal recourse.

Jean-Paul's company solved the problem by leasing the land under a 99-year lease and constructing a building that would revert to the property owner at the end of the lease term. The rent was paid in foreign currency because of the high inflation rate. This eliminated the need to have the rents adjusted monthly as the value of the Malagasy franc declined.

"Is that legal? It seems like the government keeps very close tabs on the exchange of foreign currency," Frank remarked. Jean-Paul shrugged.

VISITS TO ASSESS THE POTENTIAL FOR EXPORTING SPICES

Over the next several days, Frank tried to make appointments to speak with government officials, agricultural membership organizations, food processors, exporters, and anyone else who he thought would have valuable information about the export potential for nontraditional spices. At the Ministry of Agriculture he hoped to obtain national production statistics but soon learned that the information available was inaccurate, outdated, and incomplete. He also found out that the centralized or geographically concentrated cultivation of spices was declining in Madagascar, as the plantations once run by the French were either abandoned or extremely rundown. Some spices were grown wild and harvested by independent peasants, so yields varied from year to year. Many plants from the large plantations had succumbed to disease, and those that grew wild often were damaged by severe weather and by the rampant deforestation taking place on the island, because they were not grown in a self-contained and protected area. The wide dispersion of spices also could pose a problem for processors, as the roads and communication infrastructure were almost nonexistent in many rural areas.

On the positive side, Frank was heartened to find out that spices were not restricted export products. Initially, he feared that they might be classified as protected flora, and therefore could not be exported except by special permit due to environmental regulations. Frank did have some concerns about the quality grade of the spices and whether it was comparable to those on the world market. He found out that there were government standards, set by the Ministry of Commerce, for most types of spices. However, these standards pertained to physical characteristics, such as the length and width of the vanilla bean, rather than the quality, growing and harvesting conditions. The majority of spices grown in Madagascar were exported, with 80% going to Europe. (See Exhibit 4.) Frank hoped that boded well for the U.S. market, and that the Malagasy spices would meet U.S. standards, which are typically the highest on the world market. He thought the products of the island would stand up well against those produced in other countries (Exhibit 5).

MEETING A MALAGASY BUSINESSMAN

Frank set up a meeting with the proprietor of a Malagasy spice-processing company to learn more about the organization of spice production in Madagascar, and to gauge preliminary receptivity to the idea of forming a partnership with Summit Foods. He hoped to gain a better understanding of how the agricultural sector functioned, and what types of concerns Malagasy operators may have about working with an American importer.

Frank was early for his 2:00 p.m. appointment despite the traffic jam caused by market day in Antananarivo. He was

| EXHIBIT 4 | Countries of Destination for Exports of Nontraditional Spices From Madagascar |

Country	Quantity (kg)	Percentage	Value FOB (1,000 FMG)	Percentage
France	1,096,803	35	1,971,797	32
Germany	469,833	15	1,088,027	18
Great Britain	471,346	15	721,459	12
Belgium	149,473	5	583,252	10
The Netherlands	367,213	12	568,748	9
Soviet Reunion	68,557	2	171,382	3
Spain	87,221	3	162,850	3
South Africa	73,036	2	146,562	2
Poland	83,515	3	130,993	2
Italy	32,268	1	114,219	2
Soviet Union	12,500	0	97,170	2
Singapore	53,850	2	79,017	1
Tunisia	36,050	1	53,921	1
Nigeria	25,000	1	51,447	1
Niger	24,000	1	33,557	1
Denmark	3,730	0	28,963	0
Egypt	18,000	1	25,366	0
Comoros	22,627	1	17,536	0
Ghana	6,462	0	15,386	0
Sweden	1,259	0	7,804	0
Switzerland	300	0	4,899	0
United States	297	0	3,448	0
Austria	360	0	3,047	0
Mauritius	50	0	16	0
Malta	2	0	4	0
Monaco	1	0	1	0
Total	3,103,753	100	6,080,871	100

SOURCE: State Data Bank (BDE) Antananarivo.

NOTE: Ranked by value of freight on board (FOB), 1993. Average rates of exchange in 1993: 1 FF = 330 FMG; 1 U.S.$ = 1,900 FMG; 1 ECU = 2,200 FMG.

offered a seat in a crowded office where five employees appeared to share one telephone and one typewriter. He noticed the office workers used and reused sheets of carbon paper to make copies of their work. At 2:15 p.m., Frank asked if Mr. Rakotomanana knew he was here. The workers exchanged glances and one of them told him he should be back shortly. Frank figured he may be tied up in traffic somewhere. All of the meetings he had attended so far had begun at least 20 min late. The Malagasy took lunch from noon until 2:00 p.m., and many returned home for the noon meal with their family.

At 2:55 p.m., Mr. Rakotomanana arrived. Frank was slightly annoyed because he realized he would probably miss his next meeting, scheduled for 3:30 p.m. He asked if he could use the phone

| EXHIBIT 5 | Alternative Sources of Supply for Spices | | |

Spices	Origin	Unit	Price
Cinnamon			
Sticks	Madagascar	kg	
Pieces	Madagascar	kg	5.75–6 FF
Ground	Madagascar	kg	11–12 FF
Mace	Indonesia	ton	U.S.$2,375
	Nouvelle Guinée		
Chili pepper	Togo	kg	18–25 FF
	Central Africa		
	Republic of China		
	Madagascar	kg	35–60 FF
	Martinique	kg	35–100 FF
	Morocco	kg	8–10 FF
Peppercorn			
I. White	Sarawak	ton	U.S.$1,525–3,750
	Sarawak DW	ton	U.S.$1,525–3,750
	Muntok	ton	U.S.$1,525–3,750
	Brazil	ton	U.S.$1,900–3,300
II. Black	Lampong	ton	U.S.$1,050–1,895
	Sarawak	ton	U.S.$1,000–1,835
	Brazil	ton	U.S.$1,000–1,700
	Madagascar	ton	U.S.$1,050–1,700
Ginger	Brazil	kg	9–22 FF
	Thailand	kg	12–19 FF
Chili pepper, green	Morocco	kg	6–10 FF
	Madagascar	kg	30–60 FF
	Martinique	kg	30–100 FF

SOURCE: Marchés Tropicaux et Mediterranéens, 1993.

NOTE: Sales prices include cost, insurance, and freight.

briefly to call his next appointment. On his first few tries, there was no dial tone. One of the office workers volunteered to try calling for him so the meeting could begin.

After explaining who he was and Summit Foods' interest in spices, Frank spoke about his stay so far in Madagascar and asked for some recommendations about what tourist destinations he should visit. They discussed the weather, the local street market, and the traffic, and Frank complimented Mr. Rakotomanana on his efficient staff. Frank was interested in touring Mr. Rakotomanana's processing plant but he did not yet feel comfortable asking to do so. Mr. Rakotomanana's manner was friendly, but still quite formal. Frank finally described in detail the techniques and processes used by Summit Foods, and asked Mr. Rakotomanana some basic questions about his operations. It was about 4:00 p.m. when Mr. Rakotomanana offered to take Frank on a tour.

The tour was brief, but Frank was impressed by how much they were able to produce in such a small space with the unso-phisticated equipment they used. He almost felt as though he were in a time warp. Many of the processes they used had been used in the United States in the 1940s and 1950s. Frank then asked some questions about the company's current customers and pro-cessing capacity: "You mentioned that your customers are all domestic. What is your current production capacity?"

"Yes. We like to produce for the Malagasy market. I cannot say for certain because our capacity depends on our customers. During harvest season, we hire temporary workers and they work longer hours until the work is finished," Mr. Rakotomanana explained.

"Are you interested in possibly produc-ing for export as well?"

"Yes."

"Do you have the capacity to produce large quantities over a sustained period of time, for a large export customer such as Summit Foods, for example?"

"Yes. Of course." Mr. Rakotomanana seemed very definitive about that.

"Or would it be necessary to expand your operations, perhaps with the assistance of a partner like my company, through some sort of partnership agreement, to ensure you could meet demand?" Frank offered.

"Yes. I think that would be interest-ing," Mr. Rakotomanana eagerly replied.

"And your company would be willing to share in the capital expenses of such an expansion, if it were needed?"

Mr. Rakotomanana hesitated, and did not look back up at Frank. "I cannot say. This must be discussed with my family."

"Of course. I understand. I am only exploring the possibilities at this point. Do you think you might be interested in dis-cussing this further at a later date?" Frank asked hopefully. He did not want to push too hard, but wanted to get a clearer

indication of what this processor could do for Summit Foods, and on what terms.

"Yes. I think it would be interesting."

"I am leaving in about 3 weeks. Would you like to set up a meeting next week, after you have a chance to discuss things with your family?"

"Oh, yes."

"When would be convenient for us to get together again?" Frank inquired. He was beginning to feel his approach may be too aggressive.

"I must talk with my family."

"Can you call me at the hotel, or should I phone you later to set up a meeting?" Frank at least wanted a definitive next step, since setting up the meeting had been so difficult to begin with.

"Yes."

Frank wasn't sure which question Mr. Rakotomanana was responding to.

"You can call me at the Madagascar Hilton?"

"Oh, yes."

"Or would you prefer that I call you?" Frank felt he might have a better chance of solidifying plans if he called Mr. Rakotomanana because he had already scheduled several meetings outside the hotel the next week.

"Oh, yes. I think that would be very interesting." The men shook hands and Frank departed.

As he left the building Frank thought to himself, "He certainly was an amiable guy, but a bit hard to read. Was he being realistic about his company's capabilities? He almost seemed too accommodating." Frank was not sure how well the meeting had gone.

ASSESSING THE CREDIT MARKET

Frank ran into Jean-Paul at the Hilton on his way into the dining room, so they decided to have a drink together before dinner. Frank wanted to know about the commercial loans market in Madagascar. If he were able to set up a partnership agreement or close a long-term deal with a Malagasy processor, the processor would most certainly need to expand in order to handle Summit Foods' business. Frank preferred to deal with one or two large suppliers rather than dozens of smaller ones, and he was fairly certain there were few, if any, with enough production capacity to take on a customer such as Summit Foods while continuing to serve their current customer base.

"What can you tell me about the credit situation here?" Frank asked. "I know the national government is far outspending its receipts and I'm sure that affects the availability of credit here. Did your company finance anything locally?"

"The banks here are extremely risk averse. Even so, they still have many nonperforming loans in their portfolio. We didn't need to use any local banks for financing but we use a Mauritian-owned bank for our accounts payable and our payroll because we don't have a lot of faith in the local banking institutions. Two of the five banks are still partially owned by the Malagasy government, although they're in the process of privatizing. Until that happens, we'll stick with Union Commercial Bank."

Jean-Paul went on to explain that the prime rate was set by the Banque Centrale, which serves much the same purpose as the Federal Reserve Bank in the United States. The five commercial banks then set their rates accordingly.

"Just out of curiosity, what is the current rate to commercial borrowers?" Frank asked.

"Twenty-three percent," Jean-Paul answered, grinning. "No, really." Frank laughed.

"I'm dead serious, Frank. And they require a 50% guarantee."

"A guarantee? What do you mean? How does that work?"

Jean-Paul explained that a borrower must deposit 50% of the total amount of the loan in the bank, or commit some other type of collateral that is acceptable to the bank.

Frank was incredulous. "That's crazy. If you had the money to begin with, you obviously wouldn't need the loan."

Jean-Paul shrugged. He went on to explain that banks and other funding institutions depended a great deal on a borrower's reputation through word of mouth. There are no formal credit bureaus in Madagascar. Knowing the "right" people was essential.

Frank now understood the capital constraints firms like Mr. Rakotomanana's were facing. After Frank described his earlier conversation with Mr. Rakotomanana, Jean-Paul explained the concept of *fihavanana*, or family harmony, which was central to Malagasy culture. "It is a critical decision-making factor in all family decisions. Preserving the *fihavanana* is of great importance in this culture, and it often leads to 'uneconomic' business decisions. You are not dealing with what economic theory traditionally refers to as 'rational actors.' What makes perfect business sense to you may not even be a consideration to your Malagasy colleague."

Jean-Paul had another appointment, so Frank ate alone that night. Over dinner he considered what he had learned about doing business in Madagascar during his first week, and what additional information he would need before he left the country in 3 weeks. He was scheduled to receive a call from Martin Herlihy tomorrow morning to give him a progress report.

Madagascar was 8 hr ahead of the United States, so Martin would likely be calling around 6:00 a.m. local time. Frank wanted to think through the pros and cons tonight so he would be clear headed tomorrow morning when the call came through. He knew Martin would be interested in "the numbers," but there were so many other nonquantifiable factors that warranted as much if not more consideration than the numbers. He was not even at the stage where he could discuss production volume, profit margins, and freight costs. Frank was not sure how to present what he learned thus far because, since Martin had not visited the country, he would not easily grasp the business environment nor see both the potential opportunities and obstacles to doing business in a developing country such as Madagascar.

NOTE

a. This case was written by Valerie VinCola of Emory University under the supervision of Professor Richard Linowes of American University in Washington, DC. It is intended as a basis for class discussion rather than to illustrate either effective or ineffective handling of an administrative situation.

Case 8

CULTURE CLASH

Do International Buyouts Always Make Sense?

G. Oddou

MATT

We were back in Japan about two months and I still hadn't heard from any of my contacts. I had written them all to thank them for their time and to follow up on any potential interest. Having learned by now that Asians in general seem to prefer face-to-face communication, I wasn't totally surprised that I didn't hear from any of them. I didn't take it as a personal affront; rather, I figured it was just a difference in culture—and maybe a little lack of interest too. It might have reflected their preoccupation at the time.

In any case, the Japanese medical supplies market was blossoming fairly well despite problems in other areas of the economy. Sales had been increasing steadily for the last 16 months, averaging about a 10 percent monthly increase. We were clearly a success. I had to hand it to Muhashi. They knew what they were doing. Of course, MedTech wasn't too bad either. The quality rate had increased to about a half percent rejection rate across all the surgical instruments. Although Japan was by far MedTech's largest market to date, business was starting to pick up in the United States and we picked up hints of activity in Europe as well. In the seven months, I had made several trips back to California to help with the marketing strategy. Carl had picked up his responsibilities fairly well, but Jeff and I both thought he needed to show more leadership.

Eventually, we hired a fairly experienced marketing person away from a company one of the investors had helped fund about ten years earlier. Marc Morgan was really sharp and had some good contacts. We initially hired him on a contract basis with the explicit understanding that it would change to a full-time permanent position as soon as I returned from Japan. The logic there was that as long as no "permanent" person was hired in my place, it appeared to the Japanese that the need for me to return was still there.

One of Marc's contacts turned out to be a true gem. He eventually helped us distribute to several of the hospitals in the West owned by American Hospital Corporation.

The best contact in Europe was with a German company, Oberfeldt AG, that distributed pharmaceutical products for most

SOURCE: From *Managing internationally: A personal journey* (1st ed.) by G. Oddou. © 1999. Reprinted with permission of South-Western, a division of Thomson Learning: www.thomsonrights.com. Fax 800-730-2215.

of the largest pharmaceutical firms in Germany and some in Switzerland. Unfortunately for us, though, Oberfeldt AG was beginning to change its overall business strategy to one of acquisitions instead of just distribution. They were seeking to vertically integrate as much as possible. A new management team had come aboard Oberfeldt AG, and as the European Community became more a reality, it began to take a very aggressive stance toward what might help it be more profitable. It was in search of small firms with these four qualifications: they had already shown some success, their products had potential worldwide appeal, there was currently little to no competition in Europe, and the investment price was fairly low.

Of the four criteria, the lack of competition in Europe was an important one. Oberfeldt AG was not ready to invest capital to build a production plant in Europe if that were required. But it was fearful that if there were stiff competition in one of the EC members, particularly France, there would be a lot of pressure to stop imports or make it cost prohibitive to import the products. France, in particular, was very protective over any of its industries and generally unwilling to open itself to the possibility that a foreign firm, outside the EC, might have a clear market advantage.

Oberfeldt AG became very interested in MedTech. And although MedTech was starting to do very well and showed promise, the current investors were not necessarily interested in MedTech's long-term growth potential. As Jeff and I found out, they were more interested in getting a start-up going, attracting the interest of a larger company, selling out and making a lot of money, and then moving on to the next start-up. It seemed like the ultimate business rape to us. But there wasn't much we

could do. Jeff's position on the board didn't make any difference. The investors wanted out and Oberfeldt AG was knocking at the door and ready to pay handsomely. So what initially looked like a friendly business relationship—us as the suppliers and Oberfeldt as the distributors—was turning out to be a takeover—a hostile one to several of us at MedTech.

After some short-lived negotiations, the investors sold MedTech for a handsome price. That began the next phase of "development," as I call it. A buyout usually makes life crazy for a while and it did for us too. It did leave Jeff and me in our places, though, guaranteed for at least one year according to the terms of the agreement. The investors did that much at least.

It was harder on Jeff than me, though, in one sense. He had to deal with the Germans directly. I was thousands of miles away on my own and didn't have much direct contact with them except for the visits and a few faxes. When Oberfeldt AG first purchased MedTech, Dr. Bergman became Jeff's overseer. He was senior operations officer, a former senior scientist at Oberfeldt AG before they became primarily a distribution business. After the acquisition, for the first several months, Dr. Bergman was in California about half the time and Germany half of the time. He didn't waste a lot of time setting up various policies and procedures to bring what he called "some order and uniformity" to MedTech. A clear organizational chart—the first MedTech employees had seen—was developed and posted.

Part of his concern was standardizing certain procedures to increase the compatibility between MedTech and Oberfeldt AG. I'm not so sure compatibility should have been the goal or at least that their definition of what made us compatible was appropriate. It was obvious that

Dr. Bergman felt MedTech was too loosely run. Employees called Jeff by his first name, which wasn't very acceptable. Employees also often walked right into Jeff's office without an appointment, even sometimes when Bergman was with Jeff, which didn't go over very well either.

"How can you plan your time and follow your agenda with unexpected interruptions like that?" he would ask Jeff.

Jeff would tell him, "That's the way we've always operated and it has worked fine. When there's a problem, we do what we need to do to solve it. We go straight to the horse, and doors are always open."

Bergman countered, "But businesses are not farms. People are not horses. Horses are allowed to roam where they want. That is not very efficient for a business. In Germany, we are very efficient at solving problems also. And it is not difficult to talk directly to a manager, but some of the questions your employees ask you, one of your managers should be able to answer. They should not come to you. And if it is important, you might think about setting time aside during the day just for those kinds of calls. In addition, it seems when your employees are not asking you questions, they're often telling you things that could easily be put in a memo, which you could read at a time you have set aside for such communications." And then he added, "Having clear procedures and policies—and following them strictly—is Oberfeldt AG's way of preventing problems from occurring in the first place. It is necessary for the fine-tune functioning of any organization."

Jeff told me he didn't disagree that Oberfeldt AG was probably very efficient. They had two slightly different approaches is all: one method that Jeff liked and was used to and the Oberfeldt AG method. Oberfeldt AG didn't stop with their tinkering with just

the internal workings of the firm. They felt all Oberfeldt AG operations worldwide should be standardized in every way possible. This even included changing the dress and other habits MedTech employees had become accustomed to. Management started having to wear white shirts and ties. Staff had to dress "professionally" also. There were no more Friday "dress-down" days or late afternoon get-togethers with the entire company personnel.

"It is important to look professional at all times, especially when customers visit, and company time can be put to better use than socializing Friday afternoons," Dr. Bergman told Jeff.

Even the parking lot took on a slightly different face. Pre-Oberfeldt AG, parking was a first come, first served situation. Now there were designated spots for Dr. Bergman and an assistant of his, Karl Schmidt, who would often accompany him, for Jeff, and for the rest of upper management. They were the closest parking spots to the building entrance, of course. It really didn't change a whole lot because Jeff and the other management team were usually the first ones to arrive anyway. But this arrangement clarified any ambiguity about hierarchy.

As you can imagine, Jeff didn't accept the changes very well. We knew any buyout regardless of whether it was foreign or domestic would mean changes, and usually not for the good of the employees. Restructuring the hierarchy, the policies, and sometimes redefining the strategies were all part of the game. That was Oberfeldt AG's choice to make. Our choice was to decide whether we liked the changes or not. The bottom line for us was the changes weren't consistent with us, and we, especially Jeff, felt we were letting our employees down. Despite Jeff's efforts to explain and suggest policy, Oberfeldt

AG seemed bent on doing things their way. I can understand that, but the time comes when sometimes the "locals" know best. If MedTech were in Germany with German employees, everything probably would have been okay, but we were in the United States, California no less.

Within six months, the production manager was gone, as was the CFO. Both had been on board since MedTech's beginning. Jeff hung on as long as he could bear it, but he, too, left after another couple of months. We talked quite a while about his leaving and what that would mean for the company. Neither of us felt it was a good move for MedTech, but neither of us felt there was much choice either. When you start a company and employees have sacrificed some home life and personal recreation to put in the extra hours and sweat it takes to start a company, you feel some genuine loyalty there. Now Jeff felt as though he could no longer give something back to the employees. Oberfeldt seemed bound and determined to limit his influence to the point that it almost seemed like it didn't matter who was CEO. Everything was supposed to run according to Oberfeldt guidelines.

Before Jeff left, he asked me whether I would be interested in the position in case he were allowed to make any recommendations. The idea of being CEO was exciting—big leather chair, intercom, personal secretary, big bucks—yeah, those were the perks, just about everything Jeff didn't have! That was the image. The reality would be much different.

Question: If you were Matt, would you accept the CEO position if offered it? Why or why not?

I told Jeff that under these circumstances there was no way I wanted to take

his job, which is what he expected anyway. It turned out it wouldn't have made much difference, anyway. Bergman put his assistant, Karl Schmidt, in at the helm, which we figured was probably the plan all along. Micromanage the entrepreneurial management team until they decide to leave and then put your own people in. If that was the plan, it was working.

Jeff became CEO of a small start-up firm that one of the investors of MedTech had helped fund. That kind of thing is often done if you maintain a good reputation in the industry. Jeff seemed happy about the new position but had real regrets leaving MedTech before it had really and truly turned the corner and gone public. Going public was the big milestone for a lot of people with start-ups. That's where the real feeling of accomplishment came in (and the real money was made).

As for my situation, the visits to Tokyo became a little more frequent now that Jeff was gone. Bergman and Karl had already come and met all the Japanese connected to the partnership. They had looked over the operation and seemed satisfied in most respects. The last couple of visits were a little more serious, though. I think they both questioned whether I was needed there, and they made some hints about reevaluating the situation. By now it really didn't matter to me because mentally and emotionally I was already somewhat gone. Jan and I had already decided to return to the States as soon as either one of us could find a good job.

DISCUSSION QUESTIONS

1. What are the differences you notice between the Oberfeldt AG "way"

and the "MedTech" way? Does MedTech represent the U.S. way?

2. Do you think buying MedTech represents a wise acquisition for Oberfeldt AG? Why or why not? Would there probably be a good fit if Oberfeldt AG were to acquire a typical small firm reflecting your culture (if different from the United States)? In what areas?

REFERENCE

1. G. Oddou & C. B. Derr (1999). *Managing internationally: A personal journey* (pp. 133–137). Orlando, FL: Harcourt Brace.

Case 9

BILL KEANE

John Barnett

Keane faced three issues in managerial and personal ethics during his assignment as managing director and chairman of Szabo Diamond Company, S.A. Before describing the incidents and issues of these three ethical decisions, Bill and Szabo Diamond are described.

BILL KEANE

Bill was born in New York. His parents both worked in the business his father owned, and the family was upper middle class. Bill attended Lawrenceville School and studied government at Williams College. Following military service in the Army Signal Corps, Bill completed his studies at Williams. He became active in mountain climbing, an activity he still pursues.

Bill earned his M.B.A. from Stanford University. His initial job was with an international consulting firm. One of his first assignments was with Lyon, Churchman and Associates, West Coast importers of diamonds. After 9 months of this consulting effort, Bill joined the diamond operations of Lyon, Churchman and Associates in Los Angeles. He also was married during this period.

The wholesale distribution of diamonds is significantly controlled by DeBeers. The digging, processing, and exporting of diamonds is somewhat more open, although increasingly less so as one moves toward the wholesale customer through the DeBeers distribution system. Nonetheless, occasional opportunities arise, and Bill found himself undertaking various assignments in Brazil, Zaire, Australia, and Indonesia.

SZABO

After a couple of years, Bill became the managing director and chairman of Szabo Diamonds. Szabo, on the northeast coast of South America, became a sovereign state within the British Commonwealth, and became a republic in 1978. Its capital, Luna, then had a population of 280,000 and the country a population of 3,200,000.

Diamonds were first discovered in Szabo in the early 1930s by prospectors from the Consolidated Minerals Trust (CMT). CMT subsequently formed Szabo Trust (ST) Limited in the mid-1930s and ST negotiated a series of agreements with the government in which ST paid the government a percentage of net profits and a mineral rent in exchange for a monopoly in the mining and exportation of diamonds. The Universal Diamond Corporation (UNDICO) participated in diamond exporting and, in various ways, in CMT and ST. UNDICO sorted, graded, and marketed diamonds.

One way for the outsider to enter the diamond industry is as a diamond processor. A local Szabo processing company offered several things. First, to the outsider, it might be the only means of entry into the diamond fraternity, although one would also have to ensure a source of supply by making CMT/ST and the government of Szabo partners. Second, the processing stage would be a further means of controlling smuggling, a rampant problem throughout many stages of the diamond business. Toward this end, the Szabo government should clearly be made a partner. Thus, Szabo Diamonds, S.A.—a partnership of international interests and the Szabo government with Lyon, Churchman and Associates (LCA) as the managing partner—opened and operated a diamond-processing factory in Szabo as a foothold toward securing a portion of the overall exportation of diamonds or other natural resource development projects.

LCA made the Szabo government an interest-free long-term loan, which the Szabo government used to acquire a majority interest in Szabo Diamonds, S.A. Factory operations and all managerial decisions were controlled by LCA for a fee. Bill oversaw all the financial controls of Szabo Diamond. He stayed out of day-to-day factory operations, which were supervised by an English factory manager.

DECISION ONE

Bill's first ethical decision came in his early weeks in Szabo. Part of his duties included calling on all the government ministers connected with mining and exporting. LCA made contributions to schools and hospitals, which could be the reason for a visit to a minister or to the premier. Friendship with the ministers, partially based on mutual favors, was most helpful in both the short and the long terms. LCA wanted Bill to have considerable influence with the government of Szabo.

During his second visit to a particularly important government minister, after polite conversation about Bill's new home, tennis, and the weather, the minister said: "I have a large, 60-carat yellow diamond. On one of your trips, would you be interested in taking this out of the country for me for a fee?"

DECISION TWO

In New York, Szabo Diamond Company had hired an excellent manager, Manuel Ramon, a native of Szabo. He was the number two manager in Szabo, reporting directly to Bill Keane, who was most impressed with Manuel Ramon's ability. Bill and Manuel Ramon came to Szabo together in 1981 after both had undertaken international assignments for LCA. As typically was done by companies hiring expatriate managers, Szabo Diamond leased a local residence for use by Bill Keane and another for use by Manuel Ramon.

The political situation in Szabo was active. Occasionally, a group of politicians in and/or out of the government would put together a leadership alternative and would try to convince some of the army and others to help them overturn the existing government. While the current premier had kept control for almost a decade, there nevertheless were ongoing coalitions and plans for a coup d'etat surfacing every 2 or 3 years.

A year after Bill got to Szabo, rumors of a plot to overthrow the premier began to circulate in Luna. In the same year, Manuel Ramon's brother, Jose, who had been living outside Szabo while undertaking an assignment for the World Health Organization, returned to Szabo and to Luna. As often was done with the extended families within Szabo, Jose and his family moved into the house occupied by Manuel Ramon and rented by Szabo Diamond Company.

Jose had been a leader of the opposition to the premier, although he had never been directly proven to be a conspirator. A few of his associates had been, and they were subsequently tried and hanged for treason. Jose was widely respected and well known throughout Szabo. From Jose's return, until a few months later, the rumors of his involvement in a plot to overthrow the premier were an increasing topic of conversation among close groups and trusted individuals. Further, the house occupied by Manuel Ramon, and now by Jose, was increasingly the site of evening meetings which were presumably political.

Bill knew Manuel Ramon was important to him, to Szabo Diamond, and LCA, and that he was close to Jose. Accordingly, he was most disturbed when the minister of internal affairs, who was very close to the premier, said to Bill during his visit to the Government House:

> We, the Government of Szabo, are the majority shareholders in Szabo Diamond Company, which you manage. We are most disturbed to see our investment being used to pay rent for a house inhabited by an enemy of this government. Our house is being used for meetings plotting against us. The house is too close to a military installation. What are you going to do to correct this unacceptable condition?

DECISION THREE

Just before Christmas of the following year, Bill was compelled to participate in a smuggling investigation being conducted by a witch doctor or shaman.

The diamond factory procedure involved the Szaboan workers, of whom there were about 115, coming to a glass-enclosed area called the bench. There the worker would receive a packet of diamonds of a specified grade, never larger than one carat, to be either cut along a mark (sawed), rounded (girdled), or polished. The worker and one of the European administrators (the English manager, his English assistant, or a Dutchman also supervising operations) would count the number of diamonds (usually six to eight), agree on a total, and the Szaboan would perform the necessary step, returning the diamonds for checking.

General labor problems arose because the workers specialized as polishers, sawyers, or girdlers, and they were paid on a piecework basis. This piecework rate meant that they were relatively well paid by Szabo standards. There were frequent times, however, when the various stages of the process would become uneven. That is, there would be no girdled stones to be polished or no cut stones to be girdled, because workers in one group were slow or had been absent due to personal or tribal reasons. The workers resented these frequent shutdowns of one or more sections of the production process.

A more specific labor problem was when a difference arose between what the bench said a worker should have and what the worker said. Differences could arise because of (1) bench error; (2) worker error, such as a diamond actually flying out of the polisher as the worker failed to control the gem and the machine;

(3) smuggling; and (4) substitution, in which an inferior stone is brought into the factory and exchanged for a superior stone.

Just before Christmas the number of differences increased. The workers were unhappy about being suspected of stealing. One day the Szaboan head of the labor union came to Bill with a request that a tribal shaman investigate the matter.

Bill, who had seen shamans perform various rituals in Szabo, including healing and exorcism, agreed to the use of the shaman. Bill reasoned that such an investigation might reduce the workers' dissatisfaction and the "differences," and that it would also show some respect for tribal customs and procedures.

Thus, shortly before the end of the next workday the shaman arrived. All European and Szaboan employees participated in the investigation, led by Bill. Bill had anticipated that this shaman would follow the practice Bill had seen other shamans use, namely, going amongst the employees with a "magic" stick or broom that would only strike the guilty. This investigation, however, consisted of a different procedure, which was described to everyone beforehand by the shaman.

Bill and then every other employee lined up single file, walked up to a pot full of palm oil placed over a stone. The oil was heated to a rolling boil. Then a large rock was dropped to the bottom of the pot. Each person was to pick up the stone, lift it out of the boiling oil, and put it back in the pot. The shaman assured everyone that only the guilty persons would be burned.

Bill went first, picked up the stone, and replaced it in the boiling oil. He felt nothing. Only two persons were burned, one Szaboan and the Dutchman (they both wore bandages for several weeks). Bill was certain that some out-of-the-ordinary phenomenon occurred, and he wondered what to do. He commented:

> I was and am totally convinced that there's something behind all of this. The boiling oil wasn't even hot neither to my touch, nor to over one hundred other people's touch. While I don't go to church, and we have not had our three children baptized, I still consider myself a Christian. I've always believed in some power, and this experience probably showed some aspect of that power.

Case 10

ALTERNATIVE DISPUTE RESOLUTION AT THE PANAMA CANAL

Negotiating a Collective Bargaining Agreement Panama Canal, Panama[a]

Jeff Levon

The mediator, John Novin, could tell that Panama's so-called dry season[b] had ended: Mangos were beginning to fall and the combination of the rain, sun, humidity, and rotting fruit gave a wine smell to the air. A new season had arrived, and the promise of change inspired new hope that the Panama Canal Administration and Panama Canal Pilots Union could avoid going to arbitration over their collective bargaining agreement. The Administration had responsibility for managing the canal and the pilots who navigate the vessels through the canal (Exhibit 1). They were at odds over pay, workload, and other issues.

John arrived at the mediation session a few minutes before the meeting was scheduled to begin. The minutes passed, and he calmly took in stride the final party's half-hour late arrival. He had adapted to Panama's culture. He also felt that after 6 months of shuttling back and forth between the United States and Panama, he had finally gained the parties' confidence and trust. All those hours working together and sharing informal lunches with both sides had begun to pay off. In fact, the U.S. Federal Mediation and Conciliation Service (FMCS) could no longer send just any mediator. The Panama Canal Pilots and Administration only wanted to deal with him. He was now considered part of the group.

After a brief session of small talk, both sides began to outline their positions. Never before had John seen two positions so divergent. He knew it would be impossible to resolve the major issues at first, so he concentrated on the smaller issues at hand. After all, both sides were quite willing to go to arbitration, as they had already established a timeline and the ground rules. He had 2 months to reach an agreement before an arbitrator would take over.

Gradually, the weeks went by and John's hopes of reaching an agreement began to diminish. At least, he felt a sense of accomplishment for keeping the lines of communication open, and, in general terms, the conversations were positive. John believed a breakthrough could occur if he could just

SOURCE: These materials were developed and published by the Institute of International Education and its Emerging Markets Development Advisers Program with funding from the United States Agency for International Development.

EXHIBIT 1 Ship Crossing the Panama Canal

keep the parties talking. However, both sides remained entrenched in their positions even though both parties pulled him aside at the end of each session to quietly apologize for failing to reach an agreement. But the deadline, nonetheless, was quickly approaching. He knew this session would probably be the last before going to arbitration.

The parties arrived a little late to this negotiation and over *empenada*s and coffee, they casually talked about baseball and the upcoming elections. In spite of their differences, they were in agreement that Panamanians Ramiro Mendoza and Mariano Rivera would lead the Yankees to victory in the World Series. John was anxious to begin the session but he understood that it was important to socialize a little before conducting business in Panama. He laughed as one of the pilots joked that they always brought the better *empenada*s. He almost began to take for granted this Panamanian custom of "breaking bread" before negotiating.

John began the session by emphasizing the risks inherent in letting a neutral third party settle the dispute. He wanted both sides to carefully consider what would happen if the case were to go to arbitration. He critically looked at both sides' positions and tried to raise uncertainties about the strengths of their positions. Both parties were convinced that they would come out the winners if the case went to arbitration. After several hours of negotiation, sensing this as a final opportunity, he asked them a question: "Can we give it one more day to reach a final agreement and avoid arbitration?"

The negotiators for the Panama Canal Pilots and the Panama Canal Administration were swayed by John's plea and agreed to meet the following day. This would be a final, last chance session to avoid declaring an impasse which would result in arbitration.

Changes Proposed by the Administration Related to Panama Canal Pilots: Panama Canal Pilots Report

The Panama Canal Administration believed changes were necessary to adjust to the reality of a Panamanian-run canal, which anticipated a deficit in qualified pilots and which required a business-like operation from the government enterprise.

The Panama Canal Administration furthermore believed these issues were not subject to an arbitrator's decision. However, the Panama Canal pilots established the resolution of safety issues as a precondition to negotiations. The pilots were concerned about the additional stress of working longer hours with the less experienced pilots coming into their ranks.

For passage of a Panamax vessel the following changes would apply:

Current practice	Planned practice
Two pilots formally qualified	One pilot formally qualified
Minimum of 8 years of experience	Minimum of 6 years of experience
6 hr of labor for transit	8 hr of labor for transit
810 hr of labor per year	1,320 hr of labor per year

Panama Canal Authority Budget: December 31, 1999, to September 30, 2000

Income From Operations

Toll income	$440,727,000
Other income	164,575,000
Total income	*605,302,000*

Operating Expenses

Personal services	$238,635,000
Social security	25,805,000
Materials and supplies	15,133,000
Combustible	13,233,000
Transport, food and overseas lodging	500,000
Per diem and local travel	2,144,000
Subcontracting	29,749,000
National treasury: Rights for net ton	112,311,000
National treasury: Taxes for public services	24,000,000
Insurance	3,047,000

Reimbursement for expenses utilizing the investment reserve	(26,155,000)
Depreciation Provision	14,986,000
for accidents and disasters	6,000,000
Other operating expenses	30,195,000
Total operating expenses	489,583,000
Utility before investment program	115,719,000
Provision for investment program	85,000,000
Net utility	30,719,000

MAJOR ISSUES OF THE NEGOTIATION

(The instructor has supplemental confidential information for each negotiating party)

Compensation

The Panama Canal Pilots sought a substantial raise in salaries. The Administration sought a "cost neutral" approach: Any considered alternative should not significantly raise the costs of operating the canal. At the time, a top union pilot made about $140,000 a year.

Exhibit 2 shows how compensation to pilots had increased over the years through prior labor negotiations.

Work Rules

6/4 Work Plan. This refers to a work schedule of 6 consecutive weeks of work followed by 4 weeks off. In the beginning of Panama Canal operations, and until recently, the majority of the pilots were from the United States and most of their families resided there. The 6/4 work plan was established in order to allow the U.S. pilots the opportunity to travel home to the States to see their families. The majority of the pilots are now Panamanian and the few remaining U.S. pilots are eligible for early retirement. Piloting ships through the Panama Canal is a demanding job. Exhibit 3 shows a typical work week for a top pilot.

Manning of Ships. The size of the ship determines the number of pilots needed on board. The smaller ships require only one pilot. The larger ships in the past have utilized four, three, and now two pilots.

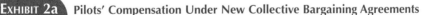

EXHIBIT 2a   Pilots' Compensation Under New Collective Bargaining Agreements

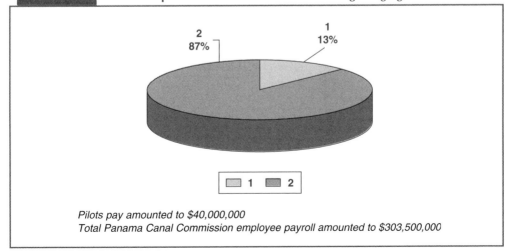

Pilots pay amounted to $40,000,000
Total Panama Canal Commission employee payroll amounted to $303,500,000

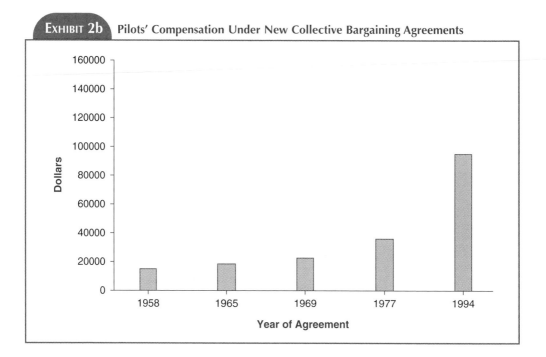

EXHIBIT 2b Pilots' Compensation Under New Collective Bargaining Agreements

EXHIBIT 3 A Week in the Life of a Top Panama Canal Ship Pilot

Day	Hours	Duration (hours)	Type of Transit	Vessel Size
Sunday	1:45 am–9:00 am	7:15	Partial	Panamax
Monday	6:45 am–7:30 pm	12:45	Full	Panamax
Wednesday	3:30 am–6:50 pm	15:20	Full	Panamax
Thursday	8:30 am–3:30 pm	7:00	Partial	Panamax
Saturday	6:30 am–6:30 pm	12:00	Full	Panamax (900+ ft)
Total Hours:	54.5			

Pilot Qualifications. In order to guide the "Panamax" vessels (largest ship that can pass through the locks), a pilot is required to have 8 years of experience.

Contracting of Pilots. This is seen as a way to remedy the shortfall of qualified pilots after the retirement of the majority of U.S. pilots.

"TRANSIT AT YOUR OWN RISK"

Standing under the hot Panamanian sun in the Canal Zone, the American EMDAP adviser[d] waited for his taxi. Every day Jeff traveled to the same place, along the same route, but with a different driver. As he opened the door and took a seat, he tried to say "Punta Paitilla"[e] with as little an accent as possible.

He did not want to sound like a tourist in order to avoid the "gringo" surcharge targeted at North Americans that was prevalent throughout Panama. The trip through El Chorillo[f] was as crazy as ever. He wondered how these cab drivers could do this for a living. In spite of the constant honking horns, sudden stops and starts, and the endless presidential campaign propaganda,[g] his thoughts wandered back to his work in labor relations at the Panama Canal Authority. He knew that his friend, John, was having a difficult time reaching an agreement with the parties. He wondered if John would be able to facilitate the negotiation over the collective bargaining agreement between the Panama Canal Administration and Panama Canal Pilots.

When he arrived at the office, he greeted the secretary, Arquelis, with a quick "Buenos dias, como te va"[h] and made his way up the stairs. Before reaching the top he realized something was terribly wrong. He heard from the next office the sound of a fist pounding on a desk and some loud profanities in Spanish. Mr. Stanziola, the director of planning, called him into his office.

Mr. Stanziola picked up one of the newspapers on his desk and asked Jeff if he had read the day's news. "Can you believe what those pilots did?! What the hell do they think they are doing?!" The headlines in *La Prensa* and *El Panama America* read, "In London and New York, Pilots Denounce Lack of Security in the Canal," "Pilots: United States Turns Over a Canal Full of Problems," "Transit at Your Own Risk: The Face of Danger in the Panama Canal." As an adviser, Jeff was aware of the other issues the Panama Canal Pilots were fighting for, namely, the 6/4 work plan and a salary increase, but now a question of security had been added as a serious issue in the negotiations. The action threw the dispute into a much wider arena, possibly tarnishing the reputation of the institution and threatening the Canal's desirability as a transportation thoroughfare.

THE PANAMA CANAL PILOT'S PERSPECTIVE

Panama Canal Pilot Jorge Rankin (Panamanian) and two other pilots had traveled to London and New York to present a report to the International Maritime Community about the new measures imposed by the Panama Canal Administration and the resulting risks to the safety of the waterway. In an interview with the radio program "Haciendo Radio," Mr. Rankin stated they had spent months trying to convince the Administration about the negative effects of these new measures, but no one had paid any attention. A letter expressing their concerns had been sent to the Administration some time ago (Exhibit 4).

EXHIBIT 4   **A Pilot's Letter to the Administrator[i]**

Ing. Alberta Aleman Z., Administrator   February 13, 1998
Panama Canal Commission
Balboa Heights, Republic of Panama

Dear Administrator Aleman:

Almost exactly 2 years ago, members of the Panama Canal Pilots Branch (PCPB) met with you over a number of topics, most important of which was our perceived estimation on the lack of available, qualified, senior pilots for the future smooth operation of the Panama Canal. We brought some rough calculations which you later sent to various offices throughout the Commission to ascertain their validity. We found out later that the Maritime Training Unit and the Chief of Pilot Division agreed in substantial detail with our figures. Both units perceived that a crisis was certainly looming.

(Continued)

(Continued)

Since our candid and mutual dialogue, the PCPB has repeatedly warned Marine Bureau officials of the impending scarcity of senior pilots. This has been done at countless meetings with the Manager of the Pilot Unit, the Manager of Canal Operations and the Manager of Maritime Operations. Indeed, their own figures show what we know to be true. Time continues to march on, and the senior pilots continue retiring at increasing rates. Over the last year or so we have said goodbye to 18 pilots. These men were not rehired or they have left. At least 7 more have indicated that they will leave before mid-1998. Countless more pilots have accrued sufficient time for retirement, and are essentially working one week at a time. They could go any day, especially if pay, standards of living, or benefits decrease.

Defying all logic in the face of this imminent crisis, the Panama Canal Commission has put rehired annuitants on short notice. These pilots are essentially working month to month, unable to make firm plans for their future.

These actions (or the lack of assertive action to retain them) only lend credence to the rumors that the Panama Canal Commission plans simply to change the manning requirements for vessels, or cancel the 6/4 Plan and magically senior pilots will once again be in sufficient quantity.

Unless timely, assertive action is taken, we foresee the Panama Canal Commission shortly implementing special measures which would mean working the remaining pilots harder and longer. It goes without saying that this is unacceptable. There are no special measures or special circumstances or emergencies involved here. This situation has been forecast for years, and the Commission has, for all practical purposes, ignored it; possibly hoping it would go away by itself.

The 6/4 Plan and the present manning of vessels are the result of an extensive negotiating process and also extensive concessions made at the bargaining table. As such, they are integral parts of our Agreement and therefore may not be changed unilaterally. But this matter goes beyond the realm of labor relations; it is a matter of common sense. Every pilot who retires and leaves creates more work for the remaining pilots. Those pilots who were thinking about retirement will think a lot faster when they see harder and longer hours facing them. This will cause more retirements earlier than was considered, which will in turn force the ever-diminishing senior pilots to work even harder. It is a vicious downhill circle with the ultimate loser being the Panama Canal.

Surely you understand that the Panama Canal Pilots Branch will not sit idly by while the pilots who remain are worked harder, more often, and longer. Over the many years we have built an unarguable reputation as some of the finest ship handlers in the world. Our reputation is in large part responsible for the success of the Panama Canal. We have every intention of keeping or even improving our hard-earned reputation. We will not have our good name and reputation tarnished by shortsighted management. As you are acutely aware, it is obvious that these transition years have created increased awareness of everything surrounding the Panama Canal. It is also obvious that the maritime community is fully expecting, at the very least, the same or better quality of service in exchange for the numerous toll increases approved in recent years.

I do not like writing this letter. It puts me in a position of saying, "I told you so." However, it is against my nature and training to allow this situation to reach the point of extremism without taking whatever action is necessary to avert a collision between the Agency that you head and the Panama Canal pilots. I feel this letter is an obvious first step in a series of actions that will necessarily follow until this issue is properly addressed. This is not a complicated issue, it is simply one that must take precedence over others such as Cut widening or Third Locks projects due to its immediate, rather than future, impact on the operation and viability of the Canal.

As always, I remain available to discuss this or other matters.

Sincerely,
Jorge A. Teran, Branch Agent

cc: Mr. Rene Van Hoorde, Marine Director, Captain George A. Markham, Manager Transit Operations Division, Captain Chet M. Lavalas, Manager, Pilot Branch

After the Panama Canal reversion on December 31, 1999, 72 U.S. Panama Canal pilots were eligible to retire early with compensation. The likelihood was that 50 of the 72 U.S. pilots would take the early retirement offer in the next few years. According to Panama Canal Pilot Jorge Lankin, the departure of these pilots would obligate the Panama Canal Administration to use people who did not have the capacity or the experience to do the job successfully. The lack of qualified pilots would obligate existing pilots to work longer hours, which would affect safety norms. Panama Canal Pilot Jorge Sanidas stated, "We are not willing to remain quiet because we are Panamanians and what is happening is the U.S. is going to return to Panama a canal full of problems with a high risk of accidents."

Frequently, ships carrying dangerous and sometimes radioactive cargo pass through the Panama Canal. One of the pilots' greatest fears was that if an accident occurred in the Culebra Cut, it could result in an ecological nightmare, since it was the primary source of potable water for most of the city of Panama. Recently, the U.S. Congress passed H.R. 3616 that stated the Panama Canal Commission would only be responsible for damages occurring in the canal that exceeded $1,000,000. This could affect the unique relationship that the Panama Canal Pilots had with the on-board Ships Masters who had to cede control of their ship when passing through the locks of the canal. They could be less willing to confide in the pilots knowing that only damages exceeding $1,000,000 would be covered.

The Panama Canal Pilots believed that the Panama Canal Commission had not had sufficient prudence to recruit Panamanian personnel to replace the U.S. pilots. The Pilots Association proposed that the U.S. pilots remain for the time necessary to cover the gap created by retirements.

THE PANAMA CANAL ADMINISTRATION'S PERSPECTIVE

Due to federal statutes that prohibit public disclosure of aspects of a negotiation when it has reached the arbitration stage, the Panama Canal Administration declined to comment. However, representatives from the very highest levels of the Government of Panama were swift to dispute the presentation in London and New York by the three Panama Canal pilots.

The Panamanian Ambassador to the United States, His Excellency Eloy Alfaro, who also presided over the Board of Directors of the Panama Canal Commission, questioned the attitude of the pilots to go abroad and make public their labor differences when arbitration was the next step in the process of reaching a collective bargaining agreement. He also questioned the fact that the pilots went abroad to publicize safety issues when they had not first informed the Panamanian public. The Ambassador believed that Panamanians abroad should give the foreign public reasons to be *confident* about the safety of the canal and capability of the administration, rather than create more doubt in the minds of the international community.

The President of Panama, Ernesto Perez Balladares, was surprised that these pilots had gone abroad to insinuate safety problems in the final stages of the reversion of the Panama Canal. He believed they tried to damage Panama by creating an insecure environment when there were no reasons to support their claims.

The Minister of the Panama Canal, Jorge Ritter, considered the actions of the Panama Canal Pilots improper and lacking patriotism. He made it clear that the Board of Directors had passed an incentive plan for voluntary early retirement but never asked any pilot to retire early. All personnel contracted before 1979 had the option of retiring under the terms of the transfer of the canal.

A source from the Panama Canal Commission stated that the safety of the Panama Canal was not at risk. On the contrary, investments in the millions, such as the expansion of the Culebra Cut, guaranteed a safer passage through the canal. In 1998, the Panama Canal had the best safety record of the last 38 years, one accident investigation for every 970 transits of the canal. A 30-year history of the traffic and accidents appears in Exhibit 5.

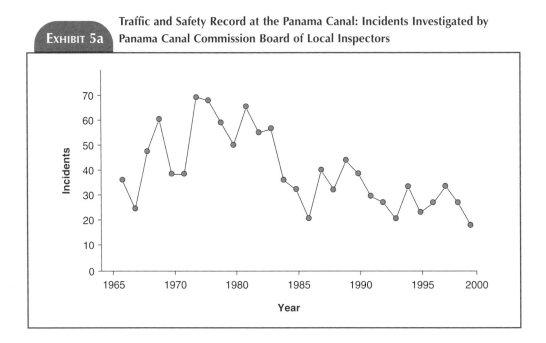

EXHIBIT 5a Traffic and Safety Record at the Panama Canal: Incidents Investigated by Panama Canal Commission Board of Local Inspectors

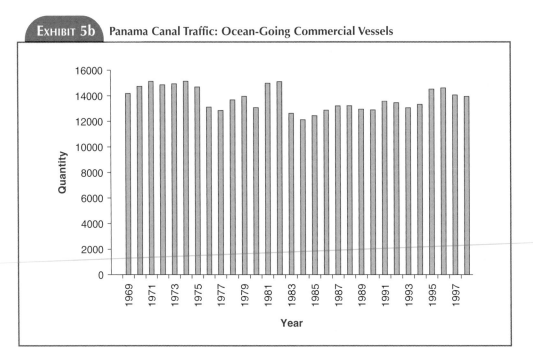

EXHIBIT 5b Panama Canal Traffic: Ocean-Going Commercial Vessels

---

Assignment

Prepare for the negotiation. Come to class prepared to serve as the exclusive representative of one of the two parties. You now have a chance to resolve this dispute. Failing to do so will result in final and binding arbitration.

APPENDIX

Background Information on Panama

Brief History of Panama

In 1501, Rodrigo Galván de Bastidas led the first expedition of the Spanish crown to discover the Isthmus of Panama by sea. The following year, the fourth voyage of Christopher Columbus, led to the establishment of a colony on the Atlantic coast in what is now Colon. In 1513, Vasco Nunez de Balboa discovered the Pacific Ocean which inspired the idea of Panama as an interoceanic region for the transport of goods and a center of commerce. Then the California Gold Rush brought to the public's attention the strategic importance of Panama's location, as 15,502 passengers passed through the Isthmus by land on their way to San Francisco, California, in 1853.

Historically, Panama was a territory of the Republic of Colombia. The failure of the Colombian Senate to ratify the Hay-Herrán Treaty on August 12, 1903, led to Panama's declaration of its independence from Colombia on November 3, 1903. This treaty would have allowed the United States to build a canal in Panama, and the revolution on the Isthmus was bolstered by a U.S. military presence.

Brief History of the Panama Canal

In 1534, Charles I of Spain ordered the first survey of a proposed canal route through the Isthmus of Panama. More than three centuries passed before the first construction was started. The French labored 20 years, beginning in 1880, but disease and financial problems defeated them.

In 1903, Panama and the United States signed a treaty by which the United States undertook to construct an interoceanic ship canal across the Isthmus of Panama. The following year, the United States purchased from the French Canal Company its rights and properties for $40 million and began construction. The monumental project was completed in 10 years at a cost of about $387 million. Since 1903, the United States has invested about $3 billion in the Canal enterprise, approximately two thirds of which has been recovered.

The building of the Panama Canal involved three main problems—engineering, sanitation, and organization. Its successful completion was due principally to the engineering and administrative skills of such men as John F. Stevens and Col. George W. Goethals, and to the solving of extensive health problems by Col. William C. Gorgas.

The engineering problems involved digging through the Continental Divide; constructing the largest earth dam ever built up to that time; designing and building the most massive canal locks ever envisioned; constructing the largest gates ever swung; and solving environmental problems of enormous proportions.

Now, more than 80 years after the first official ocean-to-ocean transit of the waterway, the United States and Panama have embarked on a partnership for the management, operation, and defense of the Panama Canal. Under two new treaties signed in a ceremony at the Organization of American States (OAS) headquarters in Washington, D.C., on September 7, 1977, the Canal would be operated until the turn of the century under arrangements designed to strengthen the bonds of friendship and cooperation between the two countries. The treaties were approved by Panama in a plebiscite on October 23, 1977, and the U.S. Senate gave its advice and consent to their ratificaton in March and April 1978. The treaties went into effect on October 1, 1979.

The Panama Canal Commission, a U.S. government agency, operated the Canal during the 20-year transition period that began with Panama Canal Treaty implementation on October 1, 1979. The Commission replaced the former Panama Canal Company, which, together with the Canal Zone and its government, was disestablished on October 1, 1979. On December 31, 1999, as required by treaty, the United States transferred the Canal to Panama.[j]

Demographics of Panama

Population: 2.7 million (July 1997 est.)

Economy: Agriculture 10%, industry 16%, services 74% (1995 est.)

Inflation: 1.3% (1996 est.)

Unemployment: 14% (1996 est.)

GDP: $14 billion (1996 est.)

GDP real growth rate: 1.5% (1996 est.)

GDP per capita income: $5,300 (1996 est.)

Key Institutions

Panama Canal Commission (PCC). A U.S. government agency that was in charge of administering and operating the Panama Canal. There were 7,500 employees of which 95% were Panamanians. There are four major unions in the Panama Canal. Based on the 1977 Carter-Torrijos treaties, this organization officially ceased to exist as of December 31, 1999.

Panama Canal Authority (PCA). The Organic Law of the Panama Canal Authority (Law 19), on June 11, 1997, established the Panama Canal Authority as the legal entity to manage and operate the Panama Canal after December 31, 1999. The Panama Canal Authority and Panama Canal Commission worked to promote a seamless transfer of the Panama Canal. The principal activities of the Panama Canal Authority are establishing regulations, environmental, labor, and fiscal.

Panama Canal Pilots. Each and every ship passing through the canal requires at least one pilot on board. There are 302 pilots (228 Panamanian, 74 U.S.) who work around a schedule of 24 hr/day, 365 days/year. These are a group of highly trained and highly paid personnel who are vital to the operations of the Panama Canal. The salary of a top Panama Canal pilot, who is required to have 8 years of training, is $140,000.

U.S. Federal Mediation and Conciliation Service (FMCS). The FMCS is a U.S. Federal Agency whose mandate is to resolve labor disputes. Since the Panama Canal Commission was a U.S. government agency, there was an interagency agreement that the FMCS would provide mediation services for labor conflicts within the Panama Canal. However, after December 31, 1999, these institutional arrangements ceased to exist, thereby creating a need for an alternative source of labor mediation services.

The New Organic Law of the Panama Canal Authority

Section 1: Personnel Relations

Article 92. To ensure that the international public service for which the Panama Canal was created is not affected, its operation may not be interrupted, neither fully nor partially, nor impaired in any way. Strikes, slowdowns, and any other unjustified work stoppages are prohibited. If any such actions occur, the Administration of the Authority shall proceed to adopt the necessary measures to immediately restore the service and shall apply the sanctions established in the Law and the Regulations, including that of dismissal.

Section 2: Labor Relations

Article 100. The administration of the Authority shall have the right to:

1. Determine the mission, budget, organization, number of workers, and internal security practices of the Authority.

2. Hire, assign, direct, dismiss, and retain workers of the Authority; suspend, remove, reduce in grade or pay, or take other disciplinary actions against the workers.

3. Assign work, make decisions with respect to contracting out, and determine the personnel needed for the activities related to the operation of the Canal.

4. Select, for hiring and promotion purposes, those candidates who have been duly evaluated and certified as the best qualified, from lists or other appropriate sources, as established in the Regulations.

5. Undertake the necessary actions to carry out the mission of the Authority during an emergency.

Article 101. The obligation of the Authority, as well as that of any exclusive representative, to negotiate in good faith shall be defined and developed in the Regulations and shall include, as a minimum, the requirement that the parties to the negotiations be represented by workers expressly empowered to enter into agreements that are binding on the parties they represent, not precluding that neither party may be compelled or obliged to accept or to agree to a proposal or to make any concession.

The Authority management, upon request, shall provide the exclusive representative with the pertinent data on the subjects discussed within the scope of the collective negotiation according to the Regulations, as long as the provision of said data is allowable under this Law.

Article 102. Negotiations between Authority management and any exclusive representative, provided they are not in conflict with this Law and the Regulations, shall deal with the following matters:

1. Those that affect the employment conditions of the workers of a bargaining unit, except those related to position classification and those expressly established by this Law or are a result of same.

2. The procedures used to implement the decisions of the administration of the Authority, pursuant to Article 100 of this Law, as well as the adequate measures applied to the worker who is adversely affected by such decisions, unless such decisions have only a slight impact on the working conditions.

3. The number, type, and grade of the workers who may be assigned to an organizational unit, project, or work schedule; the technology and the means and methods used to accomplish a job. The obligation to negotiate these matters shall be subject to the application of an interest-based method of negotiation and not the adversarial positions of the parties. This interest-based method shall be established by the Regulations. The interests of the parties should necessarily promote the objective of improving quality and productivity, service to the user, operational efficiency of the Canal, and quality of the work environment.

Article 103. For the purpose of improving the operation of the Authority, the administration of the Authority and the unions, with the participation of exclusive representatives, may work jointly as partners to improve their labor relationship, identify problems, and find solutions.

Article 104. Each collective bargaining agreement shall have a grievance procedure, including arbitration and alternate dispute resolution techniques, which shall be binding for both parties. This procedure shall constitute the exclusive administrative mechanism for the resolution of disputes.

Article 106. Arbitration is the final administrative recourse in disputes and shall be governed by the provisions of this Law, the Regulations, and the collective bargaining agreements. If arbitration is sought, the decision shall be binding. For the purposes of this Section, only the Authority or the exclusive representative may invoke arbitration. The cost of arbitration shall be divided equally between the Authority and the corresponding labor organization.

Article 107. Notwithstanding the provisions of Article 106, arbitration decisions may be appealed before the Third Section of the Supreme Court of Justice within 30 work days from the notification of the corresponding decision. Said appeal shall stay the effect of the arbitration decision, but such appeal may proceed only when based upon an erroneous interpretation of the Law or the Regulations, because of manifest partiality of the arbitrator, or noncompliance of due process in the course of the arbitration.

Notes

a. This case was written by Jeff Levon of Willamette University under the supervision of Professor Richard Linowes of American University in Washington, DC. It is intended as the basis for class discussion rather than to illustrate either effective or ineffective handling of an administrative situation.

b. The dry season in Panama lasts from December until March, and it includes lots of warm, sunny, and breezy days.

c. Budget is not a full year because in the year of the transition and thereafter, the Panama Canal Authority fiscal year would begin on October 1.

d. The EMDAP (Emerging Market Development Adviser Program) Adviser is included to provide a glimpse of the author's daily life in Panama.

e. Punta Paitilla is a wealthy neighborhood in Panama City.

f. El Chorillo is a poor neighborhood that used to be home to the headquarters for Manuel Noriega. The "barrio" suffered significant damage during "Operation Just Cause" when U.S. forces landed in Panama.

g. Mireya Moscoso became the first female president in Panama by beating the son of former strongman Omar Torrijos.

h. "Good morning, how is it going?"

i. Source: Panama Canal Pilots Web site— www.panamacanalpilots.org

j. Source: www.pancanal.com

Case 11

LEASING CARGO SPACE AT THE GRENADA AIRPORT[1]

Grenada, West Indies

Lisa Barnard

(A)
FIFTEEN YEARS AGO

It was a warm April night when the lights on the Grenada Point Salines Airport runway illuminated for the American Airlines flight coming in from Puerto Rico. Mr. Leopold Cromwell, the General Manager for the Airports Authority of Grenada (AAG), watched from his office window as the American Airlines 747 appeared past the control tower hill. It had been a long day of negotiations—labor talks in the morning and negotiations in the afternoon with Leeward Islands Air Transportation (LIAT), which was 5 months behind in payments. The next day at 8:30 a.m. he would meet people from American Airlines to discuss their need for cargo space at the airport. Despite his long day, he knew they would approach him in the meeting as if he were laidback and lazy, and as if he had slept long and well. He wondered if the Americans felt they were vacationing while in Grenada and recalled how at the last meeting Mr. Anderson, Manager of Cargo

Shipping for Caribbean and Latin America, had commented that it must be nice to live here all the time and how he had just smiled in response, not wanting to disrupt the perception of a potential tourist.

The meeting tomorrow was about leasing to American Airlines the area of the airport currently used as the airport's maintenance shop. American was currently leasing space in the bottom floor of an unattractive and unkempt building 6 miles away and on the other side of the island's principal city, St. George's. American was hoping to lease space "on-site" to reduce transportation costs to and from the airport, increase customer service by providing a nicer atmosphere and a one-stop-shop capacity, and negotiate a lower rent than what they currently pay at the other building. The AAG was looking forward to the rent income that leasing the space would provide.

Mr. Cromwell felt that he had a good hand to play in the negotiation and he was looking forward to the meeting and to facilitating American Airlines' quick move into

SOURCE: These materials were developed and published by the Institute of International Education and its Emerging Markets Development Advisers Program with funding from the United States Agency for International Development.

311

the space. He was eager to provide polite and professional customer service and to prove that the airport was happy to have American servicing the island. In addition to the funds that the rent would provide the airport, the government and Grenadian population needed the economic boost and foreign capital that would be brought by increased tourism from the U.S. American Airlines had a monopoly on all flights to the United States except for one daily British West Indies Airlines (BWIA) flight to New York City. In fact, American Airlines essentially had a monopoly on all flights to the United States from the Caribbean.[2] In addition, American Airlines provided rapid transport of cargo to the United States market and transferred 60% of the mail leaving the island.

Despite the need for tourism dollars to make the economy healthy, Grenada was better diversified than most Caribbean islands. In the 1980s the Grenadian government had taken bold steps to move away from reliance on a single source of income. Unlike the islands of Barbados or Dominica, for example, which relied almost completely on tourism and bananas, Grenada had been forced in the late 1980s to move away from a single-market economy. The banana-exporting agency had ruled in the mid-80s that Grenadian bananas were not of sufficient quality to export because the government had done little to educate farmers about proper packing procedures and consequently the fruit arrived bruised and unmarketable. Around the same time, the government stopped subsidizing fertilizers and pesticides for bananas. The island's farmers were forced to diversify their crops to cocoa (Grenada exported the finest cocoa in the world), nutmeg and nutmeg oil, fish, flowers, minor spices, and exotic fruits.

Despite the stabilized income offered by the diversified array of crops, many of the farmers left farming altogether and came to the southwest tip of the island to work in St. George's in construction, tourism, as taxi drivers, tour guides, waiters, or hotel staff. Grenada promoted diversification of services by building a very successful American off-shore medical school, promoting off-shore banking, an electronics industry, and several printers. In addition, the Tourism Board launched a successful campaign to persuade Grenadians who had been educated and worked abroad to retire in Grenada. This resulted in a construction boom and a boost to all related industries.

The Americans Check Into the Hotel

In preparation for their meeting the next day, the two American Airlines executives, Rick Anderson and Sayed Assad, checked into their hotel.

"Good night, Mr. Anderson and Mr. Assad. Please follow Richard, he will show you to your rooms," the uniformed receptionist said warmly. Rick and Sayed followed Richard past bougainvillea, a lovely pool with a swim-up bar, and a path leading off to the beach.

"This isn't bad," said Sayed.

"No, it sure isn't. That's why we service this island—it's really pretty but not a lot of people know about it yet. People just don't come here. They think of us sending the Marines in and that's about where it stops. But Grenada is building hotels, and American Airlines thinks this will become a popular destination in a few years."

"Well, you know what? Today I don't hate my job. I'm going to get in the pool and have some sort of drink with an umbrella in it," replied Sayed.

The next morning they met at 7:00 a.m. for coffee and breakfast. They waited to be served by one of the laughing employees gathered around the cash register, but no one came. Finally, Sayed got up and asked them for a menu. The request was met with an indifferent nod and the server continued his joking even as he idly picked up the menus.

"Hi, we're in a bit of a hurry—we have an 8:30 a.m. meeting," Sayed said.

"OK, sure, sure," the server said as if he understood. The group reconvened at the register and Sayed had to get up 15 min later to place the order.

"Is this fresh squeezed juice?" Rick asked when the server brought breakfast.

"No, this is from Trinidad," the server replied.

"Why don't you have juices from here?" Sayed responded.

"I don't know. We have too much from Trinidad. Everything from Trinidad or from the United States. We have beautiful fruits here, but no one is making anything out of them. Mangoes rot on the ground. You should smell it during mango season." Rick and Sayed glanced at each other. "It is a big problem here," the server continued. "We don't have the know-how to maintain the machines." The server walked back to his group around the register.

"Why do you think there are so many of them working? There are not even five guests here," Sayed said to Rick.

Meanwhile at the airport, Mr. Cromwell had arrived at 6:30 a.m. after being paged that the security manager had failed to show up for work. The security manager, Mr. Redhead, was a childhood friend of Mr. Cromwell. They had attended the same Anglican boys' school. While the smartest people Mr. Cromwell knew growing up had gone to Britain or the United States to study and work, many people employed at the airport either went to his school or attended his church. Disciplining people therefore was a problem because he knew the employees, and more often than not,

he was friends with them or their family. Mr. Cromwell knew that Mr. Redhead had problems at home and likely had overslept by accident. It would be impossible to say anything to him. If he reprimanded Mr. Redhead, the entire staff would see him as cruel and cold and would refuse to do any more than required by their basic job description. He had learned this the hard way some 2 years ago when he disciplined an employee and his staff had invented excuses to leave on a day when he needed them to stay.

Still, negotiations would be more difficult without Mr. Redhead. Security was the primary sticking point in renting the space, as far as Mr. Cromwell could tell. He could not let American Airlines cargo customers into the area that the airlines wanted to rent because of the security risk. He was afraid American Airlines would either get frustrated or believe this requirement to be unacceptable and would refuse the space. Mr. Cromwell decided he would call Mr. Redhead at home and express concern and sympathy, thereby indirectly indicating that his absence was noted and that he should be at the airport as soon as possible.

History of the Airport

Before 1984, the Grenada airport was located in Pearls on the northeast side of the island. Pearls had a 5,200-ft runway and was in the prime agricultural area of Grenada, St. Andrew's parish.

In 1983, construction began on a new airport on the southwest tip of the island, Point Salines, about 5 miles from the largest city and biggest economic center, St. George's. The space was chosen because of the relatively large expanse of flat land—however, there were many salt ponds that had been filled in to create the planned 9,000-ft runway. Most commercial airstrips are 7,500 to 12,000 ft, with the average-size strip in the Caribbean being 5,500 ft. The airport was built with the help of the Cuban government at a time when Grenada's population was leaning toward socialism. That fact, in conjunction with the unusually long runway, aroused suspicion on the part of the U.S. government about the ultimate purpose of the facility.

In October 1983, the socialist party (New Jewel Movement) had developed enough friction that civil unrest broke out and the Prime Minister, the Honorable Maurice Bishop of the People's Revolutionary Government party, was assassinated along with five other people. Ronald Reagan and the U.S. government became uncomfortable enough with the alliance of Grenada and Cuba—and with the presence of Americans in potential danger at the St. George's Medical School—that the United States sent in Marines to establish and maintain peace and democracy. Fighting lasted only 5 days, resulting in 25 Grenadian deaths. The Grenadians' reaction to the marine invasion was mixed; most were glad to have a sense of law and order preserved, but a very large minority perceived the Marines and the United States as bullies and their presence was a sign of worldwide disbelief that the Grenadian people could take care of themselves.

The New Jewel Movement fell apart after the assassinations due to infighting. A new prime minister, Mr. Geary, was selected and Grenada set to work rebuilding its damaged reputation.

The airport at the point of American intervention was about 80% completed. The Marines stayed for 1 year, and construction of the airport and its 9,000-ft runway continued during that time with American aid. The airport was finished and facilities were moved from Pearls Airport to Point Salines in October 1984.

The continued presence of the Marines for the year drew more and more opposition from Grenadians. Most Grenadians felt that the American presence lasted longer than what was necessary to maintain peace and stability.

The Meeting

The American team walked into Mr. Cromwell's office and his heart sank—the gentlemen were dressed in suits of dark colors and long sleeves. His light shirt with short sleeves and pockets seemed so different. He felt self-conscious, as he was aware of current fashions. He was angry with himself for feeling that he wasn't properly dressed. After exchanging brief greetings, the Americans launched into the business of the day. Mr. Cromwell pressed his lips together. He had wanted to start with an overview of the purpose of the meeting and to make sure everyone was clear about the agenda. He had also wanted to extend a warm welcome to his guests and show his appreciation for their coming all the way down from Miami and to make sure their accommodations were comfortable. But the Americans were clearly comfortable. Though he felt the American style of skipping formalities and not setting aside time to build relationships was rude and pompous, he let it pass.

"Leopold, we would very much like to take over the space you are currently using for your maintenance shops and rent it for use as a cargo area," Rick stated.

"Mr. Anderson, I have reviewed the documents you sent to us on March 25th and we would like to offer you 1,520 sq. ft of space for $1.75 a foot," Mr. Cromwell replied.

"We would like to rent it for $1.45 a square foot," Rick countered.

Mr. Cromwell felt that he had offered a reasonable and dignified price and was a bit taken aback that Mr. Anderson had made a counter offer. It offended him, and he felt that the Americans wanted to take advantage of him.

"Mr. Anderson, I assure you the offer of $1.75 is quite a reasonable one. LIAT and Star Agency are paying significantly more than that."

The Americans pursued their line of negotiating and Mr. Cromwell stuck to his price, but was extremely uncomfortable because he felt he was being rude. Later, the Americans stated that they would consider the offer and get back to him the next morning.

When the American delegation returned to the Rex Grenadian Hotel to discuss their options, they were relaxed. "Well, I think we should take the offer anyway," Rick said. "The only other option is for us to rent space out at the Frequente Industrial Park." (See Exhibit 1.)

"Yeh, and that doesn't sound so good. It's more space, but we have to buy trucks to move the cargo." Sayed said.

"Not to mention the time and people it will take to repack the cargo and transport it—and security," Rick stated. "I guess the positive about having the cargo space out away from the airport is that customers can come straight in."

"Nah, we should move on this offer. It's cheap and it gives us a competitive advantage in rates over LIAT and more importantly over Amerijet. Plus, their cargo facilities are WAY out of town. What is that, about 6 miles and a lot of traffic away?" asked Sayed.

"OK, so we'll accept in the morning," Rick and Sayed agreed.

The next morning, the Americans entered his office promptly at 8:30 a.m. and announced that they would accept the offer for the space. But, they added that they wanted their cargo customers to be able to enter the area and wait inside for goods as they cleared customs. Mr. Cromwell blanched. The area could not be authorized for public pedestrian traffic. It was right off the runway and inside security gates.

"I'm sorry, as you know that is part of our security area. We cannot have people

EXHIBIT 1	Grenada Industrial Parks

Grenada had two primary industrial parks, the Frequente Industrial Park located in Grand Anse just south of St.George's, and the Seamoon Industrial park, located near Grenville. In addition to these two parks, land was available for development and buildings were easily rented.

Frequente	Frequente was home to many of Grenada's manufacturers and construction companies. The complex covered almost 200,000 sq. ft and hosted 18 buildings. Other services provided by the park included 24-hr security, maintenance, daycare center, cafeteria and a lobby area for product display.
Seamoon	The Seamoon park covered 33,000 square feet and was comprised of a main building plus a four-building complex. Services available were 24-hour security, maintenance, and a T1 line and Fibre Optic cable, located near the park. Grenville was the center of agricultural activity on the island, and this park was positioned well to serve this sector.

entering and leaving that area. The cars must be checked, as well as persons inside vehicles. I can't blame you for asking, though." Mr. Cromwell began to get nervous. Grenada needed American Airlines to service the island and he couldn't tell what they would do when he said no.

Airport Physical Structure

The airport at Point Salines consisted of a departure lounge with four duty-free shops, a secondary departure lounge with a café, an immigration area and baggage claim with two luggage conveyor belts, a separate customs area with two tables, and a restaurant/bar and the administrative offices upstairs. Also located at the main building was a pilots welcome and registration area. Several souvenir shops were located in the hallway from the security area to the arrivals area. Detached from the main building and just to the right was the maintenance facility that American wanted to take as cargo space.

Outcome of the Meeting

American Airlines agreed to take the space without the capacity to allow customers into the building. Customers had to wait outside either in the airport lounge or in their vehicles. Mr. Cromwell was relieved to have the income for the airport and to avoid the blame of the government and Grenadian people for American Airlines' withdrawal from Grenada. He authorized a budget to build a new maintenance facility about ½ mile away from the airport on airport property and hired construction crews to begin immediately. He retired the next year and Mr. Donald McPhail was promoted from air traffic control to general manager.

The new building was not elaborate and did not take long to build. However,

American Airlines Grenada began having a hard time tracking employees immediately after using the building. While the building was not far away, it was behind a hill and employees drove American Airlines Grenada vehicles to get there and transport items. Employees would say that they had to go to the shop to get something and would seem to be gone for a long time. Inventory levels were also a new problem because people tended to store items both at the airport and at the new building. A phone was installed in the building, but the line was often busy. Perhaps the most frustrating problem was that employees would come back with the wrong part and then have to return to the shop to retrieve the correct one, sometimes wasting 30 min of otherwise productive time. Mr. McPhail estimated that the new building, procedures, and transportation costs to and from the shop easily cost the airport 20% more than before leasing the maintenance space to American Airlines.

FIFTEEN YEARS LATER

The airlines serving Grenada remained the same but serviced Grenada more frequently: American Airlines and British Airways had daily flights, and BWIA, LIAT, HelenAir, and Airlines of Carriacou offered many flights each day to various destinations in the Caribbean. American maintained its essential monopoly on the U.S. market, and British Airways and BWIA were the only other airlines with flights outside the Caribbean. British Airways flew one flight daily direct to London, and BWIA flew three times a week to New York City. Three cargo airlines continued to service the island: FedEx, DHL and AmeriJet. Recent tourism data appear in Exhibit 2.

The Airports Authority needed to renovate its runway, and needed to update its

EXHIBIT 2	Grenada and Caribbean Tourism			

	Statistics by Year			
	1998	**1999**	**2000**	**2001 Jan–Sept**
Total Arriving Tourists	**369,336**	**386,013**	**368,417**	**289,141**
Stayover Tourists	108,007	108,231	110,748	87,607
Cruise Ship Passengers	249,879	266,982	246,612	193,327
Same Day Visitors	11,450	10,800	11,057	8,207
Estimated Expenditures by Visitors	**155,528**	**161,064**	**160,422**	**127,189**
By Stayover Visitors	143,159	147,135	147,485	117,291
By Cruise Ship Passengers	12,369	13,216	12,207	9,384
By Excursionists		713	730	514
Stayover Visitors—Nationalities				
USA	30,033	30,380	29,320	22,569
Canada	3,920	4,205	4,977	4,124
United Kingdom	18,480	19,583	21,350	17,043
Europe	18,002	18,006	16,446	11,084
Grenadians Residing Abroad	18,145	17,030	16,922	13,852
CARICOM	14,615	14,357	16,407	14,220
Other	4,812	4,670	5,326	4,715
Facilities				
Number of Cruise Ships	446	393	323	239
Total Number of Hotels, Guest Houses & Cottages	78	78	80	83
Total Number of Rooms	1,652	1,669	1,775	1,815
Hotel Occupancy Rate, room per night	66%	59%	64%	69%

NOTE: Tourism provides an estimated EC$7 million a year to the Grenada economy.

crash, fire, and rescue (CFR) facilities to meet international standards. Mr. McPhail placed the updating of the facility as a priority. He also felt that it was important to air-condition the arrivals lounge. Grenada was fast becoming a significant tourist destination and at least 24 people a year fainted in the arrivals lounge from the heat. He realized the importance of word-of-mouth to Grenada's tourist industry and was aware that the airport was a significant first impression.

However, he was encountering significant obstacles to obtaining either Grenada government aid or bank loans to pay for renovations. The Grenadian government did not have any money allotted to give to the airport, and banks were only willing to extend a loan at a 12% interest rate, when he felt 8% should be the going rate.

Consequently, he very much wanted to renegotiate rent with American Airlines, but he felt he had little to offer as an incentive to get them to pay more for the space. While he was not afraid to ask for what he wanted, he felt that if American Airlines was unhappy with the request, they might retaliate by reducing flights to the island.

He was particularly wary of that tactic, as a short strike by the American pilots a few years before had meant outgoing mail did not leave the island for a week, and other cargo perished waiting for flight service.

Sources of Income for the Airports Authority

The airport collected rent from the airlines and also from the duty-free shops. The airport collected a percentage of gross sales from the duty-free and souvenir shops at the airport. The amount collected often ended up being three times what would be generated by a stable rent. The highest-paying shop was Colombian Emeralds, a duty-free jewelry shop, which was exempt from the percentage schedule and paid a flat rate of EC$5,000 a month.

In addition, a departure tax was collected from people leaving the island of EC$40 (approximately U.S.$15) for adults and EC$20 for children over age five. People flying to Carriacou paid a departure tax of EC$10. The airport had air-conditioned the departure lounge and did not have any major projects in the foreseeable future.

Donald McPhail wanted to renegotiate the amount of rent American Airlines was paying for cargo space but he was not sure how to go about doing so. He felt that upgrades such as air-conditioning would add to the attractiveness of the island to tourists and encourage repeat visits. He estimated the total cost for these ventures to be EC$2,000,000.

Asking but Not Expecting

Mr. McPhail called Miami to talk with Sayed late one Monday afternoon.

"Hi Sayed. I would like to arrange a meeting with you to discuss rent here in Grenada." Mr. McPhail had been educated in the United States and was comfortable using first names and dropping the "Good afternoon" customary in starting conversations in Grenada.

"What about it?" Sayed replied.

"It's been quite a while since we took a look at the price per square foot and it needs to be brought up-to-date," McPhail stated calmly.

"I'll talk with Alan, he's the new manager, and see what he says."

"I'd like to meet in 2 weeks on Monday. That will be the 17th," McPhail continued.

"I'll call you back as soon as possible, probably tomorrow morning," Sayed said.

As Mr. McPhail walked out of the airport toward his jeep to go home for the day, he stopped for a minute on the landing of the stairs to the arrivals area. He stared at the 20 ft × 15 ft sign saying "Way Out" to let arriving passengers know where to go for taxis. He wished he could walk out of the airport to find a better negotiating position, but felt the next morning would prove he had no way out—no way to raise fees to help cover the costs of the needed airport upgrade.

(B)

The American Airlines team walked in a few minutes early for the meeting. Mr. McPhail was ready to meet them. He addressed their concerns right away.

"I understand that you do not want your costs to go up, and that your pricing is very sensitive to any increases. Your competition has increased here in Grenada," he stated.

"Yes, it has," responded Sayed. "We have many more airlines to compete with in this area now."

"Then I'm sure that you will agree that we have been giving you a strong competitive advantage in providing this key storage and customer care spot. We want to continue to rent this space to you, but the price negotiated by the previous general manager is not sufficient. Let's be clear about what our needs are. We need to update our CFR so that American Airlines can continue to fly here. You need for us to update the CFR. That is going to cost a significant amount of money and I believe that we have not been charging you enough for this valuable space."

The Americans were taken aback. They became defensive. Mr. McPhail wished immediately that he had taken more time to draw them into the conclusion that the CFR would benefit American Airlines.

"Look," Mr. McPhail said, "Let's do this. We can cooperate. We can help promote American Airlines in the country, and even in the region. And you can help us improve the airport, which will also help you. Customers won't go home telling friends it was so hot that they fainted in the lobby. They will have a

better first impression and the number of return visits will increase."

They agreed upon a price of EC$4.00 a square foot, up from EC$2.34, and that the Airports Authority would promote American Airlines in the local paper and improve their check-in area first. In addition, Mr. McPhail agreed to back American in an upcoming regional meeting of airports authorities called to address the issue of American Airlines' request for heavy subsidies from the islands. He had managed to play the public relations card perfectly; he realized that American Airlines needed all the help they could get to maintain favorable relations in their Caribbean stronghold.

NOTES

1. This case was written by Lisa Barnard of the University of Maryland under the supervision of Professor Richard Linowes of American University in Washington, DC. It is intended as a basis for class discussion rather than to illustrate either effective or ineffective handling of an administrative situation.

2. Air Jamaica had daily flights from Jamaica to New York City and BWIA serviced most Caribbean islands.

PART III

Strategic and Operational

6

International Environment and Strategy

International strategic planning as a response to environmental changes and challenges, in pursuit of organizational goals, is the subject of this chapter. In general, domestic and international strategic processes are very similar, differing only in specifics. The differences are due to forces governing the international business environment. These forces include host government, political, and legal issues; currency exchange rates; competition from local business, government-supported firms, and other multinational companies (MNCs); and cultural variations among nations. Cultural differences result in variations in the strategic planning process among MNCs. For example, similar to American and European firms, Japanese MNCs prepare strategies to respond to changing environmental forces. They have, however, a different concept of strategy.

We analyze the relationships between host governments and MNCs as a major force in the process of planning a strategy. We examine the host governments' methods of dealing with MNCs and the MNCs' management of host government relations.

Notwithstanding the similarities between domestic and international strategic processes, the differences necessitate the application of specific strategies. Three different strategic choices—global integration, host country focus, and a hybrid international strategy—are described.

Chapter Vignette

Samsung Electronics is one of the Korean companies that survived the market crisis in 1997. Nowadays, it is entering the top level of the world's technology companies, being the leader in wireless technologies with devices ranging from personal digital assistants to refrigerators. Today, Samsung is the world's largest producer of memory chips and flat-panel monitors. It also has built a strong position in the manufacture of DVDs and cell phones. The Samsung Group (Chaebol) is the largest corporate entity in South Korea. It is the equivalent of what a combined IBM-Intel-Citigroup-Caterpillar-Aetna would be in the United States. It manufactures in 14 countries, employs more than 66,000 people in 50 countries, and generates 70% of its revenues outside Korea.

Many executives at Samsung Electronics are obsessed with competing against Sony. As a matter of fact, Sony is an important customer of Samsung—it buys semiconductors and displays from them. Also, Samsung is a valued partner producing components for large U.S. firms such as Dell Computer, Hewlett-Packard, IBM, and Microsoft. It has a partnership with the Sprint Corporation.

Through the application of a new strategy, Samsung achieved the goal of becoming Korea's first great global company. The new strategy focused on improving the quality of its products and polishing its image. To achieve this goal, Samsung established a new mantra of "market-driven change." In the past decade, it radically improved its manufacturing to surpass its competitors. For example, to produce a new flat-screen television, the product planners, designers, programmers, and engineers brainstormed day after day with suppliers and argued over designs and technologies. According to the head of the product planning group, for the first time, Samsung developed a television appealing to customers' lifestyles. To change its image in the world's largest market, the United States, it consolidated its 55 advertising agency accounts into one with a new, imaginative campaign of surreal advertisements. Another way in which Samsung is creating its new image is by pulling out of big discount chains such as Wal-Mart and Kmart, which emphasize price over quality, and moving into specialty stores such as Best Buy and Circuit City. It greatly improved its products' quality and designs, but it is planning to do more. It is aiming to double its sales in a few years and to become an innovation leader like Apple Computer or Sony Corporation. To promote itself as a global electronics company, it has opened up to foreign managers and appointed non-Koreans to its board. Also, foreigners own 60% of the company.

Despite all its efforts to be recognized as a global company, Samsung is firmly rooted in the Korean culture. For example, the CEO of Samsung made a trip to Japan just to apologize to Sony's CEO for a report that Samsung had commented on its intention to dethrone Sony. In Eastern cultures, these kinds of public remarks are not considered polite. Many business practices remain solidly Korean. On a business trip to the United States, for example, an entourage of 15 Samsung employees arrived at a client's office. The clients were startled and had to scramble to find a sufficient number of chairs for them.[1-4]

Introduction

Planning is the process of establishing organizational goals and the determination of methods to attain those goals. Strategic planning is the alignment of organizational capabilities with anticipated environmental changes in the pursuit of goal attainment. Because organizations are formed to satisfy societal needs, and because their survival depends on securing the resources needed to achieve these goals, understanding and awareness of environmental forces are essential to the strategic planning process. Environmental forces are not constant; they change over time. In the past, organizations faced fewer environmental changes, at a slower pace. Today, more changes are taking place at faster rates, and this trend is accelerating. The environmental simplicity and relative stability of the past have been replaced by the dynamic complexity of today. Moreover, strategic planning itself is relatively new and can be traced back to the 1970s.

According to Harry Ansoff, known as the Father of Strategic Management,[5] the predecessor of strategic planning is long-range planning (p. 13),[6] which is based on two premises. First, environmental changes are assumed to be continuous. Second, these changes are assumed to be predictable through extrapolation from historical growth patterns. Both these premises, however, pose potential problems for today's planners. When environmental conditions were simple and relatively stable, firms could expect that the future would be an extension of the past. Under those assumptions, planning was an optimistic projection of past organizational performance, with the expectation of future growth. In other words, the future was presumed to be better than the past. Environmental factors were expected to change in magnitude and not in character. Long-range planning, therefore, was the pursuit of organizational goals by matching the organization's capabilities with the economic considerations of the market.

Recent events, such as the energy crisis, proved the fallacy of those assumptions. It became evident that the past may not be a reliable predictor of the future and that many environmental changes are discontinuous. With its questionable premises, long-range planning was displaced by strategic planning.

The premises of strategic planning are different: The future may not necessarily be an improvement over the past, nor may it be extrapolated. The patterns of past events may not continue into the future. Most environmental changes are discontinuous. To succeed in such an unpredictable milieu, firms need to strategically plan and manage their present and future operations. As Figure 6.1 illustrates, the strategic planning process begins with a determination of the firm's organizational mission and goals. After establishment of the mission and goals, the process proceeds with two interdependent and simultaneous analyses: **internal assessment** and **environmental scanning**. Internal assessment provides information regarding the internal capabilities (**strengths**) and limitations (**weaknesses**) of the firm. Environmental scanning enables the firm, domestic or international, to identify existing **opportunities** and **threats** in the environment. These interdependent, simultaneous analyses should permit the firm to assess the appropriateness of its goals and, if necessary, modify them. Changes in the premises on which the firm's organizational mission and goals are based may require a modification or a total revision of those goals.

Once the appropriateness of the organizational mission and goals has been resolved, two sequential phases of strategy formulation and implementation

Figure 6.1   **Strategy Formulation Process**

begin. The formulation phase creates the plan for future activities, and the implementation phase is the execution of that plan. Based on the two simultaneous analyses discussed earlier, the firm develops a plan to accomplish its organizational goals and to exploit environmental **opportunities** through the deployment of its **strengths**. In doing so, the firm should be careful not to expose its **weaknesses** and should be prepared to face **threatening conditions** or avoid them altogether. The process is concluded when a control mechanism shows that the strategy process is being properly executed.

There are no substantive differences between the strategic planning process of a domestic company and that of an MNC. The strategic process, for both domestic companies and MNCs, entails aligning organizational capabilities with changing environmental conditions to achieve organizational goals. Regardless of the nature of the operation, the strategic management process remains basically the same for the domestic enterprise and the MNC. The fact that a firm expands abroad does not entail that there will be a different strategy formulation and implementation process. The vignette at the beginning of the chapter discussed how the application of a new strategy by Samsung propelled it from a humble position to a global leader. By expanding to foreign markets, however, the firm will encounter additional complexity from operating across national borders.

Internationalization of the firm brings about many new problems that require careful resolution. These new problems increase the burden of managing an MNC. The multiplicity of cultural, sociopolitical, legal, and economic environments creates quantitative and qualitative difficulties. Quantitatively, there are many national markets, each with its own requirements and problems that demand special attention. Qualitatively, because of historical, cultural, political, and economic variations, each national market is unique. Each changes differently and at a different pace. Confounding the problems are the interdependencies among national markets in a network of customers, suppliers, creditors, competitors, and so on that culminate in a complex global market. Additionally, geographic separation between home and host countries creates its own problems.

Much has been said about the diminishing effect of distance on international business. It is argued that the improvements in communication made possible by modern information technologies and the ease of transportation have made the world a relatively small place. But some have addressed the issue of distance in a new light.[7] This view emphasizes that the distance between home and host countries adversely affects international business. However, it maintains that distance can be viewed along four dimensions: geographic, cultural, administrative or political, and economic. The geographic dimension of distance affects the cost of communication and transportation for some businesses. Other dimensions are elaborated in the section on environmental forces. Successful MNCs learn how to deal effectively with the multiplicity of environmental conditions.

In the following sections, we discuss the cultural aspects of strategy. We learn that there are fundamental differences between the thought processes of Westerners and Easterners. These differences are reflected through the strategy formulation process. Then, we examine the environmental forces that influence international management. Each of these forces, alone or in combination with other forces, makes the job of an international manager a challenging task. Although these forces are often the source of difficulties, they have the potential to open up many opportunities for MNCs. They can hinder or help MNC operations and can improve the overall profitability or cause substantial loss.

Cultural Aspects of Strategy

The central issue in strategy formulation is identification of environmental forces that may have an influence on the organization and preparation of a plan of action to deal with them. Environmental scanning should enable the firm to identify these forces. Doing this calls for not only information gathering but also deciding what to look for, where to look, and what to select from the abundance of information available. The process is not an objective and mechanistic activity that is free of human biases. Scanning and information gathering are culturally based perceptual processes. The external environmental assessment aspect of strategy formulation has been described by Susan Schneider as a five-step process of scanning behavior, information selection, interpretation, validation, and prioritizing. Because these steps are based on culturally programmed perception processes, countrywise differences can be expected in each step.[8]

Strategy formulation and implementation also deal with internal organizational issues that center on relationships among people, such as the place of individuals and groups in society, hierarchy, power, and authority. In this section, we examine strategy implications of cultural differences relating to the environment and existing in relationships among people.

Relationship With the Environment

American and many other Western societies consider exploitation of nature a desirable action. People are considered to be masters of the world, and this belief leads to an engineering orientation toward nature. It means that the physical environment should conform to the design made by people. If there is any mismatch, it is the physical environment that should be changed to fit one's plans, and obstacles in one's path are destroyed. In contrast to this proactive and engineering view, some cultures believe in a symbiotic relationship with nature. Native Americans, for example, instead of attempting to change the environment, believe in living in harmony with their surroundings and trying to be a part of the environment, not apart from it. The mental framework used by an engineering-oriented person is very different from a symbiotic mentality. Each mentality leads to a different scanning behavior. An engineering-oriented person looks for data in support of change and intervention in the environment. In contrast, a preference to live in harmony with the environment leads a symbiotic person to search for nondestructive alternatives.

Scanning behavior is also influenced by the belief that people are able to control their environment. The fatalist beliefs of Buddhists and Muslims' conviction that events are predetermined limit their scanning behavior. If environmental forces are beyond the control of individuals or if events are preordained, what is the use of a strategy? This is not to say that Muslim or Buddhist businesses function with no plans or strategies, but it involves the acknowledgment in these cultures of the limits of human control. This is in sharp contrast with the American can-do mentality and belief in self-determination.

Strategy formulation above all is a mental exercise and a thought process. Thinking patterns among people vary. This variation is due to cultural programming that influences perception and shapes the individual psyche. In the simpler life of preindustrial societies, people were accustomed to direct contact with objects and persons. In their thinking, they relied on visual associations between events and the environment. Industrial societies have grown complex and have substituted abstract concepts for visual associations, concrete objects, and relationships (p. 423).[9] Daily life in civilized societies, therefore, relies more on conceptualization and abstraction. Cultures, however, vary in their methods of conceptualization and abstraction. There are cultural differences in the use of cognitive models of the environment for interpretation of nature and the world. An important cognitive model that greatly influences organizational life is a causation model that is used to explain events.

Research findings suggest, for example, that there is a difference between the way Americans and Japanese perceive causation.[10,11] In short, the type of information that we select from our scanning process is a function of cultural upbringing. Cultural differences result in various perceptual models that are the product of our abstraction process. Synthesizing these findings, Robert Doktor suggests that the managerial practices of Japanese and Americans are due to different views of causation. A different use of brain structure and differences in cognitive models lead to different causation maps. American thinking is shaped by Aristotelian logic, which assumes an action-reaction process, the position that events occur in "response" to one or more prior events. Most Japanese use an "environmental" model of causation. They rely on concrete data received from their primary senses. They emphasize the more concrete environmental relationships, such as group consensus, nation, and security.

Different Thought Processes

Two different approaches to the world have maintained themselves for thousands of years. These approaches include profoundly different social relations, views about the nature of [the] world, and characteristic thought processes. Each of these orientations—the Western and the Eastern—is a self-reinforcing, homeostatic system. The social practices promote the world-views; the world-views dictate the appropriate thought processes; and the thought processes both justify the world-views and support the social practices. Understanding these homeostatic systems has implications for grasping the fundamental nature of the mind, for beliefs about how we ought ideally to reason.[12]

The American cognitive model is logical, sequential, and based on an abstract concept of universal reality. Japanese cognition is based on concrete perception that relies on sense data; emphasizes particular, rather than universal, reality; is not abstract; and has a high sensitivity to environmental context and relationships. The abstract concepts used by Americans to explain organizational behavior, such as leadership, morale, and decision making, are not well-defined in the Japanese language.[13]

Western cultures, and particularly American culture, place a high value and priority on rational, objective, and factual information in support of business decisions. Aristotelian logic, used by Europeans, North Americans, and other nations, assumes the existence of an "objective" truth. Errors are considered to be the source of differences. Quite often, people attempt to reach an understanding by discarding areas of disagreements and building on the areas on which they agree. The Japanese, however, try to include multiple views and build on variations. This is similar to the variation between two different images of the same object. A three-dimensional view is the result of the differences between the two images. Discarding the variations between the two images results in a two-dimensional, flat object. For the Japanese, the objective truth of Aristotelian logic is a foreign concept, which does not have an exact equivalence in Japanese and, therefore, does not make sense. The translation of the term *objectivity* into Japanese does not quite match the meaning implied by it in the English language. The Japanese translation for the foreign word *objectivity* is *kyakkanteki*, which means the guest's point of view, and the translation for *subjectivity* is *shukanteki*, meaning the host's point of view.[14]

Richard Nisbett[12] argues that there are fundamental differences between the way Westerners and Easterners view the world (pp. 44, 45, 80–82, 100). Westerners pay more attention to objects, while Easterners focus more on the overall surroundings. Consequently, Easterners are more likely to detect relationships among events than are Westerners. Asians see the world as substances, consisting of continuous masses of matter. Westerners see a world of objects, discrete and unconnected *things*. Westerners have an analytic view, focusing on salient objects and their attributes, whereas Easterners have a holistic view, focusing on continuity in substances and relationships in the environment. Therefore, to Asians the world is understandable in terms of the whole, not in terms of the parts, and subject to collective, not personal, control. The Western view is the opposite: The world is a relatively simple place that is made up of simple objects and can be understood without undue attention to the context. It is also highly subject to personal control. This leads to Westerners' method of organizing by categorizing objects and Easterners' method of emphasizing relationships. Because of Easterners' heightened perception of the environment, they attribute causality more to the context and tend to resolve contradiction and conflict by seeking a middle option between two positions. Westerners, on the other hand, rely more on logical rules and, in resolving contradiction, insist on the correctness of one side. These differences are summarized in Table 6.1.

We can surmise from the preceding discussion that scanning behavior is a function of assumptions regarding the nature of "truth and reality" (p. 156).[8] It also brings to our attention the fact that other aspects of scanning behavior—namely, selection, interpretation, validation, and prioritization—are influenced by our mental framework and the interpretation of our observations of environmental phenomena. Observations of the managerial practices of other nations, for example, are interpreted using our cultural cognitive maps. Application of our cultural cognitive maps for understanding and evaluating the people of other cultures is also called a self-reference criterion (SRC). SRC is the unconscious reference to one's own cultural values.[15] SRC may lead us to wrong conclusions. For instance, in the past few decades, the success of Japanese business has led to the study of Japanese managerial practices, in a bid to find the "secret" of their achievements. Using SRC, we have erroneously interpreted the Japanese decision-making process as consensus. Because Japanese include input from different levels of the hierarchy and involve many employees in the process, their collective decision making has been labeled as reaching consensus. If consensus means reaching the same decision, then interpreting the Japanese approach as consensus decision making is incorrect. Japanese collective decision making can be best described as the process of informing all involved about future adjustments and paybacks. The outcome of any decision will cause inconvenience for some and benefit for others. To the Japanese, the main focus of the decision-making process is for all to make a mental note of each individual's benefits and inconveniences for future adjustment. This, therefore, calls for collective participation in the process (pp. 100–111).[14]

In the same vein, the use of SRC in the interpretation of Japanese practices has resulted in another misunderstanding. According to American cultural models, conformity implies losing uniqueness, accepting uniformity, and submission to the rule of the majority. Therefore, it is not a compliment to

Table 6.1   Differences Between Easterners and Westerners

	Easterners	Westerners
1. Pattern of attention and perception	Attention to the environment and the relationships among events	Attention to objects
2. Relation to the environment	Environmental controllability is limited	Many opportunities to control the environment
3. Change versus stability	See stability	See changes
4. Preferred pattern of explanation of events	Focus on objects and their environment	Focus on objects
5. Habits of organizing	Emphasize relationship	Categorizing
6. Resolving conflict and contradiction	Seek the middle way	Insist on the correctness of one belief versus others
7. Use of formal logical rules	Do not rely on logical rules	Rely on logical rules

SOURCE: This table is constructed based on material given in Reference 8, pp. 44–45.

call someone a conformist. *Conformity*, however, is translated into Japanese "as sharp perception of the situation, unique sense of adaptation with reality, quick orientation and reaction to cope with various situations, responding to the needs of the overall situation" (p. 109).[14] Conformity to the Japanese, using their own standards of desirability in judging behaviors, implies something desirable because it involves understanding others and the ability to comprehend situations from their viewpoints. It seems that the Japanese sense of conformity more closely corresponds to the "flexibility" of the Americans. In contrast, the American sense of conformity implies rigidity and an inability to change (p. 109).[14] Along the same lines, the most important function of job rotation for the Japanese is to make the workers think "in one another's head" and become mentally connected with others (p. 103),[14] while the purpose of job rotation in America is to reduce monotony and boredom. As a side benefit, of course, job rotation is used to build different skills among the workers, so that they can be employed interchangeably.

Relationships Among People

Managerial functions, including strategy formulation, are based on a premise involving patterns of interpersonal relationships. It is accepted that in a business enterprise, people will relate to each other in a predictable fashion. This predictability of behavior involves cultural programming such that a superior's order and a subordinate's response follow an expected pattern and agreed-on modes of behavior. The same is true for other relationships in the organization. Organizational hierarchies are established to deal with these relationships. The American work relationship is based on contractual arrangements that are based on earnings and career opportunities.[16] An American, for example, in fulfilling his or her job responsibilities, expects to receive corresponding rewards. No one is expected to make an individual sacrifice unless other employees do the same. On that basis, strategies are formulated, and environmental opportunities are considered worthwhile to pursue, if they fit this framework.

In contrast, Japanese firms have a larger assortment of alternatives for strategic choices. Employees understand that each individual may be called on to make personal sacrifices for the benefit of the company. Such sacrifices, however, are interpreted differently. Japanese employees' sacrifice for the sake of their company is ultimately for their own benefit rather than self-sacrifice. If their sacrifice makes the company prosper, it will be their gain (p. 104).[14]

At the heart of the American strategic planning process is the concept of a fully functional market. The governing force of this market is pure, albeit theoretical, competition. Fair contractual agreements provide continuity for transactions between the managers as employers and the employees. In effect, in this market the employees sell their labor for a price.[16] The strategy process and its associated scanning behaviors are bound by these rules. In contrast, the governing principle for the French organization is the honor of each class, in a society that has always been, and still is, extremely stratified. In France, "superiors behave as superior beings and subordinates accept and expect this, conscious of their own lower level in the national hierarchy but also of the honor of their own class" (p. 84).[16] Unlike the Americans, the French consider management a "state of mind." Successful French managers share a distinctive sense of belonging to the French managerial class, called *cadre*.

Most French managers come from engineering schools and see managerial work as requiring an analytical mind, independence, intellectual rigor, and the ability to synthesize information. French managers are excellent at quantitative thought and expression and the numeric aspects of strategy formulation. They believe that their achievement and high position are due to their intellectual ability. Consequently, senior French managers think that their intellectual superiority entitles them to make the most critical and important decisions. Large French organizations are characterized by a centralized decision-making, hierarchical, and compartmentalized structure. Senior managers make all the important decisions and expect to know all that happens in the firm so they can check everyone's decisions. This hierarchical arrangement is reflected in the physical structure of the typical large French firms. Often, the chief executive's office is on the top floor and the typing pool in the basement. Large public and private institutions hire the best students from top engineering schools and assign them to fast-track positions. These protégés develop an informal network that exists throughout the French managerial class. The French educational system is set up such that high proportions of the best brains from each generation are channeled into business, civil service, and government. Such a system brings close cooperation between the French government and business. The special relationship between the French education system and business, as well as French cultural attributes, create a unique managerial mentality. A simple way of explaining this uniqueness is to use the often-cited statement by a General Motors president. The French equivalent of "What is good for General Motors is good for the United States" is, "What is good for France is good for Peugeot."[17]

Management literature has begun to recognize that American management theories are not universal. The strategic management process as it was described at the beginning of this chapter is the product of management theories and practices that are rooted in American culture. Although the general framework—namely, the objective of winning in a competitive global marketplace—is universal, the methods, approaches, and orientation to it are not. Recognition of cultural differences in the strategy process enables MNCs to understand not only the competition but also the orientation and attitudes of local managers of its foreign subsidiaries. Acknowledging the influence of culture in the strategy process results in relevant and appropriate managerial practices.

International Environmental Forces _____

The difference in strategy formulation and implementation processes between a domestic and an international operation is in the degree of environmental and organizational complexities and uncertainties. MNC operations are more complex, and they face many more environmental uncertainties and complexities. In addition to all the forces that influence the strategy of a domestic business, MNCs have to deal with many more forces. The major international environmental forces include

1. cultural differences;

2. host government, political, and legal issues;

3. competition from local businesses, government agencies, and other MNCs; and

4. international finance and currency exchange rates.

We discussed cultural differences in Chapter 3. The following sections discuss host government, political, and legal issues and the competition. Financial aspects of international operations, including currency exchange rates, are the subjects of international finance.

Host Government, Political, and Legal Issues

The most influential of all international environmental forces are political, legal, and governmental. Legal and political issues could hinder an

MNC's overseas operations. A lack of understanding of local laws could cost an MNC dearly. Political turmoil that simmers under the surface may be very difficult for outsiders to detect. Yet an inappropriate response could result in substantial earning and property loss.

Host governments use their sovereign power to restrict or assist MNCs. When host countries believe that the operation of MNCs is compatible with their national goals, they may provide various incentives to attract and maintain MNC operations. If, however, the activities of the MNCs do not meet a host government's expectations, it may place many restrictions and obstacles in their paths. At the heart of this difficulty lies the difference between the objectives of host countries and those of MNCs. The major strategic goals of MNCs and host governments are summarized in Table 6.2. The challenge is to find common areas where there are mutual benefits.

Host governments have a love-hate relationship with MNCs. It is safe to say that the feeling is mutual. In general, this feeling is more intense in the case of developing nations. The power of MNCs and the fact that they operate across national borders make their operations less susceptible to influence and control by host governments. When the strategic requirements of MNCs are not compatible with a host government's economic plans, the relationship may not be very beneficial to the host country. The power, resources, and flexibility of MNCs could overwhelm most host governments' plans and render them less effective. However, MNCs are a

Table 6.2   Strategic Goals of Host Governments and MNCs

Host Governments	Multinational Corporations
National income	Return on investment
Maximization of tax revenues	Minimization of tax payments
Employment	Increased earnings
Skill diversity among the labor force	Specialization for efficiency
Economic development	Competitive advantage
Technology transfer and industry/managerial skills	Low-cost production, efficiency
Diverse economy	Cost-effective operation/control on hiring and training
Local control over business firms	Headquarters control over subsidiary
Local research and development capability	Headquarters control over research and development
Balanced industrial activities geographically	Operations in cities with adequate infrastructure and support services
Control over pattern of economic development	Freedom of trade and investment
Balance of payments	Profit repatriation

source of new technology, capital, and tax revenues. The global network of distribution channels of the MNCs could assist the host countries in reaching world markets. For many developing countries that are burdened with heavy national debts, MNCs are the only source of needed capital. While the host government relationship is a major concern for MNCs, their relationships with the governments of developing countries pose unique problems for them.

Developing Countries and MNCs

Although most countries welcome the MNCs and find the relationship with them mutually beneficial, some developing nations have expressed disappointment with the relationship. Some have argued that the needs of developing countries and the objectives of MNCs are incompatible. They view the main objectives of MNCs as exploitation of foreign markets and maximization of profit. MNCs do business with developing countries solely for economic reasons, such as cheap raw materials and untapped markets. They are not seriously concerned with the impact of their operations on developing countries. Developing countries, however, want to maximize MNCs' contribution to national goals with a minimum effect on national sovereignty.[18]

Historically, developing countries' relationships with MNCs have been marred by misunderstandings and unfulfilled expectations. Although both MNCs and developing countries believe that they can benefit from such relationships, outcomes have been less than satisfactory for some developing countries. The disappointment with MNCs, according to Peter Wright,[19] stems from dissimilar views regarding three aspects of the relationship:

1. Expectation of wealth

2. Incongruency in values

3. Technology transfer

Wealth Expectations. Developing countries expected MNCs to assist them in their pursuit of economic development. They assumed that major economic gains and technology transfer would take place through the operation of MNCs. The reality was different from the assumptions. Developing countries maintain that the benefits of the relationships accrued to the MNCs only. While the MNCs enjoyed higher sales and revenues, developing countries' quest to join the ranks of rich nations through cooperation with the MNCs did not happen. Developing countries assert that the MNCs exploited their natural resources and low labor costs without providing them with a corresponding wealth gain. MNCs and developed nations argue that the plight of developing countries may be traced to sociocultural values that are not congruent with economic growth.

Value Incongruency. There are certain inherent values that support and sustain industrialization and modernization. The most salient values of industrial societies are the utility of mass production and the economic benefits of efficiency. To operate efficiently, a mass production system necessitates adherence to certain organizational requirements. These requirements include certain man-machine ratios and specific interfaces between the person and the machine. At the micro level, for example, the efficiency of an assembly line operation is fatally damaged if it is interrupted for the daily prayers that certain religions expect. At the macro level, business decisions that are dictated by market forces are not always congruent with the political and economic priorities of host countries.

Technology Transfer. Developing nations were hoping that the operation of MNCs would result in technology transfer and would assist them in joining the ranks of industrialized nations. They were disappointed to discover that whatever transfer of technology took place, particularly in the extractive industries, such as mining, was industry specific and not applicable elsewhere. Such technology was also useless once the natural resources were depleted. Also, the viability of technology transferred in the manufacturing sector depended heavily on the MNCs. Without the provision of parts and components, for example, car manufacturing or appliance facilities in developing countries would be rendered idle.

While past relationships between developing countries and MNCs were marred by misunderstanding and dashed hopes, not many would dispute the benefits that MNCs could provide. Host governments in general, however, have a few concerns in their dealings with MNCs.

Host Government Concerns. The relationship with MNCs, particularly globally integrated MNCs, raises concerns of host governments over the following specific issues (p. 237):[20]

1. The flexibility of MNCs

2. Interdependency and control

3. Efficiency

4. The effect of MNCs on domestic strategic industries

5. Taxation

6. The MNCs' headquarters as decision centers

Flexibility of MNCs. Host governments fear that the MNC network of integrated facilities around the world could be used to the disadvantage of domestic firms. Their fear is based on MNC characteristics. First, MNCs have an information advantage over locally oriented domestic firms. Significant changes in market conditions could be detected by the global scanning capabilities of MNCs. They are able to switch out of unattractive business activities much faster than domestic firms. Second, MNCs' multiple locations around the world enable them to respond immediately to changing circumstances in the global market and shift production and manufacturing facilities to countries with a relative cost advantage. Also, because they are not particularly committed to any country, except possibly their home base, MNCs can easily relocate on short notice (p. 232).[20]

Interdependency and Control. With increased trade comes interdependence among trading partners. A decision made by one of the partners influences the other and vice versa. It compels governments to consider the ramifications of decisions made outside their national borders on their economies. Increased globalization of industry creates international interdependency among nations and exposes national economies to forces beyond the control of governments. In other words, governments lose some control over their economies, and even some of their sovereign power, to global market forces, including MNCs. Free trade brings about free movement of capital and investment. Free trade also influences labor-management relationships and restricts labor union strategies.[21] Globalization of industry and free trade pressure national economies to adjust to changes that take place globally. A change in the competitive position of an industry due to changes in the price of raw material or labor, for example, may require changing national priorities and economic programs. During the oil crisis of the early 1970s, for example, Japan realized that its high-energy-consuming aluminum industry could not compete with the American aluminum industry. The American aluminum industry could rely on domestic oil as a buffer against the high price of imported oil, while the Japanese industry had to satisfy all its needs by imports. Therefore, the Ministry of International Trade and Industry (MITI)—now called the Ministry of Economy, Trade and Industry (METI)—decided not to provide the aluminum industry with any additional source of cheap financing, causing it to wither away. In effect, the forces of the global market left the Japanese government with no choice but to watch the demise of its aluminum industry.

A Different Global Company

MTV Networks International, the music channel and its sister operations, VH1 and Nickelodeon, reach 1 billion people in 18 different languages in 164 countries. Its revenues and sales have been increasing rapidly. It owes its success to four factors. First, it draws its audience from a large pool of young people that is growing in numbers. MTV's audience, in the 10- to 34-year age-group, is expected to grow by 2010 to 2.8 billion. Second, its product, music, is a universal language, and

> rock is the universal language of young people worldwide. What MTV does is customize its offerings very successfully. Third, television ownership is exploding globally, especially in such places as China, Brazil, India, and Russia. Fourth, its management realizes that while the world's teens want American music, they really want the local music, too. To assuage the fear of Americanization, MTV's management assures host countries that they are not in the business of exporting American culture. They point out their policy of 70% local content.[22]

The competitive pressure resulting from globalization of industry as well as advancements in telecommunications and transportation has exposed the vulnerability of many domestic firms. MNCs, with a presence in many markets, have information and resource advantages over domestic firms. These advantages include capital, distribution channels, and technical and managerial expertise. MNCs can detect changes in consumer needs and purchasing patterns and learn about new technologies well before their domestic counterparts. The technology explosion of recent years has also shortened industry life cycles and has increased the cost of data gathering and analysis. The concerns of governments are heightened by the realization that information advantage, when coupled with a resource advantage, provides MNCs with a decisive edge over locally based domestic firms. These concerns are more pronounced for mature industries. Mature industries, characterized by price competition, operate in the most fiercely contested markets. Since barriers to entry are low in these industries, competition is intense and comes from many countries. Therefore, governments would like to see domestic firms branch out into emerging industries, where competitive pressures are low and the opportunities for profits are high.

Faced with the pressure of global market forces and motivated by the desire to regain control, some governments have established a much closer relationship with the industry. The cooperative relationship between MITI and Japanese industry is a good example. It has enabled Japan to reduce the cost and uncertainty for private firms in committing resources to emerging industries. Characteristically, emerging industries require heavy investments for extended periods of time. Although the eventual returns could be high, the high cost of capital and economic and technological uncertainties discourage private long-term investment in emerging industries. As Japan has demonstrated, governments can reduce the cost and uncertainties of investment and increase the participation of private firms in emerging industries.

Efficiency. On the one hand, if allowed unrestricted access to a domestic market, an MNC's competitive advantage may force less resourceful domestic businesses out of the market. On the other hand, if an MNC's participation in the domestic market is restricted or prevented, consumers may pay higher prices, and an inefficient domestic industry may unnecessarily be preserved. Even if government follows a policy of free trade, without actively encouraging the development of new and emerging industries, the country may find itself saddled with aging MNC subsidiaries. When faced with heavy competition from low-cost producers in other countries, the large-scale departure of these subsidiaries will have a harmful effect on the economy. The United Kingdom found itself in such a position several years ago. When a number of traditional plants, such as Singer's sewing machine and Caterpillar's tractor plants, lost their competitive position vis-à-vis their Asian counterparts, the impact on the United Kingdom was painful. In contrast, the government of Singapore has enjoyed the positive effects of encouraging quick adjustments to international competition and the development of emerging industries (p. 232).[20]

Effect on Domestic Strategic Industry. Globalization of business leads to specialization. If globalization is allowed to take its own course, some domestic firms may be forced out of business, while others may flourish. It is possible that the participation of MNCs in the domestic market may hinder the development of domestic industry. This is because the MNCs, with their information and resource advantage, may crowd the market and leave no room for domestic competition to evolve. Therefore, host governments believe that industries that are vital for national security should be protected from the pressure of global market forces. Without support and protection from the government, these industries may not have a chance to develop and, if they exist, may disintegrate. Even those countries that are active participants in the global market and have, therefore, accepted interdependency are very fearful of depending on outsiders in strategically important areas. To be able to control telecommunication and defense industries, for example, governments would like domestic firms to develop them exclusively. But the small size of many domestic markets for these industries raises concerns over efficiency and costs. For that reason, to make it possible to produce in large volumes and reduce costs, global arms sales present an attractive option pursued by many industrialized countries to bolster their defense industry. It is especially for this reason that efforts to curb the arms race among developing countries have not been successful. Without having modern manufacturing capabilities of their own, historically, developing countries have been eager customers for modern weaponry.

Taxation. In industries where direct costs are small and allocated costs (research and development [R&D], patents, administrative costs) are large, MNCs can manipulate the earnings of subsidiaries. Through transfer pricing, where subsidiaries are charged for their intrafirm purchases, and by allocating R&D expenditures, a subsidiary could show fewer profits to reduce its tax obligations. It is very difficult for governments to prove the actual violations and prevent them from happening. For many years, to no avail, developing countries complained about such abuses by MNCs. The inability of host countries to thwart these abuses became amply clear when, in the late 1980s and early 1990s, the U.S. government took legal actions against a few MNCs, accusing them of such practices without much success. The most recent transfer pricing dispute involved GlaxoSmithKline PLC and the U.S. Internal Revenue Service (IRS). The IRS contended that Glaxo's American subsidiary drastically overpaid royalties to its British parent for R&D costs incurred in Britain and understated its U.S. marketing costs. The disputed amount was estimated to be about $2.4 billion.[23]

The MNC Headquarters as Decision Center. An aggravating issue for host countries is that subsidiaries of MNCs may not be the real decision-making authorities. Subsidiary managers in a global firm very seldom can make an important decision all by themselves. Often, the strategic ramifications of a subsidiary's decisions for the total MNC operation compel headquarters to intervene. Subsidiary managers have to regularly consult with headquarters on any agreement made with the host government. In many cases, subsidiary managers are not even allowed to involve themselves in negotiations with the host governments. Although host government officials deal with these managers regularly, they cannot count on them to make decisions affecting the domestic market. The real decision makers are thousands of miles away in a foreign country.

Characteristics of MNC–Host Country Relationships

Until recently, many countries regarded MNCs as evil institutions that could provide some benefits. The question was whether or not their presence should be tolerated. The very same countries now assume a more practical stance and search for the best way to use MNCs to further their national goals (p. 4).[24] In the mid-1970s, for example, the government of Venezuela took over the oil industry from foreign MNCs. In the 1990s, the same government envisioned a major new role for foreign MNCs, especially oil companies such as Exxon Corporation and the Royal Dutch/Shell Group. Plans were made for these firms to participate in a $40 billion project to speed up development of Venezuela's vast energy base. Similarly, British Petroleum Company, which was nationalized in the mid-1970s by the Nigerian government, was called back in the 1990s to resume the search for oil.[25] Many host governments see the MNCs' operations as beneficial to the national economy in the development of an industrial base, creation of jobs, and generation of tax revenues.

Although there is no formal market for foreign investment, in practice, market conditions prevail. Similar to the competition among producers for the market share of consumer expenditures, countries compete for the market share of new foreign investment.[26] Firms that are looking for plant sites for international expansion are "buyers," and host governments that are offering plant locations are "sellers." In this market, the bargaining power of buyers and sellers determines the characteristics of the transactions. This issue is discussed below.

Host governments and MNCs have a very complex and interdependent relationship. Many factors determine the amount of influence that each can exert on the other. Among the factors that could dictate the nature of the relationship are (1) their relative bargaining power, (2) the type of strategy that the MNCs employ, and (3) the structure of the industry.

MNCs' Bargaining Power. An MNC's relative bargaining power increases under five conditions: first, if it has a monopolistic position; second, if it uses a technology that requires a large investment in R&D, without many viable substitutes; third, if it exports a large part of its outputs and has control over the market downstream (e.g., distribution channels); fourth, if it employs factors of production, such as unskilled labor, that are easily substitutable across countries; and fifth, if its operations require a small investment that could very easily be liquidated or moved, meaning that the operations are relatively immune from excessive pressures on the part of the host government (pp. 269–270).[26]

Bargaining Power of Host Countries. Just as there are certain conditions that increase the relative power of MNCs, there are also conditions that influence the relative bargaining power of host countries (see Table 6.3). A country in the early stages of economic development that is heavily dependent on technology importation may be in a weak bargaining position vis-à-vis MNCs. For these countries, MNCs are the only vehicle of technology transfer, and they cannot afford to alienate them; a government in dire need of hard currency can ill afford to restrict MNC operations. In general, the relative power of the host government depends on control over three factors: access to product markets, access to the domestic capital market, and access to production technology.[26]

Host governments have the power to control access to domestic markets, and they usually exercise this power. The importance of access to a domestic market is a function of one or a combination of three factors. First, the MNC may desire access to the market because of its size. China, India,

Table 6.3   Factors Influencing the Bargaining Power of Host Countries

Increasing Bargaining Power	Decreasing Bargaining Power
1. Control access to product market: Domestic market is attractive because of a. Size b. Potential for export (low labor cost) c. A regional pact member	1. Dependence on MNCs for technology 2. The need for hard currencies
2. Control access to domestic capital market	
3. Control access to production technology	

Brazil, and Mexico have large domestic markets. Their huge size and the fact that these markets cannot be supplied by locating plants in other countries make them attractive to MNCs. The low purchasing power in these countries, however, tempers their attractiveness. Control over a large domestic market gives the government a monopoly power, similar to that enjoyed by countries with desirable raw materials that are in limited supply. Second, a market may be attractive to MNCs because of its export potential. As part of its global strategy, an MNC may be interested in a country's low labor costs for setting up export-oriented manufacturing facilities. This is a major reason why some MNCs have established manufacturing facilities in China. Third, a country's domestic market could be attractive due to its membership in a regional trade pact. It could be used for entry into a market that would otherwise be difficult to access. Each of the members of the European Union, for example, could be an attractive alternative for reaching the European market.

The domestic capital market is typically controlled by governments. Host governments can generate alternative sources of capital, both internal and external, such as domestic savings and foreign commercial loans. This willingness and ability to provide or assist in securing investment finances increases the bargaining power of host governments and the attractiveness of their domestic markets. Likewise, the availability of indigenous technology or licensing agreements could improve the host government's bargaining position.

The Two Faces of Globalization in China

While China is feeding the world's appetite for consumer goods and benefits from the globalization of business, the one-time "workers' republic" is becoming a nation of haves and have-nots. The positive and negative effects of globalization are evident all over the country. Some cities, such as Wenzhou, 200 miles south of Shanghai, that benefit from China's trade with the rest of the world are quickly modernizing, and their lifestyles are changing rapidly. Some other cities are not that fortunate. Wenzhou churns out shoes, pharmaceuticals, garments, sporting goods, optics, kitchen appliances, and paint and metal work. It has an annual per capita income that is almost double the national average. It has gated communities of opulent villas occupied by residents who drive Cadillacs, Mercedes-Benzes, BMWs, and even Hummers. China's economic growth has been phenomenal. In the two decades prior to 2000, the Chinese economy quadrupled, and it is expected to become the fourth largest economy in the world in a few years.

(Continued)

(Continued)

> This growth has masked the suffering of millions who, for various reasons, are left behind and have not benefited from modernization. The socialist state suffers high levels of unemployment. Approximately 13% of China's 1.3 billion people survive on a dollar a day or less. Not only are these people suffering economically; their political situation is not much better. The government has demonstrated its contempt for basic human rights by its one-party politics, its rubber-stamp judiciary, its censored Internet and oppressed minorities, and its notorious prison system.
>
> Chinese can now afford televisions, refrigerators, and personal computers, which decades ago were considered luxuries. Many of the services that the state used to provide are, however, no longer available, and many people cannot afford to pay for them in the free market. Decades ago, the government jettisoned health care services to the free market, and rent is now about half an average worker's wages. The lower class is suffering due to these free-market changes. They used to have guaranteed employment and could afford the services that were offered by the government, albeit they were bad services. This is no longer the case.
>
> SOURCE: Reference 27.

Deterioration of Relationships. Host governments and MNCs have different strategic goals and values that may not necessarily be compatible. Sometimes, these differences many cause the relationship between the two to deteriorate. This may result in one of two possible outcomes. First, the MNC may find it necessary to withdraw its investment. Second, the host government many take certain measures detrimental to the MNC. These measures are often punitive and in the long run would not benefit the host country. The punitive measures warn other MNCs to withhold investment from the host country, which is counterproductive to the strategic goals of the host government. These measures are **nationalization, expropriation, creeping expropriation, confiscation,** and **domestication.**

1. *Nationalization*: Host governments may, for various reasons, take over the assets of MNCs operating within their borders. In legal terms, when MNCs are promptly, adequately, and effectively compensated, the takeover is called nationalization. If the seizure of the property is without compensation, it is referred to as expropriation. The right of states to nationalize foreign property is universally recognized, as long as it is done for a legitimate public purpose and is followed by adequate, prompt, and effective compensation. However, in regular usage, expropriation and nationalization are treated similarly.

There are four reasons for nationalization or expropriation:

a. The host government may suspect that the MNC is concealing profits and may want to extract more money from the firm.

b. The host government believes that it can run the business more efficiently or provide more benefits, such as managerial opportunities to citizens, by replacing the MNC.

c. Left-wing, or left-leaning governments take over MNC operations for ideological reasons.

d. For political reasons, a declining business is taken over to save jobs and win votes.

Nationalization cases were more common up to the 1970s. Host governments have used other measures to achieve the same goal of taking over MNC operations without antagonizing other foreign investors outright. In recent years, host governments have used **creeping expropriation**, or taking over the operations of MNCs through a series of restrictive administrative actions, such as the stringent application of health and safety procedures.

There are three reasons for using creeping expropriation instead of outright nationalization. First, host governments need to attract foreign direct investment and do not want to take actions that discourage foreign investors. Second, the host governments have become more sophisticated and administratively more capable. By using means other than nationalization and expropriation, they may achieve the same goals. Third, more often, international business involves joint ventures and other forms of business activities that include private enterprises as well as the host government itself.

2. *Confiscation*: Transfer of ownership of a business enterprise to the host government is called confiscation. Confiscation does not involve compensation for the MNC.

3. *Domestication*: A more subtle form of expropriation is domestication. It enables the host government to control a foreign-owned business. Domestication may be achieved through the imposition of local-content regulations or the demand that a large share of the profits be retained in the country. Local-content regulations ensure that a large share of the products is produced locally. Domestication can take place through changes in labor laws, tax regulations, and patent protection.

Political Risk. One form of risk facing the MNC is political risk. Political risk has been defined in many different ways. Often, in management research and practice, political instability has been regarded as a synonym for political risk.[28] Frequently, MNCs have avoided investing in politically unstable markets, considering such investment too risky. From a strictly financial perspective, however, a working definition of political risk refers to unforeseen host government actions that have a negative impact on a corporation's wealth. Political risk may manifest itself through nationalization, currency controls, requirements for local partnerships, restrictions on repatriation of funds, and increased regulations and changes in taxation laws. It is important to note the difference between a high-tax-rate and an uncertain-tax-rate environment. When making an investment decision in the former environment, the investor simply takes high tax rates into consideration. In contrast, the risk that the tax rates will be raised substantially after the investment is made constitutes a political risk and cannot be easily incorporated into the calculation.

Generally speaking, political risks are due to government interventions in the functioning of the economy. But not all changes will have adverse consequences for the corporation. For instance, if the corporation is operating in an industry targeted by the host government for development, then it might not only escape any discriminatory actions but also enjoy investment credits or tax concessions.

The ability to assess political risk could provide firms with a distinctive competitive advantage. Often, MNCs avoid investing in politically unstable markets, considering such investment too risky. Several models exist to analyze and forecast political risk. Some of these models are based on opinion surveys and factors such as the frequency of government changes, conflicts with other countries, and the level of violence. These models try to provide political stability indices to show how long the government will remain in power and whether it will be able to provide favorable conditions for foreign investment. Other models forecast the economic conditions of a country based on the level of inflation, interest rates, gross national product, and balance of payment figures. While the forecasting performance of these models is rather good at the country level, it is quite weak at the corporation level. These models suffer in that they implicitly assume that each firm in the foreign country faces the same degree of political risk.

Corporations react differently to the same political risk depending on their industry, size,[29] ownership structure, and level of know-how. Investments in natural resources and utilities are more apt to be expropriated than any other type of investment. Many corporations rely on consultants who specialize in predicting political risk, but they do not always come up with correct predictions. This does not mean that the corporations should ignore political risk and invest and operate blindly. It is important to analyze the likelihood of any untoward activity that may affect the corporation and to have contingency plans.

MNCs can take several steps to manage their exposure to political risk. The most important one currently practiced is to invest in countries through a joint venture agreement. This type of direct investment involves local investors in ownership and management. While the corporation loses some freedom, it gives the firm a local flavor. The company may even be perceived as owned by locals, which may help the firm in obtaining the necessary licenses and meeting the requirements and regulations, which is not easily done by a foreign company. Furthermore, this may also help avoid takeovers by the host government. There are other ways as well. The company undertakes investments in those industries that are encouraged by the local governments and fall into their national development plans. Another way would be to work with specialized technology, knowledge, and supplies that cannot be easily learned or duplicated; the local government would be hard put to take over such a firm knowing that it would do no great harm to the corporation and no great good to the local government. Attempting to raise as much capital as possible from the local financial markets or through loans from a consortium of international banks is another way to overcome political risk. Last, the company planning foreign investments may purchase insurance.

There are several agencies that offer protection against political risk and against expropriation, currency inconvertibility, war, and internal strife. These include the Foreign Credit Insurance Association (FCIA), the Export-Import Bank (Eximbank), the Overseas Private Investment Corporation (OPIC), and, most recently established, the Multilateral Investment Guarantee Agency (MIGC). All these agencies have their own unique programs and offer different premiums depending on the country and industry involved. It is possible that an MNC could follow one or the other of the above-mentioned methods and not need the insurance at all.

Managing Host Government Relations

MNCs handle government relations and respond to government demands and policy actions in many different ways. The response to government actions and demands may be centralized at headquarters, placed with the regional managers, or delegated to the country managers. The latter method, however, is not very popular with MNCs. Usually, country managers have limited authority and autonomy in their dealings with host governments. Mahini and Wells have identified four factors that largely determine the location of decision response in the organizational hierarchy and the method of handling host government relations:[30]

1. The firm's bargaining power in dealing with host governments

2. The significance of the international operations to the enterprise

3. The degree of interdependence of the subsidiaries

4. The political salience of the industry, where the industry accounts for the major part of the host country's foreign exchange earnings and the host government's revenues

Considering these factors, there are four different approaches to host government relations (see Figure 6.2):

1. Policy

2. Centralized

3. Diffuse

4. Coordinated

In the **policy approach,** the major areas of possible conflict with host governments are identified in advance and policies are devised for handling them. The policy approach might be employed where the firm is in a very strong bargaining position and the host government is dependent on the resources of the firm. Although the policies are made centrally at headquarters, the host government deals with the local MNC managers who implement them. Recent changes that were elaborated in Chapter 1 have made the use of the policy approach unrealistic.

The **centralized approach** directs and supervises government negotiations from headquarters. The difference between the policy approach and the centralized approach is in their dealing with the most important government relations matters. In the former, these issues are decided in advance by top management and are not negotiable. In the latter, headquarters is willing to negotiate on them.

Foreign subsidiaries are responsible for host government relations in the **diffuse approach.** Depending on the issues at hand, the foreign subsidiaries, the regional manager, or a functional department such as marketing might be responsible for host government relations. The diffuse approach seems to be more appropriate for firms in which the degree of interdependency between their foreign subsidiaries is minimal or nonexistent.

A middle-ground approach, between the extreme positions of the centralized and diffuse approaches, is followed by firms using the coordinated approach. The **coordinated approach** involves frontline managers while headquarters maintains some degree of centralization.

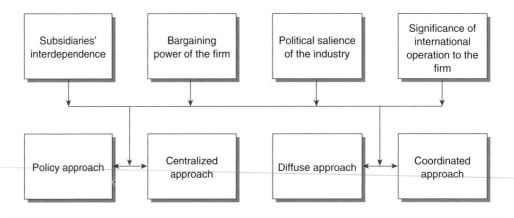

Figure 6.2   Managing Host Government Relationships

International Finance and Currency Exchange Rates

International financial management is a fascinating and, at the same time, an intricate matter. It can dramatically affect the profitability of MNCs. Unfavorable fluctuation in exchange rates may totally wipe out the operating profit of a subsidiary if those profits have to be repatriated to the home country. While international financial management is the potential source of much aggravation for MNCs, it can provide many benefits, such as multiple sources of financing. Differences in the availability and costs of funds around the world can be used to the advantage of MNCs. While domestic firms are limited to the local domestic capital markets, MNCs have the benefit of financing their worldwide operations from alternative global sources.

Exchange Rates. MNCs are concerned with exchange rate fluctuations and how they can affect the overall profitability of their corporations. Although the corporation may have undertaken a lucrative investment, exchange rate changes may result in this project offering negative returns. The currencies of major industrialized countries are traded freely in the exchange market. In such a market, the exchange rate between two currencies is determined by the supply of and demand for the currencies themselves. Factors that lead to increasing the supply of or decreasing the demand for a certain currency will bring down the value of that currency in foreign exchange markets. In the same way, those factors that result in decreasing the supply of or increasing the demand for a currency will boost the value of that currency. Broadly speaking, exchange rate fluctuations can be attributed to the following factors: inflation rates, interest rates, balance of payment surpluses or deficits, and government policies and expectations.

The Competition

A major difference between the management of MNCs and that of the domestic firm is the nature of the competition each faces. MNCs operate in a more competitive environment. In some or all aspects of their operations, many MNCs have to deal with competition from local and state-owned firms. Besides the competition from local firms, rivalry among MNCs creates very intense competitive pressure. Governments' involvement in business creates an environment of constraints and control. Through direct or indirect support and subsidies of local businesses, governments force MNCs to evaluate their strategies carefully.

Competition From Domestic and State-Controlled Firms

In the following pages, we will learn that industries may be classified along a continuum by their extent of internationalization. Multidomestic industries are at the low end of this continuum, and at the high end are "global" industries. International industries are in the middle. In multidomestic industries, where product characteristics and consumer choices are heavily influenced by local tastes and cultural norms, domestic firms can effectively challenge MNCs. In effect, in multidomestic industries, most of the advantages of being an MNC are nullified by market characteristics. Unless MNCs behave like domestic firms, they will not be able to capture much of a market share. Domestic firms have an edge over MNCs due to their insider position and familiarity with the cultural, legal, and logistical requirements of doing business. In some countries, the stigma of being a foreign company is by itself a drawback. The older generation of Japanese managers, for example, is still reluctant to deal with foreign companies. They tend to consider it unpatriotic to buy from foreigners. Some U.S. firms have capitalized on consumers' patriotic feelings as well. Wal-Mart, for example, has used its support of American suppliers, whenever these suppliers are competitive on quality and price, as an effective marketing tool.

Certain industries are considered by host governments to be strategically important for national security, and these industries receive government support to compete with MNCs. Host government policies regarding domestic strategic industries vary. In some countries, these industries are government owned. In other countries, they are the exclusive domain of domestic firms, with the government effectively controlling them. In still others, MNCs are allowed limited participation in some aspects but are barred from others. Most host governments, however, effectively tilt the competitive position of strategic domestic firms against their MNC competitors. Industries commonly controlled by governments include airlines, coal, electricity, gas, oil, automobiles, the post office, railroads, shipbuilding, steel, and telecommunications. In all countries that have modern manufacturing capabilities, defense industries are the exclusive domain of governments and domestic firms. Where private firms are allowed to participate in arms production, their sales to foreign countries are under strict government control. In addition to the benefits mentioned earlier, sales of weapons to foreign governments are an important instrument of foreign policy implementation. Global weapon sales generate huge sums annually.

Host governments can control an industry without an ownership share. A host government may be the only customer of the industry's products, and through its purchasing power, it can effectively bar MNC participation in that industry. By buying only from domestic firms, governments can create artificial entry barriers. Exclusive domestic purchasing may not be a formal government policy but a de facto practice. Nor does it have to be practiced only by the government to have an impact on MNC participation in the industry. The government of Japan, for example, only recently, and with extensive pressure from the United States, allowed American firms to participate in contract biddings for large public construction projects. Often, Japanese manufacturers restrict their purchases to domestic suppliers that are members of their Keiretsu (a Japanese-type conglomerate that is made up of a family of firms in supplier-buyer relationships, including banks and insurance companies). Such a practice makes it almost impossible for non-Japanese firms to compete in the Japanese market.

In many cases, when an MNC is successful in securing an initial contract, it can confidently expect a long-term relationship with the host government. Suppliers are abandoned only if the government becomes extremely disgruntled with their performance or technologies (p. 93).[31] For this reason, it is very difficult for a new manufacturer to break into established national markets that are controlled by governments. Only the new markets of developing countries, although small in size, offer significant opportunities for newcomers. These countries, however, rely on the advice of independent consultants and use only very reputable suppliers with proven performance in developed countries.

In obtaining a new business contract in the government-controlled industries of developing countries, MNCs that can offer new technologies have a competitive advantage over those who cannot, or are unwilling to, do so. As noted, developing countries are very interested in technology transfer. For example, CIT-Alcatel, the French supplier of switching equipment, was able to win a sizable contract from the Indian government by providing technological assistance. CIT-Alcatel agreed to set up an Indian digital telecommunication equipment industry, backed by a guarantee and agreements between the French and Indian governments (p. 103).[31]

To ensure that these industries remain responsive to national interests, some governments have demanded joint ventures with MNCs. In response to governmental demands, the MNCs have acted in two different ways. Some have established subsidiaries in each country with no interaction among them. The resulting firms are joint ventures that operate as domestic firms.

Competition From Other MNCs

Competition to MNC operation comes from other MNCs as well as domestic firms. The nature of the competition, of course, varies with industry characteristics. For the automobile and consumer electronics industries, for example, competition is not limited to MNCs in developing countries, because they employ mature technologies and have products and market characteristics that are less influenced by cultural norms. Similarities in consumer tastes and preferences provide opportunities for standardization in manufacturing and economies of scale, making them very attractive. Since these products do not require cutting-edge technologies, MNCs from newly industrialized countries, such as South Korea, Taiwan, and Malaysia, are joining the melee, too. In contrast, the leading-edge industries, such as medical technology, biomedicine, or computer chip design, are the exclusive domain of MNCs from a few advanced industrialized countries.

To encourage exports, many governments provide subsidies to domestic firms. With financial, and sometimes technological, assistance from governments, international markets are becoming the scene of very intense competition. For instance, Airbus Industries, a consortium of aviation firms from Europe backed by the French and British governments, has made successful inroads into markets that previously were exclusively served by Boeing. Airbus has used these subsidies to develop a technologically advanced passenger airplane and undercut Boeing prices. Consequently, in recent years, even some American airlines have chosen Airbus over Boeing.

In the preceding pages, we have argued that the international strategy process is the same for both domestic and MNC operations; however, the management of an international operation is more demanding and difficult. The difficulty of international management is due to the higher level of complexity and uncertainty involved in the international environment. Equipped with knowledge about the major environmental forces of international management, we now turn to the strategic choices available to MNCs.

Generic MNC Strategies

In dealing with environmental complexities and uncertainties, MNCs have a range of alternative strategic choices. Because there are some similarities as well as differences among national markets, the choice of strategy is determined by considering these similarities and differences.

An emphasis on similarities calls for producing products that can be sold globally without many modifications. To take advantage of the differences among national markets would necessitate strategies that treat each market based on its own merits. Therefore, each market is considered a unique business opportunity that requires a response to its special characteristics and demands. In terms of strategy, therefore, the choice is between global integration and national responsiveness. The old decision quandary of efficiency versus effectiveness prevails in the international marketplace too. An attempt to serve many countries with the same range of products is efficiency oriented. To serve the unique needs of each market by catering to its requirements is effectiveness oriented. Of course, the choice does not have to be between integration-efficiency and responsiveness-effectiveness. Depending on the circumstances, firms can establish a middle-ground position and lean toward either one or the other. Alternatively, a firm could combine some features of both strategies as circumstances demand. These choices are presented under three generic strategies: global integration, host country focus, and hybrid international.

Global Integration Strategy

To capitalize on the economies of scale and to take advantage of the diverse opportunities for cost reduction that the global market provides, the choice of strategy is global integration. Following a global integration strategy, MNC production and distribution facilities expand over national borders in a network of specialized operations. Firms using a global integration strategy capitalize on the similarities among the national markets and sidestep the differences. Global integration can be based on product or process specialization (pp. 12, 13).[31]

Product Specialization. MNCs using product specialization produce only part of a common global product range in each country. Each foreign subsidiary, however, offers a complete range of products in its national market. Through intrafirm trade, each subsidiary imports from other subsidiaries what it is not producing and exports to them its specialized outputs.

Process Specialization. Process specialization involves a multistage manufacturing process, where each subsidiary produces certain parts and components for a common product or product range. American semiconductor manufacturers have used this strategy by farming work out to border plants in Mexico and the Far East. The U.S. automobile industry has employed this strategy by building various cars and components in other countries.

Global integration benefits are realized through cost reduction by, for example, locating manufacturing facilities where costs of doing business are low. The emphasis on cost may come at the expense of flexibility and responsiveness to national markets. By using a global integration strategy, an MNC is compelled to find a mix of products for all its foreign markets. Standardization of products among its subsidiaries does not allow for customizing products to national criteria and tastes.

To take advantage of the large-scale operations that provide for economies of scale, manufacturing operations are centralized. The manufacturing concentration increases intercompany product shipment. If the pattern of intercompany shipments (trade) causes a country to become a net importer, it could raise the risk of host government intervention. Similar efforts to improve efficiency through centralization of R&D activities may raise the same risk. Also, large-scale centralized operations expose MNCs to foreign currency exchange risk.[32] Although MNCs face certain risks by concentrating on manufacturing and R&D activities, in general, the benefits outweigh the associated risks. Caterpillar, Ford Motor Company, IBM, and Brown Boveri have relied on global integration strategies.

Host Country Focus Strategy

If a global integration strategy could be regarded as the "efficiency" choice, the host country focus strategy is the "effectiveness" option. In a host country focus strategy, subsidiaries are treated as if they are autonomous national firms. They are allowed to respond to local demands as they see fit. The MNC's headquarters office maintains overall coordination among various subsidiaries (using some of the techniques discussed previously) in a way that maximizes the MNC's global performance. A relatively complete range of products is manufactured by each subsidiary. Since each subsidiary is responsible for its own domestic market needs, a minimum amount of trade occurs between subsidiaries. Consequently, subsidiaries are not directly responsible for the total MNC efficiency. Indirectly, however, they all are involved with the MNC's total performance.

The MNC that pursues a host country focus strategy has a different way of using its worldwide presence and resources for a competitive advantage. While MNCs with a global integration strategy compete with other MNCs, firms using host country focus vie for market share with domestic firms and the subsidiaries of other MNCs that employ the same strategy. Whereas the competitive advantage of a global integration strategy is based on corporate-wide standardization and similarities among national markets, a host country focus strategy employs the MNC's worldwide resources for a competitive edge.

In competition with their domestic counterparts, the MNC subsidiaries use the resources of their headquarters in several ways (pp. 16, 17).[31]

First, even when national subsidiaries are managed as fully autonomous profit centers, the financial umbrella of the headquarters allows more risk taking by the subsidiaries.

Second, because of the support from headquarters, lower-cost financing is available to national subsidiaries.

Third, centralized R&D activities reduce costs and can increase the benefit to the subsidiaries.

Fourth, the subsidiaries have access to a global distribution network and logistics that are beyond the reach of their domestic counterparts.

Fifth, national subsidiaries may supply their customers the same product from several sources within the MNC's global operations. Through their sister subsidiaries, they can take advantage of bilateral trade agreements among many developing countries. Such arrangements potentially make them more competitive than their domestic or globally integrated counterparts.

Finally, with central control in pricing and marketing policies by headquarters, each subsidiary can become a more resilient competitor. Instead of competing as individual firms in national markets, they can coordinate their competitive response for a better result. As an example, Goodyear's reaction to Michelin's entry into the U.S. market was a very aggressive response in Europe. If Goodyear had to respond to Michelin in the U.S. market only, it would probably have hurt itself more. In this vein, the inability to respond in the home market of their competition puts domestic firms at a competitive disadvantage versus MNC subsidiaries. This is true only if MNC subsidiaries are centrally controlled and coordinated from headquarters. However, the drawback is a reduction in flexibility (pp. 16, 17).[31]

Operating as semi-autonomous firms, the entrepreneurial flexibility and innovation of national subsidiaries enable them to identify market needs and requirements and respond to them quickly. Since national subsidiaries operate autonomously and most of their activities are carried out on a local basis, unlike global firms, they are not affected by the extreme fluctuation of currency exchange rates. Among the firms that have followed this strategy are European firms such as Unilever, Philips Electronics, and Nestlé.

Hybrid International Strategy

An attempt by MNCs to combine the benefits of global integration and host country focus strategies brings about a hybrid international strategy. In choosing a hybrid international strategy, an MNC intends not to be committed to an extreme position of global integration or host country focus. Both extreme strategies have certain shortcomings. As noted, the global integration strategy forgoes the flexibility of the host country focus, whereas the host country focus does not enjoy the economies of scale and efficiency of global integration. A hybrid international strategy aims to combine both features and, therefore, enables MNCs to decide each major situation based on its own merits and plan accordingly. For example, faced with a saturated market for soup in the United States, Campbell Soup is expanding abroad with locally responsive strategies. In Argentina, it offers split pea with ham, for the Chinese it has a watercress and duck-gizzard soup, and in Mexico it is selling Crema de Chile Poblano.[33] These locally developed products are supported by the vast marketing and financial resources of the headquarters office.

The hybrid strategy is ambiguous compared with the clarity of the other two strategies. It is an option when there is no clear-cut preference for either a global integration or host country focus strategy. It attempts to trade off the costs and benefits of the other two strategies on a case-by-case basis to maximize the overall results (p. 214).[31] Some situations may call for a host country focus strategy, with limited opportunity for global integration. Other situations may allow global integration, with moderate responsiveness to the host government's demands. Maintaining some manufacturing and R&D facilities and forming joint ventures with domestic firms in each country, for example, could satisfy host government demands yet allow for corporate-wide integration.

The hybrid international strategy requires the ability to respond quickly to changing situations and to shift different aspects of the operation among countries when circumstances change. If interventions by host governments create unacceptable conditions, MNCs should have the alternative of shifting their priorities between national subsidiaries. This strategy also calls for a close working relationship between the managers of national subsidiaries and host government officials. Headquarters, therefore, has to rely on the managers of national subsidiaries and permit their involvement in major decisions. Because of their working relationships with the local community and host government officials, these managers are in the best position to assess the need for local responses.

To benefit from the global resources of an MNC, the worldwide operations should be integrated. Integration, however, requires a global perspective and specialized resources (p. 214).[31] Local managers very seldom concern themselves with a global perspective. Similarly, specialized resources, such as a global marketing staff and manufacturing specialists, are more readily available at headquarters. Therefore, a close and supportive relationship between the subsidiaries and headquarters will improve overall corporate performance. At first, this may sound like an easy and acceptable choice. Closer scrutiny, however, reveals that it can cause problems. National subsidiaries may not be aware of, or willing to consider, the ramifications of their recommendations on the rest of an MNC's operations. Or they may out of hand reject alternatives that would enhance overall corporate performance but would require a sacrifice on their part.

Industry Characteristics and MNC Strategy _____

From our discussion of generic MNC strategies, one could surmise that the world market is made up of three industries: global, international, and multidomestic. Such a categorization is shown in Figure 6.3, which depicts the world market in two dimensions: (1) product and market requirements and (2) operational requirements of the firm.

Product requirements consist of product characteristics, such as product specifications, sizes, colors, shapes, tastes, functions, and features. Market characteristics are the attributes that differentiate among markets, such as distribution channels and service needs and expectations. Product and market requirements may be determined by market forces or dictated by the government. For example, most host governments would like to develop a national telecommunications industry and impose product specifications that effectively leave the industry in the hands of domestic firms or the autonomous subsidiaries of MNCs. Operational requirements are the factors that enable a firm to situate itself in a favorable competitive position versus other firms. These factors include, but are not restricted to, economies of scale, investment requirements in R&D, and manufacturing facilities. The characteristics of the two dimensions are summarized in Table 6.4. The interaction between these two dimensions creates three industries: multidomestic, international, and global (see Table 6.5).

Multidomestic industry has local product and market requirements and national operational requirements. Global industry is just the opposite of multidomestic industry. Global industry is characterized by worldwide product and market requirements and global operational requirements. International industry shares the worldwide product and market requirements with global industry and national operational requirements with multidomestic industry.

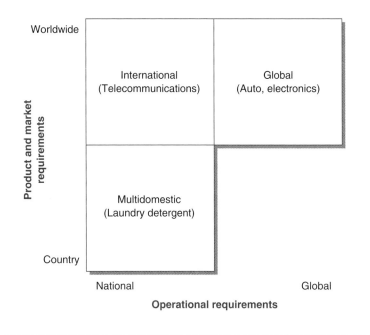

Figure 6.3   Industry Characteristics

Table 6.4   Operational and Product/Market Requirements

Product/Market Requirements	Operational Requirements
Product requirement	Economies of scale
Specifications	Investment requirement in R&D
Size	Investment requirement in manufacturing
Color	
Shape	
Tastes	
Function	
Features	
Market requirements	
Distribution channels	
Service needs	
Service expectations	

Table 6.5   Operational and Product/Market Requirements and Industry Classification

Operational Requirements	Product/Market Requirements	Industry Type
National	Local	Multidomestic
National	Worldwide	International
Global	Worldwide	Global

Table 6.6   Strategy Type and Industry Classification

Industry Classification	Strategy Type
Multidomestic	Host country focus
International	Hybrid international
Global	Global integration

The MNCs operating in each industry need to adopt the strategy suitable for that industry. In Table 6.6, industry types are matched with their corresponding generic MNC strategies. To succeed in a global industry, MNCs need a global integration strategy. A host country focus strategy is appropriate for multidomestic industry. Competitive advantage can be gained in international industry by using a hybrid international strategy. These three types of industries are discussed next.

Global Industries

MNCs' international expansion can be attributed to their ability to exploit the economies of scale and experience, location, product differentiation, process technology, and the control of distribution channels. The exploitation of some of these advantages is possible only with a global integration strategy (p. 19).[31] Certain technologies and products require a huge investment in R&D and manufacturing facilities. In such situations, organizational efficiency demands a large production run and a market share on a global scale. The efficiency imperative, therefore, creates global industries. Global industries are characterized by highly centralized large-scale manufacturing and R&D operations and standardized products. The automobile, chemical, consumer electronics, heavy equipment, commercial aircraft, supercomputer, and shipbuilding industries are considered to be global.

The global operational requirement necessitates an enormous investment of capital for establishing the global manufacturing and distribution network. R&D investment needs are large too. Economic imperatives have forced global industries toward globalization of their operations. Over the years, for example, successive technological innovations in consumer electronics have increased the minimum economic production run from 50,000 to 3 million units per year (p. 116).[32] There are no national markets with an annual absorption capacity of this size. This huge increase in the size of economic production runs has made globalization a necessity. Falling transportation and communication costs, along with relatively low restrictions on imports, have also made globalization in these industries a possibility.

In these industries, because product and market requirements are worldwide, products are produced, sold, and serviced worldwide, without many variations. In other words, consumer product needs are homogeneous across markets. For these products, national and local tastes do not vary, and there is no need to customize products to national standards. Government intervention and regulation are relatively low in global industries. Therefore, firms can locate manufacturing facilities in any place in the world that provides the most economical advantages. Manufacturing facilities for automobiles and consumer electronics, for example, are established almost everywhere—in the United States, Europe, Latin America, and Asia.

Theodore Levitt[34] has argued that technology is driving all national markets toward a converging commonality. A complete and total commonality of tastes and preferences may never arrive. In the global industries, however, this commonality has already taken place. The convergence of consumers' preference and technical standards allows the production of a narrow range of standardized products for all markets from these factories. Because rationalization and integration of these manufacturing facilities scattered worldwide requires a strong internal control, there is no premium for partnership with local firms.[35] Local partners, whose knowledge of local culture is the source of competitive advantage in multidomestic industries, have limited attraction for global firms. Therefore, global industries are dominated by MNCs that compete with each other on a global scale.

Multidomestic Industries

Multidomestic industries are characterized by local product and market requirements. National, cultural, social, and political differences lead to diverse product standards and different consumer tastes. These differences create a strong need for customized products to meet local tastes and preferences. The operational requirements of multidomestic industries are on a national scale. Therefore, separate manufacturing facilities, to serve each national market independently, are economical. There are no economies of scale in functional areas, such as R&D and marketing, beyond the national market. This means that channels of distribution, for example, are unique to each country, and R&D performed in one market cannot be duplicated in other markets. What a firm learns about the requirements of the construction industry in one country, for example, has little relevance in other countries. It also means that national subsidiaries are less dependent on headquarters for R&D.

Since benefits directly derived from headquarters are limited, national subsidiaries behave more like domestic firms. The benefits of localization and headquarters' loose control over foreign subsidiaries provide opportunities for joint ventures with local firms. In fact, some have argued that partnership with local investors is frequently a preferred option in multidomestic industries.[35] Laundry detergents, cosmetics, construction, prepared food products, and furniture are examples of multidomestic industries.

The host country focus is an appropriate strategic choice for a multidomestic industry. The need to respond quickly to local standards and changes necessitates the responsiveness that is characteristic of a host country focus strategy. If a firm correctly identifies local preference for a particular product or products with certain features or functions, it can effectively apply the host country focus strategy to that market segment. By doing so, it carves out a market segment representing domestic preferences. The example of an upstart British electronics firm, Amstrad, is a case in point (p. 113).[32] The company correctly identified the unhappiness of English consumers with the modern hi-fi equipment referred to as "music centers." The equipment had been designed to global standards and was made to be simpler and more functional. Gone were the teak exterior and complex control panel that gave the user a feeling of technical mastery and wizardry. To British consumers, the metal casing of the new global design, in silver or black, was no match for the old, warm, teak furniture look. Amstrad responded by bringing back the old exterior features and combined them with modern technology high-fidelity sound delivery. It then chose the largest discount retailer for its sales outlets. The results were that Amstrad captured the market leadership from its global competitors in England.

International Industries

The dominance of technological forces and the need to develop and distribute innovations in multiple markets are characteristics of international industries. Success in these industries depends on the ability to exploit technological forces, produce new products, and duplicate the process in different national markets. Typically, new products are developed in the home market. Then, these products and their related technologies are sequentially applied to other national markets. Since competitive advantage hinges on expensive technological development, the ability to duplicate the technology in multiple markets is an economic necessity. The imperative of the new-technology application in multiple national markets gives an impetus to the emergence of international industries.

When host governments restrict the operation of a global industry and force it to produce to national standards, international industries could emerge. As Figure 6.4 illustrates, an overlap between multidomestic and global industries characterizes international industries. When there are demands on the firm for both localization and globalization, success could come from the ability to exploit both imperatives. In the telecommunications industry, for example, forces for both globalizing and localizing are present. However, it is the ability to innovate and to adopt the innovation in national markets that differentiates the winners from the losers (p. 117).[32] General Electric, Kraft, Pfizer, and Procter & Gamble are among the U.S. firms that use this strategy.

Summary

The strategy formulation and implementation process is a plan of aligning organizational goals with environmental situations and requirements and the attempts to achieve these goals. The difference between the strategic planning

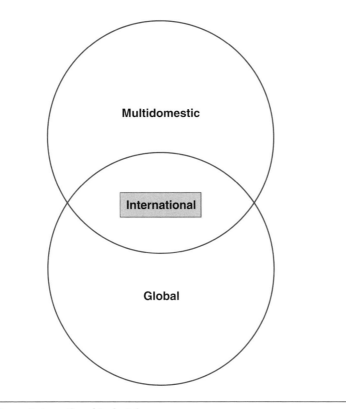

Figure 6.4   International Industries

process in a domestic firm and that of an MNC is the complexity and uncertainty of the international environment. The more demanding, complex, and uncertain the situations are, the more challenging is the strategy process.

The additional complexity, uncertainty, and challenge of international management are due to several factors, including political and legal differences; currency exchange rate fluctuations; competition from local businesses, host government agencies, and other MNCs; and the involvement of the host government in business. Each of these environmental forces is the subject of a separate chapter. In this chapter, we discussed the role of host governments and elaborated on the relationship between host governments and MNCs. This relationship is portrayed as mutually beneficial and interdependent. We learned that host governments are concerned that their relationships with MNCs may lead to dependency and loss of their sovereign power. Therefore, host governments attempt to influence the operation and strategies of MNCs so as to serve their own national priorities. Consequently, MNCs employ various methods in their governmental relationships. Variations among these methods are a function of industry characteristics and the bargaining powers of the MNCs and the host governments.

The MNC strategic choices were presented in the form of three generic strategies: global integration, host country focus, and hybrid international. We learned that industry characteristics and host government domestic policies may determine the appropriateness of each generic strategy. For instance, a global integration strategy may be effective in an industry where consumer preferences and tastes do not vary across national borders and standardized products could be sold in all markets. Also, a global integration strategy could be effective when host government involvement in the industry is at a minimum.

Besides the differences due to environmental situations, the cultural differences among countries create additional difficulties for international managers. Although strategy is a response to environmental changes and challenges, the formulation process depends on cultural values and assumptions. Since the essence of strategy formulation is perceptual and intellectual, international managers with different cultural backgrounds approach their jobs from different mental frameworks. In this vein, there are differences between the Eastern and Western strategy formulation process. A simple way to explain this difference is by the use of analogies. Cooking practices among Americans and Japanese reflect their differences in thinking and relating to the environment. There is a tendency for Americans to adhere as precisely as possible to the recipe. People of other cultures, including the Japanese, cook more by playing with the ingredients and cooking techniques as the situations demand. The Japanese tendency for situational conformity is reflected in all aspects of life, including work life. When a Japanese manager needs to get out of the office for a while, all he or she has to say to the staff is "yoroshiku tanomu," meaning "do as you think fit." The staff would keep on working without needing any other instruction. An American counterpart usually provides specific instructions for the staff before leaving the office.[36]

Discussion Questions _____

1. Explain why there are no substantive differences between the strategic planning processes in a domestic and a multinational corporation.

2. Describe the qualitative and quantitative difficulties that a firm faces as it goes international.

3. Why is there a love-hate relationship between host governments and MNCs?

4. Why have some developing countries expressed disappointment with MNCs?

5. What are a host country's major concerns when dealing with MNCs?

6. Elaborate on the argument that the relationship between a host country and an MNC is shaped by their relative bargaining powers.

7. Host countries use direct and indirect measures to influence MNCs' strategic and operational decisions. Give an example of each.

8. MNCs can handle host government relations in four different ways: the policy approach, the centralized approach, the diffuse approach, and the coordinated approach. Briefly describe each approach.

9. In their competition with domestic firms, MNCs may enjoy a superior position. What are the sources of their superiority?

10. Under what conditions could a global integration strategy be effective?

11. What are the differences between a hybrid international strategy and a host country focus strategy?

12. Describe the strategy implications of cultural differences.

13. How could the use of our cultural cognitive maps mislead us in judging other peoples' actions and decisions?

14. The American concept of the strategy formulation process is anchored to the concept of a fully functioning "market" that governs the employee-employer relationship. Is this the same in other countries?

References

1. M. Ihlwan (2006, July 3). Camp Samsung. *Business Week*, 46–47.

2. J. Solomon (2002, June 13). Back from brink, Korea Inc. wants a little respect. *Wall Street Journal*, p. A12.

3. W. J. Holstein (2002, April 1). Samsung's golden touch. *Fortune*, 89–94.

4. H. W. Choi (2002, March 22). Korea's Samsung seeks a bit more worldwide. *Wall Street Journal*, p. A13.

5. A. G. Bedeian & H. Mintzberg (2002). In memoriam: H(arry) Igor Ansoff (1918–2002). *The Academy of Management News, 33*(4), 7–8.

6. H. I. Ansoff & E. McDonnell (1990). *Implanting strategic management.* New York: Prentice Hall.

7. P. Ghemawat (2001). Distance still matters. *Harvard Business Review, September*, 137–147.

8. S. C. Schneider (1989). Strategy formulation: The impact of national culture. *Organizational Studies, 10*(2), 149–168.

9. E. J. Kolde (1985). *Environment of international business.* Boston: PWS-Kent.

10. H. Nakamura (1964). *Ways of thinking of Eastern people.* Honolulu, HI: East-West Center Press.

11. T. Tusunoda (1975). The differences of recognition mechanism toward natural sounds between Japanese and Westerners. *Medicine and Biology, 88*, 309–314.

12. R. E. Nisbett (2003). *The geography of thought.* New York: Free Press.

13. R. Doktor (1983). Some tentative comments on Japanese and American decision making. *Decision Sciences, 14*(4), 607–615.

14. M. Maruyama (1984). Alternative concepts of management: Insights from Asia and Africa. *Asia Pacific Journal of Management, 1*(2), 100–111.

15. J. A. Lee (1966). Cultural analysis in overseas operations. *Harvard Business Review, March–April*, 106–114.

16. G. Hofstede (1993). Cultural constraints in management. *Academy of Management Executive, 7*(1), 81–94.

17. J. Bardoux & P. Lawrence (1991). The making of a French manager. *Harvard Business Review, July–August*, 58–67.

18. K. Fatehi & F. Derakhshan (1982). Appropriate technology, appropriate management and international trade: An integrative proposal. *Approtech, 5*, 19–22.

19. P. Wright (1984). MNC–Third World business unit performance: Application of strategic elements. *Strategic Management Journal, 5*, 231–240.

20. Y. L. Doz (1986). Government policies and global industries. In M. E. Porter (Ed.), *Competition in global industries* (pp. 225–266). Boston: Harvard Business School Press.

21. K. Fatehi, F. Derakhshan, & J. R. Giermanski (2000). National Labour Unions' quandary: The need for internationalization. *International Journal of Human Resources Development and Management, 1*, 68–80.

22. MTV's world. (2002, Febraury 18). *Business Week*, 81–84.

23. G. R. Simpson (2002, June 11). Galxo in major battle with IRS over taxes on years of U.S. sales. *Wall Street Journal*, pp. A1, A9.

24. A. Mahini (1988). *Making decisions in multinational corporations.* New York: Wiley.

25. J. Tanner (1991, October 2). Venezuela now woos oil firms it booted in '70s nationalization. *Wall Street Journal*, p. 1.

26. D. J. Encarnation & L. T. Wells Jr. (1986). Competitive strategies in global industries: A view from host governments. In M. E. Porter (Ed.), *Competition in global industries* (pp. 267–290). Boston: Harvard Business School Press.

27. S. Glain (2006, May 26). A tale of two Chinas. *Smithsonian, 37*(2), 40–49.

28. K. Fatehi (1994). Capital flight from Latin America as a barometer of political instability. *Journal of Business Research, 30*, 187–195.

29. K. Fatehi & M. Hosssein Safizadeh (1994). The effect of sociopolitical instability on the flow of different types of foreign direct investment. *Journal of Business Research, 31*, 65–73.

30. A. Mahini & L. T. Wells Jr. (1986). Government relations in the global firm. In M. E. Porter (Ed.), *Competition in global industries* (pp. 291–312). Boston: Harvard Business School Press.

31. Y. Doz (1987). *Strategic management in multinational companies.* Oxford, UK: Pergamon Press.

32. C. A. Bartlett & S. Ghoshal (1992). *Transnational management.* Homewood, IL: Richard D. Irwin.

33. P. Engardio & J. Weber (1993, March 15). Campbell: How it's M-M-Global. *Business Week*, 52–54.

34. T. Levitt (1983). The globalization of markets. *Harvard Business Review, May–June*, 92–102.

35. F. J. Contractor (1990). Contractual and cooperative forms of international business: Towards a unified theory of modal choice. *Management International Review, 30*(1), 31–54.

36. R. Iwata (1982). *Japanese-style management: Its foundations and prospects.* Tokyo: Asian Productivity Organization.

7 Legal Issues and International Management

Although in the last few decades, we have witnessed the growth of an assortment of international agreements governing a variety of issues, the world remains primarily a community of nation-states, each with its own body of law, interests, and unique outlook. Even the European Union (EU) remains a collective of national sovereign states with their separate and unique national legal systems. This situation makes it valuable to begin the discussion of international business law with a review of the relationship between culture and law in such diverse nations and national groupings as the United States, Europe, Japan, the Islamic nations, the developing countries, and the socialist and newly independent states freed from the yoke of communism.

Even this awareness of diversity will unavoidably involve an oversimplification, since the world is considerably more complex than such groupings suggest. Within the United States there exists, for example, the federal government and 50 different state governments—all with separate legal systems. If this is true for the United States, it holds with even greater force for the national groupings just mentioned, since the nations that make them up are by no means alike.

In any analysis of law, there is also a natural division between "substantive issues" and "procedural issues." Some of the major areas of discussion in this chapter are primarily substantive, in that they deal with rules that actually govern international business conduct. It will be important, however, to remain aware of the many issues of process involving the mechanisms by which these rules are applied and by which parties seek a resolution of conflict. Even though the sections on national sovereignty, international legal issues, and multinational corporation operational disputes are largely substantive, procedural points will inescapably be intertwined with them, and it is worthwhile to pay attention to them as they arise.

It is indispensable for firms engaging in international business to seek competent legal advice in each area of concern and for each country. Nonlawyers, however, will benefit from a review of international business law as presented in this chapter by learning to recognize when to seek advice and by understanding the context to which the advice relates.[a]

Chapter Vignette

General Electric (GE) and Honeywell International Inc.

European countries used to be passive regarding antitrust regulations for mergers of large multinational corporations. In fact, they basically let the United States decide courses of actions instead of intervening directly. Lately, the European Commission, which is in charge of antitrust laws and their applications in the European Union (EU), has been more aggressive than ever in imposing antitrust regulations.

Originally, European antitrust laws were basically taken from the American regulations. Nevertheless, these laws have evolved and changed, reflecting European goals. American antitrust laws were put in place to protect customers. European regulations aim to guarantee for firms equality of business opportunities in the marketplace after a merger.

In June 2001, a 5-month negotiation between two U.S. firms, GE Company and Honeywell International, ended in collapse when the EU used its authority to disallow the pending acquisition.

There are a few explanations for the EU's action. First, what happens after a deal is approved if it does not promote competition? EU regulators do not have the luxury of legal enforcement to avoid market power abuses by merged companies. They do not have the means to restore competition. In the United States, however, litigious government entities or members of society have the right to file suits where opposition exists. The Europeans have a one-shot possibility to approve or block a merger. Once a merger has been approved, there is no turning back. This is an important reason why in making its decisions, the European Commission takes more time to investigate and puts more pressure on large mergers.

Second, unlike in the United States, in Europe, competitors to possible mergers have a considerably stronger voice. The U.S. rivals to a proposed merger seldom speak out directly against such acquisitions. They tend to focus on, and request, imposing strict limitations on mergers. In that way, they affect the outcomes.

The GE-Honeywell case shows different approaches. In the United States, a deal is approved if consumers will gain from lower prices and better purchasing conditions after a merger. Europe, on the other hand, justifies some protectionism to defend competitors as a way to guarantee competition. A concept of "bundling" has been developed in Europe. If a merger gives one company a broad range of products or business that would give it an advantage over rivals that have only limited products or lines of business, the merger would not be allowed. In the GE-Honeywell merger, for example, two different core businesses, jet engines and avionics, would be detrimental to European Rolls-Royce, an engine supplier. Europeans argue that in the short run, this kind of merger might benefit consumers, but long-run benefits should also be measured to ensure that harm on rival firms would not hurt competition.[1-3]

Introduction

The GE and Honeywell vignette illustrates a few legal issues pertinent to international business. First, it shows how the law of international business often involves commonplace issues. It undercuts the natural but usually naive assumption that international legal issues, simply by being "international," are necessarily larger than life. Second, it demonstrates how the law of other countries can be a controlling factor on issues far away from the individual national markets. Third, the case points to the extraterritorial nature of some national laws that can affect international business. Fourth, on the very same issue, national laws can be in direct opposition to the national interests of other countries. Finally, it is worth noting that there is no special tribunal available to nongovernmental entities for resolving this kind of dispute. In the absence of a globally recognized dispute settlement, the verdicts of the courts of the "host country" remain in effect. International tribunals exist for some purposes; for example, disputes arising from international treaties can be taken to the World Court. But most of the world's legal business is done by the standard courts and administrative agencies of the country exercising jurisdiction.

Cultural Heritage and Business Law

The international scene, in its effect on law, involves a mixture of diversity, born out of widely varied cultural heritages and circumstances, with certain unifying themes. The sections that follow illustrate the diversity by specific reference to certain nations and regions. More generally, however, it should be noted that countries differ widely on many aspects of law and over a vast range of issues. Some have gone quite far in the area of environmental protection, while others impose relatively few constraints. Some are strongly in favor of market competition, vigorously enforcing their antitrust laws, while others favor large-scale, protected industries. Some have extensive social and labor legislation, such as that passed in the United States dealing with employee layoffs and plant closings, while others do not.

Many reasons exist for these differences. To illustrate, consider the varied approaches to intellectual property (IP) rights. IPs represent one major form of property, the rights to which govern exclusive use of an intellectual contribution such as an invention or a work of art. The principal reason for differences in the way IPs are treated lies in the fact that developed and developing nations often perceive their interests in diametrically opposite ways. The developed nations, with their preference for economic dynamism, emphasize the importance of protecting inventors through strong patent, trademark, and copyright coverage. This is to encourage the constant improvement of technology. If IPs are given weak protection in many parts of the world, the developed countries see this as a major loss of compensation and, hence, of incentive to creative persons and firms. Certainly, this view is taken by the industrialized nations, especially the United States, which has been the world's leading supplier of technology since World War II. As developing countries advance economically, they begin to share the same perspective. This has been the case with several countries such as Korea, Mexico, and Turkey, which are rapidly industrializing and whose perspective is accordingly beginning to match that of the technologically advanced nations. In contrast, many of the poorer nations give little protection to IPs, with the result that piracy in the form of unauthorized copying and imitation runs rampant. Technically, these are not acts of piracy in countries where a patent holder has not attempted to protect a patent. The problem is in gray market goods, where the goods are legally produced in a third country—where patent protection has not been established—but sent into a country where there is protection. This difference has shown up starkly in the varied protections given to computer software. The intention of governments in the less developed countries is to benefit their own peoples, but the failure to protect IPs sometimes produces tragic results. This is apparent when those nations give little patent protection to pharmaceutical inventions, which leads to diminished R&D on, or supply of drugs against, tropical diseases by large pharmaceutical firms.

Even in the face of differences, however, certain unifying themes bind the international community together. Legal systems can be classified into "legal families," since the nations in each "family" share a common legal heritage. One of these families stems from the Romano-Germanic Civil Law System, which has a long tradition of codification—that is, of formulating law in extensive written codes. A subfamily of these nations bases its law on the Napoleonic Code, the French Civil Code of 1804. These include countries as diverse as Poland, Indonesia, and the countries of equatorial Africa. Another subfamily, which not only includes several continental European countries but also encompasses Japan and South Korea, bases its law on the German Civil Code of 1896.

A second legal family stems from the Anglo-American common law system. Here, the law was developed primarily through a gradual accretion of court decisions, built up over centuries by courts' reference to earlier precedents. A separate system of procedures and remedies known as equity was developed by a parallel set of courts. But in the 19th century, "law" and "equity" were merged into a common system in most American states and in England. The vast influence of the Anglo-American system reflects the worldwide extent of the British Commonwealth, since this family includes India, Australia, Canada, and New Zealand, among others, and the dominant influence of the U.S. systems.

The increasing role played in world affairs by Islamic nations makes it important to note the influence of Islamic law, based largely on the moral precepts laid down by Prophet Muhammad. This prevails in a large number of countries located primarily in the Middle East and southern Asia. Islamic law was frozen in content in the 13th century, and this rigidity leads to a rupture between Islamic fundamentalists, who wish to keep it as it is, and others who want to adapt it to the more secular modern world. The argument over law is merely part of the larger split among Muslims over the nature of Islam itself. The importance of Islamic law can be seen in the fact that one fifth of the earth's population embraces Islam. (For an extended discussion of the "legal families" that have formed world law, see Ref. 4, pp. 44–52; Ref. 5.)

In addition to the links forged among the legal families, ties are established through the elaborate mechanisms of international cooperation, such as conventions. A convention is an agreement, originated by an international organization, between two or more countries. This is illustrated in the area of transportation: The International Convention Concerning Carriage of Goods by Rail (CIM) applies to railroading, the Warsaw Convention spells out the extent of international airlines' liability, and the Hague Rules define the liability exposure of international water carriers. Another example is the Convention on Contracts for the International Sale of Goods (CISG), drafted through the collaboration of eight different international organizations and 62 countries.

Efforts have been made to bridge the gaps that separate nations. For example, the North American Free Trade Agreement (NAFTA) among the United States, Canada, and Mexico was approved by the U.S. Congress in 1994. In addition, since 1947 successive rounds of negotiations about tariffs and other trade barriers have been conducted under the General Agreement on Tariffs and Trade (GATT). Recently, GATT provided a base for establishing the World Trade Organization (WTO). The WTO was discussed in a previous chapter. The WTO has enforcement power over judgments it renders on international trade disputes. The agreement arising from the Uruguay Round received Congressional approval in the United States within months of the approval of NAFTA. A major development has been the extension, among many nations, of most-favored-nation status, which spreads the reduction of barriers equally to participating nations. The developed nations have gone beyond this to create a system of preferences for developing nations.

The heritage of different cultures bears strongly on the business law of individual countries, as we see in the sections that follow.

The United States

Law in the United States has primarily grown up through court decisions, reflecting its British origin. On issues of federal constitutional and statutory interpretation, the federal courts have developed a body of decisions. On issues of state law, both the state and the federal courts apply the precedents built up by the courts of the state that is governed by the law. The separate court systems for law and equity were consolidated into a single system in virtually all states after New York took the lead in 1848. England followed in 1873. Later sections of this chapter explore several aspects of American law, but some are especially worth mentioning in this preliminary discussion of cultural differences.

Although practical and political considerations unquestionably play a frequent role, weakening any generalization, it is worth noting about American policy that idealistic considerations have often been a driving force. An example is the effort to ensure the integrity of business practices regardless of the location in which they are practiced. With the Foreign Corrupt Practices Act of 1977, the United States made it a criminal violation for any American company to bribe foreign governmental officials or political candidates. The legislation followed revelations that many American companies had given bribes. To ensure compliance, large companies were required to maintain certain accounting systems and have internal accounting controls that will give reasonable assurance that a company's representatives actually comply with the law and with company policy.

This idealism is not without cost. During the years since the act's passage, concern has been voiced by the business community that the law has had a chilling effect on the ability of American firms to compete in countries where bribery is rampant. (The concern over the anticompetitive impact of the Foreign Corrupt Practices Act is expressed, for example, in Ref. 4, p. 189.) This concern, fed by the decline in the United States' competitive position, led Congress to amend the statute in 1988 to limit its scope and to make it clear that only intentional, not inadvertent, violations would be subject to prosecution.

The same idealism can be seen in the strong U.S. policy against insider trading. Such trading involves the buying and selling of securities by someone who has significant information about a company that is not known to the general public. The federal Securities and Exchange Act of 1934 prohibits insider trading. In the early 1980s, after the Supreme Court interpreted the Act narrowly, Congress went so far as to strengthen it to ensure its wider application. This reflects a prevailing view in Congress that such trading takes advantage of a less-than-level playing field, subjecting the average investor to an unfair disadvantage.

Subject to significant exceptions, such as the Smoot-Hawley Tariff, which played so major a role in deepening the worldwide depression of the 1930s, the United States has been during much of the 20th century a stalwart proponent of a legally assured competitive market. This has led to two primary results: an antitrust policy that is stricter than those of many other nations and a commitment to free trade through lower tariffs and fewer barriers to commerce. This procompetitive stance reflects the powerful influence in American history of the promarket philosophy of classical and neoclassical economics. European economic integration, however, has narrowed the differences among corporate merger cases across the Atlantic. Also, in some cases, the European courts have applied much different and stricter criteria regarding corporate mergers.[2]

During the 20th century, American business law has seen a strong movement toward uniformity, and more flexibility, by reducing the complexity that can arise if 50 different states enact separate rules. The Uniform Commercial Code (UCC) has been enacted in all states except Louisiana since the late 1950s, and it codifies rules relating to the sale of goods, negotiable instruments, stock transfers, and other commercial subjects. For the most part, the rules are more flexible than earlier law, allowing the parties more alternatives than they previously had in a number of situations. For example, if a buyer unknowingly accepts defective goods, the acceptance can now be revoked under certain circumstances.

Europe

The law of continental Europe is based on the two major systems of codification, French and German, promulgated in the 19th century. The assumptions behind each code were fundamentally the same: private property, free-market economics, and individual self-sufficiency. European history during the 19th and 20th centuries has, however, involved massive challenges to the classical liberal model on which these assumptions were based, through both nationalist and socialist critiques hostile to it. Since law reflects the enormous complexity of history and thought in a society, it is not surprising that European legal systems today involve a significant mixture of ideologies.

Grave Frustration

Dr. Su Xian, a 36-year-old anesthesiologist, migrated from China to the United States of America and established a gravestone outfit called Sinostone, Inc., in Elberton, Georgia. Her presence in Elberton is a sign that globalization has arrived in the American monument industry. She came to Elberton simply because hundreds of buyers and monument dealers meet in this city each week. A seam of rock, 6 miles wide and 35 miles long, runs underneath Elberton, which has established its position as the tombstone capital of the United States.

Despite its added transportation costs, however, the Chinese monument importer undersells its local competitors. Unlike other gravestone manufacturers, Sinostone imports gravestones directly from China at a lower production price. The tombstones are all finished, lacking only names and dates.

Many in other industries have tried to slow the process of globalization through the use of legal and procedural schemes. Su's experience is no exception. So far, she has encountered a few problems. The Granite Association, for example, declined her request to become a member; according to the association, it had "no classification" for her business. The president of the Old South Granite Co. paid her a visit. He criticized Sinostone's prices and claimed that her monuments were dyed and not genuine granite. The head of the Elberton Granite Association requested that Dr. Su provide "chemical proof" that her gravestones are granite.[6]

This complexity has most recently been expressed by two diametrically opposed tendencies: one toward European unification and another toward resurgent nationalism. The latter became evident in the 1990s civil war among the Serbian, Croatian, and Muslim ethnic groups within the former Yugoslavia and in the protests within Germany against widespread immigration. However, despite the centrifugal tendencies of nationalism, Western Europe has since World War II engaged in a gradual process of unification, with the prospect of an eventual "One Europe." The Common Market, also called the **European Economic Community** (**EEC**) or simply the **European Community** (**EC**), was formed through the **Treaty of Rome** in 1957. It purposed to eliminate tariffs and trade barriers among its member nations, unify the currency (which it did in 2001), bring about the free movement of people and investment, and stand united vis-à-vis the rest of the world. The successor to the EC is the **European Union (EU)**. With the elimination of virtually all barriers among the member nations, the EU has achieved most of these objectives. Also, it has expanded membership to include most Eastern European countries and eventually may include **Turkey**.

This new freedom of movement will be tested against ancient constraints. In Germany, for example, participation in business has traditionally required either membership in or some entrance into the society of merchants known as the "Handelskammer." In agriculture, several countries have a long tradition of protecting the small farmer. It remains to be seen how commercial freedom will work itself out within these contexts.

On the path to complete unification, the EU is facing many political, economic, and legal challenges. The inclusion of Eastern European countries has magnified these challenges. It seems, however, that legal accomplishments may precede, and smooth the way for, complete unification.

> When culture, history, language and even politics still divide member states, law has emerged as a holistic binding agent. Working behind the scenes, and cooperating in numerous ways, the EU's judges and lawyers are bringing communities together by applying similar standards and precedents.
>   . . . European law—the element that all have in common—will gradually dominate the different national laws.[7]

Japan

The history of Japan has been marked by relative isolation, cultural cohesion, a high level of energy, nationalism, and a drive toward technological advancement. These factors are reflected even in so simple a thing as contract negotiation, where dignity, harmony, and social cohesion create an expectation for patient negotiation, long-term relationships, and few written formalities.

Conflict Resolution in Japan

It is a common understanding in Japan that, except perhaps within the world of big business, it is, as Singer[8] asserts, "almost indecent to go to court. If a marriage is to be dissolved, an employee dismissed, an agreement interpreted, the proper way is to have a 'talk' and, if this is unsuccessful, to accept mediation by a go-between or a mutual friend.

(Continued)

(Continued)

> A settlement, in order to be found satisfactory, has to take into account more than the rights and duties stipulated in contract. The whole situation of all parties concerned has to be considered—the former relations between the litigants, their relative wealth or poverty, power and social standing, and above all the peace of the community of which they are members. Law has not yet emerged from the stream of common life as a sphere of its own, opposing to the fluidity and many-sidedness of common life an abstract form, rational, hard and lucid like a crystal, objective and implacable. Between law and custom, habit and convention, order of nature and order of reason, natural inclination and social duty, no rigid demarcation lines are drawn. Everything remains contingent on circumstances, subject to swift transition" (pp. 71–72). (According to Magoroh Maruyama, the famous and prolific Japanese scholar, Singer's description is accurate and applicable in today's Japan.)
>
> Disputes are seldom litigated, and there are relatively few attorneys. Sellers are almost never sued for injuries caused by goods. Japanese family life is characterized by low consumption and high rates of saving but a genuine desire for foreign goods. (For a discussion of how contract negotiations in Japan are affected by cultural influences, see Ref. 9, pp. 121–123.)

The cohesion is illustrated further by the interlocking directorates and links among Japanese firms, called Keiretsu. No parent company controls the approximately 40 companies that make up the Mitsubishi Group. Instead, each company owns part of the others, and direction is given by a "triumvirate" composed of the three leading companies. Top management from 26 companies meet at the Kinyo-Kai ("Friday Conference") (p. 159).[4] This cohesion makes new entry by competitors extremely difficult. There is a general acceptance of insider trading. Sogoshosha and Keiretsu structures, discussed in other chapters, are outstanding manifestations of those characteristics.

The government plays a major role. When a Japanese firm wants to license technology from a foreign licensor, it does so through a central licensing agency, which gives it substantially greater bargaining power than it would have if it negotiated the license itself.

Islam

The Islamic legal doctrine, or "Shari'a," prevails in several countries where there is a predominant Muslim population, such as some countries in northern Africa, the Middle East, and southern Asia. Countervailing tendencies exist between traditionalism and secularism, which affects participation in a worldwide commercial system. Secular influences have in recent years led many Persian Gulf countries to enact commercial codes. But even where such codes exist, cultural-religious traditionalism affects virtually all aspects of life. Nonmarket values rank high. In Pakistan, for example, an Islamic court banned the charging or payment of interest; the concept of *riba* bars unearned or unjustified profits; and that of *gharar* considers it gambling to make any profit that was not clearly spelled out when a contract was entered into (pp. 47–48).[9] Not merely the economic system, but the entire social system is molded by a nonsecular value system. For example, in Saudi Arabia women are barred from driving cars, and in other Muslim countries drinking alcoholic beverages is prohibited.

The Islamic religion considers interest payment or receipt as usury. It is called *riba* and is prohibited in any form. Today's business transactions, however, cannot be carried out without the use of loans. As a necessity, Islamic banks have emerged. The establishment and expansion of Islamic banks in Muslim and non-Muslim countries and particularly their growth in the member states of the Organization of Petroleum Exporting Countries (OPEC) have attracted the attention of the business community. These banks provide a full spectrum of financial services. They make loans, accept deposits, and offer fee-based retail banking services that do not involve interest payments. These services include letters of credit and guarantee, domestic and international money transfer, traveler's checks, spot foreign exchanges, investment management, mortgages, and other services. Certain adjustments have been made to match the religious requirements with the imperatives of the modern economic system. Take the case of interest payment, which is forbidden in Islam.

How can a bank operate without the use of interest? The answer is a profit- or loss-sharing system.[10–13] This should not be confused with a whole host of legal fictions devised by some financial institutions to avoid calling charges interest or *riba*. One such scheme calls interest a service charge. In a profit- or loss-sharing system, instead of guaranteeing a fixed rate of return (interest), the lender and the borrower enter into an agreement that spells out how profits or losses from the venture are to be shared between them. Therefore, in Islamic finance and banking, risk is shared by the lender, who then is encouraged to finance sound and secure ventures and avoid speculative ones. In this way, the joint ownership stakes encourage both the financier and the borrower-entrepreneur to engage in productive investments. The following example illustrates the mechanics of financing a mortgage.

Aghaa Noor-ud-Din and his wife Khorshid want to buy a house that costs $200,000. Aghaa Noor enters into an agreement with the Muslim Banking and Finance Corporation (MBF) for joint ownership of the house and puts down $40,000, or 20% of the principal. MBF finances the remaining $160,000 and leases its portion of the house to him. Aghaa Noor becomes the resident owner and pays rent based on the portion of the house that MBF owns plus a little more to increase his equity. The value of the house could be reassessed by the bank every year and rental payments adjusted accordingly. If the market value of the property has increased, the rent will increase and the amount Aghaa Noor must pay to obtain full ownership of the house increases. If the value of the house falls, so does the rent, which reduces MBF's income. In case of loan default, unlike in the conventional mortgage, Aghaa Noor does not lose his equity. MBF and Aghaa Noor split the proceeds from the sale of the property proportionately to their equity, with the result that if the value of the house has fallen to, say, $100,000, Aghaa Noor will still get back 20% of that sum, and the bank will therefore fail to recover its loan in full.

According to Islamic scholars, the essence of Islamic banking—namely, risk sharing or venture capital equity investment—is the most modern concept in finance. They assert that the United States, although not a Muslim country, in spirit and in real terms, offers more financing and investment along Islamic lines than all the Muslim countries combined. They point out that the phenomenal growth of Silicon Valley in California was in part fueled by billions of dollars in venture capital, a pure form of profit or loss sharing. Such well-known firms as Intel, Microsoft, Sun Microsystems, and Oracle were financed by the venture capital industry.[14]

Developing Countries

The underdeveloped countries, categorized with varying degrees of optimism as the "developing nations," have long been caught in the tension between needing industrial and technological growth to provide for their rapidly expanding populations and at the same time distrusting and resenting outsiders and market processes. Although these nations are participating to some degree in a worldwide move toward the privatization of enterprise, the main pattern has been central state control over societies that are often so diverse internally as to be only superficially governable.

Policies on most issues are formed out of a perception of national need. Since this need may be considerably at odds with what it takes to make a venture profitable, the policies can be self-defeating, except as judged by noneconomic criteria. To promote internal development, requirements are often placed on foreign investment, such as mandates to hire local managers, train native workers, reinvest profits, and build public utilities. Government policy is determined by a central development plan, together with what is often an intricate web of bureaucracy. In Brazil, for example, it takes an estimated 1,470 legal acts to obtain an export license (p. 482).[9]

Before an import license arrangement can be entered into with a firm in India, approval must be obtained from every government agency that will have anything to do with the product. Many requirements can seriously affect the commercial viability of the venture, such as the one that an Indian licensee must be free to export what it makes. This threatens the licensor with the possibility of "reexport," through which its own licensee becomes a competitor in the licensor's home market or in markets elsewhere around the world (p. 439).[9] In recent years, however, the fall of global communism and the failure of the command and control economic model have prompted India and many developing countries to reconsider their policies in dealing with multinational companies (MNCs).

Most developing nations place strict limits on foreign ownership and passive investments and impose restrictions on the payment of hard-currency royalties to foreigners. As noted previously, because they view innovation from their own standpoint, many of the nations believe that technology either is or should be a free good, and so they encourage, or at least do not take measures against, industrial piracy.

Attitudes and policies become more open to international trade as a nation approaches the threshold of technical development. Until recently, Mexico fit the general pattern, but in early 1990 it went from being virtually closed to technology transfer agreements to being highly receptive. Mexico's participation in NAFTA is accelerating this liberalization.

Socialist and Formerly Socialist Economies

Partly because of their relative lack of development and partly because of their ideological insistence on central governmental control, the socialist nations have had several characteristics in common with less developed countries. For example, any foreign ownership of a productive enterprise, in whole or in part, was generally prohibited. Of course, there are exceptions, such as China, which have permitted foreign corporations to share ownership of businesses with an agency of the government (p. 1276).[15] While these countries either have abandoned or are abandoning their socialist-communist past and are constructing market-based institutions, many of their practices remain basically the same. During the communist reign, all citizens, for example, were required to carry with them internal passports (permission to travel outside one's city of residence) at all times. This still is in practice in some former communist countries.

Business Contracts in China

The vast market of China is very attractive to MNCs. The potential profits are large, but so are the risks, including unresolved contract disputes. If a dispute arises, the first option—and the practical one—is to resolve it informally, by using friendly relationships that you should have established with your Chinese partner. Taking your dispute to the courts is not the best choice, because in China the rule of the law is a tenuous concept,

---

(Continued)

(Continued)

and the legal process is very slow. Moreover, the existing, outdated laws are no match for the changing business environment of China.

Chinese are not as legalistic and litigious as Americans. The number of Chinese lawyers is a fraction of the number of U.S. lawyers even though the Chinese population is many times larger. If you start your negotiations using lawyers, you may give the impression that you do not trust your partners. The advice to newcomers to China is to be patient, to take their time, and to develop personal relationships with their Chinese partners. Once a trusting relationship is established, bargain hard, and put the agreement in a contract. However, before signing it, consult a lawyer. While the courts may not be the best choice for enforcing contracts and hearing disputes, nonetheless there do exist opportunities for legal recourse. An increasingly popular option is arbitration in the China International Economic and Trade Arbitration Commission. Through the Commission, parties in a dispute choose a panel to hear their case. Foreigners are allowed to sit on the panel.

Within the former communist countries, the transition to a market economy offers both opportunities and dangers. Currency problems, inflation, the crumbling of the infrastructure, a lack of experienced managerial or entrepreneurial talent, breakdowns in supply, confused political and legal relationships, and potential civil disorder, including even potential civil war, must all be gauged by the firms that enter the field. One of the great transitions in history is under way, if it can be made successfully; but it is a difficult time for firms and individuals.

National Sovereignty

With the League of Nations and later the United Nations, the world has in the 20th century made tentative approaches toward world governance. A large number of treaties and conventions bind nations to a common policy on a multitude of subjects. Nevertheless, national sovereignty continues as the central fact on the world scene. This section explores the varied manifestations of this sovereignty in the areas of taxation, currency exchange controls, trade restrictions, government takeover of industry, and privatization.

Taxes

There are many forms of taxation. Much of the discussion here is about income taxation, but it is worth noting that value-added taxes, or VATs (a form of sales tax imposed at each level of production and distribution), have become common. In recent years, the political situation within the United States has been particularly volatile with regard to a willingness to consider differing forms of taxation, such as a flat tax on income or a removal of all taxation on capital gains.

Several small nations such as Bermuda, the Bahamas, and the Cayman Islands have made themselves tax havens by having no income tax. Others provide incentives such as tax credits, tax holidays, and favorable rates. Switzerland has long made itself a favorite by protecting the confidentiality of bank accounts (this was begun in the 1930s to shield the identity of Jewish depositors from inquiries by Nazi Germany). Since World War II, these havens have attracted a large volume of business activity. To combat this, several countries have copied the anti-tax-haven provisions, called Subpart F, of the United States' Internal Revenue Code, which applies the idea of "deemed income," imputing income to investors even though they have not received a distribution of the income from a business firm. Moreover, even where incentives are offered, business firms must scrutinize tax incentives carefully for pitfalls: Lebanon, for example, has required that if a firm receives tax benefits for 5 years, it must stay to conduct business for an equal period, a commitment that many firms would be wary to make in any event, much less under the strife-ridden circumstances in Lebanon not long ago.[16]

To reduce their taxes, some U.S. companies relocate their headquarters offshore and transfer patents, trademarks, and other intangible assets to their subsidiaries abroad. To prevent these and other corporate-accounting abuses, U.S. Treasury and Internal Revenue Service are considering various options, including prohibiting them from doing business with various federal agencies.[17]

Countries differ in whom and what they tax. Three main systems are used (for a detailed discussion of the varied systems of taxation, see Ref. 4, pp. 688–697):

1. To tax citizens or nationals of the country on all their income, no matter where they made it and without regard to where they have their residence ("nationality principle")

2. To tax legal residents within the country, regardless of where they earned the income ("residency principle"; the 66 countries that use this system also tax all income generated within their borders, even by people who are living in other countries)

3. To tax any income earned from activities within the taxing country but not income earned elsewhere ("source principle"; nationality and residency are considered for some purposes; the source principle is used by more countries than any other)

All this raises, of course, a considerable possibility of multiple taxation of the same income. The nations of the world have grappled with this in a number of ways. (The methods of handling the problem of multiple taxation are discussed in Ref. 4, pp. 704–708.) One way is for the home nation not to tax income that has been taxed by the host country (the exemption system). A second applies a tax credit, reducing the tax in one country by the amount paid in another (the credit system). A third does not give a credit, which reduces the tax dollar for dollar, but only a deduction, which reduces the declarable income (the deduction system). From the point of view of the taxpayer, the best is the exemption system, the worst the deduction system. The credit system results in the taxpayer paying whichever is the higher rate between the two nations.

Tax strategy is accordingly important to those doing business internationally. In this context, the type of business entity (i.e., partnership, corporation, etc.) used is important, since tax treatment typically varies as to the different business forms, just as it does in the United States. A pitfall is that the host country may not treat the entity as being what it appears. Many have a central registrar that categorizes the firm in terms of local law (p. 676).[4]

Most countries' income tax systems, like that of the United States, have a graduated scale of rates. But some countries, such as Jamaica and Iceland, impose a flat rate on personal income. Almost two thirds of the world uses a flat rate in taxing corporate income, varying the rate from industry to industry. A danger in less developed countries is that the government may impute a profit to a company and then tax it if the government believes that the company did not report a reasonable profit (pp. 699–700).[4]

The impact of globalization on taxes should be acknowledged. As a factor in globalization, capital and labor mobility undermine the ability of nations to set their own level of taxes. The Internet has further eroded their autonomy. In response and to preserve their sovereignty, increasingly governments will have to set multilateral rules. Only this line of action enables them to reclaim the control over national affairs that has been lost to globalization.[18]

Currency Exchange Controls

Unless the parties use barter (an exchange of goods or services for other goods or services), payment under a contract will be in the currency of some agreed-on nation. This raises two questions. First, is the currency convertible? Second, can the funds (profits) be repatriated?

The world monetary and banking system consists of a marketplace with a number of firms rather than a single comprehensive structure. People speak of a foreign exchange market, but it is not to be found in any one location because the market exists in reality in the millions of transactions conducted around the globe by a great many banks, brokers, and dealers. Custom plays a large role, as does each country's own laws and institutions, along with such world agencies as the International Monetary Fund and the Bank for International Settlements. Many of the relationships are governed by informal agreements.

A currency is considered convertible if, within this market, it can be traded freely for others at the ratios established by the market. This is done through either spot or futures contracts. Most convertibility is done on a spot basis, where money is exchanged for another currency that will be delivered to the buyer within 2 business days. A futures contract provides for a later delivery of money, normally within 30, 60, or 90 days. By locking in the exchange rate at the time the purchase is made, the buyer of the currency is able to hedge against the risk of future rate changes.

Problems exist in repatriating profits from a number of developing countries, which may require permission, place a percentage restriction on the amount that can be taken out, or specially tax such profits. If a foreign business liquidates its assets, any amount it receives over the firm's initial investment may be considered as dividend and treated accordingly. These difficulties point to the dangers of short-term investment in developing countries.

In the United States, the Overseas Private Investment Corporation (OPIC) sells insurance that applies where there is a legally existing right of convertibility. If the insured is confronted by a foreign government's denial of that right, or if conditions (such as banking procedures) change to block convertibility, OPIC will make it good. OPIC coverage is not available, however, for dealings with countries that grant no legal right to convert. (For a more complete discussion of OPIC, see Ref. 4, pp. 83–88.)

Trade Restrictions: Tariffs and Quotas

The impact of issues relating to national sovereignty on trade restrictions is well illustrated by the history of the United States. The United States was committed to free trade during the Jefferson-Jacksonian era prior to the Civil War but was heavily protectionist under the leadership of the Republican Party from the Civil War until the 1930s. The worldwide depression during the 1930s provoked a clamor within each nation to withdraw from world trade as a way to "save itself." But as the world emerged from World War II, this was generally perceived as having prolonged and deepened the depression. This perception has led to continuing efforts since World War II to negotiate a removal of trade barriers. At present, the situation is characterized by movement away from both trade restrictions and governmental intervention into expanded free trade.

Governmental intervention in trade comes in many forms, including tariffs and other constraints on imports, export controls, state subsidies, limits on foreign investment, preferences in government procurement, and countermeasures against "dumping."

Imports. As for the United States, the laws relating to imports are almost all at the federal level because under the Constitution the states have virtually nothing to do with foreign commerce. Under the "import-export clause" of the Constitution, a state cannot tax an import. The U.S. Supreme Court has accordingly been called on at various times historically to establish tests for the point at which a good loses its character as an "import" and starts being just part of the mass of property that is subject to property taxes.

Some imports are prohibited. These include such things as illegal drugs, food that is considered dangerous, and obscene or insurrectionary published materials. Sometimes the prohibition is imposed not because the item is harmful but to protect a certain industry. At other times, the prohibition is retaliatory, such as the U.S. ban on fish from a country that seizes American fishing boats. Since 1917, the U.S. "Trading With the Enemy Act" has barred imports from countries engaged in armed conflict with the United States. Quotas are sometimes imposed on imports and are less severe than outright prohibitions. The "voluntary" restrictions that a decade ago Japan had placed on its automobile exports to the United States were a substitute for the quotas that the United States had once imposed.

A tariff is an ad valorem tax, since it is based on the value of the import. Whether a tariff will apply depends on where the goods came from, how they are classified, and what value is given to them. Various practical aspects, such as the rate to be used and whether any trade restrictions apply, depend on the country of origin. If more than one country has been involved in the creation and transport of the goods, rules of origin are used to determine which is the country of origin. The main rule is the "substantial transformation test," which looks to see where the product underwent a major change. (A discussion of the country-of-origin rules appears in Ref. 9, pp. 352–359.)

Although procedures vary from country to country, it is helpful to understand the steps in the U.S. entry process (discussed at length in Ref. 9, pp. 332–340). The importer posts a bond to guarantee that the duty will be paid. Entry documents, with a complete commercial invoice telling about the shipment, are processed by the U.S. Customs Service, and the tariff is entered on an entry summary form. The importer is allowed to have the goods after a tentative duty is set. The final ruling by the Customs Service about the tariff, which by law must be made within 1 year of the goods' entry, is called liquidation. There is a right to appeal at the administrative level and then in court. If the importer wants to know ahead of time whether there will be a duty, the firm can ask for a binding ruling.

Exports. In the United States, the Constitution prohibits a tax on exports, which makes their treatment substantially different from imports. All the same, the federal government has traditionally controlled exports. A rule of thumb is that it takes permission by way of an export license to send anything out of the country.

Some exports are prohibited ("embargoed"). The reasons include ensuring the availability of goods that exist only in a small quantity, prevention of nuclear proliferation, and other foreign policy and national security goals. The United States and 16 other nations belong to the Coordinating

Committee for Multilateral Export Controls (COCOM). Violation of its constraints, such as that against selling certain types of military technology to unfriendly nations, is a criminal offense. Such a prohibition arose with regard to Iraq after its seizure of Kuwait, and exports are banned from regimes such as those of Cuba and North Korea, which remain committed to communism, or countries that are considered to support international terrorism, such as Libya. To know what is currently prohibited, an exporter should check with the Office of Export Administration, which carries out the Export Administration Act, to see what is on the "commodity control list." Other agencies can also play a role, such as the Nuclear Regulatory Commission for the export licensing of nuclear materials and the State Department for military hardware.

Because it would be easy to circumvent these prohibitions by sending the goods to an acceptable destination with the intent that they then be sent on to one of the prohibited destinations, an end-user certification is required. American law makes the exporter accountable for where the product is finally used, such as North Korea, even if the goods are sent to that location by someone else after the exporter has gotten them to a valid destination such as France (pp. 160–161).[16]

Most exports don't involve prohibited destinations. For exports in general, two kinds of licenses are issued. A general license is a blanket approval for the export of goods of a certain kind and can be issued by the exporter to itself if it complies with certain rules. A validated license is governmentally issued, looks to the nature of the goods and where they will ultimately be used, and is specific to a certain transaction (p. 160).[16]

Nontariff Trade Barriers. Governments have seemingly endless ways to restrict trade. Some of them are framed, with varying degrees of plausibility, in terms of health, safety, or environmental protection. They include the following (see Table 7.1):

- *Embargoes*: As noted, embargoes can apply to imports, exports, or both.
- *Quotas*: Again as noted, quotas limit rather than prohibit.
- *Currency controls.*
- *The imposition of unique performance, environmental, health, or safety specifications that a foreign firm may not be prepared to meet*: A commonly cited example is the EU's ban on American beef because U.S. ranchers use growth hormones.
- *Preferential treatment given to the country's own suppliers when the government is procuring supplies for its own use*: This is common in the major industrial nations. At least with regard to expensive items, there has been an effort through the Agreement on Government Procurement to limit such preferences (pp. 347–348).[4] Most military production falls into this category. Globalization, however, has even altered the nature of business in arms production. Recently, for example, the U.S. government and defense industry officials convinced

a number of European allies to agree on joint production of the radar-evading Joint Strike Fighter airplane. The interesting aspect of this deal, considered the biggest military project in history, is that other nations have accepted not only the involvement of U.S. firms in their defense industry but also the United States accepting, and in fact inviting, the other countries' participation in a U.S. military project.[19]

- *Undue red tape in customs procedures.*
- *Various internal requirements, such as that the country's own system of measurement (e.g., the metric system) be used in any specifications or that a commodity be labeled in a certain way.*
- *Government subsidies or tax preferences to a nation's own firms*: Sometimes these provoke "countervailing duties" by other nations to level the playing field for their own suppliers.
- *Constraints on "portfolio investment"*: Some nations totally bar a foreigner's purchase of securities in one of the country's firms, either in general or in certain industries. Others allow a temporary co-ownership but with the provision that at some time the ownership must come to rest entirely with the country's own nationals.

Efforts to Reduce Trade Barriers. The consensus since World War II has been that the intense national protectionism that occurred during the Great Depression was a disaster. This has led to negotiations under GATT (the predecessor of the WTO), established in 1947, as a way to reduce not just tariffs but all trade barriers. By providing an international forum, GATT made it easier for each government to resist its own producer interest groups' pressures for protectionism. Since 1947, GATT negotiations, called "Rounds," have lowered many barriers, although much remains to be done. In all, there were eight Rounds. The eighth round, the Uruguay Round, was concluded in December 1993, with a signing ceremony in January 2004 in Marakesh, Morocco. It took 7 years to conclude the Uruguay Round. It addressed,

Table 7.1	Nontariff Trade Barriers

Embargoes

Quotas

Currency control

Unique performance, environmental, health, or safety requirements

Preferential treatment to local suppliers to government, e.g., military

Undue red tape in customs procedures

Internal requirements, e.g., local measurement system

Government subsidies or tax preferences to local firms

Constraints on "portfolio investment" that bars foreign investors from purchasing certain securities

among other things, issues relating to IP rights. The most recent agreement under the WTO was the Doha Round, which started in 2001, in Doha, Qatar, and provided a mandate for negotiations, including those on agriculture and services. The Doha mandate was refined by work at Cancun in 2003, Geneva in 2004, and Hong Kong in 2005. At Hong Kong, the participating trade ministers reached an agreement that set a deadline for eliminating subsidies to agricultural exports by 2013. Also, it was argued that industrialized countries open their markets to goods from the world's poorest nations.

The WTO is the controlling agency over international trade, and it has been empowered to establish international panels to hear disputes about the decisions and laws of individual countries relating to trade. If a country does not comply with a decision after appeal, it is subject to trade sanctions or must pay compensation. For example, the WTO ruled in favor of the EU and against the United States, which was granting tax breaks on American companies' earnings from export.[20]

The central idea behind the WTO is that member nations not discriminate in their trade conduct. The normal trade relation rule (NTR), which prior to 1988 was known as the most favored nation (MFN) rule, calls for each country to give all other member nations the benefit of its lowest tariffs and least restrictive trade rules. Several exceptions have been developed, however, to allow preferential treatment for developing nations. A second rule, the national treatment rule, requires the country to give foreign goods and domestically manufactured goods equal treatment once they have entered the country. (For further information about the most-favored-nation rule and the national treatment rule, see Ref. 4, pp. 315–318.) Special rules have been worked out for free-trade areas, in which tariffs are removed among two or more nations, and for customs unions, which go a step further by setting a common tariff for countries outside the group.

The United States fought back against trade barriers with the Omnibus Trade Act of 1988, which included the "Super 301" provision, whereby a U.S. trade representative (USTR) could inform Congress if a country erected significant trade barriers against the United States or systematically discriminated against American business. In such a case, retaliation is then threatened against that country. Although successfully used against several adverse trade practices, the provision was opposed by other countries, and this experiment ended in 1991 when Section 301 was allowed to expire.

Retaliation Against Dumping. Most American states have laws against selling below cost with the intention of forcing a competitor out of business. Similar behavior, called dumping, in which imported goods are sold for "less than fair value" (LTFV), is frowned on in international trade. Fair value is determined by comparing the price with the cost of manufacture or with what the goods are being sold for at home (p. 664).[21] In the United States, the International Trade Commission, part of the Department of Commerce, investigates whether dumping has occurred and whether it has adversely affected an entire

American industry, not just individual firms. If these facts are found, a countervailing duty is placed on the goods. In recent years, the United States has experienced some friction with Japan over alleged dumping by Japan.

Expropriation, Confiscation, and Nationalization

The power of eminent domain involves a government's taking of what previously had been private property. The exercise of this power is called condemnation. In the United States, constitutional protections apply: "Taking" of private property must be for a "public purpose," and "just compensation" must be paid. In international affairs, the power was limited from the middle of the 17th to the 19th century by the doctrine enunciated in 1646 by Hugo Grotius that no government had a right to take the property of a foreigner and that if it violated this principle it would owe the foreign owner full payment. (For a discussion of the history of international legal doctrines relative to a government taking of property, see Ref. 9, pp. 453–460.)

The term *nationalization* refers to a state's assumption of ownership. Legal literature sometimes then distinguishes between expropriation, which involves meeting the tests of "a proper public purpose" and "just compensation," and confiscation, which in one or both ways does not (p. 651).[21]

Competing Doctrines. A new form of traditional theory came into being early in the 19th century. It differs from Grotius in holding that a state may lawfully take the property of a foreigner; but it elaborates on and adds to the traditional requirements by calling for a proper public purpose, an absence of discrimination against the foreign owner, and "prompt, adequate, and effective compensation." Developed countries typically treat this as established international law. The doctrine has also been gaining increasing acceptance worldwide, both among developing nations as they take on the attitudes of developed countries and among the former communist countries as they adopt market economies.

An opposing doctrine has held sway for the past century, however, among many less developed nations, which have given private property less sanctity and have often seen themselves as exploited by outsiders. These countries have embraced the Calvo Doctrine, named after a Latin American professor, which insists strongly on the right of a government to take the property of a foreign investor and sees any intervention by the investor's home state as a violation of the sovereignty of the host government. Because they strongly assert the latter's sovereignty, these nations are known as sovereign rights states. Some remove the limits of public purpose and nondiscrimination entirely; others do not go quite so far, holding merely that there need be no showing of a public purpose as long as the foreigner is not discriminated against. In all these nations, the amount and terms of compensation tend to be far less generous than in developed countries. Before allowing foreign investment, many of these countries require the investor to agree to a "Calvo clause," which says that the investor gives up the right to seek assistance from its home state.

Creeping expropriation is a business risk that has its counterpart in the United States and that has grown with the increasing sophistication of governments in less developed countries. (The term uses expropriation as synonymous with confiscation, reflecting the overall lack of consistency in the use of such labels.) This consists of the host government's gradually imposing so many controls that the property's owners lose the incidents of ownership. Although the United States has sought to have it recognized, international law does not yet acknowledge the existence of creeping expropriation (pp. 83–84).[4]

Remedies. Because of all this, there is a high level of political risk for investors in less developed countries. The remedies are limited and often ineffectual. They include suing in the courts of the country that made the seizure, suing in the home country, seeking the political support of the investor's home country, resorting to an international agency, or carrying insurance against the risk.

A lawsuit brought in the courts of a less developed country is often unrewarding, since the courts there are generally not independent and the attitudes included in the Calvo Doctrine will govern. The lawsuit may, however, be brought in the investor's home state, where the hope is to collect from property that the seizing state may have there. But this route is almost entirely blocked by legal doctrines of long standing that reflect the reluctance of one nation to invite war or international friction by interfering with another.

The Philippines' Dispute With Westinghouse

During the Marcos era, Westinghouse Electric Corporation signed a contract to build a $2.3 billion nuclear power plant in the Philippines. While the construction was under way, a popular uprising toppled the Marcos government. The uprising and the subsequent free election brought to power Corazon Aquino, the wife of the slain opposition leader, Benito Aquino, as the new president of the Philippines. Shortly after the 620-MW plant was completed, the Aquino government mothballed the plant because of safety concerns. Then, it filed suits against Westinghouse. In 1993, after it lost a bribery case against the electric company in the federal court in New Jersey, the Philippines government reached an out-of-court settlement with Westinghouse.

The terms of the agreement called for Westinghouse to build two new 100-MW gas turbines at $49.5 million. In return, the Philippines government agreed to drop a breach-of-contract arbitration case pending against Westinghouse in Geneva.[22]

One of these is the sovereign immunity doctrine. In the United States, the Foreign Sovereign Immunities Act of 1976 bars a federal court from taking a case unless the other country's actions were a form of commercial activity. In addition, there is the act of state doctrine, which declines to declare the action of a foreign government invalid, and a propensity of courts in the United States to see the other country's law as controlling in deciding the case. In the context of these intergovernmental relations, remedies for the investor are often inadequate. (For a discussion of sovereign immunity and the act of state doctrine, see Ref. 21, pp. 651–654.)

Instead of relying exclusively on a lawsuit, the investor may solicit the political help of its home state. An American investor may ask assistance from the State Department, which has the final word on whether to grant it. Subject to some exceptions, the investor must first exhaust his or her remedies within the host country. A freezing of assets, as in the case of Iran, is possible, although this does not result in immediate compensation to the investor whose property was taken. Instead, the investor must prove its claim before the Foreign Settlement Claims Commission to share in anything the American government recovers.

Resort to an international tribunal is yet another possibility. The International Court of Justice (ICJ) is, however, empowered only to decide cases between governments or cases that are instigated by agencies of the United Nations. Individuals do not have a standing to sue there. On the other hand, the International Center for the Settlement of Investment Disputes (ICSID), established at the World Bank's Washington Conference in 1965, is available to individuals and firms. About half the world's nations have ratified the convention that created the court, which handles disputes if several preconditions are met. The parties must look only to the ensuing arbitration, forgoing all court action or political assistance. (For an extended discussion of arbitration through ICSID, see Ref. 4, pp. 103–111.)

The best protection would seem to be insurance, but it is often not available. The U.S. governmental agency OPIC serves this purpose and provides risk insurance for U.S. foreign direct investment (FDI). An important limitation is that the insurance is offered only for investments in countries that have entered into an executive agreement to arbitrate any claims (doing so with OPIC itself, which will have taken as an assignment the investor's claim after paying the investor). OPIC's premium for the coverage varies with the risk. The coverage will sometimes include political violence such as terrorism, war, and revolution. OPIC is not required to insure an investment and will turn down those that are too risky. Coverage can also apply to creeping expropriation if the entire investment has been affected and if the investor agrees to abandon all rights to it. Beyond the United States, the World Bank set up the Multilateral Investment Guaranty Agency (MIGA) in 1987 to perform much the same functions as OPIC.

Privatization

The worldwide move toward a market economy in the 1970s and 1980s involved a trend that was the very opposite of nationalization. "Deregulation" and "privatization" (a government's passing of the ownership of property to individuals and firms) took hold in Europe, America, and many parts of the world. Then, when communism broke up in Eastern Europe and the former Soviet Union in the late 1980s and early 1990s, privatization became the byword for the transition of these areas to a market system.

Forms of privatization vary greatly. The state may issue scrip and auction the property, grant "concessions" to private operators but with the property remaining under the ownership of the government, pass ownership to those who had been employed at a certain facility or who were tenants, or just sell a sometimes less than controlling interest. In the semichaos that prevailed in the former Soviet Union following the fall of the Communist Party, much privatization occurred spontaneously without a controlling principle; people took over land and began farming, and the managers of industrial plants declared the plants as their own. Many of the powers of government were decentralized by a similar process as localities claimed autonomy.

Privatization does not necessarily imply an absence of governmental controls after ownership has passed into private hands. The whole range of governmental involvement, discussed earlier, remains possible.

International Implications of Legal Issues

The effect of some legal matters spills over national borders. The extraterritorial characteristics of these matters have a global impact. Among the issues with extraterritorial effects are securities regulations, labor law, banking, taxation, torts of subsidiaries, and antitrust law.

Extraterritoriality

Although each nation's law normally extends only to matters that occur within its borders, the extraterritorial application of law to events taking place elsewhere has been growing rapidly.

This has been evident in criminal law with the post–World War II Nuremberg trials, Israel's prosecutions of Adolph Eichmann and John Demjanjuk, and the United States' capture and prosecution of Manuel Noriega. The United States, applying the principles that have been developed internally by the U.S. Supreme Court relating to jurisdiction of state courts over nonresidents, has been the principal proponent of extraterritoriality. The principle has several applications to business practices, but globalization has made extraterritoriality a contentious issue.

The most contentious U.S. law with extraterritoriality implications is the 1996 Helms-Burton law. The law includes a number of provisions. Based on one of its provisions, any company that deals economically with Cuba can be subjected to legal action and that company's leadership can be barred from entry into the United States. Sanctions may be applied to non-U.S. companies that trade with Cuba. The Helms-Burton law has been very unpopular around the world. The EU, Canada, Mexico, Argentina, and other U.S. allies that have normal trade relations with Cuba have passed laws aiming to neutralize this act. These countries have argued that the law contains provisions that run counter to the spirit of international law and sovereignty.

Recent scandals and accounting misconduct by large American firms such as Enron Corporation and Global Crossing resulted in the U.S. Congress passing the Sarbanes-Oxley Act, which aimed at tightening accounting standards and restoring investors' confidence. This act will lead to profound changes in investment, banking, corporate governance, and accountancy in developed countries. Non-U.S. companies listed in the United States will have to comply with its requirements. The listed companies are required, among other things, to have an audit committee of independent directors to appoint, remunerate, and scrutinize the work of auditors. In some countries, such as Japan, independent directors are a rarity. Of course, foreign companies can delist. But by doing so, they deprive themselves of access to the biggest pool of capital on earth.[23]

The EU's commissioner for internal markets criticized this attempt, calling it "unilateralism." The reason for the criticism is that the bill requires many European companies to comply with the new rules. The act would have "extraterritorial" consequences, forcing EU auditors of European companies listed in the United States to open their books to U.S. regulators.[24] Europeans contend that certain problems may arise in implementing this law. Under German laws, for example, the management board (codetermination board, discussed in the chapter on industrial relations) takes collective responsibility. Decisions are not made by one person. Either all agree or the one who disagrees leaves the board. You cannot hold one member responsible for the decisions of the board.[25] The issues with extraterritoriality implications are discussed below (Table 7.2).

Bribery. After scandals surfaced about American firms committing bribery overseas, Congress passed the Foreign Corrupt Practices Act of 1977, which outlaws the bribing of foreign political candidates and governmental officials if the particular office exercises judgmental powers relating to the subject matter of the bribe. The act applies even though the bribe occurs outside the United States and by an individual working for an American company, who may not be an American citizen. But the act does not punish the local bribee, leaving it to the foreign state to prosecute the individual if, indeed, such a crime has taken place.

Securities Regulation. American courts have generally been willing to exercise jurisdiction over citizens of other countries, residing in those countries, to apply the American securities regulation. The federal Securities Act of 1933 relates to new issues of securities, and the Securities Exchange Act of

Table 7.2   **Issues With Extraterritoriality Implications**

Bribery
Security regulations
Labor laws
Banking
Taxation
Tort of subsidiaries
Antitrust laws
Reexportation

1934 prohibits fraud in any securities transaction and has a number of rules that apply to large companies. Extraterritoriality is exercised to prevent a circumvention of those laws.

Labor Law. Historically, the U.S. Supreme Court has refused to apply American labor law to work done outside the United States, but in recent years the federal government has pressed hard to apply such law, especially antidiscrimination principles, to American businesses abroad.

Banking. The war on drugs involves a massive struggle against the smuggling of illegal substances into the United States. The federal government, seeking to prevent foreign banks from playing a role in the laundering of profits from this and other illegal activity, has gone to court to get subpoenas to serve on the banks' branches in the United States, requiring the branches to pass on information from their parent banks. This effort has not been wholly successful, since it often incurs opposition not just from other governments but from the American courts themselves.

Taxation. The United States has a strong interest in preventing wealthy taxpayers from taking up residency in a country where taxes are lower. Most countries will not tax nonresident citizens; the United States has been the main exception to the rule.

Torts of Subsidiaries. In the 1984 tragedy at Bhopal, India, more than 2,000 people were killed and 200,000 injured by a toxic gas released by a plant operated by Union Carbide India Limited, a subsidiary of an American corporation, Union Carbide Corporation. Fifty-one percent of the Indian corporation was owned by the American company, the rest by the citizens or the government of India. The plant was built, operated, and managed entirely by Indians. The American company was sued on a newly fashioned theory known as the single-enterprise theory, which argued that parent companies that have "a global purpose, organization, structure, and financial resources" should be liable for torts (civil wrongs) committed in any country by their subsidiaries.[b] The case was settled for $470 million. Automatic tort liability for the actions of foreign affiliates, if it comes into force, will constitute a vast extension of extraterritoriality and will enormously increase the liability exposure of companies engaged in international business.

Antitrust. Antitrust law in the United States contains a per se prohibition against some restraints on trade. An act that is illegal per se is illegal "in itself," without a court's looking at extenuating factors or overall effect. Other restraints are illegal only if they violate a rule of reason (reasonableness test) or have a reasonable probability of lessening competition. Civil and criminal penalties apply, including the possibility of treble damages (a tripling of the actual damages). The principal American antitrust statutes are the Sherman Act, which prohibits monopolies and restraints on trade; the Clayton Act, which bars certain acts if they have a reasonable probability of lessening competition; and the Robinson-Patman Act, which pertains to price discrimination.

Considerable friction has existed over the extraterritorial application of antitrust laws by the United States and the EU. Largely because of the American treble damage remedy and the exemption granted to export associations, Britain has joined in the opposition voiced by many less developed countries. Some countries have adopted "blocking legislation," and courts overseas have sometimes ordered one citizen of a country not to sue another citizen on an antitrust matter in American courts.

The Foreign Trade Antitrust Improvements Act of 1982 gave a statutory basis to earlier court decisions that extended American antitrust law to the behavior of foreign entities. For a court to apply American law, it must find several things: (1) that the anticompetitive act had, or was intended to have, a substantial effect on either American exports or internal commerce; (2) that the behavior was of the sort that would violate U.S. antitrust laws; and (3) after considering the need for international comity, that the American interest in regulation outweighs the interest of the other country in governing the activity.

It is argued that uniform antitrust laws could contribute to opening world markets and limit barriers to trade. Certain limitations, however, prevent uniformity of antitrust laws. Among the limitations are considerations of sovereignty, concerns about sharing confidential information, differences in competition policy between emerging and more established economies, and the varying role of trade policies among nations.[26]

Reexportation. As we saw in the earlier discussion of governmental restrictions on trade, it is illegal to export a good on the commodity control list to an embargoed country. This takes on an extraterritorial aspect in light of the responsibility that is placed on the American exporter to see to it that the recipient in one country does not send the goods on (reexport them) to someone at a prohibited destination.

Contract Enforcement

Those engaged in international business will want to do everything possible to arrive at enforceable contracts. This requires knowledge of desirable contract provisions, the rules of law that apply, how payment is made, and the enforcement of judgments.

Contract Provisions. It is wise to include certain provisions in an international contract. One is a forum selection clause by which the parties agree on which nation's courts are to have jurisdiction over a dispute if one arises. These should be crafted with competent legal advice, since the clause will not be enforced if it seems inequitable for any of several reasons. Another is a choice-of-law clause specifying which country's law should be applied by the court hearing the dispute. The 1986 Hague Convention on the Law Applicable to Contracts for the International Sale of Goods, also known as the Choice-of-Law Convention, lets the parties freely pick the law to be applied. Along similar lines, a choice-of-language clause is desirable, to select the language in which the contract will be construed. A **force majeure** clause is also common. This provides for a party to be excused from performing if prevented from doing so by a force—such as war, expropriation, strikes, flood, embargo, and the like—that is beyond the party's control.

Law Relating to Sales. In the United States, the UCC was adopted in the early 1960s by all states except Louisiana, which derives its law from the Napoleonic Code. For international transactions, however, a source of law that is rapidly being adopted around the world is the United Nations' Convention on Contracts for the International Sale of Goods (CISG), which took effect in 1988. (The CISG is dealt with extensively in the chapter on sales in Ref. 4, pp. 422–474.) CISG preempts any given nation's law if the parties' respective countries have adopted the convention (the United States is among those that have done so). However, if the contract includes a choice-of-law clause, then the law of a member nation is applicable. CISG relates to sales between merchants, not to consumers. It speaks to issues relating to the formation of the contract and remedies, but it doesn't deal with matters of competency, lawful purpose, product liability for harm caused by goods, or the rights of third parties. These exclusions suggest that parties should continue to include a choice-of-law clause to cover those matters.

The CISG is partly based on the UCC and partly on the concepts that are inherent in European civil law. Among its principles, which frequently differ significantly from those of the UCC, are the following rules.

Way of Paying Obligations. Since the mid-1970s, rather than use the mail or telex, firms in a large number of countries have made payments of money owed to others under contracts through the Society for Worldwide Interbank

Financial Telecommunication (SWIFT), by which banks transfer funds rapidly from a buyer's bank to that of a seller.

Enforcement of Judgments. Can a judgment against an MNC be enforced in other countries besides the country where the judgment was rendered? The answer is yes, but there are caveats. Assume that one party sues another in the courts of a certain country for breach of contract and obtains a judgment in that country's courts. The collection of the judgment can possibly be obtained in yet another country through the entry of a separate corresponding judgment there. The courts of the second country generally do not require a new trial on the merits. They will recognize the foreign judgment in their country and statutorily extend comity to the judicial actions of the other nation.

This does not, however, work with perfect symmetry. While American courts will usually enforce foreign judgments in the absence of a strong public policy reason not to, many other countries attach conditions to enforcing U.S. judgments. Countries differ in the types of remedies they prefer. Specific performance is more commonly used than money judgments in many countries. In specific performance remedy cases, the court orders a party to do what it promised under a contract.

Patents, Copyrights, Trademarks, and Trade Names

As noted previously, intellectual property rights (IPRs) may constitute a valuable part of the assets of a firm doing business internationally. (See the chapter on intellectual property in Ref. 4, pp. 586–664; Ref. 9, pp. 425–452.) It becomes important to protect the exclusivity of these rights by blocking unauthorized use. One of the more effective ways to protect an IPR, where the situation fits, is to maintain an unpatented right as a trade secret. Coca-Cola, for example, for more than a century has kept its formula secret. So long as careful steps are taken to maintain the secrecy, the law of individual countries, or the law of individual states in the United States, relating to trade secrets provides remedies in case of theft.

The international registration of patents and trademarks is governed by the 1883 Paris Convention for Protection of Industrial Property. Copyrights are governed either by the Berne Convention, promulgated in 1886 (revised in 1971), or the Universal Copyright Convention. Ninety-three countries belong to one, the other, or both. The conventions are administered by the World Intellectual Property Organization (WIPO), established in 1967.

Patents, Trademarks, and Trade Names. The Paris Convention does not provide a one-time, universally valid patent, trademark, or trade name registration (although the Madrid Convention does set up such a system for trademarks and trade names among its participating nations not including the United States). Instead, a separate registration is needed within each country where protection is desired, and the laws of different countries vary widely. Patent protection starts from the time an application is filed, and if an application is filed in another member country within 1 year of the initial filing, the protection in the second country dates back to the day on which the application was filed in the first country. This 12-month rule is called the "right of priority." A similar dating back applies to trademarks if the filing in the second country is done within 6 months. Some countries, including the United States, will judicially protect a trademark on the basis of its use even if it is not registered. Subject to some exceptions, U.S. patents are good for 20 years from the day the application is filed. In other countries, the period varies from as low as 5 years to as much as 20 years.

The Paris Convention's national treatment rule requires that each member nation give foreign applicants the same protection it gives its own citizens, without discrimination. The common rules principle sets down certain guidelines for all member nations to follow, although much is then left to the nation's own laws.

Copyrights. A one-time registration of copyright is available among the nations that have subscribed to the Berne Convention, so that the claimant need not register in each country. A major issue in recent years has been the protection of computer programs, since imitation can escape copyright protection if the programming is sufficiently rearranged. The trend in the technically advanced nations is to shift to a patent rationale. A mixed system of patent and copyright has been established for computer chips. The Uruguay Round of the GATT negotiations gave considerable attention to current issues relating to all forms of IPRs.

In 1996, the WIPO in Geneva adopted two international treaties on copyright protection. It extended protection—in countries that sign on—to any kind of copyright content distributed online, such as software, music, and multimedia. It also established that countries would pass laws to make hacking into online music and film subscription services and piracy of CDs and DVDs illegal.[27]

Transfer of IPRs. The owner of an IPR may use it itself, convey it to another firm, or give a license (exclusive or nonexclusive) to one or more users. If the owner franchises the right, the owner gives a license and retains a large amount of control over its use. Many countries will grant a compulsory license to a potential user, without getting the owner's approval, if a certain period of time passes without the owner's using the IPR in the country's market.

Finally, since in effect IPRs are legally protected monopolies, given as an encouragement to invention, countries have developed a large body of law that concerns itself with anticompetitive features and specifies how the monopoly can be used. For example, most countries will treat as illegal price fixing an agreement between an IPR owner and a licensee concerning the price the licensee will charge its own customers.

International Boycott

In addition to the antitrust matters discussed in relation to extraterritoriality, it should be noted that it is illegal under the Export Administration Act of 1979 and the Internal Revenue Code for Americans either to take part in or to cooperate with an international boycott (concerted refusal to deal). Historically, the primary purpose of this provision was to prevent American participation in the Arab states' boycott against Israel. In fact, Americans are required to report to the Internal Revenue Service any request to take part in a boycott and any request to provide information about the religion or national origin of customers, employees, or suppliers. The U.S. government approves certain boycotts, however, such as the one that existed for several years against South Africa, and it is lawful to participate in those.

Many countries have merger legislation that in various ways limits acquisitions by foreign firms of part or all of a domestic company. Most particularly, developing nations want their own citizens to own at least part of each enterprise.

MNC Operational Disputes

MNCs face a number of potential operational disputes that can hamper international business.

Industrial Relations

The labor legislation that applies to international businesses is the law of the country in which employees are working, subject to certain conditions. For example, the extraterritorial effect of the law of the employees' country of origin is applicable if the employees are not natives of the host country. The International Labor Organization (ILO), an agency of the United Nations, has proposed more than 150 conventions. A convention is an agreement, sponsored by an international organization, between two or more countries. Regional treaties also exist within such areas of the world as the EC. Primarily, however, the law of a specific nation is enforceable when there is no international agreement in place or that country has persistently objected to international customary law. It is essential that an international business get to know the labor laws and customs of the nations with which it deals, since they may differ greatly from those in the United States. Most employees, for example, are employed at will in the United States, but in a nation such as Japan there is an expectation of a long-term commitment.

The ILO seeks the adoption of standards by its member nations, proposes recommendations and conventions, and conducts conferences. Its administrative tribunal hears specific cases only involving employees of intergovernmental organizations (IGOs), such as the ILO itself. (For a lengthy discussion of the ILO, see Ref. 4, pp. 259–268.)

The situation regarding collective bargaining will vary depending on the strength of union organizations, labor militancy, and the extent to which union activities such as picketing and boycotts have been under legal constraint. Various aspects of labor relations are discussed in Chapter 12, on industrial relations. Here, we will only refer to pertinent legal issues.

Many countries set limits on the right to dismiss employees and to relocate or close plants. The United States requires early notification for layoffs. In Germany, the company must work through the works council, which can insist on arbitration. The discharge of an employee often requires consultation with the union, as in Britain, or with the works council, as in Germany. In the United States, union contracts invariably provide a grievance procedure, culminating in arbitration, in cases of employee discipline.

To be employed as a foreign worker in a country, a person must obtain the necessary visa and work permits and must conform to the same laws as observed by workers of that country. In addition, myriad regulations exist regarding pay, working conditions, the percentage of foreign workers who can be employed, who will pay for their return to their home countries, and so on. Sometimes, there are prohibitions or restrictions on a worker's right to send his salary home.

Many countries have compensation systems for injury on the job. Worker's compensation, a compulsory insurance system, is prevalent in the United States, where it was copied from legislation in Bismarck's Germany. Countries generally provide for private insurance, a governmental fund, or a combination of both.

Environmental Laws

The developed nations have devoted increasing resources to protection of the environment, and most have extensive laws dealing with responsibility for and cleanup of pollution. This has not come nearly so far in the developing countries and the former communist states. Businesses, however, must be aware that as these countries improve economically, lax standards, where they exist, may soon be tightened.

Internationally, the United Nations Environmental Programme (UNEP) is actively generating a series of agreements, supplemented by guidelines. More than a hundred countries, for example, have joined the Basal Convention on Transboundary Movements of Hazardous Wastes and Their Disposal. This convention mainly addresses problems arising from one country sending wastes to another (often a less developed country) for disposal. (International environmental issues are examined in Ref. 9, pp. 517–527.)

Transfer Pricing and Earning Stripping

As discussed in previous chapters, often there are ways in which MNCs can reduce the taxes paid to host countries. Where a business has operations located in more than one taxing jurisdiction, and there are transactions among the company and its affiliates, taxes can be minimized for the enterprise as a whole. To do so, MNCs can set the charges made on the transactions so that the affiliate in the state or country with the lowest tax makes all or most of the profit. This is called transfer pricing (pp. 720–725).[4] Transfer pricing is the source of much dispute between host countries and MNCs. While flagrant cases of abuse are often detected, most subtle cases remain hidden. When, for example, MNCs use the same price for products sold both to subsidiaries and unrelated firms, these transactions may be different. Subsidiaries may receive different financing terms, warranties, advertising support, and after-sales services. In such cases, what appear to be equal and fair prices offered to both parties in fact are not.[28] It appears that foreign-owned MNCs operating in the United States are reporting significantly less profit for their U.S. operations than their U.S. counterparts. In 1987, for example, U.S.-owned firms reported an average of 2.9% return on assets, nearly four times that of their foreign competitors.[28] Since 1980, sales by foreign firms in the United States have been steadily rising, reaching more than $540 billion in 1986. Their reported profit, however, barely changed during the same period. In 1986, only 43% of 36,800 foreign-owned companies reported any taxable income. They claimed deductions of $543 billion on only $500 billion of revenues.[29]

Besides transfer pricing, there are other schemes used by some MNCs to reduce or avoid taxes. "Earning stripping" is one such scheme. Earning stripping takes place when a foreign company uses big loans instead of direct capital investment to finance its operations. The interest on the loan is a tax deduction, which reduces the taxes owed by the firm. It is estimated that foreign firms operating in the United States, using various tax schemes including transfer pricing and earning stripping, avoid more than $3 billion in taxes annually. A 1994, U.S. law closed a loophole that was allowing foreign companies operating in the United States to use earning stripping. While not totally eliminating their deduction, the law increased the cost to those companies. These companies complained that they are discriminated against compared with their U.S. counterparts, which do not face similar debt-to-equity rules.[30]

There are a couple of ways by which governments with higher tax rates can defeat this. The more common one is to apply the arm's length principle. Here, the taxing authorities use a variety of standards to adjust the prices that one entity has charged another, seeking to make them comparable with what independent firms would have charged each other. Under this principle, the taxing agencies determine what profit each entity has made.

The other approach is the unitary business rule. Here, the taxing authority starts with the total profit made everywhere by the international business and then decides what part of that profit should be attributed to the affiliate within its jurisdiction. Percentages are developed based on the relative amounts of sales, property owned, and wages paid both worldwide and locally. American law adopts the arm's length principle for the federal government, but some states use the unitary business rule.

Increased business transactions on the Internet have created a new problem. At its core is the question of jurisdictional issue. How should sales taxes, if any, be collected, and on what basis? How should they be distributed? If a dispute arises between parties in different countries, which country's law applies? While efforts are under way to create a universal set of rules, some countries have taken the matter into their own hands. For example, Australia's highest court recently shook up Internet law with a ruling that Dow Jones, the U.S.-based news group, could be sued in Australia for defamation over an article on its Web site.[31]

Research and Development

The Tokyo Round of the GATT negotiations took place between 1973 and 1979. Among other things, it produced a Product Standards Code that set up a mechanism to create internationally recognized norms for product characteristics and product descriptions. Each member nation is required to have a central standards office, which for the United States is the National Center for Standards and Certification Information, which is maintained by the Department of Commerce's National Bureau of Standards.

Technology is often transferred in international trade, and provisions are sometimes put into contracts attempting to place constraints on the recipient. Those engaged in international business need to know that such constraints are often illegal.

Most countries outlaw a transferor's placing restrictions on further research and development by the transferee, either as to the improvement of the technology itself or as to a competing technology. The United States allows restrictions where there is a legitimate business interest to be served, such as shielding the transferor from legal responsibility or safeguarding the technology's reputation.

Grant-back provisions also have legal nuances that can make them illegal. Provisions of this sort require users of technology to share the knowledge gained through the use of the technology. The provisions can be reciprocal, where both parties must share information; or unilateral, where only one (ordinarily the licensee) must. Those that are unilateral are illegal in most countries, although the United States considers them so only if, given the market situation, they have an adverse effect on competition.

Summary

This chapter touches on a great many areas of law relating to international business, but it is important to be aware that many more areas exist and are changing all the time. A single chapter leaves many topics untouched and gives only a broad outline of the law on the topics selected. Even textbooks devoted entirely to the law of international business only scratch the surface, giving a snapshot in time of the law as it existed at the time of the writing. Business firms find it necessary to go beyond a general knowledge and to master, with the aid of competent professional advice, the many specifics, often nation by nation.

The primary purpose of this chapter is to create an awareness of legal issues so that a person or firm doing business internationally will seek competent legal advice.

Discussion Questions _____

1. Is the position of the dissenting justices in the GE and Honeywell case (see the chapter vignette) similar to that of the Indian courts in the Bhopal case? Discuss.

2. What does each of the following acronyms stand for: IPRs, CISG, GATT, EEC, NAFTA, OPIC, COCOM, MFN?

3. What is a GATT round?

4. What basically did the Foreign Corrupt Practices Act of 1977 do?

5. How is the Mitsubishi Group organized?

6. Give four examples of the differences in attitude and policies between the developed and the less developed nations.

7. How does Subpart F of the Internal Revenue Code fight tax havens?

8. Describe the foreign exchange market.

9. What are the steps in the U.S. entry process for imports?

10. What is an embargo, and how can an exporter check to see whether it is lawful to export a certain item?

11. What are the two types of American export licenses?

12. Name six nontariff trade barriers.

13. What is dumping, and how is it generally handled?

14. What distinction is sometimes made between expropriation and confiscation?

15. What doctrines and court practices make it difficult to win against a host state in a lawsuit brought in a home state?

16. When is OPIC insurance available to cover the risk of confiscation by a host state? What form of relief would a claimant be entitled to?

17. What factors must a court find present to apply American antitrust law to the behavior of foreign entities under the Foreign Trade Antitrust Improvements Act of 1982?

18. What is transfer pricing, and what steps are taken to defeat it?

Notes

a. I gratefully acknowledge the contributions of Dwight D. Murphey, Wichita State University, and Karen Beyke, who taught International Business Law at Coles College of Business, Kennesaw State University for 7 years.

b. The case in which the U.S. Court of Appeals (Second Circuit) recounted the details of the Bhopal accident and held that the dispute should be heard in India, not the United States, is *In the Union Carbide Corporation Gas Plant Disaster at Bhopal*, 809 F.2d 195 (1987).

References

1. M. France (2001, June 25). Europe: A different take on antitrust. *Business Week*, 40.

2. P. Shishkin (2001, July 5). Barred merger signals U.S.-EU divergence. *Wall Street Journal*, p. A4.

3. A. Raghavan & B. Davis (2001, June 15). Uncle Sam and Mr. Monti: Tale of two trustbusters. *Wall Street Journal*, p. A11.

4. R. August (2002). *International business law: Text, cases, and readings*. Englewood Cliffs, NJ: Prentice Hall.

5. *Top ten religions of the world*. Retrieved July 24, 2002, from http://www.infoplease .com/ipa/A0904108.html and http://www.religioustolerance.org/worldrel.html

6. N. King Jr. (2002, July 23). Grave reservations: Why Dr. Su's arrival rocks Georgia Town. *Wall Street Journal*, pp. A1, A6.

7. M. Prowse (2002, December 14/15). Why a common law remains at Europe's core. *Financial Times*, p. II.

8. K. Singer (1973). *Mirror, sword, and jewel* (pp. 71–72). New York: George Braziller.

9. R. Schaffer, B. Earle, & F. Agusti (1993). *International business law and its environment*. St. Paul, MN: West.

10. S. M. Abbasi & K. W. Hollman (1990, July–September). The manager's guide to Islamic banking. *Business, 40*(3), 35–40.

11. M. A. Khan (1991). The future of Isalmic economics. *Futures, 23*(3), 248–261.

12. K. Brown (1994, April 8). Islamic banking: Faith and creativity. *New York Times*, p. D1.

13. M. Adacem (1991, May 9). Islam and the U.S. banking crisis. *Wall Street Journal*, p. A10. (A pamphlet of MSI Financial Services Corporation, circa 2000.)

14. M. Saleem (1998). Venture capital: The essence of Islamic banking. *Islamic Horizons, September/October*, 54.

15. M. B. Metzger et al. (1992). *Business law and regulatory environment.* Homewood, IL: Irwin.

16. P. J. Shedd & R. N. Corley (1993). *Business law.* Englewood Cliffs, NJ: Prentice Hall.

17. G. R. Simpson (2002, July 29). U.S. firms' overseas transfers bring an intensifying backlash. *Wall Street Journal,* p. A4.

18. P. Stephens (1999, December 3). Broken borders of the nation state. *Financial Times,* p. 15.

19. A. M. Squeo & D. Michaels (2002, July 22). Joint efforts: U.S. woos allies with unique deal on new fighter jet. *Wall Street Journal,* p. A1.

20. G. Winestock & J. McKinnon (2002, September 3). EU gets approval to impose tariffs on U.S. products. *Wall Street Journal,* p. A3.

21. R. N. Corley, O. L. Reed, & R. L. Black (1990). *The legal environment of business* (8th ed.). New York: McGraw-Hill.

22. Manila seeks end to fight over Westinghouse plant. (1993, October 5). *Wall Street Journal,* p. B13.

23. J. Plender (2002, October 7). US legislators elbow foreign watchdogs aside. *Financial Times,* p. 16.

24. EU calls U.S. bill on accounting unilateralist step (2002, July 26). *Wall Street Journal,* p. A8.

25. C. Goldsmith, W. Lambert, & M. Schroeder (2002, August 22). Europe's CEOs bite Sarbanes bullet. *Wall Street Journal,* p. A11.

26. J. B. Kobak Jr., P. Landers, & M. A. A. Warner (2002). The globalization of competition law in the new millennium. *Global Economy Quarterly, II,* 149–164.

27. M. Newman (2003, April 28). So many countries, so many laws. *Wall Street Journal,* p. R8.

28. H. Gleckman & T. Holden (1990, September 10). Can Uncle Sam mend this hole in his pocket? *BusinessWeek,* 48–49.

29. L. Chambliss (1990, May 29). Holier than thou. *Financial World, 59*(11), 20–21.

30. E. S. Browning (1994, June 14). Foreign firms fume, seek loopholes as U.S. attempts to collect more taxes. *Wall Street Journal,* p. A10.

31. N. Tait & P. Waldmeir (2002, December 11). Australia court gives landmark ruling on internet law. *Financial Times,* p. 6.

8 Organization of Multinational Operations

In Chapter 8, we present the various organizational structures of multinational companies (MNCs), and we will learn about the many factors that influence an MNC's selection of the proper organizational structure. Some of these factors are external forces and demands, such as economic conditions at home and abroad, host government policies, product-market characteristics, and information technology. Factors related to the firm itself are the history of the company, top management philosophy, nationality, corporate strategy, and the degree of internationalization. We first discuss the development of an organizational structure designed to deal with the export of products to foreign markets. The subsequent major structural designs for MNCs, including the autonomous foreign subsidiary, the international division, geographic and product divisions, and the matrix structure, are explained in this chapter. Finally, we describe the newer forms of organization, such as market-based and strategic business unit organizations, virtual corporations, and networks.

Chapter Vignette

Born Global

Internationalization used to be incremental expansion and a learning process for firms going through the successive stages of domestic, international, multinational, and global design and restructuring. Now, this norm is being revised. The unique feature of the global economy, which is dominated by the interlink between firms in the value chain covering R&D, production, logistics, marketing, and financial service, enables these firms to start from the beginning on a global mission. These firms are "born globals."

An example of a **born global** company is CMS Energy, which was a relatively small Midwest utilities firm generating electric power for the state of Michigan. In the 1990s, under new management, it began its transformation into a global operation at a very fast pace. Within a decade, it had become one of the leading companies in the world for building and operating the systems that bring energy to people. It now operates worldwide businesses in energy and power production, in natural gas pipelines and storage, and in oil and gas exploration and production. It also builds and operates power plants, power lines, and distribution companies. It provides energy marketing and management services. CMS Energy has acquired assets totaling around $16 billion throughout the United States and in 22 countries around the world. It generates revenues worth more than $10 billion. It has achieved this phenomenal growth and globalization in less than a decade.[1,2]

_____ **Introduction**

Collective endeavors, such as businesses, require a certain amount of order and organization, without which failure ensues. Organizational goal achievement depends on the effective combination of the contributions and work output of individual members. Because organizational activities are interdependent, complementary, and varied in type and timing, they require a certain degree of coordination and integration, which are facilitated through their operational proximity. Operational proximity means making allowances for the synchronization of activities in time and space. Simply put, physical proximity allows members of the organization to perform their tasks together and in a timely fashion. Organizational activities need to be grouped in a way that makes it easy for people to work together and expedites progress toward goals. Different methods and frameworks are used to arrange the operational proximity of organizational activities and tasks. The methods of organizing are based on work specialization, division of labor, and economies of scale, principles that were first articulated by Adam Smith. The frameworks used should provide for appropriate job designs, reporting and communication arrangements, authority and responsibility distribution, and the physical layout of the organization. In short, an organization needs form and structure.

Definition and
_____**Functions of Organizing**

The organizing function involves designing a skeleton and structure that delineate the nature and extent of formal relationships among various internal components, including tasks, jobs, positions, and units of the organization. It is the physical and nonphysical form the organization assumes in response to its internal requirements and external environment. It allows for the distribution of power and authority among the organization's members and the establishment of communication lines between them. The internal requirements of a firm are related to the type of technology used, the nature of tasks performed, and the type of strategy employed. The external environment is the combination of outside constituencies and forces that are influential in determining the fate of the organization. Because firms have different internal requirements and external environments, they employ various structural configurations. In other words, the structure of a firm is a tool for attainment of goals and a means to an end.

The structure of the organization defines the boundaries of the organizational components (units); the relationships among the various parts; the extent, limits, and location of authority and power; and the formal communication patterns. The architects of the organizational structure need to answer four basic questions about the firm (p. 529):[3]

1. What should the units of organization be?

2. Which components should be joined, and which should be kept apart?

3. What size and shape pertain to the different components?

4. What is the appropriate placement of and relationship between the different units?

The basic principle for organizing is to group activities that have similar characteristics and functions from the lowest levels of the firm and proceed upward. In doing so, tasks are clustered into jobs; jobs are combined to form departments; and departments are put together to create business units. Larger firms that serve multiple markets and have many product lines, consequently, have a number of different business units. These business units are organized into a corporate structure. The clustering of activities just described is commonly referred to as *departmentalization.*

There are six common bases for departmentalization or grouping of organizational activities: knowledge and skill, work process and function, time (shifts in a factory), output (products), client, and place (geographic).[4] Figure 8.1 represents organizational structures resulting from two of the most commonly used types of departmentalizations: functional and geographic.

The relationships provided by the operational necessities that we have just described are basically internally oriented. These relationships are mediated by the strategic requirements that are dictated by the nature of the competitive forces that govern the external relationships. Organizational structure is often determined by both internal requirements and external forces. However, from time to time, one element, either internal or external, exerts more influence on the shape of the organization.

The Organization of Multinationals

The fundamental structural considerations of MNCs are similar to those of domestic firms. Internal requirements and the external environments of MNCs, however, pose additional design challenges. The MNC structure should take into account physical distance, legal and governmental considerations, headquarter-subsidiary relationships, and many other factors. Because of their environmental diversity, the coordination and integration needs of MNCs are different from those of domestic firms. Therefore, the requirements of operating across national borders create additional concerns for organizing. In addition to those issues pertinent to organizing in domestic firms, there are three major concerns in the design of an MNC organizational structure (p. 5):[5]

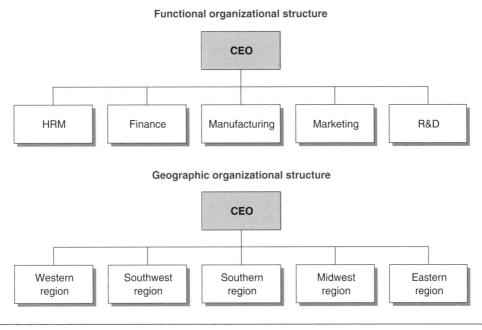

Figure 8.1   Two Types of Departmentalization

1. How to encourage a predominantly domestic organization to take full advantage of the growth opportunities abroad

2. How to blend product knowledge and geographic area knowledge most efficiently in coordinating worldwide business

3. How to coordinate the activities of foreign units in many countries while permitting each to retain its own identity

As consumers' tastes converge globally, the firms that respond to this convergence in product preferences could gain competitive advantage. MNCs respond to these changes by adopting the various strategies that were discussed in the previous chapter. Therefore, we could add another item to the above list:

4. How to exhibit local responsiveness while maintaining a global orientation

An MNC's response to these concerns is influenced by many factors, including the size and history of the company, top management orientation, product-market characteristics, and corporate strategy. As MNCs expand abroad, under the influence of these factors, their structures evolve to facilitate the accomplishment of corporate objectives. Consequently, there are many variations among MNC structures.

The organizing variations among firms are usually at a level directly below the chief executive officer. That is why we focus our presentation at this level. We also confine our discussion to managerial organization, as opposed to statutory or legal organization. To satisfy host countries' legal and statutory requirements, MNCs create legal entities that exist on paper only. The statutory entities are designed to fulfill legal obligations while promoting the MNCs' objectives of ease of operation and increased earnings. It is through these entities that the legal and ownership relationships between the headquarters and its various subsidiaries are specified. Many different statutory and legal forms link the parent company to its foreign operations, including branch offices, subsidiaries, and holding companies. The legal requirements of the host country and tax implications determine the MNC's statutory organization (p. 253).[6]

Factors Influencing the Structure of MNCs

Many factors influence an MNC's choice of organizational structure: external environmental forces, factors related to the firm itself, or a combination of both.

External Forces

The major external environmental forces that influence an MNC's structure are economic conditions, host governments, technological developments, product-market characteristics, and information technology (see Refs. 7, chap. 3; 8, pp. 97–99).

Economic Conditions. Changes in economic conditions at home and abroad create opportunities for and threats to the operation of MNCs. Unemployment and reduced purchasing power resulting from recessions and slower economic growth force adjustments in MNCs' business operations. Reduced market share and earnings in mature markets may prompt firms to diversify. Internationalization may partly be the consequence of home market saturation and maturity.

Technological Developments. In some industries, the high level of risk and huge investment required for developing new products are straining the financial capabilities of many MNCs, prompting international joint ventures between competitors. Also, because of globalization, MNCs face the same competitors in many markets. Consequently, local advantages are quickly eroded by the immediate responses of international rivals. The reality of competition between partners of international joint ventures and the need for fast response require a flexible structure and a closer integration of worldwide operations.

Technological developments are considered to be the most important factor influencing structural changes in MNCs. New product development and new manufacturing methods offer opportunities for expansion into new markets. In turn, expanded foreign operations resulting from technological advances necessitate the provision of organizational support systems and structural changes. Technological advances have increased international competition and caused the global integration of MNCs. Telecommunications and information processing technology have improved the ability of the headquarters office to monitor the performance of subsidiaries in a timely fashion. Improved communication between subsidiaries and headquarters allows the adoption of either a centralized or a decentralized mode of control. In either case, the management of information provides an opportunity to devise a proper structure.

Product-Market Characteristics. Newly industrialized countries such as South Korea and Taiwan have appeared on the international scene as competitors partly because of recent shifts in regional economic growth. The emergence of this new competition has increased market uncertainty and instability. Simultaneously, advances in manufacturing technologies, new product development, and marketing, along with the convergence of consumer tastes and preferences for certain products, have created a global market. To compete in this market, MNCs need global economies of scale and quick response. Consequently, firms require a greater degree of internal integration and coordination among their dispersed worldwide operations while allowing for local responsiveness to their national subsidiaries. Therefore, in designing a new structure, MNCs are concerned with the reconciliation of these two conflicting needs. An MNC's organizational structure should facilitate global integration and local responsiveness. Other product-market characteristics, such as diversity of product line and the nature of the competition, affect the organizing efforts of MNCs. A product division structure and a centralized decision-making process, for example, would serve well those firms that have a diverse product line and are competing with other MNCs in national markets. If competition in national markets is limited to local firms, granting more autonomy to the subsidiary would be appropriate. With competition limited to local firms, intimate knowledge of local conditions and a closer relationship with domestic businesses would be necessary.

Host Government Policies. Host government policies are influential factors shaping the strategies and, in turn, the structure of MNCs. Investment incentives offered by host governments stimulate foreign direct investment (FDI) and the expansion of MNC operations. Many forms of trade and business requirements and restrictions influence the management of MNCs. Taxes and tariffs, the need for local content, local ownership, technology transfer, local employment, and minimum exports exert pressure on foreign subsidiaries. Of course, an MNC's responses to host government policies influence headquarters-subsidiaries relationships and subsequently result in structural changes.

Company Factors

Major company factors include the company's history, top management philosophy, nationality, corporate strategy, and degree of internationalization (see Refs. 7, chap. 3; 8, pp. 97–99).

Company History. Firms in the early stages of internationalization have few managers with experience and expertise in coping with a complex worldwide operation. As the firms continue to operate abroad and learn how to manage their worldwide businesses, decisions regarding organizational structure will be affected by those years of experience in foreign markets. Therefore, when there is a small pool of managers with international experience, the most feasible structure is an international division. The use of other types of structures has to wait for more advanced stages of internationalization.

Top Management Philosophy. Top management philosophy regarding the autonomy granted to subsidiaries is reflected in various control mechanisms that the headquarters employs. Organizational structure is a means for exercising headquarters control over subsidiaries. A loose federation of national subsidiaries under the general direction of headquarters, for example, is a sign of management belief that local executives are better qualified to run their own operations.

Nationality. There are differences among the organizational designs of American, Japanese, and European MNCs. European subsidiaries, for example, tend to have more autonomy than American subsidiaries. The type of control used also varies among the MNCs of different countries. U.S. MNCs tend to exercise a higher level of output control over their subsidiaries, while Europeans usually exert a higher level of behavioral control.[9] Foreign subsidiaries of Japanese MNCs appear to have more local decision-making power. Executive selection, socialization, and acculturation of Japanese managers ensure the subsidiaries' strict compliance with the norms set by headquarters, reducing the need for other control mechanisms. Consequently, there is no need for foreign subsidiaries of Japanese MNCs to send extensive and frequent performance data to their headquarters as American subsidiaries are required to do. Another unique feature of Japanese MNCs is the structure of the *keiretsu* system. A *keiretsu* is a tight network of companies that share capital, R&D, customers, vendors, and distribution channels. *Keiretsus* are the intricate webs of relationships linking banks, manufacturers, suppliers, and distributors with the government. Major *keiretsus* have the ability to control nearly every aspect of the value chain in a variety of industrial, service, and resource sectors. Many Japanese manufacturing firms have used the *keiretsu* system. The Japanese have effectively used *keiretsu* systems to gain international competitiveness and successfully penetrate world markets.

Corporate Culture. Another factor that influences the choice of organizational structure is corporate culture. Trompenaars and Hampden-Turner[10] (p. 167) identified four types of corporate culture: the family, the Eiffel Tower, the guided missile, and the incubator. These were discussed in the chapter on culture (Chapter 3). Of course, corporate culture is a product of the national culture in which it operates. Therefore, these four types reflect the overall characteristics of their respective national cultures. Trompenaars and Hampden-Turner suggested the appropriateness of certain kinds of organizational structure for each corporate culture type. For example, matrix organizational structure may run into implementation problems in Asian countries because in these countries, the family corporate culture is a dominant form. In such a corporate culture, employees cannot give their undivided loyalty to two bosses. Superiors are regarded as fathers, and no one can have two fathers.

Corporate Strategy. Corporate strategy greatly influences the firm's structure. From the pioneering work of Chandler,[11] and subsequent research by others,[12] we have learned that the strategy of the firm sets the stage for structuring the organization. The popular phrase *structure follows strategy* suggests the link between the two. An internationalization strategy that moves the firm away from the familiar domestic market also results in structural variations. Some organizational structures employed by MNCs appear to work better with certain strategies.[13,14] For example, international division structure tends to fit a strategy that calls for a low level of foreign sales with a few products. Strategies that involve product diversity tend to be associated with product division structures.

Organizational Structure: Japanese Style

Like many other aspects of the Japanese economy, politics, and culture, there is a unique Japanese organizational form called *keiretsu*. *Keiretsus* are the outgrowth of *zaibatsus*, which dominated the Japanese economy before World War II. After the war, the occupational forces attempted to break up the monopoly of the *zaibatsus*, which had helped the Japanese government in the war. But soon, they realized that a strong Japan was needed to fight the Korean war and the expansion of communism. Substantial aid was poured into the Japanese economy, and attempts to break down the Japanese corporate structure were

---

(Continued)

(Continued)

abandoned. *Zaibatsu* companies that were broken down were free to regroup. Some regrouped around banks and trading companies that held shares in other firms too. The resultant conglomerates are the *keiretsus*. A *keiretsu* is a tight network of companies that share capital, R&D, customers, vendors, and distribution channels. *Keiretsus* also maintain ties with the government. Major keiretsus have the ability to control nearly every aspect of the value chain in a variety of industrial, service, and resource sectors.

There are two types of *keiretsus*: horizontal and vertical. A horizontal *keiretsu* is a cluster around a bank of companies from related or unrelated industries. Large horizontal *keiretsus* are found in many industries, including banking, insurance, steel, trading, manufacturing, electric, gas, and chemicals. Members use each other's products and services and are given preferential treatment. In effect, they form a production system that is distributed among many firms. Many assert that such preferential treatment and the purchasing habits of *keiretsus* are barriers to free trade and major impediments to foreign investment, products, and services. The major banks, Mitsui, Mitsubishi, Sumitomo, Fuyo, Sanwa, and Dai-Ichi Kangyo, belong to horizontal *keiretsus*.

A vertical *keiretsu* is a network of companies around a major manufacturer. The manufacturer itself may be a member of a horizontal *keiretsu*. While the members of a horizontal *keiretsu* are from diverse industries, members of a vertical *keiretsu* are from a single industry. The members consist of suppliers and distributor that serve a large manufacturer at the core. Vertical *keiretsus* include large manufacturers such as Toyota, Nissan, Honda, Matsushita, Hitachi, Toshiba, and Sony.

It appears that globalization and the changes that are taking place in the Japanese economy along with demands by foreign governments are causing *keiretsus* to drift away from a "network" model and open up to—even form alliances with—foreign business.

Degree of Internationalization. The degree of internationalization affects organizational structure through headquarters-subsidiary relationships. The foreign subsidiary's autonomy and internationalization of the firm are related. Internationalization can be defined as the number of foreign countries in which a firm has subsidiaries. As the number of foreign subsidiaries increases, so does the complexity of managing them. It is expected that MNCs with a high degree of internationalization may be forced to allow more autonomy to their subsidiaries for certain decisions, such as marketing. For other decisions, such as finance, however, they may exert more control because the intimate knowledge of local situations is more critical in marketing than in finance.

The Development of an
International Corporate Structure

As a mechanism that facilitates progress toward goals, organizational structure evolves to accommodate the implementation of strategies. Firms follow different paths to international expansion, which assumes many different forms. The organizational structure of most international operations evolves to serve the growing needs of their diverse markets. Consequently, their choice of structure depends on the type of strategy employed. An organization's structure not only signifies distribution of power and authority and a formal relationship between organizational members but also indicates the importance the company places on certain aspects of the business. A company organized on the basis of its customer groups, for example, signals emphasis on meeting the needs of its customers.

As the firm grows, so does the significance of its structure. A small business requires a simple formal organization. But as it expands, increased specialization of tasks and duties creates an additional demand for coordination and integration. A more sophisticated structure is needed to handle the complexity of the operation and the coordination and integration requirements of a large firm. Such a structure would also facilitate the efficient distribution of the firm's resources and the execution of its strategies. The structure that served the business of a domestic firm may be ill equipped to handle the diversity of the international marketplace. International expansion brings about structural changes. A three-phase evolutionary process characterizes the changes in the organizational structure of MNCs. The progression through these phases parallels the three stages of introduction, growth, and maturity of a product's life cycle (sec. 13.4).[15] The firm is thus transformed from a domestically oriented one and passes through three phases: namely, international, multinational, and global.

International Orientation. In the first phase, competition is limited to a small number of companies located in developed countries. These firms manufacture products with functions, features, and characteristics that are designed for the domestic market. International operation for these firms consists only of exports. Although exports may be an important source of revenue, they constitute only a small portion of total corporate earnings, so international operations are merely an appendage to their domestic business. At this stage, firms continue using existing domestic structures, with some minor additions to accommodate business activities across national borders.

Multinational Orientation. In the growth stage, technology diffusion and price competition, particularly from domestic firms, force firms to establish manufacturing facilities in low-cost locations abroad. As increased foreign sales make up a larger share of corporate revenues, firms enter the second phase by changing their organizational structure to include the international division structure. All international business activities are organized into a division comparable to other divisions on the domestic side of the business. There is no attempt to integrate foreign subsidiaries, and operations within each foreign country remain separate from one another. Some firms go through a transition phase before entering Phase 3, in which they attempt to learn the intricacies of the international environment through their autonomous foreign subsidiaries. A major portion of MNC earnings come from these autonomous foreign subsidiaries, which are given substantial decision-making freedom.

Global Orientation. In Phase 3, most of the corporate revenues are generated from abroad. At this stage, MNCs organize their operations on a global basis. Domestic operation becomes one aspect of their business and receives corresponding attention along with foreign operations. Various forms of organizational structure that involve the transition from a domestic form to an international structure are discussed next.

A Global Company

Asea-Brown Boveri (ABB) is a global electronic equipment company created by merging Asea, a Swedish engineering group, with Brown Boveri, a Swiss competitor, and adding on more than 70 other companies in Europe and the United States, with joint ventures in South Korea and Taiwan. ABB became very efficient by getting rid of excess capacity and eliminating duplication and reducing waste. There are no more than a dozen executives at the headquarters in Zurich, making up the executive committee that consists of American, German, Swedish, and Swiss managers. Since there is no common first language, they speak only English. The executive committee is responsible for ABB's global strategy and performance, and more than 50 business area managers report to them.

To leverage its core technologies and global economies of scale without sacrificing local responsiveness, ABB used a loose, decentralized version of the matrix organizational structure. ABB organized its operations along a matrix system of 50 or so business areas (BAs), which were grouped into eight business segments, each of which was the responsibility of a member of the executive committee. An example of a business segment is a group of five BAs that sells components, systems, and software to firms for automating their industrial processes. This business segment includes metallurgy, drives, and process engineering. Its office is located in Stamford, Connecticut.

BA managers devise strategies to optimize the BAs globally. They are responsible for cost and quality standards, allocation of export markets to factories located around the world, and sharing of expertise by rotating people across borders. National managers, who are responsible for local firms within national borders, report to BA managers. Most of the national managers are host country citizens. The local companies act as national firms and have their own boards, which may include eminent outsiders; presidents; financial reporting; and career ladders for employee advancement. The managers of local firms have a global boss, the BA manager, who sets the overall framework for the operation of the BA. They also report to the country manager, who coordinates the activities of national firms.[16-18]

The Extension of the Domestic Structure

First attempts at doing business across national borders result in some organizational changes. The firm begins to learn about other markets beyond its own familiar domestic surroundings. It carries business transactions in other currencies and learns about foreign business protocols. Foreign correspondence appears among the firm's official communications. To accommodate all these events and activities, some structural changes have to take place. None of these changes, however, require major structural modifications. Since the firm's business activities only marginally expand into the international domain, the corresponding formal changes are handled under the existing domestic structure.

At the early stage of international expansion, the firm's interest and expertise are centered on domestic operations, and its international involvement is incidental. Often, international sales are triggered by foreigners' inquiries and are insignificant compared with domestic sales. The lack of competition and the firm's superior technology lead it to export its existing products or product line without many modifications. All export jobs are contracted out to an independent agent. As sales to foreigners increase, the firm may set up an in-house export desk or export unit. An export manager, who reports to the marketing executive, is given the responsibility of handling all export activities. The export manager's position and reporting arrangement depend on the breadth of the product line. In a firm with a narrow product line, the export manager reports to the chief marketing officer. In a firm with a broad product line, the export manager reports directly to the chief executive officer (p. 82).[19]

As the volume of exports increases, the firm may establish an office abroad to handle product sales and service. Except for the addition of an export manager, the basic organizational structure of the firm at this stage remains virtually intact. The early internationalization experiences of most American firms fit this description. Japanese firms, however, have adopted a different approach. For expanding into foreign markets, the Japanese have relied on trading companies called *sogo shosha*. These trading companies perform all the necessary business functions for Japanese firms.[20,21] The only exceptions are the Japanese automobile and consumer electronics industries, which have followed a pattern of international expansion similar to that of American and European firms (p. 254).[6]

As the firm gains experience, it may get involved in other facets of international business, such as licensing and manufacturing abroad. The market matures as time passes, and local and foreign competitors enter the market. With increased competition and market maturity, local demands cannot effectively be addressed with exports only. A change in the firm's foreign involvement is also hastened due to host government demands. An increase in the volume of exports into a host country may prompt the host government's demand for local participation in the business. Export restrictions are imposed, and local content laws are passed to ensure that the MNC's operations provide benefits to the country in the form of additional jobs, improved skills, and technology transfer. A combination of market pressure and government demands forces the firm to establish local manufacturing facilities.

When the firm establishes manufacturing facilities abroad, the diversity and scope of international operations bring about a change in organizational structure. At this stage, the firm leaves behind the simplicity of the international organizational structure of an exporter and instead enters the world of managing foreign subsidiaries. It needs a control and coordination mechanism to integrate its geographically dispersed international operations.

The Transition: Autonomous Foreign Subsidiary

Initially, local subsidiaries are allowed a considerable amount of autonomy. The headquarters' lack of experience in managing a distant operation in a foreign land leaves it no choice but to grant the subsidiary managers most of the decision-making powers usually reserved for top executives. To control dispersed foreign subsidiaries, MNCs commonly use financial reporting. As long as the operations remain profitable, the headquarters follows a hands-off policy. The need to learn exceeds the desire to control (p. 20).[13]

A direct reporting relationship links the foreign subsidiary managers to the president at the corporate headquarters. These managers are fully responsible for all aspects of the subsidiary's operations. The longevity of the autonomous foreign subsidiary structure depends on two factors:

1. Its growth rate

2. The rate of international experience accumulated by the headquarters

When a subsidiary's contributions to corporate earnings become large enough to warrant closer scrutiny, headquarters begins a search for ways to exercise more control. Also, as the corporate executives become more familiar with foreign operations, they begin to feel more confident in establishing more coordination and control among foreign operations through organizational design modifications.

Sometimes, the foreign subsidiary has its own local board of directors, with the headquarters representative as a member.[22] This arrangement is more common in European firms. Two factors were influential in the creation of autonomous foreign subsidiaries by European MNCs. First, some European firms expanded into international markets before the advent of modern communication technologies. It was impossible to closely control and integrate their foreign subsidiaries. They had no choice but to allow their subsidiaries a considerable degree of self-rule. Second, starting with small domestic operations, European MNCs then found their foreign subsidiaries to be a significant part of the corporation and, therefore, treated them accordingly (p. 256).[6]

The unique relationship between European subsidiaries and their parent corporation is labeled a mother-daughter relationship. Among the many reasons given for such a relationship, three stand out.

First, European MNCs have created a strong organizational identification among their managers through a long period of acculturation and indoctrination to the norms and ways of the corporation.

Second, they have avoided joint ventures with foreign partners and assigned expatriate managers to be in charge of foreign subsidiaries. These managers could be relied on to abide by corporate norms without close supervision by headquarters.

Third, barriers to trade have kept national markets separate from one another and limited the need for cross-border communication in most European MNCs. Even without a formal system of reporting, some of these MNCs were able to achieve total worldwide standardization of policies for product mix and diversity, product quality, product design and formulas, brand names, internal or external financing, and human resource management procedures for promotions and rewards (pp. 192–193).[23]

For years, Procter & Gamble operated strong national subsidiaries in Europe. Differences in market conditions, consumer habits, and competition resulted in the creation of these subsidiaries, each of which resembled a miniature Procter & Gamble. They had their own manufacturing facilities, product development capabilities, and marketing and advertising agencies and responded to local conditions as they saw fit. Honeywell is another MNC that allowed its European subsidiaries much autonomy. Autonomous country managers were responsible for all operations in their countries. Each subsidiary sold the full line of Honeywell products, and some had manufacturing and service facilities. The headquarters in Minneapolis provided administrative and marketing support. As one executive put it, "Honeywell has always distinguished between centralized 'what-to-do' decisions and decentralized 'how-to-do-it' decisions in international areas. The philosophy is to have a tight 'what' and loose 'how' because Danes will know the business in Denmark better than the Minnesotans do (p. 535).[24]

The structure of an autonomous foreign subsidiary is better suited to satisfy the career aspirations of local nationals and is more amiable to host government demands for local ownership. Having host nationals in visible, high-level managerial positions and sharing ownership with local investors can subdue nationalist feelings against MNCs and reduce tension between MNCs and host governments (p. 257).[6] It was due to such autonomy that Benetton-Turkey (a subsidiary of the famous Italian retailer Benetton) escaped from a possible destruction of its properties in Turkey. For many years, the Kurdish minority, seeking independence, were fighting with the Turkish majority. More than 30,000 Turks had lost their lives in the war with the Kurds. The Kurdish rebel leader, Abdullah Öcalan, was a fugitive for many years. In 1999, he was forced to escape from Moscow to Italy. Immediately, the Turkish government demanded his extradition. The Italian government refused the demand, citing the fact that Turkish laws contained the death penalty. The Turkish people were outraged and reacted by taking to the streets in thousands, demonstrating against Italy and Italian businesses. Benetton-Turkey immediately reacted by removing the colorful Benetton logo from its storefronts, replacing it with black wreaths, and dressing all the mannequins in its stores in black, implying that it was in a state of "mourning." Also, it published advertisements in which it sided with the people and condemned the Italians' refusal. The Turks' response was overwhelmingly favorable, and several poems praising Benetton-Turkey were pasted on its storefront windows (pp. 116–121).[25] In this case, Benetton-Turkey's autonomy in decision-making matters had critical local implications and spared it from a sure disaster.

Advantages

Autonomous foreign subsidiaries have the freedom to operate as independent, responsible enterprises within the host country environment. MNCs use a host country focus strategy for managing these subsidiaries. (The host country focus strategy was presented in the previous chapter.) Relatively free from close supervision by the parent firm, autonomous foreign subsidiaries can integrate into the economic context of the host country and develop their own competitive posture. They gain competitive advantage by setting up local manufacturing, marketing, and purchasing. By operating as a local firm, they can tap the domestic source of cheap labor and are faced with fewer restrictions. Their independence from headquarters enables them to consider local consumers' needs in making major decisions and to be sensitive to local markets and governments. The direct relationship between the foreign subsidiary and headquarters makes it possible to present the subsidiary's problems at the highest corporate level without additional levels of bureaucracy. It also elevates the prestige of the subsidiary's managers in the eyes of host government officials and immensely improves their negotiation status (p. 257).[6]

Disadvantages

An autonomous foreign subsidiary structure has certain drawbacks. Allowing each subsidiary local decision-making power may cause subsidiaries to ignore the benefit of the corporation as a whole. As discussed in the previous chapter, certain benefits are associated with the operation of an integrated multinational. The benefits are realized by managing the firm as a whole and maximizing worldwide performance. The subsidiary manager has a local horizon, whereas the maximization of worldwide performance requires a total corporate perspective. One way to overcome this disadvantage is to tie some part of the subsidiary manager's rewards to overall corporate performance (p. 258).[6]

The International Division Structure

With increased sales and revenues from dispersed foreign subsidiaries, MNCs are compelled to impose more coordination and control. The organizational structure of an export office or the creation of independent foreign subsidiaries is inadequate to deal with the diversity of expanded foreign business. At this stage, MNCs adopt an international perspective and use international division structures (Figure 8.2).

Four factors prompt the establishment of an international division structure that enjoys sufficient organizational status on par with the other divisions (pp. 265–266).[26]

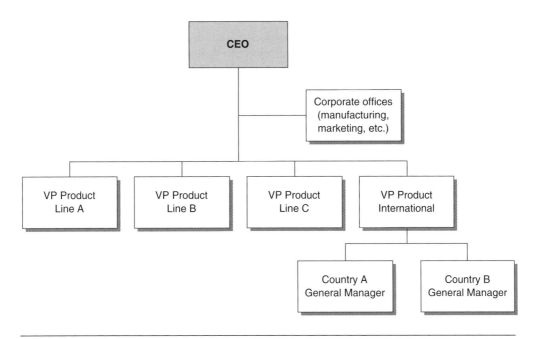

Figure 8.2   International Division Structure

First, increased international involvement, both operationally and strategically, requires the attention and involvement of a senior executive and the structure of a separate organizational unit.

Second, at this early stage of internationalization, concentration of all international activities in a single organizational unit is the best way to deal with the complexity of the global market and exploit worldwide business opportunities.

Third, there is the realization that internal specialists are needed to deal with the special features of international market opportunities.

Last, there is a desire to develop proactive global scanning capabilities to assess global opportunities and threats rather than passively responding to conditions that are presented to the firm.

In an international division structure, the management of foreign operations is coordinated by a department usually located at headquarters. Each subsidiary manager reports directly to the head of the international division. The executive in charge of the division is a member of the corporation's executive board. All activities of foreign operations are centralized at the international division, and the head of the international division is given line authority over the foreign subsidiaries. Through the international division, the MNC headquarters exercises control and coordination over foreign operations without much change in the corporation's existing structure. With the creation of an international division, the loss of autonomy of the foreign subsidiaries is matched by a corresponding measure of guidance and support from the corporate staff (see Refs. 15, sec. 13.5; 19, p. 155). In effect, the international division allows the firm to maintain separate domestic and foreign businesses and to use its limited international expertise efficiently. Since the firm basically has a domestic orientation, not many executives have international experience. Concentration of international staff in the international division allows for integration, coordination, and control of foreign subsidiaries without placing undue demands on the other executives.

The international division corporate structure is likely to be adopted by firms with a dominant domestic business, a narrow product line, limited geographic diversity, and few managers with international business expertise and experience. With the dominance of domestic business over international operations, upward mobility of executives in the corporate hierarchy is not tied to international expertise and experience. Therefore, not too many executives see the knowledge, experience, and expertise associated with international business as necessary for their career progress. Often, they see a foreign assignment as an organizational hindrance that could limit their managerial advancement. By spending a few years abroad on foreign assignments, they could become outsiders to the domestic corporate network. They could be bypassed for promotion in favor of those who are active in domestic operations and who are a part of the internal power network.

An international division structure is a manifestation of the firm's international orientation and geographic interests, which are translated into design arrangements fitting the multinational nature of its foreign operations. The firm, at this stage, considers each geographic area to be a separate market that requires differentiated business practices that are handled by foreign subsidiaries. These subsidiaries, although separate operationally, could benefit from the overall guidance and integration efforts of headquarters. There is a need to balance the self-interest of foreign subsidiaries with overall corporate performance, by standardization of the information control mechanisms of foreign subsidiaries. The structure of the international division and the associated standardization allow for the application of international corporate practices that improve corporate performance, such as transfer pricing, resource acquisition and allocation, and product distribution (sec. 13.5).[15]

Polaroid is an example of a firm that has used the international division structure. During the 1980s, nearly 40% of Polaroid's revenues came from international operations. Its international division controls all manufacturing and marketing functions outside the United States. It has three facilities, in Scotland, Ireland, and the Netherlands, that handle many aspects of manufacturing Polaroid products. It essentially sells abroad the same products as those sold in the domestic market, with some modifications to accommodate special market conditions, local regulations, and metric measures. The international division markets the full line of Polaroid products through wholly owned subsidiaries in 20 countries. It is treated as a profit center and seems to enjoy a degree of independence within the corporation that is envied by other divisions (p. 513).[27] The recent reorganization has carved the firm into three major business units—consumer, industrial, and magnetic. It seems that Polaroid is experimenting with a goal of creating a matrix organization design (p. 102).[28]

Coleman Corporation, based in Wichita, Kansas, is another firm that has employed the international division structure for many years. Coleman is the largest manufacturer of outdoor products in the world. Its product line, especially gasoline-powered lanterns and insulated coolers, has gained worldwide recognition. Coleman started its international operations in 1919 and has had an international division structure since the 1940s. The division is headed by an executive-level vice president and is located a few miles from the corporate headquarters.

The international division structure works well for Coleman, which has a rather centralized manufacturing operation and a narrow, homogeneous line of products. Coleman has its principal manufacturing sites in Wichita and Inheiden, Germany. There are other, smaller manufacturing sites in Texas, South Carolina, Utah, and Washington. Outdoor products are manufactured at the Wichita, Inheiden, and Texas sites. The Utah and South Carolina facilities make textile products, such as sleeping bags and tents. Portable generators are produced in Nebraska and water skiing equipment in Washington.

Coleman outdoor products generally need little modification for sales in foreign markets. The changes that are made are generally cosmetic, such as labeling and packaging changes. In the United States and developed countries, Coleman products are used for recreational purposes. In these countries, advertising and marketing is relatively undifferentiated. Adjustments are made for variations in the infrastructure of the markets and for differences in cultures and languages. An example is Japan, where there are many small retailers and long channels of distribution. Products are used recreationally, however, so advertising and marketing tactics are similar to those in Europe and the United States.

In developing countries, Coleman products often serve basic utility functions. Lanterns are a primary source of light, and insulated coolers are a principal source of refrigeration. Therefore, in these countries, the marketing mix is differentiated, and the distribution is through dealers with an emphasis on product promotion. Coleman does not coordinate advertising but, instead, provides free products for demonstration based on the distributor's promotion efforts.

Except for Inheiden, the international division is centralized at the headquarters. At Inheiden, Germany, Coleman manufactures products for sale to European markets. Inheiden also coordinates European sales operations and regional sales and distribution offices in Bristol, England, and Alphen aan den Rijn, the Netherlands. The international division coordinates all other regional sales and distribution offices, including Tokyo, Singapore (which covers the rest of Asia), Sydney, New Zealand, and San Juan, Puerto Rico (which includes Latin America and the Caribbean).

The international division structure at Coleman reflects the characteristics of various foreign markets and Coleman's strategic approach in serving those markets. Europe has long held business opportunities in outdoor products. The interest in outdoor recreation and the higher level of income make Europe a large market for Coleman products. Consequently, European operations are significantly larger than operations in other countries and are afforded more local decision-making power. In a sense, market characteristics determine either centralization or autonomy of the operating units.

While Europe has been Coleman's largest foreign market, Japan is its fastest growing market. During the 1980s, Coleman became the largest vendor of outdoor products in Japan. The increasing popularity of outdoor activities among the Japanese combined with the fast rate of market growth may make the Japanese market equal to that of the United States for Coleman's products. It is also expected that the market for outdoor equipment will increase in the rest of Asia and in Latin American countries. These changes in the external environment will have a structural impact on Coleman, as foreign sales surpass domestic sales. Until then, an international division structure seems to be appropriate for Coleman, based on its narrow product line and a dominant domestic business.

MNCs typically continue to use the international division structure as long as the international division remains smaller than most domestic divisions. The structure is abandoned when the international division rivals the largest domestic divisions. However, the international division structure may last longer if the rest of the MNC is organized according to a geographic structure, because there is a better fit between a geographic structure and an international division. Increased volume of business results in increased size, which in turn strains the capacity of the division to handle the MNC's product diversity and geographic dispersion. At this point, the worldwide activities need corporate direction. A very strong international division, however, hampers headquarters' direction of worldwide operations. The increased size of the international division, which is accompanied by more independence, "tends to insulate the headquarters from international operations and the corporate management from overseas problems and opportunities."[26]

The international division needs the product expertise possessed by domestic divisions. Domestic division staff, however, are reluctant to share their expertise with foreign operations due to differences in their goals. Consequently, the need to reorganize leads to one of the two forms—an international product division or an international geographic division.

Advantages

The choice of any organizational design represents trade-offs between the benefits gained and the limitations imposed on the management of the firm. International division design provides a few benefits, including adequate top management attention to foreign business, concentration of international management expertise at the headquarters, and acquisition of capital and resources worldwide (see Refs. 6, pp. 259–260; 19, pp. 85–86). Since the head of the international division is a member of the senior executive team, the firm is constantly reminded of the international implications of strategic decisions. The existence of international expertise at the headquarters expedites coordination between functional units, such as marketing, finance, production, and foreign operations. The presence of international managers at the top of the corporate hierarchy and their participation in strategy-making committees facilitate evaluation of investment decisions on a worldwide basis.

Disadvantages

The international division structure has some drawbacks (see Refs. 6, pp. 259–260; 19, pp. 85–86; 26, pp. 256–257). There is an inherent conflict between the goals of the domestic and international divisions. Almost always, products that are sold abroad are those produced for the domestic market. The international division does not have its own R&D and engineering staff. Therefore, it cannot cater to the special needs of its foreign customers. Domestic functional specialists are reluctant to give priority to foreign customers because the evaluation of their performance is based on domestic criteria. The international division, therefore, relies heavily on the cooperation of domestic functional departments, and such cooperation may not be forthcoming. There is also another source of conflict. Some activities, such as financing and resource acquisition, need to be coordinated internationally at the divisional level. Attempts at the divisional level to exercise central control over financing clash with country-level activities, such as local marketing. Domestically, the firm gives high priority to product coordination as compared with area coordination (a divisional activity). The international division, however, needs both product and area (geography) coordination.

The Geographic Division Structure

The geographic or regional structure divides worldwide operations into regional divisions. The responsibility for managing each geographic area goes to a senior-level executive (see Figure 8.3). These executives have operational and human resource management responsibilities for their regions, while the headquarters maintains strategic planning and control for worldwide corporate operations. Some regional divisions may operate as self-contained units, producing and selling all the required products locally. Other geographic divisions may rely on other divisions for some of their needs. For MNCs with the geographic division structure, the domestic market is but one of many markets worldwide. Nestlé is an example of a firm using an international division form, based on geographical grouping of its foreign subsidiaries and operations. It has 75 country managers, who report to 5 regional managers, who oversee Europe; South America and Central America; Africa and the Middle East; Asia, Australia, and New Zealand; and North America, the United Kingdom, and Ireland.[29] Another example of MNCs with a regional structure is Unilever PLC. It uses a classic regional structure that divides the world into three regions: Africa/the Middle East, Latin America and East Asia/Pacific, and Europe and North America. Yet another example is Sony Corporation, which organizes its global operations into four regions: Japan, America, Europe, and the rest of the world.[30]

Advantages

The geographic division structure is suitable for certain products and market characteristics. The advantages of the geographic division form are the possibility of regional economies of scale and the treatment of country subsidiaries as profit centers. Geographic division works well when regional similarities in customers' preferences allow for standardization and create the opportunity for economies of scale. It is also suited to situations where whole regions can be treated as a market, with modest marketing modifications for individual countries. Firms using regional structures tend to have mature businesses and narrow product lines and a greater growth prospect abroad, where their products are still new. Since these firms generate large earnings from foreign markets, they need an intimate knowledge of the

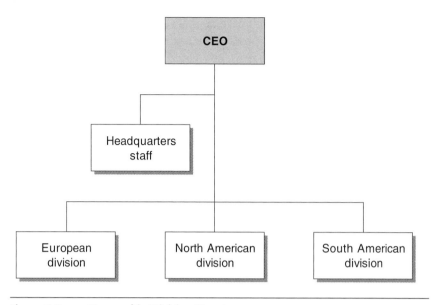

Figure 8.3   Geographic Division Structure

local environment. They generally emphasize low-cost manufacturing by establishing large plants and using stable technologies. They try to create competitive advantages through marketing techniques and price and product differentiation. The automotive, beverages, containers, cosmetics, food, farm equipment, and pharmaceutical industries have characteristics favoring the regional structure (sec. 13.7).[15]

Disadvantages

Although a regional structure simplifies the task of top management by creating regional specialists, it may cause problems (see Refs. 6, p. 264; 15, sec. 13.9). A firm with a diverse product range may find that the regional structure is inadequate to handle coordination among product lines and between the country subsidiaries. The regional structure tends to emphasize coordination and integration within an area at the expense of overall corporate integration. It may focus too much attention on regional performance, which may not necessarily optimize overall corporate interests. Rivalry among the regions may sacrifice the cooperation needed for global competition and may create too much duplication of functional and product specialists among the regions. Strong regional managers may block or delay the implementation of strategies aimed at taking advantage of global economies of scale and worldwide opportunities. MNCs using a geographic division structure may experience difficulties with the transfer of new production techniques and new product ideas from one country to another and the optimum flow of products and material from diverse sources to world markets. Firms facing this problem may respond by establishing a worldwide product manager at the corporate headquarters. This manager would be assigned responsibility for particular products or product lines worldwide. Product managers promote the development, progress, and dissemination of product ideas and production worldwide. They recommend global product strategies and act as a clearinghouse for the transfer of successful developments from one area to the rest of the MNC. This represents experimentation with the matrix structure, which is discussed later. It is likely, however, that they will encounter an ambiguous operating relationship with geographic division managers, who have line responsibilities (p. 261).[26]

The Product Division Structure

Firms using a product division structure arrange their business into product groups and assign a senior line executive total responsibility for each product division (Figure 8.4). As in a regional structure, strategic decisions within each product division that affect the operations of the MNC as a whole are made by headquarters. Products using similar technologies and having similar customers are grouped within a division. The total responsibility of serving the world market rests with each product division, which plans service strategies within the guidelines established by headquarters. These plans need headquarters' approval before they are implemented. Corporate staff provides financial, legal, technical, and other functional services and guidance to all product divisions.

Firms with diverse product lines and growth opportunities tend to use the product division structure. Their products typically have a relatively high level of technological content and different end users. Because marketing

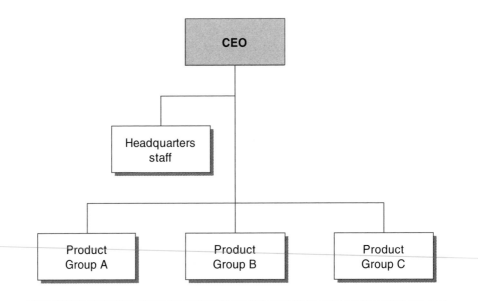

Figure 8.4   Product Division Structure

requirements for these products are varied, there is a need for product and market integration among them. The product division structure makes it easier to market such products and provides product and market integration.

Hewlett Packard has been using the product division structure to serve the world market. In 1970, Hewlett Packard established its first product groups, with four divisions. In 1975, the product groups expanded to six: electronic test and measurement instruments, computer and computer based systems, calculators, solid-state components, medical electronic products, and electronic instrumentation for chemical analysis. Each division was responsible for all aspects of business within its product group, including manufacturing, sales, and services. Product groups also prepared sales forecasts and recommended prices. The general managers of product divisions reported to two executive vice presidents, who were jointly responsible for operations. Product divisions were supported by the corporate staff reporting to the vice president for administration.[31] The recent acquisition of Compaq Computer Corporation may have, among other things, structural implications for Hewlett Packard.

Advantages

The benefits of a product division structure are realized when high transportation costs, tariffs, and other considerations favor local manufacturing of the product. By emphasizing the product market and taking advantage of advanced technology and product expertise, multinational operations are better served by this type of structure. The flexibility of division by product allows MNCs with growth strategies to add new product divisions without disturbing the rest of the organization (pp. 97–99).[8] This structure also facilitates fast response to global competitive pressures against specific product lines. The global competitive maneuvers of international rivals are spotted faster by product division executives. Therefore, an MNC can effectively concentrate and apply its resources at the location of the competitive attack.

Disadvantages

A product division structure may result in wasteful duplication of management, sales representation, and plant capacity utilization within regions (p. 262).[32] A customer, for example, may be visited by representatives from different product divisions. To eliminate duplication and waste, coordination among divisions would be necessary. Within a given geographic area, however, the coordination of different product division activities may be difficult. The addition of country managers, who do not have profit responsibility, may overcome this shortcoming. Country managers report to appropriate product divisions for their share of local activity and perhaps to a regional staff specialist for their role in maintaining local presence (see Refs. 6, p. 266; 15, sec. 13.11). In this manner, the country managers function as if they are operating in a matrix organization.

The Functional Structure

In a functional structure, the responsibilities of managing an MNC's oper-ations are organized by functions. Each business function, such as manufactur-ing, marketing, finance, R&D, and human resource management, is assigned to a top-level executive. Each executive has worldwide responsibility in his or her functional area and reports to the chief executive officer of the MNC (Figure 8.5). The manufacturing executive, for example, has line authority over, and is responsible for, all manufacturing activities, domestic and foreign, within the MNC organization. This form of structure works well in a situation where the firm has a narrow, standardized product line (p. 94)[8] and its global coverage and demand have reached a plateau, with no serious changes in the competitive challenge (pp. 259–260).[6] A functional organization allows tight centralized control with a small cadre of functional managers.

Except in raw material extractive industries, the functional form is less popular among MNCs. In a survey of 92 American MNCs, only 10 had a functional structure, and all were in raw material extractive industries.[33]

Advantages

A functional structure seems to work well in raw material extractive industries because raw materials are very homogeneous and processes do not differ substantially from one country to another. Coordination among the functions, such as exploration, production, and sales, is of strategic importance, not the introduction of new products or marketing. All major oil companies, for example, have exploration, crude oil production, trans-portation (tankers and pipelines), refining, and marketing worldwide. Functional design permits line managers to control directly all activities, at each step, globally through the process of product flow.

Disadvantages

For a firm with a multiple product line, the use of a functional structure could create problems. It puts undue demands on functional managers, which

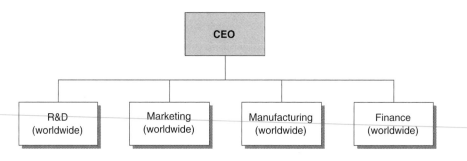

Figure 8.5   International Functional Structure

are not easily met. These managers would need expertise in multiple product lines and regions. Another problem is the inherent divergence of objectives among functional managers. The conflicts resulting from differences in objectives between functional managers, such as those in marketing and production, which cannot be resolved at the country level, need to be referred to headquarters. A headquarters overburdened with reconciling and resolving conflicts among functional divisions has less time for strategic decisions.

Mixed Structure

Some firms may find geographic and product division structures inadequate for their expanding operations. These forms are too restrictive for the ever-changing pattern of international business activities. Therefore, these organizations have opted for either a mixed design or a matrix form. The mixed or overlapping design is a combination of the other structures (Figure 8.6). One option is to combine functional and product divisions. Another choice is to mix geographic and product lines. A third version combines functional and geographic divisions.

A major reason for the adoption of a mixed structure is that other designs do not allow for optimum integration of inputs from regional, functional, and product areas. An optimum level of interaction and cross-fertilization among the three areas is necessary to gain a competitive position in the ever-changing global market. MNCs are constantly in search of a structure that combines area knowledge with product and functional skills (p. 95).[8]

Matrix Structure

Ever since its introduction, the matrix structure has been praised and criticized by both business scholars and managers. Matrix management is an organizational form in which normal hierarchy is overlaid by some form

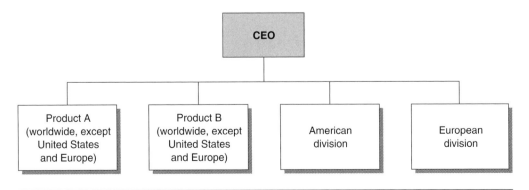

Figure 8.6   International Mixed Structure

of lateral authority, communication, and influence. A matrix organization does not follow the traditional principle of unity of command, which prescribes that each subordinate will have only one superior. It usually combines two chains of command—one along functional lines and the other along project lines (Figure 8.7). There are dual channels of authority, performance responsibility, evaluation, and control in a matrix organization.

Dow Chemical pioneered the matrix management structure in the 1960s and still uses a more flexible version of it. Dow's operations are arranged in the form of three overlapping components: functional, business, and geographic. The functional components include manufacturing, R&D, marketing, and so on. The business segment consists of product lines. The geographic part encompasses the countries where Dow has business operations.[34] Citicorp, Digital Equipment, General Electric, Shell Oil, and Texas Instruments are among the well-known firms that have used matrix design (p. 333).[35] However, some large companies, such as Xerox and Philips, have recently abandoned the matrix structure, claiming it had created a stranglehold on product development and slowed decision making.[36,37] Peters and Waterman[38] even asserted that the tendency toward hopelessly complicated and ultimately unworkable structures "reaches its ultimate expression in the formal matrix organization structure" (p. 49). They were referring to U.S. domestic operations that combine functional and product structures. The international matrix structure often combines product and regional forms.

The matrix structure could be viewed as the end product in a sequence of lateral coordinating arrangements that encompass liaison roles, task forces, teams, integration of managers, integration of departments, and finally, the matrix structure.[39] The matrix structure is a delicate system to manage. Experience indicates that firms that succeeded in building multidimensional organizations, such as those with a matrix structure, are those that begin by building an

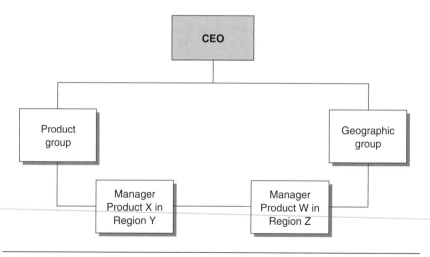

Figure 8.7   International Matrix Structure

organization instead of installing a new structure. In other words, these firms first altered their organizational psychology and built a strong organizational culture. Then, they reinforced their organizational psychology with improvements in their organizational physiology by building the proper structure.[40]

Advantages

A matrix structure offers many advantages. It enables the efficient use of organizational resources. Specialists, as well as equipment, can be shared across multiple projects or countries. It also provides a clear and workable mechanism for coordination of work across functional lines, facilitating project integration. Vertical information flow should improve in a matrix form since one role of the country manager or the project manager is to be a central communication link with top management. In addition, lateral communication is normally very strong due to the necessity of such communication. The result is improved interaction both vertically and laterally. Frequent contacts between members from different areas expedite decision making and enhance management flexibility.

Disadvantages

The matrix structure has several disadvantages. Proponents praise its efficiency and flexibility, while critics say the matrix is costly, cumbersome, and overburdening to manage. It has a built-in tension between country managers and product managers, who are in competition for control over the same set of resources. Such conflict is viewed as a necessary mechanism for achieving an appropriate balance between product issues and unique country requirements. The effect on morale, however, can be very damaging. Often, work conflicts resulting from differences in objectives and accountability, disputes about credits or blames, and infringements on professional domains spill over to a more personal level. Any situation in which equipment and personnel are shared across projects lends itself to conflict and competition for scarce resources. The time-consuming nature of shared decision making, while enhancing flexibility, also increases costs. The additional managers increase administrative overhead. The very nature of matrix structures creates situations in which "when everyone is responsible, no one is responsible." In effect, "passing the buck" is easy in a matrix organization.

Firms using the matrix structure are aware of these problems, and some have moved to minimize their impact on the organization. Dow Chemical, for example, found that instead of promoting communication, a matrix design created a labyrinth of bureaucracy, many committees, and miles of red tape. In the 1970s, to establish a more direct line of communication and to clarify authority and accountability, the firm gave ultimate authority to geographic managers. In doing so, however, a new rivalry began among the different area (geographic) managers. A series of poor investment decisions began as each manager competed with the others. To overcome the problem of rivalry and still reduce ambiguity and confusion in authority, in 1978, the company again revamped its matrix structure. It established a small team of senior executives at the headquarters to set priorities, such as return on investment, market share, expansion into a new market, or new product development, for each type of business. After establishing priorities, one of the three components of the matrix—function, product, or geography—is now chosen to carry more responsibility in the decision-making process. Of course, the component that takes the lead varies depending on the type of decision, the market, and locational considerations (pp. 55–56).[34]

Newer Forms of Organization

MNCs and domestic firms alike are in constant search for the best possible organization design. Although functions, products, and geographical areas remain the three basic models of organizational structure, each has shortcomings that limit its application. The efforts to combine the benefits of all three models while keeping the drawbacks at a minimum produced the matrix structure. Although the matrix design offers the flexibility and quick response needed in a dynamic global business environment, it is not the final answer to the organizing needs of MNCs. Many firms that were enthusiastically promoting the matrix earlier are now not quite sure of its benefits. Some have found it too cumbersome and confusing and have abandoned it in favor of market-based designs.

Market-Based Design

A market-based design takes into account market differences in structuring the firm. A market could be a group of countries that have a similar pattern of needs, purchasing behaviors, and product use. Based on these criteria, the world could be divided into a few markets that could be served with similar products and services. The advent of the Internet and modern communication technologies has reduced the problems associated with geographic separation between different units within each market. Therefore, the physical proximity that is the basis for the geographic division structure is abandoned in favor of more meaningful market characteristics. Instead of dividing the world into geographic regions, such as South America, Europe, and East Asia, for example, countries could be categorized by their level of economic development. On that basis, for example, Brazil, Mexico, South Korea, Taiwan, Turkey, and the OPEC countries could form one market (sec. 13.14).[15]

Strategic Business Units

Based on the logic of market-based design, General Electric established its planning around "strategic business units" (SBUs)—families of businesses that encompass product and geographic dimensions. The older structure serves as a supportive skeleton on which the newer structure of an SBU is overlaid. Xerox Corporation has done similarly by discarding its matrix structure in favor of SBUs (p. 58).[36] While the limitations of travel and communication over long distances coupled with the advantages of physical proximity for managing were the basis for adopting the geographic division structure, advances in telecommunications and information processing have reduced both the limitations and the benefits. Such developments have, in turn, enabled firms to use market-based and SBU structures.

Networks

There are two paths to internationalization: the traditional path and the new path. The new path is provided by the free trade system, which, with its network of participants, acts as a springboard from which firms can launch themselves directly to the global stage. In doing so, they become a part of the network and acquire network structures.

Previously, not having a large home market was a hindrance to growth and internationalization. While many European firms by necessity were engaged in cross-border businesses, their operations consisted merely of expansion to neighboring markets that were within a few hours' travel time. Today, globalization has made it possible for firms from small home markets to expand globally. Because of their small home markets, these firms are forced to use innovative strategies that consider the whole world as a market. Also, they are free to design organizational structures that are not burdened with intermittent, large-scale modifications, such as those that traditional companies had to go through—namely, progression through domestic, international, multinational, and global structures. From the beginning or at an early stage of their growth, they become global players.

Characteristically, globalization makes it possible for small and medium-size firms, as well as start-ups, to become global operators. A global market is a vast network of many firms, in many industries, with a multitude of links to each other in the form of supplier–buyer–customer, marketer–middle man–service provider, and so on. According to the United Nations, for example, there are 60,000 firms with more than 800,000 national affiliates operating in the global market.[41] This vast network is at the disposal of those with the ingenuity to use it.

Unencumbered by the organizational memory of old methods and free from organizational habits, traditions, culture, and structure that are past oriented, newcomers to the global market can move quickly and effectively. Often, it will take these firms much less time to become global players than their traditional counterparts took to reach a global status. Particularly, the development of the organizational structure of these firms follows a less cumbersome path, which takes them directly to global design. Traditionally, the organizational structure of the firm goes through successive states—namely, domestic, international, multinational, and global. But innovative newcomers, all of which have started with a much smaller size than existing global companies, acquire a global posture and structure in a short time. Because they move quickly to the global level, these firms do not use any of the conventional designs. They use an innovative, fluid, and organic structure. This structure is in congruence with the network character of the global economy.

The global economy is emerging as a worldwide web of interfirm connections (p. 41).[2] Internationalization, therefore, can be defined as the process by which firms are becoming integrated into the worldwide web of economic activities. From this perspective, the major features of the global economy—namely, its size and weblike character, the free-trade system, and the existence of global customers—push and pull firms to become global players using innovative organizational designs.

The push comes from the size of the network of the global market, which cannot be managed by conventional methods if a firm does not have a considerable resource base. Also, from their inception, most of these firms have a global mission.

The pull comes from the free-trade system, which allows cross-border transactions without many restrictions and turns far-away people into next-door customers. Even niche players, which previously did not have enough customers at home to grow, can find enough customers in distant places. The pull also results from the fact that existing global companies need suppliers to service their operations in multiple markets. These global customers pull competent and imaginative newcomers to the global stage. If the newcomers are to serve these customers and move quickly, they cannot be burdened with the rigidity of traditional forms. They devise their own forms, which do not fit into conventional designs. These firms are characterized by their connections with suppliers, marketers, and other firms and, where needed, with local governments (see Figure 8.8). We call these forms a "network" design. The network, however, is neither a solid form nor a design that has a permanent skeleton on which the organizational requirements of job design, authority-responsibility designation, communication, and relationships could be fleshed out. It is more a multidirectional organization than either a vertical or a horizontal one. It is in a permanent state of evolution and mostly involves external relationships with other firms and their own subsidiaries and joint ventures. The framework of a traditional organizational structure cannot portray a network organization because this form of organization relies on dynamic relationships. It is not a hierarchical and authority-based firm but a "hyperarchy."

The network structure is very young. It is closely tied to another form of organization, called the *virtual corporation*. In 1992, Davidow and Malone,[42] after a careful observation of the world's most advanced companies, suggested that the successful future firms of the 21st century would be the "virtual corporations." When asked what a virtual corporation would look like, they replied,

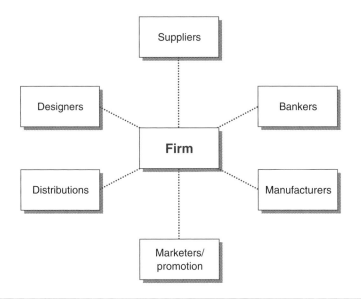

Figure 8.8   A Simple View of a Network Organization

There is no single answer. To the outside observer, it will appear almost edgeless, with permeable and continuously changing interfaces between the company, supplier, and customer. From inside the firm the view will be no less amorphous with traditional offices, departments, and operating divisions . . . [but] even the very definition of employee will change, as some customers and suppliers begin to spend more time in the company than will some of the firm's own workers. (p. 7)

Instead of asking "How does it look?" maybe we should ask "How does it work?" To describe the nature of the products and production processes of the virtual corporation, Davidow and Malone borrowed the words of the manufacturing expert Earl Hall:

The complex product markets of the twenty-first century will demand the ability to quickly and globally deliver a high variety of customized products. These products will be differentiated not only by form and function, but also by the services provided with the product, including the ability for the customer to be involved in the design of the product. . . . A manufacturing company will not be an isolated facility of production, but rather a node in the complex *network* [italics added] of suppliers, customers, engineering, and other "service" functions. (p. 6)

The virtual corporation is very tightly coupled with customers and suppliers. Customers participate in product design, and suppliers have access to most of the company's resources that previously were the exclusive domain of the firm. Suppliers, the firm, and customers are partners. In short, a virtual corporation appears "less a discrete enterprise and more an ever-varying cluster of common activities in the midst of a vast fabric of relationships" (p. 7).[42]

The network structure has been used by the apparel industry for a long time. Many clothing designers do not make their own clothes. Others can make clothes for them that are much cheaper and better. At the heart of a virtual corporation is the readiness to rely on other companies, technologies, and engineers, all of which may be scattered around the globe.[43] Flexibility, speed of response, low costs, and local connections are the obvious benefits of a virtual corporation, but there are some risks involved. First, there is a loss of control over the functions of the partners, who may not fulfill their part and may not be vigilant in safeguarding proprietary information. Second, the structure poses new and demanding challenges to managers.[44] They need to work in a less hierarchical organization, become accustomed to having less control, and accept that the top-down strategy approach is inappropriate in the global economy, where "on spot information" disperses knowledge throughout the firm, to its suppliers, customers, and other relevant businesses. This is a new reality acknowledged by the organizational theorist, who envisions even radical forms of "disposable organizations."

> As rates of change have accelerated, processes of knowledge acquisition that emphasize direct experience within a particular organization have probably become less important to competitive advantage than those processes that emphasize more analytical and broader knowledge. Research and education have become more important; individual and organizational experience have become less relevant. As a result, the comparative advantage of the individual organization as a sustained accumulator of idiosyncratic experiential knowledge has declined. (p. 430)[45]

Let us take a look at the mechanisms of two networks in practice: One is the case of Taiwanese ventures into mainland China, and the other is practiced by an American corporation.

1. *Case 1*: To take advantage of China's low labor costs and export quotas, Taiwanese companies set up intermediary firms in Hong Kong. They established links with the local government of Guandong and Fujian to set up manufacturing subsidiaries that were tied to the intermediary firms in Hong Kong.[46] These subsidiaries farmed out work to small shops in the surrounding villages. This network provided them with flexibility and enabled them to capture the advantages of costs and locations, benefit from government support services, use several countries as export platforms, and diffuse technology throughout the system (p. 173).[47]

2. *Case 2*: Cisco Systems does almost no manufacturing of its own products. Moreover, over 50% of its customer orders via the Internet go directly

to its contractors. Also, Cisco handles more than 80% of its orders and customer service issues over the Web. Cisco customers receive their orders directly from the contractor, and Cisco receives payment for those products. By not being burdened with manufacturing, Cisco concentrates on what it does best: R&D, design, engineering, information, technical support, marketing, and building a reliable network of suppliers (p. 182).[47]

With these two examples in the background, we can identify two types of organizations that have used networks: first, those that from a traditional base, by necessity and by the nature of their worldwide operations, have embraced a network structure, and second, those that from the beginning have used a network form to reach the worldwide market. Well-known MNCs such as Nike, Ford, IBM, Toyota, and Cisco Systems are in the first category. Acer, Ispat, Cemex, and Nixia International[48] belong to the second group. (The stories of Acer, Ispat, and Cemex are well documented by a number of authors, including John A. Mathews.[2])

The development of network organizations can be attributed to rapid technological changes, which have increased uncertainty and unpredictability. This in turn has made corporate flexibility a desired characteristic. Globalization has magnified the need for flexibility. Firms have been forced to abandon vertical bureaucracy in favor of a horizontal-flat design that measures performance by customer satisfaction, which requires the maximization of contact with suppliers and the customer and information availability at all levels of the organization.

The network structure is well suited to firms operating in an unstable environment, which requires quick response and innovation. Well-established relations with suppliers and distributors replace vertical integration with the benefit of added flexibility. Spreading business functions all over the world, instead of having them at a central location, exposes the organization to multiple sources of information and new trends. It enables the firm to cope with rapid technological change and increasing globalization of competition.

Sophisticated information technology provides easy access to the global network of suppliers and vendors, even to the smallest firms, at a very low cost. Low-cost information makes vertical integration more expensive as compared with the network, which is more economical. The Internet has reduced the transaction costs of doing business externally instead of relying on in-house suppliers. As formal, hierarchical controls are replaced with informal and personal relationships, internally and externally, the boundaries of firms become porous and permeable. This will lead to a blurring of the line that separates the firm from its suppliers, buyers, and competitors and creates a hospitable condition for the emerging alternative organizational form, the network. Traditionally designed and managed companies cannot operate successfully in such an environment.

With all its versatility, flexibility, and adaptability, some believe that the network structure is inherently unstable and transitional. In a case study of

Nexia International, a network of independent public accounting firms, Koza and Lewin[48] came to the conclusion that the network structure is an unstable form. Nexia has more than a 100 affiliated independent firms that pool some of their resources to gain access to a wide spectrum of competencies and respond to global changes in accounting, auditing, and consulting services. Nexia also enables members to receive referrals from its affiliates, all of which want to remain local. Some affiliates began offering their own services in other national markets, either because of their dissatisfaction with the fees they were receiving due to referral of businesses to other members or because they had gained exposure and experience in the international market. This introduced a potentially disruptive and destructive condition in the network.

It is hard to disagree with the claim that such a network is unstable. But Nexia is a contractual, alliance network, unlike a network built on equity participation and ownership, such as Acer. Established in 1976, Acer is among the world's top 10 branded PC vendors. Acer employs marketing and service operations across the Asia-Pacific region, Europe, the Middle East, and the Americas, supporting dealers and distributors in over 100 nations. In addition to offering a broad spectrum of information technology (IT) products and services, Acer is also a leading innovator of e-business, providing MegaMicro e-enabling solutions that combine IT products with a range of Micro services delivered via Acer's Mega infrastructure (http://global.acer.com/about/index.htm).

Acer's rapid international expansion into emerging markets began with its becoming a leading IT supplier, partnering with Computec in Mexico and Wipro in India. The partnership arrangement of Acer is not a network of contractual alliances. Mathews[2] describes Acer's self-propagating partnership model, which enables the firm to use an accelerated mode of internationalization through networking, as follows (p. 89):

Step 1: Firm A looks for new markets, forming links with many firms in Countries 2, 3, and 4.

Step 2: In Country 2, Firm A experiments with Firms B, C, and D for reliability.

Step 3: Firm A selects Firm C as a partner and forms joint ventures (JVs) in Country 2.

Step 4: JV AC seeks a new partnership in Countries 5, 6, and 7.

Step 5: JV AC experiments with Firms E, F, and G in Country 6.

Step 6: JV AC selects Firm F to form a new JV, ACF, in Country 6 and then looks for partners in neighboring countries.

Thus, the process of accelerated expansion is propagated from country to country. The network model of Acer, which starts with alliances and contractual agreements, ultimately transforms most of the alliances into equity position.

The astounding performance of East Asian economies during the 1970s and 1980s has prompted much research in comparative organizational theory. This research indicates that the business systems of these countries are mostly network based, although they are of a different form.[2] These firms do not follow the traditional Anglo-Saxon pattern, embedded in property rights, individualism, and separation of business and government.[49]

Networks are either centered on a major MNC or formed on the basis of alliances and cooperation between them. Most economic activities in leading industries are organized around five types of networks (pp. 5–6):[50]

1. *Supplier networks*: These include original equipment manufacturers, the subcontractor, and the links between clients and their suppliers, as well as original design manufacturers.

2. *Producer networks*: These include all involved in coproducing, enabling competing producers to broaden their portfolios by pooling their resources.

3. *Customer networks*: These include the linkage between manufacturing companies and distributors, marketing channels, value-added resellers, and end users.

4. *Standard coalitions initiated by potential global standard setters*: These try to enlist as many firms as possible into agreeing with their propriety product or interface standards.

5. *Technology cooperation networks*: These facilitate the acquisition of product design and production technology. They enable the participants to share generic scientific knowledge and R&D, and production and process development.

Small and medium-size firms with their characteristic flexibility seem to be suited for the emerging informational economy. The large companies, however, are still at the center of the new global economy. But the success of small and medium-size firms with innovative strategies and organizational structure creates doubts about the value of the traditional model of organization based on vertical integration and hierarchical functional management.

Summary

Organizational structure is a means and a tool with which the firm can accomplish its goals and implement its plans. The same basic organization design concepts used by domestic firms can be useful for MNCs. To operate on a worldwide basis, however, MNCs need to examine the organizational structures more carefully. Since their organization is spread across the globe, it is only through an effective structure that they can maintain a productive relationship between their various foreign operations and their headquarters.

External environmental conditions and circumstances, along with the firm's characteristics, determine an MNC's proper organization structure. The MNC's history, top management philosophy, nationality, corporate strategy, and degree of internationalization are attributes that affect the proper choice of an organization structure. Also, economic conditions, host government policies, product-market characteristics, and information technology are major external forces that influence an MNC's attempts to choose an organizational structure.

Five types of organizational structure are commonly used by MNCs. At the early stage of expansion into foreign markets, firms use the international division. When the revenues from foreign sales become a substantial part of corporate earnings and when the firm has gained sufficient international experience, other forms are employed. When an international division is no longer adequate for dispersed MNC operations, product division or geographic division structures are employed. Some firms go through a transition stage before establishing product or geographic divisions. In the transition stage, independent foreign subsidiaries handle almost all the MNC's business transactions. A functional organizational structure is used by firms with limited product diversity, such as firms in raw material extractive industries. Finally, the need for flexibility, coordination, and integration among their worldwide businesses prompts some MNCs to establish matrix structures. Newer forms of organization design, such as market-based designs, SBUs, virtual corporations, and networks, attempt to reduce the drawbacks of the conventional forms but benefit from the flexibility and adaptability that these forms can provide.

Discussion Questions _____

1. What are the similarities and differences of the organizing needs of MNCs compared with those of domestic firms?

2. Use the product life cycle theory to explain the development of the organizational structure of MNCs.

3. When do MNCs abandon the use of an existing domestic organizational structure and reorganize to support their international expansion?

4. In modifying a domestic organization to handle international operations, what is the most common structure employed by MNCs?

5. Describe the structure of an autonomous foreign subsidiary. What are its strengths?

6. Explain the differences between the structure of an autonomous foreign subsidiary and that of an international division.

7. Elaborate on the conditions that prompt a firm to use the international division structure.

8. Why might a firm with diverse products find a geographic organizational structure inadequate for its needs? What type of organization do you recommend for such a firm?

9. While the functional organizational structure has not been very popular among MNCs, some have used it effectively. Do you think more firms may use it in the future? Elaborate on your answer.

10. What are the advantages of using a matrix structure? Which MNCs benefit from it? How can we minimize the problems associated with using a matrix structure?

11. Discuss in detail two internal and external factors that influence an MNC's choice of organizational structure.

12. What are the differences between a *keiretsu* and a *sogo shosha*?

13. Virtual corporation and network designs differ from the conventional forms. What are their differences?

14. Is it easier or more difficult for a small firm to internationalize?

15. Do you think that small organizations threaten the domination of the global market by large MNCs? Elaborate.

References

1. CMS Energy (2001). *Annual report*. Jackson, MI: CMS Energy.
2. J. A. Mathews (2002). *Dragon multinational*. New York: Oxford University Press.
3. P. Drucker (1974). *Management*. New York: Harper & Row.
4. H. Mintzberg (1988). The structuring of organizations. In J. B. Quinn, H. Mintzberg, & R. M. James (Eds.), *The strategy process* (p. 283). Englewood Cliffs, NJ: Prentice Hall.
5. M. G. Duerr & J. M. Roach (1973). *Organization and control of international corporations*. New York: Conference Board.
6. S. H. Robock & K. Simmonds (1989). *International business and multinational enterprises*. Homewood, IL: Richard D. Irwin.
7. Organisation for Economic Co-operation and Development (1987). *Structure and organization of multinational enterprises*. Paris: Author.
8. S. B. Prasad & Y. K. Shetty (1976). *An introduction to multinational management*. Englewood Cliffs, NJ: Prentice Hall.
9. W. G. Egelhoff (1984). Patterns of control in United States, United Kingdom and European multinational corporations. *Journal of Business Studies, 15*, 73–84.
10. F. Trompenaars & C. Hampden-Turner (1998). *Riding the wave of culture*. New York: McGraw-Hill.

11. A. D. Chandler Jr. (1962). *Strategy and structure*. Cambridge: MIT Press.

12. W. Egelhoff (2002). The importance of strategy-structure relationship in MNCs. In M. J. Gannon & K. L. Newman (Eds.), *The Blackwell handbook of cross-cultural management* (pp. 99–120). Oxford, UK: Blackwell Business.

13. J. M. Stopford & L. T. Wells Jr. (1972). *Managing the multinational enterprise*. New York: Basic Books.

14. W. G. Egelhoff (1988). Strategy and structure in multinational corporations: A revision of the Stopford and Wells model. *Strategic Management Journal, 9*, 1–14.

15. S. M. Davis (1988). Organization design. In I. Walter & T. Murray (Eds.), *Handbook of international management*. New York: John Wiley and Sons.

16. C. Rappoport (1992, June). A tough Swede invades the U.S. *Fortune*, 77–79.

17. W. Taylor (1991). The logic of global business: An interview with ABB's Percy Barnevik. *Harvard Business Review, March–April*, 91–105.

18. R. Morais (2000, January). ABB reenergized. *Continental*, 47–48.

19. A. V. Phatak (1989). *International dimensions of management*. Boston: PWS-Kent.

20. D. deSilva (1991, June 6–8). Global business acumen and strategy of sogoshosha. In *Proceedings of Pan-Pacific Conference* (pp. 326–331), Kuala Lumpur, Malaysia.

21. D. deSilva (1989, June 4–7). Management forte of Japan's sogoshosha. In *Proceedings of the International Conference on Comparative Management* (pp. 46–49), Taipei, Taiwan.

22. J. Picard (1980). Organizational structure and integrative devices in European multinational corporations. *Columbia Journal of World Business, Spring*, 31.

23. L. G. Franko (1976). *The European multinationals*. Stamford, CT: Greylock.

24. F. V. Cespedes & J. King (1992). Honeywell, Inc.: International Organization for Commercial Avionics. In R. D. Buzzel, J. A. Quelch, & C. Bartelett (Eds.), *Global marketing management* (p. 535). Reading, MA: Addison-Wesley.

25. I. I. Mitroff (2001). *Managing crises before they happen*. New York: American Management Association.

26. G. H. Clee & W. M. Sachtjen (1988). Organizing for worldwide business. In J. C. Baker, J. K. Ryan Jr., & D. G. Howard (Eds.), *International business classics* (pp. 265–266). Lexington, MA: D. C. Heath.

27. H. Mintzberg & J. B. Quinn (1991). *Strategy process: Concepts, contexts, cases*. Englewood Cliffs, NJ: Prentice Hall.

28. S. Adams & A. Griffin (1990). Polaroid corporation. In T. L. Wheelen & J. D. Hunger (Eds.), *Cases in strategic management*. Reading, MA: Addison-Wesley.

29. J. A. Quelch & E. J. Hoff (1992). Nestle S.A.: International marketing. In R. D. Buzzel, J. A. Quelch, & C. Bartelett (Eds.), *Global marketing management* (pp. 407–408). Reading, MA: Addison-Wesley.

30. J. A. Byrne, K. Kerwin, A. Cortese, & P. Dwyer (1994, May 23). Borderless management. *Business Week*, pp. 24–26.

31. H. Mintzberg & J. B. Quinn (1991). The Hewlett Packard company. In H. Mintzberg & J. B. Quinn (Eds.), *The strategy process: Concepts, contexts, cases* (pp. 462–463). Englewood Cliffs, NJ: Prentice Hall.

32. D. B. Zenoff (1971). *International business management*. New York: Macmillan.

33. J. D. Daniels, R. A. Pitts, & M. J. Tretter (1984). Strategy and structure of U.S. multinationals: An exploratory study. *Academy of Management Journal, 27*(2), 292–307.

34. Dow draws its matrix again—and again, and again . . . (1989, August 5). *The Economist*, p. 55.

35. J. A. Pearce II & R. B. Robinson (1991). *Strategic management*. Homewood, IL: Richard D. Irwin.

36. How Xerox speeds up the birth of new products. (1984, March 19). *Business Week*, pp. 58–59.

37. G. Edmondson (2000, August 28). See the world erase its borders. *Business Week*, pp. 113–114.

38. T. Peters & R. Waterman (1982). *In search of excellence*. New York: Harper & Row.

39. J. Galbraith (1972). Matrix organization design: An information-processing view. In J. W. Lorsch & P. R. Lawrence (Eds.), *Organization planning: Cases and concepts* (pp. 49–74). Homewood, IL: Richard D. Irwin.

40. C. A. Bartlett & S. Ghoshal (1990). Matrix management: Not a structure, a frame of mind. *Harvard Business Review, July–August,* 140.

41. UNCTAD. World Investment Report (2001). *Promoting linkage overview*. New York: United Nations.

42. W. H. Davidow & M. S. Malone (1992). *The virtual corporation*. New York: Harper Business.

43. E. A. Gargan (1994, July 17). Virtual companies leave the manufacturing to others. *New York Times*, p. F5.

44. The virtual corporation (1993, February 8). *Business Week*, pp. 98–103.

45. J. G. March (1995). The future, disposable organizations and the rigidities of imagination. *Organization*, 2(3/4), 430.

46. Y.-T. Hsing (1996). *Making capitalism in China: The Taiwanese connection*. New York: Oxford University Press.

47. M. Castells (2000). *The information age: Economy, society and culture: The rise of the network society* (p. 173). Oxford, UK: Blackwell.

48. M. P. Koza & A. Y. Lewin (1999). The co-evolution of network alliances: A longitudinal analysis of an international professional service network. *Organizational Science, 10*(5), 638–635.

49. S. Clegg & S. G. Redding (Eds.) (1990). *Capitalism in contrasting cultures*. Berlin, Germany: Walter de Gruyer.

50. D. Ernst (1996). *Inter-firms networks and market structure: Driving forces, barriers and patterns of control*. BRIE research paper, University of California, Berkeley, CA.

9

Control of International Operations

N o organization can accomplish its goals without proper control. The imperative of organizational control is heightened when firms cross national borders and expand into unfamiliar foreign markets. This chapter is all about how international operations and foreign subsidiaries are controlled. We first look at various control mechanisms and discuss, in detail, three approaches to control. The cultural aspects of multinational company (MNC) control, which is effective in dealing with the uncertainty and complexity of the international market, are elaborated. Finally, within the context of the historical evolution of the international environment, the corresponding MNC coordination and control mechanisms are summarized. There are differences between the control of an MNC and that of a domestic firm. These differences are due to the complexity of and uncertainties surrounding the MNC environment, with a resulting potential for difficulty. The relationship with the host government creates additional problems. Following a discussion of control problems of MNCs, the influence of host government actions on MNC control is analyzed.

Chapter Vignette

During the 1980s, many developing countries experienced financial crises. Most of them were forced to block the transfer of hard currencies abroad. Multinational companies (MNCs) operating in these nations were unable to repatriate earnings or assets. In effect, the MNCs' control of these funds, and indirectly a partial control of their businesses, was subject to host government policies. Some firms used unique methods to move the blocked funds abroad. Columbia Pictures, for example, filmed a movie in Kenya to use up blocked funds generated by its parent company, Coca-Cola. In Tanzania, another firm found a creative way to spend money blocked in the country. For a while, it booked all its airline tickets for all destinations in or out of Tanzania at Dar es Salaam, the capital of Tanzania.[1]

The blocking of funds is only one way host governments interfere with the normal business operations of MNCs. Often, MNCs lose some control over their foreign subsidiaries due to host government demands. A common practice is to renegotiate contracts, often because the original agreement is so much in favor of the MNC that a renegotiation is expected. A famous example is the case of General Motors (GM), a wholly owned subsidiary in Australia in the mid-1950s. In 1954 and 1955, the GM subsidiary's profit after taxes amounted to 560% of the original investment, and the dividend paid to GM represented 8% of the Australian balance of payments.[2]

One-sided contracts are not always the reason MNCs lose control over foreign subsidiaries, nor does this necessarily happen because of renegotiations. Cases of outright takeover of foreign subsidiaries for political reasons have occurred. Whenever, and for whatever reasons, host governments initiate a rene-gotiation process, MNCs are usually reluctant participants. Consider the Papua, New Guinea, government and the three mining companies that own most of the big Porgera gold mine in that country.

The Government of Papua, New Guinea, shared ownership of the Porgera mine with subsidiaries of Placer Dome of Vancouver, Canada; Hanson PLC of Britain; and M.I.M. Holdings Ltd. of Australia. The three companies each owned 30%, and the government owned 10% of the mine, until the government decided to increase its share to 25%. This reduced each firm's stake in the mine to 25%. To finance the purchase of the additional 15% of shares, the Government of Papuas proposed that the $136 million needed for the purchase would be generated by the cash flow from the same amount from the newly acquired shares. In effect, according to a financial analyst, Papua, New Guinea, was paying the firms with their own money, at a price 20% below market value. When the government declared its intention to raise its stake, however, it suggested that production and profit from the mine had exceeded initial expectations. It claimed that the companies had withheld information and understated the mine's potential in their first negotiation.[3]

Introduction

The effective management of an organization, among other factors, depends on securing continuous and sufficient progress toward goals. Management must determine if the organization is following the right strategies and if these strategies are being implemented correctly. Sound management also involves asking whether the organization is moving in the proper direction and if the results obtained are those intended. Organizational control could provide answers to these questions. Control is needed not only for detecting problems and deviations from plans but also for anticipating problems before they occur. Simply put, control and strategic planning functions are very closely related and interdependent. A good plan has a built-in control system that monitors the implementation of the plan and provides information on goal attainment. It often involves highlighting problem areas and identifying the difficulties in carrying out the plan. Information supplied by various control mechanisms also assesses the validity and appropriateness of a strategy.

In the following pages, we introduce the major elements of the traditional control system. Using this introduction as a background, control tactics for MNCs are then discussed.

Purpose and Functions of the Control Process

Organizational control refers to the process of monitoring and evaluating the effectiveness and efficiency of organizational performance and taking corrective action when performance falls short of expectations. Based on this definition, the process of implementing control system involves four steps.

First, spell out the intended results and establish the standards against which organizational activities and accomplishments can be measured. Second, monitor and collect information on organizational activities that are aimed at goal accomplishment. Third, evaluate organizational performance and results for effectiveness. Fourth, make necessary adjustments to correct deficiencies during and after the implementation of the strategy.

Deficiencies could be due to shortcomings in implementation or flaws in the strategy. The failure of a strategy could also be related to changes in the environmental factors that were the basic premises of the strategic plan. In any case, a properly constructed control mechanism should provide information regarding the shortcomings. Therefore, control could be viewed as the last step in the strategic management process, coming after planning and implementation but with potential to feed information back into those systems as it is acquired.

Problems may arise at any point along the four stages of the control system. Inadequate information, for example, could result in inaccurate standards being established. In turn, the use of deficient standards in measuring progress toward goals could falsely indicate performance failure on the part of organizational members.

Based on the differences in time horizons and scope of coverage, planning may be either strategic or operational. Strategic planning involves the total organization, deals with its long-term survival, and requires nonroutine solutions. Routine solutions deal with recurring issues. Nonroutine solutions involve problems that are unique, and past experience is not very useful for their resolution.

Operational planning takes into account shorter-term performance requirements and deals with recurring problems that are often the domain of individual organizational units. The two types of planning have their corresponding controls, strategic and operational.

Control Mechanisms

Several control mechanisms can be used individually or in combination in an organization. Some are very formal, such as various reports from lower levels of the organizational hierarchy to higher levels. Others are informal, such as socialization and acculturation, which instill organizational values in members and create uniformity in decisions and actions. In the following section, we will review the major control mechanisms.

Input and Output Controls

Organizational activities and performance may be regarded either as inputs or as outputs. In using various control mechanisms, a firm has the choice of controlling the inputs, the outputs, or a combination of both. Input control is regarded as behavioral control, where expectations are communicated to employees in advance. Then, through personal supervision and surveillance, they are guided and directed to reach goals. Of course, rewards and punishment are the instruments that are used to induce goal-oriented behavior modification. Input control relies on feed-forward information. It works best in small organizations and where the low level of complexity allows managers to identify the desired behavior in advance. Also, input controls could be more useful at the lower levels of the organization, where activities and their outcomes are more predictable.

Output control is result oriented and uses impersonal measures such as the difference between the expected and the final outcome. It relies on feedback information to correct deviations. Output control works well for large organizations, where the complexity and heterogeneity of activities require standard objective measures of comparison. Organizations tend to use more output controls at the higher levels of the hierarchy, where there is a high level of complexity and interdependence among tasks. Output control systems are reactive, whereas input controls are proactive. Of course, the two control systems are complementary.

Locus of Decision Making

Usually, all major strategic and critical decisions are made by top-level executives. Some organizations may allow dispersion of decision-making power for other important matters among lower-level managers. *Centralization* of decision making is characteristic of a firm in which most decisions are made by top-level managers. In a centralized MNC, foreign subsidiaries have limited decision-making authority, and most important matters are decided by headquarters. The opposite is *decentralization*, where decision-making power is dispersed among more managers. Decentralized MNCs give more autonomy to their foreign subsidiaries. Centralized firms exert much tighter control over various parts of the organization than do decentralized firms.

Many factors determine the degree of autonomy granted to the subsidiary. Major factors include the nature of the decisions that need to be made and their impact on the rest of the MNC, the type of technology used, and the product and industry characteristics. In situations where the decision outcomes affect only the subsidiary and the host country market, managers are often given more autonomy. In large, globally integrated firms, decision making is more centralized so that the activities of various subsidiaries can be closely coordinated. Also, for the most important matters, such as negotiating new agreements with host governments, subsidiaries are required to clear their decisions with headquarters.

Technology and market characteristics may dictate the need for closer coordination among various subsidiaries. When products are mature, price competition is the norm in industry. Also, when product components are manufactured by a number of subsidiaries, they become very dependent on each other. Price competition and interdependency require uniformity of activities and coordination among subsidiaries. Consequently, in a mature market and when there is a higher degree of interdependencies, headquarters is more apt to exercise central control.

Decision-making autonomy also varies within the functional areas. In a study of 116 MNCs and subsidiaries in the United States, United Kingdom, Germany, Japan, and Sweden, Hedlund found that subsidiaries had the highest autonomy in matters of personnel decisions and lowest for finance decisions. For production and marketing decisions, subsidiary autonomy was in the middle.[4] A study by the Conference Board for 109 U.S., Canadian, and European MNCs reported similar findings. They found that these firms exercised stricter financial control and allowed greater local freedom for labor, political, and business decisions. Also, the home offices of these MNCs made the decisions to introduce new products and to establish R&D facilities.

Communication and Information Flow

Information collection on organizational performance is the linchpin in any control system. To assess the firm's viability and the relevance of its strategy, a variety of data must be collected from inside and outside the firm. To monitor performance, a variety of information is communicated among different parts of the organization. Strategies, goals, and expectations are communicated from headquarters to subsidiaries. Data on implementation of strategies, fulfillment of goals, and market information are sent by subsidiaries to headquarters.

Communication and information flow ranges from periodic financial and operations reports to occasional face-to-face meetings. Telecommunications technology has expanded MNCs' information-processing capability and has resulted in movements toward both centralization and decentralization. Through telephone, facsimile, electronic mail, and the Internet, headquarters is able to receive timely information from dispersed foreign operations and even remotely control equipment and machinery. Timely information allows more centralization of the decision-making process. However, decentralization efforts have also been aided by the speed and accuracy of surveillance and better control. Headquarters realize that they are well-informed and can potentially take more control, if need be. As a result, they are more amenable to granting decision-making authority to subsidiary managers. On the other hand, when circumstances call for centralization, headquarters will have more confidence in making decisions that are going to be applied in faraway operations.

Formal Reports. Formal reporting on financial and operational aspects along with local market data are essential means of subsidiary control by the

MNC. Most MNCs rely heavily on financial reports for control of foreign subsidiaries. Financial data such as return on investment and inventory turnover allow comparison with industry norms and provide information on the progress made in strategy implementation. Intrafirm business transactions and corporate tax variations among host countries make the use of financial data by MNCs more complex. This aspect of MNCs' control is the subject of conflict between host countries and the MNCs. Often, host countries claim that MNCs abuse intrafirm transactions and, through financial manipulation called transfer pricing, reduce taxable earnings and, consequently, corporate taxes.

The use of financial data for control of foreign operations has several limitations. For example, currency exchange rate fluctuations distort financial data, and strategic decisions by headquarters may limit the subsidiary manager's choice of the best possible business options. MNCs are aware of these limitations and temper the use of financial data with personal judgment.

Informal Communication. Informal communication is used along with formal communication to convey to members of the organization what the performance expectations are and to cajole them to comply with the norms. Informal communication is more subtle and indirect in enforcing organizational standards. Some firms, for example, communicate dress codes to members without making formal statements about them. Note, however, that physical distance and limited opportunities for regular face-to-face contacts with subsidiary managers compel MNCs to place greater reliance on the formal system of control.

Developing Global Control

One of the key points of international expansion is to organize and coordinate local operations with their headquarters; otherwise, confusions and misunderstandings might cause internal problems, and the possibility of growth would be diminished. Two American companies, Lincoln Electric, manufacturer of welding machines, and Gross Graphic Systems, a printing press manufacturer, faced these problems. Both companies changed recently: Lincoln changed from private ownership to being traded on the NASDAQ exchange, and Gross belonged to an important industry group and now is owned by a fund manager in New York. They came up with different approaches to solve their coordination and control problems: Lincoln began a process to customize its markets, and Gross decided to standardize development processes through a "product council."

(Continued)

(Continued)

> For Lincoln, operations around the world used to depend on the U.S. market. The first step was to level people from all over the world to the U.S. hierarchy. Then, local branches began to develop products for each specific market, considering regional differences and final usages. Another approach was transferring personnel to different locations to change American processes. Lincoln made an agreement with a Japanese control systems and robot firm to include its hardware in Lincoln's automated welding machines.
>
> On the other hand, Gross engaged in a different process because local entities developed differentiated products but were unable to take advantage of their capacity for growth and development. The company established an international "product council" that meets monthly to discuss technical and marketing strategies that would be applied by the company worldwide. New products are developed using a global platform that can be modified to fit specific local and customer needs. The platform allows differentiation between markets and customers.[5]

Organizational Structure

In Chapter 8, we discussed MNC organizational structure within the framework of the organizing function. As a tool in implementing strategy, and as a skeletal framework that regulates and channels activities in prescribed directions, organization structure is an effective control mechanism. It is within this structure that formal communication channels and superior-subordinate relationships are established.

Increased competition and changing market conditions require a timely, concerted, and uniform response from various organizational units. To increase the organizational capabilities for a proper response to competition and other market forces, firms may need to institute more central control. For example, MNCs that find themselves faced with intense competition may require tighter control and could centralize their operations by restructuring. In response to increased competition in the United States, for example, Sony consolidated its electronics and entertainment operations under one corporate umbrella headed by an American executive. When Sony bought its entertainment companies, it was hoping to capitalize on the synergies between the electronics and the entertainment businesses. The expected synergies did not fully materialize because of the strained relationship between the two divisions. The electronics executives were often critical of the huge amounts that Sony spent on its Hollywood operations. Also, there was a cultural gap between the more prosaic hardware operations and the glamorous entertainment division. With the restructuring, Sony intended to bring the two sides closer together and eliminate each division's preoccupation with its own priorities.[6]

Integrative Mechanisms

Various integrative mechanisms are used to control and manage interdependencies among different organizational units. The more common integrative mechanisms are liaison positions, cross-unit committees, integrators, and the matrix structure.[7,8] These mechanisms form a continuum from simple to complex, moving from liaison to matrix in terms of complexity. Obviously, effective control is gained by matching the level of interdependency among organizational units with the complexity of the integrative mechanisms. A low level of interdependency calls for the use of a simple integrative mechanism, such as a liaison role. A more complex integrative mechanism, such as a matrix, is appropriate for the management and control of a high level of interdependency. Therefore, it is of no surprise that some global firms with a high degree of interdependency among their worldwide operations, such as Asea-Brown Boveri, have used a matrix form.

A liaison role could be used to improve coordination among interdependent divisions and to facilitate communication between them. If the two units have to refer to a higher level in the corporate hierarchy for solving their differences and working out their interdependence, a liaison can bypass these long communication lines. Liaison roles are used more at the lower and middle levels of organizations and, therefore, are more appropriate for operational control.

To solve problems of control and interdependence, integrative roles or departments are created whose responsibility is to enable the two units to work together smoothly. Typical titles and positions are product managers, program managers, and project managers. A product manager, for example, may integrate the marketing and production activities of a product between two separate divisions. Committees are frequently used at various levels of an organization for control problems that other mechanisms cannot handle, and they can be used on either an ad hoc or a permanent basis. Many firms have permanent executive committees that handle corporate-wide strategic problems of control and integration.

Resource Allocation

The primary relationships among various units of a business organization center on economics. One way of exerting control is through resource allocation. The pattern of distribution of resources (anything that people value, e.g., money, material, promotion, knowledge, technology, vacation, a large office, etc.) indicates to the members the performances and outcomes desired by the organization. By changing the allocation of resources among subsidiaries, MNCs effectively exercise control over them. In some MNCs, the direction of resource flow is from the headquarters to the subsidiaries; in integrated MNCs, however, the flow of resources is multidirectional. A subsidiary's influence and its autonomy within the MNC is a function of the amount of resources it provides to the rest of the MNC. Ultimately, however, the headquarters determines the pattern of resource allocation and control, and it generally uses the budgeting system as the associated control system. We will elaborate on resource allocation as a control mechanism in a subsequent section on intrafirm business transactions.

Paper Tissue Control

Years ago, Jamont, a James River Corporation partnership with Italian and Finnish corporations, acquired 13 companies in 10 European countries. Through the process of integration across national borders, it learned a lot about selling toilet tissue to people of different cultures. The assumption always has been that German-speaking consumers bought strength, the French wanted soft, and Americans craved very soft. It turned out that consumers everywhere wanted both softness and strength. All these years, the manufacturers were dictating tastes instead of the consumers.

Product standardization proved to be a difficult task as well. Paper tissues were produced in different sizes in various countries, and there were other problems as well. The French, for example, were using 20 outside suppliers. That was reduced to 2. Each company used to make its own deep-colored paper tissues, a very time-consuming process. This was assigned to one plant.

Creating uniformity in measuring efficiency proved to be challenging. Some companies were counting a year with 330 days, allowing for holidays and maintenance time; others counted it with 350 days. This made the comparison between the operations of different plants a difficult task. A 95% uptime of one was not necessarily better than an 89% uptime of another.

Through consolidation, cost cutting, and instituting of control measures, revenues increased significantly and net profit doubled. These efforts made Jamont one of the largest paper producers in Europe.[9]

Budgeting System. Budgeting is the allocation of resources among various organizational units on the basis of present needs, past performance, and the projection of future needs. Budgets are standards against which actual performance can be measured. Firms use different budgets, such as a capital expenditure budget, a marketing and promotion budget, and a research and development (R&D) budget, for monitoring important activities and functions.

With a budgeting system, MNCs not only monitor subsidiaries' activities but also establish priorities that reflect corporate strategies. Increasing or decreasing the budget is an effective way to dictate the direction of a subsidiary's development and progress. Earlier in this chapter, it was mentioned that because of physical separation and the unique relationship between foreign subsidiaries and the home office, MNCs are very concerned with the performance of their dispersed global operation. One way to reduce the level of concern is to centralize the most critical decisions at headquarters. The most obvious and easily centralized decisions are those dealing with finance. Through a budgeting system, most of the activities of the subsidiaries are translated into financial reports and are available for closer scrutiny.

Control Approaches

The three approaches to control are the market approach, the rules approach, and the cultural approach. Based on the ideas of Ouchi and Maguire,[10] Lebas and Weigenstein[11] proposed that the three approaches form a triangular continuum along which organizations use a combination of two methods of control: input control and output control (Figure 9.1). The three approaches do not exist in pure form. Each, however, may be a dominant form in a given organization. Among the three approaches, as we will argue, cultural control may be needed to respond to the uncertainty and complexity of the international environment.

Market Approach

Control mechanisms employed in a market approach are external market forces. Competition, supply and demand, and contractual agreements are among the external forces that govern the relationships among organizational units. An MNC using the market approach resembles a federation of autonomous units that are free to deal with internal (other units and subsidiaries) or external suppliers. Output control is the dominant method in a market approach, which includes transfer pricing, bargaining, and management compensation. The market approach is efficient in situations where performance requirements are clearly spelled out and various goals are not compatible with one another (p. 129).[12] The market approach seems to be a more practical way to implement control in MNCs. Some researchers[13] have even advocated the use of internal markets as an ideal model of corporate management by creating what they call *the democratic corporation*, in which corporate headquarters impose minimal constraints on their profit

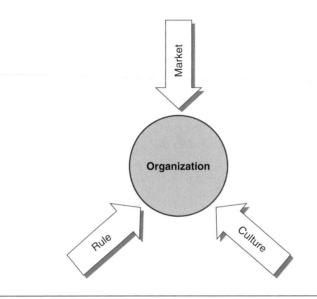

Figure 9.1   Three Control Approaches

centers or subsidiaries. The full benefit of international operations, however, can only be realized through coordination and integration of the activities of dispersed subsidiaries. This in turn necessitates the active
management of internal and external resource flows as headquarters' means
of exercising control. Resource flow as a control method will be discussed
later.

Rules Approach

In most organizations, the rules approach seems to be more visible than
other controls. A rules-oriented organization uses both input and output
controls. It relies extensively on established rules and procedures, such as
planning, budgeting, formal reports, performance evaluation, and hierarchical structure. Rules work best when both goal incongruence and performance ambiguity are moderately high and when the environment is
relatively stable. When there is less congruence among the various goals
pursued by the members, a rules-oriented control system provides a common ground for action and coordination. In a relatively stable environment,
rules provide the specifics needed to clarify goals and performance requirements. A rules-oriented system will only be viable when the environment
allows sufficient time to respond to feedback information when corrections
are needed. Of course, environmental conditions, and particularly those of
the international environment, are unstable. Often, there is not enough time
to make corrections and adjustments. Therefore, very seldom does the feedback process of error-information-correction work well for MNCs.

Cultural Approach

In a cultural approach, external rules and procedures are internalized. Instead of the supervisory surveillance that is common in a rules-oriented organization, individuals exercise self-control and abide by cultural norms and expectations. Less time is needed to respond to feedback information, and the cost of control is lower than is the case in the other two approaches. Also, culture is a vital factor in the globalization of the firm. It facilitates control over foreign operations.[14]

The most common example of the cultural approach is found in Japanese organizations. In terms of structure, Japanese organizations are generally more loosely organized. Group norms and peer pressure, as well as the desire of individuals to be good group members, are the main tools used for control. Consequently, Japanese firms have fewer bureaucratic procedures than do many of their Western counterparts.[15]

The shortcomings of other control systems make the cultural approach more attractive for MNC operations. Because of their specificity and narrow scope, and the required response time, rules-oriented controls have a narrow application and are tied to an organizational unit. There are always exceptions to the rules with which upper-level managers have to deal. Since MNCs operate in a dynamic environment, the market and rules approaches will have limited applicability, and MNCs will need to make increasing use of cultural controls. Since the efficiency of the market approach depends on clearly defined performance requirements and a high level of compatibility among various goals, the market approach cannot be very effective for organization-wide application and for dealing with the global economy in which MNCs operate.

When, through cultural controls, the norms, values, and goals of the organization are internalized, there is no need for personal supervision or formal rules. Since they are not narrow and specific, when applied to input and output controls, cultural norms are applicable on an organization-wide basis. The internalized values provide guidelines that are broad enough to cover most situations. These guidelines allow individuals to follow cultural norms where the ambiguity of the situation renders rules and established standards inappropriate—for example, in budgeting and performance criteria. People's knowledge of these broad informal rules enables them to project them into new situations and to act quickly (p. 264).[11] Therefore, compared with the market and rules approaches, the cultural approach to control provides a better ability to handle the performance ambiguity characteristic of MNC operations.

Ouchi explains the limitations of the market and rules approaches and describes the advantages of a cultural approach.[a] He builds his argument on the informational prerequisites of each approach, which are prices for the market approach, rules for the rules approach, and internalized values for the cultural approach. Prices charged for intrafirm business transactions are the basis for control in a market system. Rules and procedures form a foundation for control in a rules-oriented system. Internalized values and norms are the basis for control in a cultural approach.

> Prices are a highly *sophisticated form of information* [italics added] decision making. However, correct prices are difficult to arrive at, particularly when technological interdependence, novelty, or other forms of ambiguity obscure the boundary between tasks or individuals. Rules, by comparison, are relatively *crude informational devices* [italics added]. A rule is specific to a problem, and therefore it takes a large number of rules to control organizational responses. A decision maker must know the structure of the rules in order to apply the correct one in any given situation. Moreover, an organization can never specify a set of rules that will cover all possible contingencies. Instead, it specifies a smaller set of rules which cover routine decisions, and refers exceptions up the hierarchy where policy makers can invent rules as needed. (pp. 138–139)[12]

The amount of information required by both the market approach and the rules approach is huge. Compared with these approaches, the cultural approach has minimal informational prerequisites. Cultural norms and expectations are implicit, rather than explicit, rules that govern behavior. They prescribe performance and evaluation requirements in a general way, which must be interpreted in a particular situation. These norms, however, "in a formal organization may produce a unified, although implicit philosophy or point of view, functionally equivalent to a theory about how that organization should work. A member who grasps such an essential theory can deduce from it an appropriate rule to govern any possible decision, thus producing a very elegant and complete form of control" (p. 139).[12] The characteristics of the three approaches are summarized in Table 9.1.

Cultural control has the potential to be very effective in dealing with the diversity, complexity, and uncertainty of the MNC environment. MNCs, however, cannot totally abandon market and rules approaches. Creating culturally based controls takes a long time; cultures are not built overnight. Also, cultures change very slowly, whereas most environmental conditions are subject to sudden changes. Additionally, MNCs comprise diverse people. Diversity always

Table 9.1   Characteristics of Control Approaches

Control Approach	Dominant Method of Control	Information Prerequisite	Scope
Market	Output	Prices	Wide
Rule	Input/output	Rules	Narrow
Cultural	Input/output	Norms and expectations	Wide

makes it difficult to create uniform cultural norms. Therefore, it is impractical for the MNC not to apply other means of control and wait for the development of a corporate culture and the accompanying cultural controls. Moreover, it is important to acknowledge the influence of cultural diversity on the effectiveness of the market and rules approaches to control. In the following, we elaborate on this aspect of cultural control.

The effectiveness of various control systems is influenced by the cultural differences among nations. Because of cultural differences, for example, the usefulness of different control mechanisms could vary in the United States and in European and Asian countries. In a country such as France, for example, where hierarchical authority is more readily accepted, "a vertical organizational structure, minimal lateral relationships, dependence on chain of command, and rules and procedures set by superiors are natural control system components" (p. 266).[11] A market-oriented or cultural control system may be more appropriate in a country such as Sweden, where inequalities among the members are minimized and participative decision making is favored. In traditional societies, which avoid radical departures from established norms and where resistance to change is strong, such as in some Asian countries, people prefer the specificity of rules and regulations. Therefore, organizational hierarchy and formal authority could be an effective control system. Cultures also vary in their emphasis on the role of individuals in society. Where individualism is dominant, a market-oriented control may function better. In contrast, where the individual's concerns are subordinate to the collective interests and benefits of groups or institutions, a culture-oriented control system may be more applicable.

Cultural Aspects of MNC Control

Culture is the most effective control mechanism. Societies effectively manage and control their people by devising cultural controls. Through the socialization process, members internalize the values and norms of society, which become the criteria for judging behavior. The internalized values are also strong motivating forces that induce people to behave according to society's expectations. Organizations employ culture and socialization for control purposes too. Because MNCs operate in culturally diverse environments, the challenge, however, is to build a control system that capitalizes on the synergy of cultural diversity.

Corporate Socialization

Corporate socialization could be described as the process by which members learn what behaviors and perspectives are customary and desirable in the work environment.[16] Through the corporate socialization process, new members "learn the ropes" and are indoctrinated with the basic goals of the organization, the preferred means of goal achievement, the responsibilities of the members, the behavior pattern required for effective performance, and the rules for the maintenance of corporate identity and integrity.[17]

Corporate socialization takes place through a combination of obvious and subtle means. The obvious means of corporate socialization include job rotation, management development programs, and informal company-sponsored events. Of course, the corporate reward and compensation system is an obvious and powerful tool for shaping employee behavior and promoting the socialization process. A subtle socialization process encompasses the interaction and interpersonal relationship of top management with colleagues and the rest of the employees. The socialization process is closely related to the values inherent in the corporate culture. In this vein, corporate culture is both a reinforcing mechanism and an ever-present instrument of corporate socialization.

For a domestic firm, socialization of employees is a relatively routine process. Almost all organizations establish "the way we do things around here." Every management veteran has stories to tell about the process of breaking in new employees, a process that makes future control less troublesome. One manager's strategy of dealing with what he considered unwarranted arrogance on the part of new engineers, for example, was to demonstrate to them their lack of practical knowledge and their dependence on experienced managers.

He would ask the new engineer "to examine and diagnose a particular complex circuit, which happened to violate a number of textbook principles but actually worked very well. The new [engineer] would usually announce with confidence, even after an invitation to double-check, that the circuit could not possibly work. At this point the manager would demonstrate the circuit, tell the new [engineer] that they had been selling it for several years without customer complaint." Then, he would direct the engineer to explain why it did work. None of the new engineers he had tested were able to do it but were convinced of the need for supplementing their textbook knowledge with practical know-how. From then on, establishing a good give-and-take relationship with the new engineer would be easy (p. 214).[17]

The dispersed operations of an MNC make the socialization process more difficult and challenging. Aware of the challenge, many MNCs use job rotation to introduce employees early in their careers to the firm, the culture, and "the ropes" around their global operations. For example, to demonstrate that contrary to employees' perceptions, international experience was not a roadblock to career advancement, General Electric revamped its job rotation program. It started sending its brightest stars on foreign assignments rather than the run-of-the-mill managers it used to pick for posts abroad.[18] Motorola is another U.S. MNC with a similar program. Motorola has included foreign engineering recruits in its job rotation program. The program is designed to permit its operation in the People's Republic of China to put up to 20 top recruits into leadership training and rotate them through its worldwide operations.[19]

Evolution of Coordination
and Control of MNCs

Because of the additional coordination and control difficulties that MNCs face, they need more sophisticated control mechanisms than are used by domestic firms. The need to respond simultaneously to the different strategic requirements of foreign countries demands much flexibility. MNCs have to be flexible in order to take advantage of global opportunities while remaining responsive to local differences. This calls for developing a much more sophisticated control mechanism. Consequently, in addition to formal means of control and coordination, MNCs need to rely on a wide range of informal mechanisms,[20] including informal networks of communication, corporate culture and socialization, and career path management (p. 500).

As the international competitive environment changes, so does the MNC's strategies and operations. The implementation of new strategies and the management of new operations require different methods of coordination and control from those used in day-to-day management. As a result, the MNCs' coordination and control tactics are an evolutionary response to their environmental circumstances. The historical evolution of the international environment and the corresponding pattern of coordination and control mechanisms used by MNCs are summarized in Table 9.2. As Table 9.2 shows, over the years, emphasis has shifted from simpler to more complex coordination and control mechanisms.

The evolutionary changes in the international business environment can be divided into three periods (pp. 500–508).[20]

Period I (1920–1950) brought about political changes that discouraged international competition and were conducive to competition on a country-by-country basis. Forces that restricted international business activities included nationalist sentiments, protectionist barriers, and communication and transportation difficulties. The strategic response to environmental imperatives was the establishment of semi-autonomous businesses within each country. European firms, in particular, adopted country-centered strategies. They organized a decentralized, loosely connected federation of independent national subsidiaries. Each subsidiary served its domestic market. They did not seek to integrate local subsidiaries into a total corporate operation; these local subsidiaries were nationally responsive firms. The management of a federation of semi-autonomous firms needed little coordination and control. MNCs managed their foreign subsidiaries as a "portfolio" of investments. As long as the subsidiaries were generating earnings, they were left to the discretion of expatriate managers. These managers were the equivalent of "Roman proconsuls that were given responsibilities only after years spent absorbing the values and practices of the parent company" (p. 118).[21] Headquarters control was ensured through loyal expatriate managers who provided an informal link with subsidiaries and preserved the corporate management style even in faraway countries. Direct

Table 9.2   Historical Evolution of the International Competitive Environment and
               Corresponding Coordination and Control

Pattern of International Competition	Strategic Response of MNCs	Coordination and Control
Period I: 1920–1950		
Multidomestic (or Country-by-Country Basis)	**Country Centered**	**Limited Control and Coordination**
Competition in each country is essentially independent of competition in other countries	Direct investment in many countries	MNCs manage their activities as portfolios of subsidiaries (especially Europeans)
	Self-contained and autonomous branches	No integration
	Differentiated and responsive strategy	Decentralized federation of national subsidiaries
	Competitive advantage in mainstream value activities	Periodic financial reports
Period II: 1950–1980		
International	**International**	**Formal**
International MNC's competitive position in one country is strongly influenced by its competitive position in other countries	Concentration of production in few plants to achieve scale economies	Budgeting, standardized programs (e.g., marketing, manufacturing)
	Serve the world from these few manufacturing locations through exporting	Centralized R&D
	Centralized control of worldwide marketing activities	Structural mechanisms: product divisions, regional divisions
	Standardization of product design	Centralized "hub"
		Output control
Period III: 1980–		
Global (or Worldwide Basis)	**Global With Increasing Foreign Investment**	**Formal and Informal**
MNC's competitive position in one country is strongly influenced by its competitive position in other countries	Decentralization of production in many plants in the world, each specialized in processes and/or products, with a strong interdependence among them	Period I and II mechanisms, plus task forces, committees, integrators
	Interorganizational transfer of technology and ideas	Informal communication networks
	Simultaneous response to national interests and local needs and to economic forces toward globalization	Socialization of home-country and foreign managers
		Corporate culture

SOURCE: Adapted from Reference 20 (Tables 4a and b, pp. 504–506).

reporting of subsidiary managers to the head of the MNC was a formal means of control exercised by headquarters. Subsidiaries supplied the head-quarters with periodic financial reports, assuring headquarters that they were keeping in line with the profit objectives of the MNC.

The international environment during Period II (1950–1980) represented a reverse of the conditions in the previous period. Economic and political forces favored international competition. Advancements in production tech-nologies increased economies of scale. Decreased transportation and com-munication costs, along with economies of scale, allowed concentration of production in low-cost countries. These developments combined with the easing of protectionist barriers to increase international competition. MNCs responded by adopting an international strategy in which decision making was highly centralized and foreign subsidiaries were tightly controlled from headquarters. In terms of control, the MNCs relied on formal mechanisms, centered on budgeting, and on standardized programs in manufacturing and marketing. In addition to frequent financial reports, subsidiaries provided the headquarters with reports on all major functional areas. Formalization and standardization of policies, rules, and procedures strengthened head-quarters' tight output control over subsidiaries' operations.

Currently, MNCs are experiencing the environmental changes of Period III (1980–present), which are challenging their coordination and control capabil-ities. In the early 1980s, conflicting demands began to create a new set of pressures on MNCs. On the one hand, technological developments resulted in the globalization of business and competition in many industries. On the other hand, many governments demand that MNCs invest locally to create jobs, transfer technology, and contribute to the balance of payments. These factors plus a rise in nontariff barriers and protectionist tendencies called for local responsiveness. In turn, the contradictory demands of global strategies and local responsiveness required a higher level of coordination and control. MNCs discovered that the hands-off approach that relied on formal control and coordination mechanisms, used in the first two periods, was inadequate for Period III. Recognizing the need for flexibility and responsiveness, they instituted both formal and informal control mechanisms. In addition to the formal controls of previous periods, MNCs are now using informal and subtle means that overlap existing organizational structure and formal report-ing procedures. Included among the new control mechanisms are teams, task forces, committees, and integrators. Additionally, the free flow of informal communication among all managers—from their headquarters to subsidiaries and vice versa and among the foreign subsidiaries—supplements the formal communication channels. Philosophical changes at their headquarters allow MNCs to offer career paths that enable all managers, regardless of their country of origin, to advance to positions previously reserved for home country executives. In doing so, the MNCs create a corporate culture that effectively controls managerial actions without a reliance on formal rules and procedures. Acculturation of these managers, through continuous assignments to key positions throughout the global operation of the MNCs, works to develop a strong corporate culture and induce the internalization of organizational objectives, values, and beliefs and the corresponding policies and procedures.

Of course, this chronological progression in the application of control mechanisms is not uniform among all MNCs. Technological developments and the competitive forces of the industry, among other factors, may propel a firm to use specific control mechanisms. The trend toward globalization, however, has been compelling MNCs to abandon the less appropriate control mechanisms of earlier periods. Also, MNCs may not change their structural and formal tools of coordination and control but may additionally establish more informal mechanisms hidden under the surface. Procter & Gamble and Unilever, for example, have not significantly changed their formal coordination and control mechanisms for a long time. Instead, the internal management processes have changed. "Subsidiaries have assumed new and specific roles to respond to changing local conditions, and the headquarters' control mechanisms have evolved from ubiquitous 'company ways' to multidimensional gestalts that are applied differently to different parts of the organization" (p. 620).[22]

Control by Standardization

Prior to the advent of globalization, many MNCs, such as Whirlpool, grew in different national markets without much integration and without the benefit of standardization across products and markets. This is a luxury that globalization has made impossible to afford. Now, to compete globally, successful MNCs implement product/market standardization as a means of controlling the operations of dispersed subsidiaries. In its attempt at standardization, Whirlpool determined that its products, such as dishwashers, refrigerators, and other household durable products, had two groups of major components. The first group, which consumers did not see, consisted of subsystems and parts that were common among all, such as electric motors and fans. Because this group was culture-free and was not affected by consumer taste and preferences, it could be standardized as platforms. The second group, which consumers could see, such as size, color, and exterior design, was affected by local tastes and preferences. This group could not be standardized but could be added and built into the standardized platform. In doing so, the number of platforms worldwide was reduced from 135 to 65. As a result, annual development costs were reduced by 10% and purchasing parts by 30%.[23]

_____ Additional Control Problems of MNCs

In addition to the control problems associated with managing dispersed subsidiaries in economically and politically diverse environments, MNCs also encounter several other specific control problems:

1. Language and cultural differences

2. Geographic distance between the headquarters and subsidiaries

3. Legal differences

4. Security issues

5. Intrafirm business transactions (transfer pricing)

6. Currency exchange rate fluctuations

Currency exchange rate fluctuations were briefly discussed in the chapter on strategy. In the following, we discuss the other control problems of MNCs.

Language and Cultural Differences

Diversity in language and culture among various foreign operations is the source of many of the difficulties the MNCs' headquarters encountered. Some of the problems can be reduced by assigning expatriates who are "acculturated" at headquarters to key managerial positions in the subsidiaries and identifying local managers who are proficient in the language of the headquarters. Typically, however, most staff at headquarters have limited or no foreign language skills, and the language problem remains real. The result is that communication between much of the headquarters staff and foreign subsidiaries is limited to contacts with those subsidiary personnel who can speak the language of the headquarters. This reality reduces the amount of information the headquarters staff receives and processes. Without the ability to directly reach the sources of most information, they are at the mercy of subsidiary staff who have language skills or interpreters.

This problem is magnified if several languages are spoken by the local workforce. Such is the case in Africa and India. Even in European countries, which employ a large number of guest workers, control problems arise from the linguistic variety. In Germany, for example, many plants employ guest workers from Spain and Turkey, as well as the local German workers. The codetermination laws (covered in the chapter "International Labor Relations") require periodic meetings with workers. These meetings are held in Spanish, in Turkish, and, of course, in German. Additionally, the German subsidiaries of American firms that have American general managers hold top management meetings in English (p. 36).[24]

Language diversity often creates fewer strategic and more operational control problems. In part, it is typical for upper-level managers to be involved in strategic control, and there is a higher level of foreign language proficiency among this group of managers. In contrast, there are two reasons why language diversity creates problems in operational control, particularly in developing countries. First, and as noted, operational control affects more lower-level foreign subsidiary personnel, and they are less likely to be proficient in the MNC's home country language. Second, since language and culture reflect the level of technological development, the languages of many developing countries do not have equivalents for the technical, industrial, and commercial terms used in modern business enterprises. Often, it is impossible to translate these terms into the local language. The use of a common language, which in most cases is English, is very difficult for a workforce with minimal education and may require the MNC to institute language-training programs. To overcome the language problem for servicing its equipment, for example, Caterpillar has devised a unique method. They have developed an 800-word vocabulary called Caterpillar Fundamental English. With this tool, it is possible for local suppliers, dealers, and service personnel to work with Caterpillar equipment without the need for a translation.[25]

Even without language difficulties, cultural differences have the potential to create control problems. Cultural norms and role expectations may result in inaccurate information and misunderstanding. Criticism in public, for example, is avoided in most Asian cultures; therefore, on-the-spot suggestions for improvements may not produce the intended results. Group harmony and cohesion are very much valued in many Asian countries. Consequently, people from these cultures may not report problems to higher levels immediately, hoping instead to find a solution without unduly disturbing the group.

Geographical Distance

Telecommunication technologies and improvements in transportation facilities have greatly aided the expansion of MNC operations. Vast geographical distances between the MNCs' subsidiaries, however, pose control problems that even today's modern telecommunications and ease of travel have not been able to fully overcome. Nothing can substitute for face-to-face communication and personal visits. Written communication, telephone calls, and voice and computer messages are not the same as personal visits. Often, to travel from headquarters and visit a foreign subsidiary takes at least a couple of days and much advance preparation. Distance matters even within a host country.[26] When an MNC has a number of business operations in a country, the physical distances between them can have a negative influence on the ease with which headquarters manages them. In some cases, this added travel time permits host country staff to rig personal visits by headquarters to show a different and rosier picture of the operations. Consider the following incident.

An American paint manufacturer gave a foreign importer in an Asian country exclusive regional distribution rights. The importer was supposed to act as a middleman between the retailers and the paint company. Therefore, by contract, he was not permitted to be a retailer as well. In violation of the contract, the importer had established a full retailing operation and in effect had become a monopoly. He had set up a bogus wholesale office, separate from his main business, which would be temporarily staffed only when he was expecting a visit from headquarters. Language barriers and long physical distance allowed this masquerade to go on undetected for a few years.

Legal Differences

Although a whole chapter is devoted to the legal aspects of international management, here we briefly examine some major legal problems with MNC control. Laws and legal procedures are central to the concept of organizational control. The control of a business firm depends on the legal institutions and practices of the host country. The practices that legally are accepted or rejected in one country are not necessarily honored or rejected by another. An MNC's control of foreign subsidiaries can take place only within the confines of the legally accepted business norms of host countries. In effect, a host country's legal system may place limitations on the control that headquarters can exercise. In Germany, for example, most firms, including MNCs, are bound by codetermination laws, which require the membership of labor representatives on boards of directors. Because the law dictates power sharing and sharing of organizational control between management and labor, managers cannot unilaterally make certain decisions, such as to close a plant.

The host country's legal requirements in virtually all aspects of business operations, including labor relations, finance, marketing, and manufacturing, limit MNCs' control over subsidiaries. Some countries limit the equity ownership of domestic firms by MNCs. Equity ownership limits are more common among developing countries. In these countries, instead of direct control over the operations of the subsidiary, MNCs may assume the minority position and may have to rely on advice and persuasion. The major problems of sharing equity ownership with host countries are discussed in a subsequent section.

Security Issues

Most nations have benefited from globalization. However, increased international trade; the information explosion, including the use of the Internet; and increased immigration have also made it easier for various groups to engage in terrorism. Terrorism adversely affects international business and poses serious questions regarding control of MNC operations. For a long time, developing countries had certain concerns over the loss of control to MNCs. Now, developed countries are facing a similar dilemma, albeit of a different nature. Europeans and especially Americans are uneasy about, if not completely against, handing over to foreigners the management of firms they consider either national jewels or subject to security concerns. A number of European countries, for example, have blocked the takeover of local firms even by MNCs from other European countries.

The issue of national security as it relates to increased acts of terrorism has become a very sensitive and important matter in the United States after the tragedy of September 11, 2001. Experts have been sounding alarms about securing the nation's borders and particularly its ports.[27] The issue of port security drew a very strong uproar after the purchase of a British firm, which operated five terminals at U.S. ports, by Dubai Ports World (DPW). DPW is in the United Arab Emirates, a country south of the Persian Gulf. Some argued that this event might create, in the minds of international investors, a country risk for the United States similar to those of politically volatile developing countries. Such a development could disrupt an increasingly interdependent world economy. It might discourage foreign investment in the United States, on which the country is heavily dependent. An outcry against similar big acquisitions in Europe raised concerns about a rise in economic nationalism and a backlash against globalization.[28]

The national security issue of MNCs' control can be viewed from the perspectives of **economic benefits** and **less favored nations**.

First, from the **economic benefits** point of view, control of MNC operations grants decision-making authority and, ultimately, distribution and the use of revenues. Previously, this aspect of control was thought to be directly related to ownership rights. This assumption, however, proved to be less critical when it was tested against the sovereign power and rights of host governments. Developing countries learned that even without ownership rights, they could use their sovereignty to achieve their strategic goals. Earlier, this was discussed under the topic of creeping expropriation. This characteristic of control is more relevant to developing countries. Host governments of developing countries are interested in influencing MNC decision-making processes and steering those decisions in a desired direction that serves their strategic goals. Developed countries, however, often allow free-market forces to govern this feature of control.

Second, the **less favored nations** view is a more recent phenomenon that has attracted the attention of experts and scholars.[29,30] The rise of international terrorism has made the control of MNC operations a national security issue. International terrorism has negatively affected the operations of all MNCs. Some MNCs, however, have been more severely affected. With or without merit, MNCs with their headquarters or owners in certain countries have been negatively affected by this issue. From this perspective, certain MNCs should not be granted the opportunity to manage and control business enterprises, if such operations pose national security concerns. An example of this type of control feature was underlined when the sale of the laptop computer division of IBM went through a very rigorous examination by the U.S. Congress. Another example was the case of DPW.

It is the second perspective of MNC control that will be discussed by international scholars and security experts for years to come. In the future, this feature of MNC control will become more likely to influence host country–MNC relationships.

Intrafirm Business Transactions

Firms can use various strategies for entering into foreign markets, including exports, contractual agreements, and direct investment. An export-oriented firm is dominated by product flows from the home country to foreign markets. The flow of capital from the home country to host countries characterizes firms using investment as an entry strategy. Knowledge flows from MNCs to host countries through licensing and contractual agreements. Within this context, therefore, an MNC could be viewed as a network of resource (products and components, capital, technology and knowledge, and personnel) flow across national borders among business units controlled by the headquarters. In this network, resources flow from the MNC's headquarters located in the home country to subsidiaries in foreign countries. Additionally, there are intersubsidiary business transactions that are controlled by headquarters.

Because the flow of resources among various units of a domestic corporation takes place within national boundaries (i.e., where the firm manufactures in one area of the country but sells its products in others), it creates no special problem. The same is not true for MNCs. In some countries, MNCs cannot fully exercise their property rights. Various host government restrictions imposed on the MNCs limit the free flow of resources among subsidiaries. When repatriation of profits is restricted by host governments, for example, control and exercise of property rights on corporate earnings are limited. Some countries go even further and establish production and export requirements for MNCs, which effectively curtail operational control over their subsidiaries. China, for example, requires most MNCs to export a significant portion of their production that takes place in China.

Global Control

A couple of decades ago, Black & Decker (B&D), the U.S.-based hand tool manufacturer, was faced with competition from Makita, a Japanese company that was producing and marketing standardized, low-cost products globally. Makita was able to compete both on prices and on quality, resulting in a substantial increase in its market share. Prior to 1985, B&D had an assortment of extremely independent subsidiaries.

(Continued)

(Continued)

The British, French, and German subsidiaries manufactured products independent of one another's input and sold them locally. Standardization was nonexistent. Diversity of products, parts, and components was enormous, with over 100 different motors across the globe. This, of course, had created massive overhead.

A new strategy to control costs, improve quality, and recapture market share was implemented. The strategy focused on standardization of products among all subsidiaries for distribution around the world. Motor models, for example, were reduced to 20, with plans to reduce that number to only 5. Improvements resulted in streamlining efforts and more effective production, including time reduction for output. The company also concentrated heavily on innovative design, which resulted in worldwide design recognition. Marketing was made consistent, resulting in a global image that did not vary from market to market. B&D reduced its advertising agency network by consolidating from more than 20 to 2 principal agencies focused on coordination of advertising around the world. Together, these combined strategies resulted in a 30% increase in revenues in a few years (pp. 94–182).[31]

Resource allocation is an effective measure in support of a global competitive strategy (p. 621).[32] The complexity and mixed characteristics of MNC activities require the use of standard objective measures for comparison. These measures are characteristic of the market approach. Resources include anything of value and, therefore, comprise not only the flows of finances and products but also the flows of technology, people, and information. The pattern of resource allocation among foreign subsidiaries is an important means of control. This is particularly important when dealing with some developing countries where sociopolitical instability and capricious government policies are often the source of political risk.[33] To reduce political risk, the control of resource flow is considered an effective strategy. MNCs can exert substantial control even from a minority ownership position through the flow of technology, management know-how, and control of export-marketing channels.[34] Centralization of research and development (R&D) activities at the headquarters is a common and effective means of control that ensures the dependence of foreign subsidiaries on headquarters. For this reason, MNCs, in many cases, are very reluctant to establish R&D facilities outside their headquarters. Prior to the 1970s, oil-producing countries that had nationalized MNC operations were forced to invite the MNCs back because the local governments lacked the technological and managerial capabilities to run the very industries they had nationalized. Similarly, export-marketing channels were dominated by global oil

companies at that time. Those dominating companies effectively manipu-
lated the situation against the risk of nationalization.

Furthermore, resource flow patterns between headquarters and the subsidiaries, on the one hand, and between the subsidiaries, on the other, raise
special control issues. Although the pattern of resource flow is mostly from the
MNC headquarters to subsidiaries, increasing globalization of business and
diffusion of technology are beginning to alter this arrangement. An MNC may
find it necessary to concentrate certain aspects of its business in a particular
country. In the microcomputer industry, for example, it would be beneficial to
locate R&D facilities in Silicon Valley (San Jose, California). Proximity to, and
interaction with, a large number of firms at the cutting edge of a new technology provides easy access to a highly qualified workforce and immediate
knowledge of the latest developments. A foreign subsidiary located in Silicon
Valley could become responsible for the supply of advanced technology to the
rest of the company. The dependence of various units of the MNC on this subsidiary for technology increases the subsidiary's importance to the MNC and
along with it the amount of attention and scrutiny it receives from the company's headquarters. In fact, internal resource interdependence is believed by
many researchers to have a very important influence on decision-making
patterns within the various units of an MNC (p. 32).[35] Some even consider
headquarters' resource dependence on subsidiaries to be the most important
determinant of subsidiary autonomy (pp. 893–908).[36] Examination of the relationship pattern between a headquarters and its subsidiaries suggests that the
higher the importance of a subsidiary to the parent MNC and the rest of the
firm, the lower its decision-making authority. The more a parent company
delivers to and receives resources from a subsidiary, the more the critical decisions, such as investment and finances, that are concentrated at its headquarters. Thus, there is a negative relationship between the importance of a
subsidiary to the MNC and its decision-making authority (p. 33).[35]

The pattern of intrafirm resource flow could be used to chart the decision-
making autonomy of MNC units. Figure 9.2 illustrates the pattern of intrafirm
business transactions along a two-dimensional model (patterned after Ref.
37). One dimension of this model is the flow of resources from a subsidiary
to the rest of the MNC, and the other dimension is the flow of resources from
the rest of the MNC to the subsidiary. Four types of subsidiaries are represented in this model: net supplier, net receiver, balanced subsidiary, and marginal player. A net supplier sends more resources to the rest of the MNC than
it receives. A net receiver is just the opposite of a net supplier; it receives more
resources from the rest of the MNC than it sends to them. There is a roughly
equal inflow and outflow of resources between the balanced subsidiary and
the rest of the MNC. A minimal number of business transactions with the rest
of the MNC characterizes a marginal player.

Based on this model, there could be variations in a subsidiary's importance
and autonomy within the MNC. A subsidiary's importance to the multinational network and to the headquarters is predicated on where the subsidiary
stands on the overall pattern of resource flows. Generally, those subsidiaries

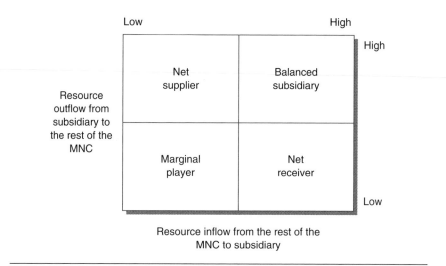

Figure 9.2   Intrafirm Resource Flow

that provide and receive a high volume and value of resources are considered more important to the MNC. Similarly, those subsidiaries that provide and receive few resources are considered marginal to the interests of the corporation. Subsidiaries that provide more than they receive and receive more than they provide have an importance in between that of the balanced subsidiary and the marginal player. Looking at this from the MNC's point of view, one may make the argument, based on standard rules and norms, that the more important type of subsidiary is the balanced subsidiary. Similarly, one may make the argument that the relatively less important type of subsidiary is likely to be the marginal player. Extending this line of thinking, the net supplier is likely to be more important than the net receiver. The reason the net supplier is more important to the headquarters than the net receiver is that an interruption of resource flow from the net supplier could affect the rest of the MNC's operations, while any interruption of resource flow to the net receiver could affect the net receiver's operations only. The net receiver, in turn, is likely to be more important than the marginal player. Both the net supplier and the net receiver are less important than the balanced subsidiary. All other things being equal, the importance of a subsidiary to an MNC's operation is directly related to the amount of resource (value and volume) inflow and outflow that occurs between the subsidiary and the rest of the MNC. On this basis, a balanced subsidiary will be more closely controlled than the other subsidiaries, and marginal players may be afforded considerable freedom from controls. Table 9.3 depicts these relationships.

Other Factors

The pattern of resource allocations and the amount of control exerted by the headquarters is determined by many factors; among them are the importance

Table 9.3   Resource Flow, Subsidiary Importance, and Headquarters Control

	Resource Flow to Subsidiary	Resource Flow From Subsidiary	Importance of Subsidiary to Headquarters	Control Exercised by MNC
Marginal player	Low	Low	Very little	Very little
Net receiver	High	Low	Some	Some
Net supplier	Low	High	Moderate	Moderate
Balanced subsidiary	High	High	Very much	Considerable

of a subsidiary to the MNC and the required relationship between the subsidiary and the host government. A subsidiary, for example, may be given more decision-making authority if it has to establish certain links with the local community and to do so, it requires more autonomy. Also, a headquarters' confidence in the managers of its subsidiaries determines the amount of central control it exercises over them. The MNC's confidence is a function of a manager's skills, experience, and nationality. More experienced and competent managers are given more decision-making authority. Also, expatriates have more autonomy than host national managers.

Ownership and Host Government Involvement

In discussing control concerns of multinational corporations, two separate, but interrelated, issues stand out. The first one is the control of organizational performance as just discussed. It deals with the activities and operation of the enterprise and provides information and assurances that the corporate plans have been accomplished. Typically, it is the control of organizational performance that comes to mind when discussing the subject of control. The second issue is the legal and ownership control that deals with business-government relationships and participation of the host country in the ownership of a foreign subsidiary. The legal and ownership issues of control are even more challenging and complex than those involving corporate strategies.

Host Government Involvement

Host governments regularly interfere in the normal business operations of MNCs and infringe on their decision-making power and control, typically getting involved with the subsidiaries rather than at the headquarters level. Consequently, the amount and type of control exercised by the headquarters over foreign subsidiaries are altered as host government involvement increases.

Host government interference falls into three major categories: financial and investment decisions, business decisions, and human resource management (pp. 13–14).[38]

Financial and Investment Decisions. The most prevalent demand by host governments is for financial participation in foreign subsidiaries. Particularly in Asia and South America, host governments pressure MNCs to share equity ownership of their subsidiaries with domestic investors or host government agencies. Under pressure, some MNCs succumb to these demands. Most MNCs do not strongly object to a minority equity ownership by locals. In fact, sharing ownership with host country investors is an effective protection against host government policy decisions that could adversely affect an MNC's operations. Some MNCs, however, have refused to do business with countries where they are not permitted to assume a majority equity ownership. From the MNCs' point of view, effective control of a business is much easier with a majority equity position.

Interference in repatriation of assets is another financial restriction imposed on MNCs. Some host governments limit repatriation of MNC assets. This limitation is considered most troublesome by MNCs because it severely curtails their investment strategies and forces them to reinvest in the host country. Reinvestment in the host country may not necessarily be the best alternative. Asset repatriation restrictions are more common among developing countries with growing markets.

Another financial decision that is a source of contention with host governments is the allocation of R&D expenses to foreign subsidiaries. Some host governments have policies limiting the amount of fees that MNCs can charge their foreign subsidiaries for R&D work carried out by their central laboratories. Another R&D issue is the location of research facilities. All countries, particularly developing nations, are very interested in technology transfer and demand that MNCs establish research laboratories in the host countries. Not only are R&D facilities a source of new technology, but they also contribute to the improvement of skills and knowledge of the local workforce.

Sharing equity ownership with host countries affects utilization, and sometimes control, of MNC's resources. Without full control over a subsidiary, an MNC may be unwilling to use the best available technology. To transfer state-of-the-art technology that could not effectively be safeguarded against pilferage and piracy is not a wise choice. It may not, however, be wise to limit technology transfer. One MNC executive expressed this dilemma in the following terms: "Local participation can interfere with the free flow of the best technology available for each market. When you slow the development of the local units this can sometimes result in the loss of management control over the decision-making process" (p. 18).[38] The requirement of a large local equity ownership may reduce an MNC's control over how it maintains and expands a business. In the extractive industries, for example, the full development of a business requires a large investment. In some countries, sufficient local capital may not be available to meet a 50%, or more, local ownership requirement. In such a case, an MNC may be forced to operate its foreign subsidiary with a less than optimum size. This is also in line with findings that indicate that in a joint ownership arrangement, an MNC's control has a significant positive impact on the survival of its subsidiary.[39]

Business Decisions. Host governments interfere with business decisions by establishing certain performance criteria for foreign subsidiaries. These criteria include local component requirements, market share limits, tie-in products, and export quotas. Local component requirements involve the demand of many host governments that products sold by MNCs in the host markets incorporate locally produced components or raw materials. The aim is to increase MNCs' contributions to the local economy and employment and to reduce hard currency spending. Host governments are also very interested in regulating domestic competition and preventing MNCs' total domination and control of local markets. Setting a limit on the local market share that foreign subsidiaries can gain ensures the viability of fledgling domestic businesses. Also, tie-in products are used to increase MNCs' contributions to the domestic economy. As a condition for allowing access to the domestic market, a host country may "tie in" by requiring that an MNC produce or sell certain products. These requirements and demands transfer partial control of the business operation from the MNC to the host country and reduce the decision-making authority of the MNC's managers.

Human Resource Management Decisions. A host government's desire to increase the employment, skills, and knowledge of its people is manifested in several ways. The host government may demand that host nationals be appointed to top managerial positions within local subsidiary operations. Compliance with this demand makes the control of local operations more difficult, especially where trust and competence become issues.

MNCs become more cautious and increase headquarters control when they are forced to appoint a host national as the head of a foreign subsidiary. Most MNCs grant more decision-making authority to expatriate managers than to host nationals, and having home country nationals at the head of foreign subsidiaries is perceived to reduce the need for other means of control. When the MNC is strategically dependent on the subsidiary, it is more likely that for control purposes, an expatriate is appointed as the subsidiary's manager.[40] An alternative effective control technique used by most MNCs is to identify local managers who have internalized corporate values. This requires constant and close monitoring of local managers' development and progress through the corporate hierarchy.

Appointments at lower organizational levels are considered less important. These and other human resource management issues, such as hiring, promotion, and negotiation with locals, are made by the subsidiary. Usually, only important and critical decisions are centralized at the headquarters.

Other matters are left very much to the discretion of the subsidiary. Those decisions that might directly affect the headquarters or other subsidiaries or might influence the profitability of the affiliates or the parent company are closely controlled. Often, these decisions are made exclusively by the parent MNC. Sometimes, subsidiaries are allowed to participate in making these decisions, but the final choice is still made by the headquarters.

Ownership and Control of Foreign Affiliates

Besides the nature of the decisions, other factors influence the centralization of decision making at the headquarters and reduce the autonomy of affiliates. We have already referred to a few of these factors, including the skills and experience of managers and their nationality. Other factors are the size and degree of internationalization of the MNC, the type of product produced by the subsidiary, the markets that the affiliate serves, and the proportion of equity owned by others. From a survey of U.S. affiliates in Mexico and France, Garnier[36] concluded that a subsidiary's autonomy is less when

1. it belongs to a large MNC that operates in many countries;

2. its products are fairly standardized;

3. the MNC is fairly integrated, with important intrafirm flow of resources;

4. besides its own home market, it serves other markets as well; and

5. a large portion of its equity is owned by the parent MNC (p. 906).

In business organizations, domestic or international, regardless of the locus of control (centralization vs. decentralization), firms are interested in the full application of the strategic decisions made at their headquarters. Compliance with headquarters' decisions will be higher when an MNC's strategy-making process is judged to be fair by the top managers of its subsidiaries.[41]

Five conditions determine the fairness of the strategy-making process:

1. Headquarters is knowledgeable about the local conditions of the subsidiaries.

2. A two-way communication exists in the multinational's strategy-making process.

3. The headquarters' decisions are fairly consistent across subsidiaries.

4. The subsidiaries can legitimately challenge the headquarters' strategic views.

5. The MNC's final strategic decisions are fully explained to the subsidiaries.[42]

A firm may prefer joint ownership with locals, at the outset of expansion abroad, due to unfamiliarity with the host country environment. At that time, an MNC may not have a majority equity ownership and, therefore, may not have full control over its foreign operations. The MNC, however, can exercise significant control through other means. As it gains experience and self-confidence, it will probably favor creating an integrated global operation that requires majority or full ownership of foreign subsidiaries (p. 32).[43] We discussed the Acer Group in Chapter 8, describing the network organization. Acer, a newcomer to global business, at the beginning of its push to become a global company, attempted to independently own and operate subsidiaries listed in the local stock markets. This vision of globalization proved to be very difficult, if not impossible, to implement. The difficulties forced Acer to reaffirm its ownership and control of these regional business units (p. 77).[44] Of course, even with majority or full equity ownership by MNCs, host governments control a wide range of subsidiaries' operating decisions, such as profit repatriation and expatriate employment.

The ownership pattern of U.S. MNCs indicates that they prefer to retain total ownership of foreign subsidiaries (pp. 32–34).[43] The management of a jointly owned foreign operation is a very difficult undertaking. Cultural differences and limited commonality among partners exacerbate the operational and strategic problems of a joint venture. Except for the learning period at the beginning of expansion into a host market, a jointly owned firm is less attractive to an MNC than a wholly owned subsidiary. Sometimes, however, as mentioned before, in a politically unstable environment, a joint venture with host country partners reduces the risk of adverse host country policy decisions. Joint ventures are inherently unstable and subject to frequent "renegotiation" imposed by the majority partner. Usually, through these renegotiations, the joint venture is converted into a wholly owned subsidiary.[45]

It is much easier to manage a firm without having to share decision-making authority with other parties. The preference for full ownership of foreign subsidiaries is therefore almost a direct result of control problems. In a marketing-oriented MNC such as Coca-Cola, for example, where commitment to certain marketing strategies for the global operation is very important and where the firm possesses special marketing skills, a wholly owned subsidiary is preferred. To implement the overall marketing strategy at the subsidiary level, headquarters needs full control. In this case, strategy implementation could be compromised if conflicts arise with the partner over centralized control. Particularly in a transition economy, the delegation of marketing matters to the local staff involves performance risk.[46]

Where control could be exercised by other means than equity ownership, MNCs have shown a considerable amount of practical flexibility. An MNC, for example, may agree to share equity ownership in a joint venture manufacturing project with a host government if it can maintain control by full ownership of sales operations. Consequently, the host government's demand is met, and headquarters maintains control over subsidiary operations.

Summary

An effective control system is needed to manage an organization successfully. In MNCs, control is a much more complex and demanding issue than it is in a domestic business. Unlike a domestic operation, a foreign subsidiary cannot, for long, subordinate its business requirements, which are often dictated by the host country, to those of the parent MNC. An effective MNC control system should allow for local adaptability and responsiveness to the host country environment. A challenging task for MNC top management is to build a control system that, while promoting the overall corporate competitive position, is beneficial to individual subsidiaries as well. In other words, if subsidiaries consider the strategy process and associated control system fair, they will accept it more readily. Subsidiaries' managers consider a corporate strategy more attractive when it includes interests important to the subsidiaries. Moreover, when subsidiaries' interests are not totally abandoned in favor of promoting corporate objectives, the strategy process will be considered to be fairer. This, in turn, provides greater incentive for compliance by the subsidiary and makes corporate control much easier.

Of course, a fair strategy-making process has a built-in control mechanism that is also fair. This means, for example, that if return on investment is used to evaluate the performance of a subsidiary manager, allowances should be made to compensate for the shortcomings of this evaluation technique. Return on investment evaluations do not reflect the impact of decisions made by the headquarters for the benefit of the whole MNC operation. Those decisions may have a negative impact on the subsidiary's earnings.

Various control mechanisms and approaches used by domestic firms are applicable to MNCs. The diversity of the international environment, however, makes it more difficult to apply these controls. Effective MNC control employs a combination of formal, informal, direct, and indirect mechanisms to account for the uniqueness of each subsidiary while addressing the total MNC strategic and operational requirements.

Discussion Questions

1. What are the differences between the control processes of MNCs and those of domestic firms?

2. Describe the various control mechanisms that MNCs could use.

3. What control mechanisms work well for an integrated MNC?

4. Why is MNC control more difficult than the control of a domestic business?

5. Does geographical distance create any difficulty for the control of an MNC?

6. What is the impact of an increase in intrafirm business transactions on control of a foreign subsidiary?

7. What attributes of managers influence the amount of autonomy granted to a foreign subsidiary?

8. Why do host governments interfere with MNC operations?

9. Which one of the three approaches to control is more appropriate for MNCs? Why?

Note

a. The terms *clan* and *tradition* used by Ouchi are very much the same as cultural traits. Since the framework of his writings was adopted by Lebas and Weigenstein to elaborate on cultural control, we too use Ouchi's argument based on "clans" and "tradition" in our discussion of cultural control.

References

1. M. R. Sesit (1984, December 3). Funds blocked abroad by exchange controls plague big companies. *Wall Street Journal*, p. 1.

2. E. T. Penrose (1956). Foreign investment and the growth of the firm. *The Economic Journal*, 66(262), 220–235.

3. L. M. Greenberg (1993, March 18). Mining firms cede portion of Porgera. *Wall Street Journal*, p. A2.

4. G. Hedlund (1981). Autonomy of subsidiaries and formalisation of headquarter-subsidiary relationships in Swedish multinational enterprises. In L. Otterbeck (Ed.), *The management of headquarters subsidiary relationships in multinational corporations* (pp. 51–64). Stockholm: Grover.

5. P. Marsh (1998, February 13). Change to global approach. *Financial Times* (London), p. 12.

6. P. M. Reilly (1993, May 25). Sony combines U.S. operations under Schulhof. *Wall Street Journal*, p. B1.

7. J. R. Galbraith (1977). Organization design: An information processing view. *Interface, 4*, 28–36.

8. D. A. Nadler & M. L. Tushman (1988). *Strategic organization design*. Glenview, IL: Scott, Foresman.

9. J. Guyon (1992, December 7). A joint-venture papermaker casts net across Europe. *Wall Street Journal*, p. B6.

10. W. G. Ouchi & M. A. Maguire (1975). Organizational control: Two functions. *Administrative Science Quarterly, 20*, 559–569.

11. M. Lebas & J. Weigenstein (1986). Management control: The roles of rules, markets and culture. *Journal of Management Studies, 23*, 259–272.

12. W. G. Ouchi (1980, March). Markets, bureaucracies, and clan. *Administrative Science Quarterly, 25*, 129.

13. R. L. Ackoff (1994). *The democratic corporation*. New York: Oxford University Press.

14. J. C. McGune (1999). Exporting corporate culture. *Management Review, December*, 52–56.

15. J. Birnberg & C. Snodgrass (1988). Culture and control: A field study. *Accounting, Organizations and Society, 13*(5), 447–464.

16. I. Van Maanen & E. H. Schein (1979). Toward a theory of organizational socialization. In B. M. Staw (Ed.), *Research in organizational behavior* (Vol. 1, pp. 209–264). Greenwich, CT: JAI Press.

17. E. H. Schein (1977). Organizational socialization and the profession of management. In B. M. Staw (Ed.), *Psychological foundations of organizational behavior* (pp. 210–224). Santa Monica, CA: Goodyear.

18. A. Bennett (1993, March 15). GE redesigns rungs of career ladder. *Wall Street Journal*, p. B1.

19. P. Engardio (1993, May 17). Motorola in China: A great leap forward. *BusinessWeek*, 59.

20. J. I. Martinez & J. C. Jarillo (1989). The evolution of research on coordination mechanisms in multinational corporations. *Journal of International Business Studies, 20*(3), 489–514.

21. L. G. Franko (1978). Organizational structure and multinational strategies of continental European enterprises. In M. Ghertman & J. Leontiades (Eds.), *European research in international business* (p. 118). Amsterdam: North-Holland.

22. S. Ghoshal & C. A. Bartlett (1990). The multinational corporation as an interorganizational network. *Academy of Management Review, 15*, 620.

23. Whirlpool's platform for growth. (1998, March 26). *Financial Times*, p. 8.

24. V. Terpstra & K. David (1991). *The cultural environment of international business*. Cincinnati, OH: South-Western.

25. Caterpillar designs easier maintenance manuals. (1973, April 6). *Business International*, p. 107.

26. P. Ghemawat (2001). Distance still matters. *Harvard Business Review, September*, 137–147.

27. J. Giermanski (2006). Boxing clever. *Cargo Security International, February–March*, 40–44.

28. G. Hitt & S. Ellison (2006, March 9). Dubai firm bows to public outcry. *Wall Street Journal*, p. 1.

29. P. Tucker (2006, March–April). Redefining national security. *Futurist, 40*(2), 6–7.

30. K. G. Busch & S. H. Weissman (2005). The intelligence community and the war on terror: The role of behavioral science. *Behavioral Science and the Law, 23*, 559–671.

31. G. S. Yip (2003). *Total global strategy II*. Upper Saddle River, NJ: Prentice Hall.

32. Y. L. Doz & C. K. Prahalad (1992). Headquarters influence and strategic control in MNCs. In C. A. Bartlett & S. Ghoshal (Eds.), *Transnational management* (p. 621). Homewood, IL: Richard D. Irwin.

33. K. Fatehi (1994). Capital flight from Latin America as a barometer of political instability. *Journal of Business Research, 30*(2), 187–195.

34. J. C. Fayerweather (1981). Four wining strategies for the international corporations. *Journal of Business Strategies, Fall*, 25–36.

35. Organisation for Economic Co-operation and Development (1987). *Structure and organisation of multinational enterprises*. Paris: Author.

36. G. H. Garnier (1982). Context and decision-making autonomy in the foreign affiliates of United States multinational corporations. *Academy of Management Journal, 25*, 893–908.

37. A. K. Gupta & V. Govindarajan (1991). Knowledge flows and the structure of control within multinational corporations. *Academy of Management Review, 16,* 768–792.

38. R. E. Berenbeim (1983). *Operating foreign subsidiaries: How independent can they be?* (Report No. 836). New York: Conference Board.

39. J. Lu & L. Hebert (1999, August). *Foreign control and survival of joint venture: An examination of Japanese IJVS in Asia.* Paper presented at the Academy of Management Annual Meeting, Chicago, IL.

40. R. A. Blderbos & M. G. Heijltjes (2005). The determinants of expatriate staffing by Japanese multinationals in Asia. *Journal of International Business Studies, 36*(3), 341–354.

41. W. C. Kim & R. A. Mauborgne (1993). Procedural justice, attitudes, and subsidiary top management compliance with multinationals' corporate strategic decisions. *Academy of Management Journal, 36,* 502–526.

42. W. C. Kim & R. A. Mauborgne (1991). Implementing global strategies: The role of procedural justice. *Strategic Management Journal, 12,* 17–31.

43. A. R. Negandhi & M. Welge (1984). *Advances in international comparative management.* Greenwich, CT: JAI Press.

44. J. A. Mathews (2002). *Dragon multinational.* New York: Oxford University Press.

45. L. L. Blodgett (1992). Factors in the instability of international joint ventures: An event history analysis. *Strategic Management Journal, 13,* 475–481.

46. J. Child, L. Chung, & H. Davis (2003). The performance of cross-border units in China: A test of natural selection, strategic choice and contingency theories. *Journal of International Business Studies, 34*(3), 242–254.

10 International Information Systems Management

AUTHOR'S NOTE: This chapter is coauthored with Mohammad Dadashzadeh, Professor of MIS and Director of Applied Technology in Business (ATiB) at Oakland University, Rochester, Michigan.

I n this chapter, the basic issues of international information systems (IS) management are introduced. The chapter discusses the characteristics of computer-based information systems (CBIS) and the benefits they will bring to the firm. It elaborates on the IS applications that enable the firm to link with its suppliers, customers, and other organizations, including the government. These include supply chain management (SCM), enterprise resource planning (ERP), and electronic data interchange (EDI), as well as the use of the Internet. The chapter explores the ramifications of internationalization on the IS function in the firm. It examines various IS options and suggests the alternatives available to multinational companies (MNCs). Also in this chapter, we learn about the impact of information technology (IT) on MNC operations. Based on MNCs' requirements and the environmental limitations that they experience, this chapter makes several suggestions for the deployment of specific IS. Finally, the impact of the internationalization of the firm on the chief information officer's (CIO's) responsibilities and duties is discussed.[a]

Rohm and Haas (R&H) is one of the world's largest manufacturers of specialty chemicals. R&H's worldwide headquarters is located in Philadelphia, Pennsylvania. With more than 17,000 employees and billions of dollars in sales, it operates approximately 140 research and manufacturing locations in 27 countries. Some of R&H's products are adhesives and sealants, automotive coatings, electronic materials, plastics additives, powder coatings, and salt.

Inadequate global information was causing R&H to spend millions of dollars carrying unwanted inventory, which was costing the company a lot of money and lost business. Its 35 production units around the world operated independently. For example, if a customer needed a product that was out of stock in France but thousands of units of the product were in storage 20 miles away, across the border in Germany, no one had access to this information. To improve its information-processing capability, R&H installed a new company-wide materials management system and a global demand-planning system. It also upgraded its manufacturing, execution, and control system and its worldwide order-entry system. These changes reduced inventory costs by $40 million and improved on-time delivery performance by 10%. This gave R&H a stronger position in the global market. Consequently, customers around the world can now receive the requested products on time even if the products are not available locally.

R&H has built a management and IT infrastructure to improve its capacity for receiving and sending the right information within its different global business units. This new management and IT infrastructure also helps researchers and marketers in extracting the information they need. With this infrastructure, R&H can standardize the software applications throughout its global organization. These applications include accounting, human resources, materials management, production scheduling, procurement, maintenance, and sales and distribution. All data are stored in a central database providing every employee the required access to the most accurate and up-to-date information. This enables R&H to make better business decisions, improve forecasting and report capabilities, and have faster and better e-commerce connections with its suppliers and customers. Another advantage is that R&H is able to close its books in 3 working days at the end of the fiscal year, a process that usually took 12 days.

IT was also used to implement the Environmental Health and Safety Management System (EHSMS) worldwide. The EHSMS, which was installed in the 1970s, provides specific requirements and guidance covering areas such as safety, employee health, and environmental protection programs for each global unit. The system enables R&H to maintain worldwide operations that protect the environment, enhance the safety and health of all employees and the public, and improve the safety and environmental impact of R&H processes, products, and services.[1-4]

Introduction

We are living in the information age. Information and IT are governing every aspect of our lives. The ever-growing reach of the Internet and the World Wide Web has brought together individuals and public and private organizations as at no other time in human civilization. The Internet, as a decentralized global network of computers, has become the de facto standard medium to transfer data, voice, and video anywhere and anytime.

Information can be considered the lifeblood of business and a strategic resource that can provide a competitive advantage. The ability to gather, store, and process information is essential for making timely decisions. As much as 80% of an executive's time is devoted to receiving, communicating, and using information in performing a variety of tasks (p. 8).[5] Because all organizational activities depend on information, systems must be developed to produce and manage them. No complex organization can function without an IS. "An information system is a set of people, data, and procedures that work together to provide useful information" (p. 8).[5] Organizational success greatly depends on effective information management and dissemination. The need for an effective management information system (MIS) function is particularly crucial for the survival and success of MNCs. Crossing national borders, MNCs are vulnerable to the uncertainties associated with the multiple political, cultural, and economic systems within which they operate. Therefore, an effective MIS is integral to the success of an MNC.

An organization's MIS is a system for obtaining, processing, and delivering information that can be used in managing the organization (p. 6).[6] The mission of IS is to improve the performance of people in the organization through the use of IT (p. 14).[7] Before the advent of computers, due to technological limitations, the bulk of MIS consisted of paper reports generated by functional areas, such as accounting, manufacturing, and marketing. Accessing this information was very slow and time-consuming. There was a time lag between the generation of information and its use. Depending on the physical distance between the source and the user of information, the time lag ranged from a few hours to weeks. As a result of the limitation in information management, greater geographical distances from the headquarters implied a higher degree of autonomy for the subsidiaries. Today, IT comprises computers and telecommunication networks that allow instantaneous access to information regardless of the physical distance between the source and the user of the information. The newfound MIS capability not only allows more timely decision making, it also enables better control of distant operations. Such a capability is especially beneficial to MNCs. IT affects MNCs in two different ways. First, it provides a coordination mechanism for geographically dispersed activities, thereby facilitating globalization. Second, it provides a mechanism for building a coalition among separate organizations, making global operation more cost-effective.[8]

Computer-Based Information Systems

CBIS play a vital role in today's businesses. The many benefits organizations seek to achieve through CBIS may be classified as follows: (1) efficiency gains, (2) effectiveness gains, and (3) competitive advantage.

Efficiency gains are concerned with doing more with the same or fewer resources. CBIS can bring about efficiency gains by automating tasks in the factory as well as in the workplace.

Effectiveness gains are concerned with doing the right things and achieving the established goals. CBIS can bring about effectiveness gains by improving internal as well as external communications and by facilitating superior managerial decision making.

Competitive advantage is concerned with providing the organization with a significant and long-term benefit vis-à-vis the competition. CBIS can bring about competitive advantage by allowing the firm to differentiate itself from its competitors, become the lowest-cost/price producer in the marketplace, or carve market niches for itself through innovative services and/or products.

It is precisely because of the major impact that IS can have on corporate strategy that today's managers must be not only computer literate but also IS literate. Computer literacy is the knowledge of computer technology. IS literacy encompasses how and why IT is applied in organizations. A knowledge of organizations, managerial levels, information needs, and decision-making approaches is an important aspect of IS literacy.

Today, no company of even modest size can operate without support from IS. But at a time when business is increasing its dependence on IT, technology is changing so rapidly that businesses are threatened by its pace. New developments arise before older ones can be assimilated, and systems purchased today are, at times, outdated even before they are put into use. It is, however, too late to stop. The use of any tool creates dependence, and computers—the most enabling tool created by man—are heavily used already. By the same account, nearly half of all capital investment in the United States is being put into IT.[9] To cease to invest, or even invest slowly, is to accept the premise that new operations and opportunities can be developed without IT support, when the old ones cannot be sustained without it! Therefore, management of IT investment has become a critical concern, because there are real risks associated with an inept organizational response to the rapid pace of developments in IT.

Information Architecture (IT)

The solution that emerged in the late 1980s to deal effectively with the rapid pace of change in IT was to build an *information architecture*—that is, to create a framework within which current as well as future organizational needs for information could be met with impunity from changing technology. The IS architect, however, must often pay dearly for the mistakes of the past. IS, like buildings and streets, have a tendency to grow haphazardly. As in a building, we do not like to break down an "outside wall," but if we cannot modify the inside walls to make the architecture useful for today's context (i.e., information needs), then there is no other choice. A well-planned information architecture should, as much as possible, obviate the need for the demolition of outside walls.[10]

Figure 10.1 depicts a model information architecture. It is based on providing infrastructures for communication integration as well as data integration on which the IT portfolio (i.e., the various application systems ranging from purchase order entry to research and development planning) would be developed.[11] Together, communication integration and data integration ensure that data are stored in a nonredundant fashion and that every authorized user can gain access to and update the required information from anywhere. These infrastructures must be provided to support the tactical deployment of IT, ensure that developing problems and opportunities can be addressed, and guarantee that catch-up time would be short and, thereby, little ground would be lost to a competitor who leads with an innovative business idea based on IT.

In addition, the above model emphasizes four application portfolios that mature IS would comprise:

1. *Institutional portfolio:* IS applications are directed at recording and reporting on business activities. Examples include transaction processing systems such as payroll, order entry, purchasing, production scheduling, and accounting IS.

2. *Professional support portfolio:* IS applications are directed at managerial problem solving and decision making, competitive intelligence, and personal productivity. Examples include critical success factor reporting systems, decision support systems, expert systems, and such tools as are used for document preparation, computer-based messaging, electronic meetings, and workgroup computing.

3. *Physical automation portfolio:* IS applications are directed at replacing manual work with IT, on the factory floor as well as in offices. Examples include computer-aided design and engineering, robotics, automated response units, and workflow automation.

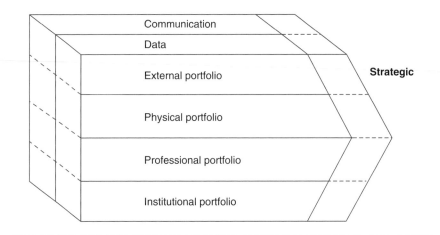

Figure 10.1   Model Information Architecture

4. *External portfolio:* IS applications are directed at linking the firm with its suppliers, customers, or other firms for the purpose of creating a strategic alliance. Examples include ERP, SCM, EDI, and interorganizational systems.

It is important to note that while the above model acknowledges that the application portfolios must address the information requirements at all levels of management, it neither assumes a particular hardware or software architectural platform nor advocates a centralized or decentralized approach to building the architecture. These choices are left to the eventual architect, who must fit the suggested architectural form to the specific context of the organization. The remainder of this chapter will use this model architecture as a backdrop to examine the ramifications of internationalization on IS architecture. However, because of the significant role that SCM, ERP, and EDI play in helping MNCs manage their worldwide operations, they are discussed subsequently.

Supply Chain Management

Supply chain management can be defined as the way a company finds the raw components it needs to make products or services, produces those products or services, and delivers them to customers. To have better SCM, most companies implement the following five basic steps.

1. *Plan:* Establish a plan to manage all the resources that go toward meeting customer demand for products or services.

2. *Source:* Choose the suppliers that will deliver the required components, materials, parts, or services. Also, develop a set of pricing, delivery, and

payment processes with suppliers and create measurements for monitoring and improving relationships with them. Then, put together processes for managing the inventory of goods and services that are received from suppliers, verifying them, transferring them to the manufacturing facilities, and authorizing payments.

3. *Make:* Schedule the activities necessary for production, testing, packaging, and preparation for delivery of the goods or provision of the services.

4. *Deliver:* Coordinate the receipt of orders from customers, develop a network of warehouses, select carriers to deliver the products to customers, and set up an invoicing system to receive payments.

5. *Return:* Create a network for receiving defective and excess products returned by customers and supporting customers who have problems with the delivered products (www.cio.com/research/scm/).

As an example, Wal-Mart has implemented a global SCM system. This system gives its major suppliers a complete view of the inventory position of their own products in each of Wal-Mart's stores. Therefore, Procter & Gamble can make Tide detergents and ship them to Wal-Mart's distribution centers based on the actual sales performance in stores. Or, similarly, a supplier in Taiwan can make DVD players and ship them to Wal-Mart as needed in what amounts to a vendor-managed inventory.

Enterprise Resource Planning

ERP's main objective is to attempt to integrate all departments and functions across a company onto a single computer system that can serve all those departments' particular needs—for example, building a single software program that serves the needs of people in the finance department as well as those of the human resources (HR) department and in warehousing. ERP creates a single, integrated system that runs on an enterprise-wide database, so that the various departments can more easily share information and communicate with each other. The integrated approach can have a tremendous payback once the organization adopts and adapts to the business processes implemented by the ERP software.

Each department typically has its own computer system optimized for the particular ways that the department operates. For instance, when a customer places an order, that order begins a mostly paper-based journey from one in-basket to another around the company, often being entered and reentered into different departments' computer systems. As a consequence, the repetition of the in-basket process and data entry causes delays and lost orders. All the data being entered into different computer systems invites errors. Meanwhile, no one in the company truly knows the status of the order at any given point, because there is no way for the finance department, for example, to get into the warehousing department's computer system to see whether or not the item has been shipped.

ERP replaces the old stand-alone computer systems in different departments with a single unified software system. The finance, manufacturing, and warehousing departments still have their own software, but now they are all linked together by an enterprise-wide integrated database. Consequently, people in the finance department can look into the warehousing records to see if an order has been shipped (www.erpcentral.com/,www.erpfans.com/).

General Motors, for example, uses ERP software to connect all its worldwide operations as well as its suppliers and dealers in a global network that permits sharing of up-to-the-minute information. An assembly plant in Atlanta, Georgia, for instance, knows exactly when it will receive body parts from the plant in Mexico and leather seat covers from China. It can also make adjustments if one of the suppliers runs into problems and faces delays.

Electronic Data Interchange

EDI[12-15] is the exchange of documents and information in standardized form between organizations in an automated manner directly from a computer application in one organization to an application in another. EDI's roots go back to the time of the Cold War. In 1948, for 1 year, the Soviet Union shut down access between Germany and the parts of Berlin that were controlled by the United States, England, and France. To deal with such a crisis, in 1949, a U.S. Army Master Sergeant, Edward A. Guilbert, and other officers developed a manifest system that could be transmitted by telex, radio-teletype, or telephone. By 1968, truckers, airlines, and ocean shipping companies were using electronic manifests and formed the Transportation Data Coordinating Committee (TDCC) to create cross-industry standards. In 1975, the TDCC published its first EDI standards.

Due to the wide range of benefits that EDI provides, it is increasingly becoming a preferred way of carrying out business transactions among trading partners. The following are some of the benefits of EDI.

- Higher processing speed, shorter turnaround time, and greater efficiency
- Less data reentry and transcription, less likelihood of error, and greater accuracy
- Lower cost and more convenience with less physical transportation of documents
- Less paper consumption due to electronic transmission and storage transactions

The automotive industry is a champion of EDI. By reducing the time taken to process orders, EDI has enabled cost savings through just-in-time management of automotive parts. Similarly, the transportation industry, which continuously exchanges routing and customs documents, has embraced EDI.

Ramifications of Internationalization
for the IS Function

The expansion of a company from a domestic corporation to a multinational one brings with it special challenges for the IS function. Consider the following ramifications of internationalization for the IS function:[16,17]

1. Although it is highly desirable to have common computer (e.g., PC) standards, local service issues and the level of support vary so widely that this seemingly straightforward issue becomes a complex one. The support and service issue notwithstanding, it may simply be overwhelmingly advantageous to improve government relationships by choosing a local brand even at the expense of the system integration problems that this may cause.

2. Although it is highly desirable to have system developers located physically close to the end users of the system being developed, the wide disparity between salaries abroad vis-à-vis the United States may make it overwhelmingly attractive to move portions of large development efforts overseas and risk coordination problems.

3. Expansion overseas also causes problems with scheduling and coordination. A business that crosses four time zones has 5 business hours that are supported in common by all portions of its operation, while one spanning more than eight time zones would have no common business hours at all. This shift in schedules can result in increased reliance on background transfers of information (such as e-mail), which do not require human interaction in real time.

4. Due to technological advances and the use of the Internet, communication costs are continuously decreasing. In general, however, communication costs increase with distance; this will hold true until the use of the Internet becomes universal. This creates an incentive to disperse data to reduce transmission costs, a strategy that can result in the loss of information control and increased security risks.

5. The use of personal data generates a wide range of sensitivities in different countries. What is seen as a consumer micromarketing information system in one country may be regarded as quite intrusive in another. Moreover, existing legislation regarding computer privacy, computer security, software licensing, and copyrights remains substantially fragmented among countries. The Internet, however, is rapidly forcing the international community to develop uniform standards.

6. Expansion into other countries also causes problems with language. Global IS must be designed to support people speaking different languages. Also, data entry as well as reporting programs must be written to accommodate different alphabets, printing directions (e.g., from

right to left instead of left to right), and collating sequences. Thus, in some countries, pages are sequenced and numbered from right to left.

7. In some countries, the installation of new telephone lines still requires a lead time of more than a year, making the planning and implementation of an adequately redundant (fault-tolerant) communication infrastructure a time-consuming ordeal.

8. Great disparities in local technical support exist between one country and another. This can lead to considerable reliance on the parent company for troubleshooting, for system development efforts, and for scanning emerging technologies that might affect the firm's operations.

As can be seen from the items listed above, the IT function, like all other functional areas, is considerably affected by internationalization. And like all other functional areas, its response to internationalization will be affected by country variables as well as company variables.

The IS Function Within the Multinational Corporation

Not surprisingly, MNCs have adopted different approaches for their IS functions. Some are centralized, some are decentralized, and some are distributed. Some are integrated but most are not.

There are several classifications of international IS. The following provides a useful starting categorization.

1. *Multinational information systems:* This most prevalent model is characterized by essentially autonomous data-processing centers in each nation-state in which the MNC operates. This approach suffers from problems of redundancy and duplication in data, applications, and operations. However, it historically represents the easiest solution available to the MNC given the conditions of national markets (i.e., regulations, language problems, facilities problems, etc., as we have discussed in previous chapters) that have encouraged the autonomy of business operations in each country.

2. *International information systems:* This model is characterized by a computer network that operates in more than one nation-state and in which data cross international borders in the process of completing a transaction. This model is now increasingly based on the Internet as its medium of data transfer.

3. *Global information systems:* This relatively new model is fundamentally characterized by the integration of data. Support for manufacturing operations that must coordinate inputs and outputs of plants located in different countries on a real-time basis has been one of several driving forces leading to the establishment of such systems.

Another impetus has been the desire to present a consistent face to a customer that may have dealings with the MNC in several countries in which it operates. However, only the recent advances in distributed database management and communication technologies have made this model a viable alternative.

Distance Is No Barrier

The new computer technology enables large corporate computing centers to serve multiple operations located in different geographic areas around the world. The computing services of global companies, however, must work within the limits of local communications capabilities. In Thailand, for example, when there was a lack of adequate data transmission and processing capabilities, Exxon-Mobil used satellites to transmit data from Bangkok to Houston for processing and back to Thailand. The distance that data had to travel from Bangkok to Houston and back added only about 1 s to the response time of the system, but it reduced computing costs at the Thailand facilities by 10%.

Telecommunications technology allows access to information regardless of the location, whether on ships at sea or at drilling rigs or production sites in remote places. With the use of modern telecommunications equipment, for example, Exxon-Mobil has been able to improve the quality and reduce the cost of ship-to-ship and ship-to-shore communications. The ships are connected to a satellite network, so they can receive and initiate instantaneous telecommunications, including voice, data, e-mail, and facsimile—just as if they were in a modern office building instead of being thousands of miles away from civilization in the middle of the ocean (based on Ref. 18).

It should be noted that the above three categories of IS follow the three strategies of host country focus, international, and global described in Chapter 6. The match between IS and strategies of MNCs is due to the fact that the information processing needs and, along with them, the IS design of MNCs vary. Decentralized MNCs will pursue independent IT operations in each country. A global or centralized firm, on the other hand, must create its IT configuration in a centralized manner.[19]

International IS Issues

IT is an important mechanism to facilitate, sustain, and promote international business. King and Sethi[20] and Keohane and Nye[21] have categorized international IS issues into intracorporate, intergovernmental, host government, and reactive international IS issues.

Intracorporate IS Issues

Intracorporate interactions provide the interface between the corporate unit (and its IS function) and its overseas subsidiary (and its IS function). In this category, there are two IS issues: (1) those pertaining to the IS function only and (2) those pertaining to the role of IS in supporting competitive strategy.

The issues pertaining only to the IS function emanate from the design of the *linkage* between the IS function at the corporate unit and the IS function in the overseas subsidiary. The linkages are of three types:

1. *Organizational linkage* design must address the organizational structure of IS at the subsidiary, its control systems and reporting procedures, and its participation in the IS function of the corporation as a whole. Both company-level variables and subsidiary-specific variables must be taken into account in designing the organizational linkage. The former includes the overall organizational structure and organizational strategy, while the latter involves the information dependency of the subsidiary, its importance (knowledge contribution), and its ownership.

2. *Architectural linkage* design must address the issues of communication integration, data integration, application portfolio, and hardware and software platforms. What is the desired level of connectivity? What is an acceptable level of standardization of codes (e.g., ethnic classification codes)? What is a tolerable level of redundancy in the databases? What is the desired degree of freedom in developing an application portfolio? And what is an acceptable level of incompatibility of equipment? The Internet has influenced all this. For this reason, at the end of this section, a brief discussion on the Internet is provided.

3. *Personnel linkage* design must address the functions of selection, staffing, appraisal, and compensation of IS personnel in subsidiaries. What is the appropriate mix of local employees, who speak the language and understand the culture and the political system, and expatriate employees, who can emphasize firmwide rather than local objectives?

The issues pertaining to the role of IS in supporting competitive strategy are influenced by industry-level variables as well as country-level variables. When MNCs in the same industry operate in the same countries, they cannot exploit comparative advantage sources (e.g., lower labor costs, raw material, etc., in one country vis-à-vis another). In such cases, the IS function must focus on maintaining firm-specific competitive advantage; for example, by transferring systems (such as order entry terminals placed at customer premises) that have created such an advantage in the home country to the host country. On the other hand, when similar MNCs operate in different countries, the IS function should focus its efforts on exploiting sources of comparative advantage.

Intergovernmental IS Issues

The interactions between the IS function and intergovernmental units are concerned with either technical issues or regulatory concerns. There are several benefits from user participation in standard-setting organizations such as the International Standards Organization (ISO). Perhaps the most important of such benefits is remaining closely informed of directions in open systems (i.e., nonproprietary) standards and technologies and assessing their impact on the corporation's IS infrastructure.

While developing coherent international standards is important for any IS function, a consistent pattern of international regulatory practices is a prerequisite to information transfers required by the global firm. As a result, we find that telecommunications and IS issues have been prominent at various international negotiations, including those sponsored by the World Trade Organization (WTO). Liberalization of global communications, in particular, can bring significant advantage to MNCs.

Host Government IS Issues

Issues pertaining to the interactions between the IS function and a host government emanate from an MNC's deployment of information technologies and the host government's reaction to it. These issues can be divided into four categories: (1) political, (2) economic, (3) technological, and (4) sociocultural.

1. Chief among the *political issues* is the concern for ownership and the sovereignty of a nation over its resources, including its information resources. IT, in the form of satellite communications, for example, can render national control of information ineffective. Similarly, it is, at times, feared that MNCs headquartered in developed countries can, through the use of IS and transborder data flow (TDF), remotely control the physical operations of their factories and potentially bring operations in a less developed country to a halt.

2. *Economic issues* have typically surfaced in the form of restrictive policies against the use of IS for fear of displacement or unemployment of workers. In addition, host government policies for the development of indigenous IS industries can force the MNCs' IS function into an unfavorable reliance on outsourcing in the host country and the deployment of less than optimal technologies.

3. *Technological issues* relate to host governments' IS-related policies regarding access to communication facilities and international networks. Host governments have a keen interest in IS through which technology transfer takes place.

4. *Sociocultural issues* deal with the stance of host governments on protecting the needs of the individual versus the needs of society. While there are no universal standards in maintaining a balance between the two, host governments often would like to see that an MNC's practices do not stir up opposition from groups or interests within the society.

Reactive International IS Issues

Often, national IS-related policies are formulated in response to changes in similar policies in other countries. These policies have an enduring impact on the IS functions of MNCs. As pointed out by the National Telecommunications and Information Administration (NTIA), "As direct beneficiaries or victims of many policy decisions, private firms have a critical stake in the nature and effectiveness of governmental decision making" (p. 25).[22] European policies on the development of standards for telecommunication services and equipment, for example, prompt corresponding decisions by the U.S. government, which in turn will have ramifications for MNCs operating in the United States.

In addition to the above four categories of IS issues, there are also intergovernment interactions as well as interactions between governments and intergovernmental bodies.[20] These interactions primarily translate into bilateral, regional, and multilateral negotiations regarding issues that directly or indirectly affect the IS function of MNCs. As an example, the North American Free Trade Agreement (NAFTA) includes computer and telecommunications service agreements to provide nondiscriminatory access, maintain existing rights of access, and limit anticompetitive practices, and it contains provisions for TDFs and access to data banks.

The Internet

The Internet is a revolutionary medium of information creation, manipulation, transmission, storage, and management that functions on a global scale. The origin of the Internet goes back to the 1960s and a daring scheme imagined by the technological warriors of the U.S. Defense Department (pp. 6–7).[23] Their aim was to prevent a Soviet takeover or destruction of American communications in the event of a nuclear war. Ultimately, the network set up by the Defense Department became the foundation for the Internet, a global, horizontal communication network of thousands of computer networks. The end result was a network architecture made up of thousands of autonomous computer networks that have innumerable ways to link up, going around electronic barriers. It is a highly flexible, self-healing, powerful medium that cannot be controlled from any center. It has been adopted for various purposes and uses, far removed from the now extinct Cold War concerns, by individuals, groups, and firms around the globe. It has spawned an industry that can be classified in four layers:

1. The first layer consists of the companies that provide the Internet infrastructure. The firms in this layer are telecommunications companies, Internet service providers, Internet backbone carriers, final access providers, and end-user networking manufacturing companies. Well-known firms such as Qwest, Corning, and Mindspring are in this group.

2. The second layer comprises the firms developing Internet infrastructure applications. These firms develop software products and services for Web transactions. Consulting and service companies designing, building, and maintaining Web sites, including portals, e-commerce sites, and audio and video delivery sites, are in this layer. Examples of companies in this layer are Oracle, Mirosoft, and Adobe.

3. The third layer is formed by companies that generate revenues not directly from business transactions on the Web but from advertising, commissions, and membership fees, in exchange for providing free services over the Web. Content providers and market intermediaries such as the news media, brokerage firms, resellers, portals, and other intermediaries are in this layer. They include such companies as Yahoo!, eBay, and E*TRADE.

4. The fourth layer consists of the companies that conduct Web-based economic transactions, such as Amazon, E-toys, Dell-Direct World, and The Street.com. *E-commerce* is the common term used for the business of these companies.

The Internet economy and the IT industries have become, qualitatively and quantitatively, the core of the U.S. economy. MNCs are among the major beneficiaries of the Internet. The Internet has enabled MNCs to coordinate geographically dispersed subsidiaries and activities economically.

With the advent of the Internet, more companies are able to expand their businesses through the development of Web sites where customers can easily download software, purchase products, obtain financial information, and get basic information. As a result, the responsibilities of corporate network managers are growing at a rapid pace. The ability to translate data into useful information, interpret it, and execute the necessary actions is important to managers. As a consequence, failure to do so regularly leads to loss of competitiveness.

The expansion and commercialization of the Internet is reshaping the roles of IS managers and IS/IT departments. Increasingly, IS and network executives are playing crucial roles in their employers' strategic business activities, gradually making IS organizations central to their companies' ongoing success.[24]

Global IS Management

The model presented in the previous section provides one means by which to organize and discuss issues pertinent to global IS management. Another approach is to undertake an empirical study to identify and rank important global IS management issues for MNCs. Two such studies will be summarized in this section.

In one study, the top IS executives of U.S.-based MNCs identified and ranked important global IS management issues.[25] They identified "educating senior personnel on the role and potential of the contribution of MIS on an international scale" as the most important issue and "export restrictions on data processing equipment and software" as the least important issue at the time of the study. Although such rankings of issues are clearly of interest, more insight is offered by classifying the issues of concern to IS executives as being in the domestic or the international arena.

Based exclusively on the rankings of the 32 issues in the study, 14 are international IS issues and 18 are domestic concerns. Of the issues that pertain solely to operating in an international arena, technological issues, such as "international protocol standards," dominate both political issues, such as "transborder data flow restrictions," and cultural concerns, such as "learning to conduct business in other countries." Those, in turn, dominate economic issues, such as "export restrictions."

Similarly, researchers have identified eight important IT management issues:[26] (1) IT transfer, (2) cultural differences, (3) international standards, (4) IT infrastructure, (5) global IT applications, (6) global IT policy, (7) global IT marketing, and (8) TDF.

The IS executives of U.S.-based MNCs considered two of the eight issues to be of most concern to them. The two issues were TDF (restrictions on the flow of data, data security vulnerabilities, and telecommunications management) and the lack of international standards (in telecommunications, software development, and computer architecture). Both TDF and the lack of international standards underline a very important issue of national security that is discussed below.

IS Security

The information explosion, including the use of the Internet, has been a boon to both big and small businesses. The use of the Internet has drastically reduced the cost of global business transactions. Outsourcing through the Internet and the availability of cheap communication services have benefited all businesses. For example, VoIP (voice over the Internet protocol), such as Skype or Vonage, substituting for regular phone services, has reduced the cost of international telecommunication, especially for otherwise heavy users of regular phone services. The information explosion has also made it easier for various groups to engage in terrorism. This adversely affects international business and poses serious questions regarding activities that involve cross-border transactions. Security of the electronic media drew the attention of scholars and the police many years ago when criminals started using them illegally. Recently, however, the illegal use of electronic information has become a national security issue.

Prior to the tragedy of September 11, 2001, almost all illegal activities on the Internet either had purely criminal profit-making origins or were acts of vandalism. Very seldom were abuses of the Internet for other purposes. Even then, while it was difficult to determine the purpose, we were reasonably sure that there were no terrorist motives behind them. For example, computer viruses that are plaguing the Internet were around even before the recent waves of terrorism.

After the tragedy of September 11, we have learned that securing the Internet and providing for safe international business transactions, through the use of secure IS, would be a very difficult task. Also, we have learned that we can use IT to thwart terrorist actions. For example, experts have proposed measures for the safety of the logistic supply chain.[27]

Terrorists, it has been suggested, may secretly use multitudes of containers going through various U.S. ports. In one of these containers, a weapon of mass destruction could enter the country undetected. To prevent such an act of terrorism, the application of radio-frequency identification (RFID) has been proposed. RFID devices can be used to electronically detect the closing and opening of a container or a trailer. As such, RFID can provide for continuous monitoring and tracking of the location of inbound shipments while in transit. It can electronically record and report any tampering with a container or trailer. However, the lack of worldwide standards for RFID is an impediment to its use.[28] The lack of global standards for RFID makes it less effective. It is also very costly, and it is impossible to construct a globally useful system. Therefore, the future of container security, according to experts, lies in a satellite solution, which by its nature avoids the limitations and infrastructure costs of a land-based system.

The preceding discussion points out the similarities between IT issues in both the domestic and the international arenas. In the next section, we present a guideline for building a global information system that addresses these issues.

Building a Global Information System

The challenge of setting up an information system spanning continents is no longer limited to the very large companies. The number of firms operating internationally—for production, distribution, or some other business function—is growing. The evidence indicates that multinational firms are earning more, and growing faster, than firms without global operations. The IS directors of the firms venturing into foreign markets quickly realize that the challenges faced by IS range from the broadest organizational issues to the most detailed programming dilemmas.[29]

Express delivery companies are using the Internet to offer better services. They are trying to integrate an online customer service technology with other SCM operations. DHL, FedEx, and UPS initially permitted customers to book shipments electronically, but now with the Internet, these companies are implementing new tools that provide accessibility to a wide range of software packages such as DHL Connect and DHL EasyShip. DHL EasyShip is targeted to meet the needs of high-volume customers. It can be installed across a shipper's network for multiuser access and shipment data transfer from the shipper's own system. Similarly, FedEx has launched a Web site called FedEx Insight where customers can create a customized view of shipment information, and they can also request detailed information about shipping events. UPS is making some changes as well. It expanded the international availability of an option to download its OnLine Tools Application from the Web. It has also teamed up with PayPal, an Internet payment service, to completely integrate the online payment process with digital tools. OnLine Tools enables companies to seamlessly integrate UPS shipping functions, such as tracking and rates, and service selection into their own Web sites, avoiding jumps from one Web site to another.[30]

Esprit's Experience

The clothing manufacturer Esprit de Corp, in San Francisco, found out the hard way that sharing software on a global basis does not always work according to plan. Faced with problems, Esprit's U.S. subsidiary adopted a production management system developed at the company's Far East affiliate. The software would track where an item was manufactured, sewn, pressed, and so on. But the software was only a moderate success in the United States because the ways of doing business are quite different in the two hemispheres. Similar to the experiences of virtually all major corporations that do business overseas, Esprit ran into a wall. It found that despite good intentions and the apparent benefits, sharing software across borders is not always the best choice. Work habits around the world are different.

Although many companies are going global and IS groups are under increasing pressure to maximize technology investments, seasoned IS experts say that not all software can or should be common everywhere. In the Far East, for example, it is standard for the shop sewing a garment to handle the other steps of finishing and washing it. In the United States, however, convention dictates that the individual steps be contracted out to different parties.

For Esprit, the end result was that the system that Hong Kong put together lacked features that would allow the U.S. operations to manage effectively the transition from factory to factory. Consequently, Esprit's U.S. Group abandoned software sharing with overseas units.[31]

When Federal Express expanded outside the United States, the cultural nuances of billing resulted in revisions of their billing system. In Britain, customers do not pay from an invoice but from a statement sent after the invoice. In Japan, the invoicing protocol calls for invoices to be sent within a specific time period after the sale and to have a specific format.

When the bicycle and race-car helmet maker Bell Sports began exporting to Europe, the IS staff back in its Rantoul, Illinois, factory ran headfirst into European safety regulations requiring statements on packages and labels inside helmets. To efficiently get the right labels on the right helmets, the IS department had to rewrite portions of its material requirement planning II (MRP-II) system (an inventory control method).

When Ikea, a large home-furnishing company from Sweden, opened its first U.S. store, the IS department had to make a variety of modifications to their store systems. For example, the IS staff had to do some "keyboard mapping" to allow the U.S. staff to prepare reports with umlauts. Also, report programs had to be adjusted to deal with American-sized paper stock. More important, however, order entry/billing programs had to be rewritten so that American customers could arrange to have furniture shipped to their homes. In Europe, the shipping company takes ownership of the order, and customers pay the shipper cash on delivery. In the United States, these procedures were unacceptable, and the programs had to be rewritten to accommodate payment in advance of delivery.

As the preceding examples illustrate, building a global information system presents a variety of challenges for the IS manager. Nevertheless, the experience of successful companies indicates that one key to success stands out: Global operation demands global information, which in turn calls for a global infrastructure in planning, data integration, communication, and information resource management.

Planning Globally

Because of the wide geographical distances separating MNCs' global divisions from their headquarters and from each other, IS play a critical role in strategic planning, implementation, and control of MNCs. Therefore, taking a reactive approach to building a global information architecture is nothing less than accepting a position of competitive defensiveness or, possibly, competitive disadvantage.[32] Nevertheless, as several studies have indicated, most senior managers do not have a clear and personal business vision for IT. To help relate business integration and technology integration, Keen[32] suggests a framework that defines the business functionality of the firm's IT facilities in terms of the two dimensions of *reach* and *range* (see Table 10.1).

In this framework, *reach* (vertical axis) determines the six locations the firm can link to: (1) locations within a single site, (2) the entire domestic operation, (3) locations abroad, (4) customers and suppliers domestically, (5) customers and suppliers internationally, and (6) anyone, anywhere.

Table 10.1   Relating Business Functionality to Data and Communication Integration

Reach Whom?	Range (What Services Can We Deliver?)			
	Standard Messages	Access to Stored Data	Single Transactions	Cooperative Transactions
Anyone, anywhere				
Customers, suppliers, regardless of IT base				
Customers, suppliers, with the same IT base				
Intracompany locations, abroad				
Intracompany locations, domestic				
Intracompany locations, single site				

The *range* (horizontal axis) determines the nature of the information that can be shared directly across systems: (1) standard messages, (2) ad hoc access to data, (3) arbitrary single transactions to be completed by one party (node), and (4) cooperative transactions to be completed by several nodes.

Reach and *range* together determine the extent of business options available to the firm. In Table 10.1, for example, the shaded cells in the bottom row signify an integrated database within a single site allowing various departments to share and update common data, while the absence of shading in the next to last row depicts the inability to process updated transactions from remote locations even within the same country. Therefore, the *reach* and *range* framework serves to translate the IT integration issues for senior management as *what option is implied by our business plans?* A firm may opt to build an enterprise-wide totally integrated IT infrastructure aiming for the maximum in *reach* and *range*. To do so, it needs to consider a variety of issues. One issue is the extent of the firm's centralization. In general, it is easier to put in place the rules and constraints of a global IT infrastructure when a corporate culture for centralization exists. Another issue is the availability of capital.

E-Commerce

E-commerce has evolved from the practice of conducting basic transactions on the Web to a complete retooling of the way partners, suppliers, and customers transact. Today, you can link dealers and suppliers online, thus reducing both lag time and paperwork. Procurement can be managed online by setting up an extranet that links directly to vendors. This cuts inventory-carrying costs and makes the firm more responsive to customers. Financial relationships with customers and suppliers can be streamlined by Web-enabling billing and payment systems.

There are enormous advantages in using Internet technology to improve relationships with customers and suppliers. The advantages are more efficiency, better services, and improved relationships. Most companies enlist the assistance of a resourceful IT partner that enables them to integrate with any of their business partners. The IT partner can provide the firm with IT solutions that have built-in flexibility in features such as content management, order management, dynamic pricing and payment, and international trading capabilities.

Increasingly, success means being first to the market. Therefore, a firm that engages in e-commerce needs options, such as outsourcing and hosting capabilities. More than ever before, customers expect and employees require access to the information anytime, anyplace. This means customized information that is tailored to a range of devices such as PDAs (personal digital assistants), mobile phones, and so on. Internet technologies enable the firms to effectively respond to these demands.[33]

Because most companies are not well centralized or awash in capital, they must rely on multiple IT architectures (each signifying a different combination of *reach* and *range*) rather than the ideal totally integrated (global) infrastructure. These multiple IT architectures are too often determined first by geography and then by function. Unfortunately, such a traditional approach usually proves counterproductive, simply because a decision in one area of the organization quite often affects other areas. A better alternative is to take a business process perspective. This means viewing a business in terms of major processes such as order fulfillment and customer service rather than functional areas. The business process perspective enables us to overcome geographical boundaries in planning for IS in a global concern.

Communication Integration in the Global Organization

Regardless of the number of business processes that a firm chooses to support with a global IT architecture, there will be a substantial cost associated with establishing and maintaining the requisite communication infrastructure. It would be a serious mistake to assume that the only difference between building a global network and building a domestic one is a matter of size.

Global communications networks, like their domestic counterparts, can provide both internal and external benefits to the firm. Internally, a global network can, at the very least, improve management control by facilitating communication among international business units and, at best, support an online, real-time, integrated database for transaction processing as well as managerial decision making worldwide. Digital Equipment Corporation, for example, reports that its global computer network helped it save $700 million in inventory-related costs over a 2-year period by increasing control over the movement of inventory between its worldwide manufacturing plants.[34]

Externally, a global network can be used to advance a company's competitive strategy. Federal Express's global network connects the U.S. network with more than 60 subsidiaries worldwide to implement the company's differentiation strategy based on real-time tracking of packages. Marriott and Scandinavian Airlines have linked their global networks to create an interorganizational system focused on providing added value (convenience) to a shared customer by checking in customers' luggage for a flight at the hotel reception desk. Despite such benefits, global networks are far from widespread for the following reasons: (1) the high costs involved, (2) the existence of politically imposed constraints, and (3) technical problems.[35]

The costs of global networks can be substantial for a combination of reasons, including the following:

1. The telephone service in other countries is considerably more expensive than in the United States.

2. Lower speeds of transmission lines in other countries mean more time spent for data transmission.

3. The cost of transmission may vary depending on the direction of data flow. For example, it costs four times as much to send data to the United States from Portugal as it does to send it in the opposite direction.[36]

4. The arrangements between telephone companies for handling international calls are based on cost sharing at each end of the link. The formulae penalize the low-cost U.S. carriers by paying, on average, 75% of the call charge to the high-cost foreign PTT (Poste Telegraphe et Telephonique). In the case of Brazil, 99 cents on each dollar of telephone charge from the United States to Brazil is paid to the Brazilian PTT.[32]

5. The PTTs are government or quasi-government monopolies for telecommunications and are very unwilling to break up their cartels, which, in turn, have controlled international telephone pricing and revenue sharing.[32]

The high costs associated with global networks are compounded by the political constraints imposed on TDF. Although some of the TDF regulation problems encountered by multinational corporations increase the cost of communication between parents and their subsidiaries, their real impact is to create a control *barrier*.[16] Examples of such barriers include the following:

- Required use of locally manufactured data-processing equipment, communication services, and software
- Restrictions on the availability of flat-rate leased lines
- Restrictions on satellite transmission, for example, to receiving data only
- Required processing of certain data locally
- Restrictions on the flow of data across national borders—for example, restriction of the export of personnel-related data
- Threat of a tax on the value of data

To deal with such TDF regulations, multinational companies can resort to one or more of the following strategies:[16]

1. Decentralization of data processing on a geographic basis

2. Preprocessing of data to filter out restricted information

3. Alternative information channels to move data to the parent company

4. Database duplication and reprocessing at the parent company to obtain the desired level of reporting and control

In addition to the high costs and political constraints associated with building global networks, there are technical problems involving the quality of services and operability that must also be overcome. Simply stated, to build an efficient global network, a company must be prepared to mix a variety of technologies and deal with compatibility issues.

In Europe, the integrated services digital network (ISDN) and cable modem are widely deployed to provide basic access to two full-duplex 64-kbps (kilobits per second) channels from the desktop. Most PTTs also offer a primary rate interface consisting of thirty 64-kbps channels capable of handling digitized voice, video, and/or data. (The definition for the primary rate interface differs in the United States and signifies twenty-three 64-kbps channels.)

As in Europe, most major cities in the United States currently offer ISDN and cable modem. Bell Atlantic (Philadelphia), Bell South (Atlanta), Pacific Bell (San Francisco), and U.S. West (Denver) are leading contenders in the deployment of ISDN. Although service offerings vary according to carrier, most services are aggressively priced. Therefore, it may not be unreasonable to expect that despite the current clamor over frame relay and asynchronous transfer mode (ATM) technologies, a great deal of telecommunications traffic between U.S. multinationals and their subsidiaries in Europe will traverse the ISDN. Where ISDN is not an option, traditional analog lines or digital lines (T-1 services operating at 1.5 million bps) or fiber-optic connections (OC-1 services operating at 45 million bps) can provide the needed connectivity even across oceans.

Digital subscriber line (DSL) has surged ahead of its rival technologies, cable modem and ISDN. DSL means high-speed Internet access up to

100 times faster than today's dial-up modems. With this new Internet connection, people can share an Internet connection across all the computers in an office or home. Besides the fast rate of data transfer, DSL has other benefits as well. The user, for example, can leave the connection open and still use the phone line for voice calls; DSL uses the same wires as a regular phone line, and the company that provides the services will supply the user with the modem as part of the installation.[37,38]

Then, of course, there are those situations where a company's only reliable means of data communication is through a wireless medium. Very small aperture terminal (VSAT) satellite networks have had the same major impact on data communication as PCs have had on computing. And it is expected that wireless networks, both spread-spectrum radio frequency and infrared, will provide a pathway in those places where a company must have a wireless link or no link at all.

Reebok Tracks Athletes

To track more than 1,000 athletes around the world, Reebok uses Lotus Notes. These athletes' endorsements of its products constitute the heart of Reebok's promotional campaign. With Lotus Notes, a groupware application, Reebok maintains a global database of the results of their endorsements. These endorsements constitute a major investment in terms of payments to the athletes, which needs to be tracked and compared with product sales. Also tied into this system is the legal department that is attempting to standardize endorsement contracts. Similarly, the company's transaction-processing systems use the Notes database for near-real-time reporting of the results of promotional activities around the world.

At Reebok, both regional and global specifications and standards are used in designing various products. With the help of Notes, Reebok designers can work collaboratively while serving their local markets. Notes enables designers to disseminate digitalized drawings and textual communications among all the company's design centers.[39]

Data Integration in the Global Organization

To understand the data integration issue, consider a global company that has determined order fulfillment to be its strategically important pacing process to be globally supported. Among other things, integrating these functions requires that information about stock availability be accessible from any of its business units around the world, and even though the customer's order has to be fulfilled by shipments from several sites, the customer is presented with a single invoice, and information about the customer is entered only once. To accomplish such data integration, a company has several alternatives.

Centralized database, centralized processing: In this approach, the database for order fulfillment resides in one location, and all processing takes place in that location, with remote sites acting as online data entry/update terminal nodes. This is similar to the traditional mainframe/dumb terminal computing model.

Centralized database, decentralized processing: A significant problem with the above alternative is that the centralized facility must be powerful enough to accommodate hundreds, or even thousands, of online terminals. In the centralized database/decentralized processing approach, although the database remains centralized, all the processing, including the handling of issues related to concurrent update of shared data and backup and recovery, takes place at remote computers. This is similar to the local area network computing model.

Centralized database, distributed processing: There are two problems with Alternative 2. First, because each remote computer must run the database management software as well as the order fulfillment application, there is still considerable computing power required of each node. Second, because the database is centralized, each remote query for, say, worldwide stock availability for a particular item requires the *entire* stock file to be transmitted to the remote site for processing the request.

In the centralized database/distributed processing approach, the order fulfillment program is broken into two components: database management system (DBMS) and user interface issues. The DBMS issues of concurrency control, backup, and recovery, as well as searching the database to retrieve or update records matching specific criteria, are delegated to the *server* component of the program, while the user interface issues of displaying data and accepting keyboard input or responding to mouse movements are handled by the *client* component. Therefore, in our example, a remote query to obtain the worldwide stock availability for a particular item is obtained by *the client program* from the user, which in turn forwards the query in a standard format such as SQL (structured query language) to *the server program*, which processes the request and transmits only that *portion* of the stock file related to the requested item to *the client program* to display it for the user. This is similar to the centralized client/server computing model.

Distributed database, distributed processing: A basic shortcoming of Alternative 3 is the absence of fault tolerance. That is, should anything go wrong with the centralized database, all database access and processing comes to a halt.

In the distributed database/distributed processing approach, the database is logically and physically partitioned. For example, each site will have its own stock file, and the customer file is divided (nonredundantly) among the various sites. As a result, there will be no single point of failure. Queries about enterprise-wide stock availability for a particular item are handled in a *location-transparent* manner by the underlying distributed DBMS. Distributed DBMS software such as Oracle and DB2 support such a distributed client/server computing model.

Global Operation Demands Global Information

"If you're really going to compete on a global scale, you'll think of your manufacturing or processing plants as one, and you'll move your capacity around the world," explains Tobey Choate, Vice President and Managing Director of IT at the consultancy Arthur D. Little in Cambridge, Massachusetts.

"You'll think of your (entire) customer base as one, and you must have a fairly uniform and detailed level of information to do that. If you're using the same manufacturing (information) system world-wide, you will get the same information, which will allow you to manage that capacity worldwide."

Most companies today do business internationally, but few have stepped up to the challenge of real globalization, according to Alan C. Stanford, National Director of IT Consulting in Ernst & Young's Chicago office. "They don't operate globally in that they do not coordinate between their (international business) units. They certainly don't align their business processes."[40,41]

Heterogeneous database processing: All the preceding alternatives assume either that the organization is initiating data processing operations at remote sites or that it is willing to scrap existing computing arrangements and reengineer them for the sake of supporting its strategically important pacing process. However, in those circumstances when a company acquires subsidiaries with established data processing and a dissimilar DBMS environment, an interim solution would be to create a heterogeneous distributed database processing environment. It is possible to create a conceptual model of the overall database and allow users and programs to formulate their requests for enterprise-wide information against this view while translating each request, behind the scenes, into a collection of cooperating transactions against various DBMs at different sites. The advent of XML (extensible markup language) allows information between disparate systems to be exchanged.

In general, retrofitting existing application systems in various countries to create a single system is more difficult than starting with a clean slate, but it is best to decide on a case-by-case basis.

The IS Application Portfolio in the Global Organization

The cardinal rule in deciding which IS applications should be made global is that not every application needs to be a global application. Accounting and payroll systems are best left to local developers and maintenance programmers. Countries such as France impose a statutory chart of accounts,[41] and each country has its own taxation laws and its own version of the United States' Internal Revenue Service with reporting forms such as the W-2, 1099, and so forth. Therefore, it is a good rule of thumb not to globalize government reporting applications. Nevertheless, there still remains a requirement for the consolidation of financial results as well as performance comparisons across subsidiaries, which must be met by developing global applications.

As already pointed out, the decision as to which applications must be supported by a global architecture must emanate from global planning for IT. A company must start with its global strategy and identify those applications that are critical to its success. Those applications then comprise the company's initial global IS portfolio.

The traditional portfolio development has followed a chronological sequence of systems development and has moved from transaction processing to management reporting, decision support executive information, and finally, workflow IS. It is interesting to note that a company's IS department might find it easier to pursue the development of a global portfolio in the reverse chronological order (Table 10.2).

That is, it appears that a greater chance of success exists if the IS department were to first bring electronic messaging and workgroup computing to the global organization. Next, it could target the development of a global executive information system that does not have to deal with the more difficult problems of providing ad hoc access to, or update of, databases. At that point, the company can move into global decision support systems that

Table 10.2   Traditional Versus Global IS Portfolio Development Order

Traditional IS Portfolio Development Order

Transaction processing systems
  Management reporting systems
    Decision support systems
      Executive information systems
        Workflow information systems

Global IS Portfolio Development Order

Workflow information systems
  Executive information systems
    Decision support systems
      Management reporting systems
        Transaction processing systems

can employ historical data as well as more or less predefined snapshots of present databases. Next, it could support ad hoc access to enterprise-wide data for reporting purposes, which would, at a minimum, require the development of a conceptual model of the organization-wide integrated database. Finally, it can begin addressing the rewriting of applications to support cooperative transaction processing and the real-time update of data at multiple sites.

Programming for International Use

When writing a program to be used by an international audience, a variety of adjustments need to be made. Language on screen and on reports needs to be translated often to character strings longer than the English equivalent, and language-sensitive input needs to be modified. For example, if a "Yes" or "No" input is needed, expecting a *Y* or *N* will not work in France, as *Oui* does not start with a *Y*. The basic program design rule is to place all constant input and output strings outside the program in a language-specific data file.

There are also other problems. Some non-European languages such as Chinese and Japanese require special video support since they use double-byte character sets. Other languages, such as Thai, use multibyte character sets; sometimes it takes one byte to get the character on screen, and at other times it may take as many as three bytes. Then, there are the Middle Eastern languages such as Arabic, Persian, and Hebrew, which are written from right to left. And in the case of Arabic and Persian, the shape of a letter depends on its position in the written word (first, middle, last, or by itself).

Currency formats and date formats need to become country specific too. And an important decision must be made regarding at which stage in a transaction currencies are exchanged.

Redefining the CIO as the Global Information Officer

The operational requirements of a truly global organization significantly increase the difficulties faced by its CIO. IT investment and coordination issues for multinational corporations are vastly more complex than for purely domestic ones, involving not only the domestic issues but also the additional difficulties discussed in this chapter. As a global information officer (GIO), the CIO's responsibilities and performance expectations are transformed—both quantitatively and qualitatively.

What are the salient attributes of an effective GIO? Let us begin with those characteristics that one would expect to find in any CIO regardless of the global scope of his or her responsibilities. First, the CIO must provide the necessary guidance for developing an information architecture. On the one hand, this requires an in-depth understanding of information technologies: hardware and software platforms, telecommunications and networking strategies, centralized and distributed database management, open systems standards, and end-user computing tools and practices. On the other hand, it requires experience in managing IS personnel and the ability to administer complex, multifaceted projects. Second, the CIO must be especially responsive to evolving user requirements and changing corporate strategy. This requires staying informed about the business and operational requirements of the firm and positioning IS to respond to evolving needs quickly. Third, the CIO cannot afford to be hands-on all the time, and thus, the actual running of networks and data centers must be delegated to others. This, of course, requires effective delegation skills.

What is needed to transform the CIO to a GIO involves more managerial skills than technical expertise. The effective GIO must master how to manage the distributed resources of the parent company and its acquisitions to align the company's IS with its strategic plan and, in doing so, address, to the extent possible, the cultural differences, language issues, business practice variations, and technology limitations of the various host countries.

Kanter and Kesner[42] identify the following as six critical success factors for the effective GIO: management style and leadership, organization and structure of the IT function, skill base, commitment to TQM (total quality management), openness to outsourcing, and technology transfer along with change implementation. It should not be surprising that the leadership qualities vital to the success of a GIO are identical to those expected from any executive officer. They include the following: (1) strategic focus, (2) flexibility in addressing tactical issues, (3) people- as well as task-oriented project management style, (4) the ability to delegate and manage through others, (5) ruling through consensus, and (6) a team approach to problem solving.

To be effective, the GIO and the IT function must be appropriately positioned within the larger organization. This means that the GIO must report to the chief executive officer and be an equal member in the top management team that deals with components of corporate strategy.

The effective GIO must have a comprehensive knowledge of the corporation, its products and services, its functional requirements, and its business processes. The GIO must understand the ramifications of emerging information technologies on the corporation and be on the lookout for disruptive technologies that can redefine the competitive marketplace. The GIO must have an understanding of the different countries and cultures in which the corporation operates to factor in the impact of the work ethics and motivation levels of people of different nationalities in optimizing global IS projects.

In a world of time-based competition, where a late system project directly affects the bottom line, the effective GIO must implement and enforce a TQM program within the IT function to ensure that projects are done right the first time. Viewing software as an engineered product subject to quality assurance and market acceptance and viability is the fundamental cultural change that such a commitment brings to the IT function.

Instead of relying entirely on in-house solutions, the effective GIO practices the wisdom of outsourcing for specific expertise or relying on the cooperation of hardware and software vendors.

Finally, the effective GIO must facilitate the discovery of appropriate new technologies; fund pilot projects; and for those that look promising, serve as the change agent for successfully implementing them in the organization.

Summary

Technological changes and innovations affect all aspects of our lives and the conduct of business, locally and globally. No technological change has had as profound an impact in a short time on modern enterprise as the advent of computers and telecommunications. The ability to send, receive, process, and otherwise manage an immense amount of information enables MNCs to exercise closer control over their foreign subsidiaries. IS management can be used not only to enhance internal operations but also to create a competitive advantage. Instantaneous information exchange among MNCs' worldwide operations drastically reduces geographical distances and brings dispersed subsidiaries closer to one another. While IS decrease the barriers to centralization, they also create opportunities for decentralization. The constant flow of information between MNCs' headquarters and their subsidiaries empowers them to operate more locally and at the same time allows their headquarters to formulate strategies globally.

Discussion Questions

1. Why is IS management critical to MNCs?

2. How do the information needs of MNCs differ from those of domestic firms?

3. What are the ramifications of internationalization of the firm on the function of its IS?

4. MNCs have adopted different IS functions. Elaborate on the reason(s) for the differences.

5. Describe intracompany IT issues.

6. Describe intergovernment IT issues.

7. Describe host country IT issues.

8. Elaborate on the internal and external benefits of communication integration to the MNCs.

9. What is supply chain management, and how can MNCs benefit from it?

10. What is enterprise resource planning, and how can MNCs benefit from it?

11. Explain how the Internet has influenced MNC operations.

12. The Internet has spawned an industry that can be classified in four layers. What are the four layers?

13. MNCs have different options for data integration. Briefly describe these options and explain the reason for their use.

14. What are the differences between the roles of chief information officer and global information officer?

Note

a. The substantive contributions of Soheil Rezai, CEO of SolutiaNet, Inc., are gratefully acknowledged.

References

1. L. H. Harrington (1997, April). The information challenge. *Industry Week, 246*(7), 97.

2. R. Mullin (2002, June). Rohm and Haas connects the dots. *Chemical Week, 164*(24), 24. (Rohm and Haas Web site www.rohmandhaas.com)

3. B. Schmitt (2002, July). Rohm and Haas expands capacity in Brazil. *Chemical Week, 164*(28), 30.

4. R. Mullin (2001, August). Top management keeps on top of IT. *Chemical Week, 163*(31), 22.

5. J. A. Senn (1990). *Information systems in management.* Belmont, CA: Wadsworth.

6. V. Zwass (1992). *Management information systems.* Dubuque, IA: Wm. C. Brown.

7. R. H. Sprague Jr. & B. C. McNurlin (1993). *Information systems management in practice.* Englewood Cliffs, NJ: Prentice Hall.

8. W. R. King & V. Sethi (1999, Spring). An empirical assessment of the organization of transnational information systems. *Journal of Management Information Systems, 145*(4), 7–28.

9. S. Roach (1985). *The new technology cycle.* New York: Morgan Stanley.

10. J. Kanter (1986). *Computer essays for management.* Englewood Cliffs, NJ: Prentice Hall.

11. D. T. Mckay & D. W. Brockway (1989). Building IT infrastructure for the 1990s. *Stage by Stage, 9*(31), 1–11.

12. J. Damsgaard & K. Lyytinen (2001). The role of intermediating institutions in the diffusion of electronic data interchange (EDI): How industry associations intervened in Denmark, Finland, and Hong Kong. *The Information Society, 17,* 196.

13. E. X. DeJesus (2001). EDI? XML? Or both. *Computerworld, 35*(2), 54.

14. F. Hayes (2002). The story so far. *Computerworld, 36*(25), 24.

15. B. Marchal (2003). Electronic data interchange on the internet. Retrieved January 16, 2003, from http://developer.netscape.com/viewsource/marchal_edata.htm

16. P. C. Deans & M. J. Kane (1992). *International dimensions of information systems and technology.* Boston: PWS-Kent.

17. F. W. McFarlan (1992). Multinational CIO challenge for the 1990s. In S. Palvia, P. Palvia, & R. M. Zigli (Eds.), *The global issues of information technology management* (pp. 484–493). Harrisburg, PA: Idea Group.

18. D. A. Zwicker (1993). The information age. *The Lamp (Exxon Corporation), 75*(4), 9–12.

19. S. L. Jarvenpaa & B. Ives (1993, May–June). Organizing for global competition: The fit of information technology. *Decision Sciences, 24*(3), 547–580.

20. W. R. King & V. Sethi (1992). A framework for transnational systems. In S. Palvia, P. Palvia, & R. M. Zigli (Eds.), *The global issues of information technology management* (pp. 214–248). Harrisburg, PA: Idea Group.

21. R. O. Keohane & J. S. Nye Jr. (1972). *Transnational relations and world politics.* Cambridge, MA: Harvard Business School Press.

22. National Telecommunications and Information Administration (1988). *Long range goals in international telecommunications and information: An outline for U.S. policy* (Committee Print, S. Prt. 98-22). Washington, DC: Author.

23. M. Castells (2000). *The rise of the network society.* Oxford, UK: Blackwell.

24. S. Girishankar (1996, April). MIS: Getting to know the Net. *Communications Week*, No. 606, p. 1.

25. P. C. Deans, K. R. Karwan, M. D. Goslar, D. A. Ricks, & B. Toyne (1991, Spring). Identification of key international information systems issues in U.S.-based multinational corporations. *Journal of Management Information Systems, 7*(4), 27–50.

26. S. Palvia & S. Saraswat (1992). Information technology and transnational corporations: The emerging multinational issues. In S. Palvia, P. Palvia, & R. M. Zigli (Eds.), *Global issues of information technology management* (pp. 554–574). Harrisburg, PA: Idea Group.

27. J. Giermanski (2006). Boxing clever. *Cargo Security International, February–March,* 40–44.

28. J. Giermanski (2006). RFID is not the one. *Cargo Security International, August–September,* 52–55.

29. A. E. Alter (1992, December). International affairs. *CIO, 6*(5), 34–42.

30. P. Hastings (2002, October 2). Global operators develop tools to help bring it all together. *Financial Times*, p. VIII.

31. J. Ambrosio (1993, August 2). Global software? *Computerworld,* 74–75.

32. P. G. W. Keen (1992). Planning globally: Practical strategies for information technology in the transnational firm. In S. Palvia, P. Palvia, & R. M. Zigli (Eds.), *The global issues of information technology management* (pp. 575–607). Harrisburg, PA: Idea Group.

33. E-Commerce (2002). Retrieved December 14, 2002, from www-3.ibm.com/e-business/overview/28210.html

34. W. A. Hall & R. E. McCauley (1987, December). Planning and managing a corporate network utility. *MIS Quarterly, 11*(4), 437–447.

35. P. J. Steinbart & R. Nath (1992, March). Problems and issues in the management of international communications networks: The experiences of American companies. *MIS Quarterly, 16*(1), 55–76.

36. D. O. Case & J. H. Ferreira (1990, August). Portuguese telecommunications and information technologies: Development and prospects. *Telecommunication Policy, 14*(4), 290–302.

37. R. Clark & V. Lewis (2002). DSL: The next generation. *Telecom Corporate, April,* 34–36.

38. J. Fausch (2002, June). A bright future for DSL. *Business Communication Review, 32*(6), 15.

39. M. Williamson (1994, June). Uniting nations. *CIO, 7*(16), 55–63.

40. M. Williamson (1994, June). World travelers. *CIO, 7*(16), 67–69.

41. M. Williamson (1994, June). Becoming a world power. *CIO, 7*(16), 40–52.

42. J. Kanter & R. Kesner (1992). The CIO/GIO as catalyst and facilitator: Building the information utility to meet global challenges. In S. Palvia, P. Palvia, & R. M. Zigli (Eds.), *The global issues of information technology management* (pp. 465–483). Harrisburg, PA: Idea Group.

Case 12

DAIMLER-CHRYSLER MERGER

André M. Everett and Pavel Štrach

The founding event for the world automobile industry is widely considered to be Karl Benz's January 29, 1886, patent application for the three-wheeled gasoline-powered vehicle he invented in Mannheim, Germany. Only 7 months later, Gottlieb Daimler patented his own four-wheeled motorized carriage, in Bad Cannstatt near Stuttgart, Germany, which today is only an hour from Benz's hometown, thanks to Benz's and Daimler's inventions, which are regarded as the direct ancestors of the nearly 1 billion motor vehicles in use worldwide today.

From tens (or even hundreds) of car producers in each industrialized country at the beginning of the 20th century, through fewer than 100 major manufacturers in the 1960s, there remain only about a dozen global players today. The manufacturer of the first patented automobile is still in business, a survivor in a graveyard littered with once-famous, once-profitable, once-independent symbols of industrial power. Its Mercedes-Benz brand has traditionally been the car of preference for heads of state, the rich, and the famous. Nowadays,

the Mercedes Car Group accounts for the bulk of the value of DaimlerChrysler, the fourth largest car maker in the world by value (fifth by volume).

However, Mercedes-Benz ran into trouble. Quality and reputation difficulties tarnished the brand, and it became conceivable that archrivals BMW and Audi would surpass the three-pointed star in sales volume. The blame for much of the problem has been put on the aftereffects of the Daimler-Chrysler "merger," in particular, the sharing of platforms, major components, and suppliers across brands. The underlying reason for sharing is cost reduction through enhanced scale and scope efficiencies, which appear advantageous until examined from a strategic perspective. Exclusivity and compatibility may well be mutually exclusive.

THE DAIMLER-BENZ ERA

Steadily increasing competition, both internationally and domestically, made life difficult for the Daimler and Benz companies. By

---

SOURCE: Used with permission and prepared for this book by André M. Everett, Department of Management, University of Otago, Dunedin, New Zealand, and Pavel Štrach, Faculty of Management, University of Economics, Prague, Czech Republic.

516

1923, over 80% of the 15 million cars existing worldwide were registered in the United States, and over half of these were Fords.[1] Production of Benz's and Daimler's cars remained at a relatively low scale of 1,382 and 1,020, respectively. Competition from 85 other German car manufacturers and the emergence of Ferdinand Porsche (who later became chief engineer at Mercedes) forced Daimler-Motoren-Gesellschaft and Benz et Cie. to form a strategic alliance in 1924, formally merging in 1926. They ceased product duplication and initiated cooperation in research and development; increasing sales and further innovations ensued.

The automobile industry in general was disrupted by World War II, and Daimler-Benz was no exception. In 1949, Daimler-Benz presented its first postwar designs, but the real revolution came in 1951 when the 300 sedan became very popular among political and industrial leaders. The company's reputation was enhanced by the 1954 gull-wing coupe, a sports car with vertically opening doors that became an instant classic worldwide. Off-road vehicles, designated G-series, were introduced starting in 1979, followed by sport-utility vehicles

(M-series) in 1989. The company assembled its millionth postwar vehicle in 1962, reaching the milestone of 10 million in 1988.

Daimler-Benz did not target more affordable market segments until the early 1980s and began to study smaller cars in the early 1990s. Its first effort involved a joint venture with the Swiss watchmaker Swatch in 1994 to build a fashionably stylish minicar. Following completion of the design phase, Swatch left the minicar partnership in 1998, and Daimler-Benz launched the Smart two-seater to European customers later that year, with introduction to the United States delayed until 2008. Internal development was used for the second, larger small car, designated A-Class—or "Baby Benz" by the press; it has not yet become a financial success, and the segment is becoming crowded with new entries by BMW, Audi, and others. (Sales figures for Mercedes-Benz cars for 1989 through 2005, distinguished by major category, are shown in Figure 1.)

On May 24, 1995, Jürgen E. Schrempp became the chairman of Daimler-Benz AG, and a colorful new era for the company commenced. Sensing that the firm's

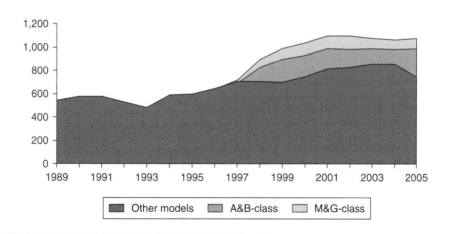

Figure 1   **Mercedes-Benz Branded Automobile Production (Thousand Units, 1989 to 2005)**

SOURCE: References 2–5.

survival depended on increased scale and broader geographic coverage (at least including the three large markets of North America, Europe, and Japan), Schrempp set the cash-rich company on a trajectory of active expansion by acquisition, focusing on markets outside its traditional European domain.

Concurrently, Chrysler (one of the "Big Three" U.S. automakers) was in a vulnerable position, with new models coming online, financial recovery under way, lean production advancing throughout its supply chain, and an ongoing hostile takeover attempt by shareholder Kirk Kerkorian in conjunction with Chrysler's former boss, Lee Iacocca. In a series of personality conflicts, executives were rolled at both Chrysler and Daimler-Benz, including some who had proposed cooperation between Mercedes-Benz and Chrysler in developing countries.

This unusual combination of circumstances, managerial egos, and dynamism of the automotive sector pointed toward future consolidation on both sides of the Atlantic, but the subsequent announcement of a merger between German Daimler-Benz and American Chrysler still came as somewhat of a shock. The largest industrial merger in history occurred on May 6, 1998, with the new company DaimlerChrysler incorporating in Germany with a market value of $75 billion.

Analysts were quick to note that economies of scale would result through coordinated purchasing, service, design, and administrative functions. The company duly announced net savings of approximately $1.4 billion from the merger itself, with expectations of ongoing savings through consolidation (e.g., reduction of power-train duplication, with Chrysler's power-train portfolio to be cut from 146 to 89 products) (p. 26).[6]

However, equally obvious was the disparity between the target markets, operating styles, and competitive advantages of the two companies; they differed substantially in strategic planning approaches, although both were founded by engineers and shared some historic similarities. Mercedes-Benz vehicles targeted the luxury market, with most sales in Europe, some in the United States, and the rest distributed globally, while Chryslers, Dodges, and Jeeps sold principally in the United States to a broad range of middle-class consumers. Daimler-Benz focused on quality, innovation, and exclusivity, while Chrysler emphasized volume, rapid decision making, and flexibility. Daimler-Benz focused on internal development and sourcing, while Chrysler led all Western automakers in outsourcing and supply chain integration. Chrysler had retained market share through acquisitions (such as Jeep and American Motors), while Daimler-Benz intentionally avoided this strategy to preclude dilution of its brand values (until merging with Chrysler).

Cultural clashes between German and American management approaches were deemed inevitable. The Mercedes car group, as the core of a larger corporation with diversified interests, including aerospace, as well as substantial global ambitions and wider intentions, saw itself as the flagship of German engineering and industry, while Chrysler's self-image was plagued by its repeated brushes with bankruptcy and status as the smallest of the Big Three U.S. car makers. Beyond the recognized cultural differences between the United States and Germany (e.g., refer to Hofstede's dimensions of culture), the organizational cultures differed—Daimler-Benz was relatively well insulated from short-term fluctuations, while Chrysler was lean in every sense, needing to respond rapidly to external changes in order to survive. The worker unions at Mercedes-Benz tended to be cooperative (and had seats on the board of directors), while those at Chrysler were frequently antagonistic (in efforts to obtain a "better deal" for their members). The two cultures could be broadly characterized as authoritative-cooperative-static versus participative-antagonistic-flexible.

The two CEOs, Jürgen Schrempp of Daimler-Benz and Robert (Bob) Eaton of Chrysler, became cochairmen of the newly established company, with Thomas Stallkamp as overall president. During 1999, Eaton (in conjunction with Schrempp) arranged Stallkamp's departure and then vacated his own job, leaving Schrempp as the sole chairman.[7] Substantial management upheavals and replacements in both the former Daimler-Benz and Chrysler occurred during the first 2 years, including relocation of some German managers to key positions in Detroit; the financial difficulties experienced by Chrysler were used to justify some of these decisions. Difficulties also arose over the deal Schrempp had brokered to acquire Nissan; when he was not backed by his own board, the deal fell through (Renault signed on the dotted line with Nissan 3 weeks later). Both German and American board members opposed the additional complications, some favoring the concept but opposing the timing.

Two years after the merger, Jürgen Schrempp told *The Financial Times* that "he never envisaged the merger as a partnership of equals" (p. 26).[6] This merely confirmed what the media had already determined:[8]

If there is anybody, anywhere within the automotive industry, who still thinks that last year's merger between Chrysler Corp. and Daimler-Benz AG was actually a merger, they should check themselves in for a brain scan. The "merger" was in reality a peaceful takeover of Chrysler Corp. by Daimler-Benz AG. (p. 66)

The year 2000 was a momentous one for DaimlerChrysler. The Mercedes brand celebrated its centennial; out of 19 million vehicles manufactured, half were believed to be still on the road, and the threshold of 1 million produced in 1 year had been attained in the preceding year.[9] DaimlerChrysler created two special divisions responsible for production and marketing of its various passenger car brands: the Mercedes Car Group for the Mercedes-Benz and Smart brands (later adding Maybach), and the Chrysler Group for Chrysler, Dodge, Jeep, and Plymouth (the latter brand being terminated at the end of 2000).

Continuing its global expansion plans, the company acquired a controlling 34% stake in heavily indebted Mitsubishi Motor Company for $1.9 billion, gaining access to Asian market share, production facilities in North America and Europe, and small engine supply. Later in the same year, Mitsubishi revealed that it had hidden customer complaints for 30 years; the firm was forced to recall some 2.5 million vehicles. (Following ongoing quality problems and a severe dearth of capital, DaimlerChrysler refused to bail out Mitsubishi and sold its stake in November 2005 for an $800 million loss. Ironically, Chrysler owned varying stakes in Mitsubishi Motors from 1971 to 1993.)

Chrysler's deteriorating performance led to DaimlerChrysler's first quarterly loss in 2001, resulting in a massive restructuring with 26,000 layoffs and six plant closures. The media speculated that either the CEO would be replaced or the company would be broken up and sold. According to an executive at General Motors, "if Schrempp was ousted, there is little doubt we would be interested in parts of the business. Of course, Mercedes and some parts of Chrysler are very attractive to any buyer."[10] Both Schrempp and DaimlerChrysler survived, with Chrysler returning to profitability faster than expected on the back of increased production and unit sales from 2001 to 2002 (revenues remained stable in dollars, but decreased in euro terms due to exchange rate effects).

Tighter integration of the Mercedes-Benz, Chrysler, and Mitsubishi brands over the next 10 years was expected to substantially cut the diversity of power trains, in line with analysts' original expectations of the merger's direction. However, the highly publicized merger across recognizedly different quality levels heightened consumer awareness of the possibilities of component sharing and outsourcing to the point that a media leak concerning Mercedes buying leather from Bulgaria (purportedly a lower-quality source) prompted a British brand consultant to take it as "an indication that they are compromising."[11]

Mercedes-Benz in the Age of DaimlerChrysler

Daimler-Benz devoted substantial attention to the deal with Chrysler, and then with Nissan and Mitsubishi, distracting it from its own developing problems and rising competition for its flagship brand. Following the merger, both Daimler-Benz and Chrysler lost substantial expertise because senior managers departed. The overall impact of the merger was deemed negative in terms of diversion of resources,[11] including strategic planning focus at the subcorporate level.

Consumer perceptions of the Mercedes-Benz brand deteriorated, perhaps fueled by media speculation but doubtless grounded on documented quality difficulties. The decline in customer satisfaction ratings was precipitous: In 1999, Mercedes-Benz came first out of 37 car brands in Consumer Reports' U.S. ranking of vehicle reliability, but 28th in 2005. The E-Class came in dead last, ignominiously designated as the least reliable passenger car in the United States. Similarly, in the J.D. Power 2005 survey of British car owners who registered new vehicles between September 2002 and August 2003, the E-Class came second to last in the executive and luxury category, with the C-Class only two places higher; the E-Class barely reached the top 100 models overall. As a manufacturer brand, Mercedes-Benz ranked below average— and below other marques such as Skoda, Daihatsu, and Vauxhall, tying for 21st place with Seat. The shift in consumer ratings of initial mechanical quality following the merger is evident from the data shown in Table 1.

Stinging from the criticism, Daimler-Chrysler and Mercedes-Benz representatives issued statements indicating that they understood the problem and were working to resolve it, acknowledging concerns that were initially downplayed. In 2004, the company announced that it would aim to again top the J.D. Power U.S. survey in 2006 but later cast doubt on this goal as being inappropriate, since the overall satisfaction index reflected American tastes rather than global values.[13] Identification of potential defects resulted in the April 2005 recall of the largest number of vehicles in Mercedes-Benz's history, 1.3 million.

Mercedes Car Group's sales fell short of targets due to a combination of currency fluctuations and product changes, and quality improvement efforts hampered production. The number of vehicles sold in 2004 declined only slightly (by 18,000, or about 1.7%), before increasing in 2005, but profits derived from the Mercedes-Benz brand dropped dramatically from 784 million

Table 1   Initial Mechanical Quality of Selected Mercedes-Benz Models

Model	1998	1999	2000	2001	2002	2003	2004	2005
C-Class	****	****	****	***	***	****	***	***
E-Class	*****	****	*****	*****	*****	**	***	****
S-Class	*****	*****	*****	*****	****	***	**	***
M-Class	****	****	****	***	**	***	****	**
Total *s	18	17	18	16	15	12	12	12
*s above minimum possible	10	9	10	8	7	4	4	4
Maximum possible = 20 *s; minimum possible = 8 *s								

SOURCE: Reference 12.

NOTE: ***** Among the best, **** better than most, *** about average, ** the rest (there is no single * rating). The initial quality study looks at owner-reported problems in the first 90 days of ownership; this score is based on problems reported with the engine, transmission, steering, suspension, and braking systems.

euros in the fourth quarter of 2003 to 20 million in the same period of 2004, leading to an operating loss of 142 million in the first quarter of 2005. By the second quarter, however, the Mercedes-Benz brand had returned to profitability, rising throughout the year, although Smart continued to drain the coffers. New lines introduced in 2005 to bolster the range included the B-Class sports hatchback and R-Class sports station wagon, resulting in 14 model lines overall (smaller hatchbacks A- and B-Class, classic sedan and station wagon C-, E-, R-, and S-Class, SLK, SL, CLK, CL, SLR, and CLS roadsters and coupes, and off-roaders M- and G-Class). In addition to passenger cars, the Mercedes-Benz star also decorates the grille of multipurpose vehicles, camper vans, vans, buses, trucks, and Unimog extreme-condition vehicles.

In July 2005, Schrempp announced his own departure, effective at the end of the year. This was hailed as momentous not only for DaimlerChrysler, but also for the German industrial organization model as a whole, signaling the end of the era of interlaced boards, banks, and labor unions. An in-depth analysis of his leadership style

determined that, contrary to the typical German model of collective leadership, as "a charismatic and overambitious leader, however, [he] presented the greatest danger to the performance and survival of [the] organization."[14] The board appointed Dieter Zetsche, head of the Chrysler Car Group, to replace him, and to serve as interim head of the Mercedes Car Group.

Meanwhile, Chrysler announced year-on-year sales increases for 18 months in a row (as of September 2005), including all-time record retail sales for a single month (July 2005),[15] and the Chrysler 300 won Motor Trend's Car of the Year award for 2005 (Chrysler had also won in 4 out of the previous 10 years).[16] The 300 was also awarded Edmunds.com's "Most Significant Vehicle of the Year," taking the honors ahead of the redesigned Ford Mustang; the review specifically mentioned systems sharing with "its more expensive Mercedes cousins."[17] The aura of Mercedes-Benz was seen as pulling Chrysler up—but it was the same shared suspension systems that Consumer Reports cited in criticizing the 300 V8 model, rated below average, along with the Mercedes S-Class.[18] For the first three quarters of 2005, Chrysler barely topped Mercedes-Benz in revenues but sold more than double the number of cars with 20% fewer employees; Chrysler was profitable, Mercedes-Benz was not. Chrysler also gained share in the U.S. market, while both General Motors and Ford dropped share and posted losses.

DISCUSSION QUESTIONS

1. How have differences between Mercedes-Benz and Chrysler affected the strategic planning conducted by the organizations throughout their histories?

2. What were the international strategic motivations affecting Daimler-Benz's pursuit of other automobile manufacturers?

3. How did the merger between Daimler and Chrysler affect the Mercedes-Benz vehicles and the brand?

4. What complications due to cultural differences should have been anticipated in this merger, and how could they have been minimized?

5. Given that the merged companies stay merged, what would you recommend as the corporate-level international strategy for the different brands?

REFERENCES

1. R. A. Wright (2001, December 3). Mercedes grew out of the rich technological age of the 1880s. *The Detroit News*. Retrieved May 10, 2005, from http://info.detnews.com/ joyrides/story/index.cfm?id=290

2. Autointell (2003). Mercedes-Benz cars and Smart: Sales and production figures. *Autointell—The Web for automotive professionals*. Retrieved May 8, 2005, from www .autointell.net/nao_companies/daimlerchrysler/ dc-business-figures/mercedes-benzsales/merc pass-car-sales-02.htm

3. DaimlerChrysler (2004). *Annual Report 2003*. Stuttgart, Germany/Auburn Hills, MI: DaimlerChrysler AG.

4. DaimlerChrysler (2005). *Annual Report 2004*. Stuttgart, Germany/Auburn Hills, MI: DaimlerChrysler AG.

5. DaimlerChrysler (2006). *Annual Report 2005*. Stuttgart, Germany/Auburn Hills, MI: DaimlerChrysler AG.

6. T. Burt & R. Lambert (2000, October 30). The Schrempp gambit. *Financial Times*, p. 26.

7. B. Vlasic & B. Stertz (2000). *Taken for a ride: How Daimler-Benz drove off with Chrysler*. New York: HarperCollins.

8. F. S. Washington (1999, November 1). Merger? What merger?—Clearly now, DaimlerChrysler is a German company. *Ward's auto world, 35*(11), 66–67. Retrieved October 30, 2005, from www .wardsauto.com/ar/auto_merger_merger- clearly_daimlerchrysler/index.htm (Now available at www.wardsauto.com/ar/auto_ merger_mergerclearly_daimlerchrysler/)

9. DaimlerChrysler (2000, December 12). *100 years of Mercedes* [Press release]. Retrieved October 29, 2005, from www .schwab-kolb.com/dcnew122.htm

10. B. Hickey (2001, January 15). GM may bid for Mercedes: Report. *Financial Times MarketWatch.com* (Europe).

11. M. Chambers (2003, November 13). Mercedes looks back to the future. *Reuters*, on XtraMSN. Retrieved November 19, 2003, from http://xtramsn.co.nz/business/ 0,,5007-2826417,00.html

12. J. D. Power Consumer Center (2005). *Compare cars*. Retrieved October 31, 2005, from www.jdpower.com/cc/index

.jsp (Now available at www.jdpower
.com/autos)

13. Reuters (2005, May 6). Mercedes may drop
goal to top quality survey, Chief says. *The
Detroit News*. Retrieved on May 9, 2005,
from www.detnews.com/2005/autoinsider/
0505/06/1auto-173641.htm

14. C. Stadler & H. H. Hinterhuber (2005).
Shell, Siemens and DaimlerChrysler: Leading
change in companies with strong values.
Long Range Planning, 38(5), 467–484.

15. DaimlerChrysler (2005). *Chrysler group
achieves 18th consecutive month of sales
gains on 4 percent rise in sales* [Press release].
Retrieved October 31, 2005, from www
.daimlerchrysler.com/dccom/1,0-5-7153-1-
548481-1-0-0-0-0-0-243-7145-0-0-0-0-0-0-
0,00.html

16. Motor Trend (2005). *Motor Trend Car of
the Year Complete Winners List*. Retrieved
October 31, 2005, from http://motortrend
.com/oftheyear/car/cotywinners/

17. Edmunds.com (2005). Most significant
vehicle of the year 2005. *Edmunds.com*.
Retrieved October 30, 2005, from www
.edmunds.com/reviews/mostwanted/2005/
103326/article.html

18. G. Tierney (2005, October 27). Asian auto
brands' reliability uneven. *The Detroit
News*. Retrieved October 31, 2005, from
www.detnews.com/2005/autoinsider/
0510/28/C01-362825.htm

Case 13

VINHDAT COMPANY LTD.

Building Effective Subcontracting Networks

Nguyen Van Thang

I t's June 15, 2000.

Good news makes Mr. Pham, the owner of Vinhdat Co. Ltd., worried. A Hong Kong–based customer wants Vinhdat to "process" 3,000 jackets in a month. But Vinhdat is already operating at overcapacity. In Vinhdat's hot and crowded manufacturing facilities, all 600 workers have already been working overtime for a month. Refusing this order, on the other hand, would push the customer to find another Vietnamese company to fulfill the order and run the risk of losing a valuable client forever. But there is another option: subcontracting the order to other Vietnamese garment companies. The questions are which companies they should subcontract the order to and how Vinhdat can ensure that these subcontractors will complete the contract on time and meet the required specifications. In addition, most garment-manufacturing companies are also operating at full capacity, so who will be willing to help?

This sort of situation has occurred more and more over the last 3 years and has been resolved on an ad hoc, case-by-case basis. Mr. Pham thinks that this issue

needs to be addressed in a more strategic and comprehensive way from now on. Indeed, perhaps it should be treated as the company's main strategic issue for the next 5 years.

BACKGROUND OF THE COMPANY

Business Idea Formulation

Mr. Pham has a background in the textile and garment industry. He began working for ATEN—a state-owned import-export company—in the 1970s. Under the former command economy system, he was in charge of making contacts and negotiating deals with foreign customers (mostly from the former Soviet Union and Eastern Europe). He learned how the garment processing business works and saw possible improvements that his company could make. However, such improvements had been very difficult to implement in a state-owned organization. In the early 1990s, the Vietnamese government issued a corporate law that legitimized the domestic private sector in the economy. Initially, Mr. Pham and a friend of his developed a proposal for a

SOURCE: Used with permission from and prepared by Professor Nguyen Van Thang.

garment-manufacturing venture, organized as a partnership, based on a seed investment of U.S.$1 million. However, Mr. Pham finally withdrew from the project. He described it as too "risky," "ambitious," and "not appropriate to the situation." Instead, he decided to set up his own company and received government approval in August 1993. Fully aware of the nascent and uncertain status of the private sector, Mr. Pham adopted a "careful, slow, but solid" development strategy for the company.

Vinhdat is located in a suburban area, 15 km north of Hanoi. In an area of about 2,000 sq. m, there are three buildings, arranged in a "U" shape. Two of these buildings are used for manufacturing, and the other is for management offices, inventory storage, and a meeting room. The main products are low-quality jackets and trousers that are sold to foreign markets. Vinhdat is a typical Vietnamese manufacturer in many ways: the manufacturing facilities are crowded, employees are low skilled, and the equipment is mostly secondhand.

Vinhdat's Evolution

Vinhdat actually started processing garments for export in August 1994. It started as a subcontractor for other private "middlemen" individuals who had contacts with Eastern European customers. But in June 1995, the first foreign customer, Zungmin (a Korean company), visited Vinhdat. They accepted the technical standards of the company and liked the company's business approach. They agreed to a contract with the company worth $30,000 in fees. This opened a new area of the company's business. In 1996, Vinhdat continued to process for Zungmin and acquired a Hong Kong–based customer (Busherlin). In addition, it still processed garments for Vietnamese companies. Up to

this point, the processing fees and profits of the company were very low.

Vinhdat continued to work under contract to foreign customers, and in 1997 it started subcontracting to other Vietnamese garment companies. The business was growing, and the number of subcontractors increased from 3 in 1997 to 15 in 1998. In 1999, the company received a loan of $60,000 from the International Finance Corporation (IFC). At that time, the government introduced a law that waved revenue tax for companies with more than 500 employees and operating in "encouraged industries" (of which the garment industry was one). The number of employees increased to 600, the company's revenues climbed to $700,000, and the company built a new three-story building. With more than 20 subcontractors, subcontracts now accounted for about 55% of the total business.

Table 1 provides some key basic background information on the company.

Vinhdat's Business

The company receives contracts from foreign customers that include product specifications and materials. A portion of this contract is manufactured in-house. The other part is subcontracted to other Vietnamese garment companies. Figure 1 illustrates the company's business model.

Despite the increase in both the quantity and the quality of the orders, neither Vinhdat's size nor its technical standards have increased since 1999. The number of employees has remained at 600 and no significant investment was made to upgrade either the equipment or employees' skills. A loan from the IFC for upgrading the building in early 1999 was the only significant investment since 1994. The owner explained as follows:

Table 1   Background Information on the Company

Name	Vinhdat Company Ltd.
Owners	Mr. and Mrs. Pham
Established	1993
Industry	Garment exports. The company has been a subcontractor to some Hong Kong and Korean customers
Number of employees (1999)	600
Location	Duong Bridge (*Cau Duong*), 15 km north of Hanoi. Very convenient to transport products to Haiphong port and Noi Bai Airport
Revenue that comes from "processing fees" paid by foreign customers	U.S.$800,000 (1999)

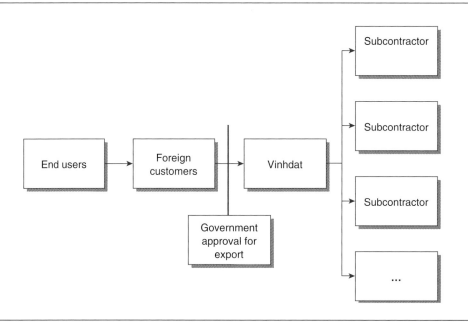

Figure 1   The Company's Business Model

Why don't I invest more money to expand the floors and upgrade the equipment? It is not that I don't see future needs for that. It's just too risky at this time. The government is giving favorable treatment to state-owned enterprises (SOEs). They merged SOEs into big corporations that dominate all important input and output markets. How can we compete with these "elephants"? Moreover, they audit too frequently any private company that they think is growing. As you observed, we have had two different auditing delegations visit us in the last two months. Each spent at least two weeks with our key managers, asking for all kinds of documents and explanations. Very disturbing. They want us to invest more of our money. At the same time, they are suspicious when we're growing. So, if big storms keep coming back, you'd better be a small tree.

Training employees to lose them? Not a good choice. Most of the employees would love to work for SOEs since private companies like ours have uncertain status. Many of my employees just wait to get better skills so that they can leave for SOEs.

In this situation, subcontracting is the solution for growing revenue without growing the company's size. Most of Vinhdat's subcontractors have difficulty accessing foreign customers. The vast majority are local SOEs, which are perceived by foreign customers to be slow, conservative, and difficult to work with. Many of them are located far from Hanoi (more than 2 hours' drive), making access to foreign customers even more cumbersome. Some of these subcontractors do not have government permission to export directly. That leaves these subcontractors dependent on other companies, such as Vinhdat, to generate export businesses.

VIETNAMESE BUSINESS ENVIRONMENT AND GARMENT EXPORT INDUSTRY

The Vietnamese Environment

Vietnam has a long history characterized by a strong wish for national independence from foreign domination, localization of the governance system that granted great autonomy to local authorities, and an uneasy relationship with China. Recently, the people of Vietnam have recognized the role of the communists in liberating the country from the French

(1885–1954) and winning the wars against the United States (1954–1975), the Cambodian Khmer Rouge (1978), and the Chinese (1979). These wars, coupled with the traditional socialist economic system, put the country in a major economic crisis in the early 1980s. This economic crisis, in combination with reform movements in China and the former Soviet Union, served as the main forces pushing Vietnam toward large-scale economic reform, known as *Doi moi*, introduced in 1986.

The economic reform program in Vietnam started formally in 1986 and underwent significant implementation during the period from 1989 to 1996. The primary aim of the reforms in Vietnam was to create a "market economy under socialist guidance."[1] The new development model was to be a multisectoral economy, in which the government, cooperative, and private sectors exist side by side, with equal rights. The government has committed itself to four key reform measures. The first was to give farmers the right to lease land from the state for a long period. Farmers' land rights were consolidated in the 1992 Constitution and in a 1993 land law. The second measure was to legitimize the private sector, which appeared in the VI Party Congress in 1986, the 1992 Constitution, and the 1993 Enterprise Law. The third was to encourage foreign direct investment, with the issue of the Foreign Direct Investment law in 1988. Last, the monobanking system, with the State Bank as the body that implemented the central credit plan, was abandoned in favor of a two-tier financial system, consisting of a central bank and multiple commercial banks.[2]

The economic reform process has been slowing down since 1996, largely because the government is concerned about the "social evils" that come with market economies. However, two key achievements of the reform in this period should be noted. In July 2000, a small stock market started trading for the first time in Ho Chi Minh City. Also in 2000, a new Enterprise Law was issued, which has helped ease the registration of private businesses. However, the private sector has yet to really achieve equal status with its state-owned counterpart.

Although a number of new laws have been issued in Vietnam, the fundamental objective of providing a level playing field for different sectors is far from being reached. In the current legal system, for example, state and private businesses are still regulated by different laws, allowing legal room for unequal competition. In two current studies, private firms found the legal procedure confusing and ineffective,[3] and none of Vietnam's enterprise managers—especially private business owners—were totally aware of the legal system relating to their businesses.[4] Indeed, the use of legal advice professionals is still alien to private business owners. Consequently, a large proportion of business transactions are conducted without being supported by the legal system.

Another characteristic of the business environment in Vietnam is the underdevelopment of intermediary professional agencies. Of these, the lack of a developed banking system is most prominent. The underdevelopment of the banking system has been an obstacle for mobilizing capital and facilitating business transactions. In a recent survey, it was seen that the public still has very low confidence in the banks, with less than 10% of the population having any direct contact with a bank. Thus, a large majority of daily transactions are still conducted using cash. In addition, private firms often find it hard to get credit from banks.

Vietnam's physical infrastructure has suffered from decades of war and years of inadequate investment. Geographically,

Vietnam is a long country, spanning 1,600 km from north to south. Recently, typhoons and floods repeatedly destroyed the infrastructure and threatened people's lives in many areas, especially in the Mekong Delta. In the early 1990s, only 10% of Vietnam's 105,600 km of roads were sealed with asphalt or concrete, and even the best roads were considered to be of low quality. Traveling and moving products between provinces are still relatively expensive and time-consuming.

The Garment Exporting Industry in Vietnam

The garment industry in Vietnam has a long tradition, yet only since the 1990s has it played a notable role in the export economy. According to the General Statistics Office of Vietnam (1999)[5] and the Vietnam Textile and Garment Corporation's report (1999),[6] Vietnam has 669 garment companies, of which 115 are SOEs, 94 are foreign and joint venture companies, and 460 are in the domestic private sector (both limited and joint stock companies).

Garment export revenues accounted for 7.6% of Vietnam's total exports in 1991 and 15% in 1998. Annual revenues have increased by about 10% per annum in the last 10 years (see Figure 2). However, the industry's main business is to "process" for foreign customers, that is, to manufacture garments according to technical specifications and materials provided by foreign customers. About 80% of the export revenue has come from processing fees for foreign customers, and 90% of the garment companies are producing for foreign customers under that kind of arrangement.[7]

The garment industry is labor intensive, and investment capital per worker is low compared with most other industries. Under pressure to create jobs, in 1998, the

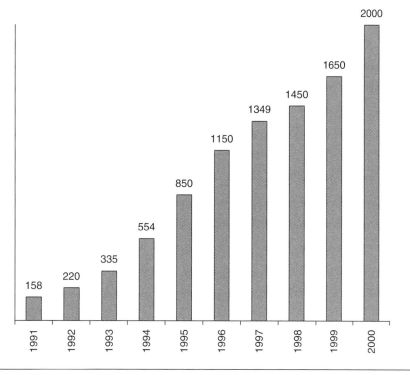

Figure 2   Export Revenue, 1991–2000 (U.S.$ Million)

SOURCE: Reference 7.

government categorized garment manufacturing as an "encouraged industry" and provided tax incentives for companies that have more than 500 employees.[7]

The industry has a high employee turnover rate of 15% to 30% per year, which has been an obstacle for companies trying to improve and maintain high technical standards. With high employee turnover and low technical standards, the industry suffers from seasonal employment fluctuations. Due to the seasonal effect of fashion and changes in the weather, different seasons require different types of products. But at the current technical level, only a few companies are capable of producing different types of products to maintain a stable business year-round. For export processing companies, the slow

season is November to April, and the busy season is May to October.

Companies are distinguished by their technical skill levels and their ability to access foreign customers. About 10% of the companies which have a higher technical level are capable of getting stable work for their employees throughout the year. They can produce and export their own products. As a result, employee turnover is low, which in turn helps maintain their high technical standards. Almost all these companies are big, traditional SOEs.

Another 30% of the companies have lower technical skills (rated 2 or 3 on a scale from 1 to 6, with 6 as the highest level), but they have direct contacts with foreign customers and have government permission for direct exports. These companies are subcontractors of foreign customers, and they can subcontract further to the remaining 60% of garment companies in Vietnam (see below). Most of these companies are located in big cities (e.g., Hanoi and Ho Chi Minh City) and have been in business for more than 5 years.

The remaining 60% of companies have about the same technical standards as those in the previous category but either do not have direct access to foreign customers or do not have the government's permission to export. Most of these companies are newly established or located far from major cities. Their main business comes from subcontracts with firms in the previous category. These firms have a competitive advantage from low labor costs in the surrounding area.

Another factor that inhibits the development of the garment industry is the poor development of supporting industries. For example, the textile industry is incapable of providing materials for the export garment industry, and almost all exported garment products require imported fabric. Without large amounts of working capital and knowledge of foreign markets, 90% of the exporting garment companies are processing for foreign customers who take on the risks of providing materials and looking for end-user markets. This way of doing business is expected to continue in the near future as supporting industries and knowledge of foreign markets will take time to develop.

THE COMPANY'S SUBCONTRACTOR NETWORK

In reviewing the various subcontractors Vinhdat has worked with, Mr. Pham favors four subcontractors: S1, S2, S3, and S4. All of them are local SOEs. Vinhdat has been working with them for at least three seasons (years). S1 and S4 are more dependent on Vinhdat for business because they do not have permission to export. The other two, although they have export permission, are located far from Hanoi (around 80 to 150 km) and do not have foreign customers. All of them have good technical standards (two of them have better technical standards than Vinhdat's) and have adequate capability (800 to 1,200 employees). The management teams of S1, S2, and S3 have a reputation for dependability, not only with Vinhdat but also with other companies in the industry. Mr. Pham also appreciates the responsiveness and market-oriented approach of S3's and S4's managers.

At the personal level, Mr. Pham and Vinhdat's managers have had a very positive experience working with people from these four subcontractors. These subcontractors' managers have been very truthful and cooperative. In 2000, when Vinhdat had too much work with a short lead time in the busy season, one of these subcontractors (S1) renegotiated with their own customers, and redirected part of their capacity to work for Vinhdat. Two others (S2, S3) had their employees work overtime.

Vinhdat also engaged in some reciprocal services to these subcontractors, such as sharing out contracts to these companies during the slow season (October to April). In 1999, one of the customers delayed paying Vinhdat for more than 6 months. As specified in the contract, Vinhdat was not obligated to pay its subcontractors before its customers made the payment. However, since one of these subcontractors (S4) was short of cash to pay its employees, Vinhdat did not wait for the payment from its customer, but instead borrowed money from several banks and paid the subcontractor. Over time, some managers of S2, S3, S4, and Vinhdat become good friends.

With these four subcontractors, Vinhdat's managers feel comfortable sharing their business information and finding new cooperative opportunities. They have already cooperated in some businesses other than subcontracting arrangements. Two examples of this are given below:

Example 1. On July 6, 2000, a director of subcontractor S4 came to discuss current subcontracts with Mr. Pham. This subcontractor was located 150 km south of Hanoi, and it was very inconvenient for him to travel to and from Hanoi. After the discussion of current subcontracts, the director of the subcontractor indicated that his company had just obtained an export quota from his local government that could result in a $4,000 profit. He asked Vinhdat's managers to help in dealing with the government bureaucracy in Hanoi. Instead of discussing the government procedure, Mr. Pham pointed out that it would not be optimal for this subcontractor to do this work in-house. A better solution would be to outsource it to someone else who could do it better (with lower labor costs and better equipment), and expend its capacity to work for Vinhdat, which could help in selling the quota for them.

Example 2. On August 16, 2000, the director of another subcontractor (S1) visited Vinhdat. This subcontractor had received some orders from a foreign customer but did not have government permission to export. Vinhdat agreed to help in dealing with all the export procedures. Thus, in all the export documents the products belonged to Vinhdat, while in fact they were really processed by the subcontractor.

Vinhdat has also done business with six other subcontractors (five of them local SOEs) for at least two seasons. All six of these subcontractors have expressed their willingness to have a long-term relationship

with Vinhdat. However, Vinhdat's managers do not feel very confident about these six subcontractors. In general, Vinhdat's managers agree that people at subcontractors S5, S6, and S7 are truthful and cooperative. The directors of S5 and S7 have been recommended to Vinhdat by highly respected officials, and the director of S6 is a close friend of Mr. Pham. At the organizational level, only S7 is dependent on Vinhdat for export business. While they are all good at communicating with Vinhdat, only S5 appears to have good technical standards.

The situations are somewhat different for subcontractors S8, S9, and S10. Business from Vinhdat has not been very significant to them. However, all of them have good technical standards, and their production capacities are very high (1,000 to 2,000 employees). Of these three, subcontractor S8 is a private company with a dynamic and market-oriented management team. Vinhdat's managers have not established strong personal relationships with managers of these subcontractors. Their experience in the last two seasons indicates that these subcontractors' managers are truthful and cooperative.

This season Vinhdat has subcontracted with another six subcontractors for the first time. All six of these subcontractors are local SOEs, located in provinces next to Hanoi (about 30 to 50 km from Vinhdat). They were established as a result of the "province division"; that is, some provinces were divided into two or three, and new provinces wanted to have their own garment-manufacturing companies. They have been in business for about 2 years. Vinhdat's managers do not know much about their technical standards or their capacity to fulfill contracts. In addition, relationships between Vinhdat and these subcontractors' managers have not been established. In the implementation of the contracts, Vinhdat has sent technical staff to supervise and support these subcontractors. Two of the six contracts were not successfully implemented. In one case, the subcontractor had technical problems and could not fulfill the contract on time. In the other, the subcontractor redirected its capacity to a more profitable contract (from another source) and did not meet Vinhdat's deadline. In both cases, Vinhdat had written contracts that clearly specified each side's responsibilities. However, Vinhdat did not take the partner to court, and no fee was charged. Mr. Pham stated the following:

> We had the option to sue them, but that would be ridiculous. You know the legal system here. There is a very small chance that the court would rule in favor of us [private companies] instead of their own "sons" [state-owned companies].

As the number of foreign customers increased, Mr. Pham decided that building the subcontracting network has become a critical task. In his mind, Vinhdat should have about 20 subcontractors with at least 6 to 8 long-term, trusted partners like S1, S2, S3, and S4. However, information on new subcontractors is scarce. Without an effective legal system, moreover, working with new subcontractors is inherently risky. Developing trusting relationships under the absence of an effective legal system and developed market institutions is a difficult task.

What criteria could Mr. Pham use to evaluate a subcontractor? What processes could Vinhdat follow to develop trusting relationships with its subcontractors? What are some inherent risks in doing so? How could Mr. Pham use personal relationships in business effectively? He needs to find answers to these questions.

REFERENCES

1. V. T. Nguyen (2005). Learning to trust: A study of interfirm trust dynamics in Vietnam. *Journal of World Business, 40*(2), 203–221.

2. V. T. Nguyen (2003). Managing change in Vietnamese state-owned enterprises: What's the best strategy? *Human Resource Management Review, 13,* 423–438.

3. R. Mallon (2004). *Managing investment climate reforms: Vietnam case study.* (Working Paper 2004-01-17). Washington, DC: World Bank.

4. Central Institute for Economic Management (1997). *Improving the macroeconomic policy and reforming the administrative procedures to promote the development of the small and medium enterprises in Vietnam.* Hanoi, Vietnam: Author.

5. General Statistics Office (1999). *Statistics year book, 1998.* Hanoi: Statistical Publishing House.

6. Vinatext (1999). *Annual report.* Hanoi, Vietnam: Author.

7. D. D. Dang & T. M. H. Ngo (1999). Hang det may xuat khau cua Vietnam: Thuc trang va giai phap (Vietnamese export garment products: Problems and solutions). *Kinh te va Phat trien (Economics & Development Review),* November–December (33), 23–27.

Case 14

LANGLEY INTERNATIONAL GROWERS, INC.

Managing a Small Business

Rae André

David Langley was the 58-year-old president of Langley International Growers, a New York-based firm with annual sales close to $4 million. Like his father and grandfather before him, Langley grew flowers for distribution to wholesale markets along the eastern coast of the United States. Domestically, he ran about 12 acres of greenhouses, putting the company among the top 10 greenhouse operations in the United States. To compete with flower growers from Latin America, Langley started a subsidiary in Santa Neuva, an island republic in the Caribbean. The following text is based on discussions with him 2 years after he successfully started the new operation.

MANAGING THE INTERNATIONAL START-UP

We first became interested in going abroad when we heard about it from one of our competitors. We had decided it might be a good idea to hedge our bets and move to a climate where there is no fuel requirement.

So we went down to Santa Neuva to see the competitor's operation, and we thought he was doing a good job. Sixty percent of the flowers used in the United States today are imported. These flowers are grown with labor at $2 a day, versus what we have to pay at minimum wage, around $3.35 per hour. We thought there was money in it.

But establishing yourself in a foreign country is not easy. There are pitfalls. The laws of these governments look like they welcome business coming in. It's all on the books: The laws are there to help you. The government itself wants you there in a lot of these countries. What they spend nationally on oil alone exceeds the money they get from exports, which constantly puts them in the doghouse international-ally. They can't buy anything outside, so they're constantly in a state of devaluation relative to everybody else. In addition to that, they have an enormous birthrate, which constantly keeps their poverty in place. (You go down there with the idea you're going to help them out from that standpoint, forget it, because they're not going to let you do it.) There's a lot of

SOURCE: This case is based on an actual company. Facts have been altered to protect the identity of those involved. Santa Neuva is a fictional country. Reprinted with permission of Rae André College of Business Administration, Northeastern University.

money to be made if you know how. You go down there and start spending your money, and then, you find out that the laws have to be administered by people, and the people are where the hang-ups come because they don't obey the law. They circumvent it to their own benefit. In other words, they make it difficult for you for various reasons. The political aims start to disappear in the bureaucracy.

For example, we have to import a lot of things into the country because they don't have them. Well, they can let that stuff sit down at that dock until some guy clears it. They let our crates of greenhouses sit there for 2 to 3 months. It threw us way back, cost us thousands of dollars. We had importers down there who knew their business. All the paperwork was right, but all that the government guy says is, "I don't think this is right," and it gets kicked back and forth. One problem is that a lot of the government income is taxes on imports, so that they're very strict, particularly if it's an American company that's shipping. This holdup means that everybody's benefiting except the poor guy who has to cut the flowers, because they've made work for the phone operator and everybody else. You're constantly checking, and checking. It's a make-work scheme, in any sense of the word, whether it's in Detroit or the Caribbean, and they're masters at it. A lot of these foreign countries, they don't operate, they make work.

For example, down where we are, the bureaucracy has increased 50% in 4 years—50% more government employees. Going through the airports, there's a guy who puts the tag on your thing, and there's a guy who takes it off, 5 feet away. You can tell them your problem, but they don't understand the problem of business having to get that money moving that's sitting there. They don't realize that they have to collect their

taxes and build their country from business. Even answering the phone, the conversations are long, the conversations are flowered. They don't get to the point, and this, of course, is frustrating if you're not used to it. And, especially, if you're paying for a long-distance phone call. It takes them a half hour to say good morning!

About 6 months ago, we needed this particular type of spreader for an insecticide, and I wanted to make sure it was there. We wanted it the following morning, and I wanted it delivered that day. And my secretary is on the phone talking to this guy 25 miles away. He kept saying, "Mañana" (tomorrow), and I kept saying, "Ayer" (yesterday). The secretary kept saying, "Mañana," and I kept saying, "Ayer." Finally, with negotiations back and forth, I got it.

So you have to tighten things. They don't respect you if they know they're getting away with it, because everybody is watching everybody else. We made that mistake. We were too easy. Of course, these people are very hungry. Their unemployment rate is tremendous. The established rate is 40%, but they don't count everybody. If they counted everybody, it's around 80%. You learn as you go, and you learn from talking to people. They don't respect softness, and yet they don't respect anybody who's going around shouting and yelling either. You've got to have them understand who the boss is. We had a guy who was coming in late all the time, so we gave him a written notice. After you hire him for 3 months, the government says you own him: It costs you money to let him go. If he's there for 3 months, you might have to give him another 3 months pay. After a year, you might have to give him another 6 months pay. The guy was late. We gave him the notice. He still was late, so we had to let him go. It didn't cost us anything. See, if he breaks the company rules and they're allowable rules according to the law, then you can get rid of him without any pay. But we had to get tougher and tougher and tougher. It's so easy to be easy because the labor's cheap. But you have to realize that any time you're not making money, it's coming out of capital, so labor's not cheap then.

We weren't knowledgeable about the culture. We assumed that they're like us—sort of like us—if you have the language. That's the mistake you make. You can hire a Neuvan to run the place, if you've got the language yourself, but you have to know the language so well that you get the innuendos, and that's something none of us have. Very few Americans have that. You could hire a Cuban, Mexican, or a Puerto Rican, but even they do not think like we do. They're more apt to identify with the person instead of identifying with the problem. They identify with their emotions and they think, "Well, poor guy."

We hadn't taken one dime out of there yet, and we were asked for a raise. They'll say, "Look at these poor people here. Don't you think they ought to be given hope?" When we went into the village, there the only means of transportation was the truck that we had bought. Now, almost everybody rides up in a new Honda motorcycle. The standard of living has gone up. We hired them, and they had 60% unemployment in the town, and yet I didn't give them hope. They're big on expectations and poor on execution down there.

You have to have an American boss, period. All those guys underneath can be Neuvans, but you got to have an American boss because you have to teach those Neuvans how you want it. If you go down there and take their way of doing it, you've lost everything you've ever had.

There was a lot of petty thievery when we built the place. A bar down the end of the street was built in the last year since we built. The owner didn't have a thing before. He's the guy who plowed our property and worked the field before we put our greenhouses up. Right after we built, he was able to build himself a bar and a dance hall from similar materials that were used to construct Langley Greenhouses. I call it Langley's bar. It's right at the end of our road. I often stop in for a cerveza.

All the foreigners do better than we Americans do. Number one, they can bribe the governments. We put strings on our businessmen that are absolutely abominable and then holler that we can't export anything. Another thing is the gringo approach. The Japanese are a new face in there, and they operate a little differently than we do. They always say, "Yes." We say, "No," but they say "Yes" and don't mean it, so it doesn't hurt as much. It's a different approach and they've sold one hell of a lot of cars. In fact, I have never driven an American car down there. If you want to go buy an American truck, just forget it. We have a little two-cylinder Japanese truck that's running up and down those hills for 50 km/gal.

LOCAL OPERATIONS

Our manager there came originally from Puerto Rico. I hired him when he was 15 or 16 years old. He has worked for me for 17 years. We usually have about 75% Puerto Ricans working for us up north. I am like a father to him. He had a child and named it after me.

I sent him down, and he's been as happy as a lark, but that's Jorge. That's not everybody. You can't generalize on Jorge.

He's doing a good job. Of course, he lost his first wife because she thought the girls were a little too loose in Santa Neuva. She wasn't wrong. She walked out on him. I don't know whether he got divorced, but he got married again. To give you just a brief insight into it, we won't allow him to hire any woman under 40. We don't want him to be passing his favors out. There's another reason for that. They'll come and work for you, but if they get pregnant, you have to give them at least a month off with pay. Sure enough, they'll come when they're already pregnant. First thing you know, you have five young ladies pregnant, nobody to do the work, and you're paying for it.

We hired the first secretary, thought she could speak English, and it took me 9 months to get rid of her. I fired her. She couldn't speak a word of English. "Yes" or "No." She had the books all fouled up. Pregnant, too. She lied to us about it. She came back and had the kid here. Now, he's an American citizen.

It's a very loose society. It's amazing, underneath. On top, if you walk into a bar or a dance hall, you can't dance with those girls in that bar, unless you know somebody who knows them. But down underneath . . . it's a different story. Jorge's getting worse, being down there. He's forgetting his English, too. He has to think twice.

We have three managers and 20 employees. That's what we call the office help—managers. We have an office manager, a pack and ship manager, and an overall manager: These people can all speak Spanish. Then, we have about 12 men and eight women. The women do the bunching. The men do the cutting, they are night watchmen, and all kinds of things. You look in that packing shed down there, and it's probably identical to this one up here, only there are no conveyers.

God forbid I ever put a conveyer down there because it'll only work about 3 hours. And that's when I'm working. The more we check up on them, the more controls we put on them in equipment, the more

apt they are to say, "This doesn't work now." It's so simple to break a computer. You spit at it or push the wrong damn buttons and it's done. We sent down one of the finest little power mowers you can buy. We started it up before it went down. It worked perfectly. It was 8 or 9 months later and three mechanical overhauls before we got that thing working.

Last year, I arrived and found 10 or 15 men cutting the fields with machetes. I'm still not sure if that isn't the cheapest. If you hire them for $2 a day, they're telling you something. They really are telling you something. You can hire their people, on certain jobs anyway, cheaper than you can use the damned equipment. You won't see a lot of bookkeeping machines in Santa Neuva. They use people, and they'll get it right. They'll have a calculator, but that's about the extent of it. You might in a very big American company but not generally.

We have parameters for the manager: checklists for his rounds, a checklist for his maintenance, a checklist for his night-man. You must be specific. You don't just walk out and say, "Clean." You've got to say, "Clean this table, clean that table, clean this." Write it down and give to him. If you don't do that, some of it will be forgotten, and some of it just won't be done. And then you can't come in and holler, because the guy will say he didn't hear you. They're really sharp this way. You have to be specific. You have to draw it step-by-step or they just won't do it. If they have a package of cigarettes, the empty packs will go onto the floor, until you tell them, "The next time you do that . . . out. We are not going to have that. This is not the way we're going to be." You go to the company next door to ours where he never enforced these things and it's a dump. It's not that he doesn't make money, but it's a dump, a literal dump. It's terrible.

We have the manager take videotape pictures around the plant every week so we see what the plants look like, see what the surroundings look like, and see what the housekeeping looks like. We also have him send all the bills, the bank balances, and the payroll up each week.

We have a problem with visitors, too. We have to keep them out. They'll just drop in and say, "Can I see the place?" and they'll take up the manager's time, and they'll take up the office time. When they get to talking, they'll talk about their grandfather, their father, their brothers, their sisters, and it's on your time. So we had to discourage that. We had to fence the place to keep the horses out, the cows out, and the people out. Just so you can keep control of the flowers. I don't know if we stopped it. If you have a fence, you have to say, "Don't crawl over the fence."

A lot of growers don't do things the way we do them, even up north. I like it written down. I hate verbal orders, unless it's just a day order. If it's a long-term deal, it should be written down and put in the policy. "This is what we do, in this way, at this particular time." We're known to have the best place in Santa Neuva, and there are a lot of flower growers. In the town, we're known as operating a very tight ship.

THE PRESIDENT'S PERSONAL INVOLVEMENT

I've spent a lot of hard times down there. When I go down there, I'm alone most of the time. There are many, many nights you're all alone. There's no one in the hotel. That's why I like to take somebody with me to play gin or to go out to eat. You're just there in the mountains, and you're all alone. It's not a bad hotel as hotels go. Jorge has a list he puts in my room for me. I have a toaster, coffee, water, coke, beer, vodka, insecticides, and other stuff. Of course, they haven't changed the linen in the 3 years we've been going there. They say that you don't go in the kitchen or you'll never eat there again. I spray the room for cockroaches and watch them wiggling. In the middle of the night, you hear them. I spray all over the room every time I go out.

The hotels are owned by the government, and they're rented from the government. It's amazing. These beautiful hotels rent for $200 to $300 a month. Anyhow you should see the way they keep it. Terrible. You can't swim in the swimming pool. It's green. It's a beautiful swimming pool, and I know how to tell them to keep it but they won't. If I were going to be down there a lot, I'd take my own chlorine and fix it. It would only cost $100 to use the pool the whole time I was there. Probably, they'd give me free drinks out of it, they'd make it up. They just don't know how to do things. They fool around.

When I was robbed at the hotel, I went to the police station and gave them a list just because I wanted it for the insurance company. Nothing happened. Nobody found anything. I didn't eat in that hotel for the next 2 months, the next two times I was there. I wouldn't go in their dining room, because I knew those guys, knew who did it. I was there alone. Somebody had to be watching, and the town is too small not to know the thief and I knew the police knew. I found out the hotel was responsible, but you can't get blood out of a stone, so I said, "All right, I want a 10% discount rate until this is paid off on my hotel room," which they went along with. After that they put a guard on me. Every night I have a guard—a private guard. They give him a peso. He's sitting right outside my door. I've never felt physically afraid, just alone, that's all.

I went down to town one night trying to negotiate for this land. Downtown at night looks like a country road. The house lights are on, but there are no street lights. I went down there negotiating with this family right in their house. (The guy who said that he owned the land just pissed me off. I had it all negotiated and later found out we couldn't get a clear title.) Anyway, I'm sitting there in this house with this family. Nobody can speak English, and I can't speak Spanish but we're negotiating. It was this guy and his son, who could speak English a little, and the whole family—his wife and relatives all come in to look at me. Everybody was just staring. All of a sudden, I started to wiggle my ears, and I'll tell you, they had a hilarious time. My wife was up in the hotel. She was worried I'd disappeared in the middle of the night down in a strange country. I didn't get home 'til 1 or 2 o'clock in the morning.

It's just a new ball game, and you should detail it right from the beginning. We should have had notebooks which was my fault. We should have had everything detailed—the duties, the laws of the country, the work rules. If I were to do it now, I would have all this stuff researched, and if we ever expand again, we'll know what the hell we're doing. And there'll be no problem. I spent quite a bit of time down there last June when we were planting, but I should have spent 2 months down there. I did spend practically that much time down there off and on, but I should have been right there and taken over the job of doing it. It's not the Neuvans' fault at all. I might lose it if I don't get down there more.

If I were going to do it over again, I wouldn't invest down there, but if I had to do it, I'd still pick that country. I didn't make a mistake in the country. We did not do that. It's probably the best of the lot. They're more democratic than most. The problem is that poverty does strange things. Poverty will turn those people into almost anything if they don't get it straightened out. That birth rate should be zero right now, but the population is going to double by the year 2000. That's why their university is a hotbed of Communism. They've got all this intelligence and they see the country like it is, and they don't know what to do.

Our government insures us if we're taken over down there because of riot or insurrection or government acquisition. Otherwise, you couldn't get any loans. You'll see people with jobs there, and you wouldn't believe it. Take the waiters in the hotels. You'll go down there today and 5 years from now and they're practically working for nothing. There's nobody in the hotels from one day to the next. Yet, they'll be there. They have no place to go. There's no place to go except the United States and there are 500,000 Neuvans working in the United States. You literally can't get a plane reservation back to the States during the first 2 weeks of January.

But it's gorgeous. It's a paradise. You couldn't believe it until you see it. Everything grows. You can have a terrific amount of flowers; I love to go there. I'm getting homesick for it. I would say they've treated us very well. After all, it's their country. It's not up to them to change . . . we're trying to take a profit out of it.

IVEY

Richard Ivey School of Business
The University of Western Ontario

Case 15

GLOBAL MULTI-PRODUCTS CHILE

Dan Campbell

INTRODUCTION

As he drove to his office in Providencia, a modern commercial and residential area in Santiago, Bob Thompson, Managing Director of Multi-Products Chile, was eagerly anticipating the upcoming week. He had spent a pleasant weekend with his family that had started well on the previous Friday afternoon with what he saw as real progress at work.

He had received an e-mail from one of the sales representatives in the North branch office reporting the minutes of the first branch sales meeting ever held in the company. Among other items, the minutes stated that the team had identified six accounts on which they were going to work together under the Integrated Solutions program and that they had chosen a team leader.

Thompson was surprised but delighted. The sales reps never knew what this type of meeting could accomplish or what they could do as a group. He had not expected these teams to function so well from the beginning. Maybe making changes in the organization would not be as difficult as he first had thought.

Upon entering his office, Thompson learned that two of his Business Unit managers were anxious to see him. The first, to whom the formally designated Integrated Solutions Manager reported, commented that he was just checking about the e-mail with Thompson and politely asked, "Have you seen the e-mail from the North? What's your opinion about the comments about Integrated Solutions? Isn't this our responsibility?"

The second Business Unit manager was more concerned and was disturbed with the tone of the e-mail: "What do you think about the note? These comments go way beyond the responsibilities of the branch people."

His earlier mood of satisfaction had turned to consternation. It appeared to him that his top executives, members of his Management Operating Committee, were suggesting a stop to his changes before they got out of hand. He found himself starting to have doubts about what he was doing. Maybe this wasn't going to be so easy after all. Should he keep pushing ahead with change when his senior management team did not appear to support it? He began to reflect on events that had led to this point.

BACKGROUND

Multi-Products Inc. was founded in the early 1900s to manufacture abrasives. The company's creation of the world's first waterproof sandpaper in the early 1920s, followed by numerous other new products, established the company's identity as an innovative, multi-product, manufacturing company. By 1998, the company manufactured and distributed over 50,000 products for a diverse range of applications. Some products were brands found in households and offices all over the world. Others became components of customer products such as computers, automobiles and pharmaceuticals. Many became the standards in their industry. All these products were the result of combining the company's core technologies in ways that solved their customers' problems.

In 1996, international sales totalled U.S.$14.2 billion, an increase of 5.8 percent over the previous year, and income from continuing operations was US$1.52 billion, an increase of 11.7 percent over 1995. International sales represented 53 percent of total sales. Multi-Products subsidiaries operated in over 60 countries outside of the United States and were the channels to sell products into almost 200 countries.

THE COMPANY VISION

According to Bob Thompson, the global growth drivers for the company were 1) technology and innovation; 2) the supply chain; and 3) a customer focus. The 1996 annual report stated the company vision this way:

> Our vision is to be the most innovative enterprise and the preferred supplier by:
>
> - Developing technologies and products that create a new basis of competition.
> - Earning our customers' loyalty by helping them grow their businesses.
> - Expanding internationally, where we already generate more than half of our sales.
> - Improving productivity and competitiveness worldwide.

TECHNOLOGY AND INNOVATION

In 1996, nearly 30 percent of sales came from products introduced within the previous four years. Those new products were derived from about 30 "technology platforms" where Multi-Products believed it possessed a competitive advantage. These technologies ranged from adhesives and fluorochemistry, to even newer technologies like micro-replication with potential in abrasives, reflective sheeting, and electronic displays.

These technology platforms were considered the path to the goal of developing products that would create a new basis of competition. The Chairman of Global

Multi-Products had high expectations for these programs:

> We have about 30 programs under way. These products serve high-growth industries and offer the potential to generate several billion dollars of new sales by the end of this decade.

Innovation in Customer Service

Historically, sales efforts were by product group. Often, sales representatives from one product group built strong relationships with customers that could benefit from products from other divisions as well. As a result, in the early 1980s, in an effort to take advantage of these opportunities, the company implemented a program referred to as "Related Sales." In 1988, this program was replaced by "Customer Focused Marketing" that sought to re-orient the sales and marketing effort around the needs of customers, instead of the company's product groups.

In the early 1990s, the process was carried a step further with "Integrated Solutions." Company documents explained the program:

> Customers rely on Multi-Products not only for innovative, high quality products, but also for solutions to other important needs. We help them develop, manufacture and merchandise their products; meet occupational health and safety standards; expand globally; and strengthen their businesses in other ways. We aim to be the first choice of customers. We strive for 100 percent customer satisfaction.

Multi-Products has an innovative way of doing business through which the client can easily access the [company's] products. The system has been labelled "Integrated Solutions" and voices the ideal of "one voice, one face, one company," which means that a single employee can provide you access to all products and solutions.

Multi-Products in Latin America

The company had a long history in Latin America. In 1996, it celebrated 50 years of operations in Brazil, and in 1997, the same in Mexico. The 1996 annual report explained:

> In Latin America, we operate in 16 countries. We've posted annual sales growth of 15 percent during the past five years. Throughout the area, Multi-Products is fulfilling the need for better roads, telecommunications systems and other types of infrastructure improvement. In addition, demand for health care and consumer products is strong. We manufacture or convert[1] products in a dozen Latin American countries.

Managing Directors in the region reported to the vice president, Latin America, Africa and Canada, who, in turn, reported to the Executive Vice President, International Operations.

Multi-Products Chile[2]

Multi-Products began operating in Chile in January 1976. With an initial investment of almost US$2 million, operations began in a large shed that served as the warehouse, production, and administration areas. In adherence to Chile's foreign investment legislation at the time, the company was required to establish a manufacturing operation as part of its investment.

Since its beginnings, Multi-Products Chile strove to project a presence throughout the country. The first company branch was created in Concepción in the south of the country during 1977; the second in Valparaíso near Santiago, two years later; and in 1982, a third branch was established in Antofagasta north of Santiago.

In 1992, Multi-Products Chile was asked to be formally responsible for the company's expansion in Bolivia. The local office enabled Multi-Products to directly satisfy the needs of the Bolivian market.

In 1997, the company's sales totalled approximately US$60 million with more than 8,000 products. Multi-Products Chile served multiple markets with multiple technologies and products, each of them with solid positions in their category. It supplied numerous manufacturing and service sectors, such as the health and first aid area (hospitals, drugstores, dentists); the industrial sector (safety products, abrasives, reflectors, packing systems, electrical and mining products, graphic communication products); the mass consumption area (cleaning, hardware and bookstore products); office, audio-visual and automobile sectors, and the large productions areas, such as forestry and construction.

Multi-Products' reputation for innovation also was recognized in Chile. El Mercurio conducted a survey in 1998 of 117 directors and general managers of medium and large-sized companies headquartered in Chile. Multi-Products Chile was ranked sixth in response to the question: "Which are the top companies in Chile in innovative capacity and incorporation of technology?"

In 1998, the company had a staff of 270 that included 80 sales representatives, nine technical support staff, 45 people in manufacturing, and the remainder in management, administrative, and maintenance positions.

CHILE: A BRIEF HISTORY[3]

In 1970 a Marxist government was elected in Chile. Soon after elections, Salvador Allende's government began a program of "economic reform." The banking, communications, textiles, insurance and copper mining industries were nationalized. Problems were soon apparent: Chile's currency reserves were gone; business groups were dissatisfied; the U.S. led a boycott against international credit for Chile; and strikes paralyzed the country. In 1973 inflation reached 300 percent.

In 1973, General Augusto Pinochet and the military took control of the country. Although General Pinochet's government was criticized for its human-rights record, it began to introduce market-oriented reforms such as reducing government's control of the economy, privatizing industries including those considered "strategic" and lowering import duties.

Sixteen years of military rule and a peaceful transition to a democratically elected government in 1990 that followed a similar economic path, provided the base for Chile's economic success. Chile boasted one of the best economies in the Western hemisphere: greater than 7 percent average growth rates, single digit inflation, a high personal savings rate (23 percent), and a fully funded pension system.

In 1998, Chile's 14.4 million inhabitants shared a per capita GDP in excess of U.S.$5,200, one of the highest in Latin America. While 60 percent of the country's population and economy was concentrated in the Santiago and Valparaíso region in the country's center, strong growth in the mining sector to the north, and the creation of a salmon fisheries industry to the south, had begun to decentralize economic activity.

Chilean Culture

Numerous Chilean managers at Multi-Products Chile shared their opinions about Chilean culture.

> Compared with the rest of Latin America, we are formal, closer to Argentina. We are the most serious people in Latin America. We often describe other Latin American cultures as less formal and see them as paying less attention to details. We are very professional at all levels and some people think Chileans are boring.
>
> We are also polite and indirect. For example, an e-mail or Lotus Notes that might be five lines from the United States, might be two pages long, on the same subject, if written by a Chilean.
>
> Many Chileans are workaholics. We work from 8am to 8pm and we often take work home with us on weekends. However, we still have scheduling problems. Time is flexible. A meeting scheduled for 10:00 may not start until 10:20.

Another manager observed:

> Why are we, as a country, not as developed as the United States over the same period of time? Chileans are more isolated from one another. I have been living in the same place for three or four years, and I don't know my neighbors. Nothing, names, number of children, nothing. In Chile, we tend to care about ourselves, our families, and maybe our friends, but that's it.

> We haven't paid enough attention to implement programs that make people work together. We haven't paid enough attention to organization development or to developing a sense of community. We don't have a tradition of taking responsibility for a wider group.

Another commented on the "silo effect" stating that, in addition to age and educational background differences, recent political history had polarized society and had not encouraged trust. He commented:

> Things are starting to change slowly, but the wounds haven't healed in 10 years. This is the biggest barrier to working in teams. People didn't trust each other, don't trust each other.

Bob Thompson

Prior to going to Chile, Bob Thompson had been an executive with Multi-Products Canada. Multi-Products Canada was a mature company with a well-trained sales force backed by good technical support that Thompson felt was the company's classic model and was essential to long-term success.

However, in 1991–92, facing a flat economy and stagnating organization, Multi-Products Canada began a change process that sought to empower managers within the organization. Thompson commented:

> The message was that we just couldn't continue with that style of management. We needed to get the best out of people. We needed to be more creative. I think the change process was successful. People felt part of the company in a much deeper way. I, personally, felt very positive about it.

In Chile, his predecessors had always come from the United States; in fact, most had spent considerable time in the head office. Thompson, on the other hand, had spent his career outside of the head office and, in keeping with the Canadian subsidiary's model of management, was more comfortable with broadly shared authority. He believed in encouraging positive risk-taking and empowerment.

Multi-Products Chile had been successful, growing at about 17 percent per year which was acceptable for a subsidiary in an emerging market. Multi-Products liked to grow at between two and four times the growth-rate of the local gross domestic product and it maintained a strong focus on incrementally improving profitability.

Although there was no crisis in Multi-Products Chile when Thompson arrived in early 1996, profitability had declined and the message to him was that it could be improved. As Thompson sized up the organization, he believed it could achieve those profitability objectives. On the other hand, he could make more substantial changes to achieve the potential that headquarters felt existed in Chile.

CUSTOMER AND DISTRIBUTION CHANNEL CHANGES

The group of retailers and distributors that Multi-Products Chile had traditionally served was changing quickly. Bob Thompson commented:

> The last five years have been dramatic. Big American retailers are here or are coming. That has meant that our organization needed to change.

U.S. superstores were rapidly changing the retail market in the country. One

manager commented that in the past, local superstores might have represented 60 percent of retail sales, with small sole-proprietorships making up the rest. This superstore segment had been growing at 8 to 10 percent per year. In 1998, he believed superstores, local and foreign, represented over 90 percent of the business.

As the level of sophistication increased among retailers, expectations of their suppliers increased as well. Purchasing managers, due to the volume of products they were purchasing, were reluctant to deal with distributors, preferring instead to deal directly with suppliers. They also expected lower prices. Multi-Products managers commented:

> Customers are asking for direct service at lower prices. With the big U.S. retailers, negotiation requirements have changed. We have lost power. Our products have traditionally had solid margins and I feel they were higher in the past. Before we might have averaged 80 percent margins. Now, it is difficult to have a different price from everyone else because communication systems like the Internet let people know the world price.

One manager recounted the entry of a new office products retailer into the Chilean market:

> They have been putting a lot of pressure on margins. We are assisting them to enter the market with special programs but it is costly. We have competitors, but Multi-Products has the most complete line of products. We try to add more value to the product. For example, our competitor may sell one kind of tape, where we will sell six.

Retailers were demanding more than just price discounts. They demanded a commitment to advertising support before they would place a product on their shelves. In the case of the office supplies retailer, Multi-Products paid 5 million pesos[4] for a photograph of its office products to be included in a supplementary catalogue. The catalogue would be followed up by a telemarketing campaign that was also a new concept for Chile.

Retailers also wanted more timely delivery to reduce inventories and better communication with their suppliers around ordering, billing and logistics. One manager commented:

> We had to learn to make the delivery and leave the invoice at the same time. As an industrial products company we were used to loading a big truck and sending it to the customer. In consumer products, we use smaller trucks and make more stops. We had to wait at the new, large retailers because the big, traditional consumer goods suppliers had more clout and were unloaded first.

Retailers wanted to reduce the number of Multi-Products sales representatives they were dealing with from four or five down to one. As a result, that sales person had to have access to information about all of the company's products being delivered to that retailer, even though they might originate from multiple product divisions.

The company also wanted to consolidate and had re-organized product responsibilities to achieve this. For example, where the Marketing Manager for Consumer Goods had been responsible for tape sales within his or her channel, responsibility for all tape sales, industrial and consumer, now resided with another manager in the Home and Office Division. This meant that the Marketing Coordinators of the Home and Office and Consumer Products Division now had to work together more closely than in the past. Cross-divisional selling had become an established fact. One manager commented:

> We have to learn to work together. They have the products and product knowledge. We have the relationship with the superstores and the skill in negotiating with them. Last year 44 percent of our division's sales were from non-consumer products to supermarkets, home centers and hardware stores.

In many instances, the company continued to use distributors, in part, because nearly 80 percent of their product sales went to industrial users. In some industries, the number of distributors had decreased after consolidation and the sophistication of the remaining distributors was increasing. Managing the relationship with distributors had become increasingly difficult as sales representatives began selling directly to end users previously serviced by a distributor.

It was not just the retail sector that had changed, but industrial products companies as well. The mining industry used to be government-controlled but large mining multi-nationals were commonplace and they operated differently. One executive commented, "Everything has been challenged. We need new skills."

NEW ROLE FOR SALES REPRESENTATIVES

Changes in the company's customer base were resulting in new responsibilities and requirements for Multi-Products' sales representatives. Generally, Chile was a fairly structured society. In business, titles conferring status in the organization were very important. The selling role was not held in the same regard as other positions, and levels of education tended to be lower. Indeed, it was often difficult for sales reps to access more senior managers in the selling process. Thompson commented that "the idea of a sales executive meeting with a client's executive does not exist commonly here."

A business unit manager described a typical sales call in the past:

> When sales representatives visited a business, they would usually sit down and have a coffee with their contact. A significant portion of their conversation would revolve around non-business-related topics such as the client's family or maybe football. The relationship was very important. Eventually, the sales representative would inspect the client's inventories and make suggestions for orders of our products.

Because of increased client sophistication and more advanced products from Multi-Products, more was required from a sales representative. Another Business Unit manager commented:

> A sales rep now needs to teach as well as to sell. In the past, they were specialists. They may have only sold simple office products. Now they need to know how to sell a multimedia projector, connect it to a notebook computer and train clients on how to use it, too! People need to be more professional in their commercial relationships and make an effort to learn. We don't sell products anymore, we sell solutions.

Instead of casual sales visits, it was not uncommon now to have a team of five or six sales people, coordinated by one single client contact, making presentations that could last two or three days. Consumer products sales reps also were now focused on visiting a given number of stores in a day and handling smaller orders faster and more frequently since there were no warehouses—just the shelves in the customers' stores. Not all the sales reps were happy with this conversion from maintaining a relationship with a store owner to being, in their view, an "ant' running all over the place.

Multi-Products Chile had started placing more emphasis on recruiting high caliber people including those for sales positions. However, most university graduates showed much greater interest in positions that appeared to offer faster mobility to executive positions such as in marketing.

INTEGRATED SOLUTIONS AND KEY ACCOUNTS IN MULTI-PRODUCTS CHILE

When Thompson arrived in Santiago, he learned that, although there was an awareness of the "Integrated Solutions" approach, little real progress appeared to have been made. He commented:

> This was our most important commercial activity globally, but it was not present in Chile. Our product line is so broad and deep, that customers were confused. "Why can't we see just one sales representative?" they would ask.
>
> The company had been organized for distribution-based selling, taking product lines to distributors. We needed to start understanding client

and business applications of products . . . acting like a consultant. This approach proved new and challenging for the organization.

Sales representatives were responsible for sales of a specific product or line of products. Performance was measured on the ability of a representative to sell certain products, and there was no incentive to sell products from other areas of the company. As a result, customers who purchased a range of products from Multi-Products were forced to deal with several different sales representatives. If the customer was a multinational, it would often have to deal with a separate sales organization in each country in which it did business.

Structural Changes

When Bob Thompson arrived at Multi-Products Chile, he found an organization that had been very successful with traditional distribution-based selling. The deeper Multi-Products "footprint" that he was used to, especially technical support groups, was limited. He added technical support positions along with a technical council to foster its development. As well, marketing, sales and manufacturing councils were added in time.

He also created the new position of Integrated Solutions Manager, reporting to the manufacturing products business unit manager. This person would be responsible for the implementation of Integrated Solutions in Chile and would coordinate the sales teams that would service large clients where the program was being implemented.

A short time later, a position of National Accounts Leader for Key Accounts was also created, reporting directly to Thompson. A new manufacturing manager was hired from Multi-Products Argentina where a more established manufacturing organization existed. See Exhibit 1 for a diagram of the revised organizational structure.

Accounts of special significance to Multi-Products Chile would now be viewed in one of two ways: Key Accounts and Integrated Solutions Targets.

Key Accounts

The Key Account concept was not new to Multi-Products Chile. However, in the past, a key account was identified as a customer with the potential to purchase large quantities of the company's products. Multi-Products Chile sold directly to these customers using programs different from distributors especially in pricing structure and logistics support, but the sales effort remained similar. Multiple sales representatives from each of the product areas selling to the client would service the account. Little, or no, coordination existed between the product groups.

Now, Key Accounts were those customers whose relationship with Multi-Products took on a strategic significance beyond a buyer/supplier relationship in that Multi-Products' technology could augment the customer's business and possibly change the basis of competition. Multi-Products Chile wanted to identify strategic partnerships with its customers where activities such as research and product development could be coordinated between the organizations, creating long-term competitive advantages for both organizations.

In 1998, this process had only been initiated, and partners, as well as the specific nature of the desired relationships with these partners, were in the process of being determined. However, the criteria for selecting Key Accounts were: a) a strong relationship with Multi-Products Chile, b) purchase potential, c) potential importance

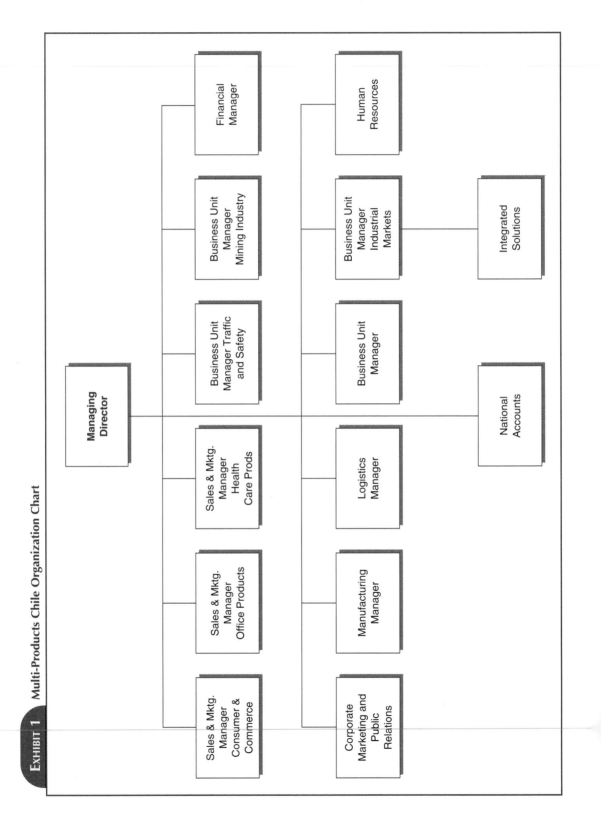

EXHIBIT 1   Multi-Products Chile Organization Chart

548

as an Integrated Solutions account, and d) an important company in Chile concerned about the environment and society and having the same values as Global Multi-Products Inc.

Multi-Products Chile was one of the first of the company's Latin American subsidiaries to create this formal Key Accounts position. The National Accounts Leader felt that his challenge was going to be to convince the other Multi-Products' companies to be consistent in their business model and prices with the Chilean company so that multinational customers could benefit from the relationship. He commented:

> This is a strategic program and will take a big change in mentality. We can't think short term, anymore. Free trade is helping to stabilize the country but we could still have big changes. This is the reason that business executives in Chile think short term.

Integrated Solution Targets

The real start of Integrated Solutions was in August 1997 with the collection of data about which customers would make the best targets for an initial effort. The idea was to discover those product divisions that had good relationships with clients and use the relationship to sell other products. Where the National Account Program, Key Accounts, was a strategic approach to link with a few very large accounts to create new products, Integrated Solutions was a broadly based tactical approach involving many more accounts.

Integrated Solutions represented an opportunity to sell products from multiple product groups to a client in a concerted effort. By early 1998, more than 30 customers had been identified as targets.

The next stage involved taking an "x-ray" of these companies to determine which

products the company was already using. A group of specialists would map a customer's business process to find opportunities for other products that might reduce a customer's costs. This process was complicated because a single company could purchase its products directly from Multi-Products Chile, although from different product groups, as well as from a range of distributors. Once managers knew what the company was purchasing, they could measure any increase in sales to those accounts and measure that against the general market to determine if the Integrated Solutions effort was succeeding.

An individual sales representative was then selected as the leader for a specific client and would act as the single point of contact for all sales to that client, including sales outside of the sales representative's own product area. These sales representatives would then request support from other representatives as required. This leader was determined by selecting the person having the best relationship with the client, who usually was obvious.

Sales Representatives and Integrated Solutions

Managers often described the Multi-Products Chile organization as silos, with individual product groups functioning independently of one another. One manager commented:

> We used to describe the situation as feudal. There were some sales reps that supported other divisions, but there was no program to formalize the activity.
>
> Salespeople feel they have ownership over their product areas. They would ask: "Why would I use my time opening doors for another sales

rep when I can use that time to visit my own customers?"

With the implementation of Integrated Solutions, it was recognized that sales staff needed to work as a team, helping one another to sell products. Everyone had not adjusted well to working with other product divisions. Some managers demanded: "Give me the products and I will sell them and earn the commission!" One manager commented:

> Not all the sales people are with the program; 15 percent are with the program, another 60 percent are with the program but are not leading it. The others are saying: "I will look after my own business and nothing else."
>
> Sales people need a change in terms of mentality. They also need to develop new sales techniques and knowledge about the products. The younger people are generally more adaptable to the change.

The increased sophistication in the buying process of some of the company's clients had also caused problems. Some sales representatives felt they had less influence in the process. They had grown accustomed to pushing new products that had been created in the US. Now marketing people were often involved in the initial process of approaching retailers with new products and negotiating the terms of sale.

Compensation also became an issue, because sales representatives usually were measured against sales targets in their product areas.

Sales Representative Compensation

When sales representatives joined Multi-Products Chile, they were given a six-month grace period during which time their compensation was 100 percent fixed. After that time, 40 percent of their compensation was fixed while the remaining 60 percent was variable or "at risk," and tied to the achievement of various targets. As a sales representative became more senior, the variable portion was reduced to 20 percent which reduced uncertainty about pay. As one manager commented, "We Latins don't like uncertainty."

The variable compensation targets were set by the sales manager, and were designed to encourage desired activity for that period. For example, 20 percent of the variable pay could be for the sale of new products. Other percentages could be used for sales calls on new clients, or sales of certain high-margin items. To accommodate Integrated Solutions, a sales manager could include sales of other product areas as a target within a sales representative's variable compensation. These targets were usually adjusted annually to meet the needs of the sales division.

Sales representatives could also receive additional pay in extra-compensation for exceeding their targets. For example, sales reps with 30 percent variable compensation could earn up to 130 percent of their salary and a senior sales rep with 20 percent variable compensation could earn up to 120 percent.

The Sales Contest

Until two years earlier, the sales contest was designed and administered by the Human Resources Department when it was transferred to Corporate Marketing. The Corporate Marketing Manager invited the Sales Council,[5] of which he was the head, to design a new program.

The new program eliminated the prizes that had been given in the past such as trips and microwave ovens which, as was clearly evident, the winners usually sold. Instead, it provided monetary rewards. If sales reps made 123 percent of their target they would get, in effect, a bonus payment of x percent. If the sales team of which they were a part met its objectives, they would get an additional y percent. And, if the Business Unit met its objectives, they could receive another z percent. In total, they could earn up to an additional $2,500.

This new sales contest presented difficulties for Bob Thompson. The Manager of Human Resources and other managers were not pleased with it. They felt that a) it was too expensive, potentially costing as much as the whole training and education budget; b) it should not have been monetarized; c) it permitted everyone to get a prize; and d) it had become part of the compensation system which was senior management's responsibility.

Thompson knew there was dissatisfaction among his managers with the new sales contest. His Human Resources Manager preferred to see changes in the plan but Thompson liked some elements of the design and since it came into effect when sales growth exceeded 23 percent it was to a degree self-funding.

INITIATING THE CHANGE PROCESS

In late 1996, soon after Thompson's arrival, a retreat was held in Iquique, a resort area north of Santiago, for senior managers from Multi-Products Chile as well as from Multi-Products Bolivia and Peru. Prior to the managers of the three countries meeting as one group, they met individually to confirm their primary mission and goals. The Chile group appeared to struggle at working together.

One of the purposes of the retreat was to establish a general mission statement for the region created by the three countries.

The discussion went poorly. Managers seemed to have trouble defining a clear mission and did not touch on broader objectives for the region. As the discussion, originally scheduled for two or three hours, entered its second day, Thompson became increasingly disappointed, not only with the group's inability to reach a conclusion, but with what appeared to him to be the quality of the discussions. Frustrated, Thompson stopped the discussion and asked the group why things were going so poorly. To his surprise, one of the Chilean managers stood up and said: "We don't trust each other."

Thompson had hired a consultant to act as a professional facilitator for the retreat. As part of his services, he later provided a report outlining his conclusions about the meeting and the group. His executive summary included the following points about the executive team:

> Generally, this appears to be a strong task- and results-oriented group. They are autonomous in doing what they do and are well adjusted to standard requirements. Because of this they are able to focus on task structure and output evaluation but are less aware of group process and its importance to productivity and teamwork. At times they seem isolated and defensive. There are also some unresolved personal conflicts with no methodology about resolving those conflicts.

This information gave Thompson some idea about the nature of the Multi-Products Chile organization, and pointed out some challenges to be met as he worked to make it more responsive to the customers and markets they served.

Additionally, the company conducted company-wide employee surveys every three years. They included information from various levels of the organization, about employees' opinions on various aspects of the company such as salaries, empowerment, and safety. As a part of the data analysis, a comparison was made of the opinions of senior managers in contrast with the opinions of lower level employees on each dimension. While opinions differed on many issues, certain areas showed senior managers having a much more positive opinion than their employees (a difference of ≥20 percent). These included: work conditions, training, job progress, pay, safety and empowerment.

About the change process, one executive observed:

> There has been resistance and conflict generated because of the changes. Maybe it has been too aggressive or too quick. People need to understand why we are changing and we are addressing this. We are in the process of changing even though not much has really changed yet.
>
> These programs promote involvement beyond your scope of responsibility. They are long-term programs, sophisticated techniques. They won't create sales tomorrow. We are measured by our results and there is no need to change. The company is doing well. There are no rewards for thinking strategically. You can be comfortable and do well not doing

these things. Thompson is doing it because he thinks it is right. It takes courage. Others do only what they are rewarded for.

Conclusion

Thompson's secretary interrupted his reflections to remind him that he had a meeting shortly with his human resources manager. Thompson thought to himself that, maybe, he had introduced enough change to Multi-Products Chile and that it was not necessary to go further. After all, business was good and things were going well.

Notes

1. "Converting" meant taking products originally received in bulk, and packaging or sealing them for consumption in the local market.
2. Much of this information was taken from company documents.
3. This section is adapted from The Economist, January 24, 1998; Santiago; What's on; Turiscom S. A., January 1998; and Chile Handbook; Charlie Nurse, Footprint Handbooks, 1997.
4. In January 1998, US$1 purchased 450 Chilean pesos.
5. The composition of this council included the corporate marketing manager, and senior sales representatives from the business units.

Case 16

ENRON IN INDIA

A Forced Renegotiation

William A. Stoever and Richard P. Teisch

During the early 1990s, India's future was looking dim . . . literally. Electricity blackouts and brownouts occurred regularly over much of the country, and power shortages and supply interruptions were limiting its economic progress. Its energy balance—the relationship between energy consumption and production—was negative and expected to worsen as the country approached the year 2000 (Table 1). The Indian government finally admitted that its policy of do-it-yourself power plant construction was not working well and, thus, decided to open up future projects to foreign bidders.

But most foreign contractors were leery of India's history of discrimination against foreign companies and its reputation as a slow, difficult, bureaucracy-ridden place to do business. Only one foreign company, Enron Corporation of the United States, was willing to enter negotiations to build a power plant there. But after committing massive resources to the development of a gigantic generating station, Enron ran into a political and financial confrontation that

threatened to ruin the project's viability. This case sets forth the history of the Enron project and the dilemma forced on the company by its Indian challenges.

INDIA'S ENERGY CRISIS

The energy shortage was due to many factors. The existing power plants were inefficient and were operating at a fraction of their designed capacity, and transmission and distribution system losses were estimated to be as much as 40%. The state-run electricity boards were losing an estimated U.S.$20 billion annually, attributed mostly to stolen electricity and to free power given to politically influential farmers. In the past, India had obtained funds for power plant construction from the World Bank, but in 1994 the bank cut U.S.$750 million from the country's allocation because the Indian states refused to stop giving free power to the farmers. Soon after the funds were discontinued, the World Bank released a report stating that India needed an injection

SOURCE: Used with permission and prepared by William A. Stoever, Keating-Crawford Professor of International Business Emeritus at Seton Hall University, South Orange, New Jersey, and Richard P. Teisch, Management Associate at Public Service Electric and Gas Company in New Jersey. Richard holds a master's degree in business administration from Seton Hall University.

Table 1   India's Energy Balance: Historical and Projected (Quadrillion BTU)

	1980	1985	1990	1995	2000	2005	2010
Consumption	4.16	5.89	7.74	10.49	13.74	17.75	21.65
Production	3.1	5.26	6.53	8.33	10.44	12.18	13.86

of U.S.$10 billion into its power industry by the year 2000, without which the daily power interruptions would persist. In 1995, electric generating capacity was estimated to be 84,000 megawatts (MW), which might have been adequate for a country the size of France or the United Kingdom with populations of 58 and 54 million, respectively. But in India, with a population of 936 million, this low level of capacity led to severe power shortages throughout much of the country.

Other factors that impeded funds flow into the country were massive corruption, red tape, poor infrastructure, and constant political struggles. These risk factors made multinational power companies hesitant to invest. Furthermore, India had a tradition of extremely inward-looking investment policies. The government practiced the Gandhian doctrine of *swadeshi* (self-reliance) and distrusted foreign companies. There was a lingering popular belief that any transactions with foreigners were either corrupt or disadvantageous to India. The country's business culture was quite different from the United States: Whereas American companies focused heavily on the "bottom line," Indians were concerned with preserving their self-respect as well as making profits. Furthermore, in keeping with its socialist ideals, the government had reserved the "commanding heights" of the economy, including power generation, for public ownership. Hence, until the early 1990s virtually all foreign power firms were prevented from entering.

However, the country's economic growth had begun to accelerate in the 1990s and picked up even faster in the following years. The growth was predicted to drive up energy demand more than 4.5% annually through 2010, the highest incremental energy demand growth of any country in the world (Table 2). The U.S. Department of Energy estimated that India would need approximately 140,000 MW of additional capacity by 2005. It became increasingly obvious that the country would never be able to supply these needs as long as it reserved power generation to the public sector. The power crisis was one of the major reasons why Congress Party leader P. V. Narasimha Rao, a longtime advocate of market-oriented reforms, was elected prime minister.

Rao's government stepped up the pace of free-market reforms that had begun under some of his predecessors, including lowering trade barriers, eliminating complicated investment-licensing laws, floating the rupee, and simplifying the tax structure. In order to attract desperately needed foreign direct investment (FDI), Rao took steps to liberalize investment in the power sector. His plan was to allow both Indian and foreign companies to build and operate privately owned power projects. However, no foreign power companies approached India with proposals since they still perceived the risks and uncertainties as too high. For example, it seemed politically desirable for foreign power companies to have local partners

Table 2   World Total Energy Consumption: Selected Regions—Historical and Projected (Quadrillion BTU)

Region/Country	1990	1995	2000	2005	2010	2015	(1995–2015)*
North America	99.9	108.3	119.0	127.8	134.7	140.2	1.3
United States	84.0	90.6	97.8	103.4	107.9	110.9	1.0
Mexico	4.9	5.6	7.3	8.8	9.8	10.9	3.4
Western Europe	61.8	64.6	70.2	74.9	79.3	83.8	1.3
Industrial							
Asia	23.1	27.3	29.7	32.3	34.7	36.8	1.5
Japan	18.0	21.4	23.7	25.8	27.8	29.5	1.6
Developing							
Asia	51.4	69.6	90.5	112.9	134.7	159.1	4.2
China	35.7	36.7	57.1	57.1	69.1	82.9	4.3
India	7.7	10.5	13.7	17.7	21.6	26.0	4.6
Total world	344.9	364.9	415.6	465.7	513.6	561.9	2.2

SOURCE: The U.S. Department of Energy.

* Average annual percent change.

even though the new guidelines did not require them; having local partners was thought to overcome the appearance of exploiting India and not giving back to the community.

Enron

Enron Corporation was formed in 1985 by the merger of several smaller power companies. It took advantage of the newly deregulated U.S. gas market to expand its market rapidly and indeed gained renown in the 1990s as the most aggressive energy company in the world. Its earnings rose at an average annual rate of 32% from 1988 to the early 1990s. However, its earnings growth slowed as U.S. gas prices declined, and the market approached saturation. Enron realized that it needed to go abroad in its quest for continued earnings growth. It started

construction of a 1,875-MW power plant in Teesside, England, a project that promised to yield phenomenal returns, and it anticipated similar successes in Argentina, China, Colombia, Guatemala, and the Philippines. These successes increased its toleration for risk in emerging markets.

Prime Minister Rao sent his power secretary, S. Rajgopal, to Washington, D.C., on a mission to attract FDI from American power companies. Enron invited Rajgopal to visit its headquarters in Houston, Texas, for a meeting with Rebecca Mark, president and chief executive officer of Enron Development Corp., the company's international energy solutions arm. The meeting with Rajgopal convinced Enron that India offered tremendous opportunities. The uncharted waters of India, the largest democracy in the world, were the type of challenge Enron thrived on. So a group of company executives flew to India to tour potential sites. After briefings on the 26 Indian states, they chose the state of Maharashtra for Enron's first investment site. With a population of over 78 million, Maharashtra was the third largest and second most literate state in India. It was known as the country's premier industrial state; was the home of the commercial capital, Bombay; and had the highest state GDP in the country. Enron selected the city of Dabhol because it was conveniently located on the western seaboard, just a few hours south of Bombay.

The Indian central government left decisions about power generation and distribution up to the individual state governments, so Enron executives entered into negotiations with Maharashtra officials. After relatively brief discussions, the Chief Minister of Maharashtra, S. Rao Naik, signed a memorandum of understanding for the construction of a 2,015-MW gas-fired power plant. At a cost of almost U.S.$3 billion, the plant would be the largest single FDI project ever committed to India. Moreover, it would be the first foreign power project ever undertaken in the country and the single largest power station in all of India.

The plant was slated to be owned by a consortium of U.S. companies. Enron's share would be 80%, while General Electric and Bechtel would each own 10%. Eventually, after the plant was up and running, Enron's plan was to sell 20% of its share to another U.S.-based energy company, Entergy. Because of the risks it perceived, Enron demanded 23% return on equity (ROE) from the project, a much higher figure than the 16% the Indian central government had approved for other domestic energy projects.

Enron took pride in being "the most reliable supplier of clean energy worldwide

for a better environment" and thus wanted the plant to use imported liquefied natural gas (LNG), a very clean burning fuel. The company calculated that the cost per kilowatt hour (kWh) would be U.S.7.4 cents, which was U.S.3.4 cents above what Indian consumers were paying other producers at that time. Enron's explanation for the high rate was that although LNG plants were cheaper to build, they were more expensive to operate. Not surprisingly, the Indian negotiators preferred to use naphtha because it was a cheaper fuel and was produced locally, thus saving on foreign exchange. Enron prevailed on this point in the initial agreement.

Once the ROE and plant specifications were agreed upon, the next step was to negotiate the power-purchase agreement (PPA). This agreement would guarantee that as long as Enron's plant met certain efficiency targets, the Maharashtra State Electric Board (MSEB) would purchase power from it. In an attempt to further ease Enron's creditors' concerns, the Indian central government offered a counterguarantee, agreeing to pay Enron and its partners for the power produced by the Dabhol plant if the MSEB failed to do so. The central government was willing to take this unprecedented step because it viewed the Dabhol project as key to meeting India's short-term requirements as well as to attracting future FDI to build power plants. The government also agreed to insert a clause allowing either party the right to pursue arbitration in a preapproved London court, thus alleviating Enron's concerns about having any potential disputes adjudicated in the Indian courts, which were notoriously slow and were believed to be subject to pressure from influential government officials.

The Backlash

While the PPA and counterguarantee were being negotiated, news of the Dabhol project leaked to the Indian public. Negative reports surfaced about both Enron and the Maharashtra government, claiming that bribery took place, no competitive bidding process was held, power rates were too high, and the ROE was astronomical. Furthermore, many were enraged with the fact that Enron's profits would be even greater when they sold the 20% share to Entergy. The tension reached a zenith when a bomb exploded at the hotel where Enron's PPA negotiation team was staying. To make matters worse, a World Bank team hired by India to conduct a feasibility study on the Dabhol project concluded that the project was not in Maharashtra's best interest. Following the bombing and several riots, Prime Minister Rao appointed his defense minister, Sharad Pawar, as the new chief minister of Maharashtra. Pawar was dissatisfied with the PPA between Enron and Maharashtra and demanded that certain terms be renegotiated. Enron agreed to lower the ROE slightly and to make other minor concessions, after which both parties signed the PPA.

Enron started work after the agreement was signed and invested substantial sums in the ensuing months. About a year later, while construction was in full swing, Indian state elections were held. The incumbent Congress Party was voted out of power in Maharashtra, and a coalition of two militant Hindu nationalist parties, the Shiv Sena and the Bharatiya Janata Party (BJP), was voted in. Although the Congress Party, which favored the Dabhol plant, remained in power at the national level, the new Maharashtra government opposed it and immediately declared its intent to review the terms. A few months later, the new Chief Minister, Manohar Joshi, announced that the Dabhol project would be cancelled. In a speech to the Maharashtra state assembly, he said,

From the speed with which the memorandum of understanding was signed, it seemed as if Enron came, it saw, and it conquered. The proposed capital investment in the project is definitely more than it should have been, and there is uncertainty about many components of the power purchase agreement, resulting in payment of an unjustified rate which is higher than other comparable projects, and therefore the project, in its current form, is not in the interest of the State.

He added, "Accepting this deal would indicate an absolute lack of self-respect and would amount to betraying the trust of the people." He decried the fact that no competitive bidding had taken place, which was indeed true, although the reason was that no other foreign power company had been willing to bid. Ex-Chief Minister Pawar later commented, "Our financial position was bad. No one was interested to come to India to invest in the power sector. No one had shown interest in the true sense except Enron."

Although the project appeared to be crucial to India's future in terms of power generation and FDI in general, the central government chose to steer clear of the dispute. Prime Minister Rao stated, "The agreement is between Enron and the state government of Maharashtra. I come into this picture only as a central government figure giving a counterguarantee (to foreign investment)."

In addition to the cancellation, a total of 24 cases were filed against Enron in Maharashtra courts, alleging everything from corruption to environmental degradation. While Enron felt they had little merit, the cases could still consume considerable time and money to contest, and they created another cloud of uncertainty hanging over the project. Some observers felt that Joshi was using the Dabhol project cancellation for his own purposes. Although the Shiv Sena/BJP coalition now controlled the state government, national elections were fast approaching. Joshi appeared to want to use the controversy over the Dabhol project to boost his party's national position. He attempted to make the Congress Party look as if they accepted bribes and were unconcerned with Indian citizens' well-being. Indian public opinion overwhelmingly supported the new Maharashtra government. One reporter said, "The theme plays nicely on the visceral distrust of foreign companies that Indian voters have felt since the colonial era."

Immediately after the cancellation, Entergy, fearing further volatility, opted not to purchase its allocated 20% share in the project, an action that caused Enron a U.S.$75 million loss. The cancellation drew much international attention. Foreign companies' confidence in India had been rising following Rao's reform package, but the cancellation made potential investors deeply wary again. U.S., British, and French government spokesmen went on record as saying that the "cancellation of the Dabhol project would have adverse consequences for India." In what seemed to be an attempt to coerce India into renegotiating, the U.S. Department of Energy issued a statement warning that canceling the Dabhol project could "adversely affect other power projects (in India)." These comments further infuriated Indian officials, who believed that the statements were an attempt to bully their country.

Other more impartial observers saw the issue differently. Pawar realized the severity of any cancellation so widely publicized, saying,

It is clearly a political stunt, totally selfish and shortsighted in its aims. By scrapping Enron's project the national economy will definitely suffer, and so will the international image of the state and the country. I strongly believe the government should not have taken this step.

Enron's Dilemma

At this point, Enron faced a number of choices, each of which carried the risk of a costly or an otherwise undesirable outcome. It could

1. attempt through negotiation to preserve the terms previously agreed to (this of course would depend on the company's assessment of its bargaining power, which might be considerably weakened in view of the large amount of money already sunk in the project and presumably nonrecoverable);

2. lower the total cost of the project;

3. lower its ROE;

4. lower the electricity prices in the PPA;

5. attempt to get the case into arbitration in the preapproved London court;

6. take whatever compensation it could get at this point and walk away from the project (perhaps on the argument of not throwing bad money after good); and

7. possibly, appease the more radical nationalists' demands if it took in a local partner, either a private power

company or a state or central government department such as the MSEB.

If it did manage to stay, Enron faced the further question of the choice of fuel: It could agree to use local, environmentally unfriendly naphtha, thus compromising the company's reputation for environmental concern, or it could insist on using LNG, which was cleaner but more expensive and was disfavored by the government.

Case 17

THE FACTORY OF CERAMIC BRICK ENTERPRISE (FCBE)

Entrepreneurial Management in a Transition Economy[a]

The former Soviet Union was a patchwork of many ethnic groups and nationalities stretching from the Baltic Sea to the Pacific Ocean. Geographically, it was the largest country in the world covering 11 time zones. There were vast historical, ethnic, cultural, and linguistic differences among these people who were all governed by the central government in Moscow. The fall of communism and the breakup of the Soviet Union in 1991 resulted in the formation of 15 independent countries, the largest of which is Russia. The Newly Independent States (NIS) carved out of the Soviet Union are split into several regions. Latvia, Lithuania, and Estonia lie in the Baltic area. Belarus, Ukraine, Moldova, and Russia, which extends into Asia, comprise the Eastern European region. Georgia, Armenia, and Azerbaijan are located in the Caucasus. Finally, Kazakhstan, Turkmenistan, Uzbekistan, Tajikistan, and Kyrgyzstan are in Central Asia.

Turkmenistan gained its independence on October 17, 1991. Shortly afterward, similar to other NIS, Turkmenistan started the privatization of its economy. Through a decree from the president and the passage of appropriate legislation, the privatization process started with the sale of a few small- and medium-size companies. The Factory of Ceramic Brick Enterprise (FCBE) was among those that were auctioned to the public in 1993. The factory had been in operation since 1938. The new owner-director, Akbabek Taganova, purchased the factory from the state. Both Akbabek and her husband were educated in law at Magytumguli Turkmen State University. She graduated in 1983 and began practicing law along with her husband in the capital city of Ashgabad.

NOTE: This case was developed in a partnership project between the Texas A&M University System and Mugtymguli Turkmen State University through a grant from the U.S. Information Agency. The Coles College of Business, Kennesaw State University, Georgia, and the International Research and Exchanges Board (IREX) financed completion of this case.

In 1997, the president of Turkmenistan, Saparmurat Turkmenbashi, issued a decree to privatize a number of state-owned companies. Shortly after the presidential decree, an auction was held in Ashgabad to sell several government-owned companies to the public. FCBE was among them. At the time that Akbabek was contemplating a bid for one of those companies, the privatization process had just begun and involved mostly the provinces. The privatization process was much slower in Ashgabad than in other parts of the country. After a careful review of the options, Akbabek came to the conclusion that Ashgabad was the best part of the country in which to operate a private business. In her opinion, there were a couple of features that made the capital city a more desirable location for private businesses. The features that made Ashgabad more desirable included a large base of potential customers and adequate infrastructure. Also, the proximity to the government agencies reduced the uncertainty involved in the early days of the privatization process. The viability of companies that the government had earmarked for privatization in other parts of the country was questionable.

In her decision to become a pioneer entrepreneur in Turkmenistan, Akbabek established a couple of criteria for her business entry strategy. First, the business had to be a manufacturing operation that could easily create value for its customers. Second, the operation should not be very complex, so she could comfortably and in a short period of time become familiar with it. Third, for the reasons already discussed, it had to be located in the capital city.

From the companies that were earmarked for privatization in 1997, two were in Ashgabad, including the brick factory. FCBE was the best candidate because it met all her criteria. After a closer examination of the factory's operation, Akbabek determined that it was a good prospective business. FCBE had many problems, none of which were beyond resolution. In fact, the existence of those problems made it a good candidate. These problems would give the impression that FCBE had a bleak future. Consequently, most prospective buyers would question the viability of the company and would be leery of bidding for it. Therefore, Akbabek hoped that there would be fewer bids on the company.

Her assessment of the situation was accurate. She did not face much difficulty in bidding and acquiring the company. However, restructuring FCBE was going to put heavy demands on management at the beginning. To solve these problems would require accepting a higher level of expenditure at the beginning before the company could turn a profit.

Taking into account all these factors, Akbabek successfully made a bid and purchased the company at 1.5 billion manats. An agreement was signed with the government that stipulated the following:

1. Pay 10% of the purchase price in cash (150,000,000 manats), with the rest borrowed from a bank. Akbabek secured a loan from the Turkmen Bank for 6 months at an interest rate of 30%.

2. The purchase price of the factory was to be paid back to the government in 9 years.

The loan was secured to enable Akbabek to run the other businesses she owned without worrying about sources of funding for their operations and allowing her 6 months time to generate more earnings. She hoped that the earnings from the other businesses and the factory itself would provide enough funds for paying back the government. The borrowing and the expenses involved in upgrading the operation resulted in an excessive financial burden on FCBE. In 1999, the company had 1.3 billion manats debt. The official exchange rate at the time was $1.00 = 5,200 manats, while the black market rate was $1.00 = 17,000 manats.

The decision to purchase FCBE was a calculated risk. From an outsider's point of view, the business did not look very promising. Even after 2 years, some considered Akbabek's decision to purchase the factory a bad choice. The Deputy Minister of Construction Material once had asked his staff, "Who is the fool who has purchased the FCBE factory?" By this comment, he implied that the factory was in very bad shape and whoever owned it would face considerable problems and could run into financial difficulties. Akbabek was pleased to hear about the comment. In her opinion, the more government agencies thought the brick factory was in bad shape, the less they would create difficulties for her, and the more favorable terms she would receive in her purchase of raw material from the state. The government bureaucrats thought that they made a good deal by selling the factory to her. In their opinion, Akbabek made a mistake purchasing a run-down factory. Indeed, the factory had been neglected for a long time and was in need of an overhaul. Most equipment needed repairs to make it fully operational. Some was beyond repair and needed to be replaced. The buildings were not well maintained and required a face-lift. All these problems, however, could be resolved with good management and careful monitoring of the cash flow. The factory had the potential of becoming a very profitable business if it could overcome financial difficulties that plague most businesses in the first few years of their operation.

THE COMPETITORS

Before purchasing FCBE, Akbabek knew that there were two other brick factories in Ashgabad. The two factories and their products and production capacities were as follows:

1. Argach Gurgoshuk (Guzel Ganat) was a state-owned and -operated factory with the capacity of producing 500,000 bricks a month.

2. BINA was a 50%–50% joint venture between an Iranian investor and a government entity called Zavot Kramichekogo Kirpicha. BINA's monthly production capacity was 250,000 bricks.

BINA had no dryers and dried the bricks in open space under the sun before baking them in kilns. Because of its lack of dryers, BINA could not operate during the winter, and the factory remained idle for more than 3 months annually. While it saved on heating oil by using the sun, this resulted in lower-quality bricks. Compared with bricks that are heat dried, sun-dried bricks are softer, lower in consistency, and have rough edges. By remaining idle for several months, BINA's production was much lower and, therefore, its allocated fixed costs and some of its variable costs were higher.

After taking over management of FCBE, Akbabek had an opportunity to physically examine and compare the products of the other two companies. Her examination confirmed her initial assumption about the lower quality of the competition. Indeed, the products of both the state-owned company and BINA were of lower quality compared with FCBE's bricks. BINA's bricks were also about 1 cm smaller, which was in violation of building codes. The lower quality was partly because BINA did not have dryers and dried its bricks under the sun. However, BINA's products were better than those of the state-owned company.

As Exhibit 1 indicates, at the time of the purchase all three plants were served by only one access road. Akbabek made sure that in the purchase agreement the access road was included as a part of the FCBE property. The three plants also shared electric service (a generator), gas supply, and water. These services were included in the purchase agreement as belonging to her. The other two plants were made to negotiate with her for purchasing services from FCBE. The FCBE purchase agreement with the government entitled her to purchase these services from the government and resell them to the two other factories. As a result of this arrangement, the cost of operating FCBE was 50% lower than that of the other two plants.

However, Akbabek was not content with the strategic and cost advantage that FCBE was already enjoying over its competitors. She seized every occasion to extend this advantage. For example, she saw an opportunity to do just that shortly after the purchase. There was a gate at the access road. This gate controlled the road that was used by the three plants for delivery and for shipping bricks to customers. When bricks were stolen from FCBE a couple of times, the thieves used the common access road through that gate. After making several reports to the police and establishing a case on the issue, Akbabek blocked the road by building a wall at its entrance. The explanation provided to the other two plants was that she had to block easy access to her property to prevent further thefts at FCBE, and she had the authority to do this because the road was on her property. Because FCBE had a separate entrance gate, the blocking of the access road did not affect its operation. However, this was very disruptive to the other two plants and particularly to the BINA factory. BINA was forced to open a dirt road through the government property. Not only was constructing this dirt road an additional financial burden to BINA; using it was much more inconvenient

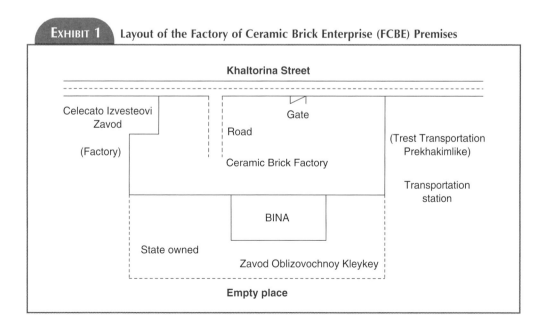

EXHIBIT 1   **Layout of the Factory of Ceramic Brick Enterprise (FCBE) Premises**

Khaltorina Street

Celecato Izvesteovi Zavod

(Factory)

Gate

Road

Ceramic Brick Factory

(Trest Transportation Prekhakimlike)

Transportation station

BINA

State owned

Zavod Oblizovochnoy Kleykey

Empty place

and time-consuming. In particular, it was very difficult to use the dirt road when it rained. Ultimately, both BINA and the government-owned factory, Argach Gurgoshuk, were forced to construct a new road. This road did not have direct access to the main street that all three plants used before FCBE blocked access to it. This was quite costly and increased the time for delivery to and from the plants, which put them at a competitive disadvantage.

In addition to buying bricks from FCBE, customers had a couple of sources from which to choose. One option was imports from Iran. Customers using the imports from Iran not only needed additional lead time due to the transportation time between Iran and Turkmenistan; they also had to pay the additional costs associated with the imports. In addition to transportation costs, there was a 10% tax on imported bricks. Therefore, importing bricks, while an option, was less practical and more expensive.

Another option was to purchase bricks from FCBE's competitors in Ashgabad, namely, BINA and Argach Gurgoshuk. Products from these two companies were often used by customers who were not well-informed about the differences in quality between the products from the three plants. Compared with the products of the other two factories, FCBE products were superior in quality and comparable in price.

The third choice was the bricks produced in other cities of Turkmenistan. These bricks were of lower quality compared with the imported bricks and those produced by FCBE. They also had the added expense of transportation costs.

SUBSTITUTE PRODUCTS

Brick has a few characteristics that make it a superior construction material. It is quite durable. The bricks used in construction in Turkmenistan during the Persian Empire, for example, have survived the ravage of ages, and many of them still are good enough to be used in construction projects today. Brick can withstand both cold and heat very well, and extreme temperature fluctuation does not damage it. It is versatile and can be used in almost any construction project. Aesthetically, it is better than competing products such as poured concrete or concrete blocks. Compared with bricks, both poured concrete and concrete blocks tend to get quite hot in summer and cold in winter. For these reasons, brick is the preferred choice in a variety of construction projects. However, bricks are more expensive than competing products.

PRODUCTION PROCESS

Brick production involves three stages:

1. Preparation of clay (raw material)

2. Producing raw brick and the drying process

3. Baking the brick in a kiln to produce the final product

The raw material, clay (a special type of soil), was purchased from the Ministry of Construction Materials (MCM). It was transported from a place about 60 km outside Ashgabad to the plants. Every day about 60 to 70 metric tons of dry clay were delivered to the plant. The MCM had a 25-year contract to exploit the land for clay. In turn, FCBE had a contract with the MCM to receive the needed clay. At the time of FCBE's purchase, MCM owed it 3,500,000,000 manats. Therefore, the clay purchase was financed from this debt. It is not clear what would happen when MCM's contract with the government expired.

There were three pits at the plant, each with a capacity of about 1,750 tons of clay. When the dry clay was brought to the plant, it was poured into the first pit and water was added slowly over a 2-month period. While the wet clay was being used from the first pit, the same process was carried out in the other two pits. The process continued in the same order.

The wet clay from the pits was carried up to the second floor of the plant by a conveyer belt. There, a machine separated gravel, stones, and other objects from the clay. A mixer on the second floor mixed 36 tons of clay a day (8 hr) to create consistent quality clay. The mixer had a capacity of 72 tons a day. But as described later, due to a bottleneck in other parts of the operation, it operated at half its capacity.

The clay was taken to the press machine on the first floor, which forced the clay into a tube with a diameter the size of a brick. As the clay moved out of the tube, a machine cut the clay into 10 bricks. Originally, the machine cut one brick at a time. Adopting BINA's invention, the machine was modified to cut 10 pieces at a time. This modification resulted in significant reduction of the cutting time and, therefore, has increased the speed of raw brick production.

Wet clay bricks were loaded in carts. The carts were slowly moved on a rail into the dryers. The quality of the bricks would have been better if they had been kept out of the dryer at room temperature for a couple of days. But because of shortages of carts, they were moved into the dryers right away. As more carts were loaded with bricks and they were moved into the dryers, the carts were pushed forward. The temperature at the entrance of the dryer was room temperature, and at the end of the dryer it was 65 to 70°C. It took about 3 days for a cart to reach the end of the dryer. At this point, the bricks were ready for the kiln (oven). Gas burners maintained the temperature at the desired level. After the bricks were cooled, they were removed from the carts and put into the kiln. Each kiln had the capacity for 800,000 bricks. For 45 days, gas burners operated on $\frac{1}{3}$ of the kiln at a time, rotating from one end of the oven to the other. Each kiln was a shell about 50 m long, 7 m wide, and 6 m high. It was constructed in the shape of a long arch with normal bricks for short-term use. A cross-section of a typical kiln was an inverted U. The kilns needed regular reconstruction due to continuous use that resulted in the deterioration of the shell. Permanent ovens could have been constructed using fireproof bricks. The time that bricks remained in the kiln could have been shortened if more gas pipes have been built into the kilns.

The plant produced 500,000 bricks per month and operated 12 months a year. BINA, on the other hand, operated 6 months a year because it did not have dryers and relied on sunshine for drying the bricks before putting them in the kilns.

At the time of the purchase, the factory owned two trucks. Shortly afterward, two additional trucks (Russian made) were purchased for $4,000 each. These trucks were used for hauling clay to the factory. The other two trucks were used for the delivery of bricks to customers. The newly purchased trucks were registered as noncommercial, which exempted them from a property tax payment.

ORGANIZATIONAL STRUCTURE AND CULTURE

The organizational structure of FCBE is depicted in Exhibit 2.

EXHIBIT 2   Organization Chart for the Factory of Ceramic Brick Enterprise

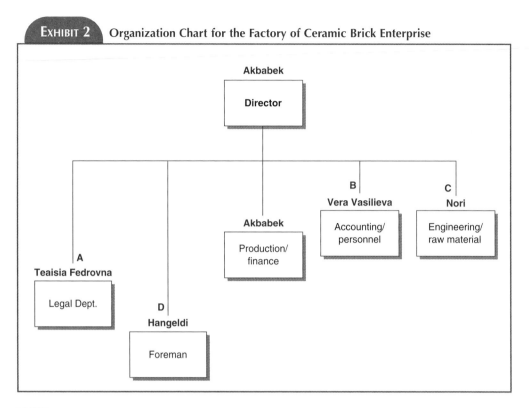

NOTE:

A. A B.S. in law from Moscow State University.

B. A Turkmen Technical School graduate with 20 years' experience in this company before privatization, with three persons reporting to her:
  1. A 50-year-old technician with a B.S. degree in engineering
  2. A 55-year-old accountant with a B.S. degree
  3. The 30-year-old head of the personnel department, with a B.S. degree

C. A 39-year-old Gopkin graduate, from Moscow Technical Academy, with 15 years of experience in the plant.

D. Foreman.

Akbabek shared the ownership of the company with her husband, but her husband did not have a formal position in the company. At the time of the purchase, the factory employed a large number of workers, many of them unskilled. Not only were these workers unproductive and their payroll a drain on the company's finances, but they also caused problems throughout the company. Often, they sat idle or engaged in talking and socializing with others. This was not only a waste of their own time; it also involved others in non-productive activities. Their work habits, expectations, and superior-subordinate relationships were shaped by years of working under the communist regime. Similarly, work rules and procedures were quite outdated, and many were irrelevant to the new competitive environment of the free-market economy. Both the organizational culture and the work rules and procedures had to be modified. The predominant, easygoing work culture was left over from the communist era but was, however, a hindrance to the implementation of new work rules.

Given that it was necessary to change the organizational culture and structure, a decision was made to reduce the workforce. Akbabek informed the employees of her decision and let it be known that only the most productive employees had a chance of remaining with the company. Those who were retained, however, would receive better pay and benefits, including paid educational expenses for their children.

Before the privatization, the factory employed 45 workers. This number was reduced to 30 shortly thereafter. Of the 30 workers, 18 were full-time, primary employees who were cross-trained and multiskilled, able to handle every task dealing with brick production. The other 12 were temporary workers who were hired as and when the need arose. Most of them were involved in nonproduction jobs such as cleaning the factory area of scraps, construction projects, and the like.

The reorganization resulted in a smaller payroll and a small staff of four people who directly reported to Akbabek. Teaisia Fedrovna, who was a graduate of Moscow State University School of Law, was responsible for the legal department. Vera Vasilieva was in charge of accounting and personnel. She was a graduate of Turkmen Technical School and had been with the company for 20 years. Vera supervised a three-person staff that included a 50-year-old technician, who had a B.S. degree in engineering; a 55-year-old accountant with a B.S. degree; and a 30-year-old head of the personnel department who also had a B.S. degree. The third person directly reporting to Akbabek was Nori. He was a graduate of Moscow Technical Academy (Gopkin).

Nori was 39 years old and had been at the plant for 15 years. Hangeldi, the foreman, was the last member of the staff. He was in charge of shop-level workers who were involved in all stages of brick production, from preparing the clay, to producing raw bricks, to maintaining the dryers and the ovens, and finally to producing the bricks. Hangeldi and his crew handled all aspects of brick production.

To Akbabek's delight, having fewer workers resulted in higher productivity and better results. The layoffs removed the less productive ones from the plant and motivated others to be more concerned with productivity and performance. The remaining workers were relatively punctual and spent less time gossiping. They paid more attention to the quality of the bricks produced and showed more interest in their work. Some even suggested certain changes in the operations that resulted in either higher efficiency or improved quality. This was a good start in changing the lackadaisical work culture.

Further steps were taken to transform the corporate culture. To foster trust and encourage open communication, for example, Akbabek established an open-door policy. She let the workers know that they could come to her office and discuss any issues of concern with her. She made a concerted effort to learn their names. She knew all her employees, although she did not remember all their names. By demonstrating an interest in their lives, she strived to create a family-like work environment. She maintained a list of their children's names to send them presents on special occasions such as birthdays and national holidays. Paid summer camps were offered for the workers' children. Such gestures were much welcomed by the workers, but not all workers took advantage of this benefit. Those who did not send their children to camp had them working at home or on their farms. The children's work, and the extra income, made a difference to the families. Akbabek knew this and sympathized with their predicament. While all of them were interested in sending their children to the summer camps, the families' financial condition did not allow it in some cases.

Another aspect of Akbabek's attempt at creating a new organizational culture was the way that she treated her staff formally. The four people who directly reported to her were considered of equal standing in the company. She wanted them to be friendly and cooperate with each other. Therefore, she treated them equally well. She made sure that no one tried to act superior to others and openly encouraged them to solve organizational problems collectively.

MARKET

Was there enough of a demand for the products or services offered by FCBE? This is the first question that any business must ask before starting its operation. The best way to answer this question is to conduct a market analysis. While no formal market analysis was performed before the purchase of the factory, Akbabek knew that there would be enough demand for the bricks. Privatization of state-owned businesses had just begun in Turkmenistan. Consequently, the country, and particularly the Ashgabad region, was poised to embark on an unprecedented process of change, renewal, and economic development. The early signs of change were already noticeable in new construction projects springing up in and around Ashgabad. Private businesses and government agencies needed office space. Housing construction would expand and quality products would be needed. This would create the

demand for construction material in general, and bricks in particular. Although public information on new construction and housing development was not available, it was clear that Ashgabad was growing and would continue to grow and become even larger. In short, the buyers of bricks were of three types:

1. Individual home owners and local companies purchased 60% of the factory's annual output.

2. Government agencies bought about 30% of the plant's output. They bartered raw material, for example, gas, water, electricity, and soil, for bricks. This part of the business was inflation free.

3. Foreign companies constituted about 10% of the sales. FCBE was interested in increasing sales to this group of customers, because they paid their bills on time, in foreign currencies, and purchased in bulk quantity.

Akbabek was counting on two groups of customers to keep the demand for bricks high. The first group of customers were all government agencies and ministries along with private businesses that needed new office space. The second group of customers constituted people who were interested in owning their own homes. Under the communist regime, people rented whatever housing the government provided them. Therefore, during the communist era there were no private housing or construction projects. Of course, all this changed under the new regime. The new government policy was to promote a market economy, and the start of the privatization process was expected to generate a robust demand for housing and construction. There was, however, a minor glitch in this rosy picture of demand projection. For aesthetic reasons, the government established a decree requiring all public buildings under construction to have marble facades. This decree eliminated a good portion of the projected demand for bricks. However, Akbabek was hopeful that discussing the issue with government officials would result in a reversal of the decree, thereby generating additional demand for bricks. She was confident that this reversal would mostly benefit FCBE and not the other two brick factories. In her opinion, given the quality of the bricks produced by the other two plants, most if not all the government orders for bricks would come to FCBE.

OTHER BUSINESS OPERATIONS

From the beginning, to guard against unexpected events that could result in the failure of FCBE, Akbabek decided to generate some additional revenues—no matter how small the amount—from other sources. For this purpose, she used the facilities of the company in ways not employed before. She diversified into other businesses by using the skills and expertise the company possessed, for example, in the production of concrete tiles and concrete bricks for sidewalks and other construction purposes. These were related businesses that the existing facilities could handle. Diversification efforts were also the result of a review of the operations to find ways of improving plant efficiency. This review, conducted shortly after the new management took over, revealed that 10% of the bricks produced at the factory were defective. The defective bricks were being discarded in a dump site outside the city at a cost of about 15,000 manats per ton. Reducing the waste would not only lower this cost but also contribute to lower overall production costs.

To reduce this cost, two separate actions were taken. First, better maintenance and repair of the machinery and equipment were necessary. This was not difficult to implement but was a long-term initiative and would also require better training of the workers. Akbabek devised such a plan and prepared a training program for all workers on the production line. A regular preventive maintenance and repair program was scheduled too. Second, instead of treating the defective bricks as waste, ways were explored to recycle them. It was learned that these bricks could be crushed in the ground form and mixed with cement to produce concrete tiles and bricks (blocks). This operation needed special equipment for grinding, which in turn required compressors. German and Canadian companies could supply the compressors at a cost of $140,000 to $170,000 each. FCBE could not afford such a high price. Two engineers who were laid off from a rubber seal manufacturing firm were hired to rig the grinding equipment. The rubber seal factory was experiencing financial difficulties. Shortly after hiring these engineers, Akbabek bought the rubber seal company. She knew that the factory had four compressors. While they were not in the best of shape, they could be repaired and put to work. The newly hired engineers refurbished the compressors at $1,000 cost per compressor. Two compressors were put to use in the rubber seal factory and the other two in the grinding of the defective bricks. As a result, the factory expanded its product line and with that increased its potential profitability. The total production cost (labor, electricity, cement, and sand) was about 300 manats per tile, and the sales price was about 1,000 manats. The factory used special machines for the production of concrete tiles and bricks. Each machine had a production capacity of 370,500 tiles and bricks per month.

Akbabek also improved and expanded a rubber-seal-making operation that was used to manufacture products for internal use at FCBE. It appeared that the rubber seal business could be expanded further. She was aware that four companies operated by the Ministry of Oil and Gas were users of rubber seals and, therefore, she could count on them for a steady demand for the rubber seals domestically. New customers were identified in Europe who needed these products and were willing to offer long-term contracts. Depending on the size, the price range of rubber seals was 7,000 to 15,000 manats each. Twenty-five items could be produced with a machine set-up time of 45 min. At the present time, the rubber seal operation was not functioning at full capacity, and packaging of products was not automated. Although the company had the capacity of 10,000 items per month, it was producing only 2,500 items.

The rubber seal products produced by FCBE were less expensive than competing products and were of comparable quality. There was no competition and the buyer at the present time was the Ministry of Oil and Gas. The demand exceeded the production capacity, and the lack of sufficient production created a delivery problem and lost sales revenue. Sales to European companies were expected to increase, especially since production costs were much lower than those of European producers. At the present time, the rubber seal business was operating at its break-even point. It was, however, expected to produce significant profit as sales to European customers increased.

There were a number of issues that concerned Akbabek. One of her concerns was the burden of property taxes. Property taxes were due annually, regardless of profitability of the company. The city was divided into various zones based on the distance from the center of the city. The farther away from the city center, the lower the property taxes. The present location of the factory was in Zone 3 and assessed 36¢ per square meter annually. FCBE had about 50,000 sq. m of property. Therefore, its property taxes added up to $18,000 annually. This put a heavy strain on revenues that could otherwise be used for improvement and modernization of the factory.

To generate additional cash flow, a vacant building on the property with 600 sq. m of space was converted into a warehouse and rented out to a Turkish firm. There were plans to build two more warehouses for leasing to other businesses. Each was about 600 sq. m. In total, the warehousing space would be about 1,800 sq. m. The prospective customers for warehouse spaces were (a) foreign companies, (b) construction firms, and (c) customs (state) agencies. The minimum rental price was $2 per square meter per month. A lower rental price was acceptable if rental space was available. In other words, Akbabek would not turn down an income-generating opportunity. Because her property tax was 36 cents per square meter per year, any amount that reduced the property tax burden would result in improved profitability of the factory.

The last diversification effort was to branch out into unrelated products. Akbabek had started a transportation and security company that offered its services to multinational companies that operated in Turkmenistan.

New Initiatives

Ashgabad was a growing city, and the brick factory was located close to its downtown area—a future site for residential housing. Thus, the government might ask Akbabek to move out of the present location. This could happen around the year 2020. Therefore, Akbabek was planning to build apartments at the location to maintain her ownership of the property. She already had a contract for water, gas, and electricity that could serve the needs of the apartments. Because FCBE would be allowed to operate, for the next 10 years, at least, at the present location, there was no need for immediate action on this issue. When and if the plant had to be relocated, Akbabek was confident that the government would welcome her constructing apartment units at the present location of the plant.

AN OPPORTUNITY

A new development was worth careful consideration. Recently, BINA had indicated an interest in selling its business and had put a price tag of $100,000 on it. Akbabek knew that BINA would not be able to sell it to anyone but her. The reasons, which have already been referred to in the previous pages, involved the limitations that hampered its successful business operations. These limitations included a lack of direct access to roads, no independent source of power and gas, and a lack of drying facilities for raw bricks. Knowing that BINA was not in a good position to command a high price, Akbabek offered to buy it for $15,000.

To compete effectively, BINA had started advertising the price of its bricks by posting a large billboard on the street. BINA's price was 300 manats per brick, which was 25% lower than FCBE's. At first, Akbabek was going to match BINA's price, but she immediately decided against it. She decided that when people learned about the large difference in prices of the two factories, they would come to the conclusion

that BINA's products were of lower quality. Construction projects (houses, office buildings, etc.) that used bricks were usually onetime, long-term investments. Not many would be foolish enough to build them with low-quality bricks that in a few years would require substantial repair. Indeed, her assumption was correct. The sales of FCBE bricks increased considerably after the billboard was erected by BINA.

IMPROVING OPERATIONS

When FCBE was privatized, it was producing only one type of brick with the dimensions of 24 cm × 12 cm × 5 cm. Two additional sizes were introduced 1 year after it was privatized. The dimensions of the two new kinds of bricks were 25 cm × 14 cm × 12 cm and 25 cm × 16 cm × 12 cm. While the original type was more popular with customers, the other two were gaining sales. Eventually, it was expected that for construction purposes the third type of brick, the largest, would capture 80% of sales, and the first type would be used for decorative purposes only.

To create a better work environment, a dining facility was constructed with a kitchen. It offered one free meal a day at lunch to employees with at least 6 months' tenure and offered the meal at 50% discount for all other employees. The quality of food was much better than what workers got in their own homes. The motivational impact of this and other benefits offered by FCBE was quite evident. Although the pay was the same as at the other factories, the additional benefits and the prospect of future pay raises created a significant demand for employment at FCBE. The workers were told that when the factory paid off all its debts, they would get a pay raise.

DISCUSSION QUESTIONS

1. Why did the present owner/manager, Akbabek Taganova, purchase FCBE?

2. What decision criteria were used in selecting FCBE for purchase from among the companies that were set aside for privatization?

3. At the time of the purchase, FCBE had a number of problems. What were these problems, and why did they not deter the present owner from purchasing it?

4. Who are the competitors of FCBE? Compare their operations and products. What are the substitute products for bricks, and how do they compare?

5. Who are the major customers of FCBE? What were their primary buying criteria?

6. What significant changes were implemented by the present owner? Evaluate the actions of the owner/manager in dealing with competition and with the employees.

7. What are the major strengths and weaknesses of FCBE?

8. What are your recommendations to solve the problems facing FCBE?

NOTE

a. This case was prepared by Kamal Fatehi and Rajaram Veliyath, Management and Entrepreneurship Department, Coles College of Business, Kennesaw State University.

PART IV

Human Resources

11 International Human Resource Management

In this chapter, we see that when a firm expands into international markets, intelligent changes must be made in its human resource management (HRM) practices. This begins with changes in managerial attitudes and corporate culture to accommodate the cultural diversity of multinational company personnel.

Certain managerial characteristics are known to increase the chances of success in a foreign assignment. These characteristics should be kept in mind when drawing up recruitment and selection criteria to help in staffing overseas subsidiaries with the right personnel. Predeparture training and preparation are crucial. Besides expatriate managers, multinational companies (MNCs) employ host country and third-country nationals, and therefore, we discuss HRM practices for dealing with foreign personnel. We conclude this chapter with a discussion on remuneration and compensation.

Motorola and the Secrets of the Orient

More than 100 years ago, Kipling said, "East is East and West is West, and never the twain shall meet." Today, however, Motorola Corporation is proving otherwise, and the meeting is providing Motorola with considerable sales growth in Asia's booming telecommunication and semiconductor markets. To ensure continuous growth, Motorola has established more than a dozen factories in several East Asian countries, including new factories in China, Malaysia, and Singapore. These countries not only produce a variety of Motorola products but are also the source of new products. Handie-Talkie, a miniature two-way radio, for example, was designed and manufactured in Malaysia. Except for one U.S. research manager, Malaysians run the whole operation. Motorola also allowed the Malaysians to design new software for cellular conference calls.

Motorola's success in Asia could be attributed to its ability to tap the human resources and brainpower of the East. It has integrated Asian managers into its corporate power structure and has granted them considerable decision-making authority. These managers often combine Asian cultural beliefs with modern management practices. Knowing well that cultural factors are the critical elements of the East-West confluence, Motorola is going to great lengths to safeguard its investment and ensure continued success: It is practicing the old adage, "When in Rome, do as the Romans do." In so doing, it is accepting cultural practices that would raise eyebrows in the United States. For instance, as a $400 million Silicon Harbor complex in Hong Kong was nearing completion, Tam Ching Ding, the president of the Asia-Pacific semiconductor division, asked his 87-year-old geomancer (diviner) to double-check the new facility's feng shui—literally, its wind and water—for good luck. The soothsayer proclaimed that the omens were favorable; the complex had water—a symbol of wealth—on three sides and was ringed by mountains—a source of power. The executive suite's layout, however, was wrong. Tam ordered a major renovation to achieve the proper alignment. Now, he can gaze over his desk, across the cobalt bay, to the towering face of Horse Shadow Mountain and boast that his office has about the best feng shui in Hong Kong.

Tam's influence extends beyond the Asian markets and into Motorola's corporate home office. When the new semiconductor headquarters was built in Phoenix, Arizona, a few changes were made at Tam's insistence. Two waterfalls were installed in the entrance to counter the forces of the city's landmark Camelback Mountain to the north. Competitors may snicker at these practices, but Motorola may have learned how to profit from the secrets of the Orient.[1,2]

Introduction

The Motorola story portrays an organization that has adopted a global perspective and uses the capabilities of its human resources all over the world. This change in perspective is an evolutionary process that begins when an organization takes its first step in expanding beyond its home market boundaries.

The Transition From a Domestic to an International Position

Most firms begin as domestic corporations. Their operations are geographically limited to the boundaries of their own home market, and they serve the customers of their home country. A saturated domestic market and intense local competition cause many firms to resort to export to compensate for a leveling off or decrease in earnings. Inquiries from interested foreign parties, the anticipation of home market saturation, and the search for cheap labor and other resources can lead to interest in foreign markets and exporting.

The firm often becomes more willing to expand abroad as it becomes more familiar with foreign markets and the procedures of exportation. It starts by establishing branches, offices, and production facilities in foreign countries in an attempt to better serve those markets and take advantage of foreign market opportunities. To bolster the market share and earnings, such a firm would recognize the need for a long-term commitment to host countries and their economic aspirations. As the markets in host countries expand, the firm prospers, grows, and gets more involved with the host countries' institutions and people. This is how the firm integrates with its host countries, which leads to the discovery that cultural and political diversity do not imply limitations and restrictions for business opportunities. National boundaries may be seen as mere geographic demarcations.[3] The advent of the Internet has shortened the time it takes for domestic firms to become MNCs, and it has enabled some firms to engage in international business from the beginning. Today, even new ventures must have some familiarity with foreign markets and cultures.

The evolution from a domestic corporation to a multinational enterprise occurs along a continuum. As Figure 11.1 shows, at one end of the continuum is the local/national orientation, where the firm is exclusively devoted to serving the home country market. At this position, the firm's business philosophy and mission reflect its home country environment. Because its managers and employees share the predominant culture of the country, few problems arise from cultural misunderstanding.

The other end of the continuum comprises the multinational phase of the firm, when it operates in many national markets and is influenced by the cultures of those countries. Consequently, managing the corporation becomes

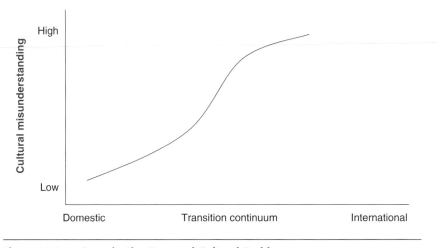

Figure 11.1   Organization Type and Cultural Problems

much more difficult and demanding. The firm may face periods of deteriorating performance due to the cultural diversity among its host countries and the lack of effective organizational policies to deal with such problems.

During its evolution, the corporation develops its corporate culture and establishes its basic HRM policies. These policies encompass employee selection, training, evaluation, rewards and compensation, and termination. The company's culture blends with the cultural environment of its markets to create new and efficient HRM practices. The management-employee relationship and how they view each other are strongly influenced by the firm's culture. The firm's culture, in turn, is determined by the national culture. As it evolves, the MNC must adopt a multicultural or cross-cultural perspective in its operations and in dealing with its employees. Managers from different cultures have different assumptions about the "ideal" way of managing and "ideal" management policies.[4] Similarly, employees from different cultures have different views about proper job-related behavior and expected management behavior. These culturally based differences in management and employee expectations can lead to conflicts and misunderstandings. Managerial practices that acknowledge the cultural diversity of the firm can reduce this conflict.

Because MNCs operate in a culturally diverse environment, their management practices, such as employee selection, career planning, performance appraisal, and compensation policies, should be adapted to fit specific countries and their cultures. For example, in some cultures, such as in the United States, career management systems represent formal, long-term human resource plans. Central to such a position is the assumption that human beings control the environment and nature. In cultures that believe human control over the environment is minimal, as in some Asian countries, such an approach is less effective. Common appraisal methods in the United States are based on employee performance and accomplishments. Such systems are ineffective in South American or

Middle Eastern countries, where lineal and personal relationships are more important than individual achievements. In the same vein, in collectivist societies, where the emphasis is on the group and not on the individual, an individual's concern with affiliation may outweigh his or her desire for recognition. Under such circumstances, a promotion that singles out an individual and separates him or her from the group may be viewed as a punishment rather than a reward.[5] There are similar variations among cultures regarding selection, hiring, training, compensation, and recognition practices.

Recruitment and Selection

Increasingly, international competitiveness is becoming a requirement for domestic success. The ability of a firm to compete in the world market may be determined by the quality of its human resources. In turn, the quality of a firm's human resources primarily depends on its HRM practices, which are shaped by the organization's staffing philosophy. Such a philosophy serves as a screening mechanism, allowing only certain types of people to join the firm.

Recruitment Philosophy

An international corporation has the option of hiring from a global pool of applicants. An objective selection process would result in choosing the best-qualified applicant. Most international staffing decisions are supposed to be based on objective criteria. Research has shown, however, that these decisions are strongly influenced by the attitudes of top executives toward the people of the host cultures. Managers' opinions and attitudes determine whether expatriates are selected for management positions in foreign subsidiaries (expatriate managers are home country managers on assignment to host countries). According to Heenan,[6] the underlying motivation behind these key decisions is the MNC's level of trust in the host country nationals and managerial perceptions of their competence (pp. 5–9). MNCs may follow any of four recruitment approaches: home country, host country, regional, or global (see Table 11.1).

Home Country Approach. Managers using the home country approach tend to staff all key positions, at the home office and abroad, with home country

Table 11.1   Recruitment Philosophy

Home country approach

Host country approach

Regional approach

Global approach

executives. They feel that this group is the most intelligent, capable, and reliable. This decision, however, may not be based on prejudice; the decision maker may lack knowledge of and experience with foreign persons and cultures. This type of attitude is most evident in firms that are highly centralized[7] and rely on low-cost production of commodity-type products for international markets.[8] MNCs are also more inclined to use expatriate managers where the political power of the host country is seen as a threat. The aim is to ensure that the objectives of the firm are not subordinated to those of the host country.[8]

Host Country Approach. Managers using a host country approach believe that the management and staffing of subsidiary firms should be left to host country nationals because they think that natives will be better able to understand the requirements of the assignment. To MNC executives, foreign operation is a mysterious undertaking best left to foreign executives. As long as the firm remains profitable and its objectives are achieved, host country executives are allowed to operate the organization in any way they see fit. This low-profile approach by headquarters results in absolute authority for the host country manager over the foreign organization.[8]

Regional Approach. Managers who use the regional approach believe that the global market should be handled regionally. For example, all European markets would be coordinated through a headquarters in France, all markets in North and South America through a headquarters in the United States, and so on. Consequently, personnel selection is carried out regionally. Although information flow and personnel transfer is high within each region, there is little or no regional crossover (p. 8).[6] This staffing style is used when products are similar all over the world but the marketing has to be tailored to meet the needs of different cultures;[8] this is often a result of strong competition from smaller, more localized organizations (p. 523).[7] While such an attitude will result in a performance appraisal based on regionwide criteria, it is not a global perspective.

Global Approach. This approach is characterized by a global systems approach to management. Managers with this perspective believe that top qualified people can come from any background and culture. They also believe that the whole world is their market. Therefore, resource allocation, staffing, manufacturing, and marketing should be done within the framework of the global economy (p. 9).[6] Locations are staffed based on overall competence, ability, and a willingness to work in different cultural settings and a global rather than an ethnic mind-set.[9] The result is an HRM system that is most appropriate for the complex and dynamic global market. In such a market, competition is not regional but consists of other MNCs that operate on a worldwide level and have similar characteristics (pp. 9–10).[8]

Selection Criteria

The success or failure of an operation hinges on the quality of home country managers assigned to foreign business operations. This is true both for firms that are new in the international market and for established MNCs with extensive experience in foreign countries. To host country personnel, these managers represent the MNC and the home country. The image they create lasts long after the initial assignment is over and they have gone home. Therefore, only the best-qualified managers should be sent abroad.

In the past, it was quite common for firms to use only managerial and technical expertise as criteria for the selection of expatriate managers. These criteria, however, are not enough for today's international assignments, and the selection of managers based only on technical and managerial expertise could result in disappointing outcomes. MNCs must work to make the expatriate assignment a positive experience for both the company and the manager. To do this, it is imperative that the selection criteria for foreign managers encompass all aspects of work and respond to the social, political, and cultural situation.

What characteristics should a manager possess to succeed abroad? What criteria should be used in selecting managers for foreign assignments? In general, all the characteristics that make a good domestic manager, such as the skills and ability to plan, organize, and direct, are necessary for an international executive, too. However, there are certain additional attributes that are essential for success in global operations. The following are characteristics crucial for any manager sent on a foreign assignment (see Table 11.2):

Technical and Managerial Skills.[10] Basic technical and managerial skills are crucial for a manager assigned to a foreign operation. In foreign assignments, managers will need all the technical, administrative, and managerial

Table 11.2   Characteristics Crucial to Managers on a Foreign Assignment

Technical and managerial skills

Maturity and emotional stability

Initiative and creativity

Communication skills

Family support

Motives and desire

Social skills, flexibility, and adaptability

Language skills

Diplomatic skills

Locally contingent factors, e.g., age and gender

skills that make them succeed at home. While past performance is usually a good indication of a person's abilities and skills, not all managers who are successful at home do equally well on foreign assignments. The novelty of the physical environment and the political, social, and cultural differences make experiences gained at home less applicable in a foreign country. Quite often, an international assignment involves novel problems that only a very astute manager can successfully solve. An international manager is usually expected to train local employees. Many of these employees are being introduced to a new method, a new process, or the use of new machinery. Support from other colleagues may not be readily available. Therefore, expatriate managers must be able to function with minimum or no support. Innovative ability and insight are crucial in assignments where the expatriate is the only expert in the organization.

As in domestic operations, the characteristics and attributes needed abroad also depend on the hierarchical position of the manager. There are four categories of assignment for an expatriate: (1) the chief executive officer responsible for the operation abroad, (2) the head of a functional department in a foreign subsidiary, (3) the troubleshooter whose responsibility is to solve specific operational problems, and (4) the operator.[11] A different set of attributes is needed for each of these positions.

Maturity, emotional stability, and respect for the laws and people of the host country are attributes required for an executive in regular contact with host country nationals. A troubleshooter needs initiative, creativity, and technical knowledge of the business. The head of a functional department must be mature and emotionally stable and also have technical knowledge of the business. The chief executive officer of a foreign subsidiary must be an effective communicator, have managerial talent, and be mature and emotionally stable.[11]

Although different characteristics are needed for various managerial assignments, all successful expatriates share certain common characteristics. In addition to managerial and technical expertise, the "ideal" expatriate must possess the right combination of interpersonal skills, intelligence, and emotional stability. To succeed, the expatriate should have a family supportive of the assignment and able to adapt to the new environment.[12]

Motives and Desire. Individuals who possess a genuine interest in foreign countries, their people, and their cultures are ideal candidates for a position abroad. Those who seek the assignment solely for extra money, added prestige, or the "boost" such an assignment might give to their careers are not as likely to be successful in expatriate situations.[13] A good indication of a manager's interest is past experience. If a manager knows foreign languages, has taken international business courses, and has traveled extensively or lived abroad, he or she is obviously interested in foreign countries and cultures (p. 115).[14]

Social Skills. Probably the most important success factor for the international manager is social skills. These are not necessarily the same social skills that lead to success at home. A person socially skilled in a domestic operation is a person who has learned the rules and norms for developing and maintaining relationships with people and knows the proper behavior for various circumstances. Because we acquire these skills by practicing them under specified rules of our own cultures, going beyond the familiar boundaries of our home culture may render our skills less effective. Naturally, understanding the host country's culture and politics and having a knowledge of the host country's history and geography are very helpful, but they may not be sufficient.

In international situations, where rules and conditions are different, managers should be flexible, adaptable, and able to accept the unfamiliar. In some cultures, but not in the United States, relationships between individuals typically develop slowly and cautiously over time. Once established, these relationships are permanent, and the obligations would not be dissolved even with the dissolution of the relationship (p. 126).[15]

International managers must be able to understand why foreigners behave the way they do. To understand people, we have to understand their culture. We perceive and interpret others' behaviors using our own cultural cues and models. A knowledge of other cultures would enable us to make correct attributions to, and predict more accurately, the behavior of people from other cultures and anticipate their reactions. This reduces the element of uncertainty in interpersonal and intercultural relations.

A very important element of any culture is language. Although we can study and learn about a culture without speaking the language, knowing the language immensely facilitates learning. The ability to speak the host country language not only allows better communication, it also minimizes differences and creates a more informal and friendly communication environment. Even when a manager is not proficient in speaking the language, a willingness to use the language shows his or her interest in interacting with the host nationals. It also indicates the manager's confidence and trust in them in taking risks and being vulnerable.

Getting out and enjoying activities such as playing in or attending sporting events, listening to or playing music, and eating out gives the expatriate the chance to socialize with locals, make friends, and learn more about their culture. It takes some of the pressure off the move to the new environment and allows the expatriate's new friends to act as teachers of the culture. Developing friendships with locals who can act as mentors in providing guidance through the maze of cultural complexities makes life much easier. Host national friends can help the manager understand people's attitudes and expectations, at work and away from work.[16]

Diplomatic Skills. On foreign assignments, international managers interact with business associates, governmental agencies, and political leaders. In most developing countries, the government assumes a larger role in business and trade than is customary in the United States. Diplomatic skills are needed to relate to government officials properly and to conduct business transactions under unfamiliar conditions. The manager serves as an ambassador, representing the company to other businesses and to host government bureaucrats (p. 114).[14] Successful managers in global companies should have the qualities of diplomats, such as patience and sharp negotiating skills, to achieve desired, favorable terms. "Global companies can no longer maintain an arm's length relationship with foreign host governments since their drive toward greater local presence has significantly expanded their exposure to local conditions" (p. 85).[17]

Maturity and Stability. Venturing into a strange environment, facing unfamiliar conditions, and dealing with unexpected situations are all part of going abroad and conducting business transactions in a foreign country. Emotionally and intellectually mature persons more readily handle the burden of foreign assignments. They recognize their own assumptions, values, motives, needs, and shortcomings. Consequently, they are in a better position to understand the attitudes and behaviors of other people, appreciate cultural differences for what they are, and be able to suspend judgment when there is insufficient understanding of circumstances. They understand the inherent logic present in different ways of life and do not overreact when they encounter unfamiliar and potentially threatening situations. These characteristics enable managers to maintain emotional equilibrium under the most demanding and difficult conditions. Therefore, they can constructively cope with adversity and handle the stress of daily life in an unfamiliar environment (p. 41).[16]

Family Factors. When evaluating candidates for foreign assignments, it is very important to review both the candidate and the family. The inability of spouses or children to adapt to their new surroundings is a major reason for failure in overseas transfers, including premature returns and job performance slumps.[18] While the expatriate manager has the relative security of a familiar work and office routine, the family must cope with an unfamiliar environment every day. To prevent failures due to family difficulties, MNCs have to address family-related issues. Ford Motor, Minnesota Mining and Manufacturing, and Exxon include spouses in their screening process for foreign assignments and/or offer educational and predeparture preparation assistance.[18]

Locally Contingent Attributes. For assignments to certain countries, attributes such as the candidate's age and gender must also be considered. Older people are respected and seniority is emphasized in many places, such as Asia and Africa. In these cultures, young representatives may have a great deal of difficulty in gaining access to important personnel and key decision makers.[19] In some countries, women encounter a great deal of resistance from superiors, subordinates, colleagues, and clients. Many high-level officials refuse to work with women and do not promote them to key decision-making positions. These people question a woman's professional competency and doubt the very legitimacy of her authority in an executive role.[20] The following incident is an example of the type of situation that women may face when they go abroad:[21]

> An American female executive was sent to negotiate a business deal with a Japanese firm because she was the most qualified person. Properly dressed in an elegant suit, she arrived on time in the board room of the Japanese corporation . . . and was prepared for a very serious negotiation. The Japanese senior executives kept asking politely where was her husband. She answered that her husband was at home in New York, taking care of their daughter. At this point the Japanese thought they finally had discovered that she was a secretary. Therefore, they asked to see her boss. To their amazement she made it clear that she was the boss! The meeting proceeded, but not with an ideal opening. Halfway through the meeting, taking a break, she asked for directions to the ladies' room. There was no ladies' room on that floor. (p. R22)

Personnel Selection Options

As it prepares to staff its foreign-based offices, the multinational firm must decide if it will fill managerial positions with expatriate, host country, or third-country managers. We discussed earlier that the attitudes of top executives toward people of other cultures influence personnel selection. Often, in the early stages of internationalization, the firm follows a home country approach in making staffing decisions. As the firm gains international experience and learns about other cultures, it may move through the host country and regional approaches to personnel selection and finally arrive at the global approach to staffing.

The selection and hiring process of MNCs is a very complex and difficult task. Each foreign office has different staffing requirements and needs. There are a multitude of other factors, such as local laws and contractual obligations, that have to be considered. In addition, the MNC's management philosophy regarding staffing plays a pivotal role in personnel selection. The prevailing managerial philosophy influences the choice among the three alternatives: expatriate, host country national, or third-country national managers.

The Expatriate Manager. An MNC may choose expatriates to fill managerial positions in its foreign offices. The selection of expatriates for foreign assignments is influenced by the ethnocentric attitudes and philosophy of the MNC's top executives. The choice may also be determined by operational needs. For example, home country managers may have a long history of service with the parent company. They possess an in-depth knowledge and understanding of the policies and procedures of the firm and are familiar with the business and industry. They may also have technical training or possess functional expertise that local managers lack. Sometimes, due to a shortage of well-trained local managers, expatriates are the only logical choice (p. 156).[22] MNCs may also select expatriates to fill foreign positions as part of their corporate managerial training program. Many MNCs view foreign-duty assignments as an indispensable part of an executive's "global" development training (p. 240).[5] General Electric, for example, is now sending its brightest stars abroad rather than the run-of-the-mill managers it once picked for foreign posts.[23] The advantages and disadvantages of selection for assignments abroad are summarized in Table 11.3.

Before accepting a foreign assignment, a prospective manager should have an intensive and in-depth meeting with his or her superior(s). The purpose of this meeting would be to agree on issues such as the expatriate's level of remuneration, the parameters and responsibilities of the assignment, and the projected home office position after the foreign assignment is over.[24] Instead of prolonged assignments for the expatriates and their families, the MNC may decide to consider short-term alternatives. In this way, expatriate managers could share their problem-solving talents and technical expertise with foreign subsidiaries while avoiding the expense and disruption that accompany expatriate relocation.

An MNC may also select individual managers or teams of managers to undertake temporary project assignments in foreign countries, typically associated with the start-up of a special project, such as the introduction of a new product line or getting an information system up and running. These assignments usually last from 3 weeks to 6 months and are an excellent way of providing the management personnel necessary to present new products, build new facilities, or introduce new management information systems (p. 166).[22]

The Host Country National Manager. In the past, many multinational firms displayed an ethnocentric view, staffing foreign offices almost exclusively with expatriate personnel. As MNCs have evolved and assumed a more global perspective, their policies for staffing foreign managerial positions have also undergone an evolutionary progression. Today, many MNCs are selecting more host country and third-country nationals to fill managerial positions in their foreign subsidiaries. This is due to the increasing costs and the high failure rate of expatriate assignments.

Table 11.3   Advantages and Disadvantages of Having Expatriate Managers

Advantages	Disadvantages
Long service with MNC	Salary costs
Familiarity with policies of MNC	Relocation costs
Familiarity with the industry	Family adapting to the new environment
Possession of technical expertise	Possibility of failure
Managerial training and development	Medical, pension, benefits, educational costs
Speaking the language of headquarters	Locals may resent the high salary and benefits

The cost of relocation can be very high for the company and the expatriate. International assignments often fail because the expatriate manager and his or her family are unfamiliar with the host culture or because they fail to adapt. The failure rate for expatriate assignments can range anywhere between 30% and 50%, and it can climb to as high as 70% in less developed countries (LDCs) (p. 171).[22] By hiring local managers, an MNC saves the cost of relocating the expatriate manager and the costs associated with his or her failure. By using local personnel, MNCs are also spared the higher salary paid to expatriates working in foreign countries. Besides their base salaries, expatriate managers also receive medical insurance, pension benefits, foreign currency adjustments, and foreign service incentives. Moreover, housing costs, relocation and transportation expenses, cost-of-living compensation, and educational allowances increase the burden on MNCs.[25] Host country personnel may resent and envy the expatriate's higher pay scale. This may eventually affect the productivity and morale of local employees.

Host country nationals may be selected because of their knowledge and understanding of local markets, consumers, and governments. Local managers may provide the company with valuable governmental contacts. These contacts can be especially helpful in dealing with governmental red tape and bureaucracy and are also useful when host governments do not trust, or are uncertain about, the presence of a foreign corporation within their borders. Some foreign governments may have regulations requiring the use of local managerial personnel (p. 171).[22] In these situations, host country managers are a better choice.

For some markets with stringent business requirements, such as Japan, hiring host country nationals is one way of breaking into those strict markets or being competitive. To recruit in such a market, MNCs may be forced to pay higher salaries than local companies and offer other benefits. For example, in Japan, foreign employers on average pay 10% more than Japanese firms and have shorter working hours, more flexibility, and merit-based promotions. MNCs are paying premium salaries in Japan because most Japanese view foreign employers as unstable, unfamiliar, and nonprestigious. An alternative, however, is available to MNCs. Since Japanese firms are reluctant to hire women, MNCs have started hiring women in larger numbers. Consequently, foreign firms, especially American firms, have been successful in attracting some top graduates of Japanese universities.[26]

Host country managers can help MNCs have a more harmonious relationship with local employees, customers, and the community. Integrating these managers into MNCs, however, is difficult because of conflicts that may arise as a result of differences between the national and corporate cultures. Certain steps can be taken to smooth their integration into MNCs and reduce the potential for conflict. MNCs should identify talented host country managers early in their careers and prepare them for future positions. The prospective candidates should be rotated to home country positions for a few years, enabling them to absorb the home country and corporate culture. This rotation also helps them develop a network of friends and colleagues who can be very helpful to them in the future. An alternative is to appoint a home country manager as a "shadow manager" for a host country candidate. The role of the shadow manager is to acclimate the host country manager to the MNC's corporate culture and to ease the communication link to the home country. NCR, Fuji-Xerox, and many other firms have used this approach.[27] Table 11.4 summarizes the benefits and drawbacks of host country staffing.

As can be seen from the table, host country staffing has many benefits. There are, however, certain caveats with this practice, particularly for smaller firms. The legal consequences of hiring a host country citizen are often complicated and costly. For instance, labor laws in many European countries require employment contracts with generous termination benefits.[28]

The selection criteria for host country national managers are similar to those used for third-country nationals.

The Third-Country National Manager. Sometimes, local managers do not have enough managerial expertise or do not wish to work for an MNC. In those situations, third-country managers may provide a viable staffing alternative. For example, because of the political tensions in Iran during the early 1980s, American firms doing business there often used British or Canadian personnel to represent their interests.[29]

Sometimes, a third-country national may simply be the best person and the right manager for the job. Third-country executives often speak several languages and know the region and its industry well. Many international hotel firms commonly employ third-country nationals. Recognizing the qualifications of these managers and their usefulness to the firm, American MNCs are hiring more third-country nationals in their foreign affiliates. For example, the ranks of third-country managers at Scott Paper swelled from a few to more than a dozen in 4 years. Another example is Pioneer Hi-Bred International, which in 5 years tripled the number of third-country managers it had in key positions in foreign operations.[30]

Table 11.4   The Benefits and Drawbacks of Host Country Staffing

Advantages	Disadvantages
No relocation and other costs	Lack of familiarity with headquarters
Lower salary	Lack of familiarity with the industry
No problem with family adjustment	Legal issues of hiring and firing
Knowledge of local language	Possible language problems with headquarters
Knowledge of local laws, customs, and culture	Possible cultural problems with headquarters
Relations with host government	Loss of training opportunity for expatriates
Relations with local customers and community	

Phase 2 is the market-orientation stage. It begins with the entrance of competition, which forces firms to focus on expanding to new markets. International expansion is an option they may choose. Initially, foreign markets are supplied by exports from the home country. Later on, assembly operations are established in countries with large domestic markets. As the emphasis shifts from product development to market development, marketing replaces R&D as the most important function.

Phase 3 is the price orientation stage. It marks the realization that competitive advantage can be achieved only by managing and controlling costs. Increased competition and standardization of products at the end of Phase 2 drives prices down and creates a need for further cost reduction. Since the market is saturated with competitors, the price falls to barely above the costs. To reduce and control costs, production is shifted to countries with the lowest production costs. By Phase 3, home country production is drastically reduced, and the home market is supplied with imports from low-cost facilities abroad.

The first three phases have their own special features and characteristics. Phase 4, however, is the culmination of the previous three phases. It is the result of dramatic changes in market forces that are best described as a progression from one stage to another, as follows.

For a couple of decades following World War II, American firms enjoyed a monopoly of power and an undisputed leadership position in world markets. For them, Phase 1 was characterized by the absence of foreign competition and a long product life cycle of 15 to 20 years. A salient characteristic of this phase was the dominance of the product development function. In the meantime, Europe and Japan rebuilt their economies and began to challenge the dominance of the United States. The consequences were increased worldwide competition and a shortened international product life cycle, leading to a much higher need for effective marketing. This was followed by technology transfer and price competition, which are the characteristics of Phase 3. By the 1980s, the international product life cycle was reduced to 3 to 5 years.

Today, we are at the beginning of Phase 4, globalization. This phase is characterized by mass customization of products designed to meet individual needs. These products are produced by assembling components that are procured worldwide. Product life cycles have been shortened further, and for some products, the life cycle is now only a few months. The emphasis is on both top-quality products and services at the least cost. Accurate identification of consumer needs and quick response to them are the hallmarks of Phase 4. Firms succeed in Phase 4 by becoming both highly differentiated and highly integrated and by combining the local responsiveness of Phase 2 with the global integration of Phase 3. In other words, firms are forced to compete simultaneously under Phase 1, Phase 2, and Phase 3 market conditions.

At each phase, the influence of cultural diversity on a firm varies. Figure 11.2 depicts the four stages of the product life cycle and the influence of culture on the organization at each stage.

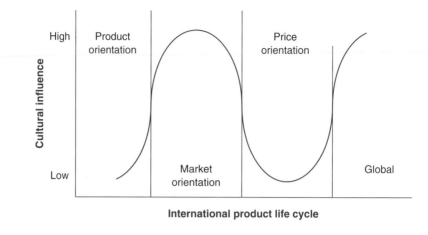

Figure 11.2   International Product Life Cycle and Cultural Influence

In Phase 1, technological superiority, product uniqueness, and monopoly power allow the firm to operate with an ethnocentric perspective and ignore the cultural differences between the home and host markets. Phase 1 firms export their products and push the cost of absorbing cultural differences to foreign buyers. In a way, these firms send a message to foreigners that says, "We will allow you to buy our products" (p. 187).[33]

A Phase 2 firm cannot operate with an ethnocentric perspective. The competitive pressure of Phase 2 does not allow firms to ignore cultural differences and expect the cost of cross-cultural mismatch between sellers and buyers to be absorbed by foreign customers. To succeed, Phase 2 firms need to take into account cultural differences and modify their operating styles to match those of their foreign customers and clients.

In Phase 3, characterized by undifferentiated products and price competition, the importance of sensitivity to most cultural differences is reduced. While in Phase 2, there may be many different ways of designing, producing, and marketing products for diverse markets, in Phase 3, only the least-cost method can succeed. In the market of undifferentiated products, the importance of market segmentation based on culture or national considerations diminishes. In other words, price competition makes the impact of cultural differences negligible.

In Phase 4, the minimum criteria for success are top-quality, least-cost products and services. Firms gain a competitive advantage by producing sophisticated mass-customized products based on global strategies. Successful market segmentation based on culture becomes a winning strategy. Phase 4 firms compete in a global market, with R&D, production, and marketing networks that are spread all over the globe and that serve very discrete market niches. Consequently, managing cultural diversity within the organization and with suppliers and customers becomes a requisite for success.

HRM Practices

Product life cycle indicates the impact of culture on the firm. It can be used to suggest corresponding HRM practices for each phase.

Firms operating in Phase 1, which produce unique products and sell them primarily to the home market, do not require much international sophistication from their employees. The firms' monopoly power insulates them from the impact of cultural differences and forces the buyers of their products to absorb the cost of the cross-cultural mismatch. Foreign customers must speak the language of the MNC, accept the MNC's cultural and managerial practices, and, after the purchase, modify products and services themselves to match their needs and requirements. Firms in Phase 1 get away with using the ethnocentric approach because their buyers and clients do not have an alternative. Personnel selection for foreign assignments, therefore, is based solely on the ability to get the job done. There is no international career or international and cultural training. For firms operating in Phase 1, not only is international experience unimportant; it may even hinder the executive's progress in the hierarchy. These firms do not send their most qualified employees to a foreign subsidiary. An executive accepting a foreign assignment falls outside the mainstream of the executive network and quite often is overlooked for promotions.

For Phase 2 firms, however, cultural adaptability and sensitivity are important, but personnel selection is still based mostly on technical competence and the willingness to accept foreign assignments. In Phase 2, firms could gain a competitive advantage by producing culturally appropriate products and services and tailoring their marketing programs to host countries' cultural requirements. These firms, besides employing expatriate managers, quite often employ host nationals in some host country positions, such as marketing and personnel. Expatriate managers of Phase 2 MNCs perform well only if they know the host country's language and understand the culture. To perform well, expatriate managers need to acquire appropriate skills and knowledge about the host culture. While on foreign assignment, they gain unique and valuable experience. On returning home, however, these expatriate managers find that their skills, knowledge, and experience are not valued much, if at all. Going abroad is not a very good career strategy for ambitious managers of Phase 2 firms. For the same reason, and because of a lack of understanding of international operations, foreign nationals very seldom rise in the hierarchy of the home country organization. Membership on the board of directors of Phase 2 firms and top executive positions are exclusively reserved for home country nationals.

Survival for a Phase 3 firm in the global market depends on price competitiveness. For geographically dispersed MNCs with a worldwide network of suppliers, manufacturers, and distributors, integration becomes an important undertaking. They become integrated primarily by standardizing their products and services and centralizing their operations and structure. International assignments are given to the best employees, and the search for managerial talent is expanded to include other nationals from the worldwide operation. While international experience is valued for career advancement, cultural sensitivity and language skills diminish in importance. Phase 3 firms attempt to integrate by assuming similarity or creating it. They assume similarity by producing generic products and services to take advantage of economies of scale and scope. These MNCs create similarity within the firm by using the home country language and by imposing home country values and cultures on their managers. They attempt to mold foreign managers in the image of home country executives. Home country or third-country national managers who get assimilated into the headquarters' corporate culture can ascend to higher-level positions. They assume that cultural differences can be either ignored through the corporate culture or minimized to reduce their impact.

Phase 4 MNCs produce and sell top-quality, least-cost, differentiated products for local tastes globally. The need for global integration and national responsiveness impels Phase 4 firms to select their best people for assignments scattered all over the globe. The home country market is no longer dominant, and the boundaries between home country, host country, and third-country managers vanish. Internally and externally, firms are faced with cultural diversity, which they cannot ignore and have to manage. Successful Phase 4 MNCs are those that can identify situations where cultural differences could be used as an asset to serve culturally differentiated market segments worldwide. To identify and respond quickly to local needs, managers need to be culturally sensitive and speak more than one language. Successful firms recognize that cultural diversity cannot be ignored. They are able to identify situations where cultural diversity can be managed as an asset and those where such diversity is a liability.

International Management and Intercultural Training and Preparation

In spite of the fact that corporations devote a great deal of time and attention to selecting the proper candidates to undertake foreign management positions, 30% to 50% of all expatriate placements do not work out. Besides the direct financial costs involved with a failed expatriate assignment, the firm may incur other costs,[34] including voided business deals, loss of valuable employees, the breakup of joint ventures, and poor relations with the host government.

The primary reason for failure is the inability of the employee or his or her family to adjust properly to the new environment and culture.[35] The failure, however, begins with selecting the wrong person. Adequate screening and proper selection procedures allow MNCs to select managers with a higher probability of success. The screening process includes interviews, tests, and the use of assessment centers. While some psychological and technical skills tests are available, these tests are not widely used by MNCs. This is because, first, there are no specific criteria for overseas success and, second, psychological tests have the potential for cultural bias and have relatively low validity (p. 536).[36] Interviews are very common for selecting prospective candidates for foreign assignments. Assessment centers offer the most promising method of selecting international personnel. These assessments include individual and group exercises, individual interviews with managers or psychologists, and perhaps some mental ability tests. After selection of a manager, predeparture preparation and training further enable the expatriate to adjust to the host country culture. Figure 11.3 illustrates the many factors that could influence an expatriate's adjustment and, consequently, contribute to the success of assignments abroad.

Japanese in London

The international expansion of Japanese firms has brought a large number of Japanese expatriates to England. A major problem for these Japanese expatriates is the education of their children. Stepping off the exams escalator at home risks sacrificing a job for life in a prestigious company. Those who have no option but to bring their children to England scramble for places in schools that teach the Japanese national curriculum. There are eight private Japanese schools and six Saturday schools attached to Japanese-owned factories.

These expatriates can choose among eight Japanese estate agents to find them a house. They look for a location that reflects their position in the social pecking order. Around London, it is St. John's Wood and Hampstead for the bosses; Finchley, Golders Green, and Ealing for the middle managers; and Croydon for the lower ranks.

The unadventurous can live as though they have never left Tokyo: reading Japanese newspapers, buying their spectacles from Japanese opticians and suits from Japanese tailors, playing mahjong in Japanese clubs, and singing in karaoke bars. London has more than 60 Japanese restaurants and eight Japanese food shops to stave off the torments of English food.

As they become more established, the Japanese are also growing more adventurous. There is plenty that they like about Britain: relatively huge houses; easy commuting; and, best of all, cheap and readily accessible golf courses. And the women enjoy their freedom and status. Japanese firms have recently started to worry that company wives may not want to go home.[37]

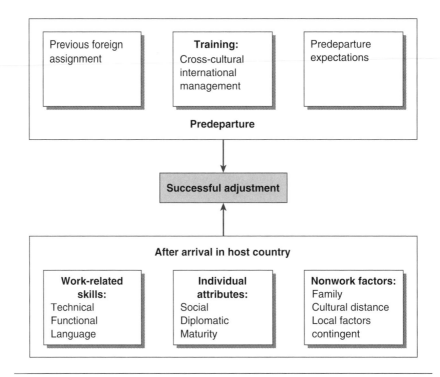

Figure 11.3   Factors Determining Expatriates' Cultural Influence

As Figure 11.3 suggests, many factors contribute to the success of expatriate managers. A proper selection process alone is not sufficient. Predeparture cultural and international management training is necessary to improve the chances of an expatriate's success. Predeparture preparation and training assist managers in preparing for most of what they may encounter in a foreign country. The preparation and training could be particularly helpful for a manager going to a culturally tough environment. The cultural toughness of the host country depends on the degree of difference between the home and host country cultures. The larger the cultural distance, the more difficult the adaptation process. Individuals may find that some cultures are far more difficult to adapt to than others (p. 43).[16] Because of the large distance between the American and Chinese cultures, American executives, for example, may experience more difficulty in China than in England.[38] For Americans, Chinese culture is tougher than British culture.

Predeparture Preparations

Predeparture preparations serve to reduce the cultural shock that foreigners experience when they enter a new culture. In particular, spouses and families benefit from participating in workshops that introduce them to the host culture. These families need more attention because they experience more cultural shock. The impact of cultural shock on managers is typically less severe than on their families because the work environment, even in a foreign country, is familiar to managers and they spend most of their time working at first. It is usually up to the spouse to find the grocery store, the doctor, the dentist, and the church; do the shopping; and so on.

Predeparture workshops may include language training and typically provide information on practical considerations such as health, safety, and medical needs, as well as information on how to handle and manage the daily routine of a household, including grocery shopping, transportation, international mail, and communication. Such information reduces predeparture apprehension and eases the entry into a new environment.

Providing employment information and helping career-oriented spouses to secure a meaningful job has an enormously positive impact on the family. Instead of viewing them as the employee's aggravating chattel, spouses should be considered as an unexpected bonus for the company. As a resource, they should be utilized to the benefit of both the employee and the MNC. For example, some MNCs emulate governments and universities and establish preferential employment policies for spouses.[39]

Mentors at home and host country offices can be very helpful to expatriates. Matching the expatriate manager and his or her family with a host country mentor helps their entry into the foreign culture. A mentor at the home country corporate office assists in the repatriation program and reentry into their home culture when the manager and his or her family are ready to return. This arrangement could make the entire expatriate experience easier for the manager and his or her family and increase the chances of success.

International and Intercultural Training

The attitudes and behaviors of managers are influenced by their culture. This influence quite often creates cultural biases. To overcome these cultural biases and achieve a truly global perspective, international managers should receive international and intercultural management training. Such training helps managers develop the skills they need to function in a variety of cultural settings and geographic locations.

International management education and intercultural training may also help managers develop global perspectives and be more receptive to and have empathy toward the cultures and customs of other nations. Such training also teaches managers not to blindly accept their own cultural norms as universal standards, and it can provide them with the understanding that no one culture, or method of managing, can consistently produce superior solutions to international managerial problems. These managers could also learn how to adapt their management styles to fit the many cultural situations they may encounter.

The purpose of international management education and training is to provide MNC managers with an awareness of the diversity of management practices around the world and to improve their understanding of the business and management philosophies and practices that exist in different countries and cultures. Through documentary programs, participation in business games, and role-playing scenarios, managers can develop a better understanding of culturally based differences in managing.

International management education and training programs can be either arranged as an in-house service or conducted at educational and training institutions. These programs could be designed to develop the understanding and skills pertinent to a specific country and culture or even a region. For example, managers could learn about the basic tenets of Japanese management and how they differ from American practices. Alternatively, training programs could focus on East Asian cultural factors influencing the management of firms. Ideally, the faculties of international management programs are made up of professional and business personnel who represent a wide variety of nationalities and cultures. A culturally diverse staff helps ensure that MNC managers are exposed to many different cultural philosophies and value systems.

Managers who are expected to have extensive contact with people of other cultures should also receive some form of in-depth intercultural training. This is useful for all MNC managers operating abroad, whether they are expatriate, host country, or third-country nationals. Intercultural training aims to develop a set of skills that will be useful to international managers.[40] These skills are listed below:

- *Self-awareness:* The recognition of personal assumptions, values, needs, strengths, and limitations and the understanding of personal response in different cultural settings
- *Culture reading:* The ability to discover and understand the inherent logic in cultural norms and expectations
- *Multiple perspectives:* The ability to suspend judgment about other cultures and appreciate others' perspectives
- *Intercultural communication:* The skill to send and receive verbal and nonverbal messages accurately in different cultures
- *Cultural flexibility:* The ability to adjust and change expectations and plans in accordance with the host country's cultural requirements
- *Cultural resilience:* The ability to handle culture shock and recover and rebound from setbacks arising from cultural differences
- *Skills in building interpersonal relationships:* The ability to develop and maintain interpersonal relations with host country people
- *Intercultural facilitation skills:* The ability to manage cultural differences and use these differences constructively

During the course of an intercultural training program, managers are provided with a wide range of information about foreign countries, their cultures and customs, and the anticipated roles the managers may be expected to assume in these cultural settings (p. 686).[35] Such intercultural exposure enhances a manager's ability to deal with the routine as well as the unexpected and unusual situations that interactions with other cultures may present.[16]

The nature and length of each individual's intercultural training are determined by several factors. These factors include

1. the type of involvement and interaction the manager will have with host cultures,

2. the manager's position in the company's hierarchy, and

3. the cultural toughness of other cultures.[16]

A typical intercultural training program provided by many MNCs follows a documentary approach. The program provides managers with printed materials on a country's history, geography, sociopolitical and economic systems, and cultural practices. This documentary information may be supplemented by lectures or films that provide practical information on day-to-day concerns such as local transportation, housing, shopping, schools, and finance (pp. 686–696).[35]

For managers who will have extensive contact with foreign cultures, a documentary program alone may not provide the higher level of intercultural sensitivity and awareness that is needed. To develop an in-depth sensitivity to a culture's mores and behavioral patterns, managers need specialized training that goes beyond a review of reports and instructions on a foreign language and culture. The scope and depth of the training should match the extent and frequency of interaction and involvement with people of different cultures. As the need for interaction with different cultures increases, training programs should assume a more interactive or affective-immersion-oriented perspective.

During affective intercultural training, managers spend a good deal of time interacting with citizens of the host country. Alternatively, they may associate with individuals who have extensive, firsthand knowledge of the host country. As a result of these interactions, managers move beyond an objective, generalized knowledge of foreign countries and gain an understanding of the subtle nuances of their cultures. For example, they will learn the proper way to listen, scold, or praise in a given cultural setting. This type of information can be invaluable to managers as they deal with people from other countries and cultures (p. 686).[35]

The Intercultural Sensitizer

A promising approach to intercultural training is the intercultural assimilator or intercultural sensitizer (ICS). The origin of the term *ICS* goes back to the efforts of Fielder, Osgood, Stolurow, and Triandis during the early 1960s to develop a computer program that could be used to give cultural training to people from different cultures. The purpose of an ICS is to teach individuals to see situations from the perspective of members of another culture.[41]

As Albert has suggested, the term *ICS* is a more appropriate name for the instrument. There is no one definitive format for constructing an ICS. Some have emphasized the major customs of the target culture, others have attempted to present the value contrasts between the two cultures, and still others have dealt with differences in interpersonal attributes between the cultures. Despite the variations, ICSs attempt to provide learners with extensive information about a target culture in a 2- to 6-hr time span. The information chosen for an ICS portrays the very important and significant differences between the two cultures. In other words, an ICS focuses on critical problems and key differences. The basic requirement for constructing an ICS is to identify two situations or critical problems and provide the learners with an active experience from which they can learn the behavior, norms, perspectives, attributes, values, and customs of the other culture (p. 189).[41]

Many American firms have realized the need for global understanding and experience among their managers. A few have already installed elaborate training and career-tracking mechanisms. Colgate-Palmolive Company, Procter & Gamble Company, General Electric, Raychem Corporation, and PepsiCo Inc., to name just a few, are among the firms that have instituted screening, selection, and training programs geared to identify young managers, early in their careers, for global operations. For example, a typical participant in Colgate's global marketing management training program holds an MBA degree from an American university, speaks at least one foreign language, has lived outside the United States, and comes with both strong computer skills and prior business experience.[42]

Training Host Country or Third-Country Nationals

In addition to generalized international management education and specific intercultural training, host country or third-country national managers who are new to an MNC should also undergo a period of introduction and orientation to the firm and its corporate culture.

In the orientation phase, the new employees are introduced to, and taught about, general aspects of the corporation's operations. They are told about the firm's overall purpose and mission, its management policies and philosophies, its marketing/sales strategies and tactics, and its financial management practices.

The second phase of the training process consists of a combination of socialization and indoctrination programs. The purpose is to make the new employees a part of the MNC by introducing them to the norms and values of the firm's corporate culture (p. 113).[22] How successful the MNC will be at implanting its "view of the world" in its new employees depends on several factors. Formal and informal organizational practices, such as salary increases, promotions, job assignments, and superior-subordinate relationships, are the most conspicuous organizational factors. The less obvious ones are personal factors, such as the importance of the managers' culture to them, how closely they adhere to the dictates of their culture, and the degree of differences between the host country national culture and the MNC's corporate culture. These factors could affect the acceptance of the corporate culture by host country or third-country nationals. The more important the managers consider their own culture, the more they adhere to their own cultural norms. The more different the MNC's corporate culture is from the host country national culture and the more the managers adhere to their own cultural norms, the more will be the difficulties these managers experience in their socialization efforts. It should be noted, however, that while the MNC's culture may affect, and even change, the way in which managers behave in work and business settings, this change in behavior may be only superficial. On a deeper level, the managers may cling to the mores and norms of their own culture (p. 233).[5]

Training Host Country Nonmanagerial Employees

Pressures from host countries are forcing MNCs to hire and train increasing numbers of local people. While MNCs may be able to manage their foreign operations with few or even no local managers, it is impossible for them to run their foreign subsidiaries without local labor. Often, in developing countries, training shop-floor employees is equivalent to managing technology transfer. Successful technology transfer requires a major commitment to train the local labor force in the use of equipment and machinery. In training local labor, a few issues require careful consideration.

First, most developing countries are short on skilled labor. An adequately trained employee may be lured away by another MNC or by host country employers. Training employees without adequate measures to maintain them is a waste of time and resources.

Second, MNCs should take into account cultural factors and differences in religion. Training a supervisor from one ethnic group to oversee workers from another ethnic group may not be a wise choice. In India, for example, Muslims may not be willing to work for a Hindu supervisor.

Third, training methods that are useful in technologically advanced countries may require extensive modifications to make them fit the needs of developing countries. Where most local labor is illiterate, training should take the form of coaching. In such situations, instead of printed material and written instructions, videos, films, and personal demonstrations should be used.

Fourth, the trainer should be aware of the cultural idiosyncrasies of training. Whereas a frank confession of personal limitations or an admission of gaps in knowledge may be appreciated by Americans, such admissions in some cultures result in loss of respect and diminish the authority of the trainer.

Finally, the teacher-student and trainer-trainee roles are not universal. While Americans are comfortable with active learning by participating in the learning process and by expressing personal opinions, the people of some other cultures are more comfortable with passive learning.

Repatriation Problems

When expatriates return home, they face problems and cultural shock similar to what they had encountered on the assignment abroad. This is particularly true after a prolonged stay abroad. Not many expatriates are prepared to deal with reentry difficulties. Repatriation issues are quite often ignored by MNCs.[43] It is assumed that coming back to the home country environment should be a very easy task that does not require much preparation. Contrary to this assumption, expatriates not only may find themselves feeling like foreigners in their own country but may also face many unpleasant surprises at work. They have to adjust and adapt to changes that have taken place during their absence.

There are many factors that cause anxiety and stress for expatriate managers returning home. The most important concern of the returning expatriate is career and job assignments. Many find that they have been left out of promotion opportunities and are treated as outsiders. To their surprise, the experience and expertise gained on international assignments may not be valued at the home office. On their return, even if they are promoted, they may experience a loss of autonomy and feel a sense of status loss. The worst case is if they have been unsuccessful in their foreign assignments. Although foreign assignments are much more difficult and challenging, to most firms, a failure is a failure, and it is unacceptable. Expatriates returning home may face financial difficulties because of the cost-of-living differences and also because the extra benefits granted to them on their foreign assignment had made living abroad much more comfortable.

These problems, of course, could be minimized by a well-planned predeparture strategy. For example, the financial burden could be eased by special agreements on real estate. Job, position, and status issues should be addressed and agreed to in advance. Symbolic events such as holding board of directors meetings abroad or arranging frequent meetings among expatriates and home office executives could reduce job-related problems.

Compensation

Executive compensation is a very important and complicated aspect of HRM. The complexity and importance of executive compensation increase as an organization expands beyond its home market. In formulating a compensation package, a domestic business has to deal with only one set of cultural, legal, financial, and structural considerations. In the construction of an international compensation package, these considerations are multiplied. Besides the issue of compensation for executives who serve the global operations, the compensation of local host country employees poses additional difficulties for MNCs.

Intercultural Merger

The merger of Daimler-Benz AG and Chrysler Corporation gave rise to some human resource management issues. The new corporation remained essentially two separate companies, one German and one American. German managers were quite comfortable with foreign assignments. Americans, however, did not like going abroad much, because, as one German manager put it, "they didn't want to leave their spacious houses for apartments or smaller houses in Stuttgart, Germany."

Chrysler paid its expatriates a lump sum worth 3 months' salary to cover miscellaneous expenses for setting up house overseas, such as moving expenses, including hotel stays and meals. Also, it paid a salary bonus if the cost of living in the new country was higher than in the United States. On the other hand, Daimler offered a cost-of-living adjustment, but it gave only a small lump-sum relocation payment, and it paid only for a hotel room, not meals.

The Americans and the Germans also had different ideas of each other. The Americans saw Germans as "running around in steel helmets and always saying, 'Yes, General!'" The Germans thought of Americans as "cowboys who shoot from the hip."

Chrysler was much less a global company than was Daimler. After the merger, Chrysler employees were encouraged to volunteer for jobs abroad. This program offered payments for housing costs abroad and for the upkeep of employees' existing homes. It also offered employees paid vacations, one plane trip back home with their families each year, assistance to the expatriate's spouse to find a new job, and reimbursement for children's school expenses.[44]

An equitable and adequate compensation package is critical in motivating and maintaining highly qualified international executives. An expatriate manager is in no position to assess the adequacy of a compensation package before arriving at a foreign location. An inadequate package can be expected to produce less than satisfactory performance from a disgruntled expatriate. Even worse, it may result in an expatriate returning home, leaving the organization with serious staffing problems (p. 35).[45] A deficient compensation system may create similar problems with host country or third-country managers. Most of these problems could be avoided with a compensation package (see Table 11.5) that has the following features (p. 36):[45]

1. When considering differences in the cost of living, additional taxes, currency fluctuations, and an incentive for going abroad, the package should not result in a significant gain or loss for the manager.

2. The package should be comparable to compensation packages offered by other MNCs in the industry.

3. The package should be equitable in comparison with the domestic compensation system and policies.

4. The package should not create problems for the firm in transferring expatriates between various foreign operations.

The first three criteria deal with the cost of the package, external equity, and internal equity. The fourth criterion addresses the relationship between the compensation and other HRM policies. For example, in a large MNC, where international assignments are requisites for promotion to higher positions, an expatriate may not be overly concerned with the exact amount of remuneration. As long as the incentives are built into the assignments, and each is perceived as a sign of progress on the way to a top corporate job, managers feel secure and accept minor inadequacies (p. 209).[22] Of course, compensation creates fewer problems for an MNC with few expatriates and operating in an industry with limited competition. In such a case, each expatriate assignment and its associated compensation package could be negotiated individually.

Compensation Methods

There are different methods of expatriate compensation. Over the years, three standard approaches have emerged:[46]

1. The headquarters scale plus an MNC's affiliate differential

2. The citizenship scale

3. The global scale

The Headquarters and Affiliate Differential Scale. Under this system, the salary scale of the home office for a particular job is used as the base. A foreign service allowance is then added to this base to cover the differences between the home and host countries. An affiliate differential (see Table 11.6) may include the following:

Table 11.5   Features of an Equitable Compensation Package

No significant gain or loss when considering all factors

Comparable to compensation packages offered by other MNCs

Equitable in comparison with domestic compensation packages

Creates no problems for transfer between subsidiaries

1. Cost-of-living allowance for housing and consumer goods differentials

2. Tax equalization adjustment for host country taxes

3. Education of children, periodic family home leaves, language training, medical care, and so on

4. Differentials for inflation, currency devaluation, and work-related legal fees

5. Expenses to comply with customary professional and social obligations

6. Hardship bonus for working abroad

The concept of differentiating salaries based on host country conditions and requirements could be taken one step further. An equitable compensation system may be devised that considers not only the hardship and extra costs but also the gains and extra benefits of an assignment. This method is called a balance sheet method. It is based on the belief that apart from the premium that the package gives for going abroad, the employee should financially neither gain nor lose from accepting the assignment (p. 34).[45]

Citizenship Compensation Scale. This compensation system was developed to deal with third-country expatriate managers. An expatriate's remuneration is based on the standard of the country of origin of the manager. An affiliate differential is added to this salary base. A German manager, for example, working for an American MNC in France is paid based on the German scale plus an additional affiliate differential. This system creates difficulties when managers of more than one nationality are assigned to similar jobs in the same subsidiary. Some have suggested using one system for all third-country personnel by employing the balance sheet concept (p. 88).[45] Such a system may create equity between third-country nationals, but it may create another problem. Offering different pay scales for the same job to home country and third-country employees creates resentment toward home country personnel. In the eyes of third-country nationals, it may also be seen as discriminatory and may become a source of dissatisfaction.

Table 11.6   The Headquarters and Affiliate Differential Scale

Cost-of-living allowance

Tax equalization

Education expenses for children

Inflation differentials

Expenses for customary professional and social obligations

Hardship bonus

Global Compensation Scale. This method is preferred by MNCs that have committed themselves to a global strategy and that have an executive rank comprising many nationalities. They offer the same salary for the same job irrespective of the executive's country of origin. An affiliate differential is added to the base salary to account for differences between countries. The global pay scale requires a global job classification and ranking. Preparing global job classifications for a large company is a formidable task. To identify and measure internationally comparable job elements and apply them to various cultural settings seems an impossible task. The technical aspect of a job may be universal and measurable, but role expectations and behavioral requirements are not. The problem is compounded when we attempt to calculate an affiliate differential. There are no reliable data sources for determining some of the items included in an affiliate differential. The difficulties of using a global compensation system are many; however, the logic and appeal of equal pay for equal jobs seem to make this system the way of the future (p. 180).[46]

Host Country Employees

Compensation of local employees in various host countries is another HRM practice that requires careful consideration. Traditionally, host country employees have been paid prevailing local wages and salaries. However, some positive differential was typically used to attract the best of the host country labor force. This differential, however, was kept at a minimum in an attempt to cause no serious upward pressure on the salary standards prevailing in the host country. The nondisruptive concept of compensation for host country personnel was defended on two grounds (p. 180).[46] First, it was claimed to be the morally correct approach. Second, any upward pressure on host country standards would inevitably lead to increased costs. Overall, this philosophy seemed equitable, because often the quality of host country personnel was not comparable to that of the MNC's staff from the home country or from other countries. In a buyer's labor market, the use of local compensation standards worked well. With the expansion of MNCs and the proliferation of technology transfer, however, there is a growing pool of qualified personnel in many host countries. In a seller's market, which characterizes most of the industrializing countries, and where there is government pressure for hiring more host country managers, the application of local compensation standards is problematic.

MNCs have grudgingly recognized the indefensibility of a salary system that pays different remunerations based on nationality for the same job. In response, they have experimented using alternative methods. Some examples are as follows (p. 181):[46]

One method allows host country personnel who meet certain performance standards to be shifted from a local to an international status. Their pay and benefits are adjusted to match the international scale. This means a qualified host country manager receives the same salary as other international managers, including the home country staff. In return, the host country manager agrees to a career as a third-country expatriate manager. Another alternative shifts all local managers above a certain level to the home country salary scale. Other managers at lower levels remain on host country compensation standards. The objective here is to motivate host country employees toward self-improvement and better performance.

Despite the methods used, the process of industrialization and economic growth is causing a strong upward pressure on the wages and salaries paid by MNCs to host country personnel, and these pressures are expected to continue.

Summary

To successfully evolve from a domestically oriented firm to a multinational or globally oriented enterprise, a firm must abandon its original one-culture viewpoint and adopt a multinational or global perspective. It should accept that there is no "ideal" way to select and evaluate personnel and no perfect way to staff foreign offices. Managerial policies have to be formed and decisions have to be made considering the cultural and environmental influences that affect the MNC's foreign operations. Managers who have a global perspective are sensitive to, and comfortable with, cultural differences. They can function effectively in different cultural settings. To maintain their sensitivity, they must receive international management education and intercultural training throughout their careers.

As a firm progresses from having a provincial, parochial outlook to a global perspective, its managers need a corresponding change in attitudes and orientation. An ethnocentric approach that assumes the universality of HRM practices for all cultures is inappropriate for a global enterprise. To succeed in the global market, managers of MNCs should act as corporate citizens of the world. They should adopt management styles that are transnational and cosmopolitan and that lack a national identity or ethnocentric prejudice.[47]

Global competition requires human resources that are broadly based and multilingual and that understand the complexity of the multicultural global market. The development of human resources to meet the challenge of global competition requires careful planning and preparation. Prospective candidates, from whatever cultural background, should be identified early in their careers. Recruits should be trained and groomed for global operation. For example, in the Coca-Cola company, to create such a pool of global talent, every one of their 21 operating divisions is expected to seek out, recruit, and develop a small group of people beyond their current needs. The excess talent can be tapped whenever a global opportunity that requires such talent arises. Coca-Cola takes the position that the company needs not only capital to invest in the global market; it needs people to invest, too.[48]

The first choice of many firms for foreign assignments is still an expatriate. But for emerging firms that view themselves as global companies, the whole world is their talent market. These firms weave an international personnel thread into their organization at the entry level. They identify prospective managers for a global career from many countries and train them for these tasks. Most of their training takes place in the host country. Some of these candidates are selected from the host country for the specific goal of host country assignments. It is cheaper to identify, recruit, and train global talent at the entry level than to recruit and hire senior-level foreign executives.[48]

Many factors influence the staffing of foreign operations. The most important factors seem to be the need to understand the uniqueness of each local market and the ability to respond to the cultural requirements of the host country. The need for local responsiveness and global competitiveness is forcing MNCs to select more cosmopolitan managers. Today, an increasing number of major U.S. firms are appointing foreign-born managers to top executive positions. Consequently, a new breed of executives is emerging in the global arena. These managers have a global perspective, are multilingual, and have extensive experience in more than one culture.

Discussion Questions _____

1. The transition from a domestic to an international position creates additional problems, particularly in HRM, for firms. Discuss the sources of these problems.

2. Some argue that MNC recruitment philosophy is based on the level of trust and perceived competence of host country nationals. On that basis, MNCs may follow four recruitment practices. Explain these recruitment practices.

3. What skills should a manager possess to succeed abroad?

4. What is the role of family members in the success of an expatriate manager?

5. Describe the locally contingent factors that determine the success of a foreign assignment.

6. Should different sets of criteria be used in the selection of host country and third-country nationals? Give reasons for your answer.

7. Elaborate on the application of the international product life cycle to HRM practices.

8. Elaborate on the attributes of a good compensation system for an international firm.

9. Identify the different international compensation systems presented in this chapter.

References

1. P. Engardio, L. Therrien, N. Gross, & L. Armstrong (1991, November 11). How Motorola took Asia by the tail. *BusinessWeek*, 68.

2. G. P. Zachary (1994, September 30). High-tech firms shift some skilled work to Asian countries. *Wall Street Journal*, pp. A1, A2.

3. S. H. Rhinesmith, J. N. Williamson, D. M. Ehlen, & D. S. Maxwell (1989). Developing leaders for the global enterprise. *Training and Development Journal, April*, 26–34.

4. A. Laurent (1986). The cross-cultural puzzle of international resource management. *Human Resource Management, 25*(1), 91–102.

5. S. C. Schneider (1988). National vs. corporate culture: Implications for human resource management. *Human Resource Management, 27*(2), 231–246.

6. D. A. Heenan (1985). *Multinational management of human resources: A systems approach*. University of Texas at Austin, Bureau of Business Research: Austin.

7. D. J. Lemak & J. S. Bracker (1988). A strategic contingency model of multinational corporate structure. *Strategic Management Journal, 9*(5), 521–526.

8. B. S. Chakravarthy & H. V. Perlmutter (1985). Strategic planning for a global business. *Columbia Journal of World Business, 20*(2), 3–10.

9. S. Green, F. Hassan, J. Immelt, M. Marks, & D. Meiland (2003). In search of global leaders. *Harvard Business Review, August*, 38–44, 143.

10. Y. Yamazaki & D. C. Kayes (2004). An experiential approach to cross-cultural learning: A review and integration of competencies for successful expatriate adaptation. *Academy of Management Learning and Education, 3*(4), 362–379.

11. R. Tung (1979). U.S. multinationals: A study of their selection and training procedures for overseas assignments. *Academy of Management Proceedings, August*, 298–299.

12. S. Overman (1989). Shaping the global workplace. *Personnel Administrator, October*, 41–44.

13. A. V. Phatak (1974). *Managing multinational corporations*. New York: Praeger.

14. A. V. Phatak (1989). *International dimensions of management*. Boston: Kent.

15. G. Fontaine (1989). *Managing international assignments: The strategy for success*. Englewood Cliffs, NJ: Prentice Hall.

16. M. Mendenhall & G. Oddou (1985). The dimensions of expatriate acculturation: A review. *Academy of Management Review, 10*(1), 39–47.

17. R. Saner, L. Yiu, & M. Sondergaard (2000). Business diplomacy management: A core competency for global companies. *Academy of Management Executive, 14*(1), 85.

18. S. Shel (1991, September 6). Spouses must pass test before global transfers. *Wall Street Journal*, p. B2.

19. E. R. Koepfler (1989). Locating and staffing offices abroad. *Systems 3X and AS World, July*, 124–126.

20. W. Q. Kirk & R. C. Maddox (1988). International management: The new frontier for women. *Personnel, March*, 46–49.

21. G. Schwartz (1990, September 21). Timely tips. *Wall Street Journal*, p. R22.

22. R. L. Desatnik & M. L. Bennett (1978). *Human resource management in the multinational company*. New York: Nichols.

23. A. Bennett (1993, March 15). GE redesigns rungs of career ladder. *Wall Street Journal*, p. B1.

24. N. J. Adler (1984). Expecting international success: Female managers overseas. *Columbia Journal of World Business, Fall*, 79–84.

25. J. S. Lublin (1989, December 11). Companies try to cut subsidies for employees. *Wall Street Journal*, p. B1.

26. R. Neff (1991, June 24). When in Japan, recruit as the Japanese do: Aggressively. *BusinessWeek*, 58.

27. W. J. Best (1992, May 11). Training Japanese leaders for Western firms. *Wall Street Journal*, p. A12.

28. M. Selz (1992, February 27). For many small firms, going abroad is no vacation. *Wall Street Journal*, p. B2.

29. C. Oakes (1988). Multinational requirement: Stick with the basics. *Management Review*, September, 55–56.

30. Firms woo executives from "third countries." (1991, September 16). *Wall Street Journal*, p. B1.

31. P. Lansing & K. Ready (1988). Hiring women managers in Japan: An alternative for foreign employers. *California Management Review, Spring*, 112–127.

32. R. Vernon (1966, May). International investment and international trade in the product cycle. *Quarterly Journal of Economics, 80*(2), 190–207.

33. N. J. Adler & F. Ghadar (1990). International strategy from the perspective of people and culture: The North American context. In A. M. Rugman (Ed.), *International business research for the twenty-first century* (pp. 179–205). Greenwich, CT: JAI Press.

34. R. O'Conner (2002). Plug the expatriate knowledge drain. *HR Magazine, 47*(10), 101–107.

35. P. C. Earley (1987). Intercultural training for managers: A comparison of documentary and interpersonal methods. *Academy of Management Journal, December*, 685–696.

36. S. Ronen (1986). *Comparative and multinational management*. New York: John Wiley & Sons.

37. Island-hoppers (1991, September 14). *The Economist*, p. 68.

38. P. Ghemawat (2001). Distance still matters in the hard reality of global expansion. *Harvard Business Review, September*, 137–147.

39. R. Pascoe (1992, March 2). Employers ignore expatriate wives at their own peril. *Wall Street Journal*, p. A13.

40. G. Shames (1986). Training for the multinational workplace. *Cornell H.R.A. Quarterly, February*, 25–31.

41. R. D. Albert (1983). The intercultural sensitizer or cultural assimilator: A cognitive approach. In D. Landis & R. W. Brislin (Eds.), *Handbook of intercultural training* (Vol. 2, pp. 186–217). New York: Pergamon Press.

42. J. Lublin (1992, March 3). Your managers learn global skills. *Wall Street Journal*, p. B2.

43. A. Jassawalla, T. Connoly, & L. Slojkowski (2002). Issues of effective repatriation: A model of managerial implications. *S.A.M. Advanced Management Journal, 69*(2), 38–46.

44. J. Ball (1999, August 24). DaimlerChrysler's transfer woes. *Wall Street Journal*, p. B1.

45. S. W. Frith (1981). *The expatriate dilemma*. Chicago: Nelson-Hall.

46. E. J. Kolde (1974). *The multinational company*. Lexington, MA: Lexington Books.

47. R. T. Moran (1988). A formula for success in multinational organizations. *International Management, December*, 74.

48. J. Laabs (1991). The global talent search. *Personnel Journal, August*, 38–44.

12

International Labor Relations

In this chapter, we address the major problems that the expansion of international business creates for both multinational companies (MNCs) and national labor unions. The chapter opens with a discussion on how MNCs divide international industrial decisions between their headquarters and subsidiaries. One of the major issues of international industrial relations is the power and flexibility of MNCs. Often, national labor unions face a dilemma in negotiating with MNCs because unions cannot cross national borders, whereas MNCs are not restricted to a particular location. This puts labor unions at a disadvantage when dealing with MNCs. Labor unions complain that while they are forced to negotiate with the local subsidiary, the real decision maker is the headquarters. There is some truth in this contention. While most of the operational decision making for local industrial relations is done by subsidiaries, strategic decisions such as locating a plant and increasing employment levels at various sites are made at the headquarters.

National laws do not permit labor unions to establish formal alliances beyond national borders. Labor unions deal with this limitation by increasing the extent of their informal alliances to counter the negotiating power of MNCs. These informal alliances involve activities such as coordination of contract negotiations, cooperation, sharing of information, and exerting pressure on MNCs on behalf of each other. Informal arrangements among national labor unions are organized through international labor institutions. These institutions are regularly employed to advance the cause of labor unions worldwide.

To demonstrate the diversity of industrial relations globally, this chapter describes a sample of practices in different countries. The discussion of diversity of industrial relations begins with a description of U.S. labor unions and then goes on to examine industrial relations in England, France, and Germany. We also see how Japanese enterprise unions stand in contrast with labor relations practices in other industrialized countries. The chapter ends with a discussion of the cultural and historical roots of Japanese labor relations.

A Dilemma

On Valentine's Day, the 500 employees of Hyster Company's forklift truck factory in Irvine, Scotland, were introduced to labor's predicament. Hyster employees faced a dilemma: accept a cut in their wages or lose their jobs. Hyster Corporation, headquartered in Portland, Oregon, had a message for them. With a grant from the British government, it was ready to invest $60 million in the plant, which would create another 1,000 jobs. This would create an overcapacity in Hyster's European facilities, however. To reduce this overcapacity, Hyster was willing to close two production lines at its Dutch factory and move them to Scotland. In return, Hyster workers and managers would have to take a 14% and 18% pay cut, respectively. They had only 48 hr to decide.

Next day, each employee received a letter from the company. It indicated that Hyster was not yet convinced that Irvine was the best of the many available alternatives for a leading plant in Europe.

At the bottom of the page, there was a ballot asking them to vote on the proposed pay cut. Only 11 people voted "No." In the words of some employees, "It was an industrial rape. It was do-or-else." Hyster's workers in Irvine were not unionized. A union would not have made a difference.

The following day, Hyster broke the news to the manager of its plant in Nijmegen, Holland. It was the first official word of Hyster's decision to reduce the workforce in the Nijmegen plant.[1]

Introduction

The dilemma that the Scottish workers at the Hyster plant faced is one of the many complexities of international labor relations. International trade makes it possible to move capital and equipment across national borders. Therefore, capital is considered mobile. For three reasons, however, labor does not enjoy such mobility. First, the movement of labor across national borders is restricted by immigration laws. Trade agreements such as the North American Free Trade Agreement (NAFTA) and the European Economic Community (EEC), however, influence cross-border labor movement. Second, even without those restrictions, labor is not as mobile as capital. Searching for new jobs in a foreign land is difficult for most workers. Also, relocation is very difficult for people. Uprooting and leaving behind family and friends is not easy and is often impractical. Third, the global demand for unskilled and semiskilled workers is very low. Starting up in a new place is much more economically feasible for well-educated workers who have special skills.

There are exceptions, however. Recent trends in some developing countries point to an increasing movement of labor across national borders. In particular, the prosperous countries of East Asia mirror the demographic characteristics that were first observed in Europe and North America. The economic gains of these nations were followed by lower birth rates and urbanization, which, combined with better living conditions, have created an aging population. To cope with a shrinking labor force, these countries are drawing immigrants from less-developed countries by offering good wages. Rapid industrialization of these countries is resulting in demographic changes that will challenge their labor relations practices and immigration laws. Already, examples of these changes can be seen in Singapore, Taiwan, and Malaysia. Singapore, which limits immigration of foreigners, is forced to relocate many industries to its neighbors. Taiwan is recruiting thousands of foreign workers from other Asian countries. In Malaysia, foreigners already hold more than 50% of the construction and plantation jobs.[2]

Compared with unskilled labor, immobility is not a serious problem for skilled labor. As workers' skill level improves, labor mobility increases. Indeed, there is a global demand for workers with higher levels of skills, and most nations welcome highly educated and skilled workers. Some labor relations experts argue that with the increasing level of education worldwide and the rising need on the part of industry for more skilled workers, the globalization of labor is inevitable.[3] An early sign of the globalization of skilled workers is the immigration of nurses from the Philippines to other countries, including the United States. By one account, nearly one quarter of all nurses in the Philippines left the country for the better wages and more attractive working environment of the United States and other developed countries.[4] With the globalization of labor comes the standardization of labor relations practices.

Two forces drive workplace standardization: companies responding to global labor markets and governments negotiating trade agreements. For a global corporation, the notion of a single set of workplace standards will eventually become as irresistible as the idea of a single language for conducting business. Vacation policies that are established in Germany to attract scientists will be hard to rescind when the employees are relocated to New Jersey; flexible work hours, which make sense in California, will sooner or later become the norm in Madrid; health care deductibles and pension contributions designed for one nation will be modified so that workers in all nations enjoy the same treatment. Typical of most innovations in corporate personnel practices, the first benefit to be standardized will be the high wages of highly valued employees, who will be the most often recruited internationally.[4]

Workplace standardization may be inevitable in the distant future. Today, however, diversity in workplace practices is the norm in international business. While there are some industrial relations practices common to most Western nations, no two countries are alike. Cultural, political, legal, and economic diversity among nations has resulted in dissimilarities in workplace practices. It is crucial to understand these practices if the foreign operation is to succeed. MNCs, particularly in the early days of entry into a market, are vulnerable to mistakes. Several Japanese firms entering the United States, for example, quickly learned that ignorance of discrimination laws and labor practices could lead to disputes and be costly. During the 1970s and early 1980s, several Japanese companies operating in the United States, including Sumitomo Shoji and C. Itoh, were sued by their American employees for race and sex discrimination. The Itoh and Sumitomo cases reached the U.S. Supreme Court, which rendered judgments against both of them (pp. 55–60).[5] In these cases, the Japanese subsidiaries had engaged in employment practices in the United States without serious consideration of their legal implications. In other words, they were victims of the "innocent abroad syndrome." Their problems were caused by their unfamiliarity with the host country's (i.e., the United States) laws and practices.

Locus of Control in
International Workplace Practices

A critical issue for any firm, domestic or multinational, is its relationship with labor. No organization can survive without a healthy relationship with its employees. Labor relations practices are particularly vital to MNCs because of the cultural, political, and legal differences among host countries.

Historical precedents, traditions, and cultural norms establish the employment practices and superior-subordinate relationships unique to each country. This diversity makes international labor relations more difficult and complex than domestic practices. On the one hand, due to the uniqueness of each country's environment, host country managers need to have the authority to handle their own labor relations. On the other hand, to function as a corporation, some form of centralized control is necessary. There are many arguments in support of each position.

Headquarters-Subsidiary Relationships

Because of the diversity of the workforce and labor management relationships, MNCs treat each subsidiary as a separate entity. Each domestic operation sets its own labor relations policies and negotiates its own labor contracts. The home office, however, maintains overall control and keeps various labor relations programs in line with corporate policies. Since MNC subsidiaries are interdependent, work disruption in one subsidiary affects others. This interdependency means that labor practices among the subsidiaries must be uniform and the home office must integrate and control these practices. Also, the implementation of MNC corporate strategies requires that various labor relations programs be integrated throughout the firm. The need for uniformity, integration, and control, therefore, compels MNCs to coordinate various labor relations programs and labor union contracts. This creates a circle of power. To counter the power and flexibility of MNCs, labor unions have begun cooperation across national borders. In turn, the movement by labor unions to cooperate internationally enforces the need for MNC control from the home office.

The Quandary of National Unions

The nature of MNCs and their vast resources offer them flexibility and power in negotiations with national unions. They can shift production across national borders and play one national union against another. Production and manufacturing facilities are opened or closed at the headquarters' discretion with little or no involvement by the labor force. In pursuit of corporate goals, MNCs allocate resources to each subsidiary according to corporate strategies. These strategies are established at and directed from the home country corporate headquarters. These actions are carried out with very little or no information shared with national labor unions. Therefore, the labor unions argue, the welfare and interests of national labor unions are of secondary importance to MNCs. National labor unions feel handicapped in dealing with MNCs. They cannot match the resources of MNCs and do not have their flexibility. Realizing their handicap, U.S. labor unions have long been in search of ways to counter the apparent advantages of MNCs. At first, U.S. labor unions, through legislative initiatives, attempted to curb any MNC operations that were considered detrimental to the unions. In 1970, Charles Levinson, secretary general of the International Chemical Foundation, asserted that "trade unions have no choice but to provide the countervailing force which is badly lacking to keep MNCs within permissible bounds."[6] Years of effort, however, have not brought about many gains.

Besides leading the legislative offensive aimed at limiting the operations of MNCs, labor unions have indicated an interest in worldwide collective bargaining with MNCs. Many years ago, Victor G. Reuther, of the United Auto Workers' (UAW), made the following prediction:

> [In the future] we will see a very significant change in the whole character of collective bargaining. To deal with MNCs, the trade unions are going to have to look beyond their narrow national views and embrace an international approach. This doesn't mean we will sit down in one room with General Motors and sign one agreement for the world but it means we need the machinery to coordinate negotiations internationally.[7] (p. 30)

Although Reuther's prediction has not fully materialized, it has not been totally false either. Global labor negotiation covering the operations of one company located in different countries is a dream of labor unions and a prospective nightmare for MNCs (p. 89).[8] Knowing that negotiating global contracts with MNCs has not been feasible, labor unions instead, realistically, aimed at increasing cross-border cooperation among national unions. The aim was the coordination of national labor negotiations with MNCs. Over the years, labor unions have had some success in promoting international labor causes.[9]

Cross-Border Labor Tactics

In supporting the labor agenda, international labor unions employ several tactics, including the following (see Table 12.1):

1. Sharing information with and providing financial assistance to each other

2. Coordinating and synchronizing activities

3. Persuading and pressuring MNCs into cooperation

Table 12.1   Cross-Border Cooperation Among National Unions

Coordinating and synchronizing contract negotiations

Sharing information

Providing financial assistance

Persuading and pressuring MNCs into cooperation

In employing these tactics, national unions use the services of international labor organizations such as the Organization for Economic Co-operation and Development (OECD) and the International Labor Organization (ILO).

Coordinating and Synchronizing. Labor unions have tried to use the timing of contract negotiations for various national subsidiaries of integrated MNCs, such as Ford Motor Company, to their advantage. To the extent that they can succeed in standardizing contract expiration dates regionally, such as in Western Europe or North America, they could chip away at the flexibility of MNCs. Such coordination brings the prospect of a regional strike into a labor negotiation contract. Standardization of contract expiration dates weakens MNCs' temptation to play one national union against another. But there are many obstacles in the way of achieving common expiration dates for international labor contracts. Among them are differences in national union structures, collective bargaining approaches, and national labor laws.

Sharing Information and Financial Assistance. While the goal of contract negotiation timing has not been realized, labor unions have succeeded in other areas. As early as 1970, labor unions began collecting and sharing data on the employment practices of MNCs. U.S. labor unions and their foreign counterparts have many opportunities to cooperate with each other. For example, United Steel Workers could inform union members in Jamaica of the financial structure of aluminum companies, assist Liberian workers in their negotiation with the local affiliate of an American steel company, or lend a jeep and a boat to a small union in South Africa.

Such informal cooperation may increase in the future, and MNCs may find the global labor market to be a much smaller arena. In Mexico, General Motors and Volkswagen have already tasted a sample of the future to come. Mexican government officials have claimed that the UAW was partly responsible for the labor strikes of the early 1990s in General Motors and Volkswagen subsidiaries because of the help the UAW gave the Mexican workers. While denying any involvement in those strikes, the UAW has acknowledged providing financial assistance to Mexican labor unions.[10] Of course, the UAW had a self-interest in those strikes. The successful negotiation of higher wages by Mexican labor could benefit the UAW members too. Higher wages could make Mexican workers less competitive against their U.S. counterparts.

Pressuring MNCs to Cooperate. Besides the sharing of information or financial assistance, American labor unions have explored other avenues to help their foreign counterparts. A few years ago, U.S. labor unions attempted to put a financial squeeze on the Costa Rican government by targeting its $300 million in annual exports to the United States. The American Federation of Labor and Congress of Industrial Organizations filed a complaint with the U.S. trade representative requesting the suspension of Costa Rica's benefits under the Generalized System of Preferences and the Caribbean Basin

Initiative.[11] It claimed that Costa Rica does not provide sufficient legal protection for labor unions.

Labor unions realize their inherent limitations as national organizations facing powerful MNCs. They understand that, at the present time, they cannot expand beyond their national borders. In the distant future, regional trade agreements, such as NAFTA, may provide labor unions with such opportunities. They have, however, been successful in pressuring intergovernmental organizations such as the OECD and the ILO to adopt a voluntary code of conduct for MNCs. Labor unions sometimes succeed in promoting their cause through informal cooperation across national borders. For example, when, in 1990, Ravenswood Aluminum Corporation permanently replaced its 1,700 workers, United Steel Workers enlisted the help of foreign labor unions. The union discovered that the billionaire Marc Rich controlled Ravenswood Aluminum. With help from labor unions in Europe, Rich's business deals came under scrutiny, and some ran into trouble. For instance, Czech unions pressured their government to reject his offer for Slovak State Aluminum. The UAW also persuaded Anheuser Busch, Miller Brewing, and Stroh Brewery not to buy Ravenswood aluminum sheets for use in their cans.[12]

European labor unions have also employed cross-border cooperation and assistance to their advantage. In the early 1990s, workers at British Aerospace (BA) went on strike demanding working hours in parity with their French counterparts at Aerospatiale, BA's French partner. The British strikers of the Amalgamated Engineering Union received financial and other tangible supports from IG Metal, the German engineering union. Their strike was coordinated by the Federation of European Metalworkers (FEM). After the strike had gone on for four months, BA granted its employees a reduction in work hours per week with productivity agreements. This proved that national unions can cooperate and pursue a common goal. Now, FEM's aim is to standardize the workweek for its 6 million members in 16 European countries.[13]

Immigrant Workers

Globalization of business creates opportunities as well as problems for both MNCs and labor unions. Recent economic expansion in Southeast Asia, for example, has resulted in the opposition to immigrant workers by labor unions. From Malaysia to Hong Kong to Japan, labor unions have expressed strong opposition to the importation of workers. They fear that with the availability of cheap migrant workers, employers who are interested in short-term quick solutions will not upgrade the salaries and working conditions of local employees. Expressing the labor unions' disapproval of imported labor, G. Rajasekaran, a leader of the Malayan Trade Union Congress, asks, "How can you develop a country by flooding it with foreign labor?"[2]

National unions need to cooperate with one another but are unable to do so formally. In almost all countries, labor strikes in support of other national unions are illegal. While national unions are restricted in their actions, multiple sourcing of labor could effectively be used by MNCs to undermine the power of national labor. In 1993, for example, several MNCs decided to relocate their operations primarily from France to England. This caused an uproar by European labor and governments alike and demonstrated that the ability of MNCs to pit one national union against another is a powerful tool. During this period, Hoover, a subsidiary of the American Maytag Corporation, announced a plan to close a vacuum cleaner plant in Dijon, France, and move the work to a plant near Glasgow, Scotland. Scottish workers had accepted changes in working conditions in exchange for job guarantees and the prospect of gaining 400 new jobs. As a consequence of this move, the French would lose 600 jobs. There was other bad news too. A unit of Rockwell International Corporation, in the United States, indicated that it was going to move 110 jobs from Nantes, France, to Britain. These announcements caused outrage in France. French labor unions and government officials contended that Britain was offering unfair incentives and taking advantage of looser labor laws and lower wages to lure away French jobs.[14]

Host Government Involvement

International industrial relations practices are made more complex by host government involvement. Regulations and legislation covering workplace practices are the basis for government involvement. The failure of J. C. Penney's expansion into Europe has been partly attributed to labor problems. J. C. Penney had acquired outdated and inefficient retail chains in Italy and Belgium in the hope of turning them around. Slashing bloated payrolls proved to be almost impossible. In both countries, government regulations and labor laws made layoffs prohibitively expensive and time-consuming. J. C. Penney was forced to get out of both countries by selling these stores at a loss. The divestiture of the Belgian chain of 52 stores alone cost J. C. Penney $16 million.[15]

The Badger Company, Inc., owned by Raytheon Company, had a similar experience. When the Belgian subsidiary of Badger, due to financial difficulties, closed its operation and dismissed its workers, the Belgian government demanded compensation for those dismissed workers but was told that funds for compensation were unavailable. The lack of compensation money in the Belgian subsidiary, the government claimed, was because the parent company had deliberately bled the finances of the Belgian operation. Therefore, it was the responsibility of the parent company to make up the shortfall in compensation funds. When several OECD governments threatened to not grant any future business to Badger, the company was forced to comply with the Belgian government's demand.[16]

Host government involvement in MNC workplace relations can be direct and formal or indirect and informal. In formal and direct cases, MNCs are obligated to comply with specific laws and follow certain procedures, as was the case with J. C. Penney. Indirect and informal cases involve demands and pressures by the host government where there is no legal basis or precedence for them. Often, for example, MNCs are forced to include more host country nationals in managerial positions. In some cases, MNCs are obligated to hire personnel from a pool designated by the host government. When China opened up to foreign investment, the first international hospitality groups that entered its market experienced the difficulty of running their hotel operations under those circumstances. They were not allowed directly to tap the local labor market for their personnel needs. The government would supply them a list of applicants from which they had to make their selections. Often, the only qualification of these workers was their membership in the Communist Party.

International Labor Organizations

International labor organizations, in their varied structures, have faced problems in their attempts to create a semblance of uniformity in their practices in dealing with MNCs. Because of cultural, political, and economic differences among nations, they have failed to create uniformity in wages and working conditions in various subsidiaries of MNCs in different countries. International union delegates, in their many meetings, have not been able to agree on the priority of many work-related issues. Agreements on these issues have been made more difficult due to the different attitudes toward work methods between the Japanese and other international labor unions. Except for wages, which are considered universally important, there is disagreement on all other issues. Besides legal obstacles, the differences in priorities among national trade unions form a major impediment to the global standardization of employee relations practices. Surveys of labor union members in different countries have revealed varying priorities. For example, among Latin American delegates, trade union rights have ranked just as high as wages. A share in determining or controlling the speed of the assembly or production line has been their Number 2 demand. The 40-hr week was the third. In contrast, in Western Europe, the main demands of English and French production workers after wages have been job security and shorter working hours. This is also the case in the United States today, where until very recently, health care and pensions were of very high priority and may again become important. Germans place the most emphasis on the job environment, stressing a desire for more relief periods. A few years ago, German metalworkers gloated over their significant breakthrough in winning 5 min of relief time in each working hour and another 3 min for personal needs, thus beating the American autoworkers' 46 min per 8-hr shift at that time. There was also a gain in controlling the pace of the production line: A minimum time allowance of 1.5 min was set for any job operation in the new plant (p. 66).[8]

Migration of Jobs

The new wave of globalization started with the migration of jobs such as the production of shoes, cheap electronics, and toys to developing countries. This was followed by the movement of simple office work such as processing credit card receipts and mind-numbing digital toil to low-cost locations. Nowadays, all kinds of jobs are being done anywhere around the world. They include computer chip design, engineering, basic research, and even financial analysis. A good example of this trend is Bank of America, which has cut thousands of jobs in back-office information technology applications by sending them to India because of lower costs.

Because of technological improvements overseas, most companies from industrial countries are moving their R&D to low-cost locations around the world and outsourcing their office work. For example, Hewlett-Packard Co. has a large number of software engineers in India. American Express, Dell Computer, Eastman Kodak, and other companies are providing round-the-clock customer care services performed by staff in developing countries. Cities in the Philippines, China, Hungary, Bulgaria, Romania, and South Africa, among other places, are tapping the global market for services and are becoming "back offices" for companies in America, Japan, and Europe.

Immigrant Asian engineers in the U.S. labs of IBM and Intel have played a big, hidden role in American tech breakthroughs for decades. Now, the difference is that Indian and Chinese engineers are managing R&D teams in their home countries. The question is whether the United States can lose these jobs and still prosper (based on Ref. 17).

At the present time, standardization of workplace practices seems an unattainable goal. Progress in other areas, however, keeps labor's hopes alive. By disseminating information and publicizing the gains made by the unions in one country, others are encouraged to emulate them. One clear benefit arising from informal agreements among national unions of different countries has been the successful negotiation of some labor contracts with MNCs. The BA strike, mentioned earlier, is an example of successful cooperation that international labor unions would like to repeat.

While host governments do not allow foreign labor unions to form legal entities within their borders, some new developments herald the birth of new practices. At the present time, the final form of these practices cannot be determined. For example, in January 2000, a new labor organization, Union Network International (UNI), which is the closest entity to a true global union, was born. According to UNI literature, it was established as a global union for skills and services, with 15 million members from 900 affiliated unions in 140 countries. UNI's head office is in Nyon, near Geneva,

Switzerland. UNI is the "trade union response to increasing economic regionalization and globalization and to the convergence of what were, in the past, separate industries" (www.union-network.org/home475.html p. 2).[18] One of the early goals of UNI is to unionize Wal-Mart operations globally.[18] With the growing impact of globalization and new technologies, many industries are fast converging. Therefore, more labor union members are working for the same global employers. UNI claims that these employers are organized too much around market values and too little around human values. UNI wants to change this and aims to ensure better behavior from MNCs, halt a race to the bottom, and increase socially responsible investment and greater accountability.[19]

International organizations concerned with labor issues can be divided into two groups: the international affiliates of labor unions and intergovernmental organizations.

International affiliates of labor unions consist of organizations that are formed and run by the labor unions. They are managed and directed by personnel drawn from the members of national labor unions. Among this group are the International Confederation of Free Trade Unions (ICFTU), the World Federation of Trade Unions (WFTU), the World Confederation of Labor (WCL), the European Trade Union Confederation (ETUC), and the International Trade Secretariat organizations.

Intergovernmental organizations are established by national governments for political and economic purposes. This group includes the ILO, the OECD, and the Centre for Transnational Corporations (CTC). (Readers interested in a comprehensive discussion of international labor organizations should consult Refs. 8, 20.) We should note that these organizations do not have any legal authority over national labor unions. As national labor unions cannot cross national borders, they attempt to cooperate informally with one another through these organizations.

International Affiliates of Labor Unions

These labor organizations are concerned with improving the wages and working conditions of their members, who are members of national labor unions worldwide. They are independent of national governments and other nonlabor institutions. They join forces in pursuit of labor objectives through regular communication and cooperation with one another. They employ the various tactics explained in the preceding discussion, including appealing to national governments.

International Confederation of Free Trade Unions. In 1949, the issue of communist domination through the representatives of Eastern bloc countries caused a split among WFTU members. National trade unions that withdrew from the WFTU formed the ICFTU. While the recent history of the ICFTU begins with the split in the WFTU, its roots go back to the 1913 Secretariat of Trade Union Federation. Surviving the two world wars, it emerged in 1945 as the WFTU and included the labor unions of communist countries too. After the split, it called itself the ICFTU. The inclusion of the word *free* in the name is an intentional reference to the members' autonomy and the lack of control by governments. The ICFTU is headquartered in Brussels, Belgium, and has 140 affiliated national centers in 99 countries with approximately 82 million members.[21,22]

The World Federation of Trade Unions. A counterpart to the ICFTU and covering the national unions of communist countries, the WFTU is headquartered in Moscow. It, however, has affiliated members in some Western bloc countries, such as France and Italy, and maintains offices in Asia, Africa, and Latin America. With the fall of communism, the future status and direction of the WFTU is doubtful.

The World Confederation of Labor. Membership in the WCL consists of Christian trade unions. Similar in political philosophy to the ICFTU, the WCL is the smallest of the international confederations of trade unions. It was established in 1920 and was called the International Federation of Christian Trade Unions. It recently changed its name to broaden its membership and avoid confusion with the ICFTU. With support from the Catholic Church, the WCL was formed to counter the liberal and socialist unions' gains among urban workers. The headquarters of the WCL is in Brussels, and it has regional centers in Asia, Africa, and Latin America.

The European Trade Union Confederation. As a regional international labor organization, the ETUC primarily deals with the European Economic Community (EEC). It is the outgrowth of the European Regional Organization (ERO), which was formed to deal with labor problems arising from the implementation of the Marshall Plan. The Marshall Plan was an economic assistance program offered by the United States to rebuild the European economies devastated by World War II.

International Trade Secretariat. The International Trade Secretariat organizations are set up along major industry lines to assist the affiliated national unions. They provide help within the same industry and within specific MNCs across national borders. They supply members with data, coordinate communication, and provide financial assistance for collective bargaining purposes. There are 16 major secretariats independent of, but associated with, the ICFTU. Three of them have been in the forefront of confrontations between labor and MNCs. These secretariats are the International Metalworkers' Federation; the International Federation of Chemical, Energy and General Workers' Unions; and the International Union of Food and Allied Workers' Associations.

Intergovernmental Organizations

These institutions are established by national governments to deal with international labor problems. The most active and well-known of these organizations are the ILO, the OECD, and the CTC.

International Labour Organization. The ILO was established by the League of Nations in 1919 and was charged with the responsibility of developing international minimum standards for industrial relations and drafting international labor conventions on human rights, freedom of association, wages, work hours, minimum age for employment, working conditions, health and safety, vacation with pay, and other work-related concerns (pp. 33–36).[23] At the present time, it is one of the agencies of the UN whose primary objective is to protect the fundamental rights of workers. It also strives to promote cooperation between workers and their employers. It encourages and supports members' programs that benefit workers. The highest priority is given to achieving full employment, improving standards of living, enhancing health care and safety in the workplace, and improving working conditions.

Each member nation appoints four delegates to the ILO, two from government, one from labor, and one from business. The 56 members of the Executive Council, which governs the ILO, are elected every 3 years. Membership in the council consists of 14 members each from labor and management and 28 government representatives. Of the 28 government representatives, 10 are from the United States, Canada, Russia, China, Japan, England, Germany, France, Italy, and India (p. 57).[8]

The ILO periodically compiles and reviews the International Labor Code, which it sends to members for their ratification. Ratification of these standards by governments is voluntary, but they have been very useful, especially in developing countries. Another noteworthy accomplishment of the ILO is the Tripartite Declaration on Multinational Enterprise and Social Policy. It covers recommendations on working conditions, training, health and safety, and other labor relations concerns. Although adherence to these recommendations is voluntary, labor unions have relied on them for curbing labor abuses (pp. 93–96).[24]

The Organization for Economic Co-operation and Development. An agency of the UN, the OECD has its headquarters in Paris, France. It was established in 1961 to promote economic growth and employment and achieve a rising standard of living in member countries.[25] In 1976, the OECD issued its Guidelines for Multinational Enterprises. Many issues pertinent to MNCs, such as investment, technology, taxes, and industrial relations, are covered in the guidelines. Among the stipulations of the guidelines are four relating to major issues of interest to labor.

First, labor has the right to unionize, and workers should be free to form or join a union without fear of reprisals.

Second, MNCs should negotiate labor contracts with the unions representing the workers.

Third, in contract negotiations, MNCs should not intimidate workers with the threat of transferring their operations to other countries.

Fourth, in addition to matters that are covered in the collective bargaining document, MNCs should regularly consult with labor unions and provide them with information on issues of mutual concern (pp. 68–69).[8]

National labor unions have used the guidelines in their contract negotiations with MNCs. Often, labor unions try to include a clause in their collective bargaining contracts that stipulates compliance with the OECD guidelines.

The Centre for Transnational Corporations. The CTC is an autonomous agency of the UN. Based in New York, the CTC was established to assist host countries, and particularly developing nations, in dealing with MNCs. It also examines the impact of MNCs on host countries' social, political, and legal environments. Of major interest to the CTC is the role of MNCs in the economic development of developing countries. The CTC assists developing countries in negotiating with MNCs for the purpose of improving their economies. It has been involved in the development of a code of conduct for MNCs that establishes standards for working conditions, provides procedures for settling disputes, and protects MNC workers. This code of conduct comprises guidelines set by different organizations, such as the OECD and the ILO, among others, defining the rights and responsibilities of MNCs. The code also contains guidelines for the treatment of corporations by host countries. It covers all aspects of international business activities, including political, economic, financial, and social affairs. It stipulates that MNCs should do the following (Table 12.2) (http://isforum.org/tobi/accountability/role-intro.aspx, www.oecd.org/EN/home/0,EN-home-93-3-no-no-no,00.html, www.cleanclothes.org/codes/overvieuw.htm#Part%20II):[26]

- They should fully take into account the established policies of the countries in which they operate and consider the views of all stakeholders.
- They should contribute to economic, social, and environmental progress, respect human rights, and encourage human capital formation.
- They must ensure that timely, regular, reliable, and relevant information is disclosed regarding their activities, structure, financial situation, and performance.
- They should contribute to the effective abolition of child labor, employ local personnel, and provide training with a view to improving skill levels.
- They must establish and maintain a system of environmental management appropriate to the enterprise, taking into account concerns about cost, business confidentiality, and the protection of intellectual property rights.

Table 12.2   A Summary of Conduct for MNCs Suggested by the Centre for Transnational Corporations

Fully take into account policies of host country

Contribute to economic, social, and environmental progress of host country

Respect human rights and encourage human capital formation

Disclose timely, regular, reliable, and relevant information regarding all aspects of the operations in host country

Contribute to effective abolition of child labor

Employ local personnel

Provide training with a view to improving skills of local labor force

Respect and protect local environment

Respect copyright and intellectual property rights laws

Do not give or receive bribes

Practice fair consumer protection measures regarding safety and quality

Do not practice anticompetitive business behavior

Pay fair share of taxes

- They should maintain contingency plans for preventing, mitigating, and controlling serious environmental and health damage from their operations.
- They should not, directly or indirectly, offer, promise, give, or demand a bribe or other undue advantage to obtain or retain business or other improper advantage, nor should enterprises be solicited or expected to render a bribe or other undue advantage.
- When dealing with consumers, they should act in accordance with fair business, marketing, and advertising practices and take all reasonable steps to ensure the safety and quality of the goods or services they provide.
- They must refrain from entering into or carrying out anticompetitive agreements among competitors and act consistently with all applicable competition laws.
- They should contribute to the public finances of host countries by making timely payment of their tax liabilities, comply with the tax laws and regulations in all the countries in which they operate, and exert every effort to act in accordance with both the letter and the spirit of those laws and regulations.

Diversity in International Labor Relations

International labor relations practices are diverse. Labor unions, organizations, and collective bargaining practices are as varied as nations. Not only are there differences in worldwide industrial relations practices, but the degree of unionization varies as well. The size of national unions, however, is not a reflection of their impact on the labor market. In Germany, for example, while union members constitute a minority of the labor force, collective bargaining agreements cover almost the entire economy. While union membership has been declining in the United States, in other countries unionization is either stabilizing or rising. We don't know a lot about developing countries because there is limited information on their union membership, and statistics for unionization in these countries are either unavailable or unreliable. Given the historical patterns of unionization in industrialized countries, it is generally expected that union membership will rise in these countries.

In what follows, we present a sample of the diversity in international labor relations by discussing labor unions in Europe, Japan, and the United States (referred to as the triad nations). Our selection is based on the fact that the bulk of foreign direct investment (FDI) around the globe is made by the triad nations. Also, the labor relations practices of the triad are often used as models for other countries. Therefore, international managers must understand these practices. We will begin with the United States and move next to Europe, specifically Germany, Britain, and France. The German model of organized labor, more than that of any other nation, has influenced European labor unions and collective bargaining practices. The labor unions of both the United States and Japan are unique. Whereas an adversarial position characterizes the American labor-management relationship, the Japanese very closely cooperate with management in their firms.

Industrial Relations in the United States

Two pieces of legislation form the legal foundation for the organization of labor unions in the United States: the National Labor Relations Act (1935), commonly referred to as the Wagner Act, and the Labor-Management Relations Act (1947), usually called the Taft-Hartley Act. These and other labor statutes gave workers the right to form, join, or assist labor organizations and to bargain collectively through their representatives with the employers. While organized labor is an integral part of American business, it does not enjoy the legal status offered to German and some other European unions. The legal status of representing workers is bestowed on a union only if it gains the majority support of the workers. Therefore, employers are not legally obligated to negotiate with a minority union. Without a majority union, there is no collective bargaining. This is a reflection of American culture, which emphasizes individualism and advocates free enterprise. In contrast, in Germany, collective bargaining covers almost the entire industry, even though the majority of German workers are not unionized.

The objectives of U.S. labor unions are very similar to those of other national unions: to improve the welfare of workers and serve as their economic agents. To accomplish these objectives, U.S. unions have mainly relied on business- and industry-level activities. At this level, organizing labor unions and using collective bargaining have been the major means of accomplishing their goals. The political route, a favorite of European labor, has not been abandoned, however. Although U.S. unions have been politically active and have sought the protection of law, they have never aspired to political prominence. There is, for example, no American equivalent of the British Labour Party. While, traditionally, the European unions have been a mainstay of politics, their American counterparts have played only a supporting role.

One of the major differences between the American labor movement and those of other nations is the U.S. approach to industrial relations. Industrial relations practices are more adversarial in the United States than in any other nation. While the United States has been a fertile ground for some of the most enlightened and progressive management theories, such as participative management, job enrichment, and management-by-objectives, there is no legal-formal instrument in the United States for joint decision making by management and labor. The works councils of Europe (discussed later), for example, are totally absent from the American scene. American businesses go to extremes to prevent unionization of their operations. Even when a business is unionized, the union can be removed through the decertification process. Also, unlike the European unions, the American unions insist on their independence in collective bargaining and lack a centralized decision-making authority.

Typically, in a collective bargaining situation, unions negotiate with a company at the local or national level. Some industry-wide bargaining occurs at the national level, as is the case in the steel industry, and at the regional level, as in the trucking industry. Usually, these labor contracts cover union recognition, management rights, job classifications, and wages. Other items included in these negotiations are seniority rights, standard work periods, the length and number of work breaks in an 8-hr work period, holidays, vacations, medical insurance and retirement benefits, grievance procedures, and the commitment to no-strike and no-lockout provisions during the contract period.

European Industrial Democracy

In the United States, since the Hawthorne studies, most of the management literature has focused on participative management. In Europe, the emphasis is on industrial democracy. Although both participative management and industrial democracy deal with the sharing of decision making and power between management and labor, their approaches are quite different. Within each approach, there are different variations in power equalization and the sharing of decision making between management and labor. The European approach, however, is a more formal-legal approach to workers' representation on the boards of directors of firms as compared with the United States' informal style.

Differences Between Participative Management and Industrial Democracy

The following is a summary of the basic differences between American participative management and European industrial democracy:[27]

1. The two methods have been adopted with different degrees of fervor and have yielded varying results in different countries. Thus, industrial democracy has appeared most often in Europe, and participative management is practiced in the United States.

2. Industrial democracy is a formal, usually legally sanctioned, arrangement of workers' representation at various levels of management decision making. Participative management, on the other hand, is an informal style of face-to-face leadership.

3. Industrial democracy is a structural approach aimed at equalizing power by joint decision making through workers' representation on ad hoc committees, permanent committees, councils, and boards at various levels of management decision making. Participative management is a voluntary behavioral approach advocated by management for informal sharing of decision making with subordinates at the workplace. Organizations try to achieve this goal through indoctrination, training, organizational policies, social pressure, and other means.

Industrial democracy has taken several forms in different European countries. The German model of worker participation, however, has exerted a powerful influence on labor movements elsewhere in Europe.[28] In particular, the German model has influenced industrial relations in the northern European countries of Denmark, Sweden, and Norway. The former Soviet Eastern European countries are likely to be increasingly influenced by this model as well. The content of today's European industrial democracy movement, if not its context, is slowly but steadily becoming similar to the German one.[28] Actually, a unique feature of European Union (EU) labor relations has been adopted from the German model. The European Company Statute allows European firms, especially those operating in several countries, to unify their organizational structure and adopt a governing board that represents workers.[29] In what follows, we examine the German model in detail.

Industrial Democracy in Germany

Decision making in any organization can be considered as a hierarchy consisting of four major levels. At the top of this hierarchy is the institutional level dealing with policy making, which is concerned mainly with the direction and the future of the organization. The middle management level deals with the implementation of decisions made at the institutional level. At the technical level, decisions are related to the actual production of the organization's output and day-to-day operations. The workers' level, which is at the bottom of the hierarchy, implements all the decisions made at the technical level (Figure 12.1).

In actual practice, the four levels of organizational hierarchy overlap. Usually, participation in decision making takes place between two adjacent levels. The extent and nature of participation, however, are always determined by the higher level. In the United States, examples of this kind of participation are committees, job enrichment programs, management by objectives, and so on, all of which involve adjacent levels (i.e., job enrichment usually involves the technical level and the workers, while management by objectives involves middle management and the technical level). However, there is a spillover effect, and the decisions made at the institutional level will have a long-lasting effect on other levels, particularly the workers' level.

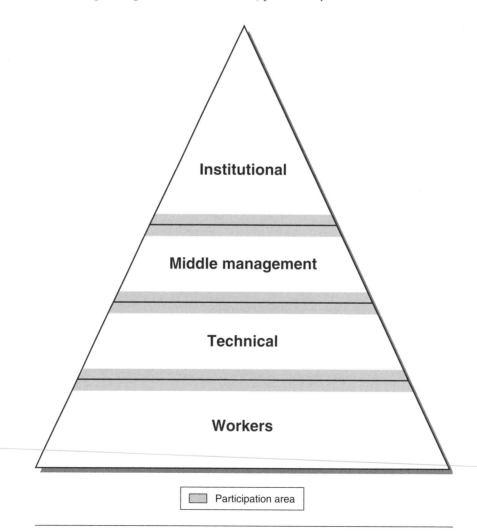

Institutional

Middle management

Technical

Workers

Participation area

Figure 12.1   Decision-Making Participation and Organizational Hierarchy

Institutional decisions require more information than do decisions made at other levels of the hierarchy. Furthermore, the information received from the lower levels of the organization is very crucial for the quality, accuracy, and, if needed, modifications of these decisions. These ideas argue for a change in the more typical adjacent-level influence-sharing processes and suggest, at least for the German model, that top management needs to find ways to share decision making with those at the worker level. Therefore, the inclusion of lower-level employees in the decision-making process of the institutional level not only is a democratic action but can also be considered an appropriate act for the sake of organizational efficiency and effectiveness.

This type of involvement in decision making has been called participation at the board level, or codetermination in Europe. More specifically, the term *codetermination* refers to the German model of industrial democracy (*mitbestimmung*). This model basically involves the participation of representatives of all employees, blue collar as well as white collar, including managers, in the two-board system of German industries. The two-board system is discussed later in this chapter.

Layoffs: The Dutch Style

In the 1980s, Dutch management and labor entered into an agreement that required companies to stay in constant communication with labor unions. Other issues included the requirement that the labor unions refrain from undue wage demands and government assurance that taxes would remain low. In return, companies agreed to hire more labor union employees and consult with the unions in major staffing decisions, including, but not limited to, layoffs. The agreement ruling, however, was to be waived in the event of a layoff of fewer than 20 employees.

The corporate culture created by this agreement was very successful in most areas. But when it came to downsizing, this culture was a major handicap because it required months, perhaps years, of negotiation between companies and unions. Thus, when a major Dutch information technology services corporation, Pinkroccade, found itself in the midst of an economic decline and needed to lay off 700 employees, it decided to take advantage of the agreement waiver, laying off 19 workers at a time. To avoid the "over 19" rule, it started laying off workers based on the location of their residence rather than their corporate location and even reclassified some. It also reassigned some young, very talented workers to secure jobs and locations to avoid laying them off. The corporate director of human resources for Pinkroccade stated that this massive layoff, while avoiding consultations with the union, was like putting together puzzle pieces that just didn't want to fit (based on Ref. 30).

Labor Unions in Germany

Industrial relations in Germany are governed by two closely related, yet separate, institutions of codetermination and collective bargaining. While co-determination allows labor to participate at the highest level of the organizational decision-making process, the German constitution provides a very general and broad framework for collective bargaining. It guarantees collective bargaining rights for labor to negotiate with the employers over wages and working conditions. German labor laws impose restrictions and limitations on labor strikes and plant lockouts. Wildcat strikes are mostly related to economic issues and not labor rights. The law has established minimum requirements for many workplace practices, such as working hours, vacations, and safety regulations. These minimums can be augmented through collective bargaining.

Industry-wide labor contract negotiations take place regionally. Some of the problems that in other countries are subject to collective bargaining are handled by works councils in Germany. Works councils, however, are not allowed to bargain for remuneration and other work-related issues that are the domain of collective bargaining. While the majority of German workers are not union members, almost all employers are members of employers' associations.[31]

Although union members are in a minority, collective bargaining contracts encompass more than 90% of workers. This is due to the widespread membership in employers' associations and the industry-wide contract negotiations. Collective agreements are negotiated on a national or area-wide industry basis and establish wage patterns for the entire specific industry. These contracts cover both unionized and nonunionized workers if the company is a member of the relevant employers' association.[31] Moreover, both unions and employers are strongly centralized, and because collective bargaining covers almost the entire German labor market, labor is included in national economic planning through collective bargaining.[32]

Background and Structure of Codetermination

Germany's experience with codetermination can be thought of as the product of two separate and independent forces. The first force was the Germans' desire for democratization of the workplace. The second force was the policy of the Allied forces, particularly the British, after World War II of strengthening the German labor movement. Allied forces wanted to prevent the resurgence of fascism, which they believed was aided by the powerful coal and iron industrialists of Germany.

German sentiment for codetermination can be traced to the social unrest and workers' demands for a greater voice in the design of work situations that arose in the first part of the 19th century. By 1905, for example, "workers' committees" had gained recognition in all mining enterprises employing more than 100 workers. The mines were legally obligated to establish workers' committees and consult with them before the introduction of any work rules or guidelines

(p. 56).[33] Democratization of the workplace gained additional momentum when the Workers' Council Act of 1920 gave managerial and bargaining power to workers' councils. The workers were given the right to have two representatives on the supervisory board. The handling of grievances and the establishment of work rules, as well as wage agreements within contracts negotiated by the unions, became the domain of workers' councils (pp. 53–54).[34]

Workers' councils were suppressed during World War II. They came to life again after the war and were given legal recognition and expanded authority by Western occupation authorities. At the Potsdam Conference, the Allied powers agreed to break up the steel and coal industries, which had exemplified Germany's military and industrial might and aided Hitler in his quest for domination. To curb the power of the managers in these industries, the Allied forces agreed to give more voice to labor.

It is ironic that the total collapse of the German political and economic systems aided the fulfillment of an old demand of the German workers. The attempts to prevent the emergence of a military industrial system, on the one hand, and the desire for a new start and consensus by all parties in Germany, on the other, provided the setting for the development of co-determination. It was the convergence of these two fundamentally different forces that resulted in the Co-determination Act of 1951, which was amended in 1956. The Workers Constitution Act of 1952 extended workers' participation to all business organizations but gave workers only one third of all the seats on the supervisory boards.[35]

Many changes have taken place since the policies of the occupation authorities reinstated workers' representation on the supervisory boards. Germany is no longer an occupied country, and its economic and political system has emerged as one of the strongest in Europe. The unions and workers have been a potent political force, constantly renewing their demands for parity with management. Finally, the Co-determination Law of 1976 granted workers full parity representation on supervisory boards and, through these boards, in the operational systems of enterprises.

Today, the 1976 legislation is in force, side by side with earlier laws, for companies with more than 500 employees. Workers and shareholders have parity representation on the supervisory boards of these companies, but the numbers vary with the size of the firm. The big companies, for instance, are divided into three categories of 2,000 to 10,000, 10,000 to 20,000, and more than 20,000 employees. The supervisory boards of these companies consist of 11, 17, and 21 members, respectively (p. 50).[35]

Although the law has given workers more power than ever before over the management of larger companies, it has fallen short of giving them full parity in decision making. If a disagreement arises between the representatives of the workers and the shareholders, the law stipulates that the shareholders' position should prevail (pp. 50–52).[35] The structural arrangements of codetermination as it stands now in Germany are depicted in Figure 12.2. The main features of codetermination are as follows (pp. 58–60):[33]

1. All private companies and profit or nonprofit organizations with five employees or more are subject to the Work Constitution Law of 1972. This law makes provision for the formation of workers' councils in each firm or in each independent unit within a company. The size of the council depends on the number of employees and can vary from 1 to 35. Where the size of the council is at least 3, blue-collar and white-collar workers vote separately and are represented on the council proportionately to their numbers. Employers and councils are encouraged to cooperate and are bound by the framework of collective bargaining.

   The functions of work councils include areas that are not regulated by collective bargaining, such as handling grievances, agreements on piece rates and wages, and working conditions that are not covered by a union contract. Furthermore, a work council is entitled to negotiate with an employer on matters such as hiring, firing of large numbers of employees, establishing plant rules, and making changes in the plant location. Also, it supervises the application of work laws and administers the welfare agencies in the plant. The members of the work councils need not be trade union members. However, in practice, more than 80% of the members of all work councils belong to trade unions.

2. Companies with more than 500 employees are governed by two boards: the supervisory board and the management board. The supervisory board is the equivalent of the board of directors of an American corporation and is a policy-making body. The supervisory board appoints the management board. The management board is responsible for the day-to-day operations of the firm. The appointment of the labor director on the management board—who represents labor viewpoints and promotes their cause—needs the approval of the majority of workers' representatives. The workers elect one third to one half of the supervisory board, depending on the size of the firm, and the employers elect two thirds to one half.

3. The election of representatives to the supervisory board is governed by an intricate and elaborate set of procedures. For example, in the case of a 10-member board, of the five workers' representatives, two are elected by the workers' council, two are elected by the union federation approved by the firm's union and the workers' council, and the fifth member is an outsider designated by the union federation. The chairman and vice chairman of the board must be elected by a two-thirds' majority of the board members. If a two-thirds' majority cannot be reached, the stockholders' representatives elect the chairman, and the vice chairman is elected by the workers' representatives.

   The chairman has the tie-breaking vote (Refs. 36, pp. 53–55; 37, pp. 117–118). The supervisory board meets at least quarterly, and besides having policy-making power and the power to select the management board, its consent is required on matters such as the purchase of land and property, mergers and acquisitions, a new plant location, important investment decisions, long-term loans, and the purchase or sales of stocks of other companies.

Opposition to Codetermination

Opposition to codetermination comes from three sources (pp. 50–52).[35] The first source of opposition is employers or their representatives. They fear that codetermination may result in the loss of management control and dilution of power and authority. They also fear that inefficiency may follow and profits may suffer if high-level decision making becomes subject to labor approval. The second group opposing workers' participation at the board level, interestingly enough, is the labor unions. They would prefer to achieve industrial democracy through the institutionalization and strengthening of collective bargaining rather than participation and representation on the board of directors. Communists and Socialists are the third source of opposition. They see participation in high-level decision making as a delay in the final victory of the proletariat. From this perspective, collaboration with capitalists will not advance the labor cause. Developments in the post-Soviet era have had an impact on the strength of this source of opposition.

Whatever the arguments are against codetermination, the opposition cannot ignore some of its benefits and impacts on the German economy. The workers' representatives have shown an understanding of "economic necessities" and consideration for the firm's long-term objectives. There is also no

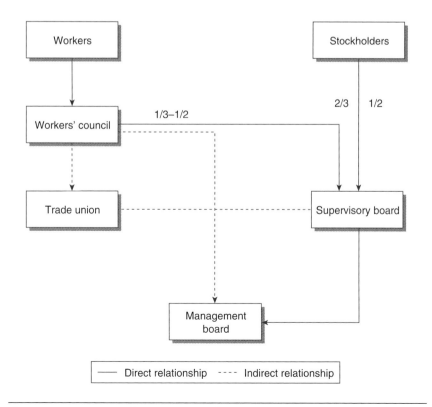

Figure 12.2   Structural Arrangement of Co-determination

evidence that these representatives have exploited their position to obtain unreasonable pay raises for the employees (Refs. 36, p. 57; 37, pp. 117–118). However, these claims were made prior to the globalization of markets. Recent economic woes and the rise in unemployment in Europe and especially in Germany, however, have been attributed to the nature of management-labor relationships.[38] Some have asserted that the recent corruption scandals in large German companies, such as Volkswagen and Daimler-Chrysler, were due to the cozy relationship between the labor members of codetermination boards and the management of these firms.[39] Faced with economic difficulties, the German government has shown interest in curbing labor benefits,[40] which may signal changes in labor-management relations.

Moreover, in response to the criticisms leveled against codetermination, Mazzolini argues that there is no basis for management's fear that codetermination may result in the dilution of management authority and control. Based on an extensive series of interviews with leading executives throughout Europe, Mazzolini provides the following explanation:[41]

> Contrary to common belief, especially in countries where there is no tradition of participation, systems such as German co-determination do not imply the downfall of the free enterprise system. . . . Experience shows that labor generally worries only about those issues which have a clear bearing on [the] working class, leaving administrative and overall policy decisions to management. While labor's influence causes firms to be more socially responsible, fears of more fundamental changes are unwarranted. (p. 80)

Most American labor unions are opposed to board-level workers' representation because they see it as a potential threat to the union's power and existence. They fear that the workers' representative on the board of directors might be independent of the union. Codetermination might also undermine the "adversary relationship" image between U.S. unions and management. American labor leaders consider codetermination rather superfluous compared with what U.S. labor has achieved through collective bargaining (p. 108).[42] They believe that unions influence more issues through collective bargaining than they could hope to affect by worker representation on the board of directors of corporations. In the words of one union officer, if unions were to share decision making with management as partners, the unions would be "most likely the junior partner in success and the senior partner in failure" (p. 110).[42] Other objections of unions to codetermination stem from the fear of losing power, the possibility of creating conflicts of interest, and the fear of disturbing the existing economic order. Traditionally, Americans favor minimum or no government involvement in business. They are reluctant to invite the government into an already complicated setting.[43] Additional opposition to codetermination comes from critics who assert that cultural differences would impede the application of codetermination in the United States.

Evidently, this skepticism is not shared by European unions. Advocates of codetermination and industrial democracy claim that union strength can be supplemented through workers' representation on the boards of directors of firms. For example, "in a system of collective bargaining alone, contract enforcement is difficult since management must be relied on for implementation. A system of workers' councils and board representation, in contrast, provides alternative institutions for contract enforcement" (p. 65).[28] According to many European labor relations analysts, collective bargaining and workers' participation at the board level are each essential to the other's continued expansion.[28]

French Labor Unions

According to Pieper, certain cultural characteristics of French society are reflected in its industrial relations (pp. 94–95):[31] The French value rationality and order, and they view authority as absolute and omnipotent. Because of its absolute nature, authority cannot be shared or compromised. Both in practical terms and symbolically, it must remain sovereign. Checks and balances of due process and countervailing institutionalized power common to American society are foreign to the French. These values have greatly influenced the fate of organized labor in France. Viewed from the upper levels of the hierarchy, the imposition of substantive rules from the top is necessary to be rational and bring about order and harmony. Viewed from the lower levels, authority is threatening and should be avoided. Achieving independence, autonomy, and security necessitates keeping a distance from superiors and not dealing with them directly. Directly dealing with one's superior leads to the acknowledgment of one's total dependence. The solution is to avoid face-to-face relationships between superiors and subordinates and to create rules. The only other alternatives are total conflict and absolute submission, neither of which is culturally acceptable. To protect one's independence and not submit to the absolute authority, one obeys the rules. In the words of Pieper,[31]

> From the top, edicting the rules affirms the capacity of sovereign power. Those rules are impersonal, which from below reinforces the sense of following an abstract order and not bowing to absolutism; and from above follows the rational model of "one best way" of ruling absolutely over one's domain without having to be bothered to make unnecessary allowances for individual peculiarities. . . . Thus the power is centralized at the top; and below, the impersonal rules define strata of subordinates with precisely defined borders . . . [in which] . . . individuals enjoy total protection and independence. . . . Therefore the power recedes higher and higher, farther and farther from the knowledge of the element necessary to take decisions. It must decide without knowing . . . and it is in the interest of the subordinates to hide or manipulate information. (p. 95)

A preference for formal, ritualistic activities and the absence of cooperation between various levels within the hierarchy produces a general climate
of apathy. The training of elite French administrators and executives con-
founds the problem. Most elite French managers are from *grandes écoles*,
the selective and prestigious universities that act as a clubby network that
doles out top positions only to its own members.

The combination of the French cultural characteristics just discussed and
a variety of historical reasons has resulted in very low unionization in
France. The large number of small firms, which are usually not unionized,
also contributes to low unionization. Moreover, French unions have held on
to a society-changing agenda much longer than most unions in the United
States and northern Europe, instead of concentrating on economic issues.[44]

Among the major European countries, union membership is the lowest
in France. By various estimates, only 7% to 10% of the labor force is
unionized (p. 191).[45]

French labor unions are highly political, ideologically oriented, and weak
in the private sector. They are, however, strong in the public sector. Their
low level of membership does not reflect the real power of French unions.
Union strength comes indirectly through the election of union candidates to
positions in firm-specific representative institutions, particularly the works
councils (pp. 181–197).[45] Their strength becomes evident when labor
strikes in the public sector disturb electricity supplies, transportation services, and civil organizations. Unions, however, enjoy public support. Even
those workers who are not union members fully support the unions in a
crisis or when they are called on to strike.

Labor Unions in Britain

Labor relations and collective bargaining in the United Kingdom have
been described as "formal" and "informal" systems coexisting in a context
of legal abstentionism.[46] In contrast to the situation in the United States and
Germany, industrial relations in Britain are characterized by a relative lack
of legal restrictions and structure. Voluntarism, a social philosophy of the
undisputed pursuit of self-interests, is a hallmark of industrial relations in the
United Kingdom.[47] Voluntarism and the lack of restriction mean that there
are no limitations on wildcat strikes or lockouts. There are also fewer restrictions on layoffs, the hiring of part-time workers, and subcontracting.
Collective bargaining agreements are considered "gentlemen's agreements,"
which are binding in honor only and not subject to legal enforcement. The
tradition of collective bargaining reflects the "grassroots" character of British
labor organizations. The shop steward has a very significant role in workplace bargaining and is as important as the unions in making and administering the rules. This is in contrast with the European system, where the
pattern and overall regulation of collective bargaining are influenced from
the top.[46] The shop steward is a unique feature of English labor relations:[8]

> Shop stewards are elected by fellow union members in the plant. Today they play a central part in helping to determine the likely reaction there to the eventual terms for a settlement. Their influence in this respect is very great and it is equally powerful at the bargaining table. The national union officials may lead the contract negotiations with employers but the stewards, by virtue of their everyday ties to the rank and file, wield almost as much, if not more, influence in the bargaining. (pp. 123–124)

Since British labor has traditionally relied on "self-help" and has preferred minimum or no legislative interference, it is not surprising that, unlike other European labor movements, British labor has opposed institutional forms of labor representation, such as codetermination. In recent years, however, the state has been getting more involved in industrial relations. The Employment Protection Act of 1975, for example, grants certain rights to unions, including access to information and consultation with management in the case of workforce reduction. It grants certain rights to unions and workers and established government agencies to provide arbitration, mediation, and conciliation for resolving industrial disputes.[48]

A unique characteristic of labor unions in Britain is their participation in politics. The historical roots of labor involvement in politics go back to the 1906 election, when a newly formed Labour party won 29 seats in the House of Commons. Over the years, the Labour party has become the political counterpart of the union movement. While in other European countries, left-wing political parties sponsored the trade unions, in Britain, the unions created the socialist political party. While the relationship between the unions and the Labour party is very strong, labor unions have not attempted to dominate the party and the government. They have always worked pragmatically with the government of the day. Even within the Labour party, major initiatives come from what might be called the intellectual rather than the union side.[48]

Japanese Enterprise Unions

Japanese labor relations practices are quite different from those of other industrialized countries. Historical precedents and cultural attributes have created a unique set of relationships between labor and management in Japan. Unlike the labor unions of other nations, Japanese labor unions are not separate entities independent of business firms. As "enterprise unions," they could be regarded as extensions of the organizations. Although Japanese labor unions are not totally independent, nonetheless, they represent the workers and play an important role in the economy.

Management practices and attitudes toward workers are important factors that shape the nature and type of industrial relations in an enterprise. The distinguishing features of Japanese management practices are lifetime commitment (employment), a seniority-based wage system, and collective decision making (*ringi*). These practices and historical developments have created the enterprise unions and industrial relations that are uniquely Japanese.

Historical Factors

After World War II, with encouragement from the Americans, the Japanese government enacted a trade union law that ensured that labor had the right to organize, bargain collectively, and strike. The economic hardships following the war made it urgent for labor unions to safeguard the living standards of workers. To achieve this objective, unions launched a joint effort, bringing together white- and blue-collar workers at the enterprise or plant level. Similarly, employers wanting to restore the balance of power in their own favor exerted considerable effort to create just such enterprise unions. To prevent the establishment of an all-powerful labor organization, however, they undertook three measures:

1. They established vertical labor organizations.

2. To bring about order in the workplace, radical workers were terminated from service.

3. They set up a new industrial relations system in every company.

These measures, particularly the vertical character of the unions, weakened their horizontal solidarity. Various levels of union organizations were established parallel to the corporate structure, such as at the head office, plant, department, and section. At each level, the unions were in constant interface with their corresponding management counterparts. Article 2 of the labor law facilitated the establishment of this unique labor-management relationship. It stipulated that all employees below the section heads, regardless of their jobs, may organize into unions. Therefore, in some large plants, supervisors are often elected as union representatives. This adds to the fragmentation of unions and increases management's influence.[49]

Management Practices

Lifetime employment and the no-layoff policy practiced by large Japanese firms increase the loyalty of workers to the firm and reduce the cost of training and turnover. Long-term relationships among employees foster an attitude of cooperation and trust and minimize conflict. Slow and orderly promotion based on seniority emphasizes the individuals and not the job titles. Knowing that they will work together for a lifetime and that there is ample time for the firm to recognize their contributions, employees learn to work for mutual benefits. Permanent employment makes rotation of workers to different jobs in the firm a practical choice. Although it is time-consuming, the *ringi* system of collective decision making and consensus building produces quality decisions that those affected by them understand and accept. The slow process of collective decision making allows enough time for everyone to adjust to the emerging decisions and commits them to the implementation of those decisions.

The Japanese Enigma

As far as outsiders can tell, most Japanese accept with equanimity all the daily demands that subordinate individual desires to those of the community. This striking communalism is, however, the result of political arrangements consciously inserted into society more than three centuries ago by a ruling elite. For centuries, statecraft in Japan has resulted from a balance between semi-autonomous groups that share power.

At the most basic level of political life, Japan is no different from any other country. The Japanese have laws, legislators, a parliament, political parties, labor unions, and a prime minister. But don't be misled by these familiar labels. The Japanese prime minister is not expected to show much leadership; labor unions organize strikes to be held during lunch breaks; the legislature does not in fact legislate (bureaucrats in ministries write the laws); and laws are enforced only if they are not too much in conflict with the interests of the powerful.[50]

More than in any other industrial country, labor relations in Japan are based on the realities of the labor market condition rather than on an open contest of power. Permanent employment and seniority-based promotion procedures enable Japanese workers to anticipate, with a high degree of certainty, how they will advance in jobs, wages, and other amenities. With assurances of job security and near certainty on career prospects, wages are the remaining major bargaining issue that could cause occasional conflict. Also, until recently, in an environment of continuous and rapid economic growth, conflict over wages could be resolved with a win-win outcome.[51]

The unique Japanese labor relations have evolved in a cultural framework of collectivism and paternalism. While modernization and global competition are eroding the foundation of lifetime employment, most large Japanese firms still follow this tradition. These firms continue to offer the welfare benefits that were established at the beginning of modernization and those that were established after World War I to eliminate the turnover of skilled employees. Now, the typical benefits offered by these firms are housing, medical and health care, recreational and sports facilities, day care for children, commuter subsidies, and meals at work.

Since employees are expected to stay with their firms for a long time, they are also expected to be team players. Instead of seeking individual gains, each member is expected to strive for collective benefits. The Japanese attribute of collectivism stands in sharp contrast to the Western ideal of individualism. While modernization and global competition are changing labor-management relationships, Japan has maintained its unique paternalistic character. Again, these relationships have cultural and historical roots:[52]

> Because industrialization was originally sparked by a dynastic elite, the idea of paternalistic concern for the welfare of subordinates is strongly rooted in Japanese management. Although the government has intervened to regulate the manager in the field of labor relations, it has nevertheless given strong encouragement to the paternalistic approach. (p. 131)

Almost all unions in Japan are enterprise unions. Because they are company specific, there are more than 74,000 of them, in 94 federations (p. 231).[53] With the tradition of enterprise unions and the collectivist orientation of the Japanese, the labor unions take a less adversarial posture against the firms. Japan has a lower incidence of labor strikes than most other industrial countries, except Germany. Many strikes do not last long, some lasting only a few hours. Most contract negotiations, and about half the strikes, take place during *shunto*, or the annual Spring Labor Offensive. Regardless of a union's affiliation or lack thereof, negotiations take place at the company level, and in their negotiations and demands for wage increases, unions consider the good of the company. A sharp public expression of conflict came from Shinichi Tsuji, the leader of the smallest and most radical of the three unions at the Japanese affiliate of Shell Oil Company. He told a newspaper reporter that his union was getting tough. The day before, they had gone on strike for 45 min, and they were planning a lunchtime multi-union demonstration so that workers would not have to miss any work.[54]

Summary

International industrial relations pose problems for both labor and management. Managerial problems are due to differences in legal practices, labor laws, and customs; host government interference with market forces; and cultural characteristics of various national markets. The problems facing national labor unions center on the erosion of bargaining power. In collective bargaining, the balance of power has shifted in favor of MNCs. Worldwide variations in wages, benefits, and industrial practices provide MNCs with the opportunity to relocate jobs to places that offer more favorable business conditions. Obviously, such moves will result in loss of jobs in areas where wages are higher and business conditions are less conducive to profit making.

While the increasing internationalization of business and the consequent interdependencies create problems for MNCs, they pose a much bigger challenge to labor unions.[9] National borders limiting workers to separate national labor markets restrict labor's options in contract negotiations with MNCs. These borders, however, are much less restrictive where MNCs are concerned. Competition among nations to attract foreign direct investment offers MNCs multiple opportunities for investment and additional munitions for fighting the demands of national labor unions. These problems will intensify with the gradual removal of trade barriers. Low trade barriers provide more opportunities to capital than labor. Because capital is much more mobile than labor, with the lowering of trade barriers, capital can relocate to countries where labor costs are low, while labor mobility is hampered due to political, social, economic, and cultural factors. Even if trade and business barriers are totally removed, labor cannot readily take advantage of the opportunities in other labor markets. Empirical evidence suggests that the removal of trade barriers undermines the power of unions in setting higher wages. While reducing barriers may eventually lead to an improved economy, initially, at least, it reduces the power of national labor unions and increases the need for international cooperation among these unions.[55]

Faced with the reality of decreasing trade barriers, national labor unions are searching for ways to counter the increasing bargaining power of MNCs. While national laws do not permit formal labor cooperation across national borders, informal methods are still available. Through international labor organizations such as the ILO, national labor unions are expanding the extent of their informal cooperation and coordination for negotiation with MNCs. A few successful examples of these types of activities have encouraged national labor unions to search for additional measures. The ultimate goal of collective bargaining with MNCs at the international level, however, might be achieved only in the distant future. Given the present circumstances and developments, we can safely predict that the future of international collective bargaining will be much more contentious and volatile.

Discussion Questions

1. What is the major problem faced by national unions negotiating with MNCs?

2. Why do the MNCs treat each subsidiary as a separate entity for collective bargaining and labor contract negotiations?

3. Why do host countries get involved in international labor relations?

4. Elaborate on the cross-border tactics used by national unions for promoting the labor agenda.

5. What is the ultimate goal of international labor unions? Do you think that this is an attainable goal?

6. What is the objective of the ILO?

7. Explain the major features of German industrial democracy (codetermination).

8. In the United States, the relationship between management and labor is called adversarial. Why?

9. French labor unions have the lowest membership rate among all European countries. What cultural characteristics explain this low membership rate?

10. What are the major characteristics of British labor relations?

11. Distinguish between European industrial democracy and Japanese enterprise unions.

12. Northern Europeans claim that their model of industrial democracy provides for smoother industrial conflict resolution than the adversarial labor-management relations of the United States. Elaborate on your acceptance or rejection of this claim.

References

1. B. Newman (1983, November 30). Single-country unions of Europe try to cope with multinational. *Wall Street Journal*, p. 1.
2. R. Pura (1992, March 5). Many of Asia's workers are on the move. *Wall Street Journal*, p. A13.
3. W. B. Johnson (1991). Global work force 2000: The new world labor market. *Harvard Business Review, March–April*, 115–127.
4. C. Prystay (2002, July 18). U.S. solution is Philippines dilemma. *Wall Street Journal*, pp. A8, A10.
5. S. P. Sethi, N. Namkiki, & C. L. Swanson (1984). *The false promise of the Japanese miracle*. Boston: Pitman.
6. R. Randal (1970, November 8). Multinational unions: Internationally organized labor tackles the corporate octopus. *Washington Post*, p. M1.
7. J. P. Gannon (1970, December 7). Worldly hard-hats: More U.S. unions help foreign workers pressure American companies overseas. *Wall Street Journal*, p. 30.
8. B. Bendiner (1987). *International labour affairs*. New York: Oxford University Press.
9. K. Fatehi, F. Derakhshan, & J. Giermanski (2000). National unions' quandary: The need for internationalization. *International Journal of Human Resources Development and Management*, 1(1), 68–80.
10. S. Baker (1992, August 31). Free trade isn't painless. *Business Week*, pp. 38–39.
11. Costa Rican unions brought back to life by AFL-CIO (1993, September 10). *Wall Street Journal*, p. A17.
12. M. Mallory & M. Schroeder (1992, May 11). How the USW hit Marc Rich where it hurts. *Business Week*, p. 42.
13. J. Parry & G. O'Meara (1990). The struggle for European unions. *International Management, December*, 70–73.

14. C. Forman (1993, February 3). France is preparing to battle Britain over flight of jobs across the Channel. *Wall Street Journal,* p. A18.

15. B. Ortega (1994, February 1). Penney pushes abroad in unusually big way as it pursues growth. *Wall Street Journal,* p. A1.

16. R. G. Blainpain (1977). *The Badger case and the OECD guidelines for multinational enterprises.* Deventer, The Netherlands: Kluwer.

17. P. Engardio, A. Bernstein, & M. Kripalani (2003, February 3). Is your job next? *BusinessWeek,* pp. 50–60.

18. K. Maher (2005, August 18). Wal-Mart tops global agenda for labor leaders. *Wall Street Journal,* p. A2.

19. Decent work for all is the global union goal (2005, August). *UNIinfo,* p. 4.

20. A. P. Coldrick & P. Jones (1979). *The international directory of the trade union movement.* New York: Facts on File.

21. J. P. Windmuller (1953). *American labor and the international labor movement.* Ithaca, NY: The Institute of International Industrial and Labor Relations, Cornell University.

22. J. P. Windmuller (1984). *Labor confronts the transnational.* New York: Labor Research Association.

23. P. R. Baehr & L. Gordenker (1984). *The United Nations: Reality and ideal.* New York: Praeger.

24. W. J. Feld (1980). *Multinational corporations and U.N. policies.* New York: Pergamon Press.

25. *OECD: History, aims, structure* (1971). Paris: OECD Publication Office.

26. M. J. Kline (2000). Business codes and conduct in a global political economy. In F. O. Williams (Ed.), *Global codes of conduct: An idea whose time has come* (pp. 39–56). Notre Dame, IN: University of Notre Dame Press.

27. B. M. Bess & V. J. Shackleton (1979). Industrial democracy and participative management: A case for a synthesis. *Academy of Management Review, 4*(3), 393–397.

28. D. G. Garson (1977). The co-determination model of workers' participation: Where is it leading? *Sloan Management Review, 18*(3), 65.

29. B. Keller (2002). The European company statute: Employee involvement and beyond. *Industrial Relations, 33*(5), 424–445.

30. D. Bilefsky (2003, July 8). The Dutch way of firing. *Wall Street Journal,* p. A13.

31. P. Conrad & R. Pieper (1990). Human resource management in the Federal Republic of Germany. In R. Pieper (Ed.), *Human resource management: An international comparison* (pp. 94–139). Berlin, Germany: Walter de Gruyter.

32. C. Summers (1989). An American perspective of the German model of worker participation. In A. Gladstone, R. Lansbury, J. Stieber, T. Treu, & M. Wiess (Eds.), *Current issues in labor relations* (pp. 113–128). Berlin, Germany: Walter de Gruyter.

33. H. J. Lux & B. Wilpert (1978). Co-determination: Worker participation in Federal Republic of Germany. In B. Wilpert, A. Kudat, & Y. Oxhan (Eds.), *Workers' participation in an internationalized economy* (pp. 56–60). Kent, OH: Kent State University Press.

34. A. Sturmthal (1964). *Works councils.* Cambridge, MA: Harvard University Press.

35. The Mitbestimmung mess-up (1978, August). *Management Today,* pp. 49–52.

36. J. E. Hebden & G. H. Shaw (1977). *Pathways to participation.* New York: John Wiley & Sons.

37. D. Jenkins (1973). *Job power*. Garden City, NY: Doubleday.

38. C. Rhods (2002, August 8). Checking out: Short work hours undercut Europe in economic drive. *Wall Street Journal*, pp. A1, A6.

39. S. Power, E. Taylor, & M. Walker (2005, July 29). After bumpy tenure at Daimler, Schremp hands over the key. *Wall Street Journal*, pp. A1, A8.

40. J. Ewing (2003, February 17). The decline of Germany. *Business Week*, pp. 44–53.

41. R. Mazzolini (1978). The influence of European workers over corporate strategy. *Sloan Management Review, 19*(3), 80.

42. J. C. Furlong (1977). *Labor in the boardroom: The peaceful revolution*. Princeton, NJ: Dow Jones Books.

43. K. Fatehi-Sedeh & H. Safizadeh (1986). Labor union leaders and codetermination: An evaluation of attitudes. *Employee Relations Law Journal, 12*(2), 188–204.

44. Unions in France: Yesterday's men (1989, February 18). *The Economist*, pp. 71–72.

45. C. Howell (1992). The contradictions of French industrial relations reform. *Comparative Politics, January*, 181–197.

46. A. C. Neal (1989). Co-determination in the Federal Republic of Germany: An external perspective from the United Kingdom. In A. Gladstone, R. Lansbury, J. Stieber, T. Treu, & M. Wiess (Eds.), *Current issues in labor relations* (pp. 128–145). Berlin, Germany: Walter de Gruyter.

47. D. Kujawa (1988). International labor relations. In I. Walter & T. Murray (Eds.), *Handbook of international management* (pp. 11/3–11/25). New York: John Wiley & Sons.

48. A. W. J. Thompson & L. C. Hunter (1978). Great Britain. In J. T. Dunlop & W. Galenson (Eds.), *Labor in the twentieth century* (pp. 85–148). New York: Academic Press.

49. Y. Takahashi (1990). Human resource management in Japan. In R. Pieper (Ed.), *Human resource management: An international comparison* (pp. 212–232). New York: Walter de Gruyter.

50. The enigma of Japanese power (1989, May 8). *Fortune*, p. 150.

51. S. B. Levine & K. Taira (1980). Interpreting industrial conflict: The case of Japan. In B. Martin & E. M. Kassalow (Eds.), *Labor relations in advanced industrial societies* (pp. 61–88). New York: Carnegie Endowment.

52. C. Kerr, J. T. Dunlop, F. H. Harbison, & C. A. Myers (1960). *Industrialism and industrial man*. Cambridge, MA: Harvard University Press.

53. R. Bean (Ed.) (1989). *International labour statistics*. London: Routledge.

54. E. S. Browning (1986, April 28). Japan's firms have a friend: The unions. *Wall Street Journal*, p. B24.

55. J. Driffil & F. van der Ploeg (1993). Monopoly unions and the liberalisation of international trade. *Economic Journal, 103*, 379–385.

Case 18

BARBARA AND WILLIAM HAROLD

A Case Study of Americans Living Abroad in Belfast, Northern Ireland

Rae André

PART A: WILLIAM HAROLD

When you first meet William Harold, he is likely to tell you that he is from Minneapolis, that he has been in the airplane business ever since he got out of the army, and that he is an engineer. "We don't know how long we will be staying here. The airplane business is like that. We have just been put back on reduced time. That means 3 days a week. Management, too, will be on 3 days a week. As it is, the Government picks up the fourth day of my salary anyhow, so that my compensation will not be drastically reduced. Our company is under some scrutiny for going to a 3-day week. The issue for the people in Northern Ireland is, Are you here on a permanent basis? Yes, I think most American companies are here to stay. At the same time, everyone is here on an approximate 10-year tax relief. Most companies, after they have run out of the tax incentive, do tend to leave." William Harold is married and has two kids going to the Belfast schools, an 8-year-old boy and an 11-year-old girl. They speak with Belfast Irish accents after having lived in Belfast for 2 years.

When you see William among his Irish friends, you can see that he is well assimilated. There is much laughter and poking fun. William will talk about the "wee nip" that he is going to have after work. He describes the neighborhood that he lives in as "all Irish," except for themselves. "We are very happy," he says. "Most of my friends are Irish. In fact, I don't pal around with the other Americans in Northern Ireland. There are about 40 at the managerial level in other companies here.

"They call this a war zone, but it doesn't feel like a war zone. The only time the violence has struck me is when the University was bombed this fall. I should have been in the classroom right below it, when the bomb went off. Barbara was in the building at the time and said that the whole building shook and that someone told her that the University had been bombed." The University had previously been bombed, before he arrived in Northern Ireland. "I do avoid certain areas of town. There are certain areas of town that I would not drive into. I would not go anywhere locally unless I know someone or am going to someone's house. I don't pay any attention to it. I don't worry about it."

SOURCE: Reprinted with permission from Professor Rae André, College of Business Administration, Northeastern University.

Barbara and William live in a large home leased for them by the company. In many ways, it is a typical Irish home of the upper middle class. What is different about it is that when you walk in the front door you are toasty warm right away. The family walks around constantly in bare feet or slippers. The doors between the hall and the living room and the hall and the kitchen are open—unlike the same situation in other Irish households, where heat is being conserved. The television, showing videotapes, is on nonstop. It is on all through the day and during dinner. There is an electric fire in the grate, whereas the Irish would have a coal fire. The house is quite nice and William likes it very much, but there are some things that they miss. For instance, in their house in Reno the family had three televisions, one for William and Barbara, one for the children, and one for the den. If anything one wanted to watch was on, each of them could scatter to their different televisions. Coming over, they had a 9,000-lb transportation limit, but of course they could not bring any of their electrical appliances. So here they all have to debate who is going to get to watch what on the television.

The house has an especially large refrigerator, and there is a freezer in the garage as well. Nevertheless, Barbara complains that they can never store enough or make enough use of their leftovers. Barbara is an excellent cook. Serving a meal to an American guest, she prepares spareribs. William suggests that the pork in Northern Ireland is absolutely superb. In fact, the local bacon is one of his favorite things. Barbara typically makes several different types of salad, much like one would have in the United States. She makes a potato salad into which she puts the local shrimp. For her guest, she also makes carrot salad and cucumber salad. A good German wine is served. Barbara comments that they cannot get California wines here, with the exception of perhaps Paul Masson or Gallo. They drink German and French wines.

The family has two cats and a longhaired chihuahua. The house is constantly full of action and talk.

The following are excerpts from a conversation with William:

What is there that I miss about the States? Nothing.

I belong to a private club. Private clubs are very popular here. I go there to play golf and squash quite a bit. It is hard to get into these clubs. This club I am in, in fact, has a 1-year waiting list. It is associated with the telephone company; it's their plant club.

I am taking my master's of science and management at the University 1 day a week from 1 p.m. until 9 p.m. They give us a lot of work. It has a 3-year program. I probably won't finish it, but I'll transfer the credits to the States. Right now I'm studying Taylor and right brain/left brain differences for a paper for a course. There really isn't that much to do around here. So I am glad to have the opportunity to go to school. And, of course, the company is paying for it.

Most people just stay home at night and watch videos. We belong to two video clubs. We go out to the movies also, but the movies only change once a fortnight or once a month. On the weekends, we just mostly watch videos. I can watch an American football game every week. Just last week we got the entire Super Bowl.

We do like to take advantage of the travel. We go all around, and we are planning to take a cruise on the Nile soon. All four of us."

There is one American restaurant in town, the only American restaurant. It is the only place you can get a hamburger and other American foods. It is quite good. The Irish food is just very plain; they do not put many spices on their food. I always eat my lunch out. I never eat in the plant cafeteria.

Every Sunday I buy all the papers.

When we first arrived here, we had two cars.

Both were stick shift, and Barbara was having trouble learning how to drive a car with a stick shift, so we traded them in and got one big car instead. Barbara makes good use of the buses.

What are the prospects for economic stability here, over the long term? Not very good, unless they get some industry in. Not big industry but small shops—eight people. That is what they need most.

It is difficult for me to get even my suppliers to come over here from England. The Irish don't like the Brits, and the Brits hear so much bad publicity—and that's just what it is, just publicity about Northern Ireland—that they are just frightened to come here. So I pick them up at the airport, and I take them to the office, and I take them to lunch, and then I take them back to the airport. That's it.

PART B: BARBARA HAROLD

We have been here a little over a year. We came in December, so we have been here now for 14 months. There is not a lot to do here.

Some time ago, we formed the Ulster American Women's Group, just because there were so many of us here, and we wanted to have something to do. So we would tour the national historic sites or go down to Dublin and meet with the American Women's Club down there.

This year I'm taking a 1-year course in health education at the University because at a certain point you just must get on with your life. I didn't want to come here and just waste my time. That is what I would have felt I was doing if I hadn't taken this course. I am a nurse and I am able to work here, so that when I finish my 1-year program I could take a job if I wanted to. I quit work several years ago and haven't worked since.

When I first came here, I had trouble finding things, things you want. I learned that you can call around and find sour cream or other things you are used to cooking with, but it takes time. When you do find it, you will only find one little bit of it. It took me 3 months to find Parmesan cheese, and when I could find it, it was only in 2-oz. containers. Everything here is small.

When we arrived here my daughter was 10. At 11½ years of age they make the children take examinations to be tracked into what is in America the equivalent of the secondary school system. She can either go into a grammar school, which is your college prep, or into the equivalent of a high school, which is less advanced. When you send your children to grammar school or high school, you have to choose which school you want to send them to. They arrange open houses at these schools to allow you to select them. How can you select a school on the basis of a 2½ hr presentation? I fought to get her exempted from that exam because she had only been in their school system for 7 months. They are allowing her to take a 4-hr psychological test instead. She is taking it next Tuesday. She is a little worried about it. But I'm not worried about her. Naturally, every American child is 1 year behind when they start school here in Northern Ireland because they start school 1 year earlier. They work the children very hard. Typically, they will have 4 or 5 hr of homework a night in grammar school. They put a lot of pressure on them that I don't think is necessary.

I don't mix very much with my neighbors. To some extent, yes. But there seem to be limits. My daughter Claire at one point took me down to meet the mother of one of the children whom she had been playing with for months. I had a frank conversation with the woman, who said, "Well, yes, I am very pleased to meet you but to tell you the truth, I am just as happy staying at home in the evenings and not going out. And I probably wouldn't take the time to come up and meet you specifically." I don't think it has always been this way, but since The Troubles people just keep to themselves more.

I was surprised at how advanced the women are in this country. Women are very aware and very eager to make something of themselves beyond being just a homemaker. But the men, sadly enough, seem to want to keep them down.

It's unusual to be invited into their homes, in my experience. At first, I thought it was me, but now I think it is them. I had been warned about this, that someone who would spend an hour on the phone talking to you would never accept your invitation back to your home to have coffee. Recently, the students at the University in my class decided that they would have a little party and since my home is right on the edge of the campus I offered it. It took me a great deal of time and effort to convince them that I was serious, that I really wanted people to come into my home. I don't know why that is, it just is.

I don't know how long I will be staying here. The airplane industry is unpredictable; it just depends. We have been moving around quite a bit. Before we came here we were in Reno for a year. (*Note*: William says that Barbara really misses her true hometown, which is Savannah. All their furniture is being stored there, and their permanent home there is being rented.)

The Irish are not very spontaneous. I would be bopping in and out of my friends' homes if I were in the States. Here, I met a woman who was telling me about her travels with a friend and said that she hadn't spoken to that friend for 6 months. I wouldn't have done that. I would have at least phoned up my friend during that 6 months' time. But that's just not the way they are here.

I think most American women here are bored. This is an outpost, there isn't much to do. If you go to the club with William . . . I don't go there because I don't like that sort of thing. You would walk in and see the women sitting together on one side of the main room, and the men sitting together on the other side.

There are some people—it is a shame—who won't let themselves take advantage of my talents, they won't let me be of use to them. There just seem to be barriers between me and them. Sometimes I just think it is because I am Black. There are just some people who can't deal with that. I'm Black and intelligent, but they don't understand that. They just don't relate to that. I judge people by who they are and how they talk to me, not by the color of their skin.

I've got used to the moving, but here I just feel like I'm camping out. There are no comfortable chairs to sit on in this house. If you go into that room there, you'll see that all the chairs are just not comfortable. The refrigerator is large by Irish standards but too small for me; I can't keep any leftovers in it. They say this is an upper middle class area, but I'm not impressed, and not just because of American standards.

PART C: BACKGROUND ON THE HAROLDS

Barbara is originally Jamaican and was brought up in London. She said she was not at all frightened to come to Northern Ireland. She had been warned that she might not get along with the Irish. She had been warned about The Troubles, but because of her previous experience in England, she said that these things did not scare her. She is a nurse and midwife.

William was formerly with the U.S. Army. Now, he is an aircraft engineer with an American company. First, the Harolds spent a year in Reno with this company, and then they were sent to Northern Ireland. The division in Northern Ireland is going to be the production facility for a jet, which is currently being built in the United States. The prototypes are being built and tested at this point. Supposedly, the plant was put on 3 days as opposed to 4 days because the testing is not going quite as perfectly as planned.

Barbara and William have some disagreements over the extent to which he has assimilated to the culture. Both of them speak fondly of their house on an island off the Georgia coast. Their children also speak fondly of the States. Both children complain that there is nothing to do here, especially the older girl, who says that sports for girls are very poor. She only has gym on Wednesdays. "The food is terrible," she says. If she were in Georgia, her daddy would drop them off to roller-skate 2 days a week, Friday and Saturday. The boy, on the other hand, is into soccer and rugby, and his team has won several championships.

DISCUSSION QUESTIONS

1. What are the issues of cross-cultural adjustment for Barbara and William? For their children? How do the problems of adjustment differ for the wage earner and the nonworking spouse?

2. What adjustment issues are especially important because these people are Americans?

3. What safety issues must the family be concerned about in this situation? In other situations, living or traveling abroad? How should their company become involved with these issues?

Case 19

AMERICAN MANAGER IN AN AUSTRALIAN COMPANY

Linda B. Catlin and Thomas F. White

"United Flight 2020 to Honolulu and Los Angeles is now boarding. Please have your tickets and boarding passes ready for the attendant at the gate."

Bob Underwood picked up his briefcase and started toward the jetway. He paused momentarily to look around the passenger waiting area and, as had been the case so often here in Sydney, he saw nothing to indicate that he was in a foreign country. Certainly, the accents were different than in the United States, but the language was English and readily understandable. This superficial familiarity, he concluded, was one of the main reasons he had had such a difficult time adjusting to his job at MedScope, Ltd., in Australia.

MedScope was one of three foreign subsidiaries owned by the parent company, MedicoSupplies, Inc., whose headquarters were in Houston, Texas. Bob was on a two-year assignment at MedScope after working in the management information systems (MIS) department in Houston for five years.

As he settled back in his seat on the plane, Bob thought back to the day he arrived in Sydney almost eight months ago. Bob and his family had left Houston on a hot, humid July day and arrived 30 hours later to find Sydney in the middle of winter. That juxtaposition of seasons probably should have alerted him that there would be many differences between the United States and Australia. Instead, during the taxi ride to their hotel through Sydney's modern buildings, everyone seemed to have the impression that they had simply arrived in a different U.S. city.

Bob's boss at MedicoSupplies had encouraged Bob to apply for the position of MIS director in Sydney. Pete Jacobs thought that this international experience would enhance Bob's chances for promotion at MedicoSupplies since he would then have knowledge of a subsidiary's operations. Reluctantly, Bob applied for and obtained the Sydney position. His wife and children had not been enthusiastic about the move to Australia. Bob's daughter, Sara, was in the seventh grade and loved her school; his son, Jim, was in the fifth grade and just had earned the pitcher's spot on his Little League team; and Bob's wife, Marie, worked part-time as a medical technician. After several long family discussions, Bob convinced Marie and the children that this move was extremely important to his career.

During the first few weeks at the Sydney office, everything seemed to go well. Bob met with his new staff during the first week and asked for their help in orienting him to the Australian operations. In this meeting, he outlined his background and industry experience, described his goals for the two years he would be managing the Australian MIS department, and assured them that he had an open door policy and was always available to talk with them on an individual basis.

"I'm looking forward to your working with me to accomplish the company's goals for Australia," he concluded. "Thank you for meeting with me today."

Bob's family had more difficulty making the transition to living in a foreign country. When they first arrived in Sydney, the family lived in a hotel apartment for three weeks while they searched for a house. When they leased a comfortable house in a Sydney suburb similar to their Houston house, Marie spent several days visiting schools and looking for the right one for Sara and Jim. Although there were state-supported schools in their neighborhood, a friend in the United States who had lived in Australia several years ago advised Bob and Marie to find a private school for the children. Deciding on schools and sorting out the equivalent grade levels and subjects proved more difficult than Marie expected, and she asked Bob to spend some time with her talking with school headmasters. Although Bob always had been closely involved in decisions regarding the children, he was reluctant to take time away from the office at the beginning of his tenure in Sydney and left these decisions to Marie.

Colleagues at MedScope organized a welcoming party for the family soon after their arrival, and Bob's boss's wife invited Marie to lunch and the theater. The family had no permanent social group at first, however, and activities that they had

enjoyed in Houston were less readily available in their new city. Jim, in particular, missed his Little League team and asked once if he could go back to Houston and live with his grandmother. Bob decided to be patient and hope that Marie and the children would adjust to their new situation after a few weeks.

Over the next six months, Bob stayed very busy learning the Australian company's MIS operations and looking for ways to improve them. Before he left Houston, the MedicoSupplies vice president of operations, Jason Blanchard, had met with Bob to discuss his assignment in Australia. Jason had made it clear that he believed MIS is a technical area and that it can and should be uniform throughout the company's subsidiaries.

"What we need to do," Jason had said, "is find the most efficient and productive methods, and then put those in place in MedicoSupplies companies, wherever they are located."

Bob's only experience in MIS was in the MedicoSupplies U.S. headquarters office and with a similar company in Dallas. His models, then, for his new assignment were U.S. models, and when he got to Sydney, he began looking for similarities and differences between the U.S. and Australian operations.

One thing Bob noted immediately was that there were fewer management levels among employees in Australia; in fact, the organizational hierarchy was remarkably flat compared to the U.S. structure. Bob found himself responding to requests and receiving information from technicians as well as managers, and from supervisors as well as heads of departments. At one staff meeting to examine the workflow design in the department, several technicians attended with their managers and participated fully in the discussions. When Bob asked one of the managers after the meeting if this was a standard procedure, the Australian manager assured him that it was.

"No one knows more about workflow design than Rob and the other technicians," the manager said. "We wouldn't have made as much progress as we did if they hadn't been involved in today's meeting. And we certainly want their support for any changes we might decide to make."

While Bob understood the manager's reasoning, he was uncomfortable having so many people involved in what he regarded as sensitive management discussions. When the same topic appeared on the meeting agenda later that month, he asked specifically that only designated managers attend. And to keep the meeting within a reasonable time frame, Bob limited the discussion on each point to 10 minutes. When this second meeting was over, he felt that much more had been accomplished with fewer participants and in less time.

About three months after arriving in Australia, Bob's boss, Emily Zortan, the general manager of MedScope, asked Bob what decision the MIS department had made regarding new software and equipment for the sales department. Bob's predecessor had amassed several files of material and information from numerous suppliers, and he had secured bids from five companies for the purchase. After reviewing the files and the bids, Bob recommended the Trujex Company in Hong Kong. Their bid was lower than three of the other companies', they promised a shorter delivery time, and Bob knew something about their product from conversations with managers in the U.S. and London offices of MedicoSupplies.

Later that month, Frank Ricardo, one of the systems analysts in Bob's department, came to Bob's office and asked if he had time to discuss a pending purchase for one of the company's departments.

"If you mean the purchase of a new system for sales," Bob said, "I've already taken care of that. Emily asked for my recommendation a few weeks ago and I told her we'd go with Trujex."

"But you didn't ask me or any of the other analysts which system we would recommend," replied Frank.

"Well, no, but I had all of the information I needed in Preston's files. He had bids from five companies, plus a mountain of information on seven or eight companies. Surely, you and the other analysts gathered that data for him, or at least recommended the companies to contact."

"Yes, we did," Frank said. "But we hadn't finished discussing the advantages and disadvantages of each system, nor had all the technicians given their opinions. Preston was planning to meet with us several times before giving Emily the department's decision."

"I think I had all the information I needed," Bob stated, with a note of finality in his voice. "I reviewed the files thoroughly and recommended Trujex, based on sound reasons. I'm sorry you and the others didn't have the opportunity to discuss it further, but I felt that a timely decision was what Emily wanted."

As Frank left his office visibly upset, Bob wondered again how Preston had accomplished anything if he had held frequent meetings with all or many of his staff members to go over seemingly straightforward procedures and decisions.

In an effort to decrease his span of control, and to achieve Jason Blanchard's objective of putting the most productive and efficient methods in place, Bob worked for the next several weeks on a reorganization plan for MedScope's MIS operations. As soon as he thought he had a good understanding of the company as a whole and of the specific functions of the MIS department, Bob put together a plan that encouraged specialization among the department's employees. He divided the group in four, assigning each of the four groups to one of the company's functional areas: administration, finance, research, and marketing. Under this scheme, each of the four groups would concentrate on the MIS needs of its designated functional area and thus become more proficient in serving that group of users. Moreover, fewer managers would report directly to Bob as head of the department and he would have more time to devote to planning.

When Bob finished the reorganization plan, he called his top managers to a staff meeting.

"The purpose of our staff meeting today," Bob began, "is to discuss an opportunity for all members of this department to hone their skills by specializing more than they are doing now. I've seen this type of plan work in other companies similar to MedScope, and I think you'll agree it has some distinct advantages over the present arrangement."

He passed out copies of the new organizational scheme and spent the next 20 minutes explaining his rationale for the plan. Bob also explained that this was still in the draft stage and that he welcomed ideas from the group on refinements and changes. Finally, he asked the managers for their comments and reactions. No one said anything.

After a few minutes of uncomfortable silence, Bob said, "I'm sure you'll want to take this plan back to your offices and give it some thought. And perhaps discuss it with some of your key people. Why don't you take a couple of days to look at it and then call or memo me with your suggestions."

Two days later, Emily Zortan called Bob to her office for a meeting. She began by saying that several people from Bob's department had called to ask her for letters of recommendation because they were applying for positions in other companies. Emily was anxious to know what Bob thought the problem might be.

"This has never happened before," Emily explained. "I've never had several people come to me with this sort of request. People leave MedScope, of course, to take better jobs somewhere else. But this is too many people all at once. What do you think is going on, Bob?"

"I don't really know," Bob said. "Actually, I'm astonished. No one has complained to me or given any indication that there's a problem. I'm pretty good about recognizing dissatisfaction among my employees, or anticipating problems which may occur. But I haven't seen any evidence of that here."

"How well do you know your employees, Bob?" Emily asked. "I realize you've only been here for eight months and that you've been busy settling in at work and at home. But have you joined them for their Friday get-togethers after work, or gone with them on some of their Saturday excursions? Preston was always talking about what a tight-knit group the MIS department is, and how many social activities they organize."

"I did go out with some of them after work a couple of times," Bob replied, "but I have been pretty busy helping Marie and the children adjust to our new situation. And I've always found that it's a good policy to maintain a certain amount of distance from one's employees."

"Oh, there is one thing that I know might be a source of irritation. Jack Strath mentioned that he had requested three weeks vacation time for a trip to Bangkok and Singapore, and that you had asked him to take only two weeks instead. Any reason for asking him to cut his trip short?" Emily asked.

"Yes," Bob explained, "I thought that three weeks is too long a time for a key manager to be away. He's working on several critical projects that need to be completed in the next three or four months."

"If I recall correctly," Emily said, "Jack has an excellent assistant who could take over in his absence. That would be good experience for a mid-level manager, don't you think?"

"I suppose so," Bob conceded, "although it's unusual for a senior manager like Jack to take three weeks off."

Emily looked puzzled. "My suggestion is that you give Jack the three weeks he requested. He's worked extremely hard this year and deserves a respite."

"And whatever the problems with other employees, I'm sure we can work them out," Emily continued. "Maybe there's just a simple misunderstanding here. Probably, you and I should have spent more time when you first got here, talking about our management style and philosophy here, and seeing if there might be some differences between Australia and the United States. Why don't you think about this and plan to meet with me after you get back from Houston in a couple of weeks."

"Right, I'll give it some thought and see if I've overlooked something. Perhaps I've stepped on somebody's toes without realizing it. I do have a tendency to get caught up in enthusiasm for projects and forget that others may not share that same enthusiasm."

"Have a good trip to Houston, Bob, and we'll talk when you get back," Emily said as she walked him to the door.

As Bob's plane left the runway at Sydney, he thought back to this conversation with Emily and began to review the events of his last eight months at MedScope. What had he done wrong? He knew he was a good manager; his previous bosses all had given him excellent performance appraisal reviews.

They always mentioned his technical expertise, his planning skills, and his department's productivity as evidence of what a good job he was doing. Yet, Emily regarded the potential department turnovers as an indication that something was seriously wrong in his department at MedScope. Bob decided he would talk with Pete Jacobs when he got to Houston and review his activities in Sydney. Maybe Pete would be able to help him see where he had made some mistakes.

DISCUSSION QUESTIONS

After carefully reading this case study, answer the following questions:

1. What do you think are the reasons several employees suddenly want to leave Bob's department? What has Bob done during his eight months at MedScope that may have contributed to these employees' dissatisfaction? Are there any cultural differences between the United States and Australia that might explain the problems Bob seems to be having?

2. What could the parent company, MedicoSupplies, have done to prepare Bob and his family for this international assignment? Outline an action plan companies might use in order to increase chances for success among their expatriate managers. Include suggestions for both the manager and members of the manager's family.

3. Articulate and evaluate your own opinion about the degree of "distance" prevalent between U.S. managers and their staffs. Who is protected by this management style? Are there any adverse organizational impacts resulting from this style?

Suggested Readings

Knotts, Rose. "Cross-cultural management: Transformations and adaptations," *Business Horizons, January* (1989): 29–33.

Mendenhall, Mark, Edward Dunbar, and Gary Oddou. "Expatriate selection, training, and career-pathing: A review and critique," *Human Resource Management,* 26, no. 3 (1987): 331–345.

Murray, F. T. and Alice Murray. "Global managers for global businesses," *Sloan Management Review,* 27, no. 2 (1986): 75–80.

Tung, Rosalee. "Selection and training of personnel for overseas assignments," *Columbia Journal of World Business,* 16, no. 1 (1981): 68–78.

———. *The new expatriates: Managing human resources abroad.* Cambridge, MA: Ballinger, 1988.

Case 20

HUMAN RESOURCE MANAGEMENT PRACTICES

A Small Business in a Transition Economy

Kamal Fatehi and Foad Derakhshan

INTRODUCTION

The South Sugar Company (SSC) was a subsidiary of the Southern Corporation, a multinational corporation. It was located in a developing country in Asia. The country had embarked on an economic development and modernization process. It was interested in becoming self-sufficient in many areas, particularly in food production. The SSC was one of several sugar companies, which together produced 60% of the country's sugar requirement. The remaining 40% was imported from other sugar-producing countries. The SSC was one of the lowest-cost producers in the country. Consequently, it was able to expand its sales and production every year. In the 4 years prior to the events described in this case, its tonnage sales had increased at an average of 20% each year, its sales in the local currency by 23%, and profits by 7.5%.

Despite this record, some managers were complaining that the SSC was not gaining its rightful share of the country's growing economy. The country had an economic development program that aimed at the modernization of agriculture as well as industrialization, financed by growing exports of raw materials and minerals. The gross domestic product (GDP) had been growing steadily for some years and was expected to continue in the future. In the sugar industry, modernization efforts were expected to result in complete self-sufficiency.

HUMAN RESOURCE PRACTICE

The SSC offered good wages and fringe benefits, including health insurance, to its employees. It also had a profit-sharing plan. Most of its employees were long-term employees. Except for department heads and agricultural specialists, most of its white-collar workers were not college graduates but had learned their work through years of experience.

The company had identified this lack of formal training and education as a problem and began hiring college graduates for administrative positions. The need for business graduates was particularly apparent, and they were hard to recruit. SSC facilities were located in rural areas, and it was especially difficult to get college graduates to leave the amenities and opportunities of modern living in the cities to live in rural locations.

The SSC had been successful, through offering a higher-than-average salary, in hiring a college graduate to be its chief accountant. This person, Byan, served successfully for 2 years. At that time, Malak, a young business school graduate, interviewed for a position as a junior cost accountant working for Byan. During an interview with Byan's supervisor, the vice president (VP) of finance, Malak was told that the VP was expecting to take a position in the home office of the parent corporation and expected that Byan would replace him.

Based on this interview, Malak decided that the SSC would provide him with opportunities for growth and progress. The company was expanding, and there seemed to be ample opportunities for promotion. Company policy on promotions was based on three criteria: education, seniority, and performance. Malak finished 3 months of training and orientation successfully. During his training, he impressed everyone with his aptitude for problem solving, his flexibility toward people, and above all, his friendly manner.

After 1 year he had proved to be an efficient and valuable employee. Consequently, he was promoted to the position of manager of the cost accounting department. Malak was pleased with his new job and with the fact that he now was the only person reporting directly to Byan. This distinguished him from other junior accountants and clerks who were not college graduates, and it was more satisfying to him personally and socially.

In his new position, Malak developed some personal relationships with the staff at the parent company, the Southern Corporation. Now and then he would receive information from his parent company contacts concerning decisions related to the firm. It was through these informal channels that he became aware of political pressure resulting in some discrimination in performance appraisals and rewards.

Although this was unpleasant, he ignored it because it did not affect him. One morning in February, Byan called Malak to his office. Byan told him that the VP of finance was about to leave for the home office and that there was a general understanding that Byan would replace him. In such a case, Malak would move up to Byan's position. Byan wanted assurance that a new accountant who had been hired recently could perform Malak's duties. Malak assured Byan that he had been training the new accountant and grooming him to assume additional responsibilities in anticipation of such an eventuality. In fact, the new accountant was doing well and could handle the job.

A couple of weeks later, the VP left for the home office, and Byan was asked to assume the vacated position. He eagerly accepted the offer and was waiting for his formal promotion. After 2 months, however, someone else from the home office was brought in as the new VP. This was a huge personal setback for Byan. It was more than he could tolerate. Disappointed and dejected, he resigned shortly thereafter. Before leaving, Byan told Malak to plan ahead so that he, too, would not become the victim of favoritism. After Byan's departure, Malak was appointed as chief accountant.

The new VP of finance was aware that Malak was concerned over what had happened. In justifying management's decision, he told Malak that it was the policy of the company to appoint its higher-level executives from the home office. The VP of finance had to be someone who had worked at the home office and had developed a working relationship and trust with the home office staff. Of course, these explanations and justifications did satisfy Malak's concerns. He was uncomfortable and unsure about his future advancement with the firm.

Malak stayed with the firm for one more year. During this time, he was convinced that chief cost accountant was as high as he could advance with the company. He began searching for other opportunities, and when he received a reasonable employment offer from another firm, he left the SSC. Before leaving the company, he had the following conversation with the personnel manager, Zamen.

Zamen: Well, we surely will miss you here. I wish you would stay with us, but I assume you have given it enough thought and are doing what is best for you.

Malak: You know, Mr. Zamen, that I would stay if I had a chance for future progress. I am not the only one who is disappointed with the firm. Look at your turnover figures.

Zamen: I can see your point, but I do not accept that everybody leaves the firm for that reason. Lots of people simply receive better offers or get tired of living in this part of the country.

Malak: Yes, I know that, but I am sure that I am not the only one who has resigned because of the company policies. I wish some day the SSC would realize what is happening around here.

The personnel manager wished him luck and left for his office. Reviewing the conversation with Malak in his mind and looking at the turnover figures for the last few years, he wondered what he could do.

DISCUSSION QUESTIONS

1. What are the consequences of a multinational company policy that allows staffing of key positions only with people from the home office?

2. Given the remote location of the SSC and its position within a foreign subsidiary, what can the personnel manager do?

3. What policy recommendations would you have? How would you deal with the trust factor?

4. Once the company had identified a lack of formal training as a problem and had hired college graduates to solve this problem, why did it deny these graduates advancement opportunities? What do you think caused this inconsistency?

Appendix A _____

Major Leadership Theories

Two streams of research, at Ohio State University (OSU) and the University of Michigan, fueled a modern debate on leadership that has persisted until today. Modern theories of leadership departed from the traditional trait theories that proposed that some people are "born leaders." According to trait theories, leaders are endowed with certain characteristics, physiological, psychological, and intellectual, that set them apart from others. All we have to do is identify people with these traits and assign them to leadership positions. Years of research, however, has shown that while certain traits increase the likelihood of a leader's success, they do not guarantee it. Researchers have found that the leader's behavior, rather than his or her traits, is more important in determining leader effectiveness. Consequently, attention has shifted toward situational demands and followers' characteristics and their influence in determining leadership effectiveness. These ideas were initially highlighted in studies that took place at OSU and the University of Michigan during the late 1940s and early 1950s. The following is a brief review of these theories. Before we proceed with our review, we should note that the "contemporary leadership field is an American product—an American seed planted in American soil and harvested by American scholars, educators, and consultants."[1]

The OSU and University of Michigan Studies

Two separate research efforts, one at OSU and the other at the University of Michigan, produced similar results. The OSU researchers identified two dimensions of leadership behavior that influence the followers' work performance. These two dimensions are *consideration* for workers and *initiating structure* or task orientation. Comparable dimensions were reported by researchers at the University of Michigan and were labeled the *employee oriented* and *production oriented* dimensions. Supportive leaders, who create a friendly environment for workers and establish their relationship on the basis of mutual trust and respect, are demonstrating concern for workers. Examples of consideration (employee-oriented behavior) are closer relationships between employees and their managers, treating subordinates as equals, doing favors and promoting the welfare of employees, giving advance notices of changes in the organization, and explaining managerial decisions. Leadership behavior that is related to task accomplishment and the efficient use of resources includes initiating structure and production-oriented behavior. Close supervision of work activities, allocating tasks, scheduling work, supplying work instruction, and generally providing the workers with direction and assistance in doing their jobs represent different aspects of this dimension.

A Synthesis of Concerns for Production and Concerns for People

The studies at the University of Michigan and OSU served as a springboard for further leadership research. In a departure from trait theories, these studies brought to our attention the fact that the leader's behavior makes a difference in the subordinates' work performance and attitudes.

While early research findings regarding the effects of these two dimensions on workers' performance have not been consistent under all conditions, certain patterns have been identified. The researchers at these universities found that, often, high consideration and employee-oriented behavior were associated with employee satisfaction, low turnover, and low absenteeism. The impact of consideration on performance, however, was low. Higher productivity and lower employee satisfaction were frequently related to high initiating structure and production-oriented behavior.[2,3]

Since concern for people and concern for production are two separate dimensions, it appears that leaders can employ a combination of both. Such a combination has actually been proposed by some scholars of leadership: In their book *Managerial Grid*, Robert R. Blake and Jane S. Mouton have suggested that by combining a concern for people with a concern for production, managers can achieve the best results.[4]

Figure A.1 depicts the results of combining the two dimensions of leadership behavior. The four quadrants in Figure A.1 illustrate four extreme variations of leadership behavior. At the lower left-hand side of the figure, Quadrant 1 represents low concern for production and low concern for people. This is the stereotypical ineffective manager who does not show much concern for either the workers or the work. The upper left-hand side, Quadrant 2, a combination of low concern for production and high concern for people, represents people-oriented behavior without much concern for the work. Quadrant 3, the lower right-hand side, is a combination of

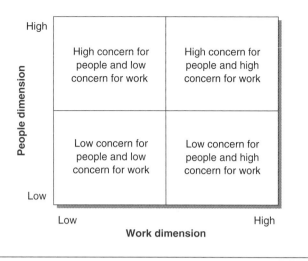

Figure A.1   A Synthesis of the Two Dimensions of Leadership

high concern for production and low concern for people, which typifies a taskmaster style. The upper right-hand side, Quadrant 4, is a mixture of high concern for workers and high concern for work. Some management scholars have suggested that this is a very effective leadership style.

Likert's Managerial Systems

Managerial leadership takes place in the organization, and it is influenced by the prevailing managerial practices. Therefore, it is not sufficient to study individual leadership behavior alone without taking into consideration the organization's norms and practices. Leadership behavior that is contrary to the prevailing managerial practices of an organization will not produce the desired results. Rensis Likert developed a questionnaire that measures an organization's management system. He proposed that there are four types of management systems: (1) exploitative authoritative, (2) benevolent authoritative, (3) consultative, and (4) participative. These systems are based on the varying degrees of trust and confidence that the manager exhibits toward his or her subordinates. The following is a brief description of the four systems.[5] Research results have been varied, but there has been some evidence of support in U.S. settings.

System 1: Exploitative Authoritative. Managers in this system have no confidence or trust in subordinates. They rely on centralized decision making from the top of the organization. Subordinates are not involved in any important decision making. In System 1 management, fear, threats, punishments, and occasional rewards are major instruments of motivation. Superior-subordinate relationships are limited to, and are based on, mistrust and fear. An informal organization develops that is parallel to the formal one. It usually resists and opposes the goals of the formal organization.

System 2: Benevolent Authoritative. The relationship between superior and subordinate in System 2 resembles a master-servant relationship. Managers express a condescending confidence and trust toward subordinates. Superior-subordinate relationships are characterized by patronizing behavior by superiors and a cautious approach by subordinates. Although most decisions are centralized at the top of the organization, within a prescribed framework some decisions are made by people at the lower levels. Rewards and punishments are used for motivating subordinates. An informal organization may develop within a System 2 organization that does not always oppose formal organizational goals.

System 3: Consultative. While managers have a substantial amount of confidence in subordinates, they still prefer to maintain control over most decisions. Strategic decisions are made by the top-level managers. Subordinates, however, are allowed to make many of the decisions affecting the lower levels. Communication flows in both directions, upward and downward. Rewards, some occasional punishment, and involvement in decision making are the major motivating tools of System 3. The informal organization that usually develops within a System 3 organization may have an ambivalent attitude toward the formal organizational goals.

System 4: Participative. The participative management system is characterized by complete confidence and trust in subordinates. Decentralized decision making differentiates this system from the other three systems. Communication flows freely between all levels of the organization. Subordinates participate in setting economic rewards, establishing goals, determining the methods of improving performance, and appraising progress toward goals. Substantial and friendly interactions between subordinates and superiors create a high degree of confidence and trust. Control is decentralized throughout the organizational hierarchy. There is a great overlap between formal and informal organizations. Often, they are one and the same.

Likert proposed that System 4 is an effective managerial leadership approach. Research studies, primarily based in the United States, tend to support his contention that participative management is associated with favorable attitudes toward the leader, open channels of communication, and group cohesiveness. Productivity and employee job satisfaction tend to be higher among System 4 organizations.

Situational Leadership

As attention turned away from the search for leadership traits and moved to efforts to find the best leadership behaviors or style, another set of factors emerged. Specifically, researchers discovered that no one particular style was effective under all situations. They concluded that the effectiveness of leader behavior is a function of the situation at hand. Situational factors such as the followers, the work, organizational culture, and other environmental factors influence the leader's effectiveness. This realization was expressed in several situational theories of leadership. The most popular situational theories are the leadership continuum and the contingency models proposed by House and Fiedler.

The Leadership Continuum

Robert Tannenbaum and Warren Schmidt[6] view leadership as a continuum. At one end of this continuum is total control by the boss (leader-manager) through the exercise of authority, and at the other end is the subordinate's autonomy to make decisions within prescribed limits. As Figure A.2 illustrates, as we move from right to left along this continuum, leader-managers play less of an authoritarian role, and the autonomy, power, and influence of subordinates increase. At the extreme right of the continuum, authoritarian leaders tend to use their power to influence their subordinates. They make decisions alone without consulting their subordinates. At the extreme left of the continuum, democratic leaders define the limits within which subordinates can make all the decisions and allow them full participation in decision making. A middle ground approach is followed by leaders who combine inputs from subordinates with the authority of the position for making decisions. Authoritarian leaders tend to be task oriented and democratic leaders tend to be relationship oriented.

Tannenbaum and Schmidt suggested that there is no one best way to lead. Leaders should use their power according to situational demands. Four situational factors could determine the appropriate use of power by a leader-manager. These situational factors are (1) subordinates' personalities, (2) subordinates' expectations about leader behavior, (3) subordinates' willingness to accept responsibility, and (4) the group's ability to accomplish its tasks. A combination of situational requirements may dictate the full use of power by the leaders. If individual subordinates are not self-directed and require close supervision, if the work group is unable to solve problems, if they are not willing to take responsibility, and if they expect the leader to take charge, then the task-oriented leadership style may be more productive. In the opposite situations, the relationship-oriented leadership style would be more appropriate. Situational factors such as time pressure, the nature and scope of the problem, and organizational circumstances also affect managers' behavior.

House's Contingency Model of Leadership

The leadership continuum as proposed by Tannenbaum and Schmidt is an acknowledgment that leadership behavior is similar to other types of behavior. It does not take place in a vacuum. Forces outside the leader have

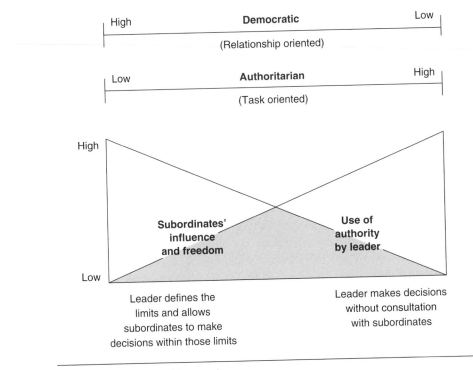

Figure A.2   Leadership Continuum

a bearing on his or her behavior. This brings to our attention the fact that leaders are not fully autonomous and are not totally oblivious to their surroundings. There are potential forces that influence leadership behavior. Robert House has pulled together elements of a number of theories to propose a contingency model of leadership called path-goal theory.[3,7] House proposes that there are three major categories of factors that affect the style the leader adopts. These factors are the nature of the subordinates, the organizational setting, and the group. The leader's style, then, changes in response to these factors. An effective leader assists his or her followers in reaching their goals and ensures that the followers' goals are compatible with the overall organizational objectives. In other words, effective leaders clarify the path for individuals to reach their goals and at the same time contribute to the attainment of overall organizational objectives. Let us take a brief look at the forces that influence leadership behavior.

Subordinates' Characteristics and Response

The subordinates' characteristics influence the leader. A leader may be inclined to closely supervise subordinates who are ill trained, lack experience, or are unwilling to assume the full responsibility of their jobs. Conversely, a leader may prefer to delegate responsibility and grant autonomy to those subordinates who have demonstrated the ability and the willingness to do the job without much external control. Like other people, leaders tend to like and trust those whose background and characteristics are similar to their own. Therefore, the amiable relationship that may exist when the leader and his or her subordinates have something in common may result in more democratic leadership behavior.

Organizational Settings

The Task. An important factor affecting employee performance is the nature of the task. Certain task characteristics reduce or eliminate the need for guidance and directions by the leader. Those who work on interesting and intrinsically satisfying tasks may not require much external motivation and persuasion. They may perform their jobs even in the absence of a leader. Under time pressure, most people, including leaders, become directive and task oriented. Faced with ambiguity, crisis, and looming work deadlines, subordinates look up to their leader for direction and expect instruction and guidance. In such situations, a leader may exhibit behavior that is more autocratic without experiencing too much resentment and resistance from his or her subordinates.

Organizational Climate. Organizational climate and the leadership philosophy of top management have a great bearing on the rest of the employees. Some organizations are known for a bureaucratic climate in which adherence to strict rules is expected. Such a climate may encourage tendencies toward more centralized, directive, and autocratic leadership behavior. Conversely, where top management demonstrates a preference for informal relations, managers are more apt to rely on such behavior in their dealings with subordinates.

We are all subject to influence by our peers, and manager-leaders are not immune to this. Individual managers are affected by the managerial style and behavioral patterns of other managers. Years of association with peers tends to create some degree of similarity in attitudes and a dominant style of leadership among managers. Deviations from the norm are frowned upon, and adherence to standards is promoted. A manager who treats his or her subordinates relatively leniently, for example, may hear objections from other managers who fear that their subordinates may demand similar treatment.

Work Groups

Groups are the primary work units within most organizations. Very seldom can individual job assignments be performed independently and outside a group setting. These assignments are usually carried out within a work group structure. The members' characteristics and the resources they bring to the work group determine the group's characteristics. The nature of the work group influences the quantity and quality of the work performed by the group's members and the effectiveness of leadership behavior. For example, when there is a high level of conflict within a group, a directive style of leadership behavior (i.e., providing work guidelines and work schedules) would be effective. By recognizing the nature of the work group and providing the type of assistance, guidance, and coaching that is needed, the leader can influence the group and individual performance.

Leadership Characteristics

Leadership behavior and the person of the leader are inseparable. Personality differences result in people behaving differently under different conditions. Motivating forces may be external or internal to an individual (see Appendix B on motivation). Those high on achievement need or power, for example, may feel more comfortable giving orders and emphasizing task accomplishment. Others who are high on affiliation need may be more interested in forming friendly relationships with people. These managers may not directly push for a higher performance. Instead, they may rely on personal relationships in fulfilling their responsibilities. A leader's philosophy regarding human nature greatly influences his or her relations with followers. As Douglas McGregor[8] proposed, some managers, called *Theory X managers*, assume that people, by their very nature, are lazy, dislike working, and avoid responsibility whenever possible. They therefore believe that people need to be controlled directly and coaxed to work hard using whatever measures may be necessary, including coercion and threats of punishment. Some other managers, called *Theory Y managers*, believe that engagement in mental and physical work is as natural to people as playing and resting. They assume that people generally like to work, do not shy away from assuming responsibility, and, under the right conditions, will perform to the best of their abilities. Therefore, the use of external control, and the threat of punishment, is not the best way to improve work performance. These two different philosophies, naturally, result in two different approaches to leadership behavior. Theory X managers tend to be more task oriented, while Theory Y managers tend to be more relationship oriented.

The above discussion on the influence of situational factors on leadership behavior highlights the interactive nature of the leadership process. It also implies that effective leaders are flexible in directing their followers and select leadership styles to fit the situation. Appropriate leader behavior is something that matches the primary demands of the situation. For example, a participative style can be used when subordinates are well trained, the job is clear-cut, and the group supports the organizational goals. In contrast, where the opposite conditions exist, a more directive or authoritarian style is appropriate. House's path-goal theory of leadership proposes that there are many forces impinging on the leader's relationship with his or her subordinates. An understanding of these forces can assist the leader-manager in selecting a proper course of action that meets the challenge of managing.

Fiedler's Contingency Model

Fred Fiedler[9] proposed a contingency model stating that both styles of leadership, namely concern for work (task oriented, similar to the OSU "initiating structure") and concern for people (relationship oriented, similar to "consideration" for OSU), could be effective under certain conditions. The conditions that influence the effectiveness of these leadership tendencies depend on a combination of three elements: task structure, leader's position power, and leader-member relations. Various combinations of these elements produce situations that are favorable or unfavorable to the leader. Leadership effectiveness depends on a match between the leader's behavioral inclinations and the favorableness of the situation.

Leader-Member Relations. Situational favorability is strongly influenced by the leader-follower relationship. A situation is favorable to the leader if the group's acceptance of him or her is high, if the group and the leader are getting along, and if there is a high degree of regard for the leader. In such a favorable situation, the group and the leader can work together, and the leader has no difficulty in leading them. A leader who is liked and respected can influence the group far beyond the limits of his or her authority.

Task Structure. A task is structured if all the requirements for performing it are known to the members of a work group. The leader has no problem determining what should be done, who should do it, how it should be performed, and the reason for doing it. Such a task leaves less room for misunderstanding and disputes. The more a task is structured, the higher the situational favorableness.

Position Power. Position power refers to the amount of power and influence that the leader has. A strong power position enables the leader to easily lead the group. No one would question his or her authority. Four types of power, legitimate (authority), expert, reward, and coercive, are the basis for the leader's position power.

Various combinations of these elements could create conditions that are either favorable or unfavorable to a leader. A favorable condition exists when the task is structured, the power position is strong, and the leader-member relationship is good. An unfavorable condition exists when there is a combination of unstructured tasks, weak position power, and poor leader-member relations. Leaders who are task oriented are more effective under both extremes of conditions: favorable and unfavorable (see Figure A.3). Relationship-oriented leaders are more effective under moderately favorable conditions. An example of a favorable situation would involve a well-respected and highly qualified head of an engineering firm for whom the tasks are structured, the power position is strong, and the leader-member relationship is good. A task-oriented leader would be able to get his or her group to work hard because they like him or her; they know the requirements of the tasks, and the leader has sufficient power to influence them. In an unfavorable situation, the only way to get the group to work hard is to demand it by setting goals, providing instructions for reaching them, and guiding and controlling the work.

Compared with task-oriented leaders, relationship-oriented leaders are not very effective in very favorable or very unfavorable situations. Their relative ineffectiveness is probably due to their lack of emphasis on production and the minimum pressure they apply for higher performance. Relationship-oriented leaders are more effective in situations that are moderately favorable. In such situations, the more directive attitude of a task-oriented leader may lead to anxiety and conflict within the group. The nondirective and permissive attitude of a relationship-oriented leader is more effective.

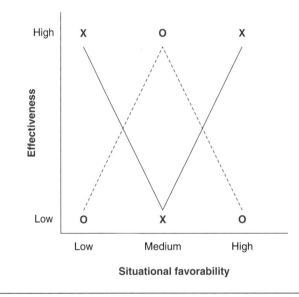

Figure A.3   Effective Leadership Behavior in Various Situations

SOURCE: Based on Reference 10.

NOTE: X = task oriented; O = relationship oriented.

References

1. B. Kellerman (2004). Leadership: Warts and all. *Harvard Business Review, January*, 44.

2. R. L. Kahn & D. Katz (1960). Leadership practices in relation to productivity and morale. In D. Cartwright & A. F. Lander (Eds.), *Group dynamics* (2nd ed., pp. 554–570). Evanston, IL: Row, Peterson.

3. R. J. House (1971). A path-goal theory of leader effectiveness. *Administrative Science Quarterly, 16*, 321–338.

4. R. R. Blake & J. S. Mouton (1978). *The managerial grid.* Houston, TX: Gulf.

5. R. Likert (1967). *The human organization.* New York: McGraw-Hill.

6. R. Tannenbaum & W. H. Schmidt (1973). How to choose a leadership pattern. *Harvard Business Review, May–June*, 162–175.

7. R. J. House (1974). Path goal theory of leadership. *Journal of Contemporary Business, Autumn*, 81–98.

8. D. McGregor (1960). *The human side of enterprise* (pp. 33–34). New York: McGraw-Hill.

9. F. Fiedler (1967). *A theory of leadership effectiveness.* New York: McGraw-Hill.

10. F. Fiedler & M. M. Chemers (1974). *Leadership and effective management.* Glenview, IL: Scott, Foresman.

Appendix B _____

Major Motivation Theories

Kamal Fatehi
Foad Derakhshan[a]

Motivation theories are classified into two groups: content theories and process theories. Content theories explore *what* motivates people. They attempt to identify items and issues that arouse and energize behavior. The most famous content theories are Maslow's needs hierarchy, Herzberg's two-factor theory, and McClelland's three-factor theory. Process theories deal with *how* people are motivated. They examine the specific steps involved in the motivation process. Vroom's expectancy theory and Adams's equity theory are well-known process theories.

Content Theories of Motivation

All the well-known content theories of motivation have been developed by American theorists whose studies involved only U.S. subjects. In the following, we briefly discuss major content theories.

Hierarchy of Needs

The cornerstone of most content theories is Abraham Maslow's concept of a hierarchy of needs.[1, 2] Maslow identified five categories of human needs, which follow a hierarchical order of importance and satisfaction. In this hierarchy, the lowest needs have to be reasonably satisfied before the next level of needs is activated. Ranging from lowest to highest, these need categories are physiological, security, social (affection), esteem (self-esteem and the esteem of others), and self-actualization. Two principles form the foundation of this theory. The *deficit principle* states that a deprived need is a motivating force. This implies that a satisfied need is not motivating. People attempt to satisfy unfulfilled needs in the hierarchy. According to the *progression principle*, people seek the satisfaction of their needs in a progression from the lower levels to the higher levels. Each level of need is activated only after the preceding lower-level needs have been sufficiently satisfied. Figure B.1 depicts this hierarchical relationship.

The early suggestion that these needs might have an instinctive origin led to a universality assumption in later interpretations of Maslow's theory. Maslow himself cautioned against overgeneralization due to a number of exceptions he had noted to the theory of hierarchical satisfaction. Many management scholars believe that in the American culture, the true motivator is the need for achievement, and its satisfaction is relatively independent of lower-level needs.

Motivators and Hygiene Factors

Herzberg identified two groups of factors, hygiene factors and motivators, that influence individual performance in work organizations.[3,4] Hygiene factors can create discomfort if they are not met, but they have no effect on motivation. These factors are external to the job (extrinsic) and include technical supervision, working conditions, pay, relations with peers, and so forth. Hygiene factors correspond to the lower-level needs in Maslow's hierarchy. Motivators include job-related (intrinsic) factors such as the work itself, achievement, responsibility, and recognition. Motivators correspond mainly to the highest needs in Maslow's hierarchy. We can portray this theory as a simplified, two-level version of Maslow's needs hierarchy, as depicted in Figure B.2.

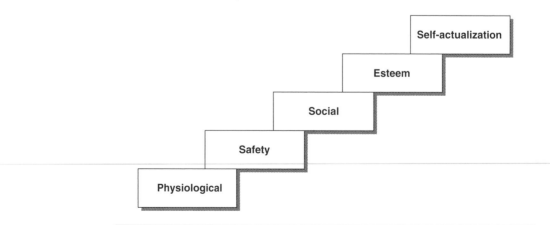

Figure B.1   Maslow's Hierarchy of Needs

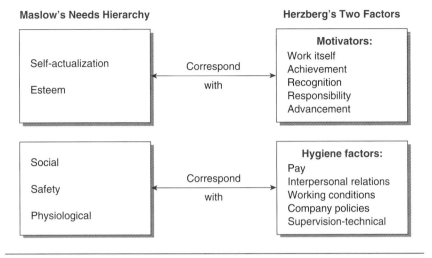

Figure B.2   The Correspondence Between Herzberg's Two Factors and Maslow's Needs Hierarchy

McClelland's Three Motives

This theory identifies three important individual drives (needs): achievement, power, and affiliation. People are motivated to satisfy these needs. McClelland[5] suggested that the need for achievement is the most important factor leading to economic success. He proposed that, at the national level, the aggregate level of this need is related to the rate of economic development. Achievement-oriented individuals seek responsibility and concrete feedback, take moderate risks, and are loners. In contrast to Maslow and Herzberg, McClelland believed that the need for achievement, and related attributes, could be taught and, in fact, that culture played an important role in socializing individuals toward these motives.[6]

Process Theories of Motivation

This section briefly examines two process theories.

Expectancy Theory

Mostly associated with the works of Victor H. Vroom, this theory proposes that motivation is a deliberate and conscious choice to engage in a certain activity for achieving a certain outcome or reward (see Figure B.3). The logic of expectancy theory has prompted some to call it the thinking person's motivation theory (p. 6).[7] Mathematically expressed, motivation (M) is the product of three variables:

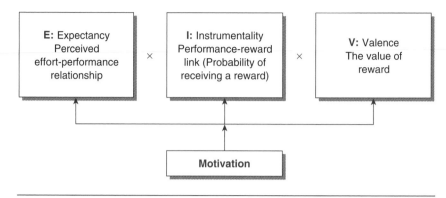

Figure B.3   Expectancy Theory

1. *Valence (V):* The *value* (attractiveness) of the *potential reward* or outcome to the individual. Potential outcome includes pay, job security, fringe benefits, job satisfaction, companionship, and the opportunity to demonstrate and apply talents and skills. In short, anything that a person can get from the job is a potential reward.

2. *Instrumentality (I):* The *performance-reward* link, which is the expectation that performance will lead to receiving the reward. Past experience forms a foundation for this linkage.

3. *Expectancy (E):* The linkage between the *effort* and *performance*, which deals with the individual's belief that exerting a certain amount of effort will lead to accomplishing the task.

$M = V \times I \times E$. The multiplicative nature of the relationship indicates that if any of the three variables is zero, then motivation will be zero.

Expectancy theory has an appeal for researchers because it expresses the motivation process as a simple mathematical relationship among three possibly measurable variables. Furthermore, its logical nature makes it appealing for those who look for a universal theory to explain motivation, independent of cultural differences.

Equity Theory

According to Adams, the individual's perception of inequity is a motivating force.[8] More specifically, a person compares the ratio of his or her compensation, that is, what he or she gets from a job (outcomes), to his or her contributions to the job (input), with the ratios of others in similar situations. Compensation comes in many different forms, including pay, job security, an interesting job, opportunity for advancement and promotion, good working relationships, and a safe and pleasant work environment. Inequity in either direction generates tension. People, however, are usually more sensitive

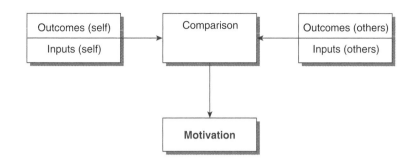

Figure B.4   Equity Theory

to a lower ratio (underreward). They respond to the perception of inequity in many different ways. These responses include filing complaints, working less, or even changing their perceptions to reestablish the equity. Figure B.4 illustrates this process.

Motivation and Learning

Motivation calls for the use of positive and negative incentives (positive reinforcement and punishment) and scheduling them in a way that will achieve the desired results. In this sense, motivation and learning become closely related. B. F. Skinner and other learning theorists assert that behavior is a function of its consequences. Behavior that is followed by desirable consequences tends to be repeated. In contrast, undesirable consequences have the opposite effect. In this way, we learn to change our behavior to experience desirable consequences and avoid the undesirable (punishment) ones.[9–12]

Note

a.   Foad Derakhshan is a professor of management at California State University, San Bernardino.

References

1. A. H. Maslow (1943). A theory of human motivation. *Psychological Bulletin, 50*, 370–382.
2. A. H. Maslow (1954). *Motivation and personality.* New York: Harper & Row.
3. F. Herzberg, B. Mausner, & B. S. Snyderman (1959). *The motivation to work.* New York: John Wiley & Sons.
4. F. Herzberg (1968). One more time, how do you motivate employees? *Harvard Business Review, January–February,* 54–62.

5. D. C. McClelland (1961). *The achieving society*. Princeton, NJ: Van Nostrand Reinhold.

6. D. C. McClelland (1962). Business drive and national achievement. *Harvard Business Review, July–August*, 99–112.

7. D. R. Hampton, C. E. Summer, & R. A. Webber (1982). *Organizational behavior and the practice of management*. Glenview, IL: Scott, Foresman.

8. J. S. Adams (1965). Inequities in social exchange. *Advances in experimental social psychology* (Vol. 2). New York: Academic Press.

9. B. F. Skinner (1971). *Beyond freedom and dignity*. New York: Alfred Knopf.

10. B. F. Skinner (1963). Operant behavior. *American Psychologist, 18*, 503–515.

11. B. F. Skinner (1961). *Contingencies of reinforcement: A theoretical analysis*. Englewood Cliffs, NJ: Prentice Hall.

12. B. M. Bass & B. M. Vaughn (1966). *Training in industry: The management of learning*. Monterey, CA: Brooks/Cole.

Appendix C _____

Charter of the United Nations

Chapter 1: Purpose and Principles

Article 1

The purposes of the United Nations are

1. To maintain international peace and security, and to that end: to take effective collective measures for the prevention and removal of threats to the peace, and for the suppression of acts of aggression or other breaches of the peace and to bring about by peaceful means, and in conformity with the principles of justice and international law, adjustment or settlement of international disputes or situations which might lead to a breach of peace;

2. to develop friendly relations among nations based on respect for the principle of equal rights and self-determination of peoples, and to take other appropriate measures to strengthen universal peace;

3. to achieve international co-operation in solving international problems of an economic, social, cultural, or humanitarian character, and in promoting and encouraging respect for human rights and for fundamental freedoms for all without distinction as to race, sex, language, or religion; and

4. to be a centre for harmonizing the actions of nations in the attainment of these common ends.

Article 2

The Organization and its Members, in pursuit of the Purposes stated in Article 1 shall act in accordance with the following Principles.

1. The organization is based on the principle of the sovereign equality of all its members.

2. Members, in order to ensure to all of them the rights and benefits resulting from membership, shall fulfill in good faith the obligations assumed by them in accordance with the present Charter.

3. All Members shall settle their international disputes by peaceful means in such a manner that international peace and security, and justice, are not endangered.

4. All Members shall refrain in their international relations from the threat or use of force against the territorial integrity or political independence of any state, or in any other manner inconsistent with the Purposes of the United Nations.

5. All Members shall give the United Nations every assistance in any action it takes in accordance with the present Charter, and shall refrain from giving assistance to any state against which the United Nations is taking preventive or enforcement action.

6. The Organization shall ensure that states which are not Members of the United Nations act in accordance with these Principles so far as may be necessary for the maintenance of international peace and security.

7. Nothing contained in the present Charter shall authorize the United Nations to intervene in matters which are essentially within the domestic jurisdiction of any state or shall require the Members to submit such matters to settlement under the present Charter; but this principle shall not prejudice the application of enforcement measures under Chapter VII.

Name Index _____

Subject Index

About the Author _____

Kamal Fatehi is Professor of International Management and former Chair of the Management and Entrepreneurship Department at Coles College of Business, Kennesaw State University. Before joining Kennesaw State University, he was Chair of the Management and Marketing Department and Interim Dean of the College of Business Administration at Texas A&M International University. Previously, he was a professor of strategic and international management at the Barton School of Business, Wichita State University, Wichita, Kansas. He has taught at Louisiana State University, Western Illinois University, Eastern Illinois University, and Texas A&M International University. At Western Illinois University, he was recognized as an outstanding scholar. He was the recipient of a Barton School of Business, Wichita State University Research Award. In 1995, he was a Fulbright Senior Scholar at Western University in Baku, Azerbaijan, and in 2004, he served as a Fulbright Senior Specialist and assisted the International Academy of Business, Almaty, Kazakhstan. In cooperation with his colleagues from Texas A&M University, he assisted Turkmen State University in establishing the first business program in Turkmenistan. In teaching and research, he draws from his years of managerial experience with industry and his service to public and private organizations as a consultant, including an assignment with the Russian Privatization Center, Moscow, Russia. Dr. Fatehi has published in journals such as the *Journal of Business Research,* the *Journal of Behavioral Economics,* the *Journal of Management, Industrial Management, Employee Relations Law Journal, Managerial Planning, Management International Review, International Executive,* the *International Journal of Management,* and the *Journal of Global Business.* He is the author of *International Management: A Cross-Cultural and Functional Perspective* (1996). He has served on the editorial board of five scholarly or professional journals.